COMPANY FINANCIAL REPORTING

COMPANY FINANCIAL REPORTING

A Historical and Comparative Study of the Dutch Regulatory Process

Stephen A. Zeff
Frans van der Wel
Kees Camfferman

A Research Study in Co-operation with the Limperg Instituut and the Council on Annual Reporting

1992
NORTH-HOLLAND
AMSTERDAM · LONDON · NEW YORK · TOKYO

ELSEVIER SCIENCE PUBLISHERS B.V.
Sara Burgerhartstraat 25
P.O. Box 211, 1000 AE Amsterdam, the Netherlands

Library of Congress Cataloging-in-Publication Data

Zeff, Stephen A.
Company financial reporting · a historical and comparative study of the Dutch regulatory process/Stephen A. Zeff, Frans van der Wel, Kees Camfferman; a research study in cooperation with the Limperg Instituut and the Council on Annual Reporting.
p. cm.
Includes bibliographical references and index.
ISBN 0-444-89525-6 (alk. paper)
1. Corporation reports – Law and legislation – Netherlands – History. 2. Corporations – Accounting – Law and legislation – Netherlands – History. I. Wel, Frans van der, 1955– . II. Camfferman, Kees, 1966– . III. Limperg Instituut. IV. Raad voor de Jaarverslaggeving (Netherlands) V. Title.
KKM1072.Z77 1992
346.492′ 06648–dc20
[344.92066648] 92–15531
CIP

ISBN: 0 444 89525 6

This book is printed on acid-free paper

Printed in the Netherlands

Foreword

A number of phenomena in the Dutch practice of financial accounting have attracted international attention. Several of these are:

- during the 1950's and 1960's, the Dutch Employers Federations published influential recommendations for the contents of annual financial statements;
- since 1971, a special Enterprise Court, a Chamber of the Court of Justice, has been operating in the Netherlands at Amsterdam. Among other things, the Court handles charges of failure to comply with the legal requirements in respect of financial statements. The verdict of the Court is applicable only to the specific case under investigation;
- also instituted in 1971 was a private body (named the Council on Annual Reporting in 1981) which does not handle specific cases but carries out its task by reviewing the accounting principles used in practice and by publishing in general terms its opinion on their acceptability within the framework of the general terms of the law. The Council consists of representatives from three interest groups, namely, the preparers (represented by the confederations of industry), the users (represented by trade unions and recently also by financial analysts), and the auditors (represented by the auditors' organization, the NIvRA);
- the application of current cost accounting in some companies for internal information on operating results and also for external information in the financial statements.

Several times, one or more of these phenomena have been discussed at international conferences, but never before has a thorough study been made of the Dutch institutional environment and of the Dutch practice of regulating the process of financial accounting.

Fortunately, Professor Stephen A. Zeff (Professor of Accounting, Rice University, Houston, U.S.A.) has now taken the initiative to make a scientific study of the Dutch regulatory process. As could be expected from an outstanding academic, Professor Zeff did not restrict himself to a superficial review. In a scientific way, he attempted to trace the conditions, the sources and the connections of the regulatory process for financial statements so that, in my opinion, a study of very high quality has been made, the result of which is recorded in this book.

A significant contribution to the study and to this book was made by Dr Frans van der Wel (Doctor of Economics and Lecturer in the Economics Faculty, Free University Amsterdam, and partner of TRN Touche Ross Netherland) and by Kees Camfferman (Lecturer in the Economics Faculty, Free University Amsterdam). Together with Professor Zeff, they formed an effective and efficient research team.

Headed by Professor Zeff, the writers did not limit themselves to describing and analyzing the Dutch process, but they also made comparisons with the standard-setting processes in the United States of America and the United Kingdom. Differences in national culture, capital market and environment are clearly exposited. Added to this is a discussion of the consequences of possible avenues for improving financial reporting.

In the final chapter of this book, the writers reflect on the results of their research. This leads them to some interesting conclusions and very useful recommendations.

In my opinion, the book gives a true and fair view of the Dutch regulatory process for company financial reporting. The description and the analysis conform to high scientific standards. It is written in a very clear and readable style, and as such it will stimulate further research on accounting and the regulatory process for financial reporting.

Professor Jan W. Schoonderbeek

Preface

This project was undertaken at the joint invitation of the Limperg Instituut and the Council on Annual Reporting (RJ, Raad voor de Jaarverslaggeving). Its object has been to provide a record of the historical development of the efforts to improve company financial reporting in the Netherlands, and to make recommendations for possible reform. Such a study, it was hoped, would be of value to a wide range of parties interested in financial reporting and the regulatory process.

The work on this study began in June 1990, and was concluded in December 1991.

The difficulty of pursuing historical accounting research in the Netherlands is considerable. First, the literature on accounting history is virtually barren. Since most accounting and auditing professors have traditionally been partners in audit firms or employed in companies or government, while serving part-time in the university, their research has typically been of a practical character. Furthermore, most of the Dutch accounting and auditing literature consists of normative argumentation, influenced in large measure by the deductive framework developed by Th. Limperg Jr. and propagated by his disciples. There has been very little empirical research, including, of course, historical research. The implication of this state of the literature for those who would conduct historical research is that there is hardly any previous work on which to build. This means that not only the data and interpretations relevant to one's own study, but also those that might have been supplied by researchers studying related questions, must both be adduced in any new undertaking. Partly for this reason, as we began the process of gathering and studying our data, we realized that this project would be much larger than we had imagined.

Second, apart from a useful card file in the library of the Nederlands Instituut van Registeraccountants (NIvRA) that goes back a number of years but is limited to the library's holdings, there is no cumulative index to the Dutch accounting and auditing literature. Nor is there an index to newspapers and magazines, except, we understand, for the last few years' issues for some papers.

In our presentation of the history, we have endeavored to provide access to the literature for the benefit of both Dutch and non-Dutch readers. Footnotes have been used extensively to supply citations and informational notes for other researchers. Since few non-Dutch readers can use the Dutch literature for additional study, we have frequently provided fuller translated quotations than would be the case if the original materials were in, say, English. At the same time, we have tried to assist Dutch readers by providing the Dutch language text of key translated words and phrases.

The sections in Chapter 1 are intended to provide an orientation for readers who are not familiar with the Dutch economy, capital market, political system, company organization, auditing profession, education for prospective auditors, professional journals, and the financial press, and the framework of financial reporting. Chapters 2 through 6 are the core of the historical study, organized mostly in chronological sequence, from the late 19th century to recent times. While we have carried the historical narrative as far as 1991, it is difficult to discern a historical perspective or insight into events and trends that have occurred in the past five or so years. Nonetheless, we have treated the more important developments that have occurred since the mid-1980's. Chapter 7 is our attempt to compare trends and developments in the Netherlands with those in the United States and the United Kingdom. In Chapter 8, we present our conclusions and policy recommendations.

In addition to consulting journals, treatises, laws, parliamentary proceedings, committee reports, company annual reports, the annual reports of other private- and public-sector organizations, court decisions, and newspapers and magazines, we were permitted access to the confidential minutes and papers of the Tripartite Study Group (TO, Tripartiete overleg), the RJ, and the Foundation for Annual Reporting (Stichting voor de Jaarverslaggeving). The Nederlands Instituut van Registeraccountants (NIvRA) allowed us to use the confidential minutes and papers of its Advisory Committee on Annual Reporting (CAJ, Commissie van Advies inzake Jaarverslaggeving), its management board, and various other committees. We are grateful to these organizations for allowing us to use these important primary resource materials.

We also conducted more than 90 interviews with key participants in, and close observers of, the regulatory process, including auditors, company executives, representatives of trade union federations, lawyers and judges, academics, staff members of the NIvRA and the Federation of Dutch Industries (VNO, Verbond van Nederlandse Ondernemingen), financial journalists, members of the financial community, functionaries in the Justice Ministry, and a member of Parliament. Included among the interviewees were 25 past or present members of the TO and the RJ, including all of the chairmen. Where they provided information and insights that went beyond documentary evidence, we have cited their interviews in the footnotes. We are deeply indebted to our interviewees, some of whom were visited more than once, for their indispensable contribution to this project.

We made extensive use of several fine libraries and archives. In particular, we wish to thank the helpful staff of the Royal Library (Koninklijke Bibliotheek), the State Archive (Rijksarchief), the *Bedrijfseconomisch* Archive (Bedrijfseconomisch Archief) of the Erasmus Universiteit Rotterdam, the Economic History Library (Economisch Historische Bibliotheek) of Amsterdam, the library of the Vrije Universiteit, and the NIvRA and VNO libraries. The minutes of the meetings of the management board of the Federation of Dutch Employers (VNW, Verbond van Nederlandsche Werkgevers), which are cited in Chapters 3 and 4, were inspected in the State Archive. We are grateful to the Ministry of Justice for granting us access to the minutes of the financial reporting subcommittee of the Verdam Commission.

There are many organizations and individuals whom we wish to thank. Foremost are the Limperg Instituut and the RJ, which supplied the stimulus and funding for the project. Touche Ross Nederland, including especially its Documentation Center, provided major support. The NIvRA and the VNO provided complete cooperation in response to our many inquiries. The Vrije Universiteit provided computers, office space and staff assistance. Rice University generously granted a special leave to enable the completion of the manuscript. J.W. Schoonderbeek was an invaluable guide throughout the project, and he and J. Klaassen kindly read the entire manuscript, and furnished us with many constructive suggestions for improvement. Others who either read parts of the manuscript or who assisted us in special ways, whom we also wish to thank, are C.A. Arnold, T. Bossert, J.C. Brezet, H.L. Brink, W. Buijink, J.A. Burggraaff, H.C. Dekker, J.F. van Dijk, H.G. Eijgenhuijsen, C. van Geffen, H. Haarbosch, W.P. Hackney, M.H.E.O. Hertzberger-van Aalst, J. van der Hoeven, K. Van Hulle, W.P. Moleveld, J.W. Muis, M.W. Noordzij, F. van Proosdij, F.P. Quax, H.J.M. van Raaij, P.P.M. van der Ree, M. Renshall, G. Rietkerk, P.J. Rutteman, H. Schreuder, R. Soeting, D. Solomons, I. Verhagen, R.G. Vingerling, O.M. Volgenant jr., and S. Zambon.

We have used the masculine form of nouns and pronouns throughout the manuscript in order to avoid cumbersome ("his or her") constructions.

None of the organizations and individuals mentioned above is responsible for the contents of this book. The authors alone are the culpable parties.

Stephen A. Zeff
Frans van der Wel
Kees Camfferman

Amsterdam
December 1991

Contents

1. Introductory notes

1.1. Aspects of the economy and the capital market

1.1.1. The economy

External trade and an open economy have always been important to the Netherlands, a small country with a limited market for finished products and a need to acquire foreign exchange to pay for imported raw materials.[1] In 1989, exports and imports of goods and services accounted for 58 and 54 percent, respectively, of Gross Domestic Product.[2] Comparable figures for the USA, UK, and West Germany for 1988 were 9 and 11 percent, 24 and 27 percent, and 29 and 24 percent, respectively.[3]

The early strength of the Dutch was in trade and shipping. In the first part of the seventeenth century, the Netherlands was the leading commercial and maritime nation in the world.[4] In 1602, the United East Indies Company (Verenigde Oost-Indische Compagnie) became the world's first company to offer shares to the public. The Amsterdam Stock Exchange (Amsterdamse Effectenbeurs) traces its origin to the launching of that famous enterprise, making it the world's oldest stock exchange.[5]

---

1 John Goodear Abert, *Economic Policy and Planning in the Netherlands, 1950–1965* (New Haven: Yale University Press, 1969), p. 1.

2 *The Dutch Economy: Recent Developments and Prospects* (The Hague: Federation of Netherlands Industry (VNO), December 1990), p. 4.

3 Department of Economics and Statistics, *National Accounts 1976–1988* (Paris: OECD, 1990).

4 *The Dutch Economy*, *op. cit.*, p. 3.

5 While the Paris Bourse had its beginnings in 1138, members of the Amsterdam Stock Exchange claim that there is no evidence that the Paris market involved the purchase and sale of shares of stock, while there is definite proof that shares were being traded in Amsterdam as early as 1602. Wilford J. Eiteman and David K. Eiteman, *Leading World Stock Exchanges: Trading Practices and Organization* (Ann Arbor, MI: Bureau of Business Research, The University of Michigan, 1964), pp. 23, 40.

For a history of the Stock Exchange Association, the governing body of the Exchange, see Prof.dr Joh de Vries, *Een Eeuw vol Effecten: Historische schets van de Vereniging voor de Effectenhandel en de Amsterdamse Effectenbeurs 1876–1976* [Amsterdam: Vereniging voor de Effectenhandel, 1976]. A 20-page résumé of this volume has been published in English, together with a 7-page update to 1990 written by E. Damen and K. Kamp, under the title *A century of stocks and shares* (Amsterdam: Amsterdam Stock Exchange, 1991). Also see *The Organization and Functioning of the Amsterdam Stock Exchange* (Amsterdam Stock Exchange, [no year]).

The Netherlands was slow to follow the British example of industrialization in the 19th century, and momentum in that direction did not begin to build until the first decades of the twentieth century. Following the interruption of World War I, the Dutch economy grew fitfully during the 1920's and was depressed during most of the 1930's, with high unemployment. During World War II, much of the relatively small pre-war industrial base was lost. After the War, there was a resurgence of industrialization within a framework of sustained economic growth, and the manufacturing sector grew to a position of considerable prominence.[6] Yet the view is still held that "Holland is a nation of traders rather than industrialists".[7]

Today, three industrial enterprises with substantial or exclusive Dutch participation are of commanding international importance: Royal Dutch/Shell Group (60 percent-owned by the Dutch holding company), Philips, and Unilever (50 percent-owned by the Dutch holding company). All three are, directly or through holding companies, listed on the New York Stock Exchange. Measured by sales turnover, Royal Dutch/Shell is the biggest enterprise in Europe (and second biggest in the world), more than half again as big as the second-place enterprise, government-owned IRI of Italy. Philips and Unilever are the 8th and 12th largest in Europe, respectively.[8] These three Dutch enterprises were among the first that could justly be called multinationals. Four other Dutch industrials, Akzo, DSM, Hoogovens, and Heineken are also of considerable international importance.

The Port of Rotterdam – Germany's major outlet to the sea – handled two-thirds more seaborne cargo in 1989 than the second largest port, Singapore. Dutch ports carry 36 percent of all of the European Community's freight.[9]

The Dutch use their resources efficiently. With 14.9 million inhabitants occupying a mere 41 864 square kilometers, the population density is one of the highest in the world, even higher than that of Japan.[10] Approximately 40 percent of the population lives in the *Randstad*, a region bounded by Amsterdam, The Hague, Rotterdam, and Utrecht, which occupies about 16 percent of the

6 P.W. Klein, "The Foundations of Dutch Prosperity", in Richard T. Griffiths (editor), *The Economy and the Politics of the Netherlands Since 1945* (The Hague: Martinus Nijhoff, 1980), pp. 1–12. Also see Steven B. Wolinetz, "Socio-economic Bargaining in the Netherlands: Redefining the Post-war Policy Coalition", in Hans Daalder and Galen A. Irwin (editors), *Politics in the Netherlands: How Much Change?* (London: Frank Cass, 1989), pp. 79–98; J.G. Berendsen, *Maatschappij, onderneming en accountant: Een onderzoek naar ontwikkelingen in de maatschappelijke positie van de openbare accountant in de jaren na 1945* (Amsterdam: VU Uitgeverij, 1990), pp. 17–29; and Johan de Vries, *The Netherlands Economy in the Twentieth Century* (Assen: Van Gorcum, 1978), pp. 63–69.

7 "Survey of the Dutch Economy", *The Economist* (London), vol. 304, no. 7515, 12 September 1987, special section, p. 3.

8 "The World's Biggest Industrial Corporations", in *Fortune* (International Edition), vol. 124, no. 3, 29 July 1991, p. 71.

9 Sara Henley, "Rotterdam Keeps Its Sleeves Rolled Up", in *International Herald Tribune*, 30 May 1991: "The Netherlands: A Special Report", p. I.

10 *The Netherlands in Brief* (The Hague: Ministry of Foreign Affairs, 1990), p. 13.

country's land-space, an area about that of Greater London.

In a society in which progress is made through consensus and compromise, the roles played by employers and employees federations have been particularly important. During World War II, Dutch employers and employees worked side by side in the resistance, and, following the War, the spirit engendered by that patriotic enterprise led to a remarkable period of cooperation by the employers federations and trade union federations in the rebuilding of the shattered economy.[11] Testimony to this new spirit was the creation of two bodies:

- the *Foundation of Labor* (Stichting van de Arbeid), a private-sector, independent, autonomous entity – bringing together industry, labor, small business, and agriculture – which was authorized to approve, reject, or modify all wage agreements;[12] and
- the *Social and Economic Council* (SER, Sociaal-Economische Raad), a 45-member public body established by the Industrial Organization Act (Wet op de Bedrijfsorganisatie) of 1950, consisting of equal numbers of employers' representatives, employees' representatives, and independent experts appointed by the Crown, which advises government at the highest level on a wide range of proposed policies and legislation relating to social and economic affairs.[13]

During the post-World War II years, the principal employers and employees federations in the Netherlands have been important participants in the development of the economy. In particular, employers federations have taken a leadership role in promoting improvements in company financial reporting. Since several of the employers and employees federations will be introduced at various stages in the discussion of efforts to improve financial reporting, the more important bodies are identified below:

Employers

- Federation of Dutch Employers (VNW, Verbond van Nederlandsche Werkgevers), founded in 1899.
- Central Social Employers Federation (CSWV, Centraal Sociaal Werkgevers-Verbond), which traces its origin to 1920.
- Catholic Federation of Employers Associations (KVW, Katholiek Verbond van Werkgeversvakverenigingen), later renamed the Dutch Catholic Employers

[11] For further discussion, see John P. Windmuller, *Labor Relations in the Netherlands* (Ithaca, NY: Cornell University Press, 1969), Chap. 3.

[12] Following 1963, when upward wage pressure from the European Economic Community combined with a very tight labor market in the Netherlands to lessen the effectiveness of the Foundation of Labor as an arbiter of wage agreements, it became less of a force in Dutch industrial relations.

[13] See Wazir Singh, *Policy Development: A Study of the Social and Economic Council of the Netherlands* (Rotterdam: Rotterdam University Press, 1972), for an extensive study of the SER.

Federation (NKWV, Nederlands Katholiek Werkgeversverbond), whose origin may be traced to 1915.
- Federation of Protestant-Christian Employers in the Netherlands (Verbond van Protestants-Christelijke Werkgevers in Nederland), which traces its origin to 1892.

In 1967, the third and fourth organizations, above, merged to form a body that was renamed in 1970 as the Dutch Christian Employers Federation (NCW, Nederlands Christelijk Werkgeversverbond). In 1968, the first and second organizations, above, merged to form the Federation of Dutch Industries (VNO, Verbond van Nederlandse Ondernemingen). Currently, about 10 000 companies are affiliated with the VNO, and about 4000 are associated with the NCW. At the national level, the VNO has been by far the more important of the two central federations.[14]

Employees

- Dutch Federation of Trade Unions (NVV, Nederlands Verbond van Vakverenigingen), founded in 1905.
- Christian National Trade Union Federation (CNV, Christelijk Nationaal Vakverbond), formed in 1909.
- Dutch Catholic Trade Union Federation (NKV, Nederlands Katholiek Vakverbond), whose origin may be traced to 1906.

It was intended that the three employees federations be merged into the Consultative Council of Trade Union Federations (Overlegorgaan Vakcentrales) in the 1970's, but, following the withdrawal of the CNV, the Consultative Council disbanded on 1 January 1976. On the same date, the NVV and the NKV began to combine their forces to form the Federated Dutch Trade Union Movement (FNV, Federatie Nederlandse Vakbeweging), a process that culminated in complete merger on 1 January 1982.[15]

[14] For a discussion of Dutch employers associations, see William van Voorden, "Employers Associations in the Netherlands", in John P. Windmuller and Alan Gladstone (editors), *Employers Associations and Industrial Relations* (Oxford: Clarendon Press, 1984), pp. 202–231.
[15] J.P. Windmuller, C. de Galan and A.F. van Zweeden, *Arbeidsverhoudingen in Nederland* (Utrecht/Antwerpen: Uitgeverij Het Spectrum, 1983), pp. 260–261.

1.1.2. The capital market[16]

The Amsterdam Stock Exchange, which is governed by the Stock Exchange Association[17] (Vereniging voor de Effectenhandel), is the only stock market in the Netherlands. Small exchanges once existed in Rotterdam and The Hague. The Exchange is subject to the Stock Exchange Act (Beurswet) of 1914, supplemented by the Act on Securities Trading (Wet Effectenhandel) of 1985, and its Rules on Securities Trading (Fondsenreglement) must be approved by the Minister of Finance. These Acts were recently replaced by two new pieces of legislation: the Act to Oversee Securities Trading (Wet Toezicht Effectenverkeer), and the Act to Oversee Investment Companies (Wet Toezicht Beleggingsinstellingen). The goals of these two recent Acts were to safeguard the investor and to strengthen the public trust in the capital market.

Historically, the Amsterdam Stock Exchange has not evinced a great deal of interest in the financial reporting practices of listed companies, although it has a strong interest in the promptness of communications by companies to the financial community.

In 1990, the Amsterdam Stock Exchange was, in terms of the US dollar value of share trading volume, the eighth largest exchange (or group of exchanges) in Europe, as follows[18]:

London	US$m	587 808
Federation of German Stock Exchanges		554 208
Zürich		400 253
Paris		127 019
Vienna		59 313
Basel		55 006
Italy		44 860
Amsterdam		44 011

[16] Apart from the items cited below, little is available in English about the Dutch capital market. Although dated, the following source may be useful: J.M. Samuels, R.E.V. Groves and C.S. Goddard, "Holland", in *Company Finance in Europe* (London: The Institute of Chartered Accountants in England and Wales, 1975), pp. 145–177.

The authors are grateful to Dr E.A.M. Elbertse, Prof.dr H.G. Eijgenhuijsen, Drs H. Haarbosch, Dr A.B. Dorsman and Dr G. Rietkerk for advice and information on the Dutch capital market, but they do not, of course, take responsibility for the authors' discussion in this section.

[17] The Vereniging voor de Effectenhandel is sometimes translated into English as the Association for Securities Trading. The authors prefer the translation used by the Exchange itself: Stock Exchange Association. See footnote 5, above, for a work on the history of the Association.

[18] *F.I.B.V. Statistics 1990* (Paris: Fédération Internationale des Bourses de Valeurs, 1991), Table 1.4.B, p. 20.

Trading volume and capitalization on the Amsterdam Stock Exchange are dominated by the "internationals": Royal Dutch Petroleum, Unilever, Philips, Akzo, and Hoogovens. During 1990, 29.0 percent of the Exchange's trading volume was in the shares of those five companies. At the end of 1990, the same five companies accounted for 54.3 percent (of which 36.4 percent was Royal Dutch alone) of the market-value capitalization of the companies whose shares are listed on the Exchange.[19]

In 1982, the so-called "Official Parallel Market" was created, enabling small companies to go public, to be listed on the Amsterdam Stock Exchange, and to facilitate the financing of future growth. Companies traded on the Parallel Market are allowed to provide somewhat less financial information in their prospectus.

The Amsterdam securities market is not an important source of new equity capital.[20] To raise new capital, the "internationals" go to other large, well-developed capital markets, such as New York and the Euro capital market, not to Amsterdam. In the Netherlands, retained earnings are a far more important source of new capital than are equity issues. Since there is no capital gains tax for individuals, such shareholders might prefer to have part of their earnings ploughed back into the business, with the prospect of an increase in the market price of the shares. Companies also offer "rights issues" (*claim emissies*), by which every shareholder can subscribe to new shares at a price below the market, and the rights are traded.

Recent studies of "market penetration" show that about 1 in 20 individuals in the Netherlands is an investor in shares.[21] The major purchasers of shares are the institutional investors, namely, pension funds, life insurance companies, and mutual funds. A substantial shareholding is in the hands of foreign investors. In a 1989 study, it was found that foreign investors held 43 percent of Dutch shares.[22]

Of the 498 companies whose shares were listed on the "Official Market" of

---

[19] *Facts and Figures 1990* (Amsterdam Stock Exchange, [1991]), pp. 16–17, and *The Amsterdam Stock Exchange in 1990* (Amsterdam Stock Exchange, [1991]), pp. 64–67. Investment and holding companies are excluded.

[20] See, e.g., Robert Parker, "Financial reporting in the Netherlands", in Christopher Nobes and Robert Parker (editors), *Comparative International Accounting* (Hemel Hempstead, Herts, UK: Prentice Hall International (UK) Ltd, 1991), p. 221.

[21] In a series of studies conducted every five years from 1979 through 1989, between 10 and 15 percent of the heads of Dutch households own shares. Assuming an average family size of 2.5, this converts to a range of between 4 and 6 percent of individuals. *De Effectenbezitter, de effectenbeurs, anno 1989* (INTOMART, June 1989), unpaginated. (This publication is available from the Exchange.)

[22] *Study on Obstacles to Takeover Bids in the European Community*, executive summary of a study conducted by Booz–Allen Acquisition Services for Directorate General XV of the Commission of the European Communities (DG XV-B-2, Direction Génerale-Institutions Financières et Droit des Societés, December 1989), p. 31. The figures are for 1987/88. The percentage of foreign ownership in Dutch shares was by far the highest in the Community.

the Exchange at the end of 1990, 260 were domestic and 238 were foreign,[23] suggesting the high degree of interest that Dutch institutional investors, as well as individuals, have in the shares of foreign companies, especially those in Anglo-Saxon countries.

The major actors in the Dutch capital market are characterized by a high degree of concentration. The three major commercial banks, together with merchant banks Pierson, Heldring & Pierson and Bank Mees & Hope, both of which are wholly owned by ABN AMRO, collectively dominate the underwriting market. During the years 1989 and 1990, they were the lead or co-lead banks in 144 of the 177 offerings.[24] The same five banks accounted for 51.49 percent of the trading of securities on behalf of clients in the Dutch capital market from 1 May 1990 to 30 April 1991.[25]

Companies obtain a listing by going to a commercial bank or a merchant bank, where the terms and the prospectus are discussed. Once these matters are settled and the prospectus has been cleared with the Stock Exchange Association, the bank begins to build up interest among institutional investors, to be confident that there will be an ample market. Then the listing is made effective and the shares are put on the market.

When institutional investors are concerned about insufficient financial information being reported by a company in which they have an investment, they might express their disquiet directly with the company management. As a result of such meetings, companies sometimes are seen to provide additional information.

A reliance on formal procedures for obtaining unavailable information may not be as necessary in the Dutch capital market as in other countries' markets that may be more widely dispersed and impersonal. "We [the Dutch entrepreneurial class] live in a small world where everybody knows everyone else and who is friends with who or was at school with who", said the late Allard Jiskoot, then the chairman of the Foundation to Oversee Securities Trading (Stichting Toezicht Effectenverkeer), a board that supervises the operations of the securities market.[26] Recently, there have been a series of steps taken to regulate insider trading. On 1 January 1987, a "model code" concerning insider trading was incorporated in the Stock Exchange Association's Rules on Securities Trading. In February 1989, the Criminal Code was revised (Art. 336a of the Wetboek van Strafrecht) to take account of the European Community's Directive on insider trading.

Most financial analysts are employed by the major commercial banks, the

[23] *The Amsterdam Stock Exchange in 1990* (Amsterdam Stock Exchange, [1991]), p. 6.

[24] This information was furnished by Bank Mees & Hope.

[25] "Groei marktaandeel grote banken op Damrak vlakt af", in *Het Financieele Dagblad*, 8 August 1991, p. 9.

[26] As quoted in David Barchard, "Regulation: New powers on the way", in *Financial Times*, 12 June 1990, Section III: "European Finance and Investment – The Netherlands", p. VI.

merchant banks, and the institutional investors. They are organized in a Society of Financial Analysts (VBA, Vereniging van Beleggingsanalisten), which was founded in 1961 and today has about 500 members. The Society has several committees, including one that deals with accounting. Since 1985, it has published a quarterly magazine, *VBA Journaal*. The Society's main activity, in the season, is to hold meetings with companies, when the members will sometimes suggest that companies consider providing additional financial information. The Society has been active in the biennial congresses of the European Federation of Financial Analysts Societies (EFFAS), which have been a forum for encouraging greater comparability of company financial statements.[27]

Since the late 1970's, Dutch financial analysts have become better organized and more professionally dedicated to investment analysis. This change was brought about, partly, because of the recent tendency by institutional investors to emphasize holdings of shares instead of bonds, with the resulting need for an effective analysis of company performance. In 1978, the Society established a three-year diploma program of part-time professional education, and those who complete the program, today numbering about 140, are called Registered Financial Analysts (RBA, Register Beleggings Analist), which is a title not regulated by law.[28]

1.2. National government and political parties[29]

In the Netherlands, the monarch and the Council of Ministers are at the apex of constitutional authority, although the monarch does not possess personal power. All formal legislation must be approved by the *Staten-Generaal*, or Parliament, which consists of two chambers. The Second Chamber, or the lower house, is much the more important chamber, and is also the larger of the two. It alone is authorized to amend legislation and to take the initiative to draft new legislation. Its 150 members are chosen in a national election, without constituent districts. Elections must be held no less frequently than every four years. The

[27] Interview with Drs R. Clement, 23 October 1990. For a discussion of the Society's work in EFFAS, see Drs H. Haarbosch, "Accounting commissie", in *VBA Journaal*, vol. 7, no. 2, June 1991, p. 40.

[28] See Drs P.J. Stephan, "VBA-opleiding", in *VBA Journaal*, vol. 7, no. 2, June 1991, pp. 44–45. Also see "Unieke opleiding voor het VBA/NIBE Diploma Beleggingsanalist", in a special section of *Het Financieele Dagblad*, 19 September 1984, for a joint version of this program, which has since lapsed.

[29] See William Z. Shetter, *The Netherlands in Perspective: The Organizations of Society and Environment*(Leiden: Martinus Nijhoff, 1987), Chaps. 13 and 14; R.B. Andeweg, Th. van der Tak, and K. Dittrich, "Government Formation in the Netherlands", in Griffiths, *op.cit.*, Chap. 9; Galen A. Irwin, "Appendix 1: Parties having achieved representation in Parliament since 1946", in Daalder and Irwin, *op.cit.*, pp. 154–160; and Ken Gladdish, *Governing from the Centre: Politics and Policy-Making in the Netherlands* (London: Hurst & Company, 1991).

First Chamber, or the upper house, is charged with discussing and reviewing proposed legislation that has passed the Second Chamber. Its 75 members are chosen by the popularly elected Assemblies of the 12 provinces.

Almost all proposals for legislation originate with the 15 or 16 ministers, who are not members of Parliament. The Council of Ministers is chaired by the *Minister-President*, or Prime Minister, who is almost always the leader of the party emerging with the greatest political leverage following the national election. Proposals for major legislation are sometimes referred to a *Staatscommissie* (government commission), which is appointed by the relevant minister. Included in the commission's final report will be a draft law together with explanatory notes. Draft laws dealing with social and economic issues are then submitted to the Social and Economic Council (see the previous section) for its reaction. Thereupon, the draft law is discussed and agreed to by the Cabinet and is then transmitted to the *Raad van State*, or Council of State, which is the senior advisory body to the Crown. After the Council of State's advice has been received, the draft law is submitted to the Second Chamber of Parliament for discussion, amendment, and approval. The Chamber forms a parliamentary preparation committee, which may call a hearing prior to sending a provisional report on the draft law to the minister. After an exchange of views between the minister and the committee, the minister forwards the draft, as modified, to the floor of the Second Chamber for debate and possible amendment. Once the draft law has been approved by the Second Chamber, it is introduced in the First Chamber, where a similar process is followed, except that, as noted above, the First Chamber must vote the measure "up or down", since no amendments are permitted. Legislation approved by both Chambers is then published, with Royal Assent, in the *Staatsblad van Het Koninkrijk der Nederlanden* (Statute Book of the Kingdom of the Netherlands). Legislation on many, sometimes important subjects has been delegated by statute to Royal Decree. Such legislation does not go through Parliament. It originates with one or more ministers and is, with Royal Assent, equally published in the *Staatsblad*.

Almost all Dutch governments are coalitions. In a given election, although as many as 15 to 20 parties may present candidates, typically about 90 percent of the seats in the Second Chamber are won by the four largest parties. This number of parties, coupled with the "proportional representation" system of allocating votes, virtually assures the absence of a majority for any one party. Since World War II, no party has received more than 35.3 percent of the vote in any national election, and usually the percentage of votes received by the leading party falls between 28 and 32. Following an election, an interim period of negotiations occurs, during which ministerial positions are apportioned among the parties taking part, according to bargaining power. Once a coalition expecting a majority of votes in the Second Chamber is formed, a government comes into existence.

Political parties span the entire spectrum of political ideologies, and a number have been historically influenced by religious principles. Although the strength of the religious influence is today not as great as it was a few decades ago, it nonetheless persists.

The major party on the left has been the Labor Party (PvdA, Partij van de Arbeid), which led the four governments from 1948 to 1958. In the 1989 election, it tallied 31.9 percent of the vote. The Catholic People's Party (KVP, Katholieke Volkspartij), a centrist party, headed coalitions from 1958 to 1971, save for a five-month period in 1966–67 when the Anti-Revolutionary Party (ARP, Anti-Revolutionaire Partij), a Protestant party, headed a caretaker government. The Anti-Revolutionary Party directed two brief governments in 1971–73, following which the Labor Party headed the government for four years.

The secular right has been represented by one major party. The People's Party for Freedom and Democracy (VVD, Volkspartij voor Vrijheid en Democratie), known as the Liberal Party, has, since World War II, received a gradually increasing percentage of the vote, from 7.9 in 1948 and 8.8 in 1952 to a range from 14.4 to 23.1 during the years from 1972 to 1989. In economic policy, the Liberal Party advocates the role of the market and freedom of enterprise, as opposed to the more interventionist Labor Party. Since the early 1950's, the Liberal and Labor Parties have alternated as the major coalition partner of the religious parties that have been represented in each of the governments.

A major party that was formed more recently is the Democrats '66 (Democraten '66), commonly known as D66. It was founded in 1966, and its members call themselves "progressive-liberals" or "left-liberals". In the 1989 election, it won 7.9 percent of the vote. It draws much of its strength from disaffected supporters of the Labor Party.

In 1975, the Catholic People's Party, the Anti-Revolutionary Party, and the Christian-Historical Union (CHU, Christelijk-Historische Unie) began a series of collaborative ventures that culminated in a merger to form the Christian Democratic Appeal (CDA, Christen Democratisch Appèl), which, being a centrist party, has headed all of the coalitions since 1977. In the 1989 election, the CDA received 35.3 percent of the vote.

1.3. Company organization[30]

Prior to 1970, there was only one kind of limited liability company in the Netherlands: the *naamloze vennootschap* (NV). As there was no Dutch equivalent of the German GmbH, company law was applicable to all companies, regardless of size, except for the publication requirement for financial statements. In 1970, a second

[30] Most of the contents of this section have been based on P. Sanders, *Dutch Company Law* (London: Oyez Publishing Limited, 1977), as updated from other sources.

legal form was created: the *besloten vennootschap met beperkte aansprakelijkheid* (BV, closed company with limited liability), whose shares are not easily transferred. Since then, the NV has been reserved for private companies whose shares may be freely traded either as bearer certificates or in registered form. So-called "large" NV's and BV's are those with assets of at least *f* 22.5m, which employ at least 100 workers, and which have a works council as required by law.[31] The remaining discussion in this section refers to the "large" NV, although many of the matters taken up are also applicable to the small NV and the BV.

Unlike companies (or corporations) in Anglo-Saxon countries, the limited liability company in the Netherlands may have as many as three boards that are entitled to designated spheres of authority in the operation of the affairs of the enterprise. The three boards are the management board (*raad van bestuur*), the supervisory board (*raad van commissarissen*), and the works council (*ondernemingsraad*). The management board consists of the company's top management, which devotes itself full-time to the running of the enterprise. Its members are known as "directors", or "managing directors", and its chairman (*voorzitter*), or president, is the company's chief executive officer.

The supervisory board, which was made mandatory for large NV's and BV's in 1971, is the panel of outside experts, such as lawyers, bankers, economists, and directors of other companies, who serve on a part-time basis to oversee the performance of management in the conduct of the affairs of the enterprise, and to provide management with advice. Appointments to the supervisory board are made by the board itself, subject to the constraint that its membership is broadly representative of the parties with an interest in the overall welfare of the enterprise. Candidates for appointment to the supervisory board may be nominated by the management board, the general meeting of shareholders, and the works council, and these candidates are to be among those considered when the supervisory board decides on new members. The shareholders and the works council (see below) have a limited right of veto in the selection of supervisory board members, on the ground that they are not representative. The supervisory board may appeal objections by the shareholders and the works council to the Enterprise Chamber (Ondernemingskamer), a special court attached to the Court of Justice at Amsterdam which hears cases on a number of aspects of company law. The works council may lodge a similar appeal.

Under the "right of inquiry", shareholders and the works council may petition the Enterprise Chamber when there is believed to have been misconduct by the management.

The members of the management board are appointed by the supervisory board after notification has been given to the general meeting of shareholders (or, if there is one, a committee of shareholders) and to the works council.

[31] Such companies are known as "*structuur*" NV's and BV's.

The supervisory board may also dismiss the directors but only after giving the shareholders meeting (or committee of shareholders) an opportunity to give its opinion, and after notifying the works council.

The supervisory board receives the annual financial statements prepared by management and decides what alterations need to be made before accepting them. The financial statements are then submitted simultaneously to the general meeting of shareholders and to the works council. The general meeting of shareholders cannot amend the annual financial statements, but is entitled only to approve or reject them. If they are rejected, a dividend cannot be distributed. Once the annual financial statements have been approved by the general meeting of shareholders, they are legally binding unless they are annulled or ordered to be revised by the Enterprise Chamber. The supervisory board is also empowered to decide whether to give its approval to certain important decisions made by the management board. Some exemptions apply to special companies.

The works council is composed of the elected representatives of the company's employees. The works council was established by the Act on Works Councils (Wet op de Ondernemingsraden) of 1950, and major amending legislation was passed in 1971. Since 1979, when the law was again amended, the membership of the works council has consisted entirely of employees' representatives. By law, one or more members of the supervisory board, together with a member of the management board, must attend a meeting of the works council at least twice a year.

A member of the management board must meet with the works council at least six times a year, and the employer is required to furnish the works council with the information necessary for the council to fulfill its functions. The employer is required to consult with the works council on certain important decisions, such as any substantial expansion, contraction or other change in the enterprise's business activities, or the termination of those activities or of any part thereof. At least twice a year, the general development of the enterprise's affairs must be discussed at a meeting of the works council. One of these meetings must deal with the financial position of the enterprise, while the other is to concern the general policy of the company toward its employees. In a limited number of areas, involving defined aspects of the company's employment policies and practices, the works council has the power of co-determination.

It is not the practice in the Netherlands for the supervisory board to have an "audit committee". The independent auditor is appointed by the general meeting of shareholders, or, in the event of its failure to do so, by the supervisory board. If the supervisory fails to act, the appointment is to be made by the management board. The auditor's report on the annual financial statements is presented to the supervisory board and the management board.

1.4. A sketch of the auditing profession[32]

As far as is known, the first firm to conduct audits in the Netherlands was "Het Bureel van Boekhouding 'Confidentia'", translated as "The Bookkeeping [or Accounting] Office 'Confidentia'", which was founded in Rotterdam on 1 January 1883. Among the functions that the firm said it performed were the keeping of account-books, "the auditing of branches in other locations and the preparation of their respective balance sheets", and "the carrying out of audits of records in which the principals have a particular interest".[33] Nonetheless, as Dijker has written, "in the main [at that time], accountants' duties confined themselves to the keeping of books, assisting in bookkeeping, and the performance of other office work".[34]

Using the establishment of the Institute of Chartered Accountants in England and Wales in 1880 as his example, E.W. Schallenberg, one of the partners in the "Confidentia" firm, founded (with four others) the Nederlandsch Instituut van Accountants (NIvA) in 1895. As there was no Dutch word that adequately captured the profession that the founders intended to launch, the term *accountant* was borrowed from Britain.

Whether the term *accountant*, as used by the Dutch during the twentieth century, has continued to mean what was intended in 1895, is not clear. While auditors writing in English language journals sometimes translate the present-day Nederlands Instituut van Registeraccountants (NIvRA) as the Dutch Institute of Registered Accountants, and almost always use the Dutch word *accountant* as the equivalent of the English word "accountant", in universities and in most other settings the Dutch terms *accountant* and *accountancy* are generally understood to mean auditor and auditing, respectively. Almost all of the usages of the Dutch term *accountant* in materials that are relevant to this study signify, in the authors' view, the meaning of auditor, not accountant.[35] There is, moreover,

---

[32] Materials of interest on the development of the auditing profession in the Netherlands are: Johan de Vries, *Geschiedenis der Accountancy in Nederland: Aanvang en Ontplooiing, 1895–1935* (Assen/Maastricht: Van Gorcum, 1985); A.L. de Bruyne, *De geschiedenis van de beroepsorganisatie der accountants in Nederland 1895–1975* (Alphen aan den Rijn: Samsom Uitgeverij b.v., 1980); Dr mr A. Sternheim, "Veertig jaren accountancy, 1895–1935", in *Gedenkboek: Nederlandsch Instituut van Accountants 1895–1935* (privately printed), pp. 7–59; *Een eeuw in balans: De wordingsgeschiedenis van Moret & Limperg, 1883–1983* (privately printed, 1983), esp. Chaps. 2–5; Berendsen, *op.cit.*; and J. Kraayenhof, "The Profession in the Netherlands: Sixty Years of Growth and Development", in *The Accountant*, vol. 133, no. 4215, 1 October 1955, pp. 382–390.

[33] See de Vries, *op. cit.*, p. 38, for an enumeration of the several functions that were mentioned in the firm's prospectus.

[34] R.A. Dijker, "Legislation for the Accounting Profession in Holland", in *International Congress on Accounting, 1929* (International Congress of Accountants, 1929), p. 133.

[35] It is true that the law applicable to *accountants-administratieconsulenten* (see below), known as the Wet op de Accountants-administratieconsulenten (Stb. 748), was approved on 13 December 1972, even though that law did not entitle *accountants-administratieconsulenten*

no precise term in the Dutch language to signify financial accounting, as that term is understood in Anglo-Saxon countries.[36] During most of its history, the NIvRA has focused almost exclusively on the role of the auditor, although in the last two decades it has devoted more of its energies to diverse aspects of accounting beyond auditing. The authors' preference is to translate the Dutch terms *accountant* and *accountancy* as auditor and auditing, respectively.

The story of the first half-century of the Dutch auditing profession may be divided into two parts: (1) the proliferation of auditing organizations, and (2) the striving to secure governmental regulation of the profession.

The Dutch penchant for individual expression has led to the founding, and eventual disappearance through merger or extinction, of so many organizations of auditors that, from the 1920's to the 1950's, there were, in most years, between ten and a dozen different such organizations competing with each other.[37] By far the most important organization was the NIvA. In 1927, for reasons that will be explained in the section on education for the profession, its major rival, the Society of Academically Trained Auditors (VAGA, Vereeniging van Academisch Gevormde Accountants), was founded. Following the War, the NIvA and the VAGA, though rival organizations, cooperated in a number of ventures. It was not until 1967, when the NIvRA was established, that only one organization of auditors, by then regulated by law, remained. At that time, the 2200 members of the NIvA, 300 of the VAGA, 100 of the Dutch Union of Auditors (Nederlandse Unie van Accountants), and 60 of the Dutch Brotherhood of Auditors (Nederlandse Broederschap van Accountants), the last surviving associations of auditors, transferred their activities to the NIvRA.[38]

In March 1967, a law enacted in June 1962 to regulate the auditing profession went into effect, as a result of which only *register accountants* could attest to the "faithfulness" ("*getrouwheid*") of audited financial statements. Previously, such representations based on audits could be made by any "expert" ("*deskundige*"),

---

to conduct audits. This is clearly an exception to general Dutch usage of the term "*accountant*", which we regard as an anomaly. See A.B. Frielink, *De GBR verklaard: Commentaar op Gedrags- en Beroepsregels Registeraccountants* (Amsterdam: Kosmos, 1974), pp. 104–105.

[36] The closest Dutch equivalents are *externe verslaggeving* and *externe berichtgeving*, both of which mean external financial reporting; *bedrijfsadministratie*, which encompasses financial and managerial accounting, including bookkeeping; and *boekhouding*, which refers to the bookkeeping (record-keeping) aspects of financial accounting.

While the Dutch language has incorporated the English terms "accountant" and "accountancy", the use of "accounting" in the Dutch-language literature is rare.

[37] A listing of the years in which auditing bodies were founded and merged during the period from 1895 to 1939, and their number of members as of 1 January 1940, was presented in a memorandum from the Ministry of Justice: "Memorie van antwoord betreffende het ontwerp van wet tot vaststelling van regelen betreffende het Accountantswezen (zitting 1939–1940; 72, no. 2)", in *Maandblad voor accountancy en bedrijfshuishoudkunde*, vol. 17, no. 4, April 1940, pp. 75–76. The authors are grateful to Willem Buijink for bringing this article to their attention.

[38] Arie L. de Bruyne, "Statutory regulation of the accountancy profession in The Netherlands", in *Journal UEC*, October 1967, p. 240.

as set forth in the Commercial Code of 1928. The absence of a law regulating the profession was a contributory factor in postponing legislation requiring companies to have their annual financial statements examined by an external auditor. It was not until passage of the Act on Annual Financial Statements of Enterprises in 1970 that Parliament imposed an external audit requirement on limited companies, although banks and insurance companies had been covered by earlier such legislation. Prior to the 1970 Act, the contents of company financial statements were unregulated, save for a 1929 law that required the separate reporting of eleven items on the asset side of the balance sheet.

The preponderance of NIvA/NIvRA's activities prior to the 1970's was directed toward the audit function: admitting new members on the basis of education and examination, setting forth the rules of professional conduct, and hearing cases of professional misconduct. In 1972, for the first time, the NIvRA approved a uniform wording and format for the auditor's report.[39]

The NIvA/NIvRA's contribution to the periodical literature of the profession has consisted of its journal, *de Accountant*, founded in 1895. Until the 1970's, *de Accountant* published few unsolicited articles, and was largely confined to examination questions and answers, committee reports, conference proceedings, speeches, official documents, the annual report and membership list of the NIvA/NIvRA, informative columns, and news notices. The NIvRA has also contributed to the serial literature, beyond periodicals. Since 1970, the NIvRA has published a numbered series of "NIvRA Monographs" (*NIVRA geschriften*), which have contained addresses and studies covering a broad range of issues of interest to the profession. Also, from the mid-1970's to 1987, the NIvRA published a numbered series of booklets, entitled *PILOT (Netherlands)*, which contained selected speeches and official documents, as well as discussions of recent developments relating to the profession, all rendered in the English language as information to non-Dutch readers.

The NIvA/NIvRA is governed by a management board whose chairman is the organization's president (*voorzitter*). In recent years, the president's term has been one year, although, beginning in December 1991, it will revert to two years. As of 31 August 1991, the NIvRA had 7593 members, including 1543 classified as non-active. Of the active members, 51.4 percent were in public practice.[40] The administrative office of the NIvA/NIvRA has always been in Amsterdam.

Each year an Accountantsdag (Auditors' Day) is celebrated, at which one or more major addresses are given on topics of professional interest before a large audience. For many years it was the practice to publish the addresses, together with the ensuing dialogue, in *de Accountant*. In fact, the first Accountantsdag, in 1907, was sponsored by the Dutch Auditors Society (NAV, Nederlandsche

[39] See "Uniforme accountantsverklaring", in *NIvRA Berichten*, vol. 6, no. 4, December 1972, p. 53.

[40] *Jaarverslag 90 91*, Nederlands Instituut van Registeraccountants, p. 26.

Accountants-Vereeniging), a body founded in 1906 by Th. Limperg Jr. and others, after Limperg had been expelled from the NIvA for defending free speech in the auditing literature. When the NAV and the NIvA agreed to combine on Limperg's terms in 1919, the Accountantsdag was continued by the merged entity.

Following the War, the NIvA's research and publication activities accelerated. In 1950, it established the Advisory Committee on Professional Matters (CAB, Commissie van Advies inzake Beroepsaangelegenheden), which proceeded to issue a series of reports on a wide array of topics of professional interest, all of which were published in *de Accountant*. In 1968–69, the CAB was replaced by three committees, one of which was the Advisory Committee on Annual Reporting (CAJ, Commissie van Advies inzake Jaarverslaggeving). The CAJ was charged with advising the management board on matters relating to company financial reporting and to prepare drafts for submission to the new Tripartite Study Group (TO, Tripartiete overleg). The TO was a body created at the suggestion of the Minister of Justice, and proceeded to issue statements of "Considered Views" on accounting principles. There were, in addition, study conferences and numerous other research initiatives.[41] In 1974, with the support of the NIvRA, the Limperg Instituut was founded, having the aim of encouraging and sponsoring research projects on accounting and auditing, and to coordinate its resources with those in the universities.

Another professional body whose members render accounting services to small and medium-sized businesses is the Nederlandse Orde van Accountants-Administratieconsulenten (NOvAA). It was founded in 1948 under the name Nederlandse Orde van Accountants, and adopted its present name in 1974. Its current membership is about 2500. The Order's members were regulated in 1972 under the Wet op de Accountants-administratieconsulenten, which also, beginning on 1 March 1974, regulated the use of the term "*accountant*". One of the most important functions of the Order's members is to compile and review the financial statements of small and medium-size companies. Members of the NOvAA are not authorized to conduct independent audits. In 1990, the Geelhoed Report was published,[42] in which recommendations were made concerning the practice rights of the members of the NIvRA and the NOvAA in the light of the Eighth Directive of the European Community.

---

[41] See de Bruyne, *op. cit.*, pp. 102–109. For a discussion in the English language, see Drs J. de Jong, "Accounting research for the profession in Holland", in *Canadian Chartered Accountant*, vol. 94, no. 2, February 1969, pp. 113–115.

[42] *Rapport van de Commissie Advisering Stroomlijning Accountantswetgeving* [Report of the Committee to Give Advice on Streamlining the Regulation of Auditors], Prof. mr L.A. Geelhoed, voorzitter, aan de Minister van Economische Zaken, 4 april 1990.

1.5. Universities, the NIvRA and education for the auditing profession

This section will deal with three topics: (1) the undergraduate programs of study in the universities, together with academic titles used in the universities; (2) the programs of study offered by the NIvRA and the universities for those who wish to enter the auditing profession; and (3) Th. Limperg's influence on accounting and auditing education, and the diminution of that influence in recent years.

1.5.1. The universities

At the present time, there are six universities that offer degree programs in economics and *bedrijfseconomie*:

- Erasmus Universiteit Rotterdam (Erasmus University, Rotterdam)
- Universiteit van Amsterdam (University of Amsterdam)
- Katholieke Universiteit Brabant te Tilburg (Catholic University of Brabant, in Tilburg)
- Rijksuniversiteit Groningen (State University of Groningen)
- Vrije Universiteit te Amsterdam (Free University, Amsterdam)
- Rijksuniversiteit Limburg (State University of Limburg)

In the Netherlands, economic science is divided into two parts: general economics (including micro and macro economics), and *bedrijfseconomie*. There is a close link between the two, and a strong foundation in general economics is considered to be essential for students of *bedrijfseconomie*.[43]

The degree program in *bedrijfseconomie* typically requires a period of four to five years of full-time study, and, at most universities, concludes with the writing of a major paper. Many Dutch educators regard the degree as being a closer equivalent to the American master's degree than to the American bachelor's degree.

[43] The term *bedrijfseconomie* is not susceptible to direct translation into English. Its closest English-language equivalent would be "business administration with a strong base of economic theory". Throughout the manuscript, *bedrijfseconomie*, the noun, and *bedrijfseconomisch(e)*, the adjective, will not be translated. In Germany and Italy, the terms "*betriebswirtschaftslehre*" and "*economia aziendale*", respectively, present similar problems of translation. For further discussion, see Anthony G. Hopwood and Hein Schreuder (editors), *European Contributions to Accounting Research: The Achievements of the Last Decade* (Amsterdam: VU Uitgeverij, 1984), pp. 7–8. Hopwood and Schreuder prefer "business economics" as the translation of "*bedrijfseconomie*". To the authors, however, "business economics" does not adequately capture the broad range of business administration-related subjects comprehended by *bedrijfseconomie*. The authors agree with Schreuder that a full appreciation of the differences between *bedrijfseconomie* and its nearest Anglo-American counterpart requires a thorough understanding of both the Dutch and Anglo-American worlds of thought. Hein Schreuder, "Accounting Research, Practice, and Culture: A European Perspective", in Barry E. Cushing (editor), *Accounting and Culture* (Sarasota, FL: American Accounting Association, 1987), pp. 19–20.

Curricula and teaching philosophies vary from university to university. Nonetheless, a sketch of the approach at the Vrije Universiteit may convey a useful impression of the scope of the degree program. The student's first year, known as the "propaedeuse", contains a strong component of micro and macro economics, and public finance and monetary theory, together with work in mathematics and statistics, financial and management accounting, and finance. In subsequent years, further work is built on these foundations, including especially accounting and finance. Courses are also offered on such subjects as law, organization theory and management, economic philosophy, marketing, and information systems. Most of the courses are taught in the lecture mode, but each student must take at least four seminars. At the conclusion of the degree program, the student completes a research thesis.

The university degree conferred upon a student who successfully completes the program of studies in *bedrijfseconomie* is known as the *doctorandus*, abbreviated as "drs", which means "candidate for a doctorate degree". Somewhat confusingly, the degree program is known as the *doctoraal*, even though it culminates in the awarding of the *doctorandus*, not the doctorate. (The same degree title is given to graduates in the other social sciences, in the humanities, and in the sciences.) Only a small fraction of recipients of this degree continue for the doctorate, which is abbreviated as "dr". In the Netherlands, the doctorate is awarded after an acceptable dissertation has been presented and defended. There is no required coursework in the program leading toward the doctorate.

Students graduating in law (an undergraduate field in Dutch universities) receive the degree *meester in de rechten*, abbreviated as "mr", which means Master in Laws. The degree title for graduates in a university course of studies in engineering is *ingenieur*, abbreviated as "ir". For graduates of engineering programs at Higher Technical Schools (Hogere Technische Scholen), the abbreviation is "ing". It is the custom in the Netherlands to place these abbreviations in front of the recipients' names, and that custom has been followed in this book. (Once the holder of a *doctorandus* obtains the doctorate degree, the "drs" is dropped and is replaced by "dr".)

Today, it is estimated that there are between 130 and 150 individuals who teach accounting and auditing in the universities. Their titles, in descending order, are *hoogleraar* (professor), *universitair hoofddocent* (equivalent to associate professor or senior lecturer), and *universitair docent* (equivalent to assistant professor or lecturer). The great majority of professors are part-time, their primary occupations being as managers or partners in auditing firms, executives in companies or financial institutions, or members of consulting firms. The vast majority of the associate and assistant professors are also part-time, as they are working on their doctoral dissertations or are employed in, or associated with, auditing firms, companies or financial institutions, or consulting firms.

1.5.2. Education to enter the auditing profession

A few years after it was formed in 1895, the NIvA (the predecessor of the NIvRA) began giving a course of part-time instruction for prospective members.[44] Since the establishment of the NIvRA in 1967, the course of studies has led to the title of Registered Auditor (*registeraccountant*), abbreviated as "RA". Typically, students enter the NIvRA program after completing secondary school or after finishing a four-year course in accounting or business administration in a higher school of vocational education. These schools, known by the acronym "HEAO", emphasize the practical aspects of accounting and business administration and place less importance on a theoretical foundation in economics. The graduates of these institutions who wish to pursue a career in auditing may, in most cases, enroll in the NIvRA program or continue their education in a university. The NIvRA requires both written and oral examinations of all students following completion of their coursework. In recent years, between 55 and 65 percent of new *registeraccountants* have gone through the NIvRA program.

In all six of the aforementioned universities, one- or two-year *post-doctoraal* programs are offered to students on a part-time basis toward fulfillment of the requirements to become a *registeraccountant*. These courses are given only on Fridays, when release time is provided by the students' employers, and they cover auditing, systems and financial reporting. Similar to the NIvRA program, the universities require both written and oral examinations of all students. The NIvRA's Examinations Bureau works to assure that the standard of pre-professional education (known as the *accountancy opleiding*) in the universities is equal to that of the NIvRA.

The first tertiary-level educational institution to offer an *accountancy opleiding* was the Nederlandsche Handels-Hoogeschool (Netherlands School of Commerce), in Rotterdam, which began such instruction in 1915, two years after the school was founded.[45] In 1936, it was renamed the Nederlandsche Economische Hoogeschool (Netherlands School of Economics), and, in 1973, it became the faculty of economics of the newly established Erasmus Universiteit Rotterdam.[46]

---

[44] For a history of the NIvA's educational program and examinations, see Drs I. Kleerekoper, "Terugblik op 70 jaar opleiding en examens", in *de Accountant*, vol. 71, no. 4, December 1964, pp. 238–245. The authors are grateful to Drs G.H. Karreman for bringing this article to their attention.

[45] The *accountancy opleiding* in the other five universities began in the following years: Amsterdam, 1929; Tilburg, 1931; Groningen, 1952; Vrije Universiteit, 1957; and Limburg, 1987.

[46] The history of the pre-university period is treated in two volumes: Dr J.H. van Stuijvenberg, *De Nederlandsche Economische Hoogeschool 1913–1963* (Rotterdam/'s-Gravenhage: Nijgh & Van Ditmar, 1963), and Dr P.W. Klein, *De Nederlandse Economische Hogeschool 1963–1973* (Rotterdam: Universitaire Pers, 1974).

1.5.3. Limperg's influence on accounting and auditing education

Th. Limperg Jr. (1879–1961), who was professor of *bedrijfseconomie* and auditing at the Gemeentelijke Universiteit van Amsterdam (Municipal University of Amsterdam, today known as the Universiteit van Amsterdam), created and developed the discipline of *bedrijfseconomie*, using a normative deductive theory constructed within a general economic framework. He was also the dominant figure in the NIvA's program of auditing studies, and he dismissed the more pragmatic, inductive approach of the Rotterdam school as being beneath the high scientific standard that he had established. Under Limperg's influence, the NIvA refused to admit Rotterdam graduates as members. Thereupon, in 1927, a group of Rotterdam teachers and graduates established their own auditing body, the Society of Academically Trained Auditors (VAGA, Vereeniging van Academisch Gevormde Accountants),[47] which was to become the principal rival to the NIvA until 1967, when the two bodies merged to form the NIvRA.

One of the effects of Limperg's influence on the NIvA program and at the Gemeentelijke Universiteit van Amsterdam, where he was in charge of the *bedrijfseconomie* program from 1922 (and, from the late 1920's, also in charge of the auditing program) until his retirement in 1949, was that many auditors became dedicated advocates of his theory of current cost (replacement value) accounting.[48] Limperg's theory was inculcated in the students in both of these programs of study, as well as at the NIvA. Through Limperg's disciples, as professors and practitioners, his theory dominated teaching, writing and practice for several decades.[49] There were opponents of his theory, and these were mainly

---

[47] For further discussion, see de Vries, *Geschiedenis*, *op. cit.*, pp. 150–155.

[48] Limperg's fundamental contribution was the theory of "replacement value" (*vervangingswaarde*) accounting, but, subsequently, this theory was refined and elaborated into his theory of current value (*actuele waarde*) accounting, embracing choices among "replacement value", exit price (*direkte opbrengstwaarde*), and present value (*indirekte opbrengstwaarde*) elements. This complex of values ordinarily reduces to the use of "replacement value" accounting. Hence, Limperg's theoretical contribution is customarily referred to as "replacement value" accounting, rather than current value accounting.

Although many Dutch authors use the term "replacement value" when writing in the English language, the term "current cost" is preferred by the authors, as being more in line with usage in the Anglo-Saxon literature.

[49] For a discussion of the role played by Limperg as well as a valuable perspective on the development of the accounting research literature in the Netherlands, see Jan Klaassen and Hein Schreuder, "Accounting research in the Netherlands", in Hopwood and Schreuder, *op. cit.*, pp. 113–131. Three useful discussions by A. van Seventer are: "Accounting in the Netherlands", in H. Peter Holzer (editor), *International Accounting* (New York: Harper & Row, Publishers, 1984), pp. 345–368; "The Continuity Postulate in the Dutch Theory of Business Income", in *The International Journal of Accounting*, vol. 4, no. 2, Spring 1969, pp. 1–19; and "Replacement Value Theory in Modern Dutch Accounting", in *The International Journal of Accounting*, vol. 11, no. 1, Fall 1975, pp. 67–94. Also see Dick H. van Offeren, "Replacement Value Accounting: Theory and Practice", in *Advances in International Accounting*, vol. 2, 1988, pp. 23–31. For an exposition of Limperg's theory by one of his strict followers, see

the teachers in Rotterdam, led by Prof.dr N.J. Polak (1887–1948).[50]

To a growing degree in the last two decades, accounting academics have come to acquire an interest in "accounting principles" as developed abroad, and in financial reporting issues such as deferred taxation, leases, pensions, goodwill, and foreign exchange. For decades, it had been believed by many academics that Limperg's theoretical formulation was a sufficient model for resolving all accounting questions.[51] But there has been a growing realization that the Limpergian construct, "value and profit" (*waarde en winst*), does not provide answers to specific accounting problems, which has led to greater attention being paid to the problem-oriented accounting literature developed in North America and the United Kingdom.[52] At the same time, company law academics have come to acquire a greater interest in accounting matters. This refocusing of interests by

---

Abram Mey, "Theodore Limperg and his Theory of Values and Costs", *Abacus*, vol. 2, no. 1, September 1966, pp. 3–23. For a profile on Limperg, see Jules W. Muis, "Wie was Limperg? Outcast who blazed the CCA trail", in *Accountancy* (journal of the English Institute), vol. 91, no. 1046, October 1980, pp. 69–70.

An English translation of four of Limperg's essays, which, together with his address given at the International Congress of Accountants in 1926, expound his "theory of inspired confidence" and his view of the role of the auditor, were published (with commentaries by David Flint and Gijs G.M. Bak) in *The social responsibility of the auditor* (Amsterdam: Limperg Instituut, 1985).

For works on Limperg in the Dutch language, see *Reflecties op Limperg*, opstellen over ontwikkelingen in onderneming, bedrijfseconomie en accountancy sinds de dertiger jaren (Deventer: Kluwer, 1979); P.J. van Sloten, "Theodore Limperg: Systeembouwer en pragmaticus", in Prof.dr A.J. Vermaat, Prof.dr J.J. Klant and Prof.drs J.R. Zuidema (editors), *Van liberalisten tot instrumentalisten: Anderhalve eeuw economisch denken in Nederland* (Leiden/Antwerpen: H.E. Stenfert Kroese B.V., 1987), pp. 157–182; the "Limperg-nummer" of the *Maandblad voor accountancy en bedrijfshuishoudkunde*, vol. 33, no. 11, December 1959; and *Herinneringen aan Limperg* (Amsterdam: Limperg Instituut, 1979).

A six-volume collection of edited notes taken from Limperg's lectures is *Bedrijfseconomie: Verzameld werk van Prof.dr. Th. Limperg Jr.* (Deventer: Uitgeversmaatschappij Æ.E. Kluwer, 1968).

[50] Prof.drs R. Burgert is the leading contemporary critic of Limperg. See his "Reservations about 'Replacement Value' Accounting in the Netherlands", in *Abacus*, vol. 8, no. 2, December 1972, pp. 111–126. At the first annual "*f*ma-congres" in June 1990, held at the Erasmus Universiteit Rotterdam, Burgert delivered a lecture on Polak's work: "De betekenis van Prof. Dr. N.J. Polak voor 'Financial Accounting' en 'Management Accounting' ", in C.D. Knoops, J. Dijksma and W.M. de Pon (editors), *fMA-kroniek 1990* (Groningen: Wolters-Noordhoff, 1990), pp. 3–20.

[51] See, for example, H.W. Hageman, "Reserve, geheime en stille", an entry in Prof. A. Goudeket, Prof. A.M. van Rietschoten and A.F. Tempelaar (editors), "Deel V: Controleleer", in Prof. Dr. A. Mey (general editor), *Encyclopedie van de bedrijfseconomie* (Bussum: Uitgeversmaatschappij W. de Haan, 1970), p. 208.

[52] Traas has argued that *bedrijfseconomie* as a whole should be reformulated. Instead of being exclusively a deductive theory constrained in a narrow cost-benefit framework, it should take greater cognizance of the legal, political and social environment in which policies are made and problems are solved in the business world. Prof.dr L. Traas, "Over de noodzaak tot heroriëntering van de (klassieke) bedrijfseconomie", in *de Accountant*, vol. 88, no. 3, November 1981, pp. 146–155.

accounting and company law academics has been influenced by a series of developments: the passage of the "modern" Act on Annual Financial Statements of Enterprises in 1970; the publication of "Considered Views" (*Beschouwingen*) by the TO beginning in the early 1970's; the increasing worldwide impact of overseas standard-setting bodies such as the Financial Accounting Standards Board and the International Accounting Standards Committee, both starting in 1973; the decisions handed down by the Enterprise Chamber (Ondernemingskamer) beginning in 1977; and the approval of the European Economic Community's Fourth Directive in 1978, followed by Parliament's approval of the adaptation law in 1983.[53]

University accounting curricula have begun to reflect a gradual restructuring of the literature along lines that have been seen in Anglo-Saxon countries, and there has been an increasing tendency to use textual materials written in the English language, especially ones originating in the United States. Thus, "value and profit" gradually began to disappear from university curricula.[54] From 1969–70 onward at the Vrije Universiteit, two leading American textbooks, *Management Accounting: Text and Cases*[55], by Robert N. Anthony, and *Accounting Theory*, by Eldon S. Hendriksen, became staples in the curriculum. In 1975, when *A New Introduction to Financial Accounting*, by Robert G. May, Gerhard G. Mueller and Thomas H. Williams, was published, it was used in place of the financial accounting portion of Anthony's textbook.[56] At the Erasmus Universiteit Rotterdam, a textbook based on the 1970 law on financial statements was published in 1972[57] and became required reading in the program of studies. In the early 1980's, a series of study units in "external financial reporting" (*externe verslaggeving*) was introduced into the NIvRA's program, replacing "value and profit".[58] The first accounting textbook with "Financial Reporting" in its title

---

[53] Interview with Prof.drs G.G.M. Bak, 20 November 1990; and A. van Seventer, "Accounting in the Netherlands", *op.cit.*, esp. pp. 358–363.

For a discussion of the evolving relation between *bedrijfseconomie* and both the auditing profession and education for the profession, see Prof.dr André J. Bindenga, *Dutch accountancy: A managerial economics based approach*, PILOT (Netherlands) 13 (Amsterdam: Nederlands Instituut van Registeraccountants, February 1983).

[54] In 1978, "value and profit" was replaced by such topical headings as "financial statements" (*jaarrekening*) and "financial reporting" (*jaarverslaggeving*) in the annual index to the leading accounting research journal, *Maandblad voor accountancy en bedrijfshuishoudkunde*, which had been founded by Limperg. "Value and profit" had been a topical heading since 1951. This was a significant acknowledgment of the changing accounting landscape in the Netherlands.

[55] Notwithstanding its title, half of the textbook dealt with financial accounting.

[56] Interview with Prof.dr L. Traas, 10 September 1991.

[57] Prof.mr P. Sanders, Prof.drs G.L. Groeneveld and Prof.drs R. Burgert (editors), *De jaarrekening nieuwe stijl* (The Financial Statements, New Style) (Alphen aan den Rijn: Samsom Uitgeverij N.V., 1972).

[58] In the mid-1970's, the NIvRA introduced elective courses for the first time. Since the NIvRA's foundation courses in financial accounting were based entirely on the "value and profit" approach, Prof.dr L. Traas, who was given charge of the elective course on *bedrijfseco-*

was published only as recently as 1987.[59]

In the last several years, perhaps reflecting the changed approach to accounting education, university accounting and auditing researchers have begun to show an interest in the kinds of research pioneered in North America and the UK during the last quarter century.

Authors have written about the "Amsterdam school" and the "Rotterdam school",[60] which flourished at their respective institutions from the 1920's to the 1970's. Yet the latter was more aptly described as an "approach" than a "school", as it was not associated with an internally consistent theory or a cohesive body of thought.[61] Rotterdam was known mainly for its pragmatic posture, a recent example of which was Prof.drs R. Burgert's "different concepts of profit for different purposes".[62] Today, however, one can no longer talk of an "Amsterdam school" or even of a distinctive "Rotterdam approach". There are no longer any disciples to carry on the tradition of the Amsterdam school, and other universities have moved closer to the Rotterdam approach.

Nonetheless, current cost continues to be an active topic of discussion, reflecting, among other things, the cumulative effect of the Limpergian literature.

---

nomie, built the course around the teaching materials being used at the Vrije Universiteit, as representing a more modern approach to the subject. Among the instructors were J. Klaassen, A.J. Bindenga and H.L. Brink. Interview with Prof.dr L. Traas, 10 September 1991.

59 Prof.dr J. Klaassen and Prof.drs G.G.M. Bak, *Externe verslaggeving* (Leiden: H.E. Stenfert Kroese B.V., 1987).

60 See Prof.dr A.J. Bindenga, "De Rotterdamse School", in *de Accountant*, vol. 96, no. 10, June 1990, pp. 578–587.

61 See Klaassen and Schreuder, *op. cit.*, p. 114, and H. Schreuder, *Economie (en) Bedrijven* (Assen/Maastricht: Van Gorcum, 1985), pp. 4–8. J. Brands reached a similar conclusion in "Amsterdamsche school der bedrijfseconomie contra Rotterdamsche school?", in *Weerspiegelde gedachten*, papers presented to Prof.dr N.J. Polak on his 25th anniversary as professor at the Nederlandsche Economische Hoogeschool, 1922–1947 (Haarlem: De Erven F. Bohn N.V., 1948), pp. 27–32.

But Muysken and Schreuder have pointed out that the attempt to construct a unified theory of *bedrijfseconomie* on the basis of deductive reasoning could only be made at a cost. They cited a number of research fields (an example was organization theory) that could not be addressed effectively within the confining framework of Limperg's *bedrijfseconomie*. By contrast, the Rotterdam approach enabled its adherents to deal with all problems encountered in a practical business environment. Prof.dr J. Muysken and Prof.dr H. Schreuder, *Economische wetenschappen: eenheid in verscheidenheid?* (Assen/Maastricht: Van Gorcum, 1985), pp. 29–31.

62 See Burgert, "Reservations", *op. cit.*, p. 124. In 1967, Burgert gave a major address at the annual Accountantsdag. The "*preadvies*" (prepared paper) that was submitted for the Accountantsdag was "Bedrijfseconomisch aanvaardbare grondslagen voor de gepubliceerde jaarrekening", which was published in *de Accountant*, vol. 74, no. 4, September 1967, pp. 153–192; Burgert's oral remarks made at the presentation, together with the discussion by Prof.dr J.L. Bouma, were published under the same title in *de Accountant*, vol. 74, no. 9, February 1968, pp. 494–523.

1.6. Professional journals and the financial press

1.6.1. Professional journals

In addition to the NIvA/NIvRA's monthly journal, *de Accountant*, mentioned in the section on the auditing profession, there are several other journals to which auditors contribute articles. Two of the journals were founded by Th. Limperg Jr. and his colleagues. The first of these was *Accountancy*, which was launched in 1903. In 1923, when Limperg resigned from the editorial board after a disagreement with the publisher, the journal changed character and lost most of its standing among auditors. The journal discontinued publication after the volume for 1936. Limperg's second journal, which became by far the more important of the two, was the *Maandblad voor accountancy en bedrijfshuishoudkunde*, which began publication in 1924 and has come to be the leading journal of accounting and auditing scholarship. In 1990, the journal adopted a more modern title, *Maandblad voor accountancy en bedrijfseconomie*, which the authors would translate as the "Monthly Journal of Auditing and *Bedrijfseconomie*". *Bedrijfshuishoudkunde* was an older and more cumbersome term for what is today known as *bedrijfseconomie*.

The NIvRA also publishes *NIvRA berichten*, a membership newsletter. It contains announcements of importance to members, and has been issued since 1967.

The *Pacioli Journaal*, begun in 1987, is published bimonthly by the Kosten en Winst Dispuut "Pacioli" (Cost and Profit Student Society "Pacioli") of the Faculty of Economics, Erasmus Universiteit Rotterdam. Although it is a student publication, faculty members serve on an advisory board. Most of its articles are concerned with accounting and auditing issues.

Articles dealing with the regulation of accounting and auditing, written by auditors as well as lawyers, are often to be found in two leading journals on company law. *De Naamlooze Vennootschap* (The Public Limited Company), was founded in 1922, and is currently published monthly. The other legal journal, *TVVS/Maandblad voor ondernemingsrecht en rechtspersonen* (TVVS/Monthly Journal for Enterprise Law and Corporate Entities), was founded in 1958 as the *Tijdschrift voor vennootschappen, verenigingen en stichtingen*. The latter, which may be translated as the "Review of Companies, Societies and Foundations", was converted to the short title of *TVVS* some years afterward.

A journal oriented toward business administration and accounting is *Maandblad voor Bedrijfsadministratie en Bedrijfsorganisatie* (Monthly Journal of Accounting and Organization), which was founded in 1894 as the *Maandblad voor het Boekhouden* (Monthly Journal of Bookkeeping).

Another journal for which auditors write articles is the *Economisch Statistische Berichten* (Economic and Statistical Reports), which is said to be the most widely read scientific magazine in the Netherlands. It has been published weekly since 1916.

1.6.2. Financial press

The leading daily financial newspaper in the Netherlands is *Het Financieele Dagblad* (The Financial Daily), which has been published since 1943, succeeding both *Het Amsterdamsch Effectenblad* (The Amsterdam Securities Newspaper) and *De Dagelijksche Beurscourant* (The Daily Stock Exchange Newspaper). Its coverage of business, finance, and economics is extensive, but it does not place much emphasis on editorial comment. (In each issue, a half-page of news summaries is presented in English, and on Saturdays an additional full page appears in English.) *FEM* (Financial and Economic Magazine) is a biweekly publication which dates from 1970.

All of the daily newspapers contain one or two pages or a regular section on business, finance and the economy, and on one day each week several papers devote an entire section to such coverage, usually on Saturday. Two daily newspapers that were founded in the 19th century mainly to serve the business community, *Algemeen Handelsblad* (General Commercial Newspaper) and the *Nieuwe Rotterdamse Courant* (New Rotterdam Newspaper), were merged in 1970 to become the *NRC Handelsblad*, which, as an evening paper, "continues the tone of mildly progressive solidity for an educated, business-oriented readership".[63] *De Volkskrant* (The People's Newspaper), originally a Catholic paper, is a well-regarded daily that espouses left-wing views. *De Telegraaf* (The Telegraph) is the daily with the largest circulation, and aims at the mass market. It is "conservative and middle-brow".[64] *Het Parool* (The Watchword) emerged out of the resistance during World War II. It supports the Socialist movement. *Trouw* (Loyalty) also had its start during the War, and was for many years a forum for the views of the Reformed Churches. But today it has a somewhat more general focus. The *Algemeen Dagblad* (General Daily) is a "middle-of-the-road morning paper attracting a large audience".[65]

The oldest of the weeklies, *HP/De Tijd*, was the result of a recent merger between the *Haagse Post* (The Hague Post), a weekly founded in 1914 by S.F. van Oss, a crusading financial journalist, and *De Tijd* (The Times), also a weekly. In the 1940's and 1950's, the *Haagse Post*, as part of its broad coverage of news

---

63 Shetter, *op. cit.*, p. 198. Shetter has been used for much of the information in the section on the financial press. An encyclopedic work covering financial journalism from 1850 to 1914 is H.G.A. Vissink, *Economic and Financial Reporting in England and the Netherlands* (Assen/Maastricht: Van Gorcum, 1985). Another useful source is Dr. Maarten Schneider in collaboration with Dr. Joan Hemels, *De Nederlandse krant 1618–1978: Van "nieuwstydinghe" tot dagblad* (Baarn: Het Wereldvenster, 1979).

64 Shetter, *op. cit.*, p. 197.

65 *Ibid.*, p. 198. Shetter also characterizes the newspaper as "mildly progressive", which the authors have reason to question.

and events, carried lively commentary on business and financial matters. *Elsevier* is a generalist weekly news magazine, and *Quote*, a monthly, was founded in 1986 and is known for its aggressive reporting, occasionally dealing with business and finance. *Intermediair*, a weekly that was begun as a source of information about job opportunities for recent graduates of the higher technical and business administration schools, also contains articles on business and finance topics. More than half of its pages are devoted to employment advertising.

In the 1950's and 1960's, the financial press followed company financial reporting with a critical eye, but since the passage of the Act on Annual Financial Statements in 1970, its coverage has been more descriptive than critical, and relatively little attention has been given to utterances by the TO and the Council on Annual Reporting (RJ, Raad voor de Jaarverslaggeving).

1.7. Some factors impinging on the framework of financial reporting

There are several factors that can influence the framework within which decisions are made on (1) the items that should be included in the body of the financial statements, and the procedures to be used when determining their amounts, and (2) the contents of the footnotes and other financial disclosures that should accompany the financial statements. The aim of this section is to discuss several of these factors that are important in a number of countries with which the Netherlands is often compared, but are not important in the Netherlands. An understanding of these differences will assist the reader in appreciating why financial reporting, and the organizational process by which decisions are taken to change financial reporting, are different in the Netherlands.

1.7.1. Irrelevance of the tax law

Unlike most other Continental European countries, the law of income taxation does not govern financial reporting in the Netherlands. Beginning with an income tax act passed in 1914, "sound business practice" ("*goed koopmansgebruik*") has been used as the gauge of proper reporting to the fiscal authority, and while the organized accounting profession has sometimes embraced the same criterion as the benchmark for company financial reporting, in actual fact the two approaches to determining a company's profit, at least for large companies, have developed independently of each other. For example, current cost, which has been used by some companies in their financial statements, has never been allowed for income taxation purposes.

Small and medium-sized companies in the Netherlands tend to use tax rules in drawing up their financial statements, chiefly to avoid keeping two sets of records. A similar practice is followed by many such companies in the United

States.

No research has been conducted in the Netherlands to explain why the Dutch are more like the British and the Irish than like their neighbors on the Continent in regard to the relationship between financial reporting and tax reporting. A suggestion by a leading Dutch tax scholar is that, perhaps, the early establishment of two very important Anglo-Dutch multinationals, Royal Dutch/Shell and Unilever, contributed to a tilting of fiscal legislation more toward the British model than the Continental model.[66] Nobes has placed the Netherlands in a class with the United States and the United Kingdom with respect to the separateness of taxation and financial reporting, since these are all "countries with an older tradition of published accounting, where commercial rules have come first".[67] One could also cite the deep-seated desire of the Dutch to remain as free of regulation as possible, and thus avoid the importation of a detailed tax law into a system of financial reporting that had been, until 1970, influenced only to a minor degree by statutory prescription. Another possible explanation is that Parliament, when enacting tax legislation, has left it to the courts to determine the meaning of "sound business practice", and it appears that the judges were not always informed about what was considered by auditors to be sound financial reporting (including the principles of *bedrijfseconomie*). The courts may also have been influenced by the desire to avoid subjective judgments in connection with tax collection policies. Whatever the explanation, one must not think of Dutch financial reporting in the same mold as that of most Continental countries as regards the influence of income tax legislation.

1.7.2. "Comparability" not a governing consideration

As will become evident in the chapters dealing with the historical development of the changes in Dutch financial reporting, the objective of promoting "comparability" among the financial statements of different companies has never been an important issue. Indeed, to many auditors of the Limperg school, it seemed natural that comparability was not a problem, since the very use of current cost accounting would, in their view, promote comparability better than would any other approach.

Since 1970, the Dutch law on financial reporting has been unique in the world by requiring that the financial statements furnish the "insight" required to enable the formation of a sound judgment into financial position and the results of operations, and, to the extent possible, into solvency and liquidity.[68] Com-

[66] Interview with Prof.dr F.H.M. Grapperhaus, 19 November 1990.

[67] Christopher Nobes, "The Causes of Financial Reporting Differences", in Christopher Nobes and Robert Parker (editors) *Issues in Multinational Accounting* (Deddington, Oxford: Philip Allan Publishers Limited, 1988), p. 37.

[68] By contrast, some companies laws, such as those in the United Kingdom and Australia, re-

parability has never been mentioned in the law on financial reporting or in the statements issued by TO and the RJ (i.e., the tripartite bodies). The implication of this position is that the financial statements are seen by auditors and legislators more as a report on stewardship than as a vehicle for providing investors with information to make decisions when choosing between the shares of different companies. The financial information is, to be sure, being furnished to investors, but, without a concern for comparability, one might argue that it is difficult to use the information when making investment decisions.

Given the historical influence of the Limperg school and this statutory premise, one can better understand the disinclination of leading members of the Dutch auditing profession to argue that the range of acceptable valuation and income determination principles should be narrowed to the point that "like things look alike, and unlike things look different", a view that was pressed by leaders of the American Institute of Certified Public Accountants (AICPA) in the 1960's,[69] and that has mirrored the thinking of the US Securities and Exchange Commission (SEC).

1.7.3. Absence of a securities commission

Since the early 1970's, a considerable number of countries have established securities commissions. The Netherlands has not been among them. In the United States, one of the most powerful forces behind the labyrinth of detail that one finds in pronouncements on accounting standards, especially those issued by the Financial Accounting Standards Board, has been the SEC. (Another force has been the specter of lawsuits in a judicially hyperactive society.) In the USA and a few other countries, securities commissions have requested that certain issues appear on the agendas of standard-setting bodies. The SEC, especially, has pressed for a prompt and definitive resolution of those issues. None of these pressures exists in the Netherlands. The tripartite body in the Netherlands has added subjects to its agenda on its own volition, and it has set its own pace for proceeding toward a resolution. It has introduced as much detail in its statements as it has thought appropriate.

---

quire that the financial statements give "a true and fair view", without saying why, and toward what end, the "true and fair view" is useful. In the United States, financial statements are to "present fairly the financial position and the results of operations, in conformity with generally accepted accounting principles", but, again, the objective to be attained by fair presentation is not mentioned. (In the United States, conformity with generally accepted accounting principles is, in the great majority of instances, the controlling factor.) In still other countries, the governing law requires that financial statements adhere to specified rules, again without a statement of purpose. Only in the Dutch law is the objective articulated, and it is the overriding criterion.

[69] See, for example, Robert M. Trueblood, "Accounting Principles: The Board and Its Problems', in *Empirical Research in Accounting: Selected Studies 1966* (Chicago: The Institute of Professional Accounting, 1967), p. 189. At the time of making the statement, Trueblood was AICPA president.

Since 1971, the Netherlands has had an Enterprise Chamber, which is a branch of the Court of Justice at Amsterdam.[70] It hears cases where companies' financial statements have been alleged to deviate from the law, and it can order companies to issue revised financial statements. In the 1960's, when consideration was given to establishing a Companies Commission in the Netherlands, with points of similarity to the SEC, it was decided instead to create a judicial organ, the Enterprise Chamber. It is the only body that can give a stimulus to the tripartite body to place particular issues on its agenda, when it announces a decision that calls into question an earlier statement of views, which does not occur frequently.

1.7.4. Absence of a "standards" program

Since 1971, the process by which the tripartite body has developed statements of views on accounting principles has been, in contrast with those in such countries as the USA, the UK, Canada, and Australia, comparatively unregulated by government. Furthermore, also unlike the regulatory climate in those countries, Dutch companies and auditors are free to accept the statements of views, or ignore them. If a company's financial statements reflect a material departure from the stated views of the tripartite body, it is virtually unknown for either the company or the auditor to draw attention to this fact, let alone quantify the effect of the departure. Owing to these significant differences in process and impact from those associated with "standard-setting programs", the authors do not use the term "standards" when discussing the program in the Netherlands. Nor do the Dutch. Since 1971, two terms have been used to describe the statements of views issued by the tripartite body: Considered Views (*Beschouwingen*) and Guidelines (*Richtlijnen*).[71] Their contents are tolerant of a greater degree of flexibility of accounting practice than is characteristic of statements of "standards" in those other countries. Moreover, they imply no imperative greater than the reasoning expressed in the statements themselves, and there is no pressure imposed by government and no force exerted by the NIvRA to see that they are actually adopted by companies. The extent of the NIvRA's actions in this direction is limited to (1) the work of a committee that contacts companies and auditors on a confidential basis to discuss apparent departures from the statements of views,

[70] See Jan Klaassen, "An Accounting Court: The Impact of the Enterprise Chamber on Financial Reporting in the Netherlands", in *The Accounting Review*, vol. 55, no. 2, April 1980, pp. 327–341.

[71] A former chairman of the tripartite body has said that "the policy of publishing the pronouncements as 'considerations' (*beschouwingen*) rather than 'standards' has eased their acceptance". Prof.drs J.W. Schoonderbeek, "The Dutch Tripartite Accounting Standards Committee", in *The Tripartite Accounting Standards Committee*, PILOT (Netherlands) 10 (Amsterdam: Nederlands Instituut van Registeraccountants, December 1980), p. 8. (The title of Schoonderbeek's paper and that of the booklet in which it appears are a rare example of the use of "standards" in the Dutch literature. One supposes that the author and editor sought to accommodate the English-language publication to usage in the English-speaking world.)

(2) the issuance every other year of a survey that reports, without disclosing company names, the degree to which the statements are actually followed by a sample of listed companies, and (3) the work of its Advisory Committee on Annual Reporting which does most of the drafting for the tripartite body.

This preference for not referring to a "standard-setting program" in the Netherlands has some historical justification. The term "standards" was formally introduced into the institutional literature to describe a program for recommending sound accounting practice in 1969–70, when the Institute of Chartered Accountants in England and Wales announced its "Statement of Intent on Accounting Standards in the 1970s".[72] Two of the essential elements in the English Institute's new program, in which all of the other major accountancy bodies in the UK and Ireland eventually joined, were "narrowing the areas of difference and variety in accounting practice" and "the disclosure of departures from established definitive accounting standards". Neither of these elements, the movement toward comparability (see above) and the required disclosure of departures, has matured as an issue in the Netherlands. The Dutch program of issuing statements of views on accounting principles has points of similarity with the English Institute's series of "Recommendations on Accounting Principles" that were issued from 1942 to 1969.[73] The tripartite body's statements of views are "the authoritative opinions of an influential private group",[74] as was the case with the English Institute's Recommendations. It was up to companies and auditors to decide whether they should be followed. But the two programs differ in two respects. First, in the UK from 1942 to 1969, the English Institute committee that did the original drafting was never permitted to select new agenda items or issue Recommendations on its own authority. New topics had to be approved by a more senior committee, and the drafts had to pass through a network of regional committees and the same senior committee before being submitted to the governing Council, which alone had the authority to decide whether they would be issued.[75] The statements of views published in the Netherlands are issued on the sole authority of the tripartite body, which deputizes a committee of the NIvRA to do most of the drafting. Second, the tripartite body has not been a committee of the NIvRA, but instead is a joint committee composed of delegations of auditors, employers/preparers, and users (formerly: employees). Since statements of views are, as a practical matter, issued only with the unani-

---

[72] See "Statement of Intent", in *The Accountant*, vol. 161, no. 4957, 18 December 1969, pp. 842–843. For a discussion of the nature of accounting standards, see T.A. Lee, "Accounting Standards and Effective Financial Reporting – II", in *The Accountant's Magazine*, vol. 79, no. 824, February 1975, pp. 74–76.

[73] Parker has also observed that "In many respects the [Dutch] guidelines are akin to the Recommendations" series. See Parker, *op. cit.*, p. 220.

[74] Schoonderbeek, *loc. cit.*

[75] Stephen A. Zeff, *Forging Accounting Principles in Five Countries: A History and an Analysis of Trends* (Champaign, IL: Stipes Publishing Co., 1972), pp. 10–13 and 22–23.

mous concurrence of all three delegations, it is not difficult to understand why a greater degree of flexibility of practice is reflected in the tripartite body's adopted positions.

1.7.5. Managers' bonuses based on profit are not a pervasive practice

In some countries, such as the United States, it is a widespread practice among larger companies to base a portion of their executives' compensation on the annual profit. In these countries, an empirical research literature has demonstrated a tendency on the part of top executives, having a clear interest in the possible impact of the level of profit on their annual bonus, to appear to use their discretion to influence the amount of profit in a way so as to maximize their bonus.[76] Executives can therefore possess a special self-interest in the proposed actions of standard-setting bodies that might adversely affect their compensation via changes in the way in which profit is to be measured, including both its amount and its year-to-year volatility. This has not been an issue in the Netherlands, as it is not a common practice for companies to link executive compensation with indices of performance in the financial statements.

[76] The *Journal of Accounting and Economics* has published a number of important articles in this line of research.

2. From the nineteenth century to the onset of World War II

2.1. Introduction

The Industrial Revolution came later to the Netherlands than to the United Kingdom, suggesting that the need for large amounts of outside capital and the consequent widespread use of the limited liability company owned by anonymous shareholders were similarly delayed. Owing largely to this slower pace of industrialization of the Dutch economy, the process of securing passage of the first elaborate company law, including specific requirements for financial reporting, began later, and culminated in legislation later, than in the UK.

The movement to regulate limited companies in the Netherlands began in the early 1870's, when the first draft law was proposed. But it was rejected by Parliament. A government commission appointed in 1879 took 11 years to render a report. The draft law recommended by the commission in 1890 was the first to propose that companies be required to publish their financial statements. Curiously, the commission's draft law recommended more extensive balance-sheet disclosures, on both the asset and equity sides, than were prescribed in the legislation that was finally approved 39 years later. But the draft law languished in a climate of inattention.

Spurred by a number of celebrated scandals in the first years of the new century, the Justice Minister presented a draft law of his own in 1910. Missing from the minister's law, however, was the specification of the contents of the balance sheet that had so ambitiously been proposed 20 years before. But owing to an impasse between the minister and Parliament, no real progress occurred until the 1920's, when several instances of "crisis and financial ruin" precipitated renewed interest in legislation. Business interests were opposed to legislation that would interfere with management's right to run enterprise as it saw fit, and auditors were divided on the need to prescribe the contents of the financial statements. In the end, laws were approved in 1928 and 1929, the first dealing (among other things) with the publication of financial statements, and the second treating the contents of the financial statements. The involvement of an auditor was suggested but not required, as the auditing profession was still unregulated.

The 1930's were a period of little further development in financial reporting. The use of secret reserves and other devices for modulating the figures in companies' financial statements apparently flourished, and the minimal disclosures required by law hardly facilitated the making of an informed judgment on meaningfulness of what was reported. Here and there, companies took steps to improve their financial reporting, but, in the main, managements disclosed no more than the law required.

2.2. Developments leading to the enactment of the 1928 and 1929 revisions of the Commercial Code

2.2.1. Provisions in the 1837 Commercial Code

The earliest indigenous Dutch company law,[1] approved in 1837, called upon every merchant to keep a journal in which a daily record is kept of

> his receivables and payables, the affairs of his trade, the drawing, acceptance and endorsement of bills of exchange and other notes, his obligations, and, in general, everything he receives and spends, regardless of its nature. In addition, [he shall keep] such accounts as are customary in the trade [*in de koophandel gebruikelijk*] but the keeping of which is not required by law (Art. 6).[2]

Article 8 obliged each merchant to "draft an inventory and balance sheet [*staat en balans*]"[3] every year, to be placed in a separate register and to be signed personally. Nothing in the law required the merchant actually to publish the "inventory and balance sheet", and there was no reference to a profit and loss statement.[4] Article 55 required the directors of limited companies to report to the shareholders annually on the "profits or losses earned or suffered during the past year". This report could be made in any of three ways: in a general meeting, by sending a statement (*staat*) to each shareholder, or by making the account (*de rekening*) available to shareholders for inspection.[5]

---

[1] From 1810 to 1837, a translation of the French *Code de commerce* was in force in the Netherlands. Article 8 in the *Code* was almost identical to Article 6 in the later Wetboek van Koophandel. Article 9 in the *Code* corresponded to Article 8 in the Wetboek, although it used the term "inventory" (*inventaire*), not "balance sheet" (*bilan*).

[2] *Wetboek van Koophandel* (Commercial Code) ('s-Gravenhage: Ter Algemeene Lands Drukkerij, 1838). Although the volume was published in 1838, the law was cited as the Wet van 10 mei 1837, Stb. 21 (Law of 10 May 1837, no. 21 in the Statute Book).

[3] J.G.Ch. Volmer, in *Handleiding bij het opmaken en controleeren van inventaris en balans* (Utrecht: W. Anton Abels, 1894), p. 7, equated "*staat*" (as used in Article 8 of the Commercial Code) with "*inventaris*", or an inventory. When values were assigned to the items in the inventory, Volmer added, the result was a "*balans*", or balance sheet (pp. 8–9).

[4] On 5 May 1922, a law was passed that changed the wording, but not the substance, of these two articles (Stb. 1922, no. 246). The law was directed at clarifying the status of accounts in legal proceedings, and at the same time modernized some of the terminology used. The substance of the requirement to keep books and draft a yearly balance sheet was not altered.

[5] The authoritative history of the Code is: Mr J.C. Voorduin, *Geschiedenis en beginselen der Nederlandsche wetboeken* (Utrecht: Robert Natan, Akademie-Boekhandelaar, 1840), vols.

2.2.2. Early attempts at reform

In 1871, a lengthy and arduous process of company law reform was set in motion. From that year until 1928–29, when the law was finally revised, lawmakers became increasingly aware that one of the effects of the Industrial Revolution was a separation of ownership from the management of enterprise.[6] Shareholders were offered no protection by way of publicity in the 1837 law, and as family companies began to seek outside capital and, eventually, a stock exchange listing, there was a growing desire to strengthen the position of the anonymous shareholders. Much of the ensuing debate centered on which companies, if any, should be required to publish their financial statements. As might be expected, the bulk of the resistance to a publication requirement came from company managements.

Between 1871 and 1929, the following stages in the process of company law reform may be discerned:

1871 The Jolles proposal, a first attempt to revise the Commercial Code, is rejected by Parliament.
1879 The Kist Commission is installed to reconsider the commercial laws.
1890 Several reports of the Kist Commission are published, dealing with company law reform.
1910 Justice Minister Nelissen issues a draft law encompassing the entire issue of company law reform.
1925 Justice Minister Heemskerk submits a revised draft law to Parliament, in reality an entirely new proposal, although it was based on the 1910 draft as amended by the comments received in 1919.
1928 Parliament enacts the draft law, with the minister's assurance that revisions will shortly be proposed.
1928–29 The Visser Commission is installed to recommend revision of the recently enacted law, and its report provides the basis for Parliament's acceptance of amendments dealing with financial reporting.

The first four of the stages enumerated above will be discussed in this section. The remaining three stages will be discussed in the next section. By the 1920's, the cumulative effect of the earlier attempts had begun to meet with a positive and sustained response, and the resulting treatment of the developments is necessarily more detailed.

VIII–X. In the context in which it is used in Article 55, *staat* refers to a statement.

6 The slow initial growth in the number of limited companies may help to explain why the process of reform was attenuated: 1850, 137; 1870, 456; 1880, 523; 1890, 957; 1910, 6874; 1927, approx. 20 000. See Prof.mr J. Valkhoff, *Een Eeuw Rechtsontwikkeling, De vermaatschappelijking van het Nederlandsche Privaatrecht sinds de codificatie (1838)* (Amsterdam: N.V. De Arbeiderspers, 1949), pp. 121–122.

2.2.2.1. The Jolles proposal – 1871

The reform process began in 1871 with a draft law forwarded to Parliament by Justice Minister Mr J.A. Jolles,[7] which was intended to replace the parts of the 1837 Commercial Code dealing with limited companies. The object of the draft was to replace the old principle of control by Royal Consent (*koninklijke bewilliging*) upon the inception of a limited company, which dated back to the days of the chartered company, with the more modern principle of control by publicity. Although the parliamentary committee that was convened to prepare the plenary discussion of the draft law agreed with this principle, it severely criticized the manner of implementation. While the draft called for publication of only (1) the articles of incorporation and (2) any losses incurred by the company in excess of a stipulated minimum (expressed as a percentage of paid-in capital), the committee considered the possibility of requiring the publication of financial statements.[8] The committee soon was confronted with a dilemma that was to occupy the minds of all involved up to 1929 (and beyond): how to assure that the required publication of financial statements would not lead to the dissemination of misleading or meaningless information? This question was predicated on the almost unchallenged assumption that companies were too diverse to enable a detailed regulation of their financial statements. In the end, the minister withdrew his draft law after hearing the criticism from the parliamentary committee.

2.2.2.2. Installation of the Kist Commission – 1879

In 1879, a government commission (*Staatscommissie*) was installed to draft proposals for the complete revision of the Commercial Code.[9] The commission was chaired by Mr J.G. Kist, a member of the Hooge Raad, or High Court, and was composed exclusively of lawyers. Among the members were J.A. Fruin and T.M.C. Asser, two highly regarded professors of civil law in Utrecht and Amsterdam, respectively. Between 1887 and 1890, the commission produced a number of reports dealing with various aspects of company law, only one of which (on company failures) led directly to a parliamentary enactment.

2.2.2.3. The Kist Commission's draft law – 1890

In 1890, the Kist Commission published a report and a draft law dealing with the limited company.[10] For reasons that are not clear, the report never left the

---

7 *Bijlagen Handelingen Tweede Kamer, Zitting 1871–1872*, no. 65, pp. 957–970.

8 *Bijlagen Handelingen Tweede Kamer, Zitting 1871–1872*, pp. 2214–2233.

9 Installed by Koninklijk Besluit [Order in Council] of 22 November 1879, no. 26, reproduced in *Ontwerpen van Wet met Memoriën van Toelichting, den Koning aangeboden door de Staatscommissie tot herziening van het Wetboek van Koophandel*, ed. Gebr. Belinfante ('s-Gravenhage, 1891).

10 *Ontwerp van een wetsvoorstel betreffende de vennootschap onder eene firma, de commanditaire vennootschap, de naamlooze vennootschap, de onderlinge waarborgmaatschappij, en de coöperatieve vereeniging*. Included in the Belinfante edition cited in footnote 9, above.

ministry in the form of a draft law submitted to Parliament, and remained in a kind of departmental limbo for 20 years. Yet the report was not overlooked by commentators on company law reform. It was mentioned frequently in the contemporary literature, as authors stated their positions for or against the commission's recommendations.[11]

Fundamental to the report was the notion of publicity, both of a company's articles of incorporation and of its financial position. In this respect, the commission saw its report as reflecting the wider European movement to replace the old system of Royal Consent and State supervision by one of private monitoring on the basis of publicity. A number of recent laws passed in the United Kingdom, France, Germany and Belgium were mentioned as sources of the commission's thinking.[12]

The commission's draft law contained the following rather ambitious proposal for extending the regulation of financial reporting:

- reporting to shareholders must take place at least once a year, by means of a balance sheet (Art. 91).
- the balance sheet must be approved by the shareholders, not by the board of supervisors (Art. 93).
- the annual balance sheet and profit and loss statement must be published, following approval by the shareholders, in the *Staats-Courant* (Official Gazette), and they are also to be available for inspection by the general public at the company's office (Art. 70). (Somewhat surprisingly, the commission did not opt for publication in the Commercial Register (Handelsregister), which was to be established under one of its other proposals.[13])

---

[11] The commission's report was discussed, for instance, in Th. Limperg's letters to the editor of the *Algemeen Handelsblad*, 8 and 9 January 1904, and in the auditing manual by J.D. Reiman and J.J.M.H. Nijst, *De Accountant als Controleur* (Zwolle: W.E.J. Tjeenk Willink, 1906), pp. 49, 59–65. In 1903–04, Limperg and Nijst were partners in the same audit firm.

[12] Explanatory Memorandum (Memorie van Toelichting) included in the commission's report, cited in footnote 9, above, pp. 85–86.

[13] The task of maintaining commercial registers was assigned to the Chambers of Commerce (Kamers van Koophandel) by the Commercial Registry Act (Handelsregisterwet) of 1918. As with many other Dutch institutions, the modern Chamber of Commerce originated in the period when the Netherlands was annexed to the French Napoleonic Empire. In 1811, Chambers of Commerce were ordered into existence by a decree that transferred all kinds of French institutional arrangements to the Netherlands. Chambers of Commerce were intended to represent regional commercial interests to the government. Their general role has been to provide the local or central government with advice, data, and proposals on all matters relating to trade and industry. They have also been assigned responsibilities by various kinds of economic legislation, including: issuance of general business licenses, regulation of seasonal sales, arbitration of certain disputes, maintenance of the integrity of weights and measures, issuance of certificates of origin, and (beginning in 1918) the keeping of commercial registers.

The Kist Commission, which was the first to propose the creation of commercial registers, was of the view that they might be kept by local courts (*cantongerechten*), but, in the end, they were given to the Chambers of Commerce. Initially, the filings in commercial registers

- the specific contents of the balance sheet were regulated by Article 69, with the following items to be shown separately:
  - initial or "other" costs not yet charged to income;
  - in separate amounts: immovables (land and buildings), machinery, rolling stock and other transportation equipment, ships, bonds, shares in other companies, treasury shares, cash and bullion, funds in current accounts and deposits, and receivables, with a separate disclosure of bad accounts;
  - both the face value of bad accounts and the provision for losses;
  - the aggregate face value of share capital authorized by the articles of incorporation, and the amount of the face value issued and to be received on subscribed shares;
  - reserves and provisions for replacement;
  - debts outstanding at face value (in the case of debt issued below par, the difference was to be shown on the asset side and amortized);
  - the face value of conditional debts, with an allowance for possible reductions shown on the asset side; and
  - the balance taken from the profit and loss statement.

The suggestion is implicit in Article 69, reflecting the predominant view of the period, that the profit and loss statement was more an adjunct of the balance sheet than a separate financial statement.

There was no provision in the Kist Commission's proposal for an audit to be performed.

According to the Explanatory Memorandum (Memorie van Toelichting) included in the commission's report, the foregoing disclosures were necessary in order to assure that the requirement that the balance sheet be published would be meaningful. The enumeration of the items to be disclosed was said by the commission to be based on Swiss law.[14]

Yet, as mentioned above, the Kist Commission's report and draft law were not acted upon for a period of 20 years. Mr dr L.E. Visser remarked ironically in a later article that this has been the fate of many reports, but he gave no reasons.[15] Th. Limperg Jr. was aware of some activity within the ministry. He mentioned that experts were consulted on the preparation of a draft law for submission to Parliament, but he offered no explanation for the long delay.[16]

were confined to such items as the articles of incorporation and the names of directors. As a result of the changes in the Commercial Code approved in 1928–29, which are discussed below, financial statements were added to the list of items to be deposited in the commercial registers.

[14] *Ibid.*, pp. 101–102.

[15] L.E. Visser, "De Naamlooze Vennootschap en de wetgever", in *Feestuitgave behoorende bij het WPNR*, no. 2947, 19 June 1926, pp. 10–12. That no reasons were given in such instances was not unusual. The standard reasons for inaction were lack of sufficient interest coupled with lack of pressure to take action.

[16] Th. Limperg Jr., "Het Wetsontwerp betreffende de Naamlooze Vennootschap en de Admin-

The Explanatory Memorandum to the 1910 draft also referred to the occurrence of such consultations.

During this interlude, the subject of company law reform continued to be discussed in the legal and financial literature. An important contribution to this literature was made in 1900 by Dr G. van Slooten. In that year, his doctoral thesis[17] became the first major Dutch treatise on the legal and accounting aspects of financial reporting by limited companies. Van Slooten was explicit about moving financial reporting away from double-entry bookkeeping. Published financial statements, he argued, should not be considered as mere extracts from a ledger, but as documents playing an important role in companies' transactions with other parties (shareholders, short-term creditors, bondholders, and employees). The use of financial statements by these groups, he said, required that their contents satisfy a dual standard of being true (*waar*) and clear (*duidelijk*). He called for the required publication of audited financial statements, to be structured along the lines of a general form or model. This model, which van Slooten described in some detail, was said to be sufficiently flexible to be applicable to all industries. General rules governed the degree of detail in which items should be reported as well as the order in which they should be presented.

2.2.2.4. Minister Nelissen's draft law – 1910

Early in the first decade of the new century, the issue of company law reform acquired greater urgency, owing to a number of financial scandals. Among the more celebrated were the collapse of the Noord-Brabantsche Bank (North Brabant Bank) in 1901 following several years' publication of misleading financial statements, and an exposé of the attempt of the Wilhelmina-Trust to issue shares in 1902 on the basis of misleading information.[18] Apparently as a result of these financial embarrassments, the Ministry of Agriculture, Industry and Trade issued

---

istratieve Contrôle – I", in *Accountancy*, vol. 8, no. 83, 15 March 1910, pp. 25–27.

[17] G. van Slooten, *Verplichte openbaarmaking van Balans en Winst- en Verliesrekening van Naamlooze Vennootschappen* [Required Publication of the Balance Sheet and Profit and Loss Statement of Limited Companies] ('s-Gravenhage, 1900). Van Slooten's degree was conferred cum laude, signifying the approving committee's high regard for his thesis. Some years later, E. van Dien, the *doyen* of the accounting profession, praised van Slooten's thesis. See E. van Dien, introductory remarks at the 5th Accountantsdag, "Accountantsdag", in *Accountancy*, vol. 10, no. 111, October 1912, p. 109.

Gooike van Slooten (1875–1932), a Frisian who took his doctorate in law at the Gemeentelijke Universiteit van Amsterdam, eventually became a member of the Court of Justice (*Gerechtshof*) in The Hague. During the first year of *Accountancy*, the journal founded in January 1903 by Th. Limperg Jr., van Slooten was a member of the editorial board. He left the board in December of that year following a difference of opinion with Limperg.

[18] The catastrophe of the Noord-Brabantsche Bank is treated in Johan de Vries, *Geschiedenis der Accountancy in Nederland: Aanvang en Ontplooiing, 1895–1935* (Assen/Maastricht: Van Gorcum, 1985), pp. 83–87 and 93, and in Reiman and Nijst, *op. cit.*, pp. 64–65. The Wilhelmina-Trust affair is discussed in S.F. van Oss, *Vijftig Jaren Journalist* ('s-Gravenhage: H.P. Leopolds Uitgeversmij. N.V., 1946), pp. 92–95. Van Oss was founder of the *Haagsche Post* and was a tireless prosecutor of fraudulent companies.

a circular in 1905, directed to all Chambers of Commerce (Kamers van Koophandel), asking for reports on their experience with abuses by limited companies and for their opinions on possible counter-measures.

On 29 June 1906, P.J. Troelstra, a socialist member of the Second Chamber of Parliament, introduced a motion in which he invited his colleagues to agree with the statement that

> the scandalous misconduct committed through the medium of limited companies, syndicates, and the like, make fundamental changes in the Commercial and Criminal Codes urgently necessary.[19]

In his speech in the Second Chamber, Troelstra discussed a considerable number of instances of willful misconduct in recent years, involving misleading prospectuses, negligent supervisory boards, shares issued against worthless property, etc.[20] Among the cases he cited were the Noord-Brabantsche Bank and the Wilhelmina-Trust. Troelstra advocated increased publicity as one of the remedies for this behavior. The Justice Minister, Mr E.E. van Raalte, said that he had no problem with Troelstra's motion, since a draft law based on the 1890 report of the Kist Commission was to be submitted to Parliament in a matter of weeks. Troelstra's motion passed without a formal vote. Yet no draft law on the subject was actually submitted to Parliament during the term of the government then in office, which ended in February 1908.

All of this led in 1910 to the issuance by the Justice Minister, Mr A.P.L. Nelissen, of a draft law[21] for revising the Commercial Code, which reflected a virtually complete revision of the law proposed by the Kist Commission. This draft, known as the Nelissen Draft (Ontwerp Nelissen), required all limited companies to publish financial statements annually in the Official Gazette, but, in marked contrast to the Kist Commission's proposal, did not specify the required contents of the financial statements. In his Explanatory Memorandum (p. 32), the minister defended his proposal by pointing to the force of public opinion, as well as to the possibility, within existing and proposed laws, that civil or criminal proceedings might be brought in the event of misleading financial statements.

A new element in the Nelissen Draft was the provision for an audit in Article 44c. The right, but not the obligation, to appoint an auditor was granted to the general meeting of shareholders.

The minister's draft law gave new life to the debate on company law reform,

---

A number of financial scandals of the period are briefly noted, with citations to further literature, in Joh. de Vries, *Lion Markus en de comptabiliteit in Nederland omstreeks 1900*, Mededelingen der Koninklijke Nederlandse Akademie van Wetenschappen, afdeling Letterkunde, nieuwe reeks, deel 46, no. 4, 1983, pp. 115–116, note 30.

19 *Handelingen Tweede Kamer, Zitting 1905–1906*, p. 2260.

20 *Ibid.*, pp. 2260–2268.

21 *Bijlagen Handelingen Tweede Kamer, Zitting 1909–1910*, no. 217.

and numerous articles were written on the subject.[22]

In 1909, the Stock Exchange Association (Vereeniging voor den Effectenhandel) made its first utterance on the financial reporting practices of listed companies. In the edition of the Association's Rules on Securities Trading (Fondsenreglement) dated 1 August 1909, the requirement was introduced in Article 5 that companies submitting a prospectus for a new issue of shares or bonds must agree to publish an annual balance sheet and profit and loss statement. Nothing was said about the contents of the financial statements, and it is not known whether the Association sought to persuade companies already listed to agree to the same undertaking.

2.3. Run-up to the 1928–29 legislation

2.3.1. Minister Heemskerk's revised draft law – 1925

The Nelissen Draft might well have been the basis for the revision that was eventually approved in 1928, but owing to a stalemate between the minister and the parliamentary preparatory committee over the matter of different treatment for "open" and "closed" companies, the draft remained bottled up in committee until 1918, and was virtually forgotten. In that year, Parliament notified the Justice Minister that a revision of company law was desperately needed. The minister, Mr Th. Heemskerk (who had been head of the government when Minister Nelissen promulgated his draft in 1910), responded that the delay was due entirely to inaction by Parliament itself.[23]

The matter that had impeded Parliament's progress on the reform legislation was to be the central issue of future debates. Many felt that companies whose shares were in the hands of a small number of investors, especially founders or directors and their families, should not be made to publish their financial statements. The problem was how to define such "closed" or family companies.

After Parliament was made aware of its forgotten task, the process started afresh. A newly constituted preparatory committee reported its views on the revived Nelissen Draft to the minister, who, with the help of L.E. Visser, made some changes in the draft on the basis of the committee's comments. As part of the revision, some of the articles were renumbered. This new version, known as the Nelissen–Heemskerk Draft (Ontwerp Nelissen–Heemskerk), or as the Revised Draft (Gewijzigd Ontwerp), was published in April 1925, together with the final

---

[22] The literature was analyzed in the doctoral thesis by B.Th.W. van Hasselt, *De literatuur over het wetsontwerp op de naamlooze vennootschappen, critisch samengevat* (Leiden: A. Vilders, 1919).

[23] This incident is related by Prof.mr E.J.J. van der Heijden in "Het wetsontwerp Nelissen–Heemskerk", in *De Naamlooze Vennootschap*, vol. 4, no. 2, 15 May 1925, p. 34.

report of preparatory committee.[24]

A further spate of scandals had refocused attention on company law reform. A member of the First Chamber used the occasion of the debate on the Justice Ministry's budget for 1923 to call for swift action on the Nelissen Draft, citing a number of recent financial scandals. He mentioned several companies that had recently drawn public attention, some because of failure, and others because of charges of mismanagement or fraud. Among the companies he cited in connection with misleading information were Marx en Co's Bank, Tabaks-Unie, Anton Jurgens' Vereenigde Fabrieken, and Algemeene Maatschappij van Levensverzekering.[25]

In 1926, L.E. Visser, after remarking on the "financial storms" that had echoed in Parliament during the first decade of the century, wrote:

> After the short post-war upswing [in the economy], stormy weather came up again; to put it differently, crisis and financial ruin repeated themselves with unprecedented force and rupture. Now, again, the desire for long-delayed action on the part of the Legislature was repeated inside and outside of Parliament [resulting in the Revised Draft of 1925].[26]

One of the more celebrated cases involved N.V. Anton Jurgens' Vereenigde Fabrieken, known simply as Jurgens. Although it eventually turned out that there was not much substance to the scandal, the episode caused quite a stir, and it succeeded in drawing public interest to financial reporting by listed companies. The affair originated with the publication in the *Haagsche Post* on 29 August 1925 of an open letter to the management of Jurgens by A.M. van Oss, accompanied by an open letter to the Justice Minister by S.F. van Oss, the editor of the *Haagsche Post* and A.M.'s brother.[27] A.M. van Oss criticized Jurgens for not paying a dividend up to the amount of its reported profits, as required by the company's articles of incorporation, while his brother accused the company of covering up genuine losses with fictitious profits. The price of Jurgens' shares plunged by 30 percent in the wake of this assault. In the next issue of the

[24] *Bijlagen Handelingen Tweede Kamer, Zitting 1924–1925*, no. 69.

[25] *Handelingen Eerste Kamer, Zitting 1922–1923*, pp. 603–605. The member who raised the issue was Mr dr M. Mendels, a well-known figure in the Social-Democratic Workers Party (SDAP, Sociaal-Democratische Arbeiderspartij), and the date of his remarks was 19 April 1923.

Another affair was the case of the "Rotterdamsche Bankvereeniging", also known as "Robaver", which was mentioned in Hartmann's 1928 article (see footnote 79, below). The matter is related in *De kroniek van Dr. A. Sternheim*, beginning at vol. 2, no. 62, 1 July 1924, p. 488.

[26] Visser, *op. cit.*, p. 11.

[27] A.M. van Oss, "Open Brief Aan het Bestuur der Naamlooze Vennootschap Anton Jurgens' Vereenigde Fabrieken", in *Haagsche Post*, 29 August 1925, pp. 1445–1448; and S.F. van Oss, "Over Jurgens – Circa Vijftig Millioen Verkapte Verliezen. Schromelijk Gemanipuleerde Balansen – Open Brief aan Z.E. den Minister van Justitie", in *Haagsche Post*, 29 August 1925, p. 1427.

Haagsche Post a week later, S.F. van Oss supplied some details in support of his allegation,[28] but, by the time Jurgens could publish a categorical rejection of the claims two weeks later,[29] the commotion seems to have died down. Neither side emerged a clear victor. Several other newspapers seized the occasion to chime in with their own views on Jurgens' financial reporting, and the bell of company law reform was rung several times.[30]

With impetus provided by the several company embarrassments, the Revised Draft attracted attention. In its articles on financial reporting, the Revised Draft reflected one substantive change from the Nelissen Draft of 1910, namely, a provision that the principles by which the fixed assets were valued should be disclosed in notes to the balance sheet and profit and loss statement. This was the first mention in a draft law of notes to the financial statements. The Revised Draft also changed the place in which the financial statements were to be published: in the commercial registers, which had come into existence under the Commercial Registry Act (Handelsregisterwet), passed in 1918, rather than in the Official Gazette. The required publication was kept in force for all companies, without exception (Article 42c), and no rules were given for the contents of the balance sheet and profit and loss statement. Articles 42 on the drafting of the balance sheet, 42a on the possible appointment of an expert to oversee the accounting process, and 42c on required publication of the financial statements were as follows[31]:

> **42**. Yearly, within eight months following the close of the financial year of the company, providing that no waiver has been granted by the general meeting of shareholders owing to extraordinary circumstances, the management [*bestuur*] shall draft a balance sheet and a profit and loss statement, which are to be presented to the general meeting for confirmation. The balance sheet and profit and loss statement are to be accompanied by notes [*toelichting*] that show the principles by which the movable and immovable properties of the company have been valued.

---

[28] S.F. van Oss, "Over Jurgens II – Hokus Pokus! *f* 55,000,000 Uit het Niet te Voorschijn! – Open Brief aan Z.E. den Minister van Justitie", in *Haagsche Post*, 5 September 1925, p. 1471.

[29] "Nota van de N.V. Anton Jurgens' Vereenigde Fabrieken aan hare aandeelhouders naar aanleiding van de campagne van Oss", in *Haagsche Post*, 19 September 1925, pp. 1579–1580.

The *Haagsche Post* continued publishing articles until early October about Jurgens' financial reporting, but without apparent effect. Some time later, a shareholder sued the *Haagsche Post* for the loss resulting from the panic selling of Jurgens' shares in September 1925. By that time, it was apparently accepted that the allegations against Jurgens were exaggerated or could not be substantiated, and it only remained to determine the liability of the *Haagsche Post* for any losses to shareholders. The outcome of the lawsuit is not known. See "De 'Haagsche Post' en de Jurgensaandelen", in *De Naamlooze Vennootschap*, vol. 6, no. 6, September 1927, pp. 177–179.

[30] See "De Jurgens-affaire", editorial in *Maandblad voor het Boekhouden*, vol. 32, no. 374, October 1925, p. 27.

[31] A summary of the principal contents of the financial reporting provisions, keyed to the several draft laws and to the 1928 and 1929 Acts, is given in Appendix 2.1.

The balance sheet, profit and loss statement and notes are to be signed by all directors and by those supervisors, if any, who are charged with overseeing the drafting of the balance sheet and the profit and loss statement.

42a. The general meeting of shareholders can, and, if such is prescribed by the articles of incorporation, shall appoint an expert [*deskundige*] in order to oversee the accounting process on a regular basis, and to report to the general meeting concerning the balance sheet and profit and loss statement, with the notes drafted by the management.

The general meeting cannot, in the matter of this appointment, be bound by any recommendation. It can discharge the expert at any time.

The expert is entitled to consult all books and documents of the limited company, the knowledge of which is necessary for a proper execution of his task. The assets of the company must be shown to him on request. He is not allowed to divulge anything that is revealed to him concerning the affairs of the company beyond the extent implied by his commission. His remuneration is to be determined by the general meeting.

Unless the articles of incorporation or a decision made by the general meeting determine otherwise, the expert will bring his report to the attention of the supervisors, if any. He will be allowed to attend the meeting called to confirm the balance sheet and profit and loss statement, and he is to have an advisory vote in this meeting.[32]

42c. The management must, within eight days after confirmation of the balance sheet and profit and loss statement, deposit completed copies, accessible for inspection by anyone, at the office of the company and in the commercial register.

Within eight days of said deposit, the management shall make this known by an announcement in the Official Gazette, and [in one of the local or provincial newspapers].

2.3.2. Reactions to the revised draft of 1925

The rash of financial embarrassments, coupled with Minister Heemskerk's apparent determination to produce legislation, led the leaders of business and the auditing profession, as well as other interested parties, to take the government's intentions seriously. They realized that the time had come for submitting their views.

2.3.2.1. General

A number of authors commented on the amount of time that had elapsed since the Kist Commission reported in 1890. Mr E.J.J. van der Heijden compared the

[32] The last sentence of the final paragraph of Article 42a was deleted in the 1927 revision and was not included in the finally approved text the following year. Minor changes were made in Article 42c as well.

Revised Draft to the "sleeping beauty", awakened by a prince who had nothing better to do at the moment.[33]

Comments on the draft were submitted by such institutions as the Netherlands Association of Lawyers (Nederlandsche Advocatenvereeniging), the Brotherhood of Notaries Public (Broederschap van Notarissen), and the Association of Directors of Mortgage Banks (Vereeniging van Directeuren van Hypotheekbanken). In their comments, they tended to concentrate on the legal aspects.

2.3.2.2. Reaction by business

The draft law provoked strong reactions from the business community. A report was issued by the Industry Council (Nijverheidsraad), an advisory body to the government composed of industrialists, in which the draft law was rejected because of the damage it would do to Dutch business.[34]

Also in 1926, the VNW published a report on the draft law by one of its committees.[35] The chairman of the five-member committee was Mr Aug. Philips, a director of Bataafsche Petroleum-Maatschappij, an important subsidiary of N.V. Koninklijke Nederlandsche Petroleum Maatschappij (Royal Dutch Petroleum). Although the committee conceded that, during the past half-century, there had been many instances of company failures owing to fraud, mismanagement and the misrepresentation of facts, and that "stupendous" sums had been lost in such ventures by the investing public (pp. 3–4), it asserted that this misconduct was due mainly to "incompetence, carelessness, recklessness or lack of policy" on the part of managements (p. 22), matters that no law can preclude from occurring.

Adopting an offensive tack, the committee rejected the draft law as impracticable and wrong in principle. Its argument is an interesting illustration of the views of business leaders on financial publicity by companies in the 1920's. The committee denied that it was possible for a law to ensure either the proper management of companies or even the publication of meaningful financial statements. Businesses were too diverse to make it possible for a statutory regulation to prevent willful avoidance (pp. 6–8). What might be useful, the committee suggested, was an obligatory audit, but that would require regulation of the audit profession (p. 8).

The committee also refused to accept the main principle on which the law was based, namely, that a healthy business needs active participation by shareholders who are endowed with suitable authority. The committee argued that the

---

33 "Doornroosje", in *De Naamlooze Vennootschap*, vol. 6, no. 1, 15 April 1927, p. 3.

34 Quoted in "De Nijverheidsraad en het Wetsontwerp op de N.V.", in *De Naamlooze Vennootschap*, vol. 5, no. 5, 15 August 1926, p. 153.

35 *Advies over het gewijzigd Ontwerp van Wet op de Naamlooze Vennootschappen, uitgebracht door eene commissie uit het Verbond van Nederlandsche Werkgevers* ('s-Gravenhage: VNW, 1926). Page citations in this section will refer to this report.

interests of the company required a strong management that can quickly make the necessary decisions, for example, in the case of takeovers (p. 12). It said that shareholders should be left free to continue their passive attitude. Holding shares without taking a detailed interest in the company was perfectly natural where share ownership was widespread (pp. 10–11). The committee recommended that the combined efforts of the Stock Exchange Association (which governs the Amsterdam Stock Exchange) and the financial press would be sufficient to make whatever improvements that are necessary. The former might, the committee said, use its influence to have audits performed and, where necessary, could effectuate changes in a company's board membership. The financial press had a role to play, the committee said, to the extent that it was "decent" and "capable" (p. 23).

Most of the Chambers of Commerce published commentaries in the press, directed to the minister and/or the Second Chamber of Parliament.[36] On the subject of financial reporting, these commentaries were unanimous on the following points: the proposed law had been drafted by lawyers without sufficient attention being paid to economic considerations, and especially its impact on business; required publicity for all NV's would be useless and even dangerous, as it would provide competitors with vital information; hence, there should be an alternative legal form to accommodate small companies, modeled on the German GmbH.

A committee was formed by leading businessmen, and headed by Dr C.J.K. van Aalst, the president of the Nederlandsche Handel-Maatschappij (a predecessor of ABN AMRO). A "Congress of Business" (Congres van de Zakenwereld) was held in The Hague on 23 September 1927 to mobilize the opposition in commercial circles to the draft law.[37] Several members of Parliament were in attendance. Most of the speakers singled out the general publication requirement as the most obnoxious feature of the draft law. The requirement would be "disagreeable", "dangerous", or "disastrous"; it would make Dutch companies prey for takeovers by foreign companies, and thus would reduce Dutch economic activity to the drawing of dividends from foreign companies; and it would cause unemployment and distress. The *Algemeen Handelsblad*, a newspaper that catered to the business community, characterized the congress as "very rare" and "gratifying". It said that the fact that the Second Chamber could accept, after only an "indifferent" defense by the Justice Ministry, a law that was so much opposed by

[36] During 1925–26, *De Naamlooze Vennootschap* quoted a number of these reports by Chambers of Commerce at considerable length. See the following places in volumes 4 and 5: 15 September 1925, pp. 186–187; 15 March 1926, pp. 376–378; 15 May 1926, pp. 55–59; and 15 June 1926, pp. 89–91.

[37] Reported in "Het congres van de Zakenwereld over het wetsontwerp op de N.V. verlangt verwerping daarvan door de Eerste Kamer", in *De Naamlooze Vennootschap*, vol. 6, no. 7, 15 October 1927, pp. 217–219. For a report in the VNW's journal, see "Een welgeslaagde demonstratie", in *De Nederlandsche Werkgever*, no. 39, 29 September 1927, pp. 512–513.

business, demonstrates the necessity for business to involve itself more heavily in politics. Luckily, it added, the First Chamber had closer ties with business and would probably pay more attention to the serious arguments made by business against the draft law.[38]

A second congress was held on 5 June 1928, also in The Hague, shortly before the debates in the First Chamber of Parliament.[39] This time, the points were made that Dutch enterprise had flourished under the old law, that the draft law represented a reactionary throwback to former days of government intervention, and that, although there had been abuses in the past, they would not have been prevented from occurring by the proposed law. The First Chamber was therefore strongly urged to reject the proposed law. Since the First Chamber was not empowered to amend proposed legislation, but only to accept or reject it *in toto*, the business community was recommending a strong measure, namely, that the First Chamber reject the entire draft law on the ground that its general publication requirement was objectionable.

In a two-part commentary following on the heels of the second congress, the *Nieuwe Rotterdamsche Courant*, while supporting a complete revision of the law, argued that the fears of publicity in the case of "closed" companies were "exaggerated". With a heavy dose of irony, the paper elucidated its point:

> The science of auditing knows the trick of publishing completely colorless balance sheets, from which no one will obtain any information. Middle-sized companies will not call upon practitioners of auditing in vain when the need arises [to obscure]. The new law can then work to the satisfaction of both parties: the minister, who will have maintained his "principle", and the middle-sized companies, who will have guarded their trade secrets.[40]

2.3.2.3. Reaction by the auditing profession

The views of auditors were not abundantly in evidence, as financial reporting was discussed only occasionally in *Accountancy* between the journal's founding in 1903 and 1925. A sampling of the subjects treated is as follows: the

[38] "Studeerkamerwetgeving", in *Algemeen Handelsblad*, 24 September 1927, evening edition, p. 1. Factual reports in the press were "Wet op de naaml. vennootschappen, het haagsche congres", in *Algemeen Handelsblad*, 23 September 1927, evening edition, p. 14; and "Bezwaren uit de practijk – Tegen 't wetsontwerp op de N.V.", in *De Telegraaf*, 23 September 1927, evening edition, p. 5.

[39] "Het tweede congres van de zakenwereld tegen het wetsontwerp op de N.V.", in *De Naamlooze Vennootschap*, vol. 7, no. 3, 15 June 1928, pp. 88–91.

[40] "De Naamlooze Vennootschap", in *Nieuwe Rotterdamsche Courant*, 5 June 1928, evening edition, p. 1. The second article in the series was "Besluit", 7 June 1928, evening edition, p. 1. Commentary following the second congress also appeared in *Algemeen Handelsblad* in a vein similar to its comments after the first congress; see "De laatste poging – bij u, over u en zonder u", 6 June 1928, evening edition, p. 1. A factual report appeared in "Het wijzigingsontwerp voor de N.V.", in *Algemeen Handelsblad*, 5 June 1928, evening edition, p. 3.

regulation of financial reporting by clauses in the articles of incorporation,[41] consolidated financial statements,[42] secret reserves,[43] goodwill,[44] and financial statement analysis.[45] From 1916 to 1918, the journal featured a regular section in which domestic and foreign financial statements were discussed.

Once the subject of company law reform was broached, financial reporting came to be discussed on a more or less regular basis. This happened not only when new drafts were issued but also in the years leading up to their issuance and at the time of the parliamentary debates. The 1910 draft by Minister Nelissen led to a series of editorials in *Accountancy* written by Th. Limperg Jr., together with an address given by J. Limburg, a member of the Second Chamber, at the Accountantsdag in 1911. J. Beerenborg, C. Miseroy, and G. van Slooten gave addresses dealing with financial reporting at the Accountantsdag celebrations in 1907, 1909, and 1912, respectively.[46]

In his Accountantsdag address, van Slooten proposed that the mandatory publication of financial statements be limited to companies (1) engaged in specific activities (savings banks and life insurance companies), (2) having a particular form of financing (when bearer bonds have been issued), or (3) that are listed on a stock exchange. His proposal was based on the assumption that the law could require publication (assumed to be detrimental to the interest of the enterprise) only if there were a significant public interest to be served thereby. (This view was at variance with that in his doctoral thesis, where he advocated that publication be linked to the legal form of the NV.) Publication, van Slooten said, should not be in the Official Gazette but in official collections of financial statements. (In

---

41 E. van Dien, "Bepalingen in Vennootschapsacten betreffende de Jaarrekening", in *Accountancy*, vol. 3, no. 29, 15 May 1905, pp. 54–55; J.G.Ch. Volmer, "De Balans", in *Accountancy*, vol. 3, no. 26, 15 February 1905, vol. 3, no. 27, pp. 14–15, and vol. 3, no. 28, 15 March 1905, p. 28.

42 "W.F.S.", "Iets over "Gecombineerde Balansen" ", in *Accountancy*, vol. 4, no. 37, 15 January 1906, pp. 4–5.

43 J.J.M.H. Nijst, "Geheime Reserves in verband met waarheid en duidelijkheid van balansen", in *Accountancy*, vol. 5, no. 48, 15 January 1907, pp. 2–4.

44 C. van Uden, "Goodwill", an account of a talk given before the "assistentenvereeniging van de N.A.V.", and recorded in *Accountancy*, vol. 8, no. 81, 15 January 1910, pp. 7–8; James Polak, "Goodwill", speech given at the 10th Accountantsdag (29 September 1918), published in *Accountancy*, vol. 17, no. 180, January 1919, pp. 2–5; vol. 17, no. 181, February 1919, pp. 13–16; vol. 17, no. 182, March 1919, pp. 25–29; and vol. 17, no. 183, April 1919, pp. 39–43.

45 B. Richters, "Beoordeeling van Jaarverslagen", a speech reported in *Accountancy*, vol. 8, no. 86, 15 June 1910, pp. 68–70; and vol. 8, no. 87, 15 July 1910, p. 86.

46 J. Beerenborg, "Openbaarheid en Unificatie van Balansen", stenographic account published in *Accountancy*, vol. 5, no. 58, November 1907, pp. 151–155; C. Miseroy, "Statuten van naamlooze vennootschappen, speciaal over administratie, balans, winst- en verliesrekening en winstverdeling", summarized in *Accountancy*, vol. 7, no. 79, 15 November 1909, pp. 125–127; G. van Slooten, "Wettelijke regeling van de publicatie der jaarstukken van Naamlooze Vennootschappen", stenographic account published in *Accountancy*, vol. 10, no. 111, October 1912, pp. 109–110; vol. 10, no. 113, December 1912, pp. 148–151; vol. 11, no. 114, January 1913, pp. 4–7; and vol. 11, no. 115, February 1913, pp. 19–20.

his thesis, he argued for publication by Commercial Registers, which would issue collected volumes of financial statements.)

He believed that a prescription of the required contents of the published financial statements would be useful, and he said that a separate law could be enacted, without awaiting a complete revision of the Commercial Code. For companies in the industrial, mining, and transport sectors, and for those with plantations, he suggested that perhaps four different sets of models could be worked out. (Here was another departure from van Slooten's thesis, where he recommended a single model to apply to all industries.) He allowed the inference that the process of agreeing upon the norms of prescription would not be difficult.

Van Slooten also advocated an obligatory external audit, and he (together with the audience) believed that the legal regulation of the auditing profession was urgently needed.

A review of the literature written by auditors yields the general impression that they were not in solid agreement on the financial reporting aspects of company law reform. The question of whether the required publication of financial statements warranted a prescription of their contents was answered in different ways. On the one hand, there were auditors like Nijst, who joined van Slooten in defending the feasibility and usefulness of prescribed contents, although they might differ on the need for having different prescriptions according to industry. Van Dien seems to have represented the view that any regulation by law was unjustified. Not prescribing the contents, he maintained, would lead to uninformative statements, and prescribing the contents was infeasible, since a law could never take proper account of differences among industries. Van Dien was of the view that shareholders who took a genuine, long-term interest in their companies would be able to press for satisfactory reporting. Speculators looking for short-term gains did not, in his opinion, have a right to be properly informed.[47]

A very different solution was presented by Prof. J.G.Ch. Volmer, a highly regarded founding member of both the Dutch Institute of Auditors (NIvA, Nederlandsch Instituut van Accountants) and the Dutch Auditors Society (NAV, Nederlandsche Accountants-Vereeniging), a founder and editor of *De Naamlooze Vennootschap*, and a professor at Delft (and later at Rotterdam as well). He also denied the feasibility of giving generally applicable legal prescriptions of the contents of financial statements, and he argued until his death in 1935 for clauses to be included in companies' articles of incorporation setting forth the accounting principles to be used. His initial comment on the Nelissen–Heemskerk Draft in *De Naamlooze Vennootschap* was rather negative. The draft, he said,

---

[47] E. van Dien, "Het nieuwe Wetsontwerp op de Naamlooze Vennootschap", in *Accountancy*, vol. 8, no. 91, December 1910, pp. 151–153; and van Dien's remarks following H. Munnik's Accountantsdag address in 1931: H. Munnik, "De publieke verantwoording der naamlooze vennootschap in het jaarverslag", in *Maandblad voor accountancy en bedrijfshuishoudkunde*, vol. 8, no. 11, December 1931, pp. 38–39.

asked too much (i.e., publication) of the small NV, and too little (i.e., there was no prescription of items to be disclosed) of the large NV's.[48] In a series of articles, Volmer discussed the desirability of excluding "closed" companies from the publication requirement, and proposed possible criteria for distinguishing "closed" from "open" companies.[49]

Limperg himself spoke out rarely on the question. His clearest remark was made on the occasion of the Accountantsdag in 1912. He argued that only in few situations were there clear grounds for the mandatory publication of balance sheets, and never for the profit and loss statement. Only when interested parties were incapable of looking after their own interests, as in the cases of insureds in relation to insurance companies and depositors in relation to savings banks, could the publication of balance sheets be justifiably prescribed by law.

Despite these differences of opinion, the NIvA succeeded in presenting its point of view on the Nelissen–Heemskerk Draft in an address to the minister.[50] In its submission, the NIvA recommended the substitution of "auditor" for the more general "expert" (*deskundige*) used in the draft law, and advanced the proposal that the permissive audit become obligatory for such classes of companies as might be determined by the minister on a case-by-case basis. In the end, neither of these two proposals found their way into the 1928–29 legislation. In Article 42a, as finally approved, the appointment of an "expert" was a matter of discretion left to the shareholders.

The NIvA also proposed an additional clause in Article 42 that would prescribe the separate disclosure of 12 balance sheet items, including both assets and liabilities. The actual phrasing of the NIvA's list, which was not entirely free of ambiguities, appears below:

> The balance sheet should show at least [the following items] separately: the value to be carried forward to expenses in the following years, fixed assets, inventories, receivables, investments in other companies, short-term securities and cash, the amount of issued and paid-in capital, the reserves and undistributed income, the value or amount of obligations to third parties, and the balance [i.e., profit or loss for the period].[51]

It is not quite clear how the NIvA report was drafted. It seems that a commit-

---

48 J.G.Ch. Volmer, "Openbaarheid en financieele aansprakelijkheid", in *De Naamlooze Vennootschap*, vol. 4, no. 2, 15 May 1925, pp. 36–38.

49 All of the articles appeared in *De Naamlooze Vennootschap*: "Vijtig jaar later", vol. 2, no. 1, 15 April 1923, pp. 2–3; "Het Wetsontwerp op Naamlooze Vennootschappen", vol. 6, no, 1, 15 April 1927, pp. 33–36; and "Balanspublicatie van besloten- en familie-vennootschappen", vol. 7, no. 5, 15 August 1928, pp. 131–132.

50 This address was not published in *De Accountant*, the journal of the NIvA, but it was reproduced under the title, "Amendement op het wetsontwerp 1925 op de naamlooze vennootschappen", in the journal of the Dutch Organization of Auditors (Nederlandsche Organisatie van Accountants), *De Bedrijfseconoom*, vol. 4, no. 8, 31 March 1927, pp. 238–243.

51 *Ibid.*, p. 238.

tee composed of J. Bosman, J. van Hamersveld, and L. van Kampen prepared an interim report that was to be discussed at a special general meeting in November 1926. The minutes of this meeting are difficult to understand, as the document on which the discussion was based was not reproduced.[52] It appears that the proposed addition to Article 42 was included in the interim report, at least in elementary form.

The NIvA report played a role in the parliamentary debate leading up to the 1928 Act. An amendment based on the report was submitted but rejected. But the NIvA's recommendation on disclosure, although not the one relating to the audit, was adopted more or less unchanged by the Visser Commission, which was charged with submitting a draft law for enactment in 1929.

2.3.3. Parliamentary course of the Nelissen–Heemskerk (1925) draft

Notwithstanding the interest expressed in company law reform outside Parliament, no action was taken on the Nelissen–Heemskerk Draft until February 1927, when, apparently as a result of the reactions registered to the draft, the minister submitted a Memorandum of Alterations (Nota van Wijzigingen), changing a number of points.[53]

On financial reporting, the only important change was made in Article 42c, in which a clause was added giving the Justice Ministry the right to exempt companies in certain industries from the publication requirement, as a step to accommodate critics of the undifferentiated treatment of "open" and "closed" companies.

2.3.3.1. Second Chamber

Even before the opening of formal debate, Mr J.R.H. van Schaik took the occasion of the Second Chamber's discussion of the 1926–27 budget for the Ministry of Justice to mention the possible establishment of a "Vennootschapskamer" ("Companies Commission"[54]) in connection with the impending consideration of the Nelissen–Heemskerk Draft.[55] Van Schaik's proposal for a Companies Com-

[52] The minutes of the meeting were reproduced in *De Accountant*, vol. 33, no. 1, January 1927, pp. 6–8.

[53] After the Memorandum of Alterations was incorporated, the draft law was usually referred to as the "Further Revised Draft" ("Nader gewijzigd ontwerp").

[54] Although the literal English translation of Vennootschapskamer is Companies Chamber, the authors prefer Companies Commission, as van Schaik's proposal refers to a regulatory commission as it is known in other countries. For the same reason, we translate Verzekeringskamer as Insurance Companies Commission, rather than as Insurance Companies Chamber.

[55] *Handelingen Tweede Kamer, Zitting 1926–1927*, pp. 762–764. Citations to page numbers in the section that treats van Schaik's proposal and the minister's reply will refer to this source.

Josephus Robertus Hendricus van Schaik (1882–1962) took his law studies at Utrecht, joined the Second Chamber in 1917 as a member of the Catholic State Party (Roomsch-Katholieke Staatspartij), and was obviously regarded as a man of substance. During the 1920's, he was a

mission was a precursor of a similar recommendation in the 1950's and 1960's, which eventually led to the establishment of the Enterprise Chamber (Ondernemingskamer), a judicial body. In making his proposal, van Schaik said that, while the draft law gave new and important rights to shareholders, they were not likely to make active use of these rights, and managements and supervisors could carry on more or less as they did before. He cited the Insurance Companies Commission (Verzekeringskamer), which had been looking after the interests of insureds since its establishment in 1922, as having proven its worth as a supervisor of the insurance companies. A comparable body, he said, should be set up to deal with other kinds of companies.

Van Schaik did not propose the specific duties of a Companies Commission, but he said,

> Please understand me correctly. I would not want a body that would need to involve itself in the management of company affairs in the economic or social sense. But a body that could do what is necessary to ensure the maintenance of the legal guarantees to shareholders and third parties (p. 763, col.1).

He added that the Companies Commission would be equipped with "a complete right of inquiry and the powers to take measures against negligent companies" (p. 763, col.1).

According to van Schaik, supervision by a Companies Commission was superior to the "fiction" of granting supreme power in a company to shareholders, as proposed by the draft law, for in the actual situation, as it has developed over time, management, not the shareholders, has assumed the de facto control. The draft law would, he said, introduce a kind of "false democracy" into company law. Shareholders and even labor should have co-determination (*medezeggenschap*), but not absolute power (p. 763, cols.1 & 2).[56] Finally, van Schaik said that the function of a Companies Commission could be performed by Chambers of Commerce if the burden were to be too much for one centralized body.

The minister, Mr dr J. Donner, said that he was not convinced of the merits of van Schaik's proposal. If, on the one hand, the Companies Commission were to be modeled on the lines of the Insurance Companies Commission, this would imply interference in the management of enterprise, because the commission had the unlimited right to ask questions, to give advice (even if it was not requested),

member of the progressive wing of his party. From 1933 to 1937, he served as Minister of Justice in the second and third Colijn cabinets, and he again served in the Second Chamber from 1937 to 1948. He was chairman of the Second Chamber during the last 15 years of his parliamentary service. During the Drees–van Schaik government of 1948–51, he was vice-Minister-President. From 1951 to 1957, he was a member of the Council of State (Raad van State). See the entry on van Schaik written by J. Bosmans, in J. Charité (general editor), *Biografisch Woordenboek van Nederland* (s-Gravenhage: Martinus Nijhoff, 1979), pp. 525–526.

[56] Although van Schaik did not say so explicitly, the Companies Commission was apparently intended to assume the role of a moderator, to observe on behalf of shareholders and others that a company had complied with the rules.

and to publish unheeded advice. Donner added that, if, on the other hand, the Companies Commission were merely to occupy itself with supervising compliance with statutory regulation, it would be assuming a task properly belonging to the public prosecutors and the courts. Besides, he said, such a Companies Commission would not be in a position to protect shareholders' interests when shareholders themselves did not actively seek to enforce them. The Chambers of Commerce, Donner said, should not be involved (pp. 822–823).[57]

The formal debates on the Nelissen–Heemskerk draft law took place on 22–25 March and 1 April 1927,[58] shortly after receipt of the minister's Memorandum of Alterations. In view of the fact that company law reform had dragged on for more than 50 years, the small interval between receipt of the minister's message and the beginning of parliamentary debate surprised most observers. It caught some interest groups, such as the NIvA and the Federation of Dutch Employers (VNW, Verbond van Nederlandsche Werkgevers), off guard, as their submissions came almost too late to influence the outcome.[59]

Prior to the debate, the VNW had published a petition to Parliament in which it recommended rejection of the draft law. A large number of companies had sent declarations of support for the VNW petition. The list of these companies in the *Proceedings* (*Handelingen*), in the section entitled "incoming mail", reads almost like a Who's Who of Dutch Industry. The list included many small and medium-sized companies (such as Koninklijke Nederlandsche Lood- en Zinkpletterijen[60]), together with such well-known, large NV's as Konink-

[57] Two reactions to van Schaik's proposal appeared in the literature, both negative. Prof. mr W.H. Drucker, after noting that van Schaik had not given many details about the operation of his proposed commission, suggested how van Schaik's proposal might work in practice, in order to enable a clearer assessment of the idea. Among the tasks that a Companies Commission might undertake, said Drucker, were: either taking over the audit implied in Article 42a or in some way assisting the auditor (e.g., by persuading management to change undesirable accounting practices); performing a limited preview of prospectuses, directed toward their completeness and clarity; advising shareholders of management proposals concerning reorganization; and, in a limited way, supervising company compliance with legal prescriptions. After elaborating on the possible role of the Companies Commission, Drucker concluded that most of the tasks of such a body could as well be performed by the auditor. A properly regulated auditing profession was much preferable to a Companies Commission, which, he said, would probably develop into a cumbersome apparatus lacking the necessary flexibility and expertise. "Een vennootschapskamer?", in *Economisch-Statistische Berichten*, vol. 12, no. 579, 2 February 1927, pp. 98–100.

In an article in its journal, the VNW predictably was not enthusiastic about van Schaik's idea. A Companies Commission created in the image of the Insurance Companies Commission was dismissed as impracticable, since a single supervisory body could not possibly possess the expertise needed to deal effectively with diverse industries and companies. "De heer van Schaik over het wetsontwerp op de naamlooze vennootschappen", in *De Nederlandsche Werkgever*, [no date indicated, but published in late November] 1926, pp. 560–561.

[58] *Handelingen Tweede Kamer, Zitting 1926–1927, p. 1775 ff.*

[59] The surprise of the NIvA was expressed in *De Accountant*, vol. 34, no. 1, January 1928, p. 9.

[60] Thirty-three years later, in 1960, J.A. Hamburger was chosen to chair a committee estab-

lijke Paketvaart-Maatschappij, Koninklijke Nederlandsche Zoutindustrie, Koninklijke Nederlandsche Hoogovens en Staalfabrieken, Werkspoor, De Steenkolen-Handelsvereeniging, Koninklijke Machinefabriek Gebr. Stork & Co, Heineken's Bierbrouwerij Maatschappij, Vereenigde Koninklijke Papierfabrieken van Gelder Zonen, and Centrale Suiker Maatschappij. Conspicuously missing from the list were N.V. Philips' Gloeilampenfabrieken (Philips' Incandescent Lamp Works) and Royal Dutch Petroleum. According to remarks made in Parliament, Royal Dutch was indirectly involved in the campaign against the law through the activities of Aug. Philips in the VNW.[61] Petitions were also sent by most of the Chambers of Commerce, also recommending rejection of the law, or at least a major modification thereof. The major point of contention in all of the petitions was the publication requirement for financial statements.

The parliamentary debates again made the familiar points: there should be a distinction between "open" and "closed" companies, and there should be a Dutch equivalent of the GmbH. A more original contribution was an amendment introduced by Dr J. van den Tempel,[62] in which he proposed an addition to Article 42, explicitly based on the NIvA suggestion, which would prescribe a number of items to be disclosed in the balance sheet. The amendment was not received favorably. Some members thought it was "too theoretical" and professed not to understand the meaning of the phrase, "the value to be carried forward to expenses in the following years".[63] One member supposed that it involved the estimation of future cash flows.[64] Others were opposed because it would be an example of excessive government intervention in the private sphere that could

---

lished by the central employers federations for the purpose of encouraging companies to be more forthcoming in their financial reporting. At the time of chairing the committee, Hamburger was managing director of N.V. Koninklijke Nederlandsche Lood- en Zinkpletterijen, having succeeded his father in that position some years earlier. As will be seen below, the Hamburger committee was created as a direct result of the government's installation of a commission to recommend company law reform. It is instructive to compare industry's response to the threat of legislation on company law reform in two very different eras: in the 1920's, calling a congress and petitioning Parliament; and in the 1960's, establishing a committee to provide constructive guidance to the government commission charged with shaping the proposed legislation.

[61] *Handelingen Eerste Kamer, Zitting 1927–1928*, p. 633.

[62] Jan van den Tempel (1877–1955) was a member of the Social-Democratic Workers Party (SDAP, Sociaal-Democratische Arbeiderspartij, the precursor of the Labor Party (PvdA, Partij van de Arbeid). Before becoming a member of the Second Chamber, he had been a prominent figure in the Dutch trade union movement and a member of municipal and provincial representative bodies. He was Minister of Social Affairs from 1939 to 1945. He wrote a number of books, including his thesis completed at the Rotterdamse Handelshogeschool, dealing with collectivist economics. In *Kapitaal en Volksinkomen* [Capital and National Income] (Haarlem: H.D. Tjeenk Willink & Zoon, 1920), he demonstrated an awareness of the effect of inflation on company profits in a section dealing with developments in income distribution in the Netherlands.

[63] The phrasing in van den Tempel's amendment was the same as in the NIvA's submission: "de waarde, toegekend aan ten laste van volgende jaren te brengen uitgaven."

[64] *Handelingen Tweede Kamer, Zitting 1926–1927*, pp. 1830–1831. Citations to page numbers in this section will refer to this source.

lead only to evasion and more regulation (p. 1830).

Minister Donner himself opposed the amendment because, he said, it would be unnecessary, as the *maatschappelijk verkeer* (the economic and social climate) could be counted on to give a clear indication of what constitutes a properly prepared balance sheet, and this would provide sufficient grounds for a prosecution of companies on the basis of the existing Article 336 and proposed Article 435 (para. 5) of the Criminal Code (Wetboek van Strafrecht), which would make the publication of misleading balance sheets and profit and loss statements a criminal offense (p. 1832). The proposed paragraph to amend the Criminal Code was included in the Nelissen–Heemskerk Draft and was being considered by Parliament at the same time as the proposed revision of the Commercial Code.

Since 1886[65], the Criminal Code had contained a provision relating to the publication of balance sheets, as follows:

> **Art. 336.** The merchant, the management or the supervisors of a limited company or cooperative society who intentionally publish an untrue balance sheet shall be punished by imprisonment for at most one year.

Yet, paradoxically, until the Commercial Code was revised in 1928, there was no statutory requirement for companies to publish their balance sheets at all. Although there were then no legally recognized criteria by which the truth of balance sheets might be judged, Volmer had written in 1914 that "Art. 336 is a blunt weapon; the falsehood must be inches thick for a verdict of guilty to be possible".[66] The Nelissen–Heemskerk proposal called for the addition of "or profit and loss statement" to Article 336 and the addition of a paragraph to Article 435, as follows:

> **5.** The management of a limited company that does not comply with the requirements imposed on it by the Commercial Code concerning the publication of the balance sheet and the profit and loss statement, together with the notes, [...] shall be punished by imprisonment for at most three months or a fine of at most *f* 1,200.

This provision did not appeal to a standard of truth, but instead relied on the specific demands to be contained in the revision of the Commercial Code. The modification of Article 336 and the addition to paragraph 5 to Article 435 were both approved by Parliament in 1928.[67]

---

[65] In 1886, the French *Code Pénal* was replaced by the Dutch Criminal Code (Wetboek van Strafrecht). The French law did not contain an equivalent to Article 336, which was introduced with the new text in 1886.

[66] J.G.Ch. Volmer, *De winstrekening en de vemogensbalans*, 2nd impression ('s-Gravenhage: G. Delwel, 1914), p. 108.

[67] This paragraph was not altered until 1970, when it was removed by the Act on Annual Financial Statements of Enterprises (Wet op de Jaarrekening van Ondernemingen), which created the Enterprise Chamber (Ondernemingskamer) to provide a civil remedy for non-

In view of Justice Minister Donner's opposition to the amendment introduced by van den Tempel, the amendment was changed to give the minister the right to prescribe the contents of the financial statements by decree, but even this version failed, by a vote of 32 to 27.

Article 42c, which had been changed by the Memorandum of Alterations to empower the minister to exempt companies in certain industries from the requirement to publish financial statements, was opposed from different sides. Two amendments were introduced: one to incorporate the exemption in the law as regards "closed companies", and another to do away with the escape clause altogether, reverting the draft law to its status before the alteration made by the minister. The latter amendment, which was submitted by Th. Heemskerk, the former Justice Minister, was carried by a vote of 42 to 25 (p. 1839). Hence, Articles 42, 42a and 42c, as presented in the Revised Draft, were approved with only minor changes by the Second Chamber.

During the debate, van Schaik had again mentioned his proposal for a Companies Commission, but it was not taken up by other members. In later years, nothing more was heard from van Schaik on the issue.

2.3.3.2. First Chamber

The draft law, as approved by the Second Chamber, was debated in the First Chamber on 13–15 and 19 June 1928.[68] Prior to the debate, the draft law had been discussed in committee. The final report, including the minister's notes in response to questions of the committee, was published in May 1928 (pp. 871–884).

The acceptance of the draft by the Second Chamber without the inclusion of an escape clause for "closed" companies led to a renewed campaign against the law by the VNW and the Chambers of Commerce.

The First Chamber was suitably impressed by the reactions of business, as expressed by the petitions and voiced at the second Congress of Business on 5 June. A number of members made the point that the Second Chamber and the minister had not paid sufficient attention to the view of the business community, because none of them had close ties or experience with companies. It was pointed out that, according to *Parlement en kiezer*,[69] none of the members of the Second Chamber who had voted in favor of the draft law had any business experience (p. 931). (The bellicose mood of these members was reinforced by the recent action

---

compliance with the law. In turn, the failure to obey judgments of the Enterprise Chamber would be penalized under the criminal law, in accordance with the Economic Offenses Act (Wet op de Economische Delicten).

[68] *Handelingen Eerste Kamer, Zitting 1927–1928*, pp. 917–989, 1013. Citations to page numbers in this section will refer to this source.

[69] "Parliament and Voter" is a yearbook containing short biographies of the ministers and of the members of the First and Second Chambers, together with the composition of all cabinets since 1848. G.G.J. Thissen (compiler), *Parlement en kiezer* (Leiden: Martinus Nijhoff, 1990).

of the First Chamber to reassert its independence from the Second Chamber by refusing to ratify an important treaty with Belgium, and so provoking a serious government crisis.)

In the end, the First Chamber agreed to the law after the minister promised that the question of "open" versus "closed" companies in relation to the publication of financial statements would be reconsidered soon after its enactment. The minister gave an early hint of this assurance in his Memorandum of Reply (Memorie van Antwoord) to the First Chamber (p. 876), when discussing the effect of the Heemskerk amendment to Article 42c. He repeated this promise more explicitly in debate, and said he would install a commission composed not only of lawyers, but also of businessmen (p. 986).

Even with the minister's assurance, the draft law was passed by only a narrow margin, 24 to 21, and was published on 2 July 1928 as no. 216 in the *Staatsblad* (Statute Book).

2.3.4. The Visser Commission and the 1929 act

On 26 July 1928, Justice Minister Donner fulfilled his promise to the First Chamber by installing a commission composed of lawyers, auditors, representatives from the business sector, a commercial banker and a representative of the stock exchanges, as follows:

- Mr dr L.E. Visser (chairman), member of the High Court, who, as adviser to Justice Minister Heemskerk, had been an active participant in the reshaping of the Nelissen draft.
- Mr W.F. Fruin, an adviser to the Justice Ministry.
- Mr G.H.A. Grosheide, a lawyer and auditor (member of the NIvA) in Amsterdam; his activity in the NIvA centered on legal matters, such as the work of the Disciplinary Council (Raad van Tucht).
- Prof. mr E.J.J. van der Heijden, a member of the Nijmegen law faculty and an authority on company law, one of the founders and current editor of *De Naamlooze Vennootschap*, in which he had made a general plea in favor of the Nelissen–Heemskerk Draft of 1925.
- Ir W.H. van Leeuwen, chairman of Nederlandsche Gist- en Spiritusfabrieken N.V., a sizable chemicals company, vice-president of the Industry Council, and one of the speakers at the Congress of Business in September 1927.
- Prof. Th. Limperg Jr., a leading auditor (member of the NIvA), a member of the department of economics of the Gemeentelijke Universiteit van Amsterdam, and founder and current editor of the *Maandblad voor accountancy en bedrijfshuishoudkunde*.
- A. Muller, a director from 1900 to 1921 of the Nederlandsche Handel-Maatschappij (a predecessor of ABN AMRO) and a former member of the

Chamber of Commerce of Amsterdam.
- J.G. van Neerven, an auditor in Eindhoven.[70]
- A.H. van Walcheren, a member of the Stock Exchange Association.

The secretary of the commission was J.B.W.P. Kickert, who was temporarily attached to the Ministry of Justice.

The Visser Commission submitted its report to the minister under date of 24 November 1928.[71] In its preliminary discussions, it was made clear that opinions were divided. Two members, presumably van Leeuwen and either Muller or van Neerven, did not want any publication requirements at all, while others favored limited publication but only when it was justified as a means of protecting the general public. This latter view meant that publication would not be linked to the legal form of the company, but to the listing of bearer shares on exchanges or to certain fiduciary activities such as banking and insurance. A third group held the opinion that publication should be tied to the legal form of the NV itself, although it was willing, for the sake of compromise, to exclude the "closed" companies if they could be satisfactorily defined. On this and other matters, the report does not reveal the identities of those who favored or opposed particular views.

Once a majority had emerged in favor of publication for "open" companies (and banks), the next question was the definition of openness. Again, opinions were divided. The final result was presented as a compromise: a proposal to amend Article 42c, making publication of the financial statements (i.e., the balance sheet, the profit and loss statement and the notes) mandatory according to a somewhat complex set of criteria that took into account the aggregate face value of bearer shares authorized by the articles of incorporation, the face value of both bearer shares and certificates of registered shares actually outstanding, whether or not the shares, certificates or bonds were listed on an exchange, and the nature of the company's activities (e.g., whether they involved banking or insurance). The practical effect of this formula was that publication was linked, in virtually all cases, with whether a company was listed on a stock exchange. The resulting proposed amendment to Article 42c was adopted by a 7–2 vote in the commission.

---

[70] Van Neerven (1892–1970) had a large reputation for drawing up the articles of incorporation of new companies, was an active figure in the Catholic Tradesmen's Association (Katholieke Middenstandsbond), and was a frequent adviser to the Minister of Economic Affairs on matters of concern to small and medium-sized business. Though a proprietor of an audit firm, he was not a member of any of the organizations of auditors. He was later the author of *Moderne bedrijfsleer voor den handelsdrijvenden en industrieëlen middenstand* (Amsterdam: N.V. H. van der Marck's Uitgevers-Mij, 1931). Interview with Prof.dr J.P.S. van Neerven (J.G. van Neerven's son), 3 October 1991. The authors surmise that van Neerven was chosen for the Visser Commission primarily as a representative of small and medium-sized business.

[71] The report was published as a supplement to the draft law presented to Parliament, in *Bijlagen Handelingen Tweede Kamer, Zitting 1928–1929*, nos. 283–284.

The commission also proposed an addition to Article 42, dealing with disclosure requirements. This issue was also controversial. Some members thought that a commission set up to lighten the burden of publication could hardly have come up with stricter measures. The proposal contained a list of 11 items that were to be shown separately on the asset side of the balance sheet. The commission defended its omission of any regulation of the equity side of the balance sheet by pointing out that there was a limit to the amount of information that the general public needed in order to secure its interests. It was assumed that the asset-side information would be sufficient for the needs of the public, supplemented by any information on the equity side that companies thought was in their interest to disclose. The lack of regulation of the contents of the profit and loss statement was not explained. The proposal to amend Article 42 was carried by a vote of 6 to 3.

In formulating its views, the commission may have been aware of the recent action of the UK Parliament to pass the Companies Act 1928, which called for particulars to be disclosed in the asset, liability and owners' equity sections of the balance sheet, and for the publication of a profit and loss statement whose contents were not prescribed. This was path-breaking legislation, and the accounting provisions of the Act were discussed and criticized in *The Economist* of 18 August 1928.[72] There was, however, no indication in the Visser Commission's report that it had taken cognizance of accounting developments in other countries.

The commission prepared a draft law embodying its proposals, which was accepted virtually without change by the minister. The draft law (and the enacted legislation) are usually referred to by the technical name of "Novelle" (New), being a change in law promised to the First Chamber in return for its approval of the original draft.

2.3.4.1. Parliamentary course of the "Visser Novelle"

Predictably, the Second Chamber protested the procedure by which, solely because of an understanding between the minister and the First Chamber, it was asked to approve a provision that it had earlier rejected.[73] Nonetheless, the Visser Novelle was passed without amendment on 15 May 1929 in the Second Chamber, and on 21 June 1929 in the First Chamber, on both occasions without a formal vote.[74] The law was published on 25 June 1929 as no. 363 in the *Staatsblad*.

The 11 items to be shown separately on the asset side of the balance sheet were included in a new, third paragraph of Article 42, as follows:

---

[72] "The New Companies Act. II – Accounts and Balance-Sheets", in *The Economist* (London), vol. 107, no. 4434, 18 August 1928, pp. 306–307.

[73] This view was expressed in the report of the preparatory committee, which was quoted in *De Naamlooze Vennootschap*, vol. 8, no. 2, 15 May 1929, pp. 54–56.

[74] *De Naamlooze Vennootschap*, vol. 8, no. 4, 15 July 1929, p. 121.

In the balance sheet of a limited company, as referred to in Article 42c, the following items are to be listed separately:

a. cash and immediately enforceable claims on banks, clearing houses and giro institutions;
b. investments [*deelnemingen*] in other enterprises and the amounts receivable from companies in which the investments have been made;
c. securities listed on an exchange, as referred to in Article 42c, in so far as the holding of them does not qualify as an investment in other enterprises;
d. securities not listed on an exchange, as referred to in Article 42c, in so far as the holding of them does not qualify as an investment in other enterprises;
e. receivables not classified under a and b;
f. movable assets [i.e., inventories] being processed or intended for processing or trading;
g. immovable assets, equipment and appliances, with their accessories and tools;
h. intangible assets, in so far as their separate disclosure is not called for by this article under some other classification;
i. the balance of revenues becoming due in future years;
j. costs and losses that are to be brought forward to the next financial year;
k. share capital issued but not fully paid.

2.3.4.2. Some reactions to the Visser Commission report and the 1929 act

Prof. Volmer, writing in the press, deplored the lack of regulation of the equity side of the balance sheet, and repeated his proposal for regulation through articles of incorporation.[75] In an unsigned article in *De kroniek van Dr. A. Sternheim*, presumably written by Sternheim, the report of the Visser Commission was dismissed as "a bitter disillusionment". The lack of any regulation of the equity side of the balance sheet was rejected as illogical.[76] Prof.mr dr H.R. Ribbius expressed satisfaction with the proposal, and judged it to be "well considered and well formulated".[77] R.A. Dijker, a prominent auditor, was moderately pleased with the proposal, although he pointed out that it could very easily be evaded by the use of holding companies, since consolidated statements were not required. He also stated that the law either should have regulated the contents of the profit

[75] Prof.dr J.G.Ch. Volmer, "De nieuwe wetgeving op de N.V.", in *De Telegraaf*, 20 February 1929, p. 13.

[76] "Wetgevers-wee, het verslag der publiciteitscommissie N.V. wet-1928", in *De kroniek van Dr. A. Sternheim*, vol. 6, no. 176, 1 April 1929, pp. 322–323. For particulars about this journal, see footnote 86, below.

[77] H.R. Ribbius, "Het wijzigingsvoorstel betreffende de nieuwe wet op de Naamlooze Vennootschappen", *Economisch-Statistische Berichten*, vol. 14, no. 686, 20 February 1929, p. 173. A commentator writing in *The Accountant*, the weekly English journal, said that, as a result of the 1929 Act, "Dutch balance sheets will be made more informative without imposing an unpractical rigidity upon their form". Dr Josef Hans, "Company Law Reform in Holland", in *The Accountant*, vol. 81, no. 2856, 31 August 1929, p. 268.

and loss statement, or should not have required its publication.[78]

An article by Dr W.J. Hartmann in the *Maandblad voor accountancy en bedrijfshuishoudkunde* was important, not for the author's argument, but for a strongly worded reply by an editor of the journal, probably Limperg, who had served on the Visser Commission. In his article, Hartmann had suggested that there was no such thing as "true financial statements" ("*ware jaarrekening*"), and that, in certain circumstances, it could be in the interests of all parties concerned with a company to hide temporary setbacks in order to preserve its credit standing. In a "Postscript" to the article, the editor wrote a reply (that was longer than Hartmann's article) in which he not only expressed abhorrence at the use of financial statements as an instrument of deception but also issued a judgment on the proposed statutory regulation:

> We know that Dutch managements of NV's will not follow Mr. Hartmann's directions. Until now, our companies have in general been well run, and their financial statements are in general completely reliable. New legal regulations were therefore not necessary to give us more guarantees. But now that such regulations have been approved, Dutch managements have nothing to fear from them [...]. And if there are any such managements that want to throw rules and traditions overboard, we count on the Dutch auditor to make this impossible. We decline to take the advice of Mr. Hartmann and to press for formal regulation of the contents of financial statements. If such regulation is intended to serve as support for the auditor, we declare that the Dutch auditor does not need that support; and if it is to give him formal protection from other demands of the law [e.g., suits brought against the auditor under civil or criminal law] then we say that the Dutch auditor does not desire such protection, because he does not intend to deviate from the code that he has followed until now, by which he cooperates in upholding the tradition of complete honesty and truth in the preparation of the financial statements of the contemporary firm.
>
> The possibility that the Dutch auditor could ever see it as his duty to validate untrue financial statements may not even be supposed.[79]

Mr E.A. Hofman welcomed Parliament's acceptance of the disclosure premise underlying the NIvA proposal of 1927.[80] The absence of a required breakdown of

---

78 R.A. Dijker, "De verplichte publicatie van balans en verlies- en winstrekening van de naamlooze vennootschappen", *De Levensverzekering*, 1929, pp. 47–55.

79 W.J. Hartmann, "De Nieuwe wet op de Naamlooze Vennootschap en de Accountant", in *Maandblad voor accountancy en bedrijfshuishoudkunde*, vol. 5, no. 8, September 1928, pp. 114–118. The "Postscript from the Editor" consumed most of page 115 and all of pages 116 to 118. Hartmann's article referred to several alleged instances in which companies or banks either delayed or obscured the disclosure of sensitive information in their financial statements, thus averting certain unpleasant consequences. This is an intriguing early reference to a phenomenon that came to be known as "economic consequences" in the 1970's. It is astonishing that an author of Hartmann's views would have submitted such an article to a journal edited by Limperg!

80 E.A. Hofman, "Het wetsontwerp betreffende de openbaarmaking van balans en winst- en

liabilities was noted, which was said to be not incompatible with the spirit of the law: as it was not necessary to explain in the notes how the liabilities were valued, it was the apparent intention of the law not to interfere with the use of secret reserves. Hofman concluded that the object of the law was not to give a "*juist inzicht in de gang van zaken en de werkelijke kracht van de onderneming*" ("true insight into the affairs and the real strength of the company"), but to protect interested parties by showing the minimum position of the owners' equity.

The VNW criticized the addition to Article 42 because of the procedure followed: the first Chamber had passed the law because of a ministerial promise to soften its impact, yet the result was a tighter regulation of companies still required to publish their financial statements.[81] The VNW called this "*een geniepige methode van wetgeving*" ("a sneaky way of legislating"), which had the effect of "*treiteren*" ("mocking") those who had opposed such legislation with serious arguments. While the VNW's criticism was directed at the procedures, its real disagreement was with the substance of the new paragraph in Article 42.

These critical remarks appear to have been a rearguard action. If one excepts reactions to the procedure followed for the Visser Novelle, there was relatively little response to this first serious attempt, in 1928–29, to regulate financial reporting. In *De Naamlooze Vennootschap*, there was no sequel to the numerous editorials that were devoted to the 1928 law. This muted reaction may have been due to a belief that the subject had, in van der Heijden's words, been "*doodgepraat, doodgeschreven en doodgerequestreerd*" ("talked to death, written to death and petitioned to death").[82]

In later years, the absence of any calls for a relaxation of the law's financial reporting provisions may be explained by an apparent lack of rigorous enforcement. In a 1936 article, J.C. van Sandick reported on a survey of companies' filings of their financial statements with the commercial registers.[83] On the basis of the sample of filings that he examined, van Sandick concluded that non-compliance with the law was widespread. He believed that a quarter to one-third of the companies that should have been depositing their financial statements were not doing so, and that this fact may have accounted for the absence for further audible opposition to the law.

verliesrekening van Naamlooze Vennootschappen", in *Maandblad voor accountancy en bedrijfshuishoudkunde*, vol. 6, no. 2, February 1929, pp. 17–20.

[81] The VNW's criticism appeared in "De Novelle inzake de naamlooze vennootschappen", in *De Nederlandsche Werkgever*, 31 January 1929, pp. 68–70.

[82] E.J.J. van der Heijden, "Doornroosje", *op. cit.*, p. 1.

[83] J.C. van Sandick, "Hoe staat het met de balanspublicatie? (Art. 42c W.v.K.)", in *De Naamlooze Vennootschap*, vol. 15, no. 8, 15 November 1936, pp. 225–227.

2.4. Developments during the 1930's

2.4.1. The state of financial reporting at the outset of the 1930's

H. Munnik, a prominent member of the NIvA, gave an address at the 22nd Accountantsdag in September 1931, in which he presented a comprehensive review of the quality of annual financial reporting by Dutch and foreign companies.[84] It was one of the very few systematic examinations of financial reporting practice to appear in the literature prior to the 1970's. His study was based on a "very large" sample of financial statements drawn from the collections of the Gemeentelijke Universiteit van Amsterdam and the Nederlandsche Handel-Maatschappij, a leading bank. Most of the statements were for financial years ending before 1930, and it is possible that many would not have reflected the 1929 law.

In general, Munnik found the state of reporting to be low. The mortgage banks and the general banks, he concluded, provided the most informative financial statements. The situation in other industries, he said, was "considerably worse" (p. 29). He complained of the failure to separate extraordinary from ordinary items, and of companies' unwillingness to disclose their sales, except, perhaps, in years when they could point to an upward trend. Although there were many commendable exceptions, Munnik concluded that

> those NV's that should, through proper publication, provide information to interested parties or to prospective interested parties (i.e., the general public), either do not do so at all, or do so in a very deficient way (p. 30).

He added that the exceptions could, to a certain extent, be explained:

> several extra-legal regulations have led to a better kind of reporting [*verslaglegging*] than was the custom until recently. As an example, I point to the conditions for admission to listing at the exchanges in Amsterdam and Rotterdam, which contributed in no small way to bringing about the above-mentioned good examples of reporting (p. 30).[85]

Munnik regarded British financial statements as only "slightly" better (p. 36). The American annual reports, while they were issued more promptly and looked attractive, did not, in his view, contain exceptional information (p. 36). The German reports, he said, were thicker than the Dutch but "they contain many

[84] H. Munnik, "De publieke verantwoording der naamlooze vennootschap in het jaarverslag", prepared paper (*preadvies*) and stenographic account of the presentation, with a record of the subsequent discussion in an appendix, *op. cit.*, pp. 26–42. Page citations in the text refer to this article.

[85] The authors are unaware of the stock exchange initiative to which Munnik referred. Beginning in 1909, the Stock Exchange Association required listed companies to publish an annual balance sheet and profit and loss statement, but the Association had not specified the contents of those statements or required that they be audited.

and exhaustive discussions of economic conditions which, as a rule, are more a source of theoretical wisdom than of facts that could be used to assess the business" (p. 31).

On the basis of his study, Munnik concluded that there was little use for formal requirements, since these do not stimulate companies to provide more than the barest necessities. Regarding the requirement in Article 42 of the 1928 law that notes should show how the movable and immovable properties were valued, Munnik found that "the legally required notes are in many cases a sham [*paskwil*]; a few meaningless phrases are given, and that's it" (p. 32). He recommended the following policy:

> I would prefer a general regulation that would require the reporting of true information [*juiste voorlichting*] and that would leave the implementation to the initiative of those who draft the financial statements, provided that the Legislature create or designate a body with disciplinary power to judge whether or not published information meets the general requirement (p. 33).

Munnik's suggestion of an arbiter of compliance was radical for the day, and it may have been influenced by the call for a Companies Commission which had been sounded by Mr J.R.H. van Schaik during the debate on the Nelissen–Heemskerk Draft in the Second Chamber in 1926–27.

Munnik believed that "limited companies that draw funds from the public market, or conduct business on the basis of public trust, should, irrespective of legal requirements, be aware of their duty to render accounts publicly [...]. When rendering an account in public, complete openness in reporting is essential. The benefit of complete openness to the public interest is so great that it outweighs, in most cases, the objections of particular NV's against publicity [...]. The auditor has a task in this as well, in the first place on the basis of his advisory function, but also by refusing to sign financial statements that seriously violate the above" (pp. 33–34).

Munnik's views were well ahead of his time. Even in the 1950's, the norms that he proposed in 1931 would have been seen by many as excessive. It was not until passage of the Act on Annual Financial Statements of Enterprises in 1970 that his progressive thinking found expression in public policy.

To be sure, there was opposition to Munnik's views in the discussion session following his presentation. Dr A. Sternheim, a NIvA auditor who founded and edited a journal devoted to the analysis of companies' financial statements,[86] pronounced himself opposed to rules of all kinds. "If businessmen want to be untrue, it is their affair, and if an auditor dares to burden his conscience with

[86] Sternheim's journal, which was published semi-monthly from 1923 to May 1940 (the last issue seen by the authors), was entitled *De kroniek van Dr. A. Sternheim*. Copies are available in the NIvRA library. (In 1933, Sternheim completed a law degree, and inserted "Mr." in the title of his journal.) Sternheim died on 10 May 1940 (*De Accountant*, vol. 46, nos. 4/5, July/August 1940, p. 3).

signing false or incorrectly grouped figures, then there are proper organs in the [auditors'] associations to take measures [...]. As a critic, one can really do no more than hope that a report will be short and to the point; "completeness" is impossible and cannot be required. Everything depends on the morals of the businessmen and their good faith" (p. 37). Others also were quick to criticize Munnik's advocacy of "complete openness". Drs A. Mey called it "wishful thinking", and E. van Dien said it would be harmful to company interests. Van Dien went on to elaborate his theory on "the shareholder as the natural enemy of the NV" (p. 39).

2.4.2. Auditors' reports

Two surveys of the frequency of appearance of audit reports in listed companies' annual reports, or of references therein to the fact that an audit had been conducted, showed a slight increase from 48 percent in 1926[87] to 55 percent in 1932.[88]

But these statistics understated the extent to which companies actually had external audits. It was the practice of some companies, apparently as late as the 1940's, not to disclose the fact that an auditor had been retained.[89] Several reasons for this practice have been given: making an audit was regarded as an internal matter, as its purpose was to inform directors and supervisors whether the accounting department was doing its work correctly; it was believed by directors and supervisors that they did not require any assistance to be trustworthy, and they held the view that shareholders did not need to know that the company had had an audit; and there was a perception by directors and supervisors that they were of a higher social class than the auditor, and that their responsibilities to report to the shareholders should not be seen as being on the same plane.[90] Underlying these views was the prevalent belief that companies

---

[87] Willem Buijink, "Some evidence on the demand for external auditing in an unregulated environment: the case of the Netherlands", paper presented at the 13th Annual Congress of the European Accounting Association, 18–20 April 1990.

[88] A. Sternheim, "Iets over den vorm der accountants-verklaring", in *De Bedrijfseconoom*, vol. 11, no. 6, December 1933, p. 67. Sternheim reported that "almost all" of his large sample of 851 companies were listed.

[89] The financial statements of N.V. Koninklijke Nederlandsche Petroleum Maatschappij (Royal Dutch Petroleum) have been audited by an outside firm every year since 1911, although it was not until the company's 1950 annual report that the existence of an external auditor was revealed. Letter to the authors from Drs J.F. Leeuwerik, dated 5 September 1991.

The financial statements of Werkspoor N.V. were audited at least as early as 1932, although the company did not disclose the existence of an external auditor until its 1954 annual report, just after its merger with Koninklijke Machinefabriek Gebr. Stork & Co N.V. was announced. A possible reason for not making the disclosure was that, until 1951, the auditor's report was qualified. Letter to the authors from J. Ringeling, director of the internal audit department, Verenigde Machinefabrieken Stork N.V., dated 16 September 1991.

[90] Interviews with Prof. A.M. van Rietschoten, 23 November 1990; with Prof.dr A.B. Frielink,

were under no obligation to disclose more than the law required. These views reflected the values and attitudes of entrepreneurs who were, in many cases, managing the companies they had founded, rather than the approach associated with the professional manager. Some of these owner-managers came from the ranks of aristocracy. By contrast, auditors often came from the middle class, and much of their early work was in the lower levels of enterprise, as bookkeepers and accountants.[91] Since an external audit was not required by law, the role of professional auditor was slower to develop than in some other countries, such as the United Kingdom.

2.4.3. Some improvements in financial reporting

In the 1930's, a small number of companies ventured to improve their financial reporting beyond the bare minimum required by law, and a few had done so even in the 1920's.

In its 1931 annual report, Philips displayed, for the first time, a consolidated balance sheet (*Concernbalans*), with the following announcement:

> At the request of many shareholders, our annual report is accompanied by a consolidated balance sheet in which we have included the figures for those companies in which we have a share of 50% or more, the other companies being shown under the heading Investments [*Deelnemingen*].[92]

During the 1930's, Philips was alone among the largest companies in presenting a consolidated balance sheet. That Philips did not also present a consolidated profit and loss statement was of no moment. Since the company reflected its share of subsidiary profits, losses and dividends in the investment accounts appearing in its parent-company balance sheet, the operating result (*exploitatieresultaat*), with which it began its parent-company profit and loss statement,[93] would have been the same as consolidated profit. Philips continued presenting a consolidated balance sheet until 1939/40, when it discontinued the practice owing to wartime restrictions on the information available from companies outside the Netherlands.

---

6 December 1990; with Prof.drs J.W. Schoonderbeek, 17 December 1990; and with A.F. Tempelaar, 18 July 1991.

[91] De Vries has remarked on the social ramifications of the transition from bookkeeper to professional auditor. Johan de Vries, *Geschiedenis der Accountancy in Nederland: Aanvang en Ontplooiing, 1895–1935* (Assen/Maastricht: Van Gorcum, 1985), pp. 78–79.

[92] Naamlooze Vennootschap Philips' Gloeilampenfabrieken gevestigd te Eindhoven, 1931 *Twintigste Jaarverslag* uit te brengen in de algemeene vergadering van aandeelhouders op 30 mei 1932, p. 7 (letter from the directors).

[93] Profit and loss statements in the 1920's and 1930's customarily began with the net profit figure, as it was rare to report any of the particulars of a company's operations. In Philips' 1931 profit and loss statement, three items appeared on the debit side: writedowns of receivables, writedowns of investments, and the distribution of profit.

Moreover, the companies outside the Netherlands were no longer subsidiaries of Philips, as they had been placed in the British and American Trusts.[94]

Philips was not the first enterprise to publish a consolidated balance sheet. Rutten's Bierbrouwerij "De Zwarte Ruiter" N.V. had published its first consolidated balance sheet as of 31 March 1928, and continued the practice in succeeding years. Wm H. Müller & Co. C.V. (Commanditaire Vennootschap-Limited Partnership) had published a consolidated balance sheet on an annual basis beginning as of 31 December 1926.[95] After the Müller partnership was reorganized as an NV in 1934, the company continued the practice of publishing consolidated balance sheets, and, beginning in 1934, added a consolidated profit and loss statement (*Geconsolideerde staat van overschot en winst en verlies*). Müller also provided considerable detail in its balance sheet and profit and loss statement. Koninklijke Nederlandsche Edelmetaal Bedrijven van Kempen, Begeer & Vos began publishing a consolidated balance sheet as of 1 July 1930, and added a consolidated profit and loss statement beginning for the year 1931–32.

In the USA, the preparation of consolidated statements by holding company groups had become commonplace by the 1910's, while in the UK, where practice was much slower to develop, a major address delivered in 1922 by Sir Gilbert Garnsey, followed by publication a year later of his celebrated book, had focused attention on the merits of consolidated statements.[96]

In general, however, Dutch financial statements in the 1930's were as abbreviated as the law would allow. The profit and loss statement typically consisted of profit for the year and a few items relating to profit distribution. The balance sheet seldom provided useful classifications, and the distinction between reserves and provisions was usually unclear. Few notes were provided. As will be discussed below, secret and undisclosed reserves were said to be used by many companies, although it was not often evident to the untutored eye whether a

---

94 The authors are grateful to Prof. H.L. Brink for a useful memorandum on Philips' consolidation policies and practices from 1931 to 1950.

95 In Bores' survey of the development of consolidated balance sheets in Europe, Müller was mentioned as one of the small number of larger companies on the European Continent that published such a statement (p. 332). Bores cited 1926 as the first year in which Müller issued a consolidated balance sheet. Wilhelm Bores, "Geschichtliche Entwicklung der konsolidierten Bilanz (Konzernbilanz)", in *Zeitschrift für Handelswissenschaftliche Forschung*, vol. 28, no. 3, March 1934, pp. 113–136; no. 4, April 1934, pp. 209–222; no. 6, June 1934, pp. 327–336.

Also see L. Polak, "De verslaglegging door holdingcompanies en enkele opmerkingen omtrent de accountantscontrole bij deze lichamen", in *De Accountant*, vol. 39, no. 7, September 1933, pp. 200–249, who mentioned that Müller's balance sheet for its holding company was drafted in accordance with English norms (p. 210).

96 See J. Kitchen, "The accounts of British holding company groups: development and attitudes to disclosure in the early years", in *Accounting and Business Research*, vol. 2, no. 6, Spring 1972, pp. 114–136; Robert G. Walker, *Consolidated Statements* (New York: Arno Press, 1978); and, for a comparative review of early practice, R.H. Parker, "Explaining National Differences in Consolidated Accounts", in *Accounting and Business Research*, vol. 7, no. 27, Summer 1977, pp. 203–207.

particular company was using them, or to what extent they were being used. It was even a rarity for companies to present comparative columns in their financial statements, despite the fact that the previous year's figures had already been reported. In 1934, Unilever began showing comparative figures, followed by Heemaf N.V. in 1937 and Philips in 1937–38. But there were few others.

In view of the state of financial reporting practice, it was not surprising that auditors were talking about promoting the uniformity of financial statements in the mid-1930's. F.F. van Doorne delivered the 1935 Accountantsdag address on "Uniformity of Financial Statements, Accounting and Product Costing".[97] At about the same time, W.C. Koppenberg Jr. argued that auditors must work for greater uniformity.[98] His preference was for complete uniformity in presentation and valuation. As a guide for preparing a uniform profit and loss statement, Koppenberg recommended *Verification of Financial Statements*, a booklet published in 1929 by the US Federal Reserve Board, which had been drafted by a special committee of the American Institute of Accountants.

2.4.4. Secret and undisclosed reserves

The earliest writings about secret reserves may be traced at least as far back as 1906.[99] There was further literature on the subject in the mid-1920's. In an article written in 1925, Volmer talked about the "social importance of secret reserves", and in subsequent articles he defended them as instruments of business policy and as beneficial influences on the business cycle.[100] The issue of secret reserves had been raised in Parliament during the debate prior to passage of the 1928 law. In reply to questions dealing with the interpretation of Article 42, especially concerning the notes on valuation principles, Minister Donner made it clear that the article was not intended to limit the allowed valuation principles in any way.

---

[97] F.F. van Doorne, "Uniformiteit in jaarrekening, boekhouding en kostprijsbepaling", in *Maandblad voor accountancy en bedrijfshuishoudkunde*, vol. 12, no. 11, December 1935, pp. 33–58.

[98] W.C. Koppenberg Jr., "Uniformiteit van de jaarrekening", in *Maandblad voor accountancy en bedrijfshuishoudkunde*, vol. 12, no. 9, October 1935, pp. 129–132.

[99] See Reiman and Nijst, *op. cit.*, pp. 152–154, for a discussion of the attitude of auditors toward secret reserves, which suggests that the issue had been addressed even earlier.

In the UK, "The creation of secret reserves, and their resurrection to augment the recorded profits in subsequent periods, were important features of company accounting in the second half of the nineteenth century and for several decades later". B.S. Yamey, "Some Topics in the History of Financial Accounting in England, 1500–1900", in W.T. Baxter and Sidney Davidson (editors), *Studies in Accounting* (London: The Institute of Chartered Accountants in England and Wales, 1977), p. 29. Also see Kitchen, *op. cit.*, pp. 121–122, and Jack Kitchen, *Accounting: A Century of Development*, An inaugural lecture delivered in the University of Hull on 18th November 1976 (University of Hull, 1978), pp. 25–28.

[100] Volmer, "Openbaarheid en financieele aansprakelijkheid", *op. cit.*, p. 38; "Balanspublicatie van besloten- en familievennootschappen", in *De Naamlooze Vennootschap*, vol. 7, no. 5, 15 August 1928, pp. 131–132; and "Stille reserves en de nieuwe wet op de Naamlooze Vennootschappen", in *De Naamlooze Vennootschap*, vol. 8, no. 1, 15 April 1929, pp. 1–4.

Its only purpose, he said, was to ensure that, whatever valuation principle was chosen, it would be properly explained in the notes. In the colloquy, Donner said that, as an example, office equipment could be valued at 1 guilder so long as it was made clear that this valuation gave rise to a reserve.[101]

The fact that secret reserves were not a burning issue during the 1930's may perhaps be inferred from the fact that they were hardly mentioned by Munnik in his comprehensive Accountantsdag address given in 1931, and in the discussion following his address. Nevertheless, the mere fact that secret reserves were defended from time to time would suggest that they were not without their detractors. Every now and then, arguments would be made against them.[102]

Drs A. Mey, a Limperg disciple, gave one of the Accountantsdag addresses in 1936 in which he mentioned secret reserves as an area in which theory could have a beneficial effect on practice. His point was that auditors should not occupy themselves with the question of whether and when to accept secret reserves in the balance sheet, but instead should persuade managements on the basis of value theory (in the Limpergian construct) to take a different attitude toward profit determination.[103]

That there remained a broad sentiment in favor of, or at least not against, secret reserves during the 1930's was made clear by two events in 1939. First, a special issue of the *Maandblad voor accountancy en bedrijfshuishoudkunde* was dedicated to views that were sympathetic to secret reserves; and, second, a revision of the NIvA's Rules of Professional Conduct (Reglement van Arbeid) appeared, in which secret reserves were explicitly accepted as part of "*goed koopmansgebruik*" ("sound business practice").

In the special issue of *MAB* (as the journal is known), three articles may be mentioned in particular. In perhaps the best-known article in the collection, T. Keuzenkamp, an auditor in The Hague, noted that there was some division in the ranks of auditors on the permissibility of secret reserves. Some auditors, he said, had taken it upon themselves to propagate the "*bedrijfseconomische*" concept of profit. Keuzenkamp said that he has adopted a more moderate position, namely, to emphasize adherence to the demands of practice. The primary function of financial statements, he said, was to assist shareholders in judging the performance of managerial stewardship. As long as there is no attempt to improve the figures by drawing from secret reserves without adequate disclosure, there is no

[101] *Handelingen Eerste Kamer, Zitting 1926–1927*, p. 878.

[102] For example, see G.K.H. Hinnen, "Stille reserves en de accountant", in *De Naamlooze Vennootschap*, vol. 8, no. 2, May 1929, p. 49, in which Volmer's position was criticized. G.H. Knap, "De publiciteit van de N.V.", in *De Naamlooze Vennootschap*, vol. 9, no. 11, February 1931, pp. 334–335, argued that the balance sheet should give a valuation of the company that was neither too high nor too low, and he expressed the opinion that the existence of secret reserves violates "honesty" and "publicity".

[103] A. Mey, "De noodzaak van een normatieve theorie der accountantscontrole als leidraad voor de beroepsuitoefening", in *de Accountant*, vol. 42, no. 7, September 1936, p. 239.

reason why management should not be allowed to present a less favorable picture of its own performance.[104]

Mr G.H.A. Grosheide, who was a member of the Visser Commission in 1928, surveyed a broad range of positions for and against secret reserves. Following his analysis, he concluded that secret reserves were part of the system of the law, and that they should remain as such, provided that proper measures were taken in the articles of incorporation to prohibit management from forming such reserves without the consent of the board of supervisors, and that adequate disclosure be given when releasing the reserves to profit.[105]

Prof.dr N.J. Polak, the intellectual leader of the Nederlandsche Economische Hoogeschool, in Rotterdam, introduced the notion of "secret reservations" (of profits). Polak had, in previous writings, accepted Schmalenbach's view on the primacy of the profit and loss statement. The balance sheet, he believed, was of limited usefulness since it could not be used as a basis for valuing the enterprise. Polak argued that one should focus on "secret reservations" (i.e., the effect of changes in the reserves on profit), rather than on their effect on the balance sheet, i.e., the amount by which the fixed assets would be undervalued. For a company with extensive and interrelated holdings of fixed assets, and which incurs sizable capital expenditures each year (and apparently on the assumption of a largely stable stock of fixed assets), Polak concluded that the "secret reservations" might not produce a significantly different effect on profit than that obtained by capitalizing and depreciating all capital expenditures. Hence, writing down fixed assets immediately to 1 guilder would lead to a profit that would not tempt companies to distribute amounts that are needed for ongoing capital expenditures.[106]

The second event in 1939 was the issuance of the report of the NIvA's Committee on the Revision of the Rules of Professional Conduct (Commissie tot herziening van het Reglement van Arbeid), which proposed a comprehensive restatement of the norms. The committee, which was chaired by Th. Limperg Jr., recommended that the benchmark of quality, "*juist beeld*" ("true picture"), used in the current set of rules, be replaced by "*goed koopmansgebruik*". No interpretation of the meaning of "*goed koopmansgebruik*" was given by the committee, except for a note in which it was stated that secret reserves were permitted, and that auditors could accept the use of such reserves in financial statements covered by their report.[107] The committee's position was not without its critics;

---

[104] T. Keuzenkamp, "Geheime en stille reserve en de accountant", in *Maandblad voor accountancy en bedrijfshuishoudkunde*, vol. 16, no. 10, November 1939, p. 195.

[105] G.H.A. Grosheide, "Juridische vraagstukken met betrekking tot de geheime en stille reserve", in *Maandblad voor accountancy en bedrijfshuishoudkunde*, vol. 16, no. 10, November 1939, pp. 195–199.

[106] N.J. Polak, "Geheime reserveringen, geheime en stille reserven", in *Maandblad voor accountancy en bedrijfshuishoudkunde*, vol. 16, no. 10, November 1939, pp. 168–170.

[107] "Rapport van de Commissie tot herziening van het Reglement van Arbeid", in *Herziening*

nonetheless, a vote in favor of preliminary approval was carried at the meeting held to discuss the report.[108]

The use of secret reserves seems to have been linked, to a certain extent, to Article 42d of the Commercial Code, which said:

> Unless the articles of incorporation determine otherwise, profit will fall to the benefit of the shareholders.

Mr G.J. Roes,[109] Prof.mr A. van Oven[110], and a committee of the Prof. Mr. B.M. Teldersstichting[111] (see Chapter 4) all have interpreted this clause, which still appears in the Civil Code (Book 2, Art. 105, para. 1), as a prohibition against declaring a dividend less than the amount of profit, except as authorized by the articles of incorporation. It would have been a simple matter to ask shareholders to give management wide powers in determining how much of the profit should be retained, and both van Oven and the Teldersstichting's committee stated that such provisions were frequently found in companies' articles. But they both made the point that such provisions were not really necessary, as managements could achieve the same end through the use of secret reserves. It may have nonetheless been the preference of many managements to regulate dividends by way of profit determination, so that it would not have been necessary to explain to shareholders at the annual meeting why a portion of profit was being withheld.[112]

2.4.5. Philips' not-so-secret reserves

Philips' decision in 1930 to bolster its annual profit by changing its treatment of secret reserves gives a vivid indication of the flexibility that companies had in

Reglement van Arbeid, Voorstellen tot vaststelling van een nieuw Reglement van Arbeid (Amsterdam: Nederlandsch Instituut van Accountants, May 1946), pp. 27–28. This volume contains the minutes of the special general meeting of the NIvA membership held on 2 December 1939 to discuss the first draft of the new Reglement.

[108] Final approval had to wait until after the War. There was at least one dissident voice: committee member G.K.H. Hinnen was opposed to the clause on secret reserves. It was stated in the report that "[committee] member Hinnen holds the view that '*goed* koopmansgebruik' precludes the formation of secret reserves". *Ibid.*, p. 26. As was noted above (see footnote 102), Hinnen wrote an article ten years earlier in which he criticized Volmer's position on secret reserves.

[109] G.J. Roes, "Wettelijke en statutaire machtsverdeeling tusschen de aandeelhouders en het bestuur eener N.V.", in *De Naamlooze Vennootschap*, vol. 9, no. 4, 15 July 1930, p. 99.

[110] A. van Oven, "Het N.V.-recht en de zelfstandigheid van de ondernemer", in *De Economist*, vol. 109, no. 12, 1961, pp. 892–894.

[111] *Open Ondernemerschap: De Groei van de Onderneming en het Vennootschapsrecht*, Geschriften van de Prof. Mr. B.M. Teldersstichting, no. 9 ('s-Gravenhage: Martinus Nijhoff, 1962), pp. 280–281.

[112] For a view that directors were concerned that shareholders might not take into account the wider interests of the company in such matters, see Dr A.C.M. van Keep, *De dividendpolitiek: Een onderzoek naar de bedrijfseconomische tendenties* (Leiden: H.E. Stenfert Kroese's Uitgevers-Maatschappij N.V., 1950), pp. 57–58.

deciding how much profit to report in a given year.[113] Philips' policy of providing more extensive disclosure in its financial statements made it possible to appreciate its change in treatment. Few other companies would have given sufficient information to allow such an analysis.

Philips had been expanding rapidly in the 1920's, investing heavily in fixed assets and in the securities of other companies, writing down all new fixed assets to 1 guilder by charges against profits, and paying regular and increasing dividends. It appears that about half of the company's capital requirements during those years was provided by the restraint on dividends resulting from the write-off policy.[114] In 1930, however, Philips would have reported its first loss if it had continued to write off capital expenditures against profit. Instead, Philips charged 50 million guilders to the "*Reserve voor uitbreiding*", which was the owners' equity account for additional paid-in capital. This reserve had been formed in the 1920's by sums received in excess of the nominal value of issued share capital. By making the charge against the additional paid-in capital account, Philips could write down the capital expenditures to 1 guilder without preventing the payment of a dividend.[115] In 1930, Philips' accounting made it possible for the company to have 5.4 million guilders available from operations for the payment of dividends. Philips repeated this practice in 1931, charging 19 million guilders to the additional paid-in capital account, and had 4.2 million guilders left over for the payment of dividends. Nothing in the Commercial Code prevented the company from writing down fixed assets against any account it wished. The audit firm of P. Klijnveld, which had taken over the Philips audit in 1930, did not even mention the change in secret reserve treatment in its lengthy, 1–1/2-page report on the financial statements![116]

[113] Pieter Lakeman discusses this episode in his *100 jaar Philips: de officieuze biografie* (Amsterdam: Lakeman Publishers, 1991), pp. 92–93.

[114] Dr G.J.M. de Gruyter, *Winstproblemen* ('s-Hertogenbosch: Teulings' Uitgevers-Maatschappij, 1930), pp. 177–179.

[115] Keus makes the point that Philips' practice was consistent with the theories of the period, which held that writeoffs (or depreciation) represented a setting aside of sums out of profit for the eventual replacement of fixed assets. In years with no profit, such sums could be transferred only from other reserves. Dr J. Keus, "Reserves bij Reserves", in *Pacioli Journaal*, vol. 4, no. 2, January 1991, pp. 14–15.

[116] For a contemporary analysis of Philips' financial reporting during this period, see the following articles in *De kroniek van Dr. A. Sternheim*: "Philips", vol. 9, no. 228, 1 June 1931, pp. 46–47; "Philips' Gloeilampenfabrieken", vol. 10, no. 251, 15 May 1932, pp. 29–32; and "Philips' Gloeilampenfabrieken", vol. 11, no. 276, 1 June 1933, pp. 34–35. The author of these unsigned articles, probably Sternheim, was less inclined to criticize Philips' accounting maneuver than to chide the company for giving its shareholders and the public nothing but optimistic and positive-sounding statements, even as late as 1929. The author wrote, "if the financial statements for 1929 and the prospectus for 1930 do indeed contain [all] that was known on those dates, what should one think of company planning that apparently could take so little account of a possible setback" (1 June 1931, p. 46).

2.4.6. General assessment of the 1930's

Notwithstanding the attempts by a few companies to improve their financial reporting, the general run of company financial statements during the 1930's was dismal. The great majority of companies disclosed no more than the law required. And the law required very little. Typically, the profit and loss statement, whose contents were not prescribed by law, was presented as a two-sided account. On the credit side, a single figure was shown, usually denominated as "*exploitatieresultaat*", which evidently meant "operating result". On the debit side, depreciation would appear, and the balance would be dedicated to dividends or, if the articles of incorporation so provided, an increase in reserves. Sometimes, interest would appear on the debit or credit side. It was commonplace for companies not to label any figure in the profit and loss statement as "profit" or "loss".

There was no concerted movement during the decade for improved financial reporting. During most of the 1930's, the economy was in the doldrums, yet beginning in 1937 it picked up somewhat with the preparations for war elsewhere in Europe.[117] Further financial reporting reform awaited the burst of energy that followed World War II.

Appendix 2.1. Proposed reporting requirements in successive stages of the Commercial Code reform

	Kist Commission Draft - 1890	*Nelissen Draft 1910*	*Revised Draft 1925*	*Further Revised Draft 1927*	*As accepted by Parliament 1928*	*Visser Commission proposals, accepted by Parliament 1929*
required publication by:	all NV's	all NV's	all NV's	all NV's, unless excepted by Order in Council	all NV's	mainly NV's with listed shares and other large NV's
required publication in:	Official Gazette	Official Gazette	Commercial Register	Commercial Register	Commercial Register	Commercial Register
audit:	not mentioned	optional	optional	optional	optional	optional
balance sheet disclosure:	asset and equity side items	none	none	none	none	asset side items only
required profit and loss statement disclosure:	none	none	none	none	none	none
notes on valuation required:	no	no	yes	yes	yes	yes

[117]See Johan de Vries, *The Netherlands Economy in the Twentieth Century* (Assen: Van Gorcum, 1978), pp. 61–62 and 86–95.

3. Developments from 1945 to 1959: Agitation for improved financial reporting

3.1. Post-World War II developments: 1945–1949

The postwar financial reporting climate changed profoundly from that of the prewar years. Prior to the war, many companies had made free use of secret reserves in order to smooth, or at least understate, their year-to-year reported profits, and the fixed assets of not a few companies were written down to 1 guilder. Following the war, this conservative practice became, for quite a few companies, no longer supportable. With the enormous expenditures that many companies had to make to repair extensive war damage, as well as to modernize and expand their operations, companies would have reported very unfavorable results if they had continued their practice of writing off virtually all such expenditures immediately – at a time when they were in search of capital to finance the large expenditures.

Following the war, attitudes toward companies' responsibilities for communicating with shareholders and the public gradually began to change. Rather than viewing financial reporting as a threat or, at best, an onerous duty, the directors of some of the largest companies came to see it as an opportunity.

In the first years following the war, Lever Brothers & Unilever N.V.[1] and N.V. Philips' Gloeilampenfabrieken (Philips' Incandescent Lamp Works) made important changes in their financial reporting. Commencing in 1945, Unilever, which had been trading on the London Stock Exchange for some years, announced that it had decided to adopt most of the recommendations of the UK government's Company Law Amendment Committee (the Cohen Committee), whose report was the basis for the Companies Act 1947.[2] Two major improvements in Unilever's annual report were the introduction of consolidated statements and a much more informative profit and loss statement. Few Dutch companies had, by

[1] The Anglo-Dutch enterprise consisted of Lever Brothers & Unilever Limited and Lever Brothers & Unilever N.V., as equal partners. The annual report issued in the Dutch language carried the name of Unilever N.V., while the annual report written in English carried the name Unilever Limited. Hereinafter, the joint enterprise will be cited as Unilever, except when particular reference is being made to either of the two holding companies.

[2] Lever Brothers & Unilever N.V., *Jaarverslag en Jaarrekening over het jaar 1945*, pp. 1–2. The Cohen Committee report was published under the title, *Report of the Committee on Company Law Amendment* (London: His Majesty's Stationery Office, 1945).

then, provided a full set of consolidated statements,[3] and no profit and loss statements of the day were as detailed as Unilever's beginning in 1945. Included in its profit and loss statement was, for the first time, a disclosure of sales turnover[4], which had not formed part of the Cohen Committee's recommendations, and was rarely practiced in the UK and the Netherlands. Moreover, Unilever provided a breakdown of sales by 9 product lines and its services sector. In 1946, the company introduced a 10-year summary of comparative financial data, and in 1947 it began presenting a geographical analysis of sales by five major regions. Few companies outside of North America were disclosing aggregate sales turnover, and virtually no companies were reporting sales breakdowns by segment. The first effective demands for "segment reporting" from the financial community and regulators were not heard until the 1960's, when conglomerate mergers were in fashion.[5]

Two men may have had much to do with the development of Unilever's financial reporting policy. As is noted below (in the section on the Rijkens report), P. Rijkens, the chairman of Lever Brothers & Unilever N.V., had a long-standing interest in accounting. Moreover, he was a progressive thinker and believed in good external relations.[6] Also, P.M. Rees, the chief accountant of Lever Brothers & Unilever Limited, the UK wing of the Anglo-Dutch enterprise, was one of the leading figures in the committee of the Institute of Chartered Accountants in England and Wales that had been drafting a series of "Recommendations on Accounting Principles". The contents of several of the Recommendations issued between 1942 and 1944 found their way into the Cohen Committee report and, in the end, the Companies Act 1947.[7]

Het Financieele Dagblad commended Unilever for its new approach to publicity:

---

3 As is discussed in the previous chapter, Philips presented a consolidated balance sheet as early as 1931, and since the company used the equity method of accounting for investments, the profit in its parent-company-only profit and loss statement would have been the same as if it had been consolidated.

4 Unilever's progressive financial reporting did not include the disclosure of cost of sales until 1961, when it took up a listing on the New York Stock Exchange, where all companies were required to report such information.

5 See A.A. Sommer, Jr., "Conglomerate Disclosure: Friend or Foe?", in Alfred Rappaport, Peter A. Firmin and Stephen A. Zeff (editors), *Public Reporting by Conglomerates: The Issues, the Problems, and Some Possible Solutions* (Englewood Cliffs, NJ: Prentice-Hall, Inc., 1968), pp. 1–16, and Appendix B (pp. 143–147). Some witnesses at the Cohen Committee hearings, however, favored a breakdown of sales and profit by product activities. See Leonard W. Hein, *The British Companies Acts and the Practice of Accountancy 1844–1962* (New York: Arno Press, 1978), p. 269.

6 Interview with Mr H.C. Wesseling, 10 July 1991.

7 See Stephen A. Zeff, *Forging Accounting Principles in Five Countries: A History and an Analysis of Trends* (Champaign, IL: Stipes Publishing Co., 1972), pp. 7–16; and Paul Bircher, *From the Companies Act of 1929 to the Companies Act of 1948: A Study of Change in the Law and Practice of Accounting* (New York: Garland Publishing, Inc., 1991), p. 235.

> Apparently, after realizing that shareholders need to be given better information [*voorlichting*], the joint board of the Dutch and English Unilever have made a very laudable, and, in our opinion, for the time being, in all respects a successful attempt – one that is unique among international approaches to publicity in the business world – to give us a clearer, better-arranged and more detailed report than has been usual until now anywhere in the world. We have the fullest praise for this approach. Confidence in [Unilever] shares will, through this openness (which the company plans to expand), undoubtedly further increase.[8]

The Economist called Unilever's 1945 financial statements "the apotheosis of holding company accounting" and "an accounting *tour de force*",[9] and characterized its 1946 financial statements as "accounting elegance".[10]

In its annual report for 1945–46, Philips abandoned secret reserve accounting and replaced it by a new policy of basing depreciation on the current cost of its fixed assets.[11] While A. Goudeket, Philips' chief internal auditor and a staunch disciple of Th. Limperg, would have argued for current cost accounting on theoretical grounds,[12] the switch probably would have appealed to Philips' management board for tactical reasons. In view of its huge postwar expenditures,

---

8 "Unilever-publiciteit – Heeft ongeëvenaard niveau van perfectie bereikt", in *Het Financieele Dagblad*, 21 November 1946, p. 1. In a further column, the newspaper referred to Unilever's statement that it had implemented the recommendations of the Cohen Committee report in the UK. The paper indicated that, in its issues of 17 and 25 July 1945, it had given extensive coverage to the Cohen Committee's recommendations. "Unilever-concern – Ontplooit groote activiteit over de geheele wereld", in *Het Financieele Dagblad*, 22 November 1946, p. 1.

If one may judge from Sternheim's assessment, Unilever was not known for the quality of its financial reporting in the 1930's. In successive issues of his journal, Sternheim criticized Unilever's financial statements for their lack of information. See, for example, "Unilever", in *De kroniek van Mr. Dr. A. Sternheim*, vol. 15, no. 370, 1 May 1937, pp. 16–17. Attitudes, however, were changing within Unilever. In his history of Unilever, Wilson referred to the emergence of a new conception of business leadership, reflecting "an increasing interest in wider economic and social problems". Charles Wilson, *The History of Unilever: A Study in Economic Growth and Social Change* (London: Cassell & Company Ltd, 1954), vol. II, pp. 381–382.

For another criticism of Unilever's reporting in the 1930's, see J.J.M.H. Nijst, "Rondom het laatste Jaarverslag der Unilever", in *De Bedrijfseconoom*, vol. 10, nos. 1/2, 31 July 1932, pp. 1–10.

9 "Business Notes: Lever and Unilever Accounts", in *The Economist* (London), vol. 151, no. 5387, 23 November 1946, p. 840.

10 "Business Notes: Unilever and World Trade", in *The Economist* (London), vol. 153, no. 5426, 23 August 1947, p. 337.

11 Although Philips has used the term "replacement value" (*vervangingswaarde*) in English-language discussions of its system, the term "current cost" is used here, as being more in line with usage in the Anglo-Saxon literature on the subject of current value/current cost accounting. Some authors, however, prefer to use "replacement value accounting" to describe Dutch practices. See, e.g., R.K. Ashton, *The Use and Extent of Replacement Value Accounting in the Netherlands* (London: The Institute of Chartered Accountants in England and Wales, 1981), and Dick H. van Offeren, "Replacement Value Accounting: Theory and Practice", in *Advances in International Accounting*, vol. 2, 1988, pp. 23–50.

12 A. Goudeket was Philips' chief internal auditor from 1938 to 1940 and from 1945 to 1964, when he retired. During the War, Goudeket, who was Jewish, was assigned to special duties

especially at a higher price level, Philips' management would have risked large operating losses if it were to have continued writing down its capital expenditures to 1 guilder. The implications for its existing shareholders and new capital suppppliers would have been horrifying. Philips' management board confessed the problem: "As further important investments [in fixed assets] are to be expected in the near future, we do not consider it fair to the shareholders still to continue the tradition of writing off to one guilder".[13] As mentioned in the discussion of secret reserves in Chapter 2, statute law has required that companies distribute all of their profit as dividends unless the company's articles of incorporation were amended to authorize the company to retain some profits in the enterprise. Companies had apparently found it more agreeable to use secret reserves to depress reported profits than make a formal request of their shareholders for permission to withhold some profits from the payment of dividends. In Philips' case, the use of current cost depreciation would have appealed to the company's management board as a means by which the financial statements would continue to give a conservative picture, but without actually showing annual losses.

Ironically, at the general meeting of Philips' shareholders in July 1947, Ir P.F.S. Otten, the company's president, said that fears had been raised that the company would weaken itself by breaking with the tradition of not paying dividends before all assets were written down to 1 guilder. Otten went to great lengths to assure shareholders that the company's balance sheet, notwithstanding the new accounting policy, gave a very conservative picture, as it still reflected enormous reserves from the past.[14]

Two other large companies also began to disclose more information. Koninklijke Luchtvaart Maatschappij N.V. (KLM Royal Dutch Airlines) started disclosing its revenues in 1946, and Albert Heijn N.V. (renamed Koninklijke Ahold N.V. in 1973), a major food retailer, began publishing consolidated statements in 1948.

In general, however, very few large companies in the 1940's even provided comparisons with the previous year's figures in their financial statements. As was noted above, Unilever, Heemaf, and Philips had begun providing such comparative information in the 1930's. Algemene Kunstzijde Unie N.V. (known as A.K.U. and which became part of Akzo N.V. in a 1969 merger) began doing so in its 1948 balance sheet.

Mr dr H.D.M. Knol, a member of the Brotherhood of Auditors (Broederschap

---

and then went underground. Memorandum dated 7 February 1980, prepared by L. Homburg, Accountantsdienst (Internal Audit Department), N.V. Philips' Gloeilampenfabrieken.

13 N.V. Philips' Gloeilampenfabrieken, *Thirty-fourth Annual Report Covering the Period from 1st May 1945 up to and Including 31st December 1946 (20 months)*, English languàge version, p. 17.

14 "Philips' Gloeilampen – Optimistische geluiden", in *Het Financieele Dagblad*, 16 July 1947, p. 1.

van Accountants), remarked that commentaries had appeared in the press on the unsatisfactory state of company financial reporting. Knol criticized the 1929 law for "not meeting its purpose, viz. to give interested parties an insight into the financial position of the NV".[15] Knol's view suggests a higher expectation of the usefulness of financial statements than was evidenced in the debates preceding passage of the 1928 and 1929 Acts, which were concerned with providing protections or guarantees to the shareholder, not with conveying "insight". Reflecting the more modern view, Knol was therefore blaming the 1929 Act for a deficiency it was not, in that earlier era, intended to repair.

In an article written in Australia, J.E. Spinosa Cattela compared Dutch financial statements with those in the United States, and complained that many Dutch companies, by making nothing more than "a terse mention of operating profit as the only figure on the credit side of the profit and loss account", failed to give an insight into the operation of the business. He concluded that an improvement in Article 42, which was silent about the required contents of the profit and loss statement, was "strictly necessary".[16]

Finally, in 1949, the Stock Exchange Association (Vereeniging voor den Effectenhandel), the body that governs the Amsterdam Stock Exchange, broke its long silence on financial reporting, and issued a circular in which it encouraged listed companies to make certain improvements.[17] In its circular, the Association was reluctant to be specific or prescriptive, although it mentioned the possibility of increasing the demands placed on companies that were already listed. It

---

[15] H.D.M. Knol, "Jaarverslagen", in *Maandblad voor Bedrijfsadministratie*, vol. 52, no. 618, September 1948, p. 98.

[16] J.E. Spinosa Cattela, "Publicatie van jaarstukken in Amerika en Nederland", in *Maandblad voor accountancy en bedrijfshuishoudkunde*, vol. 22, no. 1, January 1948, esp. pp. 17–18. Two months earlier, Spinosa Cattela had written a brief article commenting on the use in Australia and the United States of the vertical format of the balance sheet, leaving an inference that it represented a more modern approach to financial reporting. "Een nieuwe vorm van publicatie van de jaarbalans", in *Maandblad voor accountancy en bedrijfshuishoudkunde*, vol. 21, no. 10, November 1947, pp. 324–326.

Spinosa Cattela, formerly a senior member of Philips' internal audit department, was the author of *Inleiding tot de leer van de accountantscontrôle* (Leiden: H.E. Stenfert Kroese's Uitgevers Maatschappij, N.V., 1948), and *Diccionario de Contabilidad, Administración, Control y Ciencias Afines* (Buenos Aires: Selección Contable, 1943). He was the father of R.C. Spinosa Cattela, who is mentioned later in this Chapter and in Chapters 5 and 6.

[17] Since 1909, the Stock Exchange Association had required listed companies to publish an annual balance sheet and profit and loss statement. In 1958, it added the stipulation that both consolidated and separate financial statements must be made available unless the Association were to waive this requirement. It also provided, beginning in 1958, that the annual financial statements should give a "faithful picture" (*getrouw beeld*). But the Association has never specified the contents of the annual financial statements or required that they be audited. (It was not until 1970 that the law required that the annual financial statements of such companies be audited.)

It should be noted, however, that in 1958 the Stock Exchange Association did begin to require the inclusion of an auditor's report in new-issue prospectuses, although this requirement could be waived by the Association's executive committee.

complained that "some limited companies do not always provide information to the public that is needed to form a well-founded judgment about the course of affairs and financial position of these companies".[18] Yet, because of the differences among companies and the uncertainty over what information was relevant for inclusion in financial reports, the Association concluded that "it is difficult to find any general formulas in the matter".[19]

The Association did express the view that the publicity demanded in the public interest would not interfere with the interests of the companies concerned,[20] evidently in an effort to allay the fears of some managements over the wisdom of disclosing additional information. Even the timeliness of annual reports was an issue. The Association reminded companies that a provision in Article 42 of the Commercial Code required that annual reports were to be published within eight months of the end of the financial year.

As the 1940's ended, there was growing disquiet over the adequacy of the legal requirements that were last revised two decades earlier. Companies were more aware of the importance of the securities market as a source of capital, and of the need to provide shareholders with more than the barest essentials from one side of the balance sheet. Commentators used such terminology as "insight" and "a well-founded judgment" in a company's operations. Financial statements had come to be viewed as a source of information about the position and profitability of a company, rather than merely a first line of protection for shareholders against possible mismanagement by the directors.

3.2. Private-sector initiatives to improve financial reporting: 1950–1959

3.2.1. The Stock Exchange Association takes a more aggressive tack

In October 1951, the Stock Exchange Association issued a second circular, in which it mustered the courage to advance several recommendations. Evidently, its gentle persuasion was not working. It noted that "a number of companies persist in publishing defective information, which damages not only the public interest but also the interest of the companies themselves".[21] It nonetheless observed that a policy of encouraging voluntary compliance was to be preferred over mandatory prescriptions if only because the latter could apply only to newly listed companies. (The Association had reconsidered the suggestion made in its

---

[18] Mededelingen no. 270 van het Bestuur aan de Leden, Vereeniging voor den Effectenhandel (Bedrijfsgroep Effectenhandel), dated 15 January 1949, p. 1.

[19] *Ibid.*

[20] *Ibid.*

[21] Mededelingen no. 285 van het Bestuur aan de Leden, Vereeniging voor den Effectenhandel (Bedrijfsgroep Effectenhandel), dated 15 October 1951, p. 1.

1949 circular that the demands placed on companies already listed might be increased.) In its second circular, the Association asked its members to bring the following items to the attention of listed companies:

- the timely publication of annual reports;
- an interim report, to be published not later than the ninth month of the financial year, containing a general discussion of its course of affairs;
- the inclusion in annual reports of comparative figures from the previous year;
- a listing in annual reports of investments,[22] together with as many amplifying details as possible (in lieu of consolidated statements); and
- the inclusion in annual reports of an analysis of the distribution of income to the several classes of shareholders.

In 1952 and 1954, the NIvA's Advisory Committee on Professional Matters (Commissie van Advies inzake Beroepsaangelegenheden) also issued a pair of reports on comparative figures.[23] But both reports dealt exclusively with the auditor's responsiblity for comparative figures and not with whether such information was a useful addition to the financial statements.

3.2.2. Independent audits

A curious omission from the Stock Exchange Association's list was a reference to the examination of company financial statements by an independent auditor. Two surveys conducted in 1948 and 1951 found that between 56 and 72.6 percent of listed companies had an independent audit.[24] In a study conducted by the authors of the annual reports of 33 major companies from 1935 to 1960, it was

[22] The term *deelnemingen*, which is rendered as "participations" or "participating interests" in many translations from the Dutch language into English, is here translated as "investments". According to the Explanatory Memorandum attached to the Act on Annual Financial Statements of 1970, *deelnemingen* are "understood to be a relationship with another enterprise that is meant to be lasting and which results from the ownership of a certain part of the share capital [presumed to be at least 25 percent] of the latter enterprise... : the participating company itself has an interest in the activities of the dependent enterprise and thus usually a certain influence on its management". *Wet op de jaarrekening van ondernemingen/Act on Annual Accounts of Enterprises*, NIVRA geschrift nummer 6 (Amsterdam: Nederlands Instituut van Registeraccountants, 1972), p. 67.

[23] "I. Vergelijkende cijfers in een jaarrekening", in *de Accountant*, vol. 59, no. 3, November 1952, pp. 219–221; and "Nader rapport der C.A.B. aan het Bestuur betreffende vergelijkende cijfers in een jaarrekening", in *de Accountant*, vol. 60, no. 9, March 1954, pp. 479–481.

[24] In 1948, Lafeber published a study of 263 companies, and found that 72.6 percent at least mentioned an audit. He omitted from his sample a large number of companies with affairs in Indonesia that had not recently published financial statements. See A.F. Lafeber, "Een onderzoek naar aanwezigheid van accountants-verklaringen in jaarverslagen van naamloze vennootschappen, welker aandelen of obligaties officieel genoteerd zijn", in *Maandblad voor accountancy en bedrijfshuishoudkunde*, vol. 22, no. 5, May 1948, pp. 140–145.

In 1951, a survey taken by the NIvA found that, of 559 companies listed on the Amsterdam Stock Exchange, 315 (56 percent) had independent audits. See J. Kraayenhof, "The Profession in the Netherlands: Sixty Years of Growth and Development", in *The Accountant*, vol. 133,

found that 14 still did not disclose the existence of an independent auditor as late as 1952.[25] Those omitting a reference to an independent auditor in 1952 were the following[26]:

- Algemene Kunstzijde Unie N.V. (A.K.U.)
- N.V. Koninklijke Paketvaart-Maatschappij*
- Werkspoor N.V.
- Koninklijke Java–China Paketvaart Lijnen N.V.*
- N.V. Nederlandsche Kabelfabrieken
- Koninklijke Papierfabrieken van Gelder Zonen N.V.
- N.V. Koninklijke Zwanenberg–Organon*
- Albatros Superfosfaatfabrieken N.V.*
- Koninklijke Nederlandsche Gist- en Spiritusfabriek N.V.*
- N.V. Werf "Gusto"
- Koninklijke Demka Staalfabrieken N.V.
- N.V. P.F. van Vlissingen & Co's Katoenfabrieken
- N.V. Magazijn "De Bijenkorf"
- Blijdenstein & Co N.V.

Five of the companies in the foregoing list (marked with an asterisk) did not indicate the existence of an independent auditor as late as 1959.

Even though the internal audit departments in a number of the largest companies conducted full-fledged financial audits, this practice does not explain the frequency of independent audits in the Netherlands. When internal audit departments carried out a financial audit, the independent auditor would rely to a considerable degree on the work done internally. Philips' internal audit department was, especially during the postwar period when A. Goudeket and P.C. Louwers were its heads (1945–1978), a base of considerable power in the company. During that era, the company's financial administration was not authorized to initiate communications with Philips' independent auditor, Klynveld, Kraayenhof & Co.,

no. 4215, 1 October 1955, p. 388.

The difference between the Lafeber and the NIvA findings may have been attributable, at least in part, to the treatment of companies with affairs in Indonesia. The direction of the difference is especially curious since the NIvA study refers to companies that had audits, and the Lafeber study refers to companies that mentioned the audit in their annual reports. As was discussed in the preceding chapter, it was known that some companies that had audits did not disclose the fact of such audits in their annual reports. One would have therefore expected a higher percentage in the NIvA study than in the Lafeber study, other things being the same.

[25] See Appendix 1 for the list of companies included in the authors' study. English translations of the companies' Dutch names are also supplied in the appendix.

[26] N.V. Koninklijke Nederlandsche Petroleum Maatschappij (Royal Dutch Petroleum Company) did not reveal an auditor for its parent company financial statements until its 1953 annual report, and therefore might be included in this list. Yet the joint auditors of the Koninklijke/Shell Groep (Royal Dutch/Shell Group) had been disclosed, together with their report, since the publication of the Group's 1950 annual report.

but only with the internal audit department.[27] The internal audit department, in turn, dealt with the independent auditor. Beginning in 1984, Philips' internal audit department no longer carried out financial audits. It is understood that, in the 1980's, the internal audit departments of a number of other major companies discontinued the practice of conducting financial audits. The reason given by Philips, which may be applicable to other companies that have dropped internal financial audits, was the desire to reduce the cost of the internal audit activity.[28]

As reported in Chapter 2, Werkspoor N.V. actually had an independent audit since the 1930's, but it was not the company's policy to disclose this fact. Several likely explanations for this policy were given in Chapter 2, one of which was that some independent-minded company managements believed that their accountability to shareholders did not require the publication of an auditor's report, even when an independent audit had actually been conducted.[29] That this practice may have continued to occur in the 1950's was suggested by a provision in the Rijkens report issued by the employers associations in 1955 (see below) which, after expressing the desire that an auditor's opinion on the financial statements be obtained, found it necessary to add that the auditor's report should be published in the company's annual report.

3.2.3. Comment in professional publications

Remarks on the state of financial reporting continued to appear in professional journals. In 1951, H.D.M. Knol repeated his complaint that the financial statements of large companies left something to be desired, and he remarked that "this complaint is uttered [in other journals] not infrequently".[30] Comparing Dutch financial reports with those published in the United States, Knol claimed that, among the arguments arrayed against more expansive reporting in the Netherlands, the fear of informing one's competitors was, on the basis of US experience, "a bit exaggerated".[31]

In the view of Mr P. Sanders, a lawyer in private practice and a leading figure in the Labor Party (PvdA), the efforts of the Stock Exchange Association to promote improved financial reporting were having little effect. In a 1952 article in which he alleged a lack of openness in the affairs of limited companies, Sanders said, in relation to financial reporting:

> [Managements] view it as a sport to make the annual financial statements as

---

[27] Interviews with Prof. H.L. Brink, 9 August 1990; with H.H.A. Appelo, 12 September 1990; with R.C. Spinosa Cattela, 13 November 1990; and with J. Uiterlinden, 18 July 1991.

[28] *Ibid.*

[29] Interview with Prof. A.M. van Rietschoten, 23 November 1990.

[30] H.D.M. Knol, "Nauwkeurige verslaggeving", in *Maandblad voor Bedrijfsadministratie*, vol. 55, no. 652, July 1951, p. 105.

[31] *Ibid.*

> meaningless as possible, and there is hardly a trace of interim reporting, despite the good efforts of the Stock Exchange Association to change this situation.[32]

Sanders' article was better known for his advocacy of a "Companies Commission" (Vennootschapskamer), which would be given supervisory powers over the financial reporting of limited companies.[33] It would operate very much like the Insurance Companies Commission (Verzekeringskamer), which has regulated the activities of insurance companies since 1922. Prior to the writing of his article, Sanders had taken a trip to the United States, where he had become acquainted with the work of the Securities and Exchange Commission (SEC) and an admirer of its operation. Ten pages of Sanders' 34-page article were used to explain how the SEC works.

Sanders' argument attracted comment in the literature, as well as in the financial press, and it became a topic of nervous discussion among those concerned with company management and supervision, in part because many found it hard to believe that regulation by a government agency (such as the proposed Companies Commission) would actually be confined to financial reporting.[34]

A recurring theme in articles during the early and middle 1950's was the comparison of the American standard of financial reporting with Dutch practice, and J. Brands, a leading member of the Society of Academically Trained Auditors (VAGA, Vereeniging van Academisch Gevormde Accountants), wrote in 1953 that the comparison was having an effect:

> It may be said that, in recent years, one can observe on the part of some of the biggest companies a clear aim toward more openness, which can be seen in the growing care they bestow on [profit and loss statements]. The examples from across the ocean will no doubt have worked as a stimulant in this regard.[35]

R.J. Ovezall, an auditor in public practice, made a plea for individual and collective action by auditors in the matter of secret reserves.[36] He described an international trend (citing the US and UK experiences as examples) in the direction of

[32] P. Sanders, "Verantwoording van het bestuur in de publieke naamloze vennootschap", in *Rechtskundige opstellen*, essays dedicated to Prof.mr R.P. Cleveringa (Zwolle: N.V. Uitgevers-Maatschappij/W.E.J. Tjeenk Willink, 1952), p. 338.

[33] As Sanders acknowledged, Mr J.R.H. van Schaik had, in 1927 as a member of the Second Chamber of Parliament, made a similar suggestion during the debate over revision of the Commercial Code. See *ibid.*, pp. 352–354. A discussion of van Schaik's proposal is presented in the section, "Parliamentary course of the Nelissen–Heemskerk (1925) draft", in Chapter 2.

[34] See, e.g., Mr A. Schadee, "Een Vennootschapskamer?", in *De Naamlooze Vennootschap*, vol. 32, no. 1, April 1954, pp. 1–4. For commentary in the financial press, see Justus Meyer, "De N.V.-wet moet op de helling", *Haagse Post*, 17 January 1953, p. 20, and Justus Meyer, "Toezicht op naamloze vennootschappen", *Haagse Post*, 8 May 1954, p. 18.

[35] J. Brands, "Het Jaarverslag van de Naamloze Vennootschap", in *De Naamlooze Vennootschap*, vol. 30, nos. 11/12, February/March 1953, p. 213.

[36] R.J. Ovezall, "Enige aspecten van het vraagstuk der stille en geheime reserves voor de accountant", in *Maandblad voor accountancy en bedrijfshuishoudkunde*, vol. 27, no. 4, April 1953, pp. 167–176. Page citations in the text refer to this article.

better financial reporting, and also saw signs in the Netherlands: the continuous attention by the financial press, the statements by the Stock Exchange Association, and the fact that the UK Companies Act 1948 (which consolidated the 1947 Act with previous legislation) had "made its influence felt" in the Netherlands through the international character of many large companies (p. 174). Ovezall feared that the auditors would be left behind if they did not take an active role. He said,

> Must the Dutch auditors take a completely passive attitude toward this development? This creates the risk that others will occupy themselves with this question and will try to move it toward a solution. Yet it has to be stated that this is typically a matter in which the auditor is competent, a question in the sphere of accounting and auditing, areas in which the auditor is preeminently expert. It detracts, in my view, from the honor of the auditors profession if it is not *they* who take the lead in striving toward financial statements that can be considered to give a correct picture [*juist beeld*] of the financial position and income of the enterprise (p. 174).

Ovezall called for attention to be given to the problem of secret reserves in Accountantsdag addresses, in the press and in the professional journals, and in the work of the NIvA's Advisory Committee on Professional Matters (p. 176).

Drs G.L. Groeneveld, the external auditor of Philips, in an important Accountantsdag address in October 1953, "New Trends in Published Financial Statements", drew attention to two significant developments in financial reporting: the increasing use of current cost accounting (of which he was an ardent advocate), and the tendency to publish financial statements with less delay after the end of the financial year.[37] The more widespread use of current cost accounting was discussed almost entirely in connection with the declining use of secret reserves. The use of current cost accounting, Groeneveld argued, was a more precise and theoretically defensible instrument than blunt conservatism (i.e., the use of secret reserves) to prevent the paying out of dividends when it would not be in the interest of the company as a going concern to do so (p. 8). It was also, he argued, a more proper way to guide both management and investors through the swings of the business cycle (p. 14). In view of the clear superiority of current cost, Groeneveld concluded, he would question whether auditors should continue to accept financial statements prepared on the basis of historical cost (p. 20). Groeneveld ascribed the trend toward the earlier publication of financial statements to "a development in the direction of a situation like that in America" (p. 21).

In a 1954 article, J.M. Vecht, a member of the NIvA, wrote, "It is almost impossible to read any treatise dealing in any way with the limited company

[37] G.L. Groeneveld, "Nieuwe tendenties in de gepubliceerde jaarrekening", in *de Accountant*, vol. 60, no. 1, September 1953, pp. 3–35. This was the *prae-advies*, i.e., the paper prepared and distributed in advance of the Accountantsdag. Page citations in the text refer to this article.

without finding the complaint that financial reporting by the NV is seriously deficient". To illustrate his point, Vecht catalogued several recent criticisms of financial reporting by authors writing in professional journals: "meaningless document", "meaningless notes", "puzzle", "too little information" and "hardly to be taken seriously". He added:

> When formulated with somewhat more precision, the [authors'] objections concern the limited breakdown of items in profit and loss statements, as well as the smoke-screen that covers the valuation and composition of the assets and liabilities in balance sheets. The same complaints are heard about prospectuses that issuing companies typically publish.[38]

Yet Vecht rejected the argument that more information for shareholders was necessarily better. He identified a number of stakeholders in the enterprise, and he said that their interests must be balanced against that of the enterprise itself. It was not clear, Vecht said, that American companies have not been damaged by extensive disclosures in their financial reports, and he wondered whether the elimination of secret reserve accounting, in the light of the balance he would strike, was justified. Vecht characterized companies' financial reporting policies more as a matter of "business politics" [*bedrijfspolitiek*] than the result of scientific demonstration.[39]

3.2.4. Some evidence of improved reporting

During the first half of the 1950's, some companies took steps to improve their financial reporting at a time when there were pockets of concern in the financial press about the lack of informativeness of company reporting. In 1951, Philips unveiled its integrated reporting system based on current cost accounting[40] (the company had been depreciating on a current cost basis since 1945–46).

---

[38] J.M. Vecht, "De verslaggeving van de Naamloze Vennootschap", in *Maandblad voor Bedrijfsadministratie*, vol. 58, no. 685, April 1954, p. 57.

[39] *Ibid.*, pp. 57–60.

[40] See Philips' annual report for 1951 and the following papers: A. Goudeket, "An Application of Replacement Value Theory", in *The Journal of Accountancy*, vol. 110, no. 1, July 1960, pp. 37–47; R. Vangermeersch, "An Historical Analysis of the Financial Reporting Practices of Philips Industries of the Netherlands for Tangible Fixed Assets and Inventory 1915–1981", Working Paper No. 57 (January 1983), Academy of Accounting Historians, pp. 7–11; Adolf J.H. Enthoven, *Current Value Accounting: Its Concepts and Practice at N.V. Philips Industries, the Netherlands*, International Accounting Research Study # 3 (Dallas: The University of Texas at Dallas, 1982); and H.L. Brink, "Stelselkeuze en stelselwijzigingen: de 'Philips-case'", in *Pacioli Journaal*, vol. 3, no. 6, September 1990, pp. 26–27. For a comment on current cost accounting as practiced by Dutch companies, see Jules W. Muis, "Current Value Accounting in the Netherlands: Fact or Fiction?", in *The Accountant's Magazine*, vol. 79, no. 833, November 1975, pp. 377–379.

For comment in the financial press on Philips' integrated current cost system, see "Sterke reservepositie van Philips-concern", in *Het Financieele Dagblad*, 13 May 1952.

Perhaps prompted by the Stock Exchange Association's circulars, 19 of the large companies in the authors' 33-company survey began displaying two-year comparative figures in their balance sheet and profit and loss statement between 1951 and 1953, as follows:

- Heineken's Bierbrouwerij Maatschappij N.V., beginning in its annual report for 1950–51
- N.V. Koninklijke Nederlandsche Petroleum Maatschappij (Royal Dutch Petroleum Company), 1951; comparative figures were shown as early as 1950 in the Koninklijke/Shell Groep (Royal Dutch/Shell Group) consolidated statements
- N.V. Koninklijke Paketvaart-Maatschappij, 1951
- Werkspoor N.V., 1951
- Koninklijke Java–China Paketvaart Lijnen N.V., 1951
- N.V. Nederlandsche Kabelfabrieken, 1951
- N.V. Koninklijke Zwanenberg–Organon, 1951
- Koninklijke Nederlandsche Gist- en Spiritusfabriek N.V., 1951
- Koninklijke Demka Staalfabrieken N.V., 1951
- Albert Heijn N.V., 1951
- N.V. Magazijn "De Bijenkorf", 1951
- Koninklijke Nederlandsche Hoogovens en Staalfabrieken N.V., 1951–52
- Albatros Superfosfaatfabrieken N.V., 1951–52
- N.V. Borneo Sumatra Handel Maatschappij, 1952
- N.V. Hollandsche Kunstzijde Industrie, 1952
- N.V. P.F. van Vlissingen & Co's Katoenfabrieken, 1952
- Willem Smit & Co's Transformatorenfabriek N.V., 1952
- N.V. Koninklijke Maatschappij "De Schelde", 1953
- Blijdenstein & Co. N.V., 1953

Only four of the 33 companies surveyed had not begun showing comparative figures by 1953; all four added the comparative column to their financial statements by 1955.

Gradually, companies began presenting multi-year summaries. KLM introduced a five-year profit and loss statement in 1950. Beginning in 1951, Philips provided a five-year summary and A.K.U. gave comparative information at five-year intervals back to 1920. As already noted, Unilever began presenting a 10-year summary in 1946, but it was not until 1954 that the Royal Dutch/Shell Group provided its first multi-year summary. One company, Billiton Maatschappij N.V., became so enamored of multi year comparisons that, in its 1951 annual report, it presented a three-page, year-by-year exhibit of net income and general reserves for the 92 years going back to 1860! The company's zeal was brought under control the following year, when the multi-year summary was confined to the past 25 years.

The reporting of comparative figures in the financial statements was, to be sure, only a modest improvement in financial reporting, as the previous year's figures had already been disclosed.

3.2.5. Comment in the financial press

Groeneveld, in his 1953 Accountantsdag address, referred to the efforts of the Stock Exchange Association and cited the pressure from journalists for improved company reporting. He said,

> Already voices have been raised repeatedly in the press for quarterly publications and even quarterly dividends, following the American trend, and now that A.K.U. has taken the lead with the publication of quarterly results, one may assume that similar publications will follow from other companies.[41]

Again reflecting the weight of American example, Brands wrote in 1953, "When the American annual reports arrive, one can sometimes read in the financial press that the sight of [such reports] makes many blush who are concerned about the well-being of Dutch enterprise".[42]

In the columns of the financial press, there were occasional complaints of inadequate financial information, but no one was the equal of Justus Meyer, of the weekly *Haagse Post*, for penetrating commentary coupled with wit and sarcasm.[43] A good example of Meyer's style were his comments on Royal Dutch Petroleum's 1949 and 1950 annual reports. Meyer characterized the 1949 report as composed of "Royal crossword puzzles", while the much-improved 1950 report was "an apparently serious attempt to give, for once, something more than chit-chat and one impenetrable profit figure".[44]

De Volkskrant took the occasion of P.F.S. Otten's speech (discussed below) to comment on the climate in company-shareholder relations:

> The [provision of] information to shareholders by the managements of their companies has always been a sensitive issue in the Netherlands. On the one hand, most managements have displayed, and continue to display, considerable reticence in their communications to the factual owners, while, on the other hand, shareholders have not shown as much interest as might be expected of owners. In fact, they are often silenced by the meaningless answers to questions they ask at shareholders meetings. It can be acknowledged that, since the last war, things have been improving in this area.[45]

---

41 Groeneveld, *op. cit.*, p. 21.

42 Brands, *loc. cit.*

43 See, e.g., the following columns by Meyer: "Het Jaarverslag der Heemaf", 18 March 1950, p. 16; "Royal Dutch en Standard Oil", 9 June 1951, p. 12; "Onaantrekkelijk", 23 August 1952, p. 14; "Pers, publiciteit en het bedrijfsleven", 22 May 1954, p. 20; and (for a favorable commentary on Philips' reporting) "Met zevenmijlslaarzen door jaarverslagen", 1 May 1954, p. 13.

44 "Koninklijke Kruiswoordraadsels", in *Haagsche Post*, 17 June 1950, p. 18; and "Royal Dutch en Standard Oil", in *Haagsche Post*, 9 June 1951, p. 12.

45 "Voorlichting", in *de Volkskrant*, 15 May 1954, p. 2.

The financial press took an enterprising initiative in 1954 when Hendrik A.H. Sijthoff, the publisher of *Het Financieele Dagblad*, the country's leading financial newspaper, established the Henri Sijthoff Prize for the best annual report of a listed company. Although a similar Annual Award had been instituted the previous October by *The Accountant*, the British journal,[46] the founder of the Sijthoff Prize has cited an annual award given by a magazine in the United States as the inspiration of his enterprise.[47] The panel of judges for the Sijthoff Prize was composed of the presidents of the three Dutch associations of securities exchanges. The president of the Stock Exchange Association has always served as chairman of the panel. No one with expertise in accounting served on the panel until 1974, when Prof.drs R. Burgert, of Erasmus Universiteit Rotterdam, became a member. To be eligible for service on the panel, an individual could not be a member of companies' supervisory boards and must not, in the case of the person with accounting expertise, be a practicing auditor.[48]

Although the norms used for judging the annual reports were not published until late 1956,[49] a two-part article commenting on the deficiencies in annual reports appeared in *Het Financieele Dagblad* on 6–7 January 1955, on the occasion of the announcement of the prize-winning 1953 annual reports, almost as if the article were the summarized comments of the judges.[50] In a speech delivered at the awards ceremony, William Schrikker, president of the Stock Exchange Association and chairman of the panel of judges, gave a sketch of the primary criteria used by the judges:

1. the interval between the end of the financial year and the publication of the annual report should not exceed 3 to $4\frac{1}{2}$ months, depending on the company's industry group;
2. the amount of the income tax expense should be disclosed; and

---

[46] "Reports of Public Companies", *The Accountant*, vol. 129, no. 4115, 31 October 1953, p. 489. Of the seven judges, five were qualified accountants, one was a barrister, and one was editor of the journal. *The Accountant*, vol. 129, no. 4122, 19 December 1953, p. 700.

[47] Interview with Hendrik A.H. Sijthoff and H.B.G. Sijthoff, 6 December 1990. The American magazine was *Financial World*, whose annual award of "Oscars" for the best company annual reports had originated in the early 1940's. In 1959, KLM Royal Dutch Airlines became the first European company to receive an Oscar. "Annual Report Awards Section", in *Financial World*, vol. 112, no. 18, 28 October 1959, pp. 57–95.

[48] Interview with Hendrik A.H. Sijthoff and H.B.G. Sijthoff, 6 December 1990.

[49] *Normen voor de beoordeling van Jaarverslagen opsteld voor de Henri Sijthoff-prijs*, dated December 1956.

[50] "Financiële publiciteit I: Duidelijk opgaande lijn, Verdere verbetering blijft mogelijk" and "Financiële publiciteit II: Meer inzicht door beter cijfermateriaal, Gebaseerd op realiteit", in *Het Financieele Dagblad*, 6 January 1955, p. 1, and 7 January 1955, p. 1, respectively. The first article to appear in *Het Financieele Dagblad* about the Sijthoff Prize was the announcement of the winning annual reports for 1953: "Henri Sijthoff-prijs: Voor het beste jaarverslag, Door de Heer William Schrikker uitgereikt", 8 January 1955, p. 1. The newspaper's reporter who was most directly concerned with the administration of the Sijthoff Prize and who wrote the foregoing articles was Th.M. Ram. Interview with J. Hanekroot, 18 September 1990.

3. comparative figures should be included in the balance sheet and profit and loss statement, and multi-year summaries were encouraged.[51]

3.2.6. The Philips challenge

Also during 1954, the president of Philips, Ir P.F.S. Otten, declared his views on the role of enterprise leadership in providing good information disclosure to shareholders. In his annual address to the Philips shareholders on 14 May, which was extensively covered in the press,[52] Otten defined a satisfactory annual report as one whose financial statements give an "acceptable picture" (*aanvaardbaar beeld*) of a company's financial position and operating results. On the controversial subject of secret reserves, he ruled out their use only when they might distort this picture. Otherwise, they belonged to "sound business practice" (*goed koopmansgebruik*).[53] Otten listed four "demands" that must be satisfied for an acceptable picture to be given:

> **1.** An explanation must be given of the overall income so that one may acquire an insight into the enterprise's activities and the way in which the income was obtained.
> **2.** A specification must be given of the net assets and the capital components so that an insight may be acquired into solvency and liquidity.
> **3.** The principles by which operating income is calculated and the capital components are valued must be stated, because without this explanation the furnished data can not be judged.
> **4.** Every change in the makeup of the figures and in the principles must be stated, because the comparability over time can be upset by such changes (pp. 6–7).

A pivotal term in Otten's points 1 and 2 was "insight", reflecting less a conformity with legal prescription than a quality of informativeness of the financial statements. As noted above, "insight" had begun to be used in discussions of financial reporting in the late 1940's. It was to reappear in several important

[51] "De Henri Sijthoff-prijs: Het beste jaarverslag, Gevraagd om formulering van normen en wensen", in *Het Financieele Dagblad*, 10 January 1955, p. 1.

[52] *De Telegraaf* called Otten's speech "powerful" and "impressive". "Krachtig pleidooi voor goede verslaggeving, Kwartaalcijfers moeten vaste gewoonte worden", in *De Telegraaf*, 15 May 1954. *De Volkskrant* viewed the speech as an important step down the road toward improved financial reporting. "Voorlichting", in *de Volkskrant*, 15 May 1954, p. 2. See also "Ir P.F.S. Otten over public relations; ook ten opzichte van de aandeelhouders", in *Het Financieele Dagblad*, 14 May 1954, p. 5; "Ir Otten gaf college over een goede voorlichting", in *Algemeen Handelsblad*, 14 May 1954, p. 13; "Jaarverslag moet aanvaardbaar beeld van de onderneming geven", in *De Maasbode*, 14 May 1954, p. 9; and "Voorlichting", in *Elseviers Weekblad*, 22 May 1954, p. 15.

[53] *Het beleid van Philips ten aanzien van de voorlichting van aandeelhouders*, speech by Ir P.F.S. Otten, chairman of the management board (i.e., president) of N.V. Philips' Gloeilampenfabrieken, to the general meeting of shareholders, 14 May 1954. In this section, citations in the text to page numbers will refer to this booklet.

reports published in the 1950's and 1960's, and in 1970 it was approved by Parliament as the standard by which the quality of companies' financial reporting was to be judged. Yet its first influential expression was in Otten's speech.

Otten said that point 3 in his statement of demands "has especial meaning not alone for the judgment placed on the annual financial statements themselves but also for the so-called intercompany comparisons that will facilitate a comparison of the position of a particular enterprise with that of other enterprises" (p. 7).[54] This aspect of intercompany comparability was not accorded any attention in the subsequent reports that drew heavily on the demands synthesized in Otten's speech.

Much of Otten's speech was, one may be sure, drafted by A. Goudeket, who was Philips' chief internal auditor and the company's unquestioned authority on accounting and auditing matters.[55] The Philips challenge, as it might be called, played an important role in subsequent efforts to raise the standard of financial reporting by Dutch companies.

The founder of the Sijthoff Prize has said that there was no relationship between the Otten speech and the inception of the Prize.[56] Although the Sijthoff Prize was established sometime in 1954, the first public mention was not made until 8 January 1955.[57]

3.2.7. Philips, A.K.U. and Royal Dutch enter the New York securities market

In 1953–54, Philips, A.K.U. and Royal Dutch Petroleum became the first Dutch companies to be publicly traded in the New York securities market. Philips' shares began to be traded in New York in 1953, in the form of American Depositary Receipts on the over-the-counter market. In 1954, A.K.U. and Royal Dutch (the dominant holding company in the Royal Dutch/Shell Group) took up listings on the American Stock Exchange and the New York Stock Exchange, respectively. (KLM Royal Dutch Airlines and Unilever N.V. began trading on the New York Stock Exchange in 1957 and 1961, respectively.)

All three companies, therefore, became subject to the jurisdiction of the US Securities and Exchange Commission (SEC) in one way or another. In the 1950's, the SEC's policy toward foreign registrants was in its infancy, and evidently

---

[54] Eight years later, at the Eighth International Congress of Accountants, Otten took a stronger view. He said that one area in which "uniformity of public financial reporting ... is of essential importance" was "the principles of the calculation of capital and profit and the demonstration thereof in the annual report". He emphasized that his reference was to principles, not details. P.F.S. Otten, "Bedrijfsleven en Accountants", in *Maandblad voor accountancy en bedrijfshuishoudkunde*, vol. 36, no. 11, December 1962, p. 456.

[55] Interviews with H.H.A. Appelo, 12 September 1990; with R.C. Spinosa Cattela, 13 November 1990; and with J. Uiterlinden, 18 July 1991.

[56] Interview with Hendrik A.H. Sijthoff and H.B.G. Sijthoff, 6 December 1990.

[57] See footnote 50, above.

exceptions from the strict regulations applicable to US companies were allowed.[58] Foreign companies traded over-the-counter in New York were permitted to use their home-country financial reporting practices and customs. Notwithstanding these relaxations in the SEC's rules, foreign companies knew that they would be competing against US companies for capital, and they realized that their reporting might be open to suspicion if they did not provide as much disclosure as US companies.

In his speech, therefore, Otten announced that Philips would shortly be issuing its first quarterly report, following a "transitional period" in which it had been publishing half-yearly reports. In 1954, Philips became the second major Dutch company to issue quarterly reports. A.K.U. had commenced quarterly reporting in 1953,[59] and the Royal Dutch/Shell Group began issuing quarterly reports in 1955.[60] Quarterly reports were required of companies listed on the

---

[58] The extent to which the SEC imposed US reporting requirements on foreign companies in the early to middle 1950's is somewhat open to question. In 1953, the SEC accepted a prospectus for A.K.U., which sought to offer some of its shares to US investors (through depositary arrangements), without challenging the company's use of current cost accounting for inventories and depreciation expense, since it was reported as being "acceptable" in the Netherlands. Yet the SEC did not allow US companies under its jurisdiction to depart from historical cost accounting in the body of their financial statements. See Carman G. Blough, "The 'A.K.U.' Prospectus", Accounting & Auditing Problems, in *The Journal of Accountancy*, vol. 97, no. 4, April 1954, pp. 483–484. The 1960's were apparently a pivotal decade for the requirements imposed on foreign issuers. See Andrew Barr, "The International Harmonization of Accounting Principles" (1967), in *Written Contributions of Selected Accounting Practitioners-Volume 3: Andrew Barr* ([Champaign, IL:] Department of Accountancy, University of Illinois at Urbana-Champaign, 1980), pp. 473–475. The authors are grateful to Andrew Barr (who served as SEC Chief Accountant from 1956 to 1972) for bringing the Blough article to their attention.

Louis H. Rappaport, at that time the leading authority on SEC accounting, wrote that the SEC insisted that foreign registrants disclose the effects of departures from US generally accepted accounting principles. Louis H. Rappaport, *SEC Accounting Practice and Procedure* (New York: The Ronald Press Company, 1959), pp. 429–430.

The SEC did not impose a quarterly reporting requirement on registrants until 1970. Prior to then, half-yearly reports were required. George J. Benston, *Corporate Financial Disclosure in the UK and the USA* (London: Saxon House/Lexington Books, 1976), p. 70.

[59] See "A.K.U. werkt op volle capaciteit, Bevredigend resultaat verwacht", in *De Telegraaf*, 19 June 1953, p. 7; and "De A.K.U. publiceert kwartaalcijfers – Lopende jaar tot nu toe bevredigend", in *Het Financieele Dagblad*, 19 June 1953, p. 1. In the latter, the reporter stated, "shareholders, who had virtually no criticism of [and had made no demands for] information concerning the annual financial statements [were surprised] by the publication of a nicely presented quarterly report .... Here we have, then, the first quarterly report published by a large Dutch concern in imitation of American custom".

[60] Royal Dutch/Shell had begun issuing half-yearly reports in 1954. *The Economist* noted that Royal Dutch/Shell's decision to publish quarterly reports stemmed directly from a share listing on the New York Stock Exchange. It then asked, "Could not other oil companies – and, indeed, some of the leviathans in other industries – follow this lead without the help of a special spur?" "Business Notes: Royal Dutch-Shell Earnings", in *The Economist* (London), no. 172, no. 5796, 25 September 1954, p. 1007.

KLM Royal Dutch Airlines began issuing cumulative three-, six- and nine-month reports in 1957, the year of its listing, and in the third quarter of 1959 the company began issuing reports

New York Stock Exchange, although foreign companies were sometimes granted an exemption.[61] Although Philips was not required to issue quarterly reports, the company would have been sensitive to the fact that virtually all other major companies trading in the New York capital market were reporting on a quarterly basis.

As they prepared to enter the New York capital market, A.K.U., Royal Dutch Petroleum, and Philips began adopting financial reporting practices that were being used by American companies that were subject to regulation by the SEC. In 1952, A.K.U. began disclosing sales in absolute amount, following a year in which only indexes had been provided. In 1953, it began disclosing its cost of sales, and in 1954 A.K.U. presented consolidated statements for the first time. In 1950, the Royal Dutch/Shell Group published consolidated financial statements for the first time, and in 1952 it started disclosing its sales and cost of sales. Philips, however, had published a consolidated balance sheet from 1931 through 1937–38. In 1948, it resumed publication of a consolidated balance sheet, and followed two years later with a consolidated profit and loss statement.[62] Philips began reporting its sales in 1951, followed a year later by the first disclosure of its cost of sales. Among other large Dutch companies during the early and middle 1950's, the disclosure of sales and cost of sales and the use of consolidated statements were rare.

By the summer of 1954, therefore, the financial community had taken steps to encourage improvements in financial reporting, and a number of large companies had amplified their reporting. In addition, the president of a leading company, Philips, had declared a set of norms as a guide for responsible financial reporting to shareholders. And Philips, together with A.K.U. and Royal Dutch Petroleum, had entered the New York capital market, which served as a stimulus to their financial reporting. Finally, the leading financial newspaper had, sometime during 1954, established a prize for the best annual report of a listed company, to serve as an incentive for improved financial reporting.

A sector from which very little institutional advice was seen to come was the auditing profession. The NIvA and the VAGA, the two most important bodies of auditors, were almost wholly preoccupied with the educational preparation

---

for each quarter. Unilever began issuing quarterly reports in 1964, under an agreement made in 1961 when the listing of the shares of both Unilever N.V. and Unilever Limited was approved by the New York Stock Exchange. "Shorter Notes", in *The Economist* (London), vol. 201, no. 6170, 25 November 1961, p. 834. Unilever had begun issuing half-yearly reports in 1957.

[61] See the New York Stock Exchange's *Company Manual*, dated 1 September 1953, Section A-2 (Listing Agreements), p. A-26.

The New York Stock Exchange required quarterly reports of listed companies at least as early as 1939. Exceptions to this requirement were made "only upon presentation of convincing reasons that such reports would be impracticable or misleading". *Bulletin*, New York Stock Exchange, vol. 10, no. 8, August 1939, back page.

[62] The authors are grateful to Prof. H.L. Brink for a useful memorandum on Philips' consolidation policies and practices from 1931 to 1950.

of auditors and the standards of auditor performance. Above all, they sought parliamentary recognition for the auditing profession (which was not achieved until the 1960's). Two reports emanated from the NIvA's Advisory Committee on Professional Matters on comparative figures in financial statements, but, as indicated above, they were confined to matters of concern to the auditor.

3.2.8. The Rijkens Committee report

3.2.8.1. General

In the summer of 1954, the executive committee of the management board of the Federation of Dutch Employers (VNW, Verbond van Nederlandsche Werkgevers) invited the three other employers federations to enter into the joint sponsorship of a committee to study the annual reporting of "open", i.e., listed, limited companies. The committee was chaired by Dr P. Rijkens,[63] the chairman of Unilever, one of the country's most important companies, and a highly respected industrialist.

Formation of the committee was the idea of Dr M. Weisglas, who had joined the VNW and the other major employers federation, the Central Social Employers Federation (CSWV, Centraal Sociaal Werkgevers-Verbond) in 1951 as their public relations adviser. His charge was "to bring Dutch industry to the public", as the employers federations realized that, following the War, they were "very inward-looking, and we should be outward-looking".[64] Weisglas believed that the cooperation of the member companies themselves, and especially those listed on the stock exchanges, was necessary to improve the public image of Dutch enterprise.[65] In particular, he felt that more should be done with their annual report to shareholders – "not just pictures and layout, but they should be 'reliable' and 'informational' as well as 'food for the press' ".[66]

In a memorandum dated 10 March 1954 to the executive committee of the VNW's management board, Weisglas acknowledged that the largest companies have, through their financial reporting, sought to inform a wider audience than their own shareholders and have gone beyond legal requirements to reach public opinion through the financial press.

> But [he added] middle-sized companies – still the most important part of Dutch industry – have mainly limited themselves to a strictly formal type of financial reporting .... It should certainly be possible, without releasing trade secrets, to

[63] Rijkens' doctorate was an honorary degree awarded in 1948 by the Nederlandsche Economische Hoogeschool, which today forms part of the Erasmus Universiteit Rotterdam.
[64] Interview with Dr M. Weisglas, 31 August 1990.
[65] For Weisglas' views on the place of annual reports in a company's public relations program, see Dr M. Weisglas, *Public relations: een terreinverkenning* (Amsterdam: Elsevier, 1955), Chap. 4.
[66] Interview with Dr M. Weisglas, 31 August 1990.

make these financial reports more interesting reading for the outsider, by means of which industry could enhance its goodwill [with the public].

Since members of the VNW have shown much interest in public relations, they would appreciate more information on the possible use of financial statements in this respect from the management board [of the VNW]. This could be in the nature of an informative report or internal brochure, which would, of course, not be binding.

To prepare [such a report], the management board should consider installing an ad hoc working group .... The committee would be chaired by the leader of an enterprise that is actively involved in financial reporting, while the other members would be drawn from middle-sized companies.

It is our thought that Dr P. Rijkens, chairman of the management board of Unilever, might be suggested as chairman of the proposed committee, because he has a known interest in this matter and because his company has a good track record [in financial reporting]."[67]

With a chairman of Rijkens' stature, Weisglas believed, it would be possible to convince others to serve.

Another reason for the committee surfaced in the discussions of the VNW's executive committee, namely, anxiety over the discussions in the press and elsewhere on the possible creation of a Companies Commission.[68] There was a feeling that, if companies did not seek to reform their ways, a call for government to intervene might gather momentum. This concern was set against the backdrop of the ongoing discussions within the Labor Party-led government coalition over a possible revision of company law with a view toward facilitating the co-

---

[67] "Eventuele instelling werkcommissie ad hoc jaarverslaggeving" (DB-679), dated 10 March 1954, memorandum attached to the agenda for the meeting of 16 March 1954 of the executive committee of the management board of the Federation of Dutch Employers.

Although Weisglas' proposal was conveyed more than two months prior to P.F.S. Otten's forward-looking speech to Philips shareholders on 14 May, the decision by the VNW's management board to establish the Rijkens committee was not taken until 10 June, by which time Otten's widely reported speech may have made an impact on the directors of other large companies.

[68] At the meeting on 3 March 1955 of the liaison committee ("Contactcommissie") of the four employers federations, where approval was sought for publication of the Rijkens report, Weisglas stressed the necessity of publication by mentioning "far-reaching plans at the Finance ministry regarding standards to be set on financial reporting". Minutes of the Contactcommissie, 3 March 1955 (CC-645). (In their research, the authors have seen no evidence that the Ministry of Finance was interested in taking any initiatives in financial reporting.) Shortly before publication of the Rijkens report, Weisglas told the VNW's executive committee that he "is convinced that publication of the report will have a favorable effect and should forestall the establishment by government of a companies commission". Minutes of the management board of the Federation of Dutch Employers, meeting of 15 March 1955, p. 6. With an eye toward maximizing the impact of the report, Weisglas arranged for it to be presented by Rijkens himself at a press conference on 1 April 1955. Rijkens also gave a talk on the report as one of a series of lectures by businessmen on a radio program entitled "Uit het Bedrijfsleven". See "Openhartige jaarverslaggeving, Radiorede van dr P. Rijkens', in *De Nederlandse Industrie*, August 1955, pp. 399–400.

determination by workers in enterprise.

Rijkens accepted the chairmanship, and it was he who succeeded in arranging for the study to be conducted under the auspices of all four of the employers federations.[69]

In the end, the committee was composed of 16 members: 11 company directors (from companies of varying size), two auditors, a commercial banker, a financial journalist, and Weisglas. A member of the VNW staff served as secretary. One of the members was a finance subdirector of N.V. Koninklijke Maatschappij "De Schelde", whose 1953 annual report had been presented by Weisglas to the VNW executive committee as an example of progressive financial reporting. Weisglas had known, and thought highly of, the chairman of De Schelde and of his company. The sharp-tongued critic Justus Meyer, of the *Haagse Post*, did not share Weisglas' assessment of the quality of De Schelde's annual reporting. Two years later, Meyer issued the ironic pronouncement that the company's 1955 annual report "is once again a mockery of the most elementary demands set forth in the renowned report of the four employers associations on 'the annual report' [i.e., the report of the Rijkens committee]".[70]

The two auditor members, A. Goudeket and J. Kraayenhof, were obvious choices. Goudeket was the chief internal auditor of Philips, a company that was known for its progressive financial reporting. Otten's widely reported speech of 14 May 1954 served to reinforce that reputation. Kraayenhof was the managing partner of Klynveld, Kraayenhof & Co., which was the auditor of Philips, A.K.U., and Royal Dutch Petroleum (and joint auditor of the Royal Dutch/Shell Group), three of the most important companies in the country. Kraayenhof himself maintained a close touch with all three engagements.[71] Weisglas esteemed Kraayenhof, who had been president of the NIvA in 1944–47, as a "big name" in the auditing profession.[72] Additionally, Goudeket and Kraayenhof had more international contacts than any Dutch auditor, Goudeket through the worldwide Philips organization, and Kraayenhof through his firm and the NIvA. Both would have been in a position to be aware of the best financial reporting practices elsewhere in the world.

The financial journalist serving on the committee was A.C. Winninghoff, of the Catholic daily, *De Maasbode*, in Rotterdam. Winninghoff, like the chairman of De Schelde, was one of Weisglas' support group, and was someone in whom he had confidence. He described Winninghoff as the country's "most senior reputed financial editor".[73] The inclusion of a journalist fitted in with Weisglas' public

---

[69] Unsigned memorandum, "Werkcommissie ad-hoc Jaarverslaggeving" (DB-733), dated 2 June 1954, attached to the agenda for the meeting of 10 June 1954 of the executive committee of the management board of the Federation of Dutch Employers.

[70] Justus Meyer, "Kon. Schelde hoont kapitaal", in *Haagse Post*, 18 February, 1956, p. 9.

[71] Interview with G. Timmer, 4 September 1990.

[72] Interview with Dr M. Weisglas, 31 August 1990.

[73] Interview with Dr M. Weisglas, 31 August 1990. Weisglas' evaluation of Winninghoff was

relations strategy.[74] Judging from the financial section of *De Maasbode* of those years, the paper would have been known more for its straight reporting than for criticism. When it became known to the VNW management board that a financial journalist was to placed on the committee, one member expressed anxiety, as he had just read one of Justus Meyer's thrusts in the *Haagse Post*. He was advised that the journalist who was being invited to serve on the committee was "a very able man".[75]

The committee began deliberations in November 1954, and its report was presented to the press on 1 April 1955.[76] It completed its work with dispatch. The report ran to 18 pages, plus specimen layouts for financial statements, and, as will be seen, was said to have had a noticeable influence on companies' financial statements, an assertion for which there is a measure of evidential support.

The report was addressed to "open" limited companies, and mainly those in the industrial field (p. 5). Emphasis was placed on reporting not only to shareholders and creditors but also to "other groups, such as potential new capital suppliers, important business relations, the government, and in a larger sense also the public as such" (p. 5). A principal conclusion was that "the factual demands that are placed on modern annual reporting go beyond what is called for in the current provisions of the Commercial Code" (p. 5).

The committee went to pains to make clear that its "guidelines and recommendations ... do not have binding force" (p. 7). Without this caveat, the members could have agreed only on platitudes. In fact, the decision that the committee's recommendations would not be binding was made by the VNW's executive committee even before it finally resolved to appoint the committee.[77] The objective was to give advice and to encourage managements to hold their reporting performance to a higher standard.

While it is possible that the members of the Rijkens committee were influenced by financial reporting practices in the USA and the UK, no references to other countries' practices or writings were included in the report.[78] The committee

shared by Dr J.C. Brezet, who knew Winninghoff well. Interview with Dr J.C. Brezet, 13 September 1990.

[74] See Weisglas, *op.cit.*, pp. 158–159.

[75] Minutes of the management board of the Federation of Dutch Employers (VNW), meeting of 15 June 1954, p. 7.

[76] *Het jaarverslag* (The Annual Report), report of the Annual Reporting Committee (Commissie Jaarverslaggeving) of the Federation of Dutch Employers (VNW, het Verbond van Nederlandsche Werkgevers), the Central Social Employers Federation (CSWV, het Centraal Sociaal Werkgevers-Verbond), the Catholic Federation of Employers Associations (KVW, het Katholiek Verbond van Werkgeversvakverenigingen), and the Federation of Protestant-Christian Employers in the Netherlands (VPCWN, het Verbond van Protestants-Christelijke Werkgevers in Nederland) ('s-Gravenhage, March 1955). In this section, all citations in the text to page numbers will refer to this report.

[77] Minutes of the meeting of 6 April 1954 of the executive committee of the management board of the Federation of Dutch Employers.

[78] By 1955, only two Dutch enterprises, A.K.U. and Royal Dutch Petroleum (the dominant

simply stated that its recommendations were based on "general notions that came up during the discussions of the committee" (p. 7).

In the development of the committee's views on annual reporting, Goudeket and Kraayenhof surely played major, if not dominant, roles. Goudeket was said to be a "strong man with strong convictions and an ability to convince others of his views", and was regarded as the most important internal auditor in the country. Kraayenhof "was a very strong, able, and convincing man".[79] Of the two, Kraayenhof was more the pragmatic negotiator. He was not "a theoretical man".[80] Moreover, they were the only members of the committee with accounting or auditing expertise, although Rijkens himself had studied accounting and had worked in an accounting capacity early in his career. Accounting was one of his hobbies.[81] Evidence of Rijkens' active interest in accounting-related issues was his addresses to Unilever shareholders in 1948 and 1949, in which he argued for the adoption of a measure of "real profit" for income taxation purposes.[82]

Telling evidence of Goudeket's influence in the committee, and of the general respect for Philips as a progressive enterprise, was the inclusion early in the report of four "general demands" (*algemene eisen*) that had to be satisfied if the financial statements were to give a "faithful picture" (*getrouw beeld*) of the enterprise's course of affairs and the composition of net assets. The demands were strikingly similar to those contained in Otten's important speech in May 1954. As rendered in the committee's report, they were as follows:

> **1.** a specification of operating income in such a manner as to enable an insight into the composition thereof and into the rate of return on the enterprise's invested capital.

---

holding company in the Royal Dutch/Shell Group), were listed in New York, but neither of the two companies was represented on the Rijkens committee. Of importance, however, was the fact that Kraayenhof's firm, Klynveld, Kraayenhof & Co., was the auditor of both A.K.U. and Royal Dutch Petroleum (as well as joint auditor of the Royal Dutch/Shell Group), and, as has been noted above, Kraayenhof himself was closely involved with both sets of audits. He would therefore have had good reason to be well informed about US accounting and reporting practices.

Moreover, Goudeket had overseen Philips' entry into the New York over-the-counter market in early 1954, and he would have become fully aware of financial reporting practices in the USA. Interview with R.C. Spinosa Cattela, 13 November 1990. Kraayenhof was in close touch with the Philips audit as well.

[79] Interviews with Drs I. Kleerekoper, 22 August 1990, and with J.A. Burggraaff, 10 September 1990.

[80] Interview with G. Timmer, 5 September 1990.

[81] See Paul Rijkens, *Handel en wandel: Nagelaten gedenkschriften 1888–1965* (Rotterdam: Ad. Donker, 1965), p. 15; and interview with Dr M. Weisglas, 31 August 1990.

[82] See *De instandhouding van het Bedrijfsvermogen*, speech by Paul Rijkens, chairman of the management board of Lever Brothers & Unilever N.V., to the general meeting of shareholders, 26 August 1948 (Rotterdam: Lever Brothers & Unilever N.V., August 1948); and *Rede door de heer Dr. Paul Rijkens, voorzitter van de Raad van Bestuur van Lever Brothers & Unilever N.V., uitgesproken in de algemene vergadering van aandeelhouders op 11 augustus 1949* (Rotterdam: Lever Brothers & Unilever N.V., August 1949).

2. a specification of the assets and liabilities in such a manner as to enable an insight into solvency and liquidity.
3. the principles followed in the calculation of operating income and by which the assets and liabilities are valued, in order to make it possible to pass judgment on the published figures.
4. mention of possible changes relating to the previous year in regard to these principles and in the composition of the figures, if possible with an indication of the influence thereof on the figures, in order to allow comparability with previous periods (p. 8).

Point 4 contained a novel disclosure: "if possible with an indication of the influence thereof on the figures". Such a reconciliation was seldom seen in the Netherlands, and would not have been all that common overseas. Conspicuously missing from the committee's discussion of the four points was the emphasis that Otten placed on intercompany comparisons. The committee focused, as in Otten's speech, on the importance of acquiring an "insight" into one or another facet of an enterprise's operations and into its solvency and liquidity. Its aim was more to promote a report on stewardship than than to facilitate a comparison among enterprises.

3.2.8.2. Getrouw beeld

The committee's use of the term *getrouw beeld*, "faithful picture" (or "image"), is of historic importance. It was the term's first appearance in an authoritative publication. In 1972, it was to become the key phrase in the recommended form of the auditor's report,[83] signifying the professional standard of quality in a company's financial statements (equivalent, for example, to "true and fair view" in UK usage).

The first use of *getrouw beeld* in a published auditor's report was in the report given by the London firms of Cooper Brothers Co. and Price, Waterhouse & Co. on the annual financial statements of Unilever for 1932. In Unilever's 1931 Dutch-language annual report, the joint auditors' report was given in the English language, and "true and correct view", which was the terminology stipulated in the UK Companies Act then in force, was used in the auditors' report. But in Unilever's Dutch-language annual report for 1932, the joint auditors' report was, for the first time, rendered in Dutch, and "true and correct view" became *getrouw beeld*. The two auditors continued to use *getrouw beeld* in their joint report on the Unilever financial statements even after the UK Companies Act 1948 altered the required terminology from "true and correct view" to "true and fair view".

In auditors' reports appearing in companies' annual reports during the 1930's, 1940's and 1950's, a diversity of terminology was used, as the organized audit-

[83] See "Uniforme accountantsverklaring", in *NIvRA berichten*, vol. 6, no. 4, December 1972, p. 53, in which the NIvRA's management board, for the first time, officially approved a uniform wording and format for the auditor's report.

ing profession had not recommended a standard form of the auditor's report (the NIvRA finally did so in 1972). The key phrases found in auditors' reports of the period included *akkoord* [also spelled *accoord*] *bevonden*, which may be translated as "found correct"; *juist bevonden*, "found correct"; *in orde bevonden*, "found in order"; *juist weergeeft*, "correct rendering"; *aanvaardbaar beeld*, "acceptable picture"; *betrouwbaar beeld*, "reliable picture"; and *getrouw en juist beeld*, "faithful and correct picture". In some annual reports, the auditor signed the financial statements without giving a report.[84]

Getrouw en juist beeld appeared for the first time in the report of Price, Waterhouse & Co., Rotterdam, in the 1934 annual report of Wm H. Müller & Co. N.V., and this terminology continued in use until just after World War II (even though a new auditor had taken over in 1938). By far the most influential adoption of auditor's report terminology, however, was in the 1953 annual report of Royal Dutch Petroleum. Prior to 1953, the holding company's annual report did not indicate the involvement of an auditor. In the company's 1950 annual report, the financial statements of the Royal Dutch/Shell Group had been published for the first time, and Turquand, Youngs & Co., London, and Klijnveld, Kraayenhof & Co.,[85] The Hague, were shown as joint auditors; in their report, *aanvaardbaar beeld* was cited as the standard of quality. In the 1953 annual report of Royal Dutch Petroleum, two auditors' reports were shown. The report on the financial statements of Royal Dutch Petroleum, signed only by Klynveld, Kraayenhof & Co., used the term *getrouw beeld*. As the Royal Dutch/Shell Group was in the process of becoming listed on the New York Stock Exchange, it was felt necessary to append an American-style auditor's report to the Group's financial statements. That report, signed by Klynveld, Kraayenhof & Co., The Hague; Turquand, Youngs & Co., London; and Price Waterhouse & Co., New York, used the following terminology (unprecedented in a Dutch annual report): "*geven ... een getrouw beeld ... op basis van algemeen aanvaarde administratieve beginselen*", which was a direct translation of "present ... fairly ... in conformity with generally accepted accounting principles". The translation into Dutch of this standard American phrasing was not easily accomplished. The suggestion of *getrouw* was inspired by a Biblical passage.[86] J. Kraayenhof and a close associate

84 Limperg maintained that no auditor's report could be more "eloquent" than a simple signature beneath the words, "the Auditor". Th. Limperg Jr., "Eenige beschouwingen over het accountants-rapport", part II, in *Accountancy*, vol. 2, no. 19, 15 November 1904, p. 125.

85 The spelling of Klijnveld was anglicized to Klynveld three years later, when three of the firm's clients (A.K.U., Royal Dutch, and Philips) were in the process of entering the New York capital market.

86 De Jong has attributed the suggestion that *getrouw beeld* be used in the auditors' reports covering the 1953 financial statements of Royal Dutch Petroleum and the Royal Dutch/Shell Group to the suggestion of a colleague who had remembered the term *getrouw dienaar*, "faithful servant", from the Bible, and thought that *getrouw* could serve as the Dutch equivalent of "fair". Yet, apparently unknown to de Jong and his colleague (and to the Kraayenhof firm), *getrouw beeld* was, as noted above, used in the auditors' report contained in the Unilever annual

in his firm, G. Timmer, were uncertain whether *administratieve beginselen* was the proper rendering of "accounting principles", a concept that had not been translated into Dutch in the literature on accounting or auditing. They even approached Drs R. Besançon, the NIvA president in 1954–55, for his opinion of their translation.[87] Of significance was the fact that a figure as important as Kraayenhof became convinced that *getrouw beeld* was the proper rendering of both "true and fair view" (the terminology specified in the UK Companies Act 1948) and "[present] fairly" (the standard American terminology), and therefore that it was to be recommended for general usage in the Netherlands.[88] The term shortly began to appear in his firm's auditors' reports in the annual reports of two of the major clients with which Kraayenhof maintained close contacts, A.K.U. and Philips, beginning in 1954 and 1955, respectively.

Owing, therefore, to Kraayenhof's influence in the Rijkens committee, the sentence introducing the four "demands" in its report gave prominence to *getrouw beeld*: "The financial statements are meant to give shareholders and others a faithful picture of the affairs of the company during the financial year and of the composition of the company's capital at the end of the year" (p. 8). *Getrouw beeld* was used at several other places in the Rijkens report to denote the standard of quality of financial information.

3.2.8.3. Current cost

Reflecting the influence of Goudeket, the Rijkens committee took a strong position in support of current cost accounting. Although only Philips had, by then, adopted the integral approach to current cost accounting, i.e., in both the balance sheet and the profit and loss statement, the courses of instruction in accounting and auditing at both the Gemeentelijke Universiteit van Amsterdam and at the NIvA had been propagating the Limperg teachings in favor of current cost. Hence, many auditors were educated in the current cost school of thought. It is testimony to the persuasiveness of Goudeket (who had taken his studies through the NIvA) that the Rijkens committee endorsed current cost accounting so strongly:

> [The committee] is convinced that depreciation on the basis of current cost is necessary for the determination of net income. Otherwise, the enterprise would

---

report since 1932 as the Dutch equivalent of "true and correct view" and then of "true and fair view". See Drs J. de Jong, "Over 'getrouw beeld' en 'voldoen aan de eisen van de wet'", in the "Kruidnagels!" department of *de Accountant*, vol. 82, no. 2, October 1975, p. 71. The authors are grateful to Prof.drs J.W. Schoonderbeek for bringing de Jong's article to their attention.

[87] Interview with G. Timmer, 5 September 1990.

[88] See J. Kraayenhof, "Spiegel Historiael", in the "Kruidnagels!" department of *de Accountant*, vol. 82, no. 8, April 1976, p. 431.

Zeff has argued that "present fairly" is not a proper English language translation of "geeft een getrouw beeld". See Stephen A. Zeff, "The English language equivalent of 'geeft een getrouw beeld'", in *de Accountant*, vol. 90, no. 2, October 1990, p. 83.

> run the risk of being drained of its financial resources ....
>
> Moreover, the committee recommends a revaluation of fixed assets in the balance sheet according to the current price level, after a period of significant changes in this level. Revaluation of assets needs to take place only when actual replacement is to be expected ....
>
> Also in regard to other than fixed assets [the evident reference is to merchandise inventories], the committee is of the view that the failure to apply current cost accounting must be considered to be dangerous as well (p. 11).

Current cost accounting was an attractive cause since, in times of rising prices, it offered the prospect of a conservatively stated net income, albeit not nearly as conservative as by the unrestricted use of secret and undisclosed reserves.

3.2.8.4. Secret reserves

"Secret and undisclosed reserves", said the committee, "are acceptable only within such limits that the faithful picture [*getrouw beeld*] of the composition of capital and of income is not clouded. The committee considers the often-used principle of the 'minimum position' [i.e., when the actual state is no worse than is shown] ... to be out of date."(p. 9) Following the view expressed in Otten's speech to the Philips shareholders, the committee said that there was still a place for such reserves:

> Circumstances may arise in which it will be necessary to use reserves for coping with unforeseen contingencies, as in the case of [down]turns in the business cycle. In these cases, the formation of "undisclosed reserves" can be justifiable (pp. 9–10).

While there was some evidence in companies' annual reports that the incidence of use of secret reserves may have begun to decline in the years following the War, they were apparently still widely used and were the object of critical comment in the financial press. One financial journalist took the committee to task for compromising its position by saying that it is not possible to draw a clear line between the use of secret reserves that are acceptable and those that are not (p. 9).[89]

3.2.8.5. Other topics

When a more accelerated rate of depreciation was used for income tax purposes than for financial statement purposes, the committee favored the use of a provision for deferred tax liabilities. If no provision was made in such circumstances, the omission had to be explicitly mentioned in the notes (p. 10).

The committee recommended use of a consolidated balance sheet and profit and loss statement when it was not practicable to show separate financial statements for all subsidiary companies (p. 13). Subsidiary companies were defined

[89] "Hoe kan men de jaarverslaggeving verbeteren?", in *Algemeen Handelsblad*, 1 April 1955, p. 11.

as those in which the investor held, directly or indirectly, at least 50 percent of the common shares and voting rights (p. 13).

While favoring the disclosure of gross sales, the committee recognized that such disclosure may be "detrimental" to the interests of the business. "In this case", the committee said, "it is desirable that the notes provide insight into the activities in some other way"(p. 17). As to the reporting of cost of sales, the committee said that the disclosure of wages and depreciation was considered to be "effective" (p. 17).

The committee deemed it "desirable" that an auditor should give an opinion on the financial statements, and that the auditor's report should be published in the company's annual report (p. 18).

The committee recommended that the directors' report should give insight into the commercial, technical, financial, and social developments during the year, and include information on the company's competitive position, the trend in its profit margins, research and development expenditures, actual and planned capital expenditures, liquidity, employment conditions, and the dividend proposal (pp. 19–20). The committee added that, where appropriate, this information be given for the company's important product lines. The committee also recommended that directors supply "prospective information" (*vooruitzichten*) concerning the outlook for the near future (p. 20). These were far-reaching recommendations for the 1950's. Few companies anywhere in the world were providing such information in their annual reports to shareholders, and no professional accounting bodies had even recommended that such information be supplied.

Finally, the committee recommended the publication of comparative figures in the annual financial statements, and supported the dissemination of interim information (pp. 12,16,22). Under the heading of "Tables and Graphs", the committee recommended that, in order to provide a "better insight into the continuity of the course of affairs of the enterprise", companies should publish a summary of some important items for a period of, say, five years (p. 21).

On behalf of the Rijkens committee, Weisglas presented the final draft of the report to the VNW's management board, and it was approved with only a single alteration. In the original version, a sentence in the Introduction (quoted above) read, "Thus viewed, the factual demands that are placed on modern annual reporting go far beyond what is called for in the current provisions of the Commercial Code" (p. 5). In the management board, the adverb "far" was removed so as not to imply that the gap was immense.[90]

The Rijkens report appeared at a time when companies were emerging from an era when, generally speaking, they did not feel they owed a full reporting obligation to shareholders.

---

[90] Minutes of the management board of the Federation of Dutch Employers (VNW), meeting of 15 March 1955, p. 5.

In comparison with the experiences in other countries, an initiative taken by a federation of employers to improve the standard of financial reporting to shareholders was truly unusual. Typically, the first step in a campaign to improve financial reporting has been motivated by the threat of government intervention, as in the United States and the United Kingdom in the 1930's and 1940's, respectively.[91] The instrument of improvement has usually been a series of recommendations issued by a committee of a professional accountancy body. More often than not, employers have been viewed as the source of resistance to proposals for enlarged financial reporting.

3.2.9. Press reactions to the Rijkens report

The financial press generally complimented the report published by the employers federations, but not without some misgivings. In a three-part article, *Het Financieele Dagblad* discussed the contents of the Rijkens report at length, and said that "we wholeheartedly welcome the initiative. For years, we have worked for an improvement in financial reporting both by word and deed [the latter in reference to the Sijthoff Prize]".[92] At the same time, the paper spoke disapprovingly of the compromises and lack of clarity evident in the report.

Algemeen Handelsblad, *De Telegraaf*, *Trouw*, the *Haagsche Courant*, and the *Haagse Post* complained that the Stock Exchange Association was not officially represented on the committee.[93]

Several of the journalists were critical of the lack of firmness in the committee's recommendations. Justus Meyer, in the *Haagse Post*, while praising the

[91] See Stephen A. Zeff, *Forging Accounting Principles in Five Countries: A History and an Analysis of Trends* (Champaign, IL: Stipes Publishing Co., 1972), pp. 7–20, 129–139 and 309–310. The setting up of the English Institute committee in 1942 that drafted "Recommendations on Accounting Principles" seems to have been motivated, if only in part, by the desire by accountants employed in industry to anticipate the major changes that were expected in the forthcoming revision of company law.

Although, in the Netherlands, there was some concern about the possible establishment of a companies commission, it was not a significant factor in the decision to create the Rijkens committee.

[92] "Werkgeversverbonden over jaarverslagen: Aanbeveling aan industrie, Maar ook aan anderen", "De wijze van afschrijven, Bedrijfseconomische en fiscale belasting", and "Balans moet een juist inzicht geven, In liquiditeit en solvabiliteit", in *Het Financieele Dagblad*, 2 April 1955, p. 4; 4 April 1955, p. 1; and 5 April 1955, p. 3, respectively. The quotation is taken from the first article.

[93] "Hoe kan men de jaarverslaggeving verbeteren?", in *Algemeen Handelsblad*, 1 April 1955, p. 11; "Werkgeversbonden geven richtlijn jaarverslagen, Lofwaardig initiatief", in *De Telegraaf*, 1 April 1955, p. 13; "In de beursspiegel: Jaarverslagen", in *Trouw*, 2 April 1955, p. 21; "Financiele Kroniek: Betere voorlichting in de jaarverslagen", in *Haagsche Courant*, 9 April 1955, p. 2; and "Het goede jaarverslag", in *Haagse Post*, 16 April 1955, p. 11. Further coverage, essentially descriptive, was "Richtlijnen voor Jaarverslaggeving, Rapport Commissie der Werkgeversbonden", in *De Maasbode*, 1 April 1955, p. 15; and "Behartenswaardige studie over het jaarverslag, Rapport van commissie uit werkgeversverbonden", in *Haagsche Courant*, 1 April 1955, p. 35.

initiative, said, in his accustomed manner, "Unfortunately, there are so many reservations and 'escape clauses' that countless ill-intentioned managements may well find loopholes in order to hide or misrepresent things in the so-called interest of their enterprise".[94]

De Volkskrant said that the report "is clear proof that in circles of company managements the overall deficiency of financial reporting is acknowledged". Alluding to the report's carefully constructed compromises, it added,

> One would like to see more outspoken and clear language in the report, the more so as Dutch managements prefer to say nothing rather than something to their shareholders. It is to be feared that they will quite readily count themselves under the [report's] exceptions.[95]

In an article entitled "A Praiseworthy Initiative", *De Telegraaf* wrote, "At last there is an initiative in the chaotic situation in the field of financial reporting in the Netherlands ... , but the report loses value because of several compromises .... Now it should be the task of the Stock Exchange Association to undertake a standardization of financial reporting; in this regard, it should consult with industry, but the final result should not itself be drafted by industry".[96]

The references in several newspapers to "compromises" and "escape clauses" was probably unfair comment. The report represented the first attempt by the employers federations to speak out on a topic that, not many years earlier, would have been treated perfunctorily. The committee's avowed framework of providing "insight" argued against the use of strict rules. Financial reporting was clearly controversial in the 1950's, and a committee composed of mainly company directors could hardly have been expected to issue a unanimous report without the use of qualifying language.

In another commentary, the *Nieuwe Rotterdamse Courant* said that, while the Rijkens recommendations were "useful", they could not be used as a substitute for actual legislation.[97]

Het Binnenhof, a daily paper published in the region of The Hague, said that an action by the employers federations to propose recommendations that exceeded the current demands of the Stock Exchange Association conferred the "big advantage" of taking the wind from those who would press for more extensive legal regulation. At the same time, the paper remarked that the Stock

---

94 Justus Meyer, "Het goede jaarverslag", in *Haagse Post*, 16 April 1955, p. 11. For a similar view, see "Richtlijnen voor N.V.'s bij jaarverslaggeving", in *Het Parool*, 1 April 1955, p. 17.

95 "Verslaggeving", in *de Volkskrant*, 1 April 1955, p. 2. An accompanying, descriptive article was entitled "Commissie Jaarverslaggeving: Maatschappij verslagen moeten een getrouw beeld geven, Voorzichtig met stille reserves".

96 "Werkgeversverbonden geven richtlijn jaarverslagen, Lofwaardig initiatief", in *De Telegraaf*, 1 April 1955, p. 13.

97 "Richtlijnen voor de moderne jaarverslaggeving, Initiatief van de vier werkgeversverbonden", in *Nieuwe Rotterdamse Courant*, 1 April 1955, p. 15.

Exchange Association "does not always act with such forcefulness as is required by the interests of shareholders and the general public".[98]

Prof.dr J.L. Meij, of the Rijksuniversiteit Groningen, writing in *De Tijd*, saw the real significance of the Rijkens report as evidence of the increased sense of social responsibility among employers rather than in its actual recommendations.[99]

3.2.10. A personal view from Rijkens

In 1960, shortly after the government had installed a commission on company law reform, Dr P. Rijkens issued a belated reply to the press reactions. He wrote as follows:

> At the time, the main criticism of the press concerning the report was directed at the occasionally vague phrases in which the recommendations were wrapped. I can agree with this criticism. But the committee adopted the point of view, rightly, I believe, that, if at all possible, it would have to come up with recommendations that would acceptable to all members of the committee, especially those representing business.
>
> Therefore, although it was possible to reach agreement on the most important principles, it nevertheless needed to be pointed out that exceptions to the principles had to be considered permissible. It was naturally difficult for some members to distance themselves from the reporting practiced by their company at that moment, and on which they did not have the final say.[100]

Rijkens went on to relate his own views on proper financial reporting:

- the publication of audited financial statements should be mandatory for a circle of companies substantially in excess of those that are listed.
- secret reserves should be classified as "not allowable", although undisclosed reserves should be tolerated only for banks and insurance companies.
- current cost accounting was to be strongly advocated, as historical cost information might conflict with the demands of a "*getrouw beeld*"; also, allowance should be made for the use of current cost for tax purposes.
- disclosure should be made of sales, and comparative figures should be mandatory.[101]

[98] "Jaarverslag moet aan vele eisen voldoen, Drang naar 't verkrijgen van beursnotering gevaarlijk", in *Het Binnenhof*, 2 April 1955, p. 9.
[99] Prof.dr J.L. Meij, "Waarheid en klaarheid in de jaarrekening", in *De Tijd*, 9 April 1955, p. 4.
[100] "Herziening ondernemingsrecht (V)-Publieke verantwoording van de naamloze vennootschap", in *Algemeen Handelsblad*, 16 November 1960, p. 11.
[101] *Ibid.*

3.2.11. Effect of the report on company practices

The impact on companies themselves is hard to judge, for any observed improvements in their financial reporting might have occurred in the absence of the Rijkens proposals. In one case, however, that of Koninklijke Papierfabrieken van Gelder Zonen N.V., several salient improvements could be directly attributed to the report. Mr F.H.A. de Graaff, a member of the company's management board, was a signatory of the Rijkens report as well as chairman of one of its four sponsoring employers federations. In the directors' report included in the company's 1954 annual report to shareholders, which was issued just as the Rijkens report was being published, the following passage appeared:

> The growing interest in the publications of Limited Companies has caused us to modify our usual reporting practices by adjusting them to the demands that are consistent with modern concepts.
>
> Not only will more data be furnished in the future regarding the operations, but also the balance sheet will be drawn up in a way so that a better insight into the financial position and profitability of our enterprise may be obtained.[102]

True to its word, the company styled its 1954 report more attractively than its predecessor, and for the first time it provided a five-year comparison of selected financial data. Furthermore, the company adopted current cost accounting for its fixed assets and raw materials inventories. Two years later, in its 1956 report, the company disclosed the existence of an external auditor for the first time, and the auditor used the terminology favored in the Rijkens report, *getrouw beeld*.

As regards other companies whose directors served on the Rijkens committee, a few showed noticeable improvement, while others continued practices that were found by the Rijkens committee to be less than sound. In its 1955 annual report, Willem Smit & Co's Transformatorenfabriek N.V. presented consolidated statements, an indexation of the sales values of finished goods, and order backlogs, all for the first time. Albert Heijn N.V.'s 1955 annual report was more colorful than in previous years, but no other improvements were evident. In its 1956 annual report, Koninklijke Nederlandsche Hoogovens en Staalfabrieken N.V. adopted current cost accounting for both asset valuation and depreciation expense (the "integral" approach), introduced a 10-year comparative summary of selected financial statistics, and disclosed sales for the first time. Albatros Superfosfaatfabrieken N.V. disclosed sales for the first time in its 1954/55 annual report but failed to disclose the existence of an external auditor throughout the 1950's. In

[102] *1954 Jaarverslag* (Annual Report) of Koninklijke Papierfabrieken van Gelder Zonen N.V., p. 7. This was the only company annual report in the authors' sample (see Appendix 3.1) in which a reference to the call for improved financial reporting could be found. For a contemporary reaction to the company's 1954 annual report, see Prof. J. Brands, "Het Jaarverslag van de open Naamloze Vennootschap", in *De Naamlooze Vennootschap*, vol. 33, no. 2, May 1955, p. 24.

its 1954 annual report, A. Hooimeyer en Zonen N.V. began showing comparative figures in the balance sheet (but not in the profit and loss statement until after 1960) as well as a five-year summary of balance sheet information. It did not report sales during the 1950's. On the other hand, the annual reports of N.V. Koninklijke Maatschappij "De Schelde" (the company whose 1953 annual report was held up to the VNW executive committee as an example of progressive reporting) and Blijdenstein & Co N.V. seemed to be unaffected by the Rijkens report. Indeed, the latter continued to show its transportation equipment at 1 or 2 guilders into the 1960's, and its 1955 annual report was issued more than two months later than the previous year's report.

In regard to large companies in general, improvements were noticeable here and there. A few companies, such as Hollandsche Kunstzijde Industrie and N.V. Koninklijke Zwanenberg-Organon, began to disclose sales and cost of sales in their 1955 annual reports. The former disclosed the absolute amount of its sales, while the latter employed an index. But the majority of large companies continued their practice of not reporting either sales or cost of sales.

Perhaps influenced by the Rijkens committee's (and the Sijthoff Prize judges') advocacy of multi-year summaries, a number of companies began to insert such exhibits in their annual reports in the middle 1950's, covering a diversity of time periods. Among the enterprises reporting such a summary, together with the first year in which it was provided, were: Koninklijke Demka Staalfabrieken N.V. (1954), N.V. Koninklijke Zwanenberg-Organon (1955), and Wm H. Müller & Co. N.V. (1955). The Demka multi-year summary gave comparative figures at five-year intervals going back to 1916–17.

A few companies began to present consolidated financial statements in their 1955 annual reports (e.g., N.V. Billiton Maatschappij and Willem Smit & Co's Transformatorenfabriek N.V., the latter for its balance sheet only). As already noted, Unilever, Albert Heijn and the three companies that entered the New York capital market in 1953–54 had begun issuing full consolidated statements in the 1940's and early 1950's. But during the decade of the 1950's, comparatively few large companies published consolidated statements. From information in the companies' unconsolidated financial statements, it was seldom possible to determine whether their investments represented a majority interest in the shares of other enterprises; hence, one could not say with confidence that consolidated statements would have been justified by the circumstances.

Overall, the Rijkens report was having an effect on large companies' financial reporting, although, to be sure, momentum toward improved reporting had actually commenced some years earlier. Several of the largest companies had begun to improve their financial reporting in the years immediately after the War, followed by a number of others in the early 1950's. Yet the tradition of secrecy in companies that had been family enterprises not that many years before was slow to die out. Most companies were accustomed to giving no more than the law required, and most of what the Rijkens committee had recommended went beyond legal prescriptions.

3.2.12. Commentary in professional publications

In speeches and articles, several auditors asserted that the Rijkens report was a significant document and was having an effect. Drs I. Kleerekoper, in a 1959 address to the Summer School of The Institute of Chartered Accountants of Scotland, quoted extensively from the report and said, "I consider this report to be highly important because it provides a gauge of what business life thinks [is] necessary for the annual report".[103] Prof.dr A.Th. de Lange, writing in 1962, said that "the recommendations of the committee have exercised considerable influence".[104] J.H.M. van Vlerken said in 1965 that "the influence of [the Rijkens] report was considerable, which is easy to understand since the recommendations originated within the circle of the entrepreneurs themselves".[105] Prof. J. Brands, of the Nederlandse Economische Hogeschool, wrote, "Probably, the influence of the report will be great, and a general improvement of financial reporting will follow".[106] Drs A.C.J. Jonkers, like Brands a leading member of the VAGA, wrote, "The influence of the [Rijkens committee's] Recommendations is plainly discernible in the annual reports".[107]

J. Kraayenhof, a member of the Rijkens committee, wrote in 1960 that "the report has had a great beneficial influence; it is still consulted by management and by members of our profession as well".[108] He added that "it may be taken for granted that the report would have been of far less importance if it had been issued by accountants only".[109] By way of corroboration, Drs F. Graafstal later wrote, "It should be considered whether, in view of the fact that the primary responsibility for financial reporting rests with the management, the making of public recommendations (exclusively by accountants) is at all efficient".[110] Company managements, it has been claimed, did not then regard auditors as

---

[103] I. Kleerekoper, "Some Aspects of Accounting and Auditing in the Netherlands", in the *Seventh Summer School Booklet*, The Institute of Chartered Accountants of Scotland, 1959, p. 48.

[104] A.Th. de Lange, "Accounting in the Netherlands", in *The Canadian Chartered Accountant*, vol. 81, no. 4, October 1962, p. 339.

[105] J.H.M. van Vlerken, "Financial Reporting in Holland", in *The Canadian Chartered Accountant*, vol. 87, no. 5, November 1965, p. 347.

[106] Brands, *op.cit.*

[107] A.C.J. Jonkers, "A Netherlands View on Auditing Standards", in *Maandblad voor accountancy en bedrijfshuishoudkunde*, vol. 36, no. 11, December 1962, p. 489.

[108] Jacob Kraayenhof, "International Challenges for Accounting", in *The Journal of Accountancy*, vol. 109, no. 1, January 1960, p. 36.

[109] *Ibid.*

[110] "Harmonisation of Accounting Principles and the Concept of Profit", in *Maandblad voor accountancy en bedrijfshuishoudkunde*, vol. 42, nos. 1/2, January/February 1968, p. 90.

their social equals.[111] Hence, if managements were to be persuaded to alter their opinions, a recommendation made by company directors would be the most likely to succeed.

K. Soesbeek, a director of A.K.U. (eleven years later he became chairman of A.K.U.'s management board, and he presided over the merger that produced Akzo in 1969), wrote in 1955 that the favorable reception given to the Rijkens report by the press was due to the realistic approach taken by the committee.[112] Yet he argued that the report did not go far enough. Soesbeek believed that the committee might have taken a stronger stance on disclosure. He argued that the requirement for showing the current cost of assets should be included among the four "general demands" that must be met in order to give a *getrouw beeld*. This disclosure was necessary, he said, in order to be able to make a correct assessment of the return on capital (which formed part of one of the "general demands" in the report).[113] Soesbeek also argued that interim reporting, which the Rijkens committee had supported, should be in the format of complete quarterly profit and loss statements, which A.K.U. had been providing since 1953. Also of interest, especially in an article written by a company director, was Soesbeek's recommended disclosure in the directors' report of an indication of the relative importance of different product lines. Soesbeek's article was a reflection of A.K.U.'s progressive approach to financial reporting.

On the other hand, H.D.M. Knol considered the Rijkens report to be a repetition of much that had already been said in the journals in the last several years, and he criticized the committee for compromising its position on sales disclosure, so as not to inform competitors. Knol saw the particular composition of the committee, with a heavy representation of company directors, as the explanation for this posture.[114]

Of the several auditors who testified that the Rijkens report was having an impact, none offered any data on particular companies to support their generalizations. If they were thinking of the multinationals that had recently begun share trading in New York, it was not the Rijkens report, but the demands of the New York capital market, that had stimulated the improvements in their financial reporting. Among the other large companies, as we have seen, improved reporting had occurred, but it was limited to a few items and to a few companies.

---

[111] Interviews with Prof.drs J.W. Schoonderbeek, 17 December 1990, and with Drs F. Graafstal, 27 June 1991. For a discussion of the relative social standing of company directors and auditors, see Johan de Vries, *Geschiedenis der Accountancy in Nederland: Aanvang en Ontplooiing, 1895–1935* (Assen/Maastricht: Van Gorcum, 1985), pp. 78–79 and esp. 203.

[112] K. Soesbeek, "Het jaarverslag", in *Maandblad voor accountancy en bedrijfshuishoudkunde*, vol. 29, no. 6, June 1955, pp. 255–257.

[113] A.K.U. had been reporting depreciation expense on a current cost basis since 1947, and inventories and cost of goods sold on a current cost basis since 1953.

[114] H.D.M. Knol, "Een rapport inzake de jaarrekening en het jaarverslag", in *Maandblad voor Bedrijfsadministratie*, vol. 59, no. 699, June 1955, pp. 97–99.

That most of the auditors were addressing foreign audiences may have led them to express themselves more expansively than otherwise.

Nonetheless, the seed had been planted. The Rijkens report was read intently by auditors, and was discussed by the auditors with their clients. In the universities, lecturers referred to the report, and it was read by students. By the end of the 1950's, it had become influential.[115]

3.2.13. A NIvA committee draws on the Rijkens report

In 1956, the NIvA's Advisory Committee on Professional Matters issued a report written by one of its subcommittees which cited the Rijkens report with favor.[116] The subject of the report was *"obligo's"*, which was the general name given to a number of legal liabilities that were customarily not disclosed in the financial statements. Examples were orders for fixed assets, leasing agreements, forward contracts in commodities or currencies, discounted bills of exchange, guarantees, letters of credit, and licensing agreements.

The subcommittee undertook the study in order to place the question of *obligo's* in the wider perspective of the changing demands being placed on financial reporting. That those demands have changed, said the subcommittee, can be seen by comparing the report of the Visser Commission, which led to passage of the 1929 amendment to the Commercial Code, with the Rijkens report (pp. 397–398). Financial statements, the subcommittee said, are supposed to give a "picture" (*beeld*) of the amount and composition of the financial position and income (p. 398). But, in the course of time, the "economic and social climate" (*maatschappelijk verkeer*) changes its conception of what is merely useful, and what is necessary, in order to give such a "picture" (p. 399). The subcommittee then proceeded to cite the 1949 and 1951 circulars of the Stock Exchange Association; the Groeneveld article, published in 1953, on "New Trends in Published Financial Statements" (cited in footnote 37, above); P.F.S. Otten's 1954 speech to Philips shareholders; the articles of 6 and 7 January 1955 in *Het Financieele Dagblad* on financial reporting (cited in footnote 50, above), and the Rijkens report.

In view of these indicators of changing demands, the subcommittee said that, notwithstanding the traditions of financial reporting, companies should recognize that the choice of legal form does not govern the proper accounting treatment of transactions. It is not the form that dictates disclosure, the subcommittee said,

---

[115] Interview with Prof.drs J.W. Schoonderbeek, 10 September 1991. "The auditors had something in their hands, and they could say to their clients, 'It was done by the employers' ". *Ibid.*

[116] "Rapport van de Commissie van Advies inzake Beroepsaangelegenheden over het vraagstuk van het al dan niet verwerken van obligo's in de verslaglegging", in *de Accountant*, vol. 62, no. 6, April 1956, pp. 395–409. In this section, citations in the text to page numbers will refer to this report.

but the effect on financial position and income (pp. 401, 406). The subcommittee said that the auditor should press for disclosure when the effect is material (p. 406).

The subcommittee also cited recent developments in the USA, the UK, and West Germany regarding commitments and contingent liabilities (pp. 407–408).

The tenor of the report suggests that the subcommittee chose to write on *obligo's*, at least in part, as a vehicle for contributing to the dialogue on the important changes it had been observing in the demands being placed on financial reporting. Drs J.W. Schoonderbeek was the secretary-*rapporteur* of the five-member subcommittee.

A.B. Frielink, a member of the NIvA, criticized the subcommittee for appealing to a subjective criterion, i.e., to give a "picture", when determining what should be disclosed in financial statements. This criterion, he argued, was insufficient as a practical tool and could easily lead to unlimited demands for more information. Frielink maintained that disclosure was necessary only if it served a concrete purpose in the context of the specific audience to which a set of financial statements was directed.[117]

3.2.14. Sijthoff Prize: Announcement of the norms of good financial reporting

While the first Sijthoff Prize for "the Best Annual Report" was awarded to A.K.U. for its 1953 report (in the category of industrial companies), and the prizes for the 1954 annual reports were awarded to Philips and to Koninklijke Papierfabrieken van Gelder Zonen, the norms used for judging reports were not published until December 1956.[118] The 11-page booklet containing the norms reflected the influence of the Rijkens report, although it did not mention the report. The Sijthoff norms were developed by a panel of judges, consisting of the president of the Stock Exchange Association and the presidents of the other two associations of securities exchanges. Two of the three panel members had been educated as lawyers.

The term "insight", which had figured prominently in Otten's speech of 1954 as well as in the Rijkens report, was used no fewer than 17 times in the explication of the Sijthoff norms. "The purpose of the balance sheet", according to the norms, "is to give a correct insight into the invested capital, the financial structure and liquidity"(p. 5), and "the purpose of a profit and loss statement is to give a clear insight into the economic profit from operations"(p. 3).

[117] A.B. Frielink, "Het al dan niet verwerken van obligo's in de verslaglegging", in *Maandblad voor accountancy en bedrijfshuishoudkunde*, vol. 32, no. 7, July, 1958, pp. 295–299. Frielink's article contains a particularly clear exposition of the *obligo* question.

[118] *Normen voor de beoordeling van Jaarverslagen opsteld voor de Henri Sijthoff-prijs*, dated December 1956. Also see footnote 50, above. In this section, all citations in the text to page numbers will refer to this booklet.

Although the panel of judges said that current cost depreciation would "increase the insight into income during the year" and that balance sheets on the basis of current cost accounting would be "valuable" (*waardevol*), they decided that the absence of this information should not reflect adversely on the quality of annual reports, since it was being provided by so few companies. Companies that do not give current cost balance sheets could, the panel said, give an indication of insured values in the notes (pp. 5–6). Comparative figures were deemed to be imperative, and the Stock Exchange Association's circular of 15 October 1951 was cited (p. 3). Moreover, the panel advocated the reporting of balance-sheet and profit-and-loss-statement figures covering a series of years (p. 3).

While the statement of norms specified that, in general, all reserves should be disclosed separately in the balance sheet, it acknowledged the existence of cases in which the "interest of all parties concerned" made the formation of secret reserves necessary (p. 9). A consolidated balance sheet was recommended when a significant fraction of the owners' equity was invested in majority holdings, but the desirability of a consolidated profit and loss statement was only mildly suggested (pp. 9–10). The statement affirmed that it was "of interest" that an auditor's report be included in the annual report (p. 12). Many of the disclosures recommended by the Rijkens committee, such as sales (in absolute amount or indexed), cost of sales, and other subtotals in the profit and loss statement, were also enumerated in the Sijthoff norms (pp. 10–12). Where the Rijkens committee was content to encourage the publication of interim reports during the year, the Sijthoff norms called specifically for half-yearly and even quarterly information (p. 12).

In general, the Sijthoff norms were similar to the recommendations in the Rijkens report in regard to information disclosure, but they reflected less of an interest in how the figures in the financial statements were to be measured. Nowhere in the statement of Sijthoff norms was there a suggestion that the accounting principles used by the company, together with a notation of any changes therein, should be disclosed. This disclosure relating to the companies' accounting principles had occupied a central position in both the Otten speech and the Rijkens report.

One should not underestimate the importance of the Sijthoff Prize as a factor in promoting improvements in companies' financial reports. It has been an award that is coveted by the managements of large and medium-sized companies,[119] and it is fair to assume that the published norms for the judging of annual reports were studied by company directors with considerable interest.

In an article published in 1957, an auditor, H.J. Reyn, attempted a comparison between the Sijthoff norms and the Rijkens report.[120] While he praised the

[119]Interviews with G. Timmer, 5 September 1990; with J. Hanekroot, 18 September 1990; with Drs H. Haarbosch, 12 November 1990; and with Drs G. Verhagen, 27 November 1991.

[120]H.J. Reyn, "Twee publicaties over het jaarverslag", in *Maandblad voor accountancy en*

support given to current cost accounting in both reports, he found it unfortunate that the strength of the Sijthoff panel's support was not as great as that reflected in the Rijkens report. That both reports advocated current cost accounting led Reyn to conclude that this principle was accepted by the business world as a "sound business practice" (*goed koopmansgebruik*). If, in the auditor's opinion, the use of current cost accounting were necessary in order to present a "correct picture" (*juist beeld*), Reyn said that the auditor must insist on clear notes to the financial statements to provide the additional information.

3.3. Review of the postwar period to 1959

The postwar agitation for improved financial reporting was in marked contrast to the serenity of the 1930's. Changes in economic conditions played a large role in this development. Drs W. van Bruinessen, a leading auditor who served as the NIvRA president in 1970, referred to "major changes [that] occurred in the structure of industry and trade as well as in the opinions on enterprises as constituent parts of economic and social life":

> Following, *inter alia*, post-war technological developments, many enterprises experienced a large need for funds that could not be met from the traditional sources (profits retained in the business and savings made by the owners). Moreover, for maintaining their relative position at the market, enterprises were often obliged to expand their business. This, again, increased the need for additional funds that could not be met by either the owners or the profitability of the enterprise. After the loss of the previous colony Indonesia [in 1949], traditionally a dependable market for the Dutch industry, new and unknown markets had to be found and developed and, naturally, such activities can be better embarked upon by a large enterprise than by a smaller one. Finally [in 1957] Dutch industrial enterprises were confronted with a developing European Common Market and, consequently, with competition from far greater German and French enterprise ....
>
> For the problem of accounting principles, the aforementioned structural developments since 1945 were of major significance in one respect: the markedly increased share in the financing taken by long-term and short-term loans made available by third parties, together with the increasing segregation of management and ownership, gave rise to an expansion of the duty to render an account on the management's stewardship up to an extent that, prior to 1940, could hardly be imagined in the Netherlands.[121]

---

bedrijfshuishoudkunde, vol. 31, no. 8, September 1957, pp. 340–342.

[121] W. van Bruinessen, "Accounting Standards and Rules – Voluntary or Regulatory Determination?", in *Maandblad voor accountancy en bedrijfshuishoudkunde*, vol. 49, no. 1, January 1975, p. 7.

Van Bruinessen's mention of "the opinions on enterprises as constituent parts of economic and social life" referred to the growing influence of trade unions during the 1950's as an important stakeholder in enterprise. The effects of this development will become evident in the

The effects of these structural changes were palpable. Auditors and lawyers writing in the professional journals, as well as reporters writing in the financial press, began to place higher demands on financial reporting. Some companies began to depart from their conservative attitudes toward financial reporting, and became somewhat more generous providers of information. Initially, as with a reluctant swimmer trying out the water, modest innovations were attempted. At first, companies began furnishing comparative figures and multi-year summaries. At the same time, auditors' reports began to appear more frequently in companies' annual reports. Some companies began to introduce more substantive improvements, such as consolidated statements, the disclosure of sales, and more expansive profit and loss statements. Unilever, which had been trading in London, and A.K.U., Royal Dutch Petroleum, and Philips, which began trading in New York in 1953–54, led the field in innovative reporting, but they may have been responding more to competitive pressures in overseas securities markets than to the movement for better financial reporting in the Netherlands.

Domestic stimuli for improved reporting began to come from several sources: first, from the financial community (including the financial press); second, from the president of a major company; and third, from the employers federations. A common thread passing through all of these initiatives was the importation of overseas reporting practices, especially from the USA. *First:* The Sijthoff Prize, while it was based on norms developed by a panel of judges consisting of the presidents of the three Dutch securities associations, indirectly propagated US financial reporting practices, as the awards for five of the first seven years, from 1953 to 1959, were given to the three companies that began trading in New York in 1953–54 and whose reports reflected American standards of reporting. *Second:* At the very time when Philips' president enunciated its financial reporting philosopy, the company's shares had just begun to be traded in New York, where companies competing in the same market were disclosing much more information than was customary in the Netherlands. *Third:* The two auditor members of the Rijkens committee, Goudeket and Kraayenhof, had recently been heavily involved with American reporting practices owing to former's work in Philips and the latter's close association with the audits of all three companies, including Philips, that had just entered the US capital market. All three initiatives were influential in their own ways, but there is reason to believe that the decisions by the Sijthoff panel were watched with special interest by companies.[122]

---

next chapter.

[122] Burgert has written that, as a result of the international companies going overseas for capital, "more and more [Dutch] accountants became involved in foreign accounting standards. As a reaction purely national companies also engaged themselves for more and better disclosure". Prof.drs R. Burgert, "Current Accounting Practice in the Netherlands", in *Maandblad voor accountancy en bedrijfshuishoudkunde*, vol. 55, nos. 2/3, February/March 1981, p. 53. Burgert was a member of the panel of judges for the Sijthoff Prize from 1974 to 1984.

The 1950's were a period in which a wide circle of commentators, including auditors, lawyers, financial journalists, leaders of the investment community, and company directors, began the process of discussing how financial reporting could be adapted to the changing economic times. Beginning in 1959, as will be seen in the next chapter, the cause of improved financial reporting became part of the larger collection of issues surrounding the democratization of private enterprise.

Appendix 3.1. Companies surveyed

The following list includes the full names of the companies whose financial statements are referred to in this chapter. The rank number refers to a listing of all quoted companies according to total assets (consolidated when available), compiled from the 1954 edition of *Van Oss' Effectenboek*. It should be noted that this ordering is of limited value as an unambiguous indication of size, as some companies valued their assets using current cost, while others still used secret and undisclosed reserves.

Of the fifty largest companies, a number were omitted from the survey because their financial statements were not available in the Bedrijfseconomisch Archief (Archive) of the Erasmus Universiteit Rotterdam. Another reason for omitting certain companies was to avoid the inclusion of a disproportionate number of shipping companies, which figured more importantly in the asset ranking than their role in economic life would suggest, and which, by their secretive disclosure practices, would have distorted the general picture in regard to manufacturing companies.

1. N.V. Philips' Gloeilampenfabrieken (Philips' Incandescent Lamp Works)
2. N.V. Koninklijke Nederlandsche Petroleum Maatschappij (Royal Dutch Petroleum Company)
3. Unilever N.V.
4. Koninklijke Nederlandsche Hoogovens en Staalfabrieken N.V. (Royal Dutch Blast-Furnaces and Steelworks)
5. Algemene Kunstzijde Unie N.V. (General Artificial Silk United)
6. N.V. Koninklijke Paketvaart-Maatschappij (Royal Steam-Packet Company)
7. Werkspoor N.V.* [An engineering conglomerate centered on transportation equipment]
11. Domaniale Mijn-Maatschappij N.V. (Territorial Mining Company)
15. Koninklijke Machinefabriek Gebr. Stork & Co N.V.* (Royal Machine Manufacturing – Stork Bros. & Co)
17. N.V. Koninklijke Maatschappij "De Schelde" (Royal "De Schelde" Company) [Shipbuilding]
18. Koninklijke Java–China Paketvaart Lijnen N.V. (Royal Java–China Steam-Packet Lines)

20. Wm H. Müller & Co. N.V. [Shipping company]
24. N.V. Nederlandsche Kabelfabrieken (Dutch Cable Factories)
25. Koninklijke Papierfabrieken van Gelder Zonen N.V. (Royal Paper Mills van Gelder & Sons)
26. N.V. Centrale Suiker Maatschappij (Central Sugar Company)
27. N.V. Borneo Sumatra Handel Maatschappij (Borneo Sumatra Trading Company)
29. N.V. Koninklijke Zwanenberg–Organon [Chemicals]
30. N.V. Billiton Maatschappij [Mining]
34. Heineken's Bierbrouwerij Maatschappij N.V. (Heineken's Brewery Company)
35. Albatros Superfosfaatfabrieken N.V. (Albatros Super Phosphate Works)
36. N.V. Hollandsche Kunstzijde Industrie (Dutch Artificial Silk Industries)
37. Koninklijke Nederlandsche Gist- en Spiritusfabriek N.V. (Royal Dutch Yeast and Methylated Spirits Factory)
38. N.V. Werf "Gusto" v/h firma A.F. Smulders ("Gusto" wharf)
41. Koninklijke Demka Staalfabrieken N.V. (Royal Demka Steel Manufacturing)
43. Albert Heijn N.V. [Food retailing]
44. N.V. P.F. van Vlissingen & Co's Katoenfabrieken [P.F. van Vlissingen & Co's Cotton Mills)
45. N.V. Magazijn "De Bijenkorf" [General retailing]
46. N.V. Heemaf [Electrical engineering]
47. Willem Smit & Co's Transformatorenfabriek N.V. (Willem Smit & Co's Transformer Manufacturing)
48. Koninklijke Nederlandsche Maatschappij voor Havenwerken N.V. (Royal Dutch Port Works Company)

* In 1955, Stork and Werkspoor merged to form Verenigde Machinefebrieken N.V. (United Machine Manufacturing).

Three companies were included in the sample in addition to the ones mentioned above:

- Koninklijke Luchtvaart Maatschappij N.V. (KLM Royal Dutch Airlines) was included in the sample as a major Dutch company, although its first listing was in the 1955 edition of *Van Oss' Effectenboek*.
- The financial statements of Blijdenstein & Co N.V. [shipping] and A. Hooijmeijer & Zonen N.V. [food processing] were surveyed as well, because members of their management board (i.e., directors) took part in the Rijkens committee. The ranking of Blijdenstein would have been 93, and that of Hooijmeijer would have been higher than 200.

4. Developments from 1959 to 1970: The swift political current toward a new company law

4.1. Introduction

In 1959, the discussion about improvements in financial reporting vaulted into the political arena. On center stage was the highly charged debate over the role that employees should be given in company management. Windmuller has sketched the thinking behind the movement as follows:

> After many decades of struggle, a workable parliamentary democracy had emerged. Through its institutions, workers had gained their rightful voice in national affairs. The logical next step was the extension of equal rights from the body politic to the workplace. Shared decision making through appropriate institutions built into the enterprise was the proper answer to demands for worker participation in management. The right of free workers to a voice in industrial management was the true counterpart of the right of free citizens to a voice in political government.[1]

The cause of workers' co-determination in enterprise may be traced to the prewar years. Following the War, the workers joined with employers, as social partners, in a cooperative effort to reconstruct and develop the war-torn Dutch economy. The Labor Party (PvdA, Partij van de Arbeid) emerged in February 1946 out of a restructuring of the Social-Democratic Workers Party (SDAP, Sociaal-Democratische Arbeiderspartij) and several breakaway groups from other parties, and in the same year it entered into a center-left coalition with the Catholic People's Party (KVP, Katholieke Volkspartij), which was to govern the country until 1958. But in 1950, when Parliament passed the Act on Works Councils (Wet op de Ondernemingsraden), under which every employer with 25 or more employees was required to set up a works council, stiff employer resistance to giving employees an actual voice in management prevented the works councils from having more than a consultative or advisory role.[2] The issue of workers' rights in enterprise festered during the 1950's, and by the end of the decade the general question of the democratization of enterprise, including the right of

1 John P. Windmuller, *Labor Relations in the Netherlands* (Ithaca, NY: Cornell University Press, 1969), p. 408.
2 *Ibid.*, pp. 408–411.

shareholders, employees and the public to receive adequate financial information about the company affairs, rose to the level of national debate.

A blow was struck in 1959, when the Labor Party issued a report on the restructuring of enterprise, containing major proposals for company law reform. Shortly afterwards, it became known that the recently elected center-right government led by the Catholic People's Party, with the Labor Party in opposition,[3] had decided to install a commission to recommend a revision of company law. The Labor Party manifesto and the government's decision immediately led to calls for two additional studies: one by the employers federations, as a follow-up to the Rijkens report of 1955; and one by the Liberal Party (VVD, Volkspartij voor Vrijheid en Democratie) which was part of the government coalition. The reports of the two studies were published in 1962, and both were filled with arguments against most of the reforms favored by the Labor Party. All three reports – those by the Labor and Liberal Parties, and the one from the employers federations – treated financial reporting as an important issue in company law reform. Everyone awaited the report of the government's Verdam Commission, which was impaneled in 1960. The press, of course, was alive to the escalating political significance of these developments, and the coverage, especially of the Verdam Commission report, was extensive.

When the Verdam Commission report became known in early 1965, it was clear that the country was heading inexorably toward company law reform, and financial reporting occupied a significant place in the proposed law. Following the receipt of advice on the Verdam recommendations, the Justice Ministry submitted a draft law to Parliament. After an exchange of views with the minister and a consideration of several amendments, Parliament passed the Act on Annual Financial Statements of Enterprises (Wet op de Jaarrekening van Ondernemingen) in 1970, which was the first legislation on company financial reporting since 1928–29. In 1971, Parliament approved the Act on Works Councils (Wet op de Ondernemingsraden), which fortified the 1950 Act by granting works councils a measure of co-determination in management decisions.

These developments, as they relate to company financial reporting, are examined in this chapter.

---

[3] Although the Catholic People's Party (KVP) obtained the largest vote, 31.6 percent, in the 1959 election, the Labor Party (PvdA) received only slightly less, 30.4 percent. In the 150-seat Second Chamber, the KVP held 49 seats (augmented by 45 from its coalition partners), and the PvdA had 48. G.G.J. Thissen (compiler), *Parlement en kiezer* (Leiden: Martinus Nijhoff, 1990), pp. 39, 133, 136.

4.2. Further private-sector initiatives

4.2.1. The Dr. Wiardi Beckman Stichting report on the restructuring of enterprise

In 1959, the "think tank" of the Labor Party, known as the Dr. Wiardi Beckman Stichting (Dr. Wiardi Beckman Foundation), published a book entitled *De hervorming van de onderneming* (The Restructuring of Enterprise),[4] in which most of a chapter, about 10 percent of the 175-page book, was devoted to the "revision of the regulation of financial reporting".

The Dr. Wiardi Beckman Stichting had appointed a study committee in 1953, stemming from a request made in 1948 to the Foundation of Labor by the then Minister of Justice, Mr G.H. van Maarseveen (a member of the Catholic People's Party, but serving in a government coalition headed by the Labor Party), for advice regarding the revision of company law with a view toward giving a role to labor as a participant in industrial enterprise. One of the considerations entering into labor's participation was the access to company financial information. An issue, therefore, was the nature and scope of company financial reporting. Of the 14 members of the study committee, eight were lawyers. The chairman was Prof.mr J. Valkhoff, who lectured in civil and commercial law at the Gemeentelijke Universiteit van Amsterdam. The only member with an accounting background was Prof.dr A. Meij, of the same university, who was a strict Limperg disciple.[5]

The study committee saw the need for "opening up", or democratizing, large enterprise, with a view toward making it more accountable to capital suppliers as well as to workers and the general public (Chapter 1). Successive chapters were devoted to the interests of shareholders, employees, and the public in the affairs of large enterprises. It was proposed that the board of supervisors (*raad van commissarissen*) be broadened to reflect a tripartite constituency representing shareholders, employees and the general interest (Chapter 6). The employees' involvement was discussed in the context of "co-determination" (*medezeggenschap*) by workers in enterprise, which was a major political issue of the day. The study committee made the controversial recommendation that employees should be represented in a newly constituted supervisory board that would be less responsive to shareholders.

Among the members of the study committee was Prof.mr P. Sanders. The

---

[4] *De hervorming van de onderneming* (Amsterdam: N.V. de Arbeiderspers, 1959). In this section, all citations in the text to page numbers and chapters will refer to this report.

[5] See, for example, Abram Mey, "Theodore Limperg and his Theory of Values and Costs", in *Abacus*, vol. 2, no. 1, September 1966, pp. 3–23; and Abram Mey, *On the Application of Business Economics and Replacement Value Accounting in the Netherlands*, International Business Series No. 8, Studies in Accounting (Seattle: International Accounting Studies Institute and the Graduate School of Business Administration, University of Washington, 1970), esp. ftn. 8.

committee made a case for the establishment of a Companies Commission (Vennootschapskamer) along the lines suggested in Sanders' 1952 article.[6] It was patterned on both the US SEC and the Dutch Insurance Companies Commission. The committee believed that a Companies Commission, coupled with improvement in the regulation of financial reporting, was necessary to:

- ensure a wider share ownership in society,
- enable the general public to form an opinion on the affairs of large companies that have grown to be public institutions, and
- provide trade unions with the necessary information during wage negotiations (p. 119).

In its argument for the proposed revision of company law, the study committee referred at several places to the 1955 report of the Rijkens committee. Although, as noted above, several prominent auditors had asserted the favorable effects of the Rijkens report on company financial reporting, it was the study committee's view that, while the Rijkens report was "a happy attempt at improving financial reporting, ... it is disappointing that only a few enterprises have responded in a positive way to its suggestions, judging from recent annual reports" (pp. 46–47).

The provisions in the company law dealing with financial statements were lacking in significance, the study committee said, because of the virtual absence of disclosure requirements. "The result has been", it said, "that most of the financial statements of our major corporations have, with a few favorable exceptions, excelled in vagueness. The protests that have been uttered against this [practice], especially by the financial press, have not been able to bring about more than limited improvement" (p. 46). Yet the study committee seemed to be less interested in recommending norms for financial reporting than in designing a mechanism, namely, the Companies Commission, for its regulation.

Owing to differences of opinion among experts in *bedrijfseconomie*, the study committee said, it would be infeasible to prescribe a uniform valuation principle, although it might be possible to require the disclosure of a "test" figure, such as the insured valuation (p. 122). By contrast, the Rijkens committee had come out strongly for current cost accounting.

Going further than the Rijkens committee's position on secret and undisclosed reserves, the study committee declared that "the camouflaging of the real financial position, which takes place on a large scale, should be ended" (p. 122).

The study committee's recommendation on consolidated statements was more categorical than the hedged position in the Rijkens report: consolidated statements should be drawn up whenever there were majority investments (p. 122). Sales should be disclosed, the study committee said, adding that experience in

[6] P. Sanders, "Verantwoording van het bestuur in de publieke naamloze vennootschap", in *Rechtskundige opstellen*, essays dedicated to Prof.mr R.P. Cleveringa (Zwolle: N.V. Uitgevers-Maatschappij/W.E.J. Tjeenk Willink, 1952), pp. 329–362.

the United States demonstrated that there was no basis for fearing that a company's competitive position might possibly be endangered thereby (pp. 122–123). Interim reports, it said, should be prescribed when reliable figures could be supplied, which meant that, for the time being, they should be required only of the largest companies (p. 123). Finally, it was recommended that a report by the non-managing directors, i.e., the supervisors, should be attached to the financial statements, giving their views on the company's affairs and on the policies followed (p. 123).

In view of the clearer picture of the company's affairs that would be provided by financial statements containing the information called for in the report, the study committee thought it desirable that a "dispensation" be inserted in the regulations, stating that the Minister of Economic Affairs could waive certain of the regulations when there was good reason to believe that the disclosure would seriously damage the interests of a company. This exemption was provided even though the study committee noted that the experience of the US Securities and Exchange Commission suggested that the effect on competitiveness of increased disclosure was limited (p. 124).

The study committee's recommendations on the contents of financial reports were spelled out in the space of less than two pages. The Rijkens committee, since it was concerned solely with financial reporting, had been much more elaborate in the range of topics treated and in its discussion. It paid more attention to the development of a framework ("insight") for its proposals, and to a number of disclosures not addressed by the study committee, such as deferred taxes, pension liabilities, and assorted information about trends in the company's operations. The Rijkens report had confined its recommendations to "open" companies. By contrast, the Dr. Wiardi Beckman Stichting study committee was prepared to extend the public reporting requirements to the largest "closed" companies having shareholders' equity of more than 1 million guilders. The study committee's reasons for including these companies were as follows:

1. These companies seriously affect the general interest, even though the number of their shareholders is small.
2. They compete with "open" companies of the same size, and would enjoy a certain competitive advantage if they were not required to publish their financial statements.
3. Extending the publication requirements to such companies might remove a psychological obstacle to their going public (pp. 124–125).

Attaching an auditor's report to the financial statements could be required as soon as the auditing profession were to be properly regulated. In the meantime, the study committee said, only the largest companies should be required to publish an auditor's report, but the Companies Commission would have to give its consent to the auditor chosen in order to guarantee a certain standard of quality (p. 127).

The proposed Companies Commission would consist of five members appointed by the Crown, and would operate under the Ministry of Justice.[7] Only large companies would be required to file their reports with the Companies Commission, irrespective of their listing status. Government-owned companies as well as banks and insurance companies, which already had their own supervisory entities, would be omitted. The study committee estimated that the total number of companies reporting to the Companies Commission would not exceed 1500. The Companies Commission would examine in detail only about ten percent of the financial statements filed each year, while submitting the remainder to a more general test. It would order the amplification or amendment of missing or incorrect information (pp. 129–131).

4.2.2. Press reactions to the report

Commentators in the press said little about the position of the Dr. Wiardi Beckman Stichting study committee on financial reporting. By then, there was an effective consensus on the need to strengthen the regulation of financial reporting, although there was considerable disagreement over the means.

In the main, the press reacted to the committee's recommendations on the restructuring of enterprise.[8] There were, however, two exceptions. The *Haagse Post*, in an unsigned article reminiscent of Justus Meyer, endorsed much of the committee's criticism of financial reporting.[9] And the reporter in *Het Financieele Dagblad* said:

> Increased supervision and the duty to render an account will not, in general, encounter much criticism. The employers associations have for years been pressing for better reporting, and most NV's are being audited.[10]

Articles appearing in the journals of the two leading employers federations, the VNW and the CSWV, were, as might be expected, critical of the Dr. Wiardi

---

7 As in Sanders' 1952 article, analogies were drawn with the Securities and Exchange Commission and the Dutch Insurance Companies Commission (Verzekeringskamer).

8 See "Medezeggenschap in bedrijven", in *de Volkskrant*, 3 September 1959, p. 2; and "Van Nozem tot Commissaris", in *De Telegraaf*, 4 September 1959, p. 5.

9 "De hervorming van de onderneming, Een socialistische, constructieve bijdrage", in *Haagse Post*, 5 September 1959, pp. 3–4.

10 "Hervorming van de onderneming I: Wanbegrip van de ondernemersfunctie-Studie van de dr Wiardi Beckman Stichting", in *Het Financieele Dagblad*, 12 September 1959, pp. 1, 5 (quotation is from p. 5). The other two parts of the newspaper's coverage of the report were devoted to refuting the demands for a restructuring of the supervisory board. "Hervorming van de onderneming II: Politieke tegenover economische concentratie", 14 September 1959, pp. 1, 8; and "Hervorming van de onderneming III: Constructieve acties-Als tegenwicht voor politieke activiteiten", 15 September 1959, pp. 1, 2.

Beckman Stichting report.[11] A conference was organized by the Dr. Wiardi Beckman Stichting in October 1960 to discuss the report, at which the idea of a Companies Commission was generally rejected, as it was believed that its proposed task might well be carried out by the Stock Exchange Association.[12] Yet the writer in the *Haagse Post*, reflecting on the committee's proposal for an SEC-like body in the Netherlands, opined that people could not cherish any hope that the Stock Exchange Association was interested in investor protection, as the Association was founded not to protect investors, but to further the interests of its members.[13]

Government consultations on the possible restructuring of enterprise had been going on throughout the 1950's, and in the first Budget Speech following the 1959 national election, following which the Catholic People's Party (KVP) assumed charge of the government coalition, the intention to form a State Commission on the revision of company law (which was to become known as the Verdam Commission) was announced.[14] That company law reform was indeed a concern to all political parties was made evident by the fact that the government of Dr J.E. de Quay was the first postwar coalition without Labor Party participation and was, at the time, regarded as a "shift to the right".

The report of the Dr. Wiardi Beckman Stichting study committee, which appeared in the late summer of 1959, played a role in placing the issue of the restructuring of enterprise, including the sub-issue of financial reporting by companies, on the plane of national political debate.

4.2.3. Commentary in professional publications

As the centerpiece in his judicious and sympathetic review of the Dr. Wiardi Beckman Stichting report, J.M. Vecht comprehensively examined the arguments for and against the Companies Commission (Vennootschapskamer), including the earlier articles by Drucker and Sanders,[15] as well as comments by other authors

---

[11] "Een aanval op het vennootschapsrecht", in *De Nederlandse Industrie* (house organ of the Federation of Dutch Employers (VNW, Verbond van Nederlandsche Werkgevers)), 21 June 1959, pp. 577–579; and "Het rapport van de dr. Wiardi Beckman Stichting over de hervorming van de onderneming", in *De Onderneming* (house organ of the Central Social Employers Federation (CSWV, Centraal Sociaal Werkgevers-Verbond)), 26 September 1959, pp. 746–748. These employers federations were the two leading sponsors of the Rijkens report.

[12] "De hervorming van de onderneming: Conferentie van de Dr. Wiardi Beckman Stichting", in *De Onderneming*, 29 October 1960, pp. 791–792. Also see "P.v.d.A.-aanval op rechtsvorm van de ondernemingen, Overheid en arbeid als commissarissen in n.v.", in *De Telegraaf*, 17 October 1960.

[13] "De hervorming van de onderneming, Een socialistische, constructieve bijdrage", in *Haagse Post*, 5 September 1959, p. 3.

[14] The announcement as part of the Budget Speech was published in the *Nederlandse Staatscourant*, 15 September 1959, p. 7.

[15] J.M. Vecht, "Naar een vennootschapskamer?", in *Maandblad voor accountancy en bedrijfshuishoudkunde*, vol. 34, no. 2, February 1960, pp. 42–49. The other two articles mentioned

on the proposal by Sanders and the advocacy of a Companies Commission in the Dr. Wiardi Beckman Stichting report. Vecht rejected the argument by Schadee[16] that the Stock Exchange Association had an important role to play in regulating financial reporting: the Association may have good intentions, said Vecht, but one could not expect a body set up to further the interests of securities traders to take initiatives that might be antithetical to those interests. Vecht discarded as irrelevant the idea that a Companies Commission would be unnecessary if shareholders were to buy shares only from companies that provided sufficient information, since, in his view, shareholders did not make investment decisions by such a criterion: they valued stocks mainly on the basis of dividends. After weighing all the arguments, Vecht concluded that the notion of a Companies Commission deserved serious consideration, and he inclined toward favoring the proposal.

Prof.mr A. van Oven rejected the idea advanced in the study committee's report that "co-determination" and social accountability had already reached the status of *de facto* legal norms. They were, he said, merely attractive ideas that were in conflict with other established (legal) norms, especially the exercise of free enterprise.[17] Van Oven accepted that improvements in financial reporting were necessary, but that they could be achieved only to a limited degree by regulation. Nonetheless, he favored a more elaborate stipulation in the law of the required contents of financial statements. Van Oven agreed with the study committee that the current law did not adequately supervise the correctness and completeness of companies' financial statements. But unless it was proven that this supervision could not be achieved through regulation of the audit profession and an obligatory audit, the idea of a Companies Commission should be rejected.

4.2.4. The Hamburger Committee report

With the Dr. Wiardi Beckman Stichting report and the government's announcement of a formal inquiry into company law revision serving as stimuli, the Council of Dutch Employers Federations (Raad van Nederlandse Werkgeversverbonden), composed of the four employers federations that had jointly sponsored the Rijkens report, led by the VNW, decided in 1960 to appoint a follow-up committee to Rijkens. The theme of the last part of the preceding decade had been the "opening up" of enterprise, of making it accountable to a larger community than just shareholders. The interests of workers and the public as a whole had been emphasized.

---

were: W.H. Drucker, "Een Vennootschapskamer?", in *Economisch-Statistische Berichten*, vol. 12, no. 579, 2 February 1927, pp. 98–100; and Sanders, *op. cit.*.

[16] "Een Vennootschapskamer?", in *De Naamlooze Vennootschap*, vol. 32, no. 1, April 1954, pp. 1–4.

[17] "Het N.V.-recht en de zelfstandigheid van de ondernemer", in *De Economist*, vol. 109, no. 12, 1961, pp. 878–905.

Contrary to the more relaxed climate in which the Rijkens committee deliberated, "co-determination" was in the air in 1960, and quite a few directors of large companies eagerly sought appointment to the new committee.[18] By the time the committee was being formed, the government's Verdam Commission on the revision of company law had already been appointed, and the objective of the employers federations was to "try to influence as much as possible the political outcome and the political thinking at a very early stage".[19] In particular, there was a desire to issue a strong reaction to the Dr. Wiardi Beckman Stichting report and to influence the Verdam Commission.[20] If the committee could come up with a set of unanimous recommendations, then its report would be published because of the influence it would carry. But if the committee were to be seriously divided, it is likely that the report would not have been published.[21]

The new committee was similarly constituted as its predecessor, with members drawn primarily from the ranks of company directors, and included experts from the banking and securities world, from the auditing profession, and from the financial press. The committee, which was chaired by J.A. Hamburger, a member of the VNW executive committee and a director of N.V. De Koninklijke Nederlandsche Lood- en Zinkpletterijen, a "closed" NV in Utrecht, commenced work in October 1960, and its report was published in September 1962.[22] The report ran to 47 pages, and was, in point of content, about three times the length of the Rijkens report.

The Hamburger committee, as it came to be called, was composed of 24 members, half again as many as were on the Rijkens committee. One-third of the members of the Hamburger committee, including Rijkens himself, were carried over from the earlier committee. Two financial journalists were included this

---

[18] Interview with J.A. Hamburger, 29 August 1990.

[19] *Ibid.*

[20] In meetings of employer groups, a constructive stand in favor of improvement in financial reporting was seen as a way by which the employers could take the momentum away from the reformers. See the Minutes of the meeting of 7 March 1961 of the executive committee of the management board of the Federation of Dutch Employers, p. 10, and the reports of the joint "regional meetings" of the Federation of Dutch Employers and the Central Social Employers Federation (DB 130), attached to the agenda for the meeting of 5 September 1961 of the executive committee of the management board of the Federation of Dutch Employers.

[21] Interview with J.A. Hamburger, 29 August 1990.

[22] *Verslaggeving verantwoording en voorlichting door de besturen van naamloze vennootschappen* (Reporting, Rendering an Account and Providing Information by the Managements of Limited Companies), a report published by the Council of Dutch Employers Federations (Raad van Nederlandse Werkgeversverbonden), composed of: The Federation of Dutch Employers (VNW, Het Verbond van Nederlandsche Werkgevers), The Central Social Employers Federation (CSWV, Het Centraal Sociaal Werkgevers-Verbond), The Dutch Catholic Employers Federation (NKWV, Het Nederlands Katholiek Werkgevers Verbond), and The Federation of Protestant-Christian Employers in the Netherlands (VPCWN, Het Verbond van Protestants-Christelijke Werkgevers in Nederland) ('s-Gravenhage, July 1962). In this section, all citations in the text to page numbers will refer to this report.

time: A.C. Winninghoff, who had served on the Rijkens committee, and B. de Smalen, of *Trouw*.[23] Both Prof. A. Goudeket[24] and J. Kraayenhof, two influential members of the Rijkens committee, played important roles on the Hamburger committee, Goudeket's influence being most conspicuous in the section dealing with current cost accounting.[25] Also serving on the committee were Prof.dr A.Th. de Lange, a Limperg disciple at the Gemeentelijke Universiteit van Amsterdam, and Prof.dr B. Pruijt, of the Nederlandse Economische Hogeschool, in Rotterdam.[26] Both specialized in finance at their respective institutions, although de Lange was also a partner in a small Amsterdam auditing firm and in 1958–59 had served as president of the NIvA.

The committee membership consisted of 13 company directors, three auditors (one of whom was also a professor of finance), another professor of finance, two financial journalists, an economist in the employe of the VNW, an investment banker, a commercial banker, and the full-time secretaries of two of the sponsoring employers federations. Among the companies represented were Unilever, Hoogovens, Philips, and A.K.U.,[27] reflecting the interest of the largest industrial companies in the committee's task.

The investment banker serving on the committee, J.C. van Marken, of the banking firm of Pierson, Heldring & Pierson N.V., had been a member of the Stock Exchange Association's management board since 1941. In 1961, midway through the Hamburger committee's deliberations, van Marken was appointed president of the Association,[28] a position he held until 1973. By the inclusion of

---

[23] Some years later, de Smalen wrote a book on the securities market which included a chapter on financial statements. See B. de Smalen, *Effectenbeurs, effectenbedrijf en effectenverkeer* (Amsterdam: J.H. de Bussy, 1975); see esp. Chap. 5, "Belegger en jaarrekening".

[24] In 1956, Goudeket became a part-time professor of auditing at the Nederlandse Economische Hogeschool, in Rotterdam. He continued to serve as chief internal auditor of Philips until 1964, when he retired. Goudeket died in 1969. For a biographical sketch of Goudeket, see P.C. Louwers, "In memoriam: Professor A. Goudeket (1903–1969)", in *de Accountant*, vol. 75, no. 6, February 1969, p. 256.

[25] Interview with J.A. Hamburger, 29 August 1990.

A NIvA committee, known as the "Commissie Kastein", after its chairman, Mr A.Th.E. Kastein, had been set up in 1958, and, among other things, served as a kind of support committee for auditors who were members of committees outside of the NIvA. The committee reviewed drafts prepared by Goudeket and Kraayenhof prior to their formal presentation to the Hamburger committee. The authors are grateful to Prof.drs J.W. Schoonderbeek for furnishing them with the minutes of the Kastein committee.

[26] In January 1962, Pruijt resigned his professorship to become a member of the management board (i.e., a director) of Steenkolen-Handelsvereeniging N.V. (SHV), of Utrecht, having served as an adviser to the company previously. From 1966 to 1975, Pruijt served as SHV's president.

[27] The A.K.U. director serving on the Hamburger committee was K. Soesbeek, who had written five years earlier that the Rijkens report had not gone far enough in the direction of reform. See the section, "Commentary in professional publications", following discussion of the Rijkens report in Chapter 3.

[28] The presidency of the Stock Exchange Association implied that the incumbent was also president of the Amsterdam Stock Exchange.

an investment banker of van Marken's standing on the Hamburger committee, the employers federations were probably reacting to criticism by the financial press that an official representative of the Stock Exchange Association had been omitted from the Rijkens committee in 1954–55.[29]

The committee's charge, as stated in its report, was to look into "whether it is desirable that new guidelines be developed with respect to the annual reporting of industrial limited companies – especially in the light of the modern questions surrounding the structure and legal form of enterprise" (p. 7).[30] Emphasis was placed on "industrial" companies because the representatives of the commercial banks, insurance companies, and sea transport companies (both on and off the committee) would not commit themselves to the recommendations. To achieve a unanimous result, therefore, it was necessary to confine the recommendations to industrial enterprises.[31]

In the Preface to the report, written by H.J. de Koster, chairman of the Council of Dutch Employers Federations, it was stated that "the report cannot have any binding force" and "is intended merely to serve as a general recommendation within its own constituency" (p. 3). A similar disclaimer had been included in the Rijkens report.

The report was divided into two main parts. The first dealt with ideological and strategic issues, while the second, consisting of slightly more than half of the report, identified the desirable contents of financial reports intended for shareholders.

The principal ideological issue arose from the efforts by trade unions and the Labor Party to broaden the public reporting responsibility of enterprise beyond the traditional accountability to shareholders. The employers federations were also concerned over the mounting discussion, e.g., in the report of the Dr. Wiardi Beckman Stichting's study committee, of the possible establishment of a Companies Commission to regulate the financial reporting of limited companies.[32]

---

[29] In 1958, the *Haagse Post*, in an unsigned article, had advocated stronger legislation to govern financial reporting, and called upon the Stock Exchange Association to adopt more stringent listing requirements. "Effecten en publiciteit: Betere verslaggeving dringend gewenst", in *Haagse Post*, 28 February 1958, pp. 4–5.

[30] Within the committee itself and the management board of the Federation of Dutch Employers, the committee charge was still being debated even after the committee began its deliberations, and agreement on the charge was not achieved until the spring of 1961. The question was raised whether the committee should address the issue of "public accountability" or whether it should prepare a "rump" report dealing only with financial reporting from a strictly *bedrijfseconomische* point of view. See the Minutes of the meetings of 7 February 1961 and 7 March 1961 of the executive committee of the management board of the Federation of Dutch Employers, pp. 13 and 10–11, respectively.

[31] Interview with J.A. Hamburger, 29 August 1990.

[32] It seems that some of the representatives of the Federation of Protestant-Christian Employers in the Netherlands, one of the four participating employers federations, had fewer reservations over the prospect of a Companies Commission. Minutes of the meeting of 15 May 1962 of the executive committee of the management board of the Federation of Dutch Employers, p. 6.

The overriding strategic aim was to prevent the inclusion of onerous provisions in any revision of company law.

In the opening chapter, the committee took strong exception to the view, expressed in the Dr. Wiardi Beckman Stichting report and in the Justice Minister's charge to the Verdam Commission (delivered on 20 June 1960, and discussed below), that the limited company owes an "accountability" to the public. On the contrary, the committee argued, the rendering of an account by the management of a limited liability company "must be understood to mean the making of an account to those [namely, the shareholders] who have entrusted the management of their capital to others" (pp. 8–9). Although "public accountability" was occasionally used to signify an assumed obligation to report to "designated groups in economic and social life, other than shareholders", the committee held the view that such reporting "runs not to the rendering of an account on the conduct of capital management, but rather to the response to the needs of various groups and of 'the public at large' for information concerning what has occurred in the enterprise" (p. 9). The distinction drawn by the committee between "rendering an account" (*verantwoording*) and "providing information" (*voorlichting*) would have found little support among the reformers of the day, especially the leaders of the Labor Party.

In a chapter largely drafted by Pruijt,[33] the committee acknowledged and welcomed the greater public interest in information about enterprise affairs, and it said that the spread of some knowledge of business affairs was of considerable importance to the companies themselves. But a part of this demand for information, it said, was based on feelings of discomfort with, or even mistrust of, the managers of enterprise (p. 10). In order to remove this distrust, and because it is in the interest of businesses that the general public possess some insight into their affairs, the committee recommended "that the management boards of limited companies pay considerable attention to the desirability of as great a degree of openness as is possible about the affairs of the business" (p. 11). In this connection, the committee mentioned the provision of information to employees, possibly through works councils (*ondernemingsraden*). But, as regards the public, the "information" requirement could be met by a broader distribution of the report addressed to shareholders (p. 11).

An enterprise's "rendering an account" to shareholders, the committee said, took the form of the annual report presented at the annual meeting of shareholders, according to current law (Articles 42 and 49 of the Commercial Code) (p. 14). This accountability, it said, had increased in importance to become a system of multi-tiered accountability that had grown, in stages, out of certain customs in the "economic and social climate" (*maatschappelijk verkeer*). The succession of tiers – the audit, supervision by non-managing directors (*commissarissen*),

[33] Interview with J.A. Hamburger, 29 August 1990.

judgment by the financial press, the annual meeting of shareholders, and the right of inquiry (*het recht van enquête*[34]) – all took as their starting point, to a greater or lesser extent, the annual report, which, therefore, was the cornerstone of the accountability process (pp. 14–18).

The committee joined the political debate over the democratizing of enterprise, although it limited its discussion to financial reporting by arguing against the legal regulation of "the providing of information". Such regulation was rejected on three grounds: impracticality, owing to the diversity among businesses; undesirability, as it would hamper the free development of reporting practices; and that it was not based on law, as the public did not have, according to current law, a "right" to information (p. 23). Furthermore, the committee said, the right to an accountability should not be enforced by new institutions, such as a Companies Commission. Current procedures, it said, enabled every shareholder to maintain his rights. Although the committee conceded that current legislation did not provide a useful specification of the contents of financial reports, a gradual broadening of the scope of rendered accounts had nonetheless occurred, which had led many companies to issue financial reports that went beyond legal requirements. While it might be possible to codify in the law the demands of this more or less informal system, this should not be allowed to block the continued free development of financial reporting or make financial reporting a mere formality (pp. 23–25). In the committee's view, "the broad characterization of the contents of financial reports that the legislature envisaged in 1929 should continue to be the guiding principle" (p. 25).

The committee was therefore strongly in favor of retaining a general law to govern financial reporting, rather than see the introduction of detailed prescriptive legislation.

Following the initial chapters on ideology and strategy, the remainder of the report dealt with the specific contents of financial reports. The Hamburger committee stated at the outset of this discussion that it sought a "close correspondence" with the Rijkens report (p. 29). This link was particularly evident in the Hamburger report's sections on balance-sheet items to be disclosed (Part II, Chapter 2), which were virtually copied from the Rijkens report.

4.2.4.1. Role of the financial statements

The committee's description of the central position which the financial statements occupy in the annual report closely followed the view of the Rijkens report:

[34] The right of inquiry referred to the right to ask a court to appoint investigators to inquire into the possible misconduct of an enterprise's management. Under then-existing law, this right was restricted to shareholders having at least 20 percent of the voting shares of the company's capital stock.

> The profit and loss statement should provide insight into the size and composition of the income earned by the company during the fiscal year; the balance sheet should give a picture of the financial position at the end of the year, i.e., of the size and composition of capital and of the kinds of assets in which it has been invested (p. 30).

The committee followed the Rijkens committee in requiring that the accounting principles used for purposes of asset and liability valuation as well as income determination be enumerated (p. 32). Also following Rijkens, it recommended that any changes in those principles, especially including any change in the basis of valuation, be mentioned, and that the comparative figures be calculated using the new principles. The notes should, the committee stated, indicate the effect of any changes on the income for the year or on the financial position, or both (p. 31).

4.2.4.2. Getrouw beeld

Curiously, the term *getrouw beeld* was used only twice in the report (pp. 32, 35). In the section on the auditor's report, the term *aanvaardbaar beeld*, "acceptable picture", was invoked as the key criterion by which the company's operating income and financial position were to be shown (p. 50). Evidently, a difference of opinion arose within the committee over the proper terminology.

4.2.4.3. Current cost

Under the strong influence of Goudeket, the committee firmly endorsed current cost accounting,[35] as follows:

> It is emphatically urged that [asset] valuation and income determination take place in a sound *bedrijfseconomisch* way, which, in many cases, implies the application of some form of current cost accounting. This [opinion] is based on the conviction that a good insight into the operating income and the financial position can be obtained only in this way. The principles must in any case adhere to norms that are accepted as reasonable in economic and social life. In other words, they should not violate "sound business practice" [*goed koopmansgebruik*] (p. 32).

The mention of "a sound *bedrijfseconomisch* way", through the link with current cost, referred to the teachings of Limperg. The committee's decision, however, to refer to "sound business practice" reflected a terminological confusion which, at that time, had not yet been resolved. The phrase "sound business practice" had been referred to in the NIvA's Rules of Professional Conduct (Reglement van

[35] Interview with J.A. Hamburger, 29 August 1990. Hamburger added that other members of the committee could accept current cost accounting because they knew the committee's recommendations were not binding; furthermore, they realized that it would be difficult, if not impossible, to incorporate current cost accounting in the law.

Arbeid) since 1939 as the principal standard of quality to be used by the auditor when judging financial statements. But the term had also been used, since the imposition of the 1914 Income Tax, as an important qualitative standard in tax legislation. In order to discourage the inference that income for tax accounting and income for financial accounting were alike, the committee stated in a footnote that the term "sound business practice" was not intended to refer to practice acceptable for income tax purposes (p. 32).

When current cost accounting was not used, the committee added, the notes to the financial statements should, where the difference is material, provide the following information:

> the approximate depreciation on fixed assets for the year computed on a current cost basis, as well as what effect the changes in the price and cost ratios of raw materials have had on operating income, ... and the current cost of the several classes of assets (pp. 32–33).

4.2.4.4. Secret reserves

Compared with the Rijkens report, the Hamburger committee took a much more categorical position against the use of "secret and undisclosed reserves", as follows:

> [Secret and undisclosed reserves] are no longer acceptable from a *bedrijfs-economisch* point of view, both because of the influence on income of unseen additions to the reserves and because such reserves distort the insight into the capital position. The opinion that is still current in certain circles that simply showing the so-called "minimum position" (namely, that capital and the operating income are no lower than the figures show) will suffice to make financial statements acceptable is considered to be out of date (p. 34).

Any reductions of reserves that increase income or net assets were to be disclosed and commented upon in the notes (p. 33).

By 1960, few of the largest companies still seemed to be employing secret and undisclosed reserves. Yet the subject of secret reserves continued to be a matter of discussion and controversy during the 1950's and into the 1960's, suggesting that the practice was still believed to be used by many companies.[36] Nonetheless, by the early 1960's there had been a growing belief within companies and among auditors that secret and undisclosed reserves were "indefensible".[37] One of the

[36] In 1957, Groeneveld wrote, "In drafting the annual accounts there is a noticeable tendency to strive for an equalization of profits and distributed profits". He argued against the use of secret reserves, implying that the practice was still being followed. G.L. Groeneveld, Introduction to the session on "Ascertainment of Profit in Business", in *Verslag van het Zevende Internationaal Accountantscongres 1957* (Amsterdam: Seventh International Congress of Accountants, 1957), p. 579 (p. 568 in the Dutch version of the paper).

[37] Interview with J.A. Hamburger, 29 August 1990.

BALANSEN HEEMAF N.V. HENGELO

	31 december 1962		*31 december 1961*	
Gebouwen en terreinen	f 1	—	*f 1*	—
Machinerieën	1	—	*1*	—
Gereedschappen	1	—	*1*	—
Instrumenten	1	—	*1*	—
Modellen	1	—	*1*	—
Kracht- en lichtinstallatie	1	—	*1*	—
Centrale verwarming, gas- en waterleiding	1	—	*1*	—
Telefoon- en klokinstallatie	1	—	*1*	—
Vervoermiddelen	1	—	*1*	—
Inboedel	1	—	*1*	—
Afd. Zwakstroom	1	—	*1*	—
Laboratorium	1	—	*1*	—
Totaal vaste activa	f 12	—	*f 12*	—
Patenten	1	—	*1*	—
Deelneming Smit	9.032.727	84	—	—
Overige deelnemingen	1	—	*1*	—
Depots bij derden	13.139	48	*12.033*	*74*
Goederen	18.195.266	91	*16.694.169*	*74*
Debiteuren	7.886.096	91	*7.409.461*	*54*
Gedane vooruit- en termijnbetalingen	98.615	16	*470.188*	*05*
Effecten	2.826.818	12	*4.045.522*	*50*
Gelden à deposito	9.400.000	—	*9.600.000*	—
Kas, giro en bankiers	1.913.199	55	*705.571*	*25*
	f 49.365.877	97	*f 38.936.960*	*82*

	31 december 1962		*31 december 1961*	
Aandelenkapitaal	f 11.497.500	—	*f 7.800.000*	—
Diverse reserves	12.042.552	72	*11.719.520*	*76*
Reserves Smit	5.335.227	84	—	—
Dividendreserve	18.231	10	*11.607*	*36*
Voorzieningen	2.511.100	—	*1.919.060*	—
Crediteuren	8.638.863	08	*8.061.045*	*28*
Personeelsfondsen	77.774	49	*58.615*	*10*
Ontvangen vooruit- en termijnbetalingen	7.161.196	—	*7.886.792*	*70*
Saldo winst	2.083.432	74	*1.480.319*	*62*
	f 49.365.877	97	*f 38.936.960*	*82*

De raad van commissarissen

J. DE WILDE
W. H. KRUYFF
H. A. M. KROESE
H. ALBARDA
J. H. GISPEN
E. A. GELDERMAN
H. M. FOKS
L. C. SMIT

Hengelo, februari 1963

De directie

H. J. BUTTINGER
J. L. BONEBAKKER
J. VAN DER WATEREN

larger companies made no attempt to hide the fact that it was making extensive use of secret reserves: Heemaf N.V., whose 31 December 1960 balance sheet continued to display a column of *f* 1's for its 12 categories of fixed assets. (See the accompanying reproduction.) One of the reasons why interest had focused on secret and undisclosed reserves was that company profits entered into the macro calculations under the government's "Guided Wage Policy".[38]

4.2.4.5. Other topics

On the subject of deferred tax liabilities, the Hamburger committee's recommendation followed closely that of the Rijkens committee (p. 33).

Consolidated statements were proposed as the most efficient way of presenting information on majority investments (p. 35). A much greater discussion of the classification and valuation of financial interests in other companies appeared in the Hamburger report than in the Rijkens report, which had been concerned only with the dividing line between majority and minority holdings. Such a financial interest was to be classified as an "investment" (*deelneming*) rather than as other shareholdings, when the business activities of the investor and investee were similar and where the length of the holding period and the relative size of the interest reinforced the view that the interest was a significant, long-term investment (p. 38). The valuation of investments by the "intrinsic value" (*intrinsieke waarde*) method was recommended (p. 39).[39]

The Hamburger committee's positions on the disclosure of sales and cost of sales were similar to those in the Rijkens report (pp. 45–46).

Whether the annual report was seen in an accountability context, or as fulfilling a more general information function, the judgment of an independent expert was required, the committee said. In this regard, a reference was made to the expectation that, within a few years, the auditing profession would be regulated by law (p. 50).[40] In late 1957, the Stock Exchange Association had changed its requirements for prospectuses in connection with new issues (as set forth in its Rules on Securities Trading, or Fondsenreglement), with effect from 1 January 1958, to call for the inclusion of an auditor's report except in cases where the Association's executive committee were to grant dispensation.

The recommendations on the directors' report and comparative figures were

[38] *Ibid.*

[39] "Intrinsic value" was understood to mean the aggregate of the assets of the subsidiary minus the aggregate of the liabilities, in which all components were valued according to the valuation principles in use by the parent company (p. 39). This may or may not equal the initial amount recorded under the "equity method" of accounting, as it is known in the United States. Subsequently, under both methods, the initial valuation would be adjusted for the parent company's share of the subsidiary's profits and dividends.

[40] A 1960 study by Vecht showed that about 90 percent of industrial and transport companies disclosed an auditor's report. J.M. Vecht, "De accountantsverklaring in gepubliceerde jaarverslagen van Nederlandse naamloze vennootschappen", in *Maandblad voor accountancy en bedrijfshuishoudkunde*, vol. 34, no. 3, March 1960, pp. 100–108.

virtually identical to those in the Rijkens report, although the Hamburger committee cautioned that the directors' report should not contain items that belong in the notes (pp. 31, 48–49). Of interest was the committee's recommendation that information on funds flow (*de herkomst en de besteding van de middelen*) be included in the directors' report (p. 49).

When the committee's report was placed before the Council of Dutch Employers Federations and the management board of the VNW in June 1962, a number of relatively minor changes were recommended. Once these were entered, the report was published in September. H.J. de Koster, chairman of the Council and a director of Meelfabriek "De Sleutels" N.V., a "closed" NV in Leiden, was a forceful leader and believed it was important to have the report published.[41]

4.2.5. Reactions to the Hamburger report

The report was extensively covered in the financial press. Lengthy articles, mostly descriptive, appeared in *Het Financieele Dagblad*, *De Telegraaf*, *Algemeen Handelsblad*, *de Volkskrant*, *De Tijd-Maasbode*, and *Trouw*, among others.[42] The *Haagsche Courant* said the report's conclusions were welcomed, and viewed the statement on secret reserves as "the most important conclusion in the report".[43]

In a column appearing in *Trouw*, which was probably written by de Smalen, the following perspective was furnished:

> The days are gone when companies such as Royal Dutch Shell, Philips, Unilever and AKU informed shareholders about the course of their affairs in a miniscule booklet, and while a very detailed and accurate balance sheet was published, it was not possible to acquire a clear insight into the company's financial position. Nowadays, the big companies publish thick volumes in which a wealth of data

[41] Interview with J.A. Hamburger, 29 August 1990.

[42] "Commissie Nederl. Werkgeversverbonden: Voor jaarverslaggeving geen nieuw controlerend orgaan, Pers was reeds grote stimulans voor niveau verslaggeving", in *De Telegraaf*, 13 September 1962, p. 15; "Verslaggeving en verantwoording door N.V.'s: Commissie Werkgeversverbonden staat positief tegenover voorlichting aan het publiek, Vraagstuk leent zich niet voor een wettelijke regeling", in *Algemeen Handelsblad*, 13 September 1962, p. 11; "Commissie van werkgevers: Jaarverslagen verbeteren het best in vrijheid", in *de Volkskrant*, 13 September 1962, p. 2; "Ruimer rapport Commissie Jaarverslaggeving: Pleidooi voor openhartigheid over ondernemingsgebeuren, Ontwikkeling in vrijheid van het grootste belang" in *De Tijd-Maasbode*, 13 September 1962, p. 11; and "Raad van Nederlandse Werkgeversverbonden: Vennootschapskamer zou geen reden van bestaan hebben, Jaarverslag is niet naar starre formulering samen te stellen", in *Trouw*, 13 September 1962, p. 11. Also see "Rapport werkgeversverbonden: Openhartigheid gewenst in jaarverslaggeving, Toenemende behoefte aan voorlichting", in *Nieuwe Rotterdamse Courant*, 13 September 1962, p. 11.

As can be seen, the papers emphasized different aspects of the report's conclusions in their headlines.

[43] "Commissie Jaarverslaggeving van werkgeversverbonden: Onzichtbare reserves niet aanvaardbaar geacht, Vervangingswaarde als grondslag", in *Haagsche Courant*, 13 September 1962, p. 21.

> is included about the performance of the company in which the shareholders invested their money. The annual report has, as a result, taken on a larger role than before, when it provided information for the shareholders alone.
>
> When more and more data are provided, the need for enlightenment and information rises. In spite of the enormous progress in the field of financial reporting, to which the [Rijkens] report of 1955 contributed importantly, various other groups have pressed for an expansion of the enlightenment.[44]

In his concluding remark, the writer referred to the demands coming, in the main, from the trade unions and the Labor Party.

In the professional literature, there was considerable comment. A double issue of *De Naamlooze Vennootschap* contained a dozen short articles on the theme of "Reporting, Rendering an Account, and Providing Information" ("*Verslaggeving, verantwoording en voorlichting*"), the three key terms in the title of the Hamburger report. It was a diverse collection of articles with widely dispersed views, ranging from solid endorsement by F.J. Phillips to rather severe criticism by W. Hessel.[45] Hessel took the Hamburger committee to task for defining the obligation to "render an account" too narrowly. In another article, E.A. Brouwer took exception to the Hamburger committee's position on legal regulation, which he regarded as weak. The function of the capital market, he said, was of such strategic importance to the national economy that its performance could not be guided by voluntary actions on the part of companies. Some kind of regulation was necessary, he argued, and this had to be of a legal kind owing to the failure of the Stock Exchange and the auditors to correct the deficiencies in financial reporting.[46] I. Kleerekoper, a member of the NIvA, said that the importance of the report for auditors lay in the fact that it made more explicit the demands inherent in the key terms "economic and social climate" (*maatschappelijk verkeer*) and "sound business practice" (*goed koopmansgebruik*).[47]

J.M. Vecht compared the Hamburger and Rijkens reports in some detail, and concluded that the Hamburger report "is especially important because modern terminology and modern conceptions of annual reporting are brought together in a nice, readable, and, in all respects, responsible way ... ".[48] In the article, he

[44] "In de beursspiegel: Rekening en verantwoording", in *Trouw*, 13 September 1962, p. 11.

[45] F.J. Phillips, "Het probleem van verslaggeving, verantwoording en voorlichting door de besturen van naamloze vennootschappen bezien vanuit het gezichtspunt van de grote publieke N.V.", in *De Naamlooze Vennootschap*, vol. 40, nos. 8/9, November/December 1962, pp. 117–120; and W. Hessel, "Behoefte aan informatie of recht op rekenschap?", *De Naamlooze Vennootschap*, vol. 40, nos. 8/9, November/December 1962, pp. 134–135.

[46] E.A. Brouwer, "De grote belegger en de verslaggeving van NV's", in *De Naamlooze Vennootschap*, vol. 40, nos. 8/9, November/December 1962, pp. 125–128.

[47] I. Kleerekoper, "Een beoordeling van het rapport van de commissie Jaarverslaggeving dd juli 1962 vanuit het gezichtspunt van de openbare accountant", in *De Naamlooze Vennootschap*, vol. 40, nos. 8/9, November/December 1962, pp. 137–141.

[48] J.M. Vecht, "Jaarverslaggeving: een nieuw rapport", in *Maandblad voor accountancy en bedrijfshuishoudkunde*, vol. 37, no. 3, March 1963, pp. 120–121.

recommended that a study be conducted, perhaps along the lines of the annual US survey, *Accounting Trends & Techniques*, so that the record of progress in annual reporting might be more easily monitored.

Drs W. van Bruinessen said that "It is self-evident that Dutch colleagues regard this report as a milestone in the development of views on reporting".[49] A staunch advocate of current value accounting, van Bruinessen drew attention to two positions that the committee adopted "categorically and unequivocally":

> (i) by means of the annual accounts the management is to render an account on its stewardship during an elapsed period, and
> (ii) the bases of valuation underlying that account be actual values, i.e. those on which the determination of the management's policy during the period should have been based.[50]

Prof.dr J.F. Haccoû criticized the Hamburger committee for failing to respond with the right arguments and with sufficient clarity to the outside demands for legal reform, especially the call for a Companies Commission. To Haccoû, there was only one argument: that a Companies Commission would be incompatible with a market economy based on free enterprise.[51]

4.2.6. Reports by two NIvA subcommittees

In 1962, subcommittees of the NIvA's Advisory Committee on Professional Matters issued lengthy and thoughtful reports on two controversial subjects: secret and undisclosed reserves, and deferred tax accounting.[52] Both reports carried the standard disclaimer that they were not binding on members of the NIvA, and were intended to serve only as a guide to thinking on the topics under discussion.

4.2.6.1. Secret reserves

The subcommittee that prepared the 17-page report on secret and undisclosed reserves was of the view that many of the arguments formerly used to justify

---

[49] W. Van Bruinessen, "Accounting Standards and Rules – Voluntary or Regulatory Determination?", in *Maandblad voor accountancy en bedrijfshuishoudkunde*, vol. 49, no. 1, January 1975, p. 9.

[50] *Ibid.* The term *verantwoording* (e.g., as used in the title of the Hamburger report) may be translated as either "accountability" or "stewardship". Van Bruinessen, whose article was written in English, translated "actuele waarde" literally; the translation preferred by the authors is "current value".

[51] J.F. Haccoû, "Verslaggeving, verantwoording en voorlichting door de besturen van N.V.'s", in *TVVS*, vol. 5, no. 6, October 1962, p. 121.

[52] "De gevolgen van stille en geheime reservering voor de goedkeuring der jaarrekening door de accountant", in *de Accountant*, vol. 68, no. 9, May 1962, pp. 531–547; and "De vraagstukken, welke samenhangen met de invloed van de latente belastingverhoudingen op de jaarrekening van de naamloze vennootschap", in *de Accountant*, vol. 69, no. 1, September 1962, pp. 40–51. In this section, citations in the text to page numbers will refer to these reports.

such reserves had lost their validity in the course of time (pp. 532–535). The recent rethinking of the function of financial statements had placed primary emphasis on their informational content, leading to the view that net income should not be determined on the basis of statutory demands or with an eye toward competition or shareholder relations, but on the basis of sound economic principles (pp. 535–538). This interpretation, the subcommittee argued, leads to the conclusion that financial statements should provide an insight into the enterprise's capital structure and net income. They should give an "acceptable picture" (*aanvaardbaar beeld*) so that shareholders could form a judgment on profitability and financial position (p. 538).

The subcommittee made no secret of its advocacy of current cost accounting, and even suggested that a decision not to adopt current cost accounting would lead a company unwittingly to create a secret reserve, owing to the consequent understatement of assets (pp. 538–540).

Citing a paragraph in the Rijkens report, the subcommittee agreed that secret and undisclosed reserves were not justified when their use would cloud the "faithful picture" (*getrouw beeld*) of the composition of capital and income (p. 541).

The subcommittee concluded that the auditor should withhold his approval of the financial statements if income and financial position were shown at significantly lower amounts than would be calculated on a *bedrijfseconomische* basis, or if income were significantly increased by a drawing down of secret reserves without adequate explanation (p. 546). Two of the subcommittee's eight members were Prof.drs G.L. Groeneveld, a partner in Klynveld, Kraayenhof & Co. who was in charge of the Philips audit, and Prof.dr J.L. Mey, of the Rijksuniversiteit Groningen. Both had been students of Limperg, although Mey departed in a number of respects from Limperg's teachings.

4.2.6.2. Deferred taxes

Drawing on the principle that financial statements should reflect accountability to shareholders, the subcommittee said that they should provide insight into the enterprise's financial position, and should show its income (p. 44). Taxation, the subcommittee argued, should be seen as an element of income determination, not of income distribution, which implied that the tax expense should be related to reported income and not be the amount of taxation actually falling due during the year (p. 45).

The general rule, the subcommittee said, was that differences between taxation based on fiscal and *bedrijfseconomische* principles should be shown as provisions or deferred claims so long as future realization is reasonably certain (pp. 46–47).

The subcommittee recommended disclosure guidelines for deferred liabilities and deferred claims. The netting of liabilities against claims was not favored, and the subcommittee said that it doubted the usefulness of showing deferred items at present value (pp. 48–51).

These two reports, together with the report of the subcommittee on *obligo's* in 1956, were the only institutional initiatives undertaken by the NIvA to partake in the increasing dialogue over financial reporting in the latter half of the 1950's and the early 1960's. Both of the reports issued in 1962 were published prior to the release of the Hamburger report.

4.2.7. The Teldersstichting report: The Liberals reply

The challenge issued by the Dr. Wiardi Beckman Stichting report in 1959 was met by an even lengthier report published in 1962 by the Prof. Mr. B.M. Teldersstichting (Prof. Mr. B.M. Telders Foundation), the "think tank" of the Liberal Party (VVD). Entitled *Open Ondernemerschap: De Groei van de Onderneming en het Vennootschapsrecht* (Open Entrepreneurship: The Growth of Enterprise and of Company Law), the hefty, 407-page volume was published at virtually the same time as the Hamburger report.[53] The Teldersstichting report rejected the call for a Companies Commission and instead proposed a revision to Article 42 of the Commercial Code that represented a cautious expansion of companies' reporting responsibilities.

Only a relatively small fraction of the Teldersstichting report, less than 20 percent of its contents, dealt with financial reporting and its argument against the proposal for a Companies Commission. The major issues treated were, as with the report of the Dr. Wiardi Beckman Stichting's study committee, co-determination, the right of inquiry, and, in general, the democratizing of enterprise.

The Teldersstichting chose a 14-man committee to prepare the report. Its chairman, Prof.dr H.J. Witteveen, a prominent member of the Liberal Party, was an economics professor at the Nederlandse Economische Hogeschool. Ten of the committee's 14 members were lawyers. Several of the members were active in business, and one of the lawyers, Mr J. de Wilde, was a director of the Bataafsche Hypotheekbank. Witteveen and de Wilde were also members of the First Chamber of Parliament. The only auditor on the committee was Prof. A.M. van Rietschoten, who was a partner in the important Amsterdam firm of Frese & Hogeweg. In 1949, van Rietschoten had succeeded Limperg in the auditing chair of the Gemeentelijke Universiteit van Amsterdam, and in 1956–57 he served as president of the NIvA. Th.H. Joekes served as the committee's *rapporteur*. Working closely with the committee's secretary, Mr H. Hülsmann, Joekes drafted the report. He recalled that van Rietschoten "set the tone" for the section on financial reporting.[54]

---

[53] *Open Ondernemerschap: De Groei van de Onderneming en het Vennootschapsrecht*, Geschriften van de Prof. Mr. B.M. Teldersstichting, no. 9 ('s-Gravenhage: Martinus Nijhoff, 1962). In this section, citations in the text to page numbers will refer to this report.

[54] Telephone conversation with Th.H. Joekes, 17 October 1990.

One of the members of the Teldersstichting's committee, Mr E. Bloembergen, a director of Albatros Superfosfaatfabrieken N.V., was also serving on the executive committee of VNW's management board, and he kept the latter apprised of the course of the committee's deliberations.[55]

As the Hamburger committee had drawn a distinction between "accountability" (*verantwoording*) and "information" (*voorlichting*) in order to define the limits of the public reporting responsibility of enterprise, the Teldersstichting's committee distinguished between "information" (*voorlichting*) and "publicity" (*publiciteit*). The choice of terminology was different, and the meanings attributed to the terms were different, but the objective was the same.

The Teldersstichting's committee confined the right to "information" to the following interested groups:

a. the shareholders, whose right to "information" was derived from their legal function in the company (i.e., supervision and decision making) which could not be performed without information. Included in this information set was the balance sheet, the profit and loss statement, and the directors' report.
b. potential shareholders, who were entitled to "information" (in the prospectus) as a form of protection for their funds. (Necessarily, this "information" would also lead to "publicity".)
c. members of the board of supervisors.
d. employees, whose right to "information" was embodied in the 1950 Act on Works Councils (Wet op de Ondernemingsraden). In practice, the committee said, the quality of this information had varied from company to company.
e. creditors of banks and insurance companies.
f. the general public, whose right to "information" was limited to the aggregated data assembled by the government's Central Bureau of Statistics (Centraal Bureau voor de Statistiek) (pp. 308–314).

In contrast to the right to "information", which was founded upon the express or implied obligation of the law, "publicity" was open-ended and was "accessible to everyone – the press, the 'man in the street', and competitors" (p. 302). The committee took a firm position on the limit of the public's "right to know":

> It is our firm conviction that the "public opinion" as such does not have a right to be informed about the financial position and income of individual limited companies . . . .
>
> Those who want to exercise a right to information must have a proven interest, like a shareholder. If there is no such interest, it cannot be established by pointing to the general interest . . . (p. 314).

In order to promote an expansion in the financial information to be given by

[55] Minutes of the meeting of 15 May 1962 of the executive committee of the management board of the Federation of Dutch Employers, p. 6.

"open" limited liability companies, the committee recommended several amendments to Article 42 in the Commercial Code. In the first paragraph of the Article, the term "financial statements" (*jaarrekening*) would be inserted to encompass the balance sheet, the profit and loss statement, and the notes – perhaps to make the point that the two financial statements were on an equal footing, rather than perpetuate a view that seemed to have currency in the 1920's that the profit and loss statement was an appendage of the balance sheet. A new paragraph would be added, containing the four-point statement of "general demands" set forth in the Rijkens report (which in turn had been borrowed from P.F.S. Otten's address to Philips shareholders in 1954). The order in which the Rijkens report presented the four points was altered, and two of the four points were slightly amended, as follows:

> The financial statements must satisfy the following general requirements:
>
> 1. a specification of the assets and liabilities in such a manner as to enable an insight into solvency and liquidity [identical to 2 in Rijkens].
> 2. mention of the principles followed in calculating the operating result and by which the assets and liabilities were valued ["mention of" was added, and the "in order to" phrase was deleted; otherwise, identical to 3 in Rijkens].
> 3. mention of possible changes relating to the previous year in regard to these principles and in the composition of the figures, with an indication of the influence thereof on the figures, insofar as these changes have a substantial effect on the figures ["if possible" and the "in order to" phrase were deleted, and an ending phrase was added; otherwise, identical to 4 in Rijkens].
> 4. a specification of the operating result in such a manner as to enable an insight into the composition thereof and into the rate of return on the enterprise's invested capital [identical to 1 in Rijkens] (pp. 325–326).

The qualifier "if possible", which was omitted in requirement 3, was said to be unnecessary "because in the notes a broad indication is all that is needed so long as general requirement 4 is followed" (p. 326). The committee did not offer any comments on the other alterations from the Rijkens wording, except for the two "in order to" phrases, which would have been out place in a proposed law.

The third paragraph in Article 42, being a required breakdown of assets, would be retained, but with a few additions, e.g., the definition of an "investment" (*deelneming*) as a holding of 5 or more percent of the shares of another company. Another new paragraph would include a required breakdown of owners' equity and liabilities (not included in Article 42), which was said to be based on the Rijkens report (p. 327). A further new paragraph would specify the required items to be disclosed in the profit and loss statement, namely, the amount of income tax, changes in statutory reserves, and extraordinary items (p. 329). The committee was of the view that, if the law were to require the disclosure of sales, it could seriously affect the interests of some companies (pp. 328–329).

Finally, another new paragraph would call for the publication of consolidated financial statements or, alternatively, separate financial statements for majority investments (p. 330).

The report was noncommittal on the choice of a valuation principle. Companies should be free, the committee said, to choose their own valuation principle, provided that they enable an insight into both solvency and the rate of return (requirements 1 and 4). The notes should be used to clarify any serious departure from the "actual magnitude" of the owners' equity (pp. 331–332), an allusion to the formation of secret reserves.

In regard to new securities issues, the committee recommended that the Stock Exchange Association require that prospectuses always contain financial statements covering a five-year period and that an auditor's report always accompany the financial statements. The committee took note of the Stock Exchange Association's revised Rules on Securities Trading (Fondsenreglement), which took effect in 1958, requiring the appointment of an auditor in connection with new-issue prospectuses. But, as the committee pointed out, the regulation permitted a dispensation of this requirement by the Association's executive committee (pp. 341–343).

Overall, most of the information disclosure recommendations by the Teldersstichting's committee were comparable to those in the Rijkens and Hamburger reports, although the committee's recommendations on how to measure those figures were less firmly developed. In two important respects, the Hamburger report went further than the Teldersstichting report: it rejected secret reserves, and it favored the disclosure of sales. Also, deferred taxes, which figured prominently in both the Rijkens and Hamburger reports, was not mentioned in the Teldersstichting report, and a definitive position was not taken on the choice of a valuation principle (probably owing to the absence of Goudeket!). Moreover, both the Rijkens and Hamburger reports were more expansive in their discussion than was the Teldersstichting report. These differences may be explained by several factors. First, the differing backgrounds of the auditors serving on the committees: Goudeket and Kraayenhof were, owing to their work in Philips and Klynveld, Kraayenhof & Co., respectively, conversant with the financial reporting practices of the overseas capital markets. Van Rietschoten, by contrast, was one of the leading partners in a large firm whose clients did not include any multinationals with overseas listings. Van Rietschoten did have international contacts, but they were not as extensive as Kraayenhof's. Second, the Teldersstichting's committee was composed predominantly of lawyers, in contrast to the mix of company directors, auditors and representatives of the press and the financial community on the Rijkens and Hamburger committees. Finally, the Teldersstichting's committee had a political mission: not to encourage the Verdam Commission, which was meeting at the same time, to be too prescriptive.

In its discussion of the possible establishment of a Companies Commission, the Teldersstichting's committee argued that the reason for reviewing company law at this time could not be attributed to scandal or abuse. The Netherlands, it said, had a long tradition of dependable trading dating back to the 17th century. This fact, said the committee, explained both the slow development of company law up to 1929 and the success with which Dutch companies passed the test of the Depression.[56] Those who had been holding up the US Securities and Exchange Commission as an example to be emulated by the Dutch were therefore making an error of judgment (pp. 302–308). Furthermore, the SEC was installed to deal with specific US problems such as the difficulty of harmonizing the regulations of the various states, as well as the "rougher and tougher" business culture compared with that in the Netherlands (pp. 345–346). The example of the Insurance Companies Commission, the committee said, was also inappropriate. That body was set up to protect small, risk-avoiding creditors (i.e., the insureds), while a Companies Commission would be protecting the interests of shareholders who were willing to take risks and may therefore be expected to take care of themselves (p. 346). The committee was of the belief that the Stock Exchange Association was competently handling new issues of securities, and did not require the assistance of a Companies Commission (pp. 346–347). Finally, it said, the requirement of an audit for all "open" companies would make a Companies Commission unnecessary (p. 350).

4.2.8. Reactions to the report

The Teldersstichting report was extensively covered in the press, but the commentators devoted most of their attention to the "hot" political issues, especially co-determination.[57] A few gave some attention to financial reporting issues and, in particular, to the rejection by the Teldersstichting's committee of a Companies Commission.[58]

[56] The Teldersstichting's committee ventured the following observation: "Resounding scandals in the area of the limited company, as known in other countries, cannot be found in our history" (p. 307). This was evidently a view seen through rose-colored glasses. In Chapter 2, the authors drew attention to the collapse of the Noord-Brabantsche Bank and the Wilhelmina-Trust affair in 1901–02, the frenzy of claims and counter-claims in the Jurgens episode in 1925, and other celebrated embarrassments in the 1920's. Of course, the Teldersstichting's committee was trying to make a case against the need for establishing a Companies Commission. But its assertion that the history of Dutch limited companies was free of "resounding scandals" is not supported by the record.

[57] See "Behoudend Rapport", in *Haagsche Courant*, 5 October 1962, p. 2, and "Liberale Telderstichting [sic], Medezeggenschap laat werknemers koud", in *de Volkskrant*, 4 October 1962, p. 2.

[58] See "Prof. mr. B.M. Teldersstichting: Rapport over de onderneming en het vennootschapsrecht, 'Open ondernemerschap'", in *Nieuwe Rotterdamse Courant*, 4 October 1962, p. 11; "Teldersstichting wenst verbetering n.v.-recht, Fundamenteel is structuur evenwel gezond", in *De Telegraaf*, 4 October 1962, p. 17; "Open ondernemersschap [sic]: Prof. Teldersstichting bepleit sterker positie aandeelhouders, Geen vennootschapskamer en werknemerscommissarissen", in

P. Sanders, who was on the Dr. Wiardi Beckman Stichting's study committee and was also serving on the Verdam Commission (which was still deliberating when the Teldersstichting report was published), said that, in the case of the "open" NV, no distinction could be drawn between (1) a company's obligation to render an account both to shareholders and others with a "right" to information, and (2) the report it prepares for the public. Even if, as the Teldersstichting's committee claimed, the public had no "right" to receive an account, management at least had the obligation to render one, since "every form of unsupervised authority is an abomination".[59] On the subject of the Companies Commission, which he had advocated as early as 1952, Sanders said that the arguments made against the Commission by the Teldersstichting's committee were not convincing. Even if the Securities and Exchange Commission was created to deal with much more serious wrongs in the United States than had occurred in the Netherlands, the existence of rules required a compliance mechanism other than "social forces". Also, the committee's fear that the Commission might usurp even greater powers could be handled by a proper organization and specification of its functions (pp. 196–197). The auditor, Sanders said, could not perform the function of a Companies Commission, although he would remain indispensable under such a system. There would always be arguments about the interpretations of rules, and auditors would, because of the competition among members of their profession, always be inclined to interpret them according to the wishes of their clients (p. 197). If one were to reject a Companies Commission, as the Teldersstichting's committee did, Sanders concluded that the logical alternative was "a central judicial authority". This alternative, he said, would do as well, so long as there would be a single source of judicial decisions, leading to the accumulation of authoritative jurisprudence. Reliance on the Stock Exchange Association, however, would not be justified, because any supervising body must be independent. "It is therefore no coincidence that the Association has not been active in this matter, except for the case of the prospectus" (p. 198).[60]

De Tijd-Maasbode, 4 October 1962, p. 11; and "Teldersstichting over vennootschapsrecht: Nederland mag niet fundamenteel afwijken van het buitenland, Te stringente voorschriften leiden tot andere rechtsvormen", in *Trouw*, 5 October 1962, p. 13.

See also the article in the VNW's house organ: "Open ondernemerschap", in *De Nederlandse Industrie*, 15 October 1962, pp. 775–777.

59 "De Jaarrekening der Naamloze Vennootschap en de Verantwoording van het Bestuur", in *De Naamlooze Vennootschap*, vol. 40, nos. 11/12, February/March 1963, p. 196. Citations in the text to page numbers refer to this article.

60 Sanders was serving as chairman of the Verdam Commission's financial reporting subcommittee. As will be shown below, in the discussion of the Verdam Commission, the subcommittee had decided by September 1962 to adopt a judicial alternative to the Companies Commission.

4.2.9. Report of the Society for Investor Protection

In March 1963, the Society for Investor Protection (Vereniging Effectenbescherming), a body that had been established in 1924 to look after the interests of shareholders, issued a 68-page report entitled *De aandeelhouder en de herzieningen van vennootschaps- en belastingwetgevingen* (The Shareholder and the Revision of Company and Taxation Law).[61]

There is no evidence in the report that its authorship was other than the Society's eight-man management board, which was listed on the inside front cover of the publication. None of these board members was associated with any of the other reports of the 1950's and 1960's on the reform of financial reporting or company law. It is likely that one of its number, W.C. Posthumus Meyjes, a well-known journalist, had a large hand in the writing of the report.[62]

In its report, the Society cited the Rijkens and Hamburger reports, as well as the reports of the Dr. Wiardi Beckman Stichting and the Teldersstichting, and indicated its awareness that the Verdam Commission on the revision of company law had been sitting since 1960 (p. 13). As part of its function to protect the interests of shareholders, the Society said that it had the task of publishing its opinions on company and taxation law. This task, it said, was especially important in the light of the proposed comprehensive revision of the Commercial and Civil Codes (Het Nieuw Burgerlijk Wetboek),[63] the deliberations of the Verdam Commission, and the extensive debate in the industrial world and in politics (pp. 3–4). In regard to company law, the Society said that the accountability of managements to shareholders must be assured, and "As it is sufficiently clear

---

[61] *De aandeelhouder en de herzieningen van vennootschaps- en belastingwetgevingen* (Den Haag: Vereniging Effectenbescherming, March 1963). In this section, citations in the text to page numbers will refer to this report.

In 1987, the Society changed its name to the Society of Securities Owners (Vereniging van Effectenbezitters).

[62] In 1960, Posthumus Meyjes had written a 61-page booklet entitled "The Annual Meeting and the Annual Report": *Jaarvergadering en jaarverslag* (Laren (Nh.): Uitgeverij Andries Blitz, [1960]).

[63] In 1947, Prof.mr E.M. Meijers accepted an assignment to draft a new Civil Code that would incorporate, among other things, the sections of the Commercial Code dealing with the NV. In 1954, Meijers published his first installment, known as the ontwerp-Meijers (Meijers Draft), which contained a slightly altered version of the articles on financial reporting in the Commercial Code. See *Ontwerp voor een Nieuw Burgerlijk Wetboek*, opgesteld door Prof.mr E.M. Meijers ingevolge opdracht verleend bij koninklijk besluit van 25 april 1947, no. 20 (Den Haag: Staatsdrukkerij- en Uitgeversbedrijf, 1954). In regard to Article 42 of the Commercial Code, Meijers' draft provided that the specification of the contents of the balance sheet and profit and loss statement should be regulated under a General Administrative Order (i.e., by decree), rather than by the law itself. In general, commentators were opposed to that recommendation. Both the Dr. Wiardi Beckman Stichting's study committee (p. 48) and the Teldersstichting's committee (p. 319) said that such matters were too important not to be treated in the law itself. Since Meijers' death not long afterwards, the work has been carried on by a team of lawyers. The project is still in process.

that persuasion is not sufficient to reach this goal, the Society considers legal and more extensive regulation of financial reporting to be desirable" (p. 4).

In proposing a series of revisions to the section of the Commercial Code dealing with financial reporting, the Society drew heavily on the report of the Teldersstichting's committee, which had appeared only six months before. Indeed, most of the Society's proposed revisions were *verbatim* copies of those contained in the earlier report, with no acknowledgment of the source. The Society began with the same four-point statement of requirements that the Teldersstichting's committee had borrowed from the Otten speech by way of the Rijkens report (pp. 33–34). It followed with an enumeration of the breakdown of assets and liabilities and capital that was identical to that in the Teldersstichting report (pp. 34–35). The recommendation of the Teldersstichting's committee on the treatment of majority investments was also copied without change (p. 35). In an original recommendation, the Society said that companies' financial statements should be accompanied by a report from an independent registered auditor on the "correctness" (*juistheid*) of the data (p. 34). The Society also went beyond the Teldersstichting report to call for the separate reporting of several items in the profit and loss statement, including sales, cost of sales, and the separate disclosure of depreciation and labor costs (p. 35).

The Society expressed its agreement with the Hamburger committee's distinction between "accountability" and "information" (p. 20). It also agreed that the claim by managements that secrecy is needed in order not to inform competitors is exaggerated. "They mislead not the competition", the Society said, "but their own shareholders" (p. 19).

While the Society supported the call for legal regulation, since it did not think that the employers federations could force their members to follow the Rijkens committee's recommendations, it did not think it was necessary to create a separate supervisory body such as a Companies Commission. It was not sanguine that the Stock Exchange Association would be a suitable regulator, even though its articles of association required it to act in defense of shareholder interests, since the weight of a penalty against a company would fall most heavily on its shareholders (pp. 19–20).

The Society disliked the use of secret and undisclosed reserves, because they clouded the real value of the enterprise, obscured the real rate of return, and might make management less alert to possible improvements (p. 20). It also recommended that the valuation of assets be in accordance with "sound business practice" (*goed koopmansschap* [sic]) (p. 20). Quarterly and half-yearly financial information was considered to be desirable (p. 21).

4.3. Public-sector initiatives

4.3.1. The Verdam Commission report

Following the 1959 general election, the new government coalition was headed by the Catholic People's Party (KVP), with the Liberal Party (VVD) and the Christian-Historical Union (CHU) as participants. In the latter part of 1959, the government decided to appoint a commission to recommend a revision of company law, with particular attention to the democratization of enterprise, including workers' co-determination therein. The commission was established by ministerial decree on 8 April 1960, and its inaugural meeting was held on 20 June 1960. The chairman of the 16-man commission was Prof.mr P.J. Verdam. As is the custom with such commissions, the selection of members was carefully balanced according to their party affiliations. Four members each represented the two largest political parties, the KVP and Labor Party (PvdA). Three came from the VVD, and two each were drawn from the CHU and the Anti-Revolutionary Party (ARP). Most were major figures in their respective parties. Additionally, a civil servant in the Ministry of Justice attended as a full member. All four Labor Party representatives, plus the civil servant, had been members of the Dr. Wiardi Beckman Stichting's study committee, and two of the three Liberal Party representatives were serving at the same time on the Teldersstichting's committee, which completed its work in 1962.

Eleven of the 16 members were lawyers. Two of the eleven, Prof.mr W.C.L. van der Grinten and Prof.mr P. Sanders, were authorities on company law. There were two commercial bankers but no one from the auditing profession on the commission.[64] One member was a professor of economics, and another was a professor of psychology. Four of the commission members were then serving on the Social and Economic Council (SER, Sociaal-Economische Raad), a 45-member tripartite body that advises the government at the highest level, and Verdam himself was named to the SER the following year. Three of the members had served as ministers in previous governments, and one, Prof.dr H.J. Witteveen, was appointed Minister of Finance in July 1963, and was replaced on the commission by J.A. Hamburger, who had chaired the committee whose report was published in September 1962 by the Council of Dutch Employers Federations. Three members were in Parliament, and two other members took up seats in Parliament three months after the commission began its work. One of the commission's members, Drs J.M. den Uyl, who was director of the Dr. Wiardi Beckman Stichting from 1947 to 1962, would serve as Minister-President (i.e., Prime Minister) from 1973 to 1977. Another member, Mr W.F. Lichtenauer, was named

[64] The commercial banker, A.A. van Sandick, died in May 1962 and was replaced by Prof.ir L.H. de Langen, who was a director of A.K.U. De Langen's academic field was mechanical engineering.

in 1961 to the Council of State (Raad van State), the senior advisory body to the Crown. The commission membership was, by any standard, distinguished.[65]

The Verdam Commission, as it came to be called, submitted its 129-page report on 26 November 1964, and it was published in January 1965.[66] That more than four years were required to complete the work of the commission was said to have been due to the political complexity of the co-determination question.[67] Sixty pages of the report contained draft articles for the revision of the Commercial Code of 1928–29 and the 1950 Act on Works Councils, including the commission's memoranda thereon. The remainder of the report consisted of textual discussion. The names of the members who dissented to particular recommendations were duly disclosed.

In his installation address to the commission, Mr A.C.W. Beerman (CHU), the Minister of Justice, drew attention to the previous government's Declaration of Intent of 23 October 1956 in which the prospect was held out of an inquiry "into the question of revising company law with a view to participation by workers in, and the public accountability of, open limited companies" (p. 2). He indicated that the preparation of that inquiry had been under way since that year. The Verdam Commission, he said, was being given an even broader charge. It was "to launch an investigation into the question of the need for revision of the legal form of enterprise, and thereby to pay particular attention to the management and supervision of the large enterprise, as well as to the public accountability of enterprise" (p. 2). Only a few sentences of the Minister's 1900-word charge to the commission dealt with financial reporting, as follows:

> From different quarters, it has been argued that it should be possible to improve annual reporting. In connection with the important role played by the larger enterprises in the economic life of our country, it is of great significance that the annual financial statements – especially the balance sheet and the profit and loss statement – give a clear picture [*duidelijk beeld*] of the course of affairs of the limited company. A committee constituted by the four employers associations put forward suggestions in that regard some years ago. The question on this point, however, is whether it is sufficient to rely entirely upon the insights from the business sector and, in this domain, whether this might not justifiably be a task for legislation. The means by which compliance with further statutory provisions might be assured deserves particular attention. The question of whether

[65] For biographical sketches of the commission members, see "Commissie-Verdam (na 5 jaar studie): Ondernemingsrecht behoeft veel wijziging", in *Het Parool*, 19 January 1965, p. 13.

[66] *Herziening van het ondernemingsrecht* (Revision of Enterprise Law) ('s-Gravenhage: Staatsuitgeverij, 1965). In this section, citations in the text to page numbers or chapters will refer to this report.

[67] Interview with Mr B.C. de Die, 5 September 1990. De Die, who was educated in economics and law, was head of the department concerned with the revision of the civil code in the Ministry of Justice during the 1960's and the 1970's. De Die was also assistant secretary to the Verdam Commission and regularly attended the meetings of its financial reporting subcommittee.

> or not a companies commission should be set up to supervise compliance is to be considered by you as well (pp. 2–3).

The eight chapters of the report dealt mainly with the restructuring of enterprise, including the "right of inquiry" by shareholders and employees into the conduct of enterprise affairs, the co-determination by employees into enterprise decision making, and the role of the board of supervisors in limited companies. These were the heavy political issues.[68]

Financial reporting, including the question of whether a Companies Commission should be established, was covered in one chapter of nine pages of textual discussion and 22 pages of draft articles and the commission's notes thereon, constituting one-fourth of the report.

A subcommittee was set up to deal with financial reporting. The members were Sanders, chairman; van der Grinten; Witteveen; Verdam; A.A. van Sandick, who was president of Nederlandsche Handel-Maatschappij N.V. (which, in a 1964 merger, became part of Algemene Bank Nederland N.V.); Dr J.R.M. van den Brink, a former Minister of Economic Affairs who was a director of the Amsterdamsche Bank N.V. (which, in a 1964 merger, became part of the Amsterdam-Rotterdam Bank N.V.); Mr L. de Vries, secretary to the Verdam Commission and a full voting member; and three individuals who were not themselves members of the Verdam Commission: Mr P.F.J. de Kok, president of the Stock Exchange Association; Dr B. Pruijt, a professor of finance at the Nederlandse Economische Hogeschool until January 1962, when he became a member of the management board of Steenkolen-Handelsvereeniging N.V. (SHV); and J. Kraayenhof. Sanders and de Vries had been members of the Dr. Wiardi Beckman Stichting study committee. Witteveen was, at the same time, chairing the Teldersstichting's committee. Both Pruijt and Kraayenhof were contemporaneously serving on the Hamburger committee, and, in the end, they made major contributions to the committee's report. Kraayenhof had been suggested for the subcommittee by Sanders,[69] and, as a past-president of the NIvA, president of the 1957 International Congress of Accountants, and chairman of one of the most important auditing firms in the Netherlands, Kraayenhof was the foremost auditor in the country.[70] Kraayenhof, it was said, was accepted by the government and by non-auditors as one who had "deep insight".[71]

The work of the subcommittee on financial reporting was probably the least

---

[68] In a press interview more than twenty-five years later, Verdam recalled, "The bell of co-determination was tolling every moment". M.A. Goudswaard and H. Maarsen, "Commissaris kan tot regent verworden-Mr dr Verdam ziet zelfbenoemingsrecht als schoonheidsfoutje in de structuurwet", in *Het Financieele Dagblad*, 15 May 1991, p. 13.

[69] Interview with Mr B.C. de Die, 5 September 1990.

[70] For an obituary on Kraayenhof (1899–1982), see H.C. Treffers, "In memoriam J. Kraaijenhof", in *de Accountant*, vol. 88, no. 7, March 1982, p. 409.

[71] Interview with Prof.dr A.B. Frielink, 6 December 1990.

controversial of the questions facing the Verdam Commission.[72] It was, as one member of the commission recalled, "absolutely a sideline", since the commission's principal concern was, "how should the company law be modernized?"[73] The subcommittee's proposals were accepted by the commission with hardly any discussion.[74]

4.3.2. The Commission's conclusions on financial reporting

In one quintessential respect, the role of the Verdam Commission differed from that of the Rijkens and Hamburger committees, namely, that it was a ministerial commission charged with recommending legislation. The Rijkens and Hamburger committees, by contrast, were private-sector initiatives for the purpose of counseling "open" limited companies on the best financial reporting practices, and both committees made it clear that their advice was not binding. The Verdam Commission was not in a position to enjoy the luxury of such a disclaimer. The commission did say that it "had been able to take advantage of" the Rijkens and Hamburger reports (p. 34).

The Verdam Commission drew a distinction between "reporting" (*verslaggeving*) and "publicity" *(publiciteit)*, which, on the surface, resembled the dichotomy in the Hamburger report between "rendering an account" and "providing information". The Hamburger committee and the Verdam Commission were in agreement on the two audiences for company information, shareholders and the general public, and on the fact that financial statements were addressed primarily to shareholders. The Verdam Commission went on to define "publicity" as making these same financial statements available to the public, and to require such publicity by law. The Hamburger committee, however, had in mind an obligation to the general public that was significantly less than that to the suppliers of capital. A schism also divided the Teldersstichting's committee and the Verdam Commission, since the former maintained that the general public was entitled only to aggregated data as might be supplied by the government's Central Bureau of Statistics.

In the choice of a regulatory approach for financial reporting, the Verdam Commission said that it opted for a "middle course" between the US preference for a fairly general law that is implemented through the detailed rules of a securities commission, and the German preference for a highly specific and prescriptive regulation embodied in statute law. It favored

> regulation by law through a few rather general statements which, on the one hand, show companies with sufficient clarity the norms to which financial reporting

[72] Interview with J.A. Hamburger, 29 August 1990.
[73] Interview with Prof.mr P. Sanders, 24 August 1990.
[74] Interview with Prof.mr W.C.L. van der Grinten, 14 August 1990.

should conform, but, on the other hand, leave sufficient leeway to adapt the implementation to the circumstances in every industry (p. 35).

The Verdam Commission's draft articles were divided into three chapters: Chapter 1, definitions, general principles, measurement issues, and some disclosure matters; and Chapters 2 and 3, other disclosure matters.

4.3.2.1. General principles of financial reporting

Articles 2 and 3 in the legislation proposed by the Verdam Commission set forth the "general principles" for financial reporting. The two articles drew heavily on the Rijkens and Hamburger reports, for, indeed, they were drafted by Kraayenhof.[75] The draft articles were stated as follows:

Article 2

The financial statements shall give, in accordance with the requirements of this law, an insight such that a well-founded opinion can be formed concerning the financial position and return on invested capital of the enterprise, as well as concerning the solvency and liquidity.

Article 3

1. The balance sheet, with the notes thereto, shall present faithfully and consistently the amount and composition of the financial position of the enterprise at the end of the financial year.
2. The profit and loss statement, with the notes thereto, shall present faithfully and consistently the amount and composition of the net income of the enterprise during the financial year (p. 42).

The use of the term "faithfully" (*getrouw*), which figured so prominently in the Rijkens report but which was mentioned only twice in the Hamburger report, was once again accorded a preeminent role, together with "consistently" (*stelselmatig*), which could be traced, via the Rijkens report, back to point 4 in Otten's speech to Philips shareholders in 1954. Kraayenhof believed that, since another term that had gained some favor in such discussions, "sound business practice" (*goed koopmansgebruik*), was firmly implanted in income tax law, it would not be suitable for financial reporting.[76] The term "insight", which had occupied a central position in Otten's speech, and was picked up in the Rijkens report, the norms announced in 1956 for the Sijthoff Prize, and the Hamburger report, also depicted the overriding criterion in the Verdam Commission's "general principles".

In the commission's remarks, it was stated that these two articles formed the "core" of the financial reporting provisions of the proposed law. "Article 2", the commission said, "presupposes that one can form a responsible, well-founded

[75] Interview with Mr B.C. de Die, 5 September 1990.
[76] Interview with Mr B.C. de Die, 5 September 1990.

judgment on the basis of financial statements, although it will necessarily be incomplete" (p. 52).

4.3.2.2. The valuation principle

It was easier for the Rijkens and Hamburger committees, whose recommendations were not binding, to come out strongly for current cost accounting, a valuation principle that was applied by only a relatively small number of companies. The presence of Goudeket on the two committees virtually assured that such a recommendation would appear in the final report. But the Verdam Commission was concerned with legislation, and, moreover, Goudeket was not a member of the financial reporting subcommittee. Kraayenhof did not believe that thinking on the question was mature enough to justify the inclusion of a prescribed valuation principle in the law.[77] (In this respect, the commission found itself in essential agreement with both the Dr. Wiardi Beckman Stichting study committee and the Teldersstichting's committee.) Article 5 of the draft legislation permitted, as a result, alternative approaches to valuation:

1. The principles used in valuing the assets and liabilities shall satisfy norms that are considered to be acceptable in the economic and social climate.[78]
2. A change in valuation principles, if material, shall be shown explicitly, together with the impact of the change on net income and financial position.
3. The notes to the balance sheet shall give an explanation of the valuation principles (p. 43).

In the commission's view, Article 5 would ensure a valuation that was neither excessively low (too conservative) nor too optimistic. The commission believed that, while *bedrijfseconomie* gave important guidelines, it did not offer a ready-made solution for all cases.

---

[77] *Ibid.*

[78] This was the first usage of a terminology that was to play a central role in the Act on Annual Financial Statements of 1970: "are considered to be acceptable in the economic and social climate" *(in het maatschappelijk verkeer als aanvaardbaar worden beschouwd)*. The term "the economic and social climate" *(het maatschappelijk verkeer)* had appeared once in the Hamburger report, in the section on current cost accounting. Reflected in the term was the endeavor to infer the relevant economic choices and societal values, inevitably a highly subjective judgment. The addition of "are considered to be acceptable in" *(als aanvaardbaar worden beschouwd)* in the Verdam Commission's draft articles was apparently intended to call upon a judgment of what was appropriate in the circumstances, rather than what was actually done. A distinction was therefore drawn between "acceptable in the economic and social climate" and the American standard terminology, "generally accepted accounting principles". The former was normative and broad, while the latter was, at least in its wording, descriptive and technical. In actual fact, however, the American term "accepted" has been interpreted by American authorities as meaning "acceptable" to the SEC or to the standard-setting body on which it relies.

According to de Die, the terminology was suggested by Kraayenhof. *Ibid.*

4.3.2.3. Secret reserves

The Verdam Commission condemned secret and undisclosed reserves as "one of the main reasons why the picture that financial statements give is troubled" (p. 53). Its principal attempt to prevent such "unacceptable" valuation was contained in Article 5. Its counterpart, as regards secret reserves, was Article 20, which prescribed that "provisions" could be made only against specific risks, and that it was therefore not possible to form reserves for general purposes by charges against profit. Furthermore, it was stated in Article 6 that any changes in reserves must be disclosed in order to give a *getrouw beeld*.

The Commission made an exception for banks, as it did not consider the valuation of a bank building at 1 guilder to be unacceptable, and it explicitly exempted banks from complying with Article 20.

4.3.2.4. Consolidated financial statements

Article 12, paragraph 3, and the commission's accompanying notes indicated that, in the case of majority investments, and taking into account both direct and indirect holdings, the parent company may elect to issue separate, combined, or consolidated financial statements (pp. 44, 55–56). By 1960, most major industrial companies were not publishing consolidated statements. It is not usually clear, however, from a reading of companies' financial statements whether their investments in other companies constituted a majority holding. Nonetheless, it would appear that there existed a reluctance to issue consolidated statements. No more than cautious support had been given for consolidated statements in the Rijkens and Hamburger reports. In view of this state of affairs, the Verdam Commission preferred to allow alternative ways of displaying the financial statements of the parent and subsidiary companies.

4.3.2.5. Valuation of investments

Departing from the Hamburger committee's advocacy of the "intrinsic value" (*intrinsieke waarde*) method, the Verdam Commission favored the disclosure of information about the value of investments, and of changes therein, but did not suggest a particular method of accounting. All holdings of 25 percent or more of the investee's outstanding shares were considered to be "investments", as distinguished from other shareholdings (Art.12, para.1). Smaller holdings might qualify as investments as well, if they were not intended to be temporary. The general principle of Article 3, "faithfully" (*getrouw*), was invoked as the essential criterion to be observed in the valuation of investments (pp. 44, 55–56).

4.3.2.6. Changes in accounting principles

Apart from the references to "consistently" in Article 3, and the prescription in Article 5, paragraph 2, relating to changes in valuation principles, nothing was said about the treatment of changes in accounting principles. That the draft provisions of the proposed law did not require a disclosure of the impact of such changes on financial position and net income, other than for changes in valuation principles, constituted a retreat from the strong recommendations contained in the Rijkens and Hamburger reports.

4.3.2.7. Disclosure of sales

In Article 25, which dealt with the question of reporting a measure of revenue, neither the terms "sales" nor "revenue" actually appears. In order to be comprehensive of all fields of endeavor, including banking and insurance, the commission employed a generalized formulation, as follows:

> The extent of the affairs of the enterprise during the last financial year shall be shown by the usual measures of the industry, expressed either in absolute numbers or in proportionate figures with respect to the last financial year (Art.25, p. 47).

In the notes, the commission expressed the view that the fear of competition that is occasionally heard in connection with this disclosure was "exaggerated". It added that "... completely hiding the sales figure does not meet even the most elementary demands of accountability" (pp. 58–59). As was observed above, the majority of large companies did not report their sales by the beginning of the 1960's. The Rijkens and Hamburger committees had espoused positions similar to that taken by the Verdam Commission.

4.3.2.8. Disclosure of cost of sales

The only reference in the draft articles to an item of cost to be disclosed was the depreciation of "durable goods" (*duurzame goederen*) (Art.26). There was no discussion of this subject in the commission's notes. Both the Rijkens and Hamburger committees favored the separate disclosure of depreciation and wage cost. As was indicated above, few large companies disclosed their total cost of sales by the beginning of the 1960's.

4.3.2.9. Disclosure of profit-and-loss-statement items

In addition to depreciation, the following items were to be disclosed in the profit and loss statement or in the notes:

income from investments,
income from shareholdings,
provision for taxation, and
extraordinary gains and losses (Art.26).

4.3.2.10. Deferred income tax accrual

In Article 26, paragraph d, it was stated that the provision for income taxes was to be disclosed in the profit and loss statement, but nothing was said about the recognition of deferred income taxes, notwithstanding the support given to their recognition in the Rijkens and Hamburger reports. The commission probably was of the belief that deferred income taxes was too technical a subject to be mentioned in legislation.

4.3.2.11. Appointment of an auditor

In Article 34, paragraph d, the commission stated that companies whose financial statements must be published in accordance with the law were required to have an audit performed by a registered auditor, and paragraph f said that the report must be published together with the financial statements. (In 1962, the Registered Auditors Act (Wet op de Registeraccountants) had been approved, although it did not take effect until 1967.) As regards "closed" companies, the commission decided to reaffirm Article 42a of the Commercial Code, under which the general meeting of shareholders was entitled to appoint an auditor, if it wished to do so (pp. 43, 49, 61–62). While the Rijkens committee had said it was "desirable" that an auditor be retained to give an opinion on the financial statements, the Hamburger committee was of the view that, both for purposes of accountability and the providing of information, the judgment of an auditor was necessary. The reports of both committees were intended to apply only to "open" companies.

4.3.2.12. Directors' report

The directors' report was not regulated by the commission's proposed articles, because it was felt that there was no "apparent need" for such regulation (p. 42). Both the Rijkens and Hamburger committees had recommended that management's views about current and prospective developments relating to the enterprise should be recited in the directors' report.

4.3.2.13. Comparative figures

This matter was not mentioned in the commission's report. Both the Rijkens and Hamburger committees had called for the reporting of comparative figures. By the mid-1960's, most large companies were already disclosing comparative figures in their balance sheet and profit and loss statement.

In the Verdam Commission's financial reporting subcommittee, van den Brink raised the question whether the draft articles should require that comparative figures be presented. But Kraayenhof was opposed. He believed that they would lead to excessive attention being paid to short-term developments. He was, however, willing to provide for comparative figures in the context of four- or five-year summaries, but such a requirement, he said, could not be imposed by legislation.[79]

[79] Report of the 13th meeting of the financial reporting subcommittee (Subcommissie Publiciteitsvraagstukken) of the Verdam Commission, 4 September 1962, p. 2.

4.3.2.14. Interim reporting

This topic was not mentioned by the commission, perhaps in the belief that it was more of a concern to the Stock Exchange Association.[80] Both the Rijkens and Hamburger committees had favored some kind of interim reporting.

In a report that was marked by dissent in many of its sections (dealing with co-determination, etc.), the foregoing recommendations on financial reporting all secured the commission's unanimous approval.

4.3.3. The Commission's advocacy of an "Enterprise Chamber"

In a section of the report entitled "Administration or judge", the commission unanimously favored a judicial over an administrative approach to securing compliance with the financial reporting provisions. A Companies Commission, it argued, was costly, as it would be charged with reviewing all annual reports. An administrative agency would also raise many questions concerning its composition and mode of operation. Inspired by a suggestion from Prof.mr A. Mulder and Prof.mr Ch.J. Enschedé,[81] two experts on criminal law who were consultants to the commission on the form that sanctions should take in relation to the prescriptions for financial reporting, the commission proposed the creation of a new branch of the Court of Justice at Amsterdam, to be known as the "Enterprise Chamber" (Ondernemingskamer). Mulder and Enschedé had suggested either of two alternatives: a board of independent experts, or a special branch of the judiciary. The commission's financial reporting subcommittee, with which Mulder and Enschedé conferred, preferred the "judicial" alternative, which was, in the end, adopted by the commission.[82]

[80] In fact, the Stock Exchange Association amended its listing requirements in 1971 to call for the publication of half-yearly reports.

[81] Interview with Mr B.C. de Die, 5 September 1990, as well as two memoranda: "Note on the meeting of 29 August 1962 with Prof. Enschedé and Prof. Mulder relating to the sanction on the prescriptions for financial reporting" ("Nota naar aanleiding van de bespreking van 29 augustus 1962 met Prof. Enschedé en Prof. Mulder betreffende de sanctie op de voorschriften omtrent de jaarrekening"), written by Sanders; and "Brief note regarding the regulation of the sanctions in the preliminary draft of a law on the annual financial statements of enterprises (with reference to the letter from the chairman of the financial reporting subcommittee dated 10 July 1962)" ("Notitie over regeling van de sancties in het voor-ontwerp van een wet op de jaarrekening van ondernemingen (verwijzing naar brief voorzitter sub-commissie publiciteit dd.10 juli 1962)"), written by Mulder. (These documents were furnished by the Ministry of Justice.)

[82] The financial reporting subcommittee adopted the "judicial" alternative at its meeting on 4 September 1962. Secretary de Vries proceeded to compose a section of the commission's report together with draft articles. In his draft, de Vries introduced the plan that the court would be composed of three justices and two experts drawn from a panel. De Vries coined the term "Ondernemingskamer" for the judicial alternative in place of "Vennootschapskamer", the term used by Mulder and Enschedé for the chamber of independent experts and also associated in the literature with the controversial proposal for a Companies Commission, an administrative

The new court was said to be analogous to the Chamber for Leasing Disputes of the Court of Justice at Arnhem (Pachtkamer van het gerechtshof te Arnhem), which, since its founding in 1958, had been dedicated to applying the law to the pricing of leased land. The Enterprise Chamber would also be a specialized tribunal, and would include among its members two experts on *bedrijfseconomie* and auditing. Cases could be brought to the court by interested parties and by the Attorney-General (Procureur-Generaal) attached to the Court of Justice at Amsterdam. The court would have the injunctive power to direct the defendant company to issue a revised financial report in the event that the financial report originally issued was found to contravene the law. Through its opinions, the Enterprise Chamber would accumulate a body of law (*jurisprudentie*), which would provide guidance in future cases. The Chamber's established procedures would contribute to a greater degree of certainty in comparison with the decrees of an administrative agency (pp. 39–41).

As an organ of the judiciary having exclusive jurisdiction over companies' financial reporting, the Enterprise Chamber was without precedent, not only in the Netherlands but in any other country.

4.3.4. Other issues addressed by the Commission

The matters discussed above were probably the least controversial in the commission's charge. The most disputed topic, and the one that prolonged the commission's deliberations, was the co-determination by employees in the affairs of enterprise. The commission recommended that works councils be given additional powers, including the right (1) to be consulted on all proposed measures seriously affecting employees, (2) to determine, up to certain limits, the content of information that management must provide on the enterprise's economic affairs, and (3) to receive and discuss the company's annual financial statements (pp. 92–95). Under the proposed articles, works councils were also authorized to invite outside experts to participate in their discussions (pp. 91–92). Finally, works councils could enforce their rights by application to the new Enterprise Chamber.

As a further step in the restructuring of enterprise, the commission arrived at a heavily compromised recommendation (with nine of the commission's 16 members voting in favor) on the powers and composition of the board of supervisors. Employees were to be given the right to propose one or two supervisors, depending on the size of the board, in the case of listed companies. The board was to be empowered to appoint and remove members of the management board, to approve the financial statements, and to ratify certain important decisions by the

agency with features adapted from the US Securities and Exchange Commission and the Dutch Insurance Companies Commission. "Explanation" ("Toelichting"), dated 12 September 1962, document in the file of the financial reporting subcommittee.

management board or the shareholders' meeting, such as the issuance of shares or bonds, obtaining a stock exchange listing, and engaging in mergers or acquisitions. The independence of the board of supervisors was to be guaranteed by protection from arbitrary dismissal (Chapter 8). The "right of inquiry" by shareholders and employees also received the commission's attention. This right (as regards only shareholders) had come into existence in an elementary form in the 1928 revision of the Commercial Code, which provided for recourse in the county courts (*arrondissementsrechtbank*). As the right had seldom been exercised, the commission proposed some modifications. The right was to be extended to trade union federations and to smaller minorities in the shareholders' meetings. As newly defined, the right pertained to instances of alleged misconduct or abuse of authority by the management board or the board of supervisors, and it was to be enforceable in the Enterprise Chamber (Chapter 5).

4.3.5. Press reactions to the report

The commission's report was far-reaching, and it was covered extensively in the press. Most of the press commentary dealt with subjects other than financial reporting: creation of the Enterprise Chamber, the strengthening of the works councils, the redefinition of the board of supervisors, and the expansion of the right of inquiry.

Het Financieele Dagblad ran a series of five lengthy, mostly descriptive articles on the Verdam Commission report from 27 January to 1 February 1965. The paper's capsule comment on the financial reporting provisions was as follows:

> The norms agree in general with the opinions that a financial analyst holds on reasonable reporting. It is important that [the commission] has attempted to take into account the specific circumstances of different industries. This is evidence of realism. Nevertheless, the proposals will, if they are enacted, amount to a great step [forward] for many businesses, and will lead to a substantial change in financial reporting.[83]

Het Parool regarded the proposal relating to financial reporting, including establishment of the Enterprise Chamber, as one of the key recommendations in the commission's report. The paper drew particular attention to the expanded disclosure requirements in comparison with existing law, the full disclosure of changes in reserves, and the requirement for an independent audit.[84]

---

[83] "Rapport Commissie Verdam IV: Jaarverslaggeving II-Norm: verantwoord inzicht in vermogen en rentabiliteit-Omzetcijfer niet verplicht", in *Het Financieele Dagblad*, 30 January/1 February 1965, p. 3. Note that the headline highlights the fact that sales figures are not to be required.

[84] "Commissie-Verdam (na 5 jaar studie): Ondernemingsrecht behoeft veel wijziging", in *Het Parool*, 19 January 1965, p. 13.

De Telegraaf considered the proposed Enterprise Chamber and the changes in the works councils to be the most important elements in the report.[85] In an adjoining article, the paper discussed the reactions of the trade unions and employers federations. They were said to be "not dissatisfied" with the report. The vice president of the Dutch Federation of Trade Unions (NVV, Nederlands Verbond van Vakverenigingen) thought that the section on financial reporting could be implemented in short order because of the agreement in the business world on the subject. The Dutch Catholic Trade Union Federation (NKV, Nederlands Katholiek Vakverbond) said that it was "happy" with the sections of the report on financial reporting, the Enterprise Chamber, and the right of inquiry.[86] Like *Het Parool*, the *Haagsche Courant* mentioned the commission's proposal relating to secret reserves.[87]

Extensive discussion of the report also appeared in the *Algemeen Handelsblad*, *de Volkskrant* and the *Nieuwe Rotterdamse Courant*, but only perfunctory attention was given to the recommendations on financial reporting.[88] *Trouw* reported the cautious reaction to the report by H.J. de Koster, the president of the Federation of Dutch Employers. He was reported to have said that the proposed changes did not all show the same degree of insight into enterprise practice. Most of the proposals, he said, would have a profound impact on the current situation.[89]

4.3.6. Commentary in the professional literature[90]

There was an outpouring of articles in professional journals on the many recommendations of the Verdam Commission, not only because they were on highly contentious subjects but because they portended a change in the law.[91]

---

85 "Commissie-Verdam stelt voor: Ondernemingskamer en betere positie ondernemingsraden, Oneens over benoeming van werknemerscommissaris", in *De Telegraaf*, 19 January 1965, p. 13.

86 "Rapport-Verdam niet ongunstig ontvangen", in *De Telegraaf*, 19 January 1965, p. 13.

87 "Commissie-Verdam bracht rapport uit, Ernstige meningsverschillen over medezeggenschap, Meer aandacht voor ondernemingsraad?", in *Haagsche Courant*, 19 January 1965, p. 13.

88 "Commissie-Verdam bepleit instelling van een ondernemingskamer, Ruimere publikatie van en betere voorlichting in jaarverslagen nodig geacht", in *Algemeen Handelsblad*, 19 January 1965, p. 11; "Meer rechten voor ondernemingsraad, Commissaris verantwoordelijk voor algemeen belang", in *de Volkskrant*, 19 January 1965, p. 2; and "Commissie-Verdam wil taak ondernemingsraden vergroten, Verdeeldheid over werknemerscommissarissen", in *Nieuwe Rotterdamse Courant*, 19 January 1965, pp. 1, 7.

89 "Reactie van heer de Koster op rapport-Verdam, Niet alle ontwerpen geven blijk van inzicht in onderneming-praktijk, Over consequenties moet beslist niet te licht worden gedacht", in *Trouw*, 20 January 1965, p. 11.

90 Page citations in the text refer to pages in the article being discussed.

91 Among the many publications responding to the section of the commission's report dealing with financial reporting that are not discussed below are: Prof.dr W. Hessel, "Een goed uitgangspunt voor een voort te zetten discussie", in *TVVS*, vol. 7, no. 11, March 1965, pp. 232–236; J.P. Coelingh, "De jaarverslaggeving uit het gezichtspunt van een ondernemer" in *De*

One of the most impressive commentaries was by Prof.drs R. Burgert, of the Nederlandse Economische Hogeschool, who was a member of the Society of Academically Trained Auditors (VAGA, Vereniging van Academisch Gevormde Accountants).[92] Burgert traced the gradual movement toward greater openness in the financial affairs of companies. In an earlier day, he wrote, internal financing was managed through secret reserves, which were sometimes reinforced by interposing holding companies between the shareholders and operating subsidiaries. Over the decades, the owner-manager ("*ondernemer-regent*", or "entrepreneur-oligarch", in Burgert's words) was replaced by the professional manager, who was more accustomed to rendering an account of his stewardship. Burgert referred to the American influence, via the SEC, as "a shining example", which shone even brighter when the largest Dutch companies found it necessary to raise capital in New York (pp. 264–265). Given the presence of these "natural forces", Burgert wondered whether the rationale for further legislation, to persuade the last unwilling companies to improve their reporting, was valid. He would rather rely on market pressures, although, he said, this would require a change in the status and independence of the stock exchange authorities.

In commenting on specific provisions in the draft law, Burgert found it strange that, if reliance could no longer be placed on social forces, these same forces could be expected to regulate income determination and valuation (in Article 5). More attention, he thought, should have been given to the valuation principles and to the disclosure of the income determination principles. He said it would have been better to include in the law a number of currently accepted or proposed income determination and valuation systems, with the requirement that the company explain its choice in the notes. At the very least, he said, there should be a requirement to disclose the income determination principles (in tandem with the requirement for valuation principles in Article 5(3)) (p. 269). As will be seen in the next section, the NIvA and the VAGA made the same suggestion in a communication to the Ministry of Justice, and their proposal was accepted.

Burgert was not optimistic that a judicial body such as the Enterprise Chamber would be a fruitful source on which accounting principles or practices were "acceptable in the economic and social climate". Then he added:

> This is probably the core of the problem: the weak link in the current procedure

Naamlooze Vennootschap, vol. 43, nos. 1/2, April/May 1965, pp. 5–6; Drs A.B. Westra, "De jaarverslaggeving van ondernemingen", in *Economisch-Statistische Berichten*, 7 July 1965, pp. 623–626; J.M. Vecht, "Het rapport van de commissie-Verdam en de jaarrekening", in *Maandblad voor Bedrijfsadministratie en -Organisatie*, vol. 69, no. 823, October 1965, pp. 357–359; Drs H.H.J. Nordemann, *Wensen en Grenzen-Enige beschouwingen over de jaarrekening van ondernemingen* (Deventer: Æ.E. Kluwer, 1967); and Prof. A. Goudeket, "De toelichting als onderdeel van de jaarrekening", in *Maandblad voor accountancy en bedrijfshuishoudkunde*, vol. 41, no. 10, November 1967, pp. 438–444.

[92] R. Burgert, "De jaarrekening van ondernemingen-Hoofdstuk IV van het rapport van de Commissie-Verdam", in *TVVS*, vol. 7, no. 11, March 1965, pp. 263–270.

of accountability is that the management of an NV finds itself confronted with unequal opponents, but with an inert mass, in which the interests of each individual are relatively small. One should aim for an adequate representation of these interests, and the exchange authorities, provided they are properly organized and sufficiently independent, would be a suitable body for this [task] (p. 270).

Burgert placed considerable emphasis on an emerging role for the stock exchange authorities, yet the Stock Exchange Association's low profile over the years on matters having to do with financial reporting suggested little likelihood of any interest in such a proposition.

A.F. Tempelaar delivered the 1965 Accountantsdag address on "The Financial Reporting by Limited Companies", and addressed his remarks specifically to the Verdam Commission report. In an appendix, he reviewed a number of previous writings, including H. Munnik's Accountantsdag address in 1931 (discussed in Chapter 2), the Otten speech of 1954 and the Rijkens report (discussed in Chapter 3), and the Dr. Wiardi Beckman Stichting, Hamburger and Teldersstichting reports (discussed earlier in this chapter). After referring to some American publications on "uniformity" in financial reporting, which was a burning issue in the USA during the mid-1960's, Tempelaar suggested its relevance to the Dutch setting and advised his colleagues that the organized profession must take a much more active role in providing informed guidance to those who prepare and use financial statements. In his *preadvies* (prepared paper), he wrote as follows:

Undoubtedly, there must be an attempt to make principles themselves, the ground rules, as uniform as possible, especially the rules on valuation ... .

Thus far, the professional organization of auditors as such in our country has taken no initiative to make known its proposals and thoughts in suitable publications to the business world. Individually, auditors have contributed much to the developments, some in important committees of business life, but they were there on a personal basis.

With Goudeket and others, I am of the opinion that we as a professional organization have to operate more as an institute, as a group – either with or without cooperation from other bodies – in the domain of providing information and recommendations concerning financial reporting, and in that way cooperate in giving a concrete meaning to the *general demands* that the legislature will make.[93]

At that point, Tempelaar, who was to become the NIvA's president two years later, warned of the consequences of inaction by the Institute:

If we leave this to others, matters that lie within our expertise, or, more strongly put, which belong to the most important elements in our profession, will

[93] A.F. Tempelaar, "De jaarverslaggeving van Naamloze Vennootschappen", in *de Accountant*, vol. 72, no. 1, September 1965, pp. 43–44.

be decided without us. We cannot assume that the government or business life will wait for us to take the initiative. I don't think that we have "missed the boat", as Goudeket puts it, but we are not really on time.[94]

In the discussion following Tempelaar's presentation, Prof.dr A.Th. de Lange, who had served on the Hamburger committee, disagreed with Tempelaar. He said that auditors had done enough collectively in the form of Accountantsdagen, study meetings and reports of the NIvA's Advisory Committee on Professional Matters. De Lange argued that auditors had a good knowledge of the accounting principles that were accepted within the profession, and he said he did not miss a codification of such principles in a way that would make them binding for auditors (p. 285). Tempelaar replied that, while auditors had indeed conducted discussions of accounting principles, it was nonetheless important that these principles be stated not only in internal NIvA documents but also in publications accessible to business (p. 289).

Prof. A. Goudeket, in the article to which Tempelaar referred, had lamented that the profession had done little to crystallize the meaning of "sound business practice" ("*goed koopmansgebruik*"), i.e., the principles to be used in the preparation of financial statements. As a result, audited financial statements did not always convey the insight that might be expected. As evidenced by their diverse reactions to the Verdam Commission's report, auditors had shown a marked difference of opinion on important accounting questions. Government intervention might have been avoided if the profession had taken steps to formulate rules concerning the contents of financial statements.[95]

Prof.drs G.L. Groeneveld, who had served as the NIvA president in 1964, liked the Verdam Commission's proposal for an obligatory audit. Recent research, in fact, had shown that most companies already were being audited, so the idea was hardly radical. Groeneveld referred to a NIvA study in 1958 which found that 331 out of 481 companies published an auditor's report. A more recent survey conducted by Groeneveld himself showed that 340 out of 402 listed companies had audits.[96]

Groeneveld found the draft law's general principles (Articles 2 and 3) to be "completely responsible" ("*volledig verantwoord*"). A Limperg disciple and the partner in charge of the Philips audit, Groeneveld lamented the Verdam Commission's assertion that a reference in the law to the principles of "*bedrijfseconomie*"

[94] *Ibid.*, p. 44. Citations in the text to page numbers refer to the discussion following Tempelaar's presentation ("De jaarverslaggeving van Naamloze Vennootschappen", in *de Accountant*, vol. 72, no. 5, January 1966, pp. 271–292).

[95] A. Goudeket, "Goed koopmansgebruik", in *Maandblad voor accountancy en bedrijfshuishoudkunde*, vol. 39, no. 8, September 1965, pp. 282–289.

[96] G.L. Groeneveld, "De jaarverslaggeving volgens het rapport van de Commissie Verdam, bezien vanuit het gezichtspunt van de accountant", in *De Naamlooze Vennootschap*, vol. 43, nos. 1/2, April/May 1965, pp. 6–10; the results of Groeneveld's survey were presented on p. 8.

was not possible owing to differences of opinion among experts in the field. The assertion was not valid, he said, because current cost accounting was generally recognized as being theoretically superior (pp. 9–10).

Prof. A.M. van Rietschoten, an auditor who had served on the Teldersstichting's committee, noted the large area of agreement between the general principles expressed in the Rijkens and Verdam reports, and ventured the observation that the philosophy underlying the 1928 law, namely, free choice of accounting principles coupled with required explanation in the notes, had been retained in Verdam's Article 5.[97] Noting that secret reserves were restricted by Articles 5, 6 and 20, he said that such reserves were "one of the most important obstacles to achieving effective financial reporting. It remains to be seen to what extent opponents [of these articles] will be able to lessen their impact before some law comes from this proposal" (p. 217). Van Rietschoten liked the idea of an Enterprise Chamber, as it would leave the autonomy of companies intact for as long as possible, but would permit far-reaching measures to be taken against those that are recalcitrant (pp. 214, 224).

There was considerable comment in the journals over the use of "are considered to be acceptable in the economic and social climate" ("*in het maatschappelijk verkeer als aanvaardbaar worden beschouwd*"), in Article 5, as opposed to the more traditional "sound business practice" ("*goed koopmansgebruik*"), which had been mentioned in the Hamburger report. Each of the terms implied a subjective standard for determining which specific accounting principles or practices were appropriate in a given set of circumstances. There was also controversy over two almost synonymous terms: "faithfully" ("*getrouw*"), as used in Article 3, and "faithful picture" ("*getrouw beeld*"), as used in the Rijkens and Hamburger reports. These latter two terms also appealed to subjective standards, but they were typically used when referring to whether financial statement as a whole had been properly prepared.

In regard to the first set of terms, Burgert declared that the substitution of "*maatschappelijk verkeer*" for "*goed koopmansgebruik*" was "definitely not an improvement". The latter at least had the advantage of a long history; the former would contribute to legal uncertainty. Until the meaning of the former becomes evident, "everyone will need to take counsel with himself in order to find out what norms are considered as 'acceptable in the economic and social climate'. For the economic and social climate is not equipped with a mouthpiece".[98] Mr Th.S. IJsselmuiden also concluded that the new term was not an improvement, and pointed out that recent court decisions had narrowed the gap between profit for taxation purposes and profit for financial accounting purposes; hence, he said,

---

[97] A.M. van Rietschoten, "Een voorontwerp van een wet op de jaarrekening van ondernemingen", in *Maandblad voor accountancy en bedrijfshuishoudkunde*, vol. 39, no. 6, June 1965, pp. 213–224; the discussion recapitulated in the text appears on pp. 216–217.

[98] Burgert, "De jaarrekening", *op. cit.*, p. 266.

"*goed koopmansgebruik*", which was generally associated with tax accounting, could well have been continued in use for financial reporting. He also remarked that the international trend had been toward a closer integration of fiscal and "commercial" profit determination.[99] H.H.M. Foppe, a member of the NIvA, in an effort to understand the meaning of "*maatschappelijk verkeer*", referred to the Hamburger report, where the term was equated with "*goed koopmansgebruik*". He therefore concluded that Verdam did not rule out "*goed koopmansgebruik*" and all of its associated bad valuation practices, including secret reserves. "The traditionalists can be content", he said.[100] Prof.dr H.J. van der Schroeff, the leading exponent of Limpergian theory, reached the conclusion that, even though "*maatschappelijk verkeer*" was used instead of "*goed koopmansgebruik*", the content of the two terms could be none other than the same.[101]

Groeneveld said he was comfortable with "*getrouw*", since the term had come to be used more and more in auditors' reports.[102] Foppe was of the view that only current cost accounting could truly give a "*getrouw beeld*". Since he had discovered in a recent survey of 81 listed companies that only 27 were using current cost, he argued that it would be unsatisfactory, given the new terminology, to leave existing valuation principles unchanged.[103] Prof. A.B. Frielink wrote that "*getrouw*" actually meant something that the Verdam Commission did not intend. According to his view, "*getrouw*" meant "exactly like the original, without any distortion", while the Verdam Commission probably meant something like "without serious or disturbing deviations". In that case, he argued, one might better use the term "*juist weergeven*" or "*juist beeld*", which would mean "as it should be" or "in a proper way" ("*zoals het moet zijn*").[104]

Clearly, there was a remarkable disparity of views about both sets of terms.

4.3.7. Reaction of the Social and Economic Council

As was normal in such matters, the Social and Economic Council (SER, Sociaal-Economische Raad) submitted a memorandum of its views on the Verdam Com-

---

99 Th.S. IJsselmuiden, "Enige opmerkingen over het voorontwerp van een wet op de jaarrekening van ondernemingen", in *De Naamlooze Vennootschap*, vol. 43, no. 7, October 1965, pp. 95–100; vol. 43, no. 8, November 1965, pp. 113–118; and vol. 43, no. 9, December 1965, pp. 136–141; the discussion recapitulated in the text appears on p. 98.

100 H.H.M. Foppe, "Het getrouwe beeld in de gepubliceerde jaarrekening", in *Economisch-Statistische Berichten*, 27 October 1965, pp. 991–993.

101 H.J. van der Schroeff, "Het rapport van de commissie-Verdam en de rapporten van de werkgeversverbonden inzake de verslaggeving van ondernemingen", in *Maandblad voor accountancy en bedrijfshuishoudkunde*, vol. 39, no. 6, June 1965, pp. 225–231; the discussion recapitulated in the text appears on p. 229.

102 Groeneveld, "De Jaarverslaggeving", *op. cit.*, p. 9.

103 Foppe, *op. cit.*, p. 993.

104 A.B. Frielink, "Enkele misvattingen in en rond hoofdstuk IV van het rapport Verdam", in *Maandblad voor accountancy en bedrijfshuishoudkunde*, vol. 40, no. 4, April 1966, pp. 138–144; the discussion recapitulated in the text appears on p. 144.

mission report. The comments were drafted by the SER's 19-member committee on company law, and were published in 1966, together with appended communications received from the Minister of Justice and interested organizations.[105] The discussion in this section will be confined to the comments relating to the commission's recommendations on financial reporting and the Enterprise Chamber.

The Minister of Justice reported that

> The government has, in general, favorably received the proposals on financial reporting. The government is convinced that the current regulations on this matter are deficient. The more extensive regulations proposed by the commission will be a substantial improvement (p.I-1).

The SER said that it supported the general principles in the commission's report: regulation by law, rather than by decree (as proposed in a recent draft of a new Civil Code[106]); regulation by fairly general principles, rather than by a detailed prescription; and a system of sanctions through the Enterprise Chamber; and added,

> The SER is of the opinion that the draft law proposed by the Verdam Commission generally codifies in a very satisfactory way the demands that, at the least, must be met in order for the financial statements to serve their purpose (p. 4).

The SER said that it saw the general structure of the law to be in two parts, as follows: the general requirements of Chapter I, mainly Articles 2, 3, and 5 (quoted above), which contained the actual demands to be placed on financial statements (i.e., the insight to be provided); and Articles 9 and onward (Chapters II and III), which represented applications of the general principles, or minimum requirements. In the SER's view, the financial statements could not be said to have met the criteria of the law by complying only with the specific demands set forth in Article 9 and subsequent articles. In every instance, the SER said, it remained to be seen whether more disclosure was needed to provide the required insight. If this interpretation was correct, the SER said, the relationship between the two sets of articles should be clarified either in the draft law itself or in the minister's Explanatory Memorandum (Memorie van Toelichting) (p. 5).

As regards Article 2, the SER feared that the expression "well-founded opinion" (*verantwoord oordeel*) might give rise to excessive expectations or demands. Financial statements were, by their nature, limited in the insight they could give in matters such as liquidity and return, and this view should be acknowledged

---

[105] *Advies inzake de wetgeving over de jaarrekening van ondernemingen*, uitgebracht aan de Minister van Justitie, 1966, no. 4 (Uitgave van de Sociaal-Economische Raad). In this section, all citations in the text to page numbers will refer to this memorandum.

[106] Refer to footnote 63, above, for a brief discussion of the proposed overhaul of the Civil Code.

in the law. The SER therefore proposed the following insertion (italicized) in Article 2:

> The financial statements shall give ... an insight such that, *given the nature of the statements*, a well-founded opinion can be formed ... (p. 8).

The SER endorsed the suggestion by the Stock Exchange Association, contained in a communication included as Appendix V(A), that comparative figures be shown in the financial statements. The SER recommended that this additional demand be inserted in Article 3 (p. 9).

It was reported that a large minority of the SER would like to see an additional criterion for distinguishing between "investments" and other shareholdings, namely, that, in order to qualify as an investment, the holding must "in a durable way be linked functionally to the investor company" (p. 14). This additional criterion was an echo of a suggestion made in the Hamburger report.

While the Verdam Commission was content with making few prescriptions for the contents of the profit and loss statement in Articles 24–26, the SER recommended that a series of subtotals as well as several additional items be disclosed. The sequence of recommended subtotals was:

operating income,
other revenues and costs,
income before taxes,
addition to the tax provision, and
net income.

The additional items to be disclosed were:

amortization of intangible assets,
interest revenue,
interest expense, and
wage and social security expense.

Furthermore, it said, the extraordinary gains and losses should be reported separately, and not netted against each other (p. 21).

The SER said that it was not correct for the Verdam Commission to reaffirm the principle of 1928–29 that only "open" companies must publish their financial statements. Given that one of the commission's charges was that it consider the interests of employees, the SER believed that publication should be required of the largest "closed" companies (with issued shares having a face value of at least *f* 500 000, with or without registration of shareholders). Several members of the SER took issue with this view (pp. 22–26).

The Stock Exchange Association, in its communication to the SER, said that the law should leave no doubt whether it is necessary to publish the holding company's financial statements in addition to the consolidated statements. It did not issue a brief for either interpretation, but only that the law should be unambiguous on the point (pp. V-3,V-8). The SER assumed that the text of the draft law was sufficiently clear to avoid the misunderstanding signaled by the Association, and therefore did not propose any alterations (p. 17).

4.3.8. Advice from the NIvA and the VAGA

In 1966, shortly after publication of the SER's memorandum, the management boards of the two most important professional bodies of auditors, the NIvA and the VAGA (which were to merge the following year), issued a joint set of comments on the Verdam Commission report.[107] Apart from the NIvA's submission in 1927 on the proposed company law (see Chapter 2) and three reports by NIvA subcommittees published in 1956 and 1962, this was the first official utterance by any auditing body on the possible improvement of companies' financial reporting practices. Indeed, the joint report might not have come out at all. The NIvA's Advisory Committee on Professional Matters (CAB, Commissie van Advies inzake Beroepsaangelegenheden) counseled the NIvA management board in December 1965 against issuing a public statement on the financial reporting provisions of the Verdam Commission report, since "the socio-political aspect plays too great a role in this matter" (CoKas 183).[108] The board then thought it would convene a study meeting so that the views held within the auditing profession could become known without any commitment by the board (CoKas 185). Sometime in April 1966, however, the board decided that a memorandum had to be drafted before the end of June, and be made ready for presentation together with the VAGA (CoKas 203). The apparent reason for the board's change of heart was the hint dropped by L. de Vries (of the Justice Ministry) that "the silence of the auditing profession on the report of the Verdam Commission has been noticed" within the ministry, and that some statement by the NIvA and the VAGA would be considered "useful" (CoKas 194).[109]

[107] "Nota van de besturen van het Nederlands Instituut van Accountants en van de Vereniging van Academisch Gevormde Accountants inzake het voorontwerp van de commissie Verdam van Wet op de jaarrekening van ondernemingen", in *de Accountant*, vol. 72, no. 11, July/August 1966, pp. 583–595. In this section, all citations in the text to page numbers will refer to this article.

[108] Extract from a letter sent by the CAB to the NIvA management board, contained on page 183 ("CoKas 183") of the minutes of the "Commissie Kastein" ("Kastein Committee"), which had been set up within the NIvA in 1958 to study the possible consequences of the Meijers draft on the proposed New Civil Code. It met on an occasional basis to study financial reporting in general, and it served as a kind of support group for auditors serving on non-NIvA committees, such as Goudeket and Kraayenhof on the Hamburger committee, and van Rietschoten on the Teldersstichting's committee. The chairman was Mr A.Th.E. Kastein, who, according to his stationery, was an "Advocaat en procureur" as well as an auditor.

[109] The Kastein Committee, which was charged with preparing the report that was to serve as the basis for the joint submission, had to work feverishly throughout May and June to complete the report on time.

In their introductory remarks, the two boards observed that financial reporting had improved considerably in recent years, notwithstanding the lack of legal guidance. While not wishing to question the desirability or necessity of regulation by law, they nonetheless cautioned that any regulation must not hinder the future development of financial reporting (pp. 583–584).

They agreed with the SER that regulation by law was superior to regulation by decree (p. 584).

In the boards' view, the entire proposed law was a valuable formulation of current opinion on financial reporting. They added that, while they would have desired that the proposed law be limited to general principles only, in order to avoid creating a straitjacket of detailed rules, such a strategy would run the risk that "other, unfounded" opinions than those laid down in the articles dealing with applications might find their way into practice. Furthermore, without the articles on applications there would be an absence of proper guidance for the Enterprise Chamber, possibly resulting in incoherent court decisions. In view of the current state of development of financial reporting, and after weighing the foregoing considerations, the two boards concluded that the disadvantages of having only general principles outweighed the advantages (p. 584).

Once it was decided that the articles on applications should be retained, the two boards agreed with the SER's recommendation that the relationship between Articles 1–8 (the general principles) and Articles 9 and onward (the applications) be clarified (p. 584).

Most of the boards' remaining comments dealt with the wording of the Verdam Commission's draft law.

The boards agreed with the SER's proposed modifications of Articles 2 and 3. In addition, they suggested that the term "return on invested capital" (*rentabiliteit*) in Article 2 be replaced by "income" (*resultaat*) (p. 585). (As will be seen below, this suggestion was adopted in the draft of the proposed law announced in 1968 by the Ministry of Justice.)

The boards also suggested that "the principles used in income determination" (*de grondslagen van de winstbepaling*) be included among those that must be "acceptable in the economic and social climate". (This suggestion was incorporated in the 1968 draft.) The suggestion was also made that "the economic and social climate" should be narrowed to "the economic climate", else general usage might interpret this phrase more broadly than was intended (pp. 586–587). (This suggestion was not adopted in the 1968 draft law.)

The boards pleaded for the inclusion in the law of further qualitative criteria for determining when shareholdings were to be classified as investments (pp. 589–591).

The SER's suggestions for the elaboration of the requirements for the profit and loss statement were, for the most part, accepted by the NIvA and VAGA boards. But they recommended that a consolidated profit and loss statement that met the requirements of revised Articles 25 and 26 should not need to be accompanied by a profit and loss statement for the holding company (p. 594). (This suggestion was adopted in the 1968 draft law.)

The SER's proposal for the publication of the financial statements of the largest "closed" companies evoked the suggestion that such companies, when they were the subsidiaries of other companies, should be excluded from the requirement (p. 595). No comment was offered on the Verdam Commission's proposal for a required audit, as this matter was to be treated in a forthcoming study by the boards (p. 595). In 1967, the boards published two letters to the Minister of Justice, one recommending that foreign auditors be allowed to practice with a permit from the Minister of Economic Affairs, and the other proposing the stipulation that the Enterprise Chamber hear the views of the auditor before it reaches a verdict on the propriety of financial statements.[110] (Both recommendations were adopted in the draft law promulgated in 1968.)

It is curious that the NIvA and VAGA management boards did not express an opinion on the wisdom of the Verdam Commission's proposal for an Enterprise Chamber.[111] It is likely that the commission's judicial alternative to the Companies Commission that had been endorsed by the Dr. Wiardi Beckman Stichting's study committee was seen as much the lesser of two evils.

4.3.9. Drafting of the Act on Annual Financial Statements

Once the report of the Verdam Commission was received, the Minister of Justice followed the established practice of appointing a small committee to prepare a draft of the proposed law to be considered by Parliament. Minister Dr I. Samkalden, a member of the Labor Party (which had been the sponsor of the Dr. Wiardi Beckman Stichting report of 1959, discussed above), selected three draftsmen: J. Kraayenhof, who had played a major role in the formulation of the draft articles on financial reporting in the Verdam Commission's report; Prof.mr P. Sanders, who had served as chairman of the Verdam Commission's financial reporting subcommittee; and Drs S.C. Bakkenist, who was vice-president of N.V. Koninklijke Zwanenberg-Organon N.V. (which, through a succession of mergers in 1967 and 1969, became part of Akzo) and, in 1970, was to become president of the Federation of Dutch Industries (VNO, Verbond van Nederlandse Ondernemingen).[112]

---

[110] The letters were dated 25 January 1967 and 8 March 1967, respectively, and were published under the title, "Voorontwerp van wet op de jaarrekening van ondernemingen", in *de Accountant*, vol. 73, no. 7, March 1967, pp. 319–322.

[111] It was said that the auditing profession, as a whole, was opposed to a Companies Commission. Interview with Drs I. Kleerekoper, 22 August 1990.

[112] The VNO was formed in January 1968 upon the merger of the Federation of Dutch Employers (VNW) and the Central Social Employers Federation (CSWV), the two main sponsors of the Rijkens and Hamburger reports of 1955 and 1962, respectively. In 1967, the Dutch

The three-man drafting committee was assisted by Mr B.C. de Die and Mr L. de Vries, who were senior civil servants in the department of the Ministry of Justice concerned with civil code revision, and who had participated in the work of the Verdam Commission's financial reporting subcommittee. In view of the fact that the Verdam Commission, which was broadly representative of the political spectrum, had adopted the draft articles on financial reporting unanimously, and that the points raised by the SER and the NIvA and the VAGA did not strike at fundamental issues, it was no surprise that the draft law submitted by the committee adhered closely to the draft articles in the commission's report. Once it was approved by the Ministry of Justice, the committee's draft, together with minister's Explanatory Memorandum (Memorie van Toelichting), and the draft prepared separately on the right of inquiry, were transmitted to Parliament under the date of 13 May 1968.[113]

By this time, Mr C.H.F. Polak, a member of the Liberal Party (which been the sponsor of the Teldersstichting report of 1962, discussed above), had become the Justice Minister.

4.3.9.1. Changes in the draft law

A number of substantive changes were made when the draft articles in the Verdam Commission report were converted into the draft law submitted in 1968. Perhaps the most important of the changes was the insertion of "and the de-

Catholic Employers Federation (NKWV) and the Federation of Protestant-Christian Employers in the Netherlands (VPCWN), the two other sponsors of the Rijkens and Hamburger reports, combined to form a federation which, in 1970, adopted the name, Dutch Christian Employers Federation (NCW, Nederlands Christelijk Werkgeversverbond). Hence, the VNO and the NCW became the two central employers federations. See William van Voorden, "Employers associations in the Netherlands", in John P. Windmuller and Alan Gladstone (editors), *Employers Associations and Industrial Relations: A Comparative Study* (Oxford: Clarendon Press, 1984), Chap. 8, esp. pp. 204–213.

[113] *Bijlagen Handelingen Tweede Kamer, Zitting 1967–1968,* "Wettelijke bepalingen met betrekking tot de jaarrekening van ondernemingen" (9595) (nos.1–3), "Wijziging van de artikelen 53–54c van het Wetboek van Koophandel" (Herziening van het enquêterecht) (9596) (nos.1–3).

Parliamentary materials are published in four series. The stenographic recordings of the parliamentary debates are published in a series designated as *Handelingen*. These are published separately for both chambers, and cited as *Handelingen Tweede Kamer* (Second Chamber) and *Eerste Kamer* (First Chamber), respectively, followed by the year of session (*zitting*) and the page number.

The documents circulating during the course of these sessions, such as drafts, memoranda, letters and amendments, are published for both chambers separately in the series *Bijlagen Handelingen Tweede* and *Eerste Kamer,* respectively. Within these series, the documents are keyed primarily to the number of the draft law to which they pertain. Documents relating to a particular draft law are numbered chronologically. Lastly, the parliamentary year during which each document is issued is usually indicated. As the number of the draft law is the same for all cases in the following discussion (no. 9595), it is not included in subsequent citations.

The four series thus distinguished will be cited by abbreviation in the following discussion by "H" and "B" for *Handelingen en Bijlagen*, respectively, followed by "1" or "2" to indicate the first or second chamber.

termination of income" (*en de bepaling van het resultaat*) in Article 5, para. 1, which, with the addition, read as follows:

> The principles used in valuing the assets and the liabilities and the determination of income shall satisfy criteria that are considered to be acceptable in the economic and social climate. (*De grondslagen waarop de waardering van de activa en de passiva en de bepaling van het resultaat berusten, voldoen aan normen die in het maatschappelijk verkeer als aanvaardbaar worden beschouwd.*)

In Article 13, intermediate subsidiaries were exempted from the obligation to consolidate or to give separate financial statements for all of their investments (*deelnemingen*). In a new Article 14, holding companies were required to disclose the names and locations of subsidiaries and of other significant investee companies, subject to a materiality constraint, all of which was softened somewhat by a provision suggesting the possibility of a ministerial exemption from this requirement. Article 14 was inspired by a recommendation from the SER. In Article 15, also new, it was provided that foreign subsidiaries could be omitted from the consolidation, so long as their financial statements were shown separately or were deposited with the commercial registers. In the article on owners' equity, the drafting committee added a paragraph requiring the splitting up of reserves into share premium, revaluation, and retained earnings (B2, 1967–1968, no. 2).

Among the changes in the "miscellaneous provisions" was a reduction in the time period in which companies must publish their financial statements from eight to five months following the close of the financial year. The Verdam Commission had retained the eight-month period from the 1928 Act, but the minister shortened it to five. He observed that a "great majority" of companies already published their financial statements within five months, and, in his view, the statements would lose much of their information value by being published as late as eight months after the close of the financial year (B2, 1967–1968, no. 3, p. 22).

The draft law was more explicit in regard to the required disclosures in the profit and loss statement. Various subtotals were added to the list of disclosed items: operating income, other profits and losses, income before taxes, and estimated taxes on income. Wage expense and social security expense were also to be separately reported, although not necessarily in the profit and loss statement itself. Finally, the drafting committee took into account the recommendation of the SER by calling for a more detailed breakdown of items in the profit and loss statement, as follows:

depreciation of fixed assets,
amortization of intangible assets,
profits or losses on investments,
profits or losses on other shareholdings,

interest revenue,
interest expense,
extraordinary gains, and
extraordinary losses (Art.29).

One significant change in wording, which had been recommended by the NIvA and the VAÇA, was to replace "return on invested capital" by "income" in the Article 2.

4.3.9.2. Procedure

Once a draft law is published, the next step in the process of passing legislation is to assign it to a parliamentary preparation committee, which may call a hearing and, after initial deliberation, submits a provisional report to the minister. Thereupon, the minister and the committee exchange comments and replies until it is decided that the proposed legislation, possibly modified by the minister, should be transmitted to Parliament for debate and possible amendment.

A 17-member parliamentary preparation committee was formed under the chairmanship of M.W.J.M. Peijnenburg, with representation from all of the major, and most of the minor, political parties. Among the members was Th.H. Joekes, who, prior to entering Parliament, had served as the principal draftsman of the Teldersstichting report.

The committee held a hearing on 19 November 1968. The interested parties that made presentations were the following: the Society for Investor Protection, the National Council of Cooperatives, the Society of Financial Analysts, the Royal Netherlands Alliance of Smaller Companies, the Council of Dutch Employers Federations, the Consultative Council of Trade Union Federations, and the NIvRA. Curiously, the Stock Exchange Association was not among the interested parties. The report of the hearing was published on 17 December 1968 (B2, 1968–1969, no. 4). The committee's provisional report was presented to the minister on 20 January 1969 (B2, 1968–1969, no. 5), and the minister submitted his memorandum of reply (B2, 1968–1969, no. 6), accompanied by a memorandum of alterations (Nota van Wijzigingen) in the draft law (B2, 1968–1969, no. 7), on 14 July 1969. A further letter was submitted by the minister, comparing the legal systems in a number of other countries (B2, 1969–1970, no. 8). A further memorandum of alterations was submitted by the minister on 13 October 1969 (B2, 1969–1970, no. 9), followed by a letter from the minister in which a number of open matters were discussed (B2, 1969–1970, no. 10).

Not satisfied with the minister's replies, the committee held a meeting with the minister, attended by de Die, on 4 November 1969. The report of this meeting served as the committee's final report, dated 30 December 1969 (B2, 1969–1970, no. 11). This meeting led to the third and final memorandum of alterations from the minister (B2, 1969–1970, no. 12).

The next step was the debate. The draft law, as modified, was discussed in the Second Chamber in three sessions, on 7, 8 and 14 April 1970.[114] In the First Chamber, a similar but less elaborate procedure was followed. At the outset, the draft law was transmitted to Parliament.[115] A preparatory committee rendered a provisional report on 3 June 1970 (B1, 1969–1970, no. 118a), which was followed by a memorandum of reply from the minister dated 17 July 1970 (B1, 1969–1970, no. 118b). The debate in the First Chamber took place on 8 September 1970,[116] where the law was passed without a formal vote (which is not unusual) and without changes. The First Chamber does not have the right to make amendments.

4.3.9.3. Content of the discussion and debate

In his Explanatory Memorandum which accompanied the initial version of the draft law, Minister Polak referred to the favorable reception of the Verdam Commission report in wide circles, and said that the draft law was explicitly based on the report. He added that the SER and professionals in the fields of company law and auditing had generally accepted the outline and the main principles, although they had criticized the draft on details (B2, 1967–1968, no. 3, p. 7). He pointed out that the general principles set forth in the draft law formed the basis for a series of concrete provisions that were to be interpreted as minimum requirements. A company, he said, was not discharged from the duty to give more information than the minimum when the "insight" into the financial statements would otherwise be harmed (idem, pp. 7–8).

A lesson to be learned from the experience of laws in foreign countries, the minister said, was that detailed regulation carried the danger of rigidity (*verstarring*), and of hindering new developments. Furthermore, it would be difficult to cater to every industry by giving detailed rules. The advantages of the proposed law, he said, could be summarized as follows:

> In this way, through the combination of general guidelines, concrete rules for normal cases, and a sanction, a system results that combines certainty before the law with flexibility, is applicable in practice, and does not require an elaborate supervisory apparatus (idem, p. 8).

In his commentary on Article 5, dealing with the valuation principles, the minister issued his call for what was to become the Tripartite Study Group on

---

[114] *Handelingen Tweede Kamer 1969–1970*, pp. 2856–2896, 2901–2931, and 2941–2948. Subsequent citations to this debate will be inserted in the text by page number, preceded by the series indicator (H2).

[115] *Bijlagen Handelingen Eerste Kamer, Zitting 1969–1970*, 9595, no. 118. In the discussion that follows, textual citations will be given to the series (B1), the year of sitting, and the number assigned to the pertinent document. The number 9595 will not be repeated.

[116] *Handelingen Eerste Kamer 1969–1970*, pp. 1087–1098. Subsequent citations to the debate will be inserted in the text by page number, preceded by the series indicator (H1).

accounting principles:

> I expect that organized business [*georganiseerd bedrijfsleven*] in collaboration with the organization of auditors will consider it to be their task to make an inventory of these principles used in the economic and social climate [*het maatschappelijk verkeer*], as intended in Article 5, and to judge them on the basis of what, in their opinion, can be considered as acceptable in the economic and social climate and as fulfilling the demands in Articles 2 and 3. The resulting publications concerning acceptable principles will meet a clear need on the part of enterprise managements, and can serve as a point of reference as well for the Enterprise Chamber when a case in this area is brought before it (idem, p. 14).

The idea that a committee drawn from "organized business" and the "organization of auditors" be charged with undertaking an inventory of valuation principles has been traced to Kraayenhof, who, as was indicated above, did not believe that the thinking on the subject of valuation principles was sufficiently well developed to justify a prescription in the law.[117]

This remark by the minister was not a matter of discussion in the preparatory stage. Its implications may have escaped the committee, which may explain the committee's somewhat persistent demand for "model financial statements". During the parliamentary debate, only the minister and Kraayenhof referred to it, when making the case that such "models" were not necessary.

In the debate in the Second Chamber, the active participants were, with a few exceptions, the members of the preparatory committee. In both chambers, most of the speakers displayed a good understanding of the issues. Two of the most active speakers, R. van den Bergh, of the Labor Party, and C. Boertien, of the Liberal Party, could quote from articles in the financial press and from journals such as the *Maandblad voor accountancy en bedrijfshuishoudkunde*. Van den Bergh had studied law at the Gemeentelijke Universiteit van Amsterdam and had practiced in a private law firm prior to entering Parliament. Boertien had served as an assistant secretary to the NIvA from 1952 to 1960, and from 1960 to 1965 was a lawyer at Philips. Both were members of the committee. H. van Rossum, a representative of the Political Reformed Party (Staatkundig Gereformeerde Partij), the second-smallest party in the Second Chamber, showed a surprising insight into accounting matters, although he was not a member of the preparatory committee and had been educated as an engineer. He asked a

[117] Interview with Mr B.C. de Die, 5 September 1990. G. Timmer, who was a close colleague of Kraayenhof's, is also of the belief that the suggestion can be attributed to Kraayenhof. Interview with G. Timmer, 5 September 1990. In April 1967, a year before the Justice Minister announced his suggestion that "organized business" and "the organization of auditors" collaborate in the taking of an inventory of valuation principles, Kraayenhof discussed such a plan and gave every indication that it was his idea. "Rede van de heer J. Kraayenhof", at the "Eerste bijeenkomst van de ledenvergadering van de Orde Nederlands Instituut van Registeraccountants", in *de Accountant*, vol. 74, no. 1, May 1967, pp. 16–19.

number of questions on issues such as the valuation of intangibles, accounting for leases, and the valuation of building contracts (percentage of completion v. completed contract) (H2, 1969–1970, pp. 2877–2878).

During the debates, Kraayenhof served as an adviser to the minister and occasionally replied to questions in accordance with a special clause in the rules of procedure.

As the draft law had already been discussed rather thoroughly in the preparatory committee of the Second Chamber (where it had been received favorably), most of the articles were accepted on the floor without a formal vote. On certain issues, however, amendments were proposed that caused further debate and an occasional vote.

A summary of the major points made during the parliamentary debate may be usefully organized in the following subsections.

4.3.9.4. General appreciation of the law

During the preparatory stage and the general debate, most members of both chambers expressed their satisfaction with the draft law as a whole, notwithstanding certain reservations as to particulars.

Through van den Bergh, the Labor Party declared that it was "moderately pleased" with the law: it would be an improvement, although it did not go far enough (H2, 1969–1970, p. 2858). The Liberal Party, whose view was stated by J.G. Rietkerk, also a member of the committee, considered the draft law to be a proper intermediate position which took into account the interests of all concerned. The Liberal Party did, however, consider some of the concrete requirements to be a bit too detailed (H2, 1969–1970, p. 2864). The Catholic People's Party spokesman, Peijnenburg, also emphasized the balanced nature of the draft. It set a good standard, he said, for companies with deficient reporting, while at the same time not encouraging the progressive companies to fall back to the minimum requirements (H2, 1969–1970, p. 2866).

A favorable comparison with the approaches in the United States and West Germany was drawn by several members of Parliament. Their systems were considered to be too stringent and detailed (H2, 1969–1970, p. 2872; p. 2877).

The only criticism of the draft as a whole was voiced by H. Wiebenga, a member of the committee representing the small Pacifist Socialist Party (Pacifistisch Socialistische Partij). He saw the draft as a mere correction of some excesses of a system of "unsupervised positions of power". The Justice Ministry could, he said, use this draft law and the one on the right of inquiry as political propaganda in support of its progressiveness, while at the same time maintaining the current system virtually intact by escape clauses (H2, 1969–1970, pp. 2893–94).

In his first speech in the Second Chamber, Minister Polak again sketched the favorable development of financial reporting despite the lack of extensive regulation. One of the factors promoting this development, he said, was the "powerful influence" of the Stock Exchange Association (H2, 1969–1970, p. 2904). In the First Chamber, the minister claimed a major role for the proposed law in the process of easing tensions between employees and employers, and ensuring the social confidence in enterprises, a process that was to be continued with other laws emanating from the Verdam Commission report (H1, 1969–1970, p. 1092).

Kraayenhof expressed his expectations for the law as follows:

> When we speak of financial statements in general, we usually think of the financial statements belonging to a few hundred companies that do it well, and we forget that, especially in the case of many closed companies, shareholders are not always properly informed, and certainly not according to the demands of this law. In the case of these thousands [of companies], the law will bring considerable improvement. In the case of, say, 400 (although I think this is expecting too much) that do it well already, there won't be much to improve. I hope and expect that a large number of leading enterprises will continue to go beyond the requirements of this law, especially in their information and in the way they make the profit and loss statement understandable, and that more and more enterprises will join that group. We will have to wait to see whether that will eventually give rise to more extensive demands in the law (H1, 1969–1970, p. 1097).

4.3.9.5. Small enterprises

An issue that provoked some resistance was the fact that the draft did not distinguish among several classes of enterprise, but instead prescribed the same reporting for all companies. This matter was mentioned by the employers during the hearing (B2, 1968–1969, no. 4, p. 5), and was taken up by the preparatory committee in its initial report (B2, 1968–1969, no. 5, p. 3) and in its meeting with the minister (B2 1969–1970, no. 11, pp. 1–2). Especially in Articles 16 (inventories), 17 (receivables), and 28 (revenues), it was argued that there should be an escape clause for small, undiversified companies. The minister did not accept this proposal, as, he said, it would lead to a serious loss of insight and would burden the Ministry with many requests for dispensation.

An amendment was therefore proposed during the parliamentary debate by a group of members from the Catholic People's Party, the Liberal Party, and the Christian-Historical Union that would give the Minister of Economic Affairs the right to grant dispensation on request when vital interests were at stake (amendment no. 20, later superseded by no. 22). This amendment, which did not contain a specific reference to small enterprises, was adopted by one of the few individual votes taken during the entire debate, 59 votes to 56 (H2, 1969–1970, p. 2943).

4.3.9.6. Comparative figures

The subject of comparative figures did not figure importantly in the work of the preparatory committee, but it was taken up by most speakers in the first round of parliamentary debate. Since the demand for this disclosure was expressed by a large majority of members, the minister accepted one of the two proposed amendments on the subject (amendments no. 14, by van den Bergh, and no. 18, by Boertien; the latter was accepted). Boertien defended his amendment by quoting A. Goudeket[118] and the Hamburger report (H2, 1969–1970, p. 2872). The minister repeated, before conceding, that the argument he had been defending had come from "several experts" (H2, 1969–1970, p. 2904).[119]

4.3.9.7. Sales disclosure

Apart from the objection from small companies, this issue was of concern to large companies as well. A general requirement for sales disclosure was requested at the hearing by both the Society for Investor Protection and the Society of Financial Analysts (B2, 1968–1969, no. 4, pp. 2, 4). Members of the preparatory committee also called for sales disclosure (B2, 1968–1969, no. 5, p. 11).

During the parliamentary debate, therefore, two somewhat contradictory amendments were being discussed at the same time: one providing for an exemption even for the required disclosure of indices, and one, submitted by van den Bergh (no. 16), calling for the disclosure of sales by all companies covered by the law. Van den Bergh defended his amendment by emphasizing the importance of sales in evaluating all other figures, and also by citing (H2, 1969–1970, p. 2929):

- a speech by J.C. van Marken, president of the Stock Exchange Association, in which he called for more sales disclosure;
- an article in *Het Financieele Dagblad*, in which it was shown that the newspaper could calculate the sales revenue of a non-disclosing company by methods such as counting the number of trucks leaving the gate; and
- the Hamburger report, which had dismissed the competitiveness argument as invalid in most cases (p. 45 of the report).

Other members expressed sympathy for the idea of preventing an unnecessary hiding behind index figures, but pointed out that, in the European context, the amendment might cause problems for Dutch companies. They thought it would be more prudent to await collective action in the European Economic Community on the matter. The minister agreed, and he advised against the van den Bergh amendment, which was, in the end, rejected. It was supported only by the left-wing parties: the Labor Party, the Democrats '66, the Pacifist Socialist

[118] The reference was to A. Goudeket, "De toelichting als onderdeel van de jaarrekening", in *Maandblad voor accountancy en bedrijfshuishoudkunde*, vol. 41, no. 10, November 1967, pp. 438–444.

[119] As noted in the discussion of the deliberations of the Verdam Commission's financial reporting subcommittee, above, the question of comparative figures had been raised by van den Brink but had been opposed by Kraayenhof.

Party, the Communist Party, and the so-called "Aarden Group" (H2, 1969–1970, p. 2943).

4.3.9.8. Comparability and financial statement models

The idea of promoting uniformity and comparability by prescribing models of financial statements to be followed by companies had been suggested during the hearing by the Society of Financial Analysts, which pointed to legislation in West Germany, France, and the UK, and proposed a model drafted by the European Federation of Financial Analysts Societies as a substitute for the articles in the law dealing with the profit and loss statement (B2, 1968–1969, no. 4, p. 4). The idea was advocated during the preparatory stage by a number of committee members, but it was rejected by the minister, since, he said, it would lead only to "apparent" comparability (B2, 1969–1970, no. 11, pp. 2–3). It came up for the last time during the initial debate in Parliament (by van den Bergh, among others), but it did not lead to any amendments.

Related to this general question was an issue raised by van Rossum. The essence of his argument was that the criterion in Article 5, "principles acceptable in the economic and social climate", would leave room for many calculations of income. This would, he said, cause large differences among companies that would dilute the quality of insight. Furthermore, he contended, it would place considerable power in the hands of the Enterprise Chamber when deciding what treatments were "acceptable". It would also, he added, cause the income concepts used in financial reporting and income tax determination to "drift further apart", which he regarded as undesirable (H2, 1969–1970, p. 2879).

Kraayenhof spoke at length on this subject, as he felt that some members might not have a complete understanding of the position of the law in such matters. In his view, the law was not intended to ensure "perfect" financial statements or even completely comparable financial statements. The actual goal was somewhat more modest:

> The main point of this law is really that the faithful picture [*getrouwe beeld*] of the financial position means: no hidden and also no secret reserves, and a rendering of the correct income is required; therefore, [improper transfers to and from] secret or hidden reserves must be abandoned (H2, 1969–1970, p. 2911).

A number of the points raised by the members that were not addressed in the law would, said Kraayenhof, need to be dealt with by the committee representing organized business and auditors. In this way, Kraayenhof declined to pronounce his views on the questions asked by van Rossum, but referred them to the committee envisaged by the minister (H2, 1969–1970, p. 2912).

4.3.9.9. Directors' report

The 1928–29 amendments to the Commercial Code had provided that the directors were to make a statement on the affairs of the company on the occasion when the financial statements were presented. The general meeting of shareholders could vote that the directors' report be in writing. The Verdam Commission and the 1968 draft law had left this requirement basically unchanged, apparently because, according to the minister, current practice was regarded as satisfactory (B2, 1967–1968, no. 3, p. 23).

Van den Bergh proposed a written report in all cases (amendment no. 17 I) and a partial prescription of the contents of the report (amendment no. 17 II and no. 20 revised). According to his proposed amendments, information on developments since the end of the financial year and information on the financing of new capital construction had to be given. Although members from the other parties were sympathetic to the idea, they rejected the proposals on the grounds that

- there was no need to prescribe what the shareholders could easily demand for themselves if they so desired, and
- it was impracticable to give rules for such a general document as the directors' report. Such rules might easily be interpreted as an acceptable minimum requirement by companies (H2, 1969–1970, pp. 2945–2946).

The first amendment was rejected by 61 votes to 56, and the other found only the left-wing parties voting in favor.

4.3.9.10. Interested parties before the Enterprise Chamber

Some members of the preparatory committee in the First Chamber wanted a more explicit listing of "interested parties" who would have standing before the Enterprise Chamber. In reply, the minister said that shareholders and holders of certificates of shares should always be recognized as interested parties in regard to the entire contents of the financial statements. For other groups, such as creditors and employees, he said that the circumstances of the case and the nature of the claim would be decisive (B1, 1969–1970, no. 118b, pp. 1–2). During the debate, the Labor Party asked for general recognition of employees as interested parties, while the Liberal Party argued for limitations on their standing in the case of hostile takeovers (H1, 1969–1970, p. 1089). It was argued that, when a company seeks to take over another company, the former should not be allowed to demand fuller information in court simply because it had bought a few shares.

The draft law, as amended, was passed by Parliament and was published, with Royal Assent, in the Statute Book of the Kingdom of the Netherlands on 24 September 1970.[120] Its official title was the Act on Annual Financial Statements

[120] *Staatsblad van Het Koninkrijk der Nederlanden*, no. 414 (1970).

of Enterprises (Wet op de Jaarrekening van Ondernemingen). The law was made effective by an Order in Council (Koninklijk Besluit) dated 30 October 1970,[121] and took effect on 1 May 1971. All financial statements for a financial year closing after that date were to meet the new statutory requirements.

4.3.10. Other laws resulting from the Verdam Commission report

As was mentioned above, by far the most politically charged issues that were discussed by the Verdam Commission were those dealing with the democratization of enterprise, including the enhancement of the employees' role in company management. Apart from financial reporting, the Verdam recommendations led to parliamentary consideration of three draft laws that were eventually approved in 1970–71, as follows:

- A law expanding the "right of inquiry" by shareholders, extending the right to trade unions, and assigning a role in the procedure to the Enterprise Chamber (1970, Stb. 411[122]).
- A law on works councils, replacing the 1950 Act, which aimed to make the installation of the works council obligatory for large companies, and provided more safeguards for its independence (Wet op de Ondernemingsraden, 1971, Stb. 54).
- A law transferring important powers from shareholders to supervisors in certain large companies, and governing the composition of supervisory boards in such companies (1971, Stb. 289).

4.3.11. Introduction of the BV

Also in 1971, a law was enacted to establish the Besloten vennootschap met beperkte aansprakelijkheid (BV, Private Company with Limited Liability).[123] The introduction of a Dutch equivalent to the German GmbH had been proposed repeatedly as part of the company law reforms of 1928 and 1929. Instead, the NV (Naamloze vennootschap, Limited Liability Company) was retained as the sole legal form for limited liability companies, but, as regards financial reporting, the 1929 Act set forth criteria by which companies would be classified as either "open" or "closed". "Open" companies had to publish their financial statements, while "closed" companies did not.

The recognition of the BV in Dutch law was the direct result of the First Directive of the European Economic Community, which had been approved on 9 March 1968. The Directive would require the publication of the financial statements by all NV's, without exception. Hence, it became necessary to accommo-

[121] *Staatsblad van Het Koninkrijk der Nederlanden*, no. 533 (1970).
[122] "Stb." is the abbreviation for the *Staatsblad* (Statute Book).
[123] Wet op de Besloten Vennootschap, Stb. 286.

date the large number of "closed" companies that existed under the 1929 Act. Under the 1971 Act, which became part of the Commercial Code, all NV's were required to publish their financial statements, but all BV's were exempted from this obligation, save for (1) those exceeding a specified size limit defined in terms of number of employees and asset value, and (2) financial institutions.

4.3.12. Sijthoff norms are changed to reflect the draft law

In December 1969, when the Sijthoff Prizes for 1968 were awarded, the panel of judges announced several alterations in the norms used to evaluate companies' financial reports, both to take into account the draft law that was nearing final approval, and to signal a desirable expansion of the reporting obligation.[124] The two changes that were based on the draft law were (1) a five-month time limit for publication of a company's financial statements, and (2) publication of an auditor's report. The latter became one of the primary criteria that had to be met if a company's annual report was even to be eligible for consideration. The time period allowed for publication, which previously was eight months, was already one of the primary criteria.

Two other additions to the norms reflected the panel's view of desirable reporting: (1) inclusion of a statement discussing future developments, and (2) publication of a half-yearly "quantified insight into the results", together with a forecast of the result for the full year. Both of these two items were also designated as primary criteria.

The changes were announced by J.C. van Marken, chairman of the judging panel as well as president of the Stock Exchange Association. He regarded the Sijthoff Prize as the principal medium by which the Stock Exchange Association could contribute to the improvement of company financial reporting.[125] Eighteen months later, the Association formally changed its Rules on Securities Trading (Fondsenreglement) to require the publication of half-yearly reports, to take effect on 1 July 1971.[126]

4.3.13. Concluding comment

It is doubtful that reform legislation would have been approved on company financial reporting in the absence of the larger political controversy over the opening up of enterprise. It seems very unlikely that the comparatively few public allegations of insufficient financial information in company annual reports would, in and of themselves, have led to new legislation. In a real sense, there-

---

[124] "Totale publiciteit staat nu centraal-Nieuwe normen Sijthoff Prijs", in *Het Financieele Dagblad*, 11 December 1969.

[125] Interview with J.C. van Marken, 2 November 1990.

[126] The Association's announcement appeared in circular 71–17.

fore, the passage of the Act on Annual Financial Statements of 1970 owed much to the movement to restructure enterprise and to give employees a greater voice in company management.[127] It was described as a "liberal law", one which prescribed no strict valuation rules and which, "in approximately 40 rather short articles indicates what information must be disclosed as a minimum about assets and liabilities and revenue and expense".[128]

Imbedded in the Justice Minister's Explanatory Memorandum to the draft law in 1968 was a suggestion, probably noticed only by the affected parties, that led to the first ongoing program in the Netherlands to recommend improvements in company financial reporting. It was the minister's way of avoiding a decision on the controversial question of which valuation principles should be used in financial statements. Limperg's disciples had no difficulty defending current cost accounting, together with the determination of profit predicated on the continuity postulate, as an integral part of the deductive framework of *bedrijfseconomie*. But only a minority of companies actually practiced current cost accounting,[129] and there was also disagreement among leading auditors.[130] Limperg's dictum did not find favor at the Nederlandse Economische Hogeschool, in Rotterdam. If there had been any doubt in earlier years about the prevailing belief at the Rotterdam school, the stronghold of the VAGA, it was dispelled in 1967, when Prof.drs R. Burgert delivered the annual Accountantsdag address under the auspices of the newly established Dutch Institute of Registered Auditors (NIvRA, Nederlands Instituut van Registeraccountants), which resulted from the merger of the NIvA and the VAGA earlier in the year. One of Burgert's major points was that Limperg's postulate of continuity presupposed a policy decision by a company's management with respect to the appropriate capital maintenance concept and its implications for the calculation of distributable profit. Since, he said, such policies varied from one company to another, and since companies' financial statements performed different roles for different audiences, an argument could be made for more than one concept of profit, rather than just the one implied in the Limperg doctrine. Burgert also argued that the measure of a

[127] Burgert has written, "we obtained our law on the annual accounts in 1971, not because there were serious complaints about reporting practices, but as part of a general revision of company law creating employees' participation in management". Prof.drs R. Burgert, "Current Accounting Practice in the Netherlands", in *Maandblad voor accountancy en bedrijfshuishoudkunde*, vol. 55, nos. 2/3, February/March 1981, p. 53.

[128] *Ibid.*

[129] In a survey conducted a few years earlier, Foppe had found that 27 of a sample of 81 listed companies were using some form of current cost accounting. Of the 27, only 13 were using current cost accounting in both their balance sheet and profit and loss statement. Foppe, *op. cit.*

[130] For a review of the published opinions of auditors on current cost accounting from the late 1950's onward, see G.L. Groeneveld, "Ontwikkeling van afwijkende opvattingen over winst en waarde", in Part II, "Ontwikkelingen na Limperg", in Limperg/Groeneveld, *Waarde, Winst en Jaarrekening* (Deventer: Kluwer, 1979), esp. pp. 205–218.

company's distributable profit could be influenced as well by an explicit consideration of changes in the general price level (as distinguished from relative price changes), which did not form part of Limperg's theory.[131]

The next task in the continued development of financial reporting was the organization of the Tripartite Study Group (TO, Tripartiete overleg), resulting from the minister's suggestion. The organization and work of the TO, together with the impact of the early verdicts of the Enterprise Chamber, will be discussed in the following chapter.

[131] For the paper prepared in advance of the Accountantsdag, see R. Burgert, "Bedrijfseconomisch aanvaardbare grondslagen voor de gepubliceerde jaarrekening", in *de Accountant*, vol. 74, no. 4, September 1967, pp. 153–192. Burgert's oral presentation of his paper and the discussion by Prof.dr J.L. Bouma were reported under the same title in *de Accountant*, vol. 74, no. 9, February 1968, pp. 494–523. Several years after his Accountantsdag address, Burgert wrote "Reservations about 'Replacement Value' Accounting in the Netherlands", in *Abacus*, vol. 8, no. 2, December 1972, pp. 111–126. For a discussion of the controversy surrounding Limperg's views, see Jan Klaassen and Hein Schreuder, "Accounting research in The Netherlands", in Anthony G. Hopwood and Hein Schreuder (editors), *European Contributions to Accounting Research: The Achievements of the Last Decade* (Amsterdam: VU Uitgeverij, 1984), pp. 121–124.

5. The decade of the Tripartiete overleg

The period from the late 1960's to the early 1970's was one of major ferment in the accounting principles programs in the USA, Canada, and the UK. In the USA, the Accounting Principles Board gave way to the Financial Accounting Standards Board in 1973 amid criticisms that the former had lost its way. In Canada, the Canadian Institute of Chartered Accountants unveiled its *CICA Handbook* in 1968 and then, in 1972, following an embarrassing case in which a major audit firm had used unwarranted discretion in interpreting generally accepted accounting principles (GAAP), the provincial securities commissions publicly declared that the *CICA Handbook* would be accepted as GAAP for their purposes. And in the UK, criticism in the press of the undue flexibility of accounting principles led the Institute of Chartered Accountants in England and Wales to announce a completely reorganized and strengthened program of setting accounting standards.

In the Netherlands, a suggestion made by the Justice Minister in 1968, in the course of the parliamentary debates leading up to passage of the Act on Annual Financial Statements of 1970, prompted the creation of the first ongoing program of giving public advice on company financial reporting. This chapter treats the inception and development of the program, and the tribulations in its later stages until, at the end of the 1970's, it became evident that pressures were mounting for a reconsideration of its status and authority and a restructuring of the program itself.

5.1. Origins and early work of the Tripartiete overleg

5.1.1. Kraayenhof's early notice of the minister's suggestion

A year prior to the suggestion by the Justice Minister, in his Explanatory Memorandum to the draft law, that "organized business" and the "organization of auditors" should take an inventory of valuation principles used in "the economic and social climate", as well as judge their acceptability, NIvRA President A.F. Tempelaar and J. Kraayenhof, the father of the suggestion, advised the NIvRA membership that this novel form of collaboration was in the offing and represented an important step forward.

The occasion for these remarks was the inaugural membership meeting of the NIvRA on 28 April 1967, following its official designation as the regulatory body for the auditing profession. Tempelaar, whose presidential term bridged the winding up of the NIvA and the formation of the NIvRA, advised the assembled members that the auditing profession would be expected to play a more activist role in interpreting the new regulation. He spoke as follows:

> A new legal regulation of financial reporting is in the making. This constitutes an appeal to the profession to formulate its opinions clearly on the questions concerned and to make them known both collectively and individually. The auditing profession must pay sufficient attention to the developments that will follow from this legal regulation. Concerning aspects of this legal regulation on which consultation or even guidance from the auditing profession may be expected, [the profession] should be able to meet these expectations fully.
>
> One of the important questions being accentuated by the coming legal regulation of financial statements is the shaping of the demands that the financial reporting must meet, concerning both their contents and presentation (sometimes simply referred to as the question of "accounting principles"). In cooperation with business and the universities, the auditing profession will have to play a leading role.[1]

Kraayenhof, who followed Tempelaar on the podium, was more explicit and direct. He was, after all, a member of the three-man committee appointed by the Justice Minister to propose a draft law based on the Verdam Commission report, and he had been an influential adviser to the financial reporting subcommittee of the Verdam Commission. He spoke as follows:

> The chairman [Tempelaar] has, in connection [with the expected legal regulation of financial reporting], pointed out that the auditing profession, in cooperation with business, shall have to play a leading role in shaping the demands placed on financial reporting. Especially, he pointed out the problem of the so-called "accounting principles", which signify the valuation principles and other guidelines for companies' financial statements. I do not merely want to underscore this task lying before the profession, but state as my conviction that this should be given high priority.[2]

After noting that "a very important and urgent task for the boards of companies" was "to choose from the alternative methods ... that fall within the norms implied by the law", Kraayenhof remarked,

> It cannot be other than that the auditor must be closely involved with this choice.

1 "Rede van de voorzitter van het N.I.v.R.A., de heer A.F. Tempelaar", at the "Eerste bijeenkomst van de ledenvergadering van de Orde Nederlands Instituut van Registeraccountants", in *de Accountant*, vol. 74, no. 1, May 1967, pp. 10–11.

2 "Rede van de heer J. Kraayenhof", in *ibid.*, p. 17. Page numbers cited in the text refer to this speech.

> Now, where will the two parties find sufficient guidance in the literature concerning the acceptable alternatives? Even auditors will have to rely to a considerable extent on the insight acquired from their continual and numerous contacts with questions of financial reporting, and on this ground give a more or less objective judgment, without, however, being able to show their clients publications that give adequate guidance from professional sources. My conclusion is that the encouragement of pronouncements in this area, supported by leading organs of business life and a representative organ of the Institute, should be seen as an urgent task for both business and the auditing profession. In my opinion, the course to be followed would be that a committee created by the Institute would make an inventory of the valuation principles and other guidelines followed in the [economic and social] climate, and that the criterion of acceptability would be applied in combined consultation between a committee appointed by the Council of Employers Federations and the committee of the Institute.
>
> I think that this is of preeminent importance, especially in connection with the circumstance known to you that, on the basis of the draft law, an Enterprise Chamber of the Amsterdam Court can be called upon to give a verdict on disputes in this area. In such a case, how will the two proposed "expert members" of that Chamber be able to test their opinion objectively concerning "acceptability in the economic and social climate" and to make it plausible to their fellow lawyer-members [of the Chamber] (p. 18)?

Kraayenhof appended an ominous note: "There is a danger that the much-desired freedom and scope for development in this matter will be lost in a rigidity that will unintentionally force itself upon us" (p. 18). The possible threat to the auditor's professionalism inherent in the new order being imposed on auditors and companies may well have been a concern to a number of those in Kraayenhof's audience. Less than six months earlier, Prof. A.M. van Rietschoten had suggested, in his Accountantsdag address, that the Enterprise Chamber could place the auditor on the defensive:

> After the auditor has declared that the financial statements are correct, a court decision might be taken to the effect that the financial statements nevertheless do not meet the requirements of the law.
>
> The diminution of the authority of the auditor's report that might result from this must be avoided by the auditors as much as possible.[3]

G.L. Groeneveld, writing in late 1966, concurred with van Rietschoten's specter of concern.[4]

Since the draft law had not even been presented to Parliament at the time of Kraayenhof's speech, many in the audience may not have appreciated the

---

[3] A.M. van Rietschoten, "De accountantscontrole in het Nederlandse bedrijfsleven anno 1966", in *de Accountant*, vol. 73, no. 1, September 1966, p. 9.

[4] G.L. Groeneveld, "'Goed koopmansgebruik' of bedrijfseconomisch beginsel in de jaarrekening", in *Stramien – Een bundel opstellen rond de beroepsregelen voor accountants* (Deventer: N.V. Uitgeversmaatschappij Æ.E. Kluwer, 1967), pp. 237–238.

full gravity of his message. The occasion on which Kraayenhof appeared before the large audience was for the purpose of celebrating, after decades of ceaseless striving, the legal regulation of the auditing profession. The passage of major legislation on financial reporting, while widely expected, may not have preoccupied many minds on that day.

5.1.2. The minister's prompting suggestion and the NIvRA's response

In May 1968, Justice Minister C.H.F. Polak inserted a suggestion in his Explanatory Memorandum to the draft law, which sent reverberations throughout the auditing profession. It dealt with Article 5, on valuation and income determination principles, and was as follows:

> I expect that organized business in collaboration with the organization of auditors will consider it to be their task to make an inventory of these [valuation] principles used in the economic and social climate, as intended in Article 5, and to judge them on the basis of what, in their opinion, can be considered as acceptable in the economic and social climate and as fulfilling the demands in Articles 2 and 3. The resulting publications concerning acceptable principles will meet a clear need on the part of enterprise managements, and can serve as a point of reference as well for the Enterprise Chamber when a case in this area is brought before it.[5]

The minister's recommendation represented a confirmation of the proposal so strongly endorsed by Kraayenhof at the NIvRA membership meeting in April 1967. The NIvRA made known in its first annual report, issued in the latter part of 1968, that it was setting up an Advisory Committee on Annual Reporting (CAJ, Commissie van Advies inzake Jaarverslaggeving) "to conduct research concerning opinions and insights into the matter of financial reporting of enterprises in the Netherlands and abroad. Furthermore, the committee is to study financial reporting insofar as it results from current or expected legal regulation in order to contribute, as a professional body, to the shaping of the requirements that financial reporting must meet". It was added that "consultations are in progress on the manner by which, in due course, a form of cooperation between organized business and the NIvRA can be realized".[6]

The CAJ was installed on 19 June 1969, and Drs J. Los, the NIvRA president, pointed out that the creation of the committee marked the start of a new phase in the life of the profession, which coincided with the new public status of the NIvRA following passage of the Registered Auditors Act (Wet op de Registeraccountants) in 1962. In the past, Los said, it was a consistent policy of the NIvRA

[5] *Bijlagen Handelingen Tweede Kamer, Zitting 1967–1968*, no. 3, p. 14. Articles 2 and 3 of the 1970 Act dealt with general principles. For further particulars, see the sections on the Verdam Commission report and on the drafting of the Act on Annual Financial Statements, in Chapter 4.

[6] *Jaarverslag, periode 28 april 1967 tot en met 31 augustus 1968*, Nederlands Instituut van Registeraccountants, p. 13.

to be "introverted" ("*introvert*") in its focus. Los chose to view the committee's assignment in broad terms, as follows:

> This charge [contained in the minister's Explanatory Memorandum] does therefore not only include the making of an inventory of, and evaluating, the current norms and usages, but, as well – and I would like to say even with emphasis: luckily – a possibility for the development of new norms in our fast-developing society. In this way, [there will be a continuation of the] leeway that has benefited Dutch business life and the Dutch auditing profession in the past, as a result of which [financial] reporting in our country compares favorably in many respects with that abroad .... In many countries, detailed prescriptions are being given for the preparation of financial statements, and professional organizations in those countries have published "accounting principles" in which a certain preoccupation with details, and therefore rigidity, cannot be denied. I hope and trust, completely, that your committee will succeed in producing such publications, in concert with organized business, that will guarantee the necessary flexibility in the application of principles.[7]

The CAJ's founding chairman, Prof. A.M. van Rietschoten, a senior partner in the audit firm of Frese, Hogeweg, Meyer & Hörchner, was a former president of the NIvA who, as noted above, had raised a concern over the impact of the Enterprise Chamber on the credibility of the auditor's report. Van Rietschoten was a respected elder of the profession. The other members of the nine-man committee reflected diverse backgrounds:

F. Tiebout, secretary, a partner in the audit firm of Vereenigde Accountantskantoren
P.C. Breek, a member of Philips' management board
Drs J. Broertjes, the chief internal auditor of Hoogovens
Prof.drs R. Burgert, of the Nederlandse Economische Hogeschool
J.A. Burggraaff, a partner in the audit firm of Doornbos, De Brey, Spits & Co.
A. van Dongen, chief internal auditor in the Ministry of Finance
Drs H.F. Oosterholt, a partner in the audit firm of Moret, De Jong & Starke
D.J. Wiersma, a partner in the audit firm of Dijker, Bianchi en Vink.[8]

---

[7] Rede, uitgesproken door de heer drs. J. Los, voorzitter van het N.I.v.R.A., bij de installatie van de C.A.J. [19 June 1969] (CAJ 63). The reference "(CAJ 63)" is to a minute book from the files of the NIvRA.

In the speeches by Tempelaar, Kraayenhof and Los, the Anglo-Saxon term "accounting principles" was not translated into Dutch, but instead was cited in its original English, within quotation marks, underscoring the novelty of this concept in the Dutch literature. Even today, when there has been extensive Dutch experience with "accounting principles", the term continues to be rendered in English (but without quotation marks).

[8] These were the affiliations shown in the *Ledenlijst 1968* of the NIvRA. H.M. Jorritsma, an employee in van Rietschoten's firm, was attached to the committee as a supplementary secretary.

While the career of the CAJ was thus launched with a suitable expression of optimism, the auditing profession had, save for the reports of three subcommittees of the NIvA's Advisory Committee on Professional Matters in 1956 and 1962 (see Chapters 3 and 4), no tradition of giving advice to its members, let alone also to companies, on accounting principles. As Los accurately stated in his installation speech, the historical position of the NIvA on such matters had been "introverted". Auditors did not see it as their responsibility to make rules, but only to audit according to the rules made by others.[9] There was also a feeling among auditors that, as they all possessed the required expertise, there was no need for formal guidance. The CAJ, therefore, represented an entirely new institutional role for auditors, one that was created only because the Justice Minister had issued an invitation that could not be ignored.

5.1.3. Important players in the field of financial reporting

When discussing the events from 1969 onward, it is important to understand the roles that were played by several institutions and organizations. Shortly, it will be important as well to appreciate the roles played by key individuals. The initiative taken by the Justice Minister eventually led to the formation of the Tripartite Study Group (TO, Tripartiete overleg),[10] which was composed of delegations of employers, employees and auditors.

As mentioned above, the minister wanted to stimulate a form of cooperation between "organized business" and "the organization of auditors". Only one ele-

---

9 Interviews with J.A. Burggraaff, 10 September 1990, and with Prof.drs J.W. Schoonderbeek, 17 December 1990. Also see J.W. Schoonderbeek, "Wet op de jaarrekening van ondernemingen, Het accountantsberoep en de", entry in Prof. A. Goudeket, Prof. A.M. van Rietschoten and A.F. Tempelaar (editors), "Part V: Controleleer", in Prof. Dr. Abram Mey (general editor), *Encyclopedie van de bedrijfseconomie* (Bussum: Uitgeversmaatschappij W. de Haan, 1970), p. 270.

10 The English language equivalent of the uniquely Dutch word "*overleg*" is ordinarily rendered as consultation or deliberation. A resulting translation of "Tripartite Consultation", to describe a committee or group, makes for awkward syntax. Most Dutch commentators, when writing in English, have translated "Tripartiete overleg" as either Tripartite Study Group or Tripartite Accounting Study Group. Since the term "accounting" does not appear in the Dutch title, the authors would prefer the former. As a simplifying device, the authors hereafter refer to the Tripartiete overleg as the TO. In quoted material, the same usage will be followed. Prior to August 1971, when the TO came into existence, the study group was bipartite, consisting of auditors and employers delegations only. In referring to the bipartite study group, the authors will use the term "study group".

In October 1981, an English language version of the accumulated "Considered Views" (the final statements issued by the TO), as rewritten in 1980 by Prof.dr J. Klaassen and retitled as "Guidelines", was published under the title, *Netherlands Accounting Guidelines*, by "The Tripartite Accounting Standards Committee". In the authors' view, a translation of "Tripartiete overleg" as Tripartite Accounting Standards Committee does not suitably capture the authority position of the TO, since the term "standards" as employed in the national standard-setting programs in the USA and the UK has implied degrees of specificity and obligatoriness that have never been associated with the "Considered Views".

ment of "organized business" was involved all of the time, namely, the employers. In general, one can say that the employers delegation, representing the Council of Dutch Employers Federations (Raad van Nederlandse Werkgeversverbonden) did not initiate proposals to expand the contents of financial statements or of the associated disclosures, but instead reacted to the initiatives taken by the auditors.[11] The employees delegation, representing the Consultative Council of Trade Unions (Overlegorgaan Vakcentrales) was involved, but not with the same degree of intensity as that of the employers. This differential degree of interest is understandable, because the issues to be raised struck at the freedom and privacy of company managements, while financial reporting was a relatively low priority of employees and their organizations.

The NIvRA took an active role from the beginning, and its newly established committee, the CAJ, took the lead in preparing drafts for consideration by the TO.

The Justice Minister himself adopted a rather passive position. He did not take any other initiatives, but awaited the results of the collaboration he had inspired. He conveyed the government's views to the European Economic Community (EEC) concerning the contents of the Fourth and Seventh Directives, and once these were approved, he managed the process by which legislation was proposed to adapt Dutch law to the Directives. During the parliamentary debates leading up to passage of the Act on Annual Financial Statements in 1970, J. Kraayenhof served as the first accounting adviser to the Justice Ministry. Successive accounting advisers have been H.C. Treffers, Mr P.A. Wessel and, since 1 January 1990, Prof.drs G.G.M. Bak.

Another important body was the Enterprise Chamber (Ondernemingskamer), a branch of the Court of Justice at Amsterdam, which was created by the Act on Annual Financial Statements. A novel tribunal in the Netherlands, and unexampled in other countries,[12] it has exclusive jurisdiction over all judicial proceedings brought against companies on the ground that their financial statements have deviated from the law. Each case is heard by three full-time judges and two experts, usually auditors, drawn from a panel maintained by the Chamber. The first decisions on financial reporting were announced by the Enterprise Chamber in 1977. Many lawsuits were filed by SOBI (Stichting Onderzoek Bedrijfs-Informatie-Foundation to Investigate Company Reporting), a social pressure group founded in 1976 by Drs Pieter T. Lakeman, whose university degree was taken in econometrics. Its purpose was to improve financial information in the Netherlands,

[11] One should recall that, in 1955 and 1962, the employers federations took very significant initiatives. In those years, the reports of the Rijkens and Hamburger committees, respectively, were published, containing progressive proposals for the improvement of company financial reporting. See the discussions of the Rijkens report in Chapter 3, and of the Hamburger report in Chapter 4.

[12] Interview with Prof.mr P. Sanders, 24 August 1990.

and its primary activity was to bring companies before the Enterprise Chamber when their financial statements were believed to fall short of what the law required.[13] After SOBI was successful in several lawsuits, it was considered as a player to be reckoned with in the field of financial reporting.[14]

5.1.4. Organization and early work of the CAJ and the TO

5.1.4.1. Preliminary discussion by the NIvRA

At its meeting on 27 March 1968, the management board (Raad van bestuur) of the NIvRA, with Tempelaar as president, discussed the setting up of contacts with the employers about accounting principles. According to Tempelaar, it was not the board's intention that strict decisions be made, but rather that guidelines be provided to the Enterprise Chamber. Some members of the board wanted the employees to be involved, else the NIvRA might seem to have made a choice favorable to the employers. But Tempelaar was of the view that the preparation of financial statements was a matter of concern to the companies alone. In the discussion, the Social and Economic Council (SER, Sociaal-Economische Raad) was suggested as a possible party to the discussion group, because it would assure a role for the employees (B Not 254–255).[15] In the end, on 10 December 1968, a delegation of the NIvRA board met with four representatives of the Consultative Council of Trade Unions. The union representatives took the position that the NIvRA should begin the process of developing memoranda, following which it should engage in consultation with the employers and employees (WV 163).[16] On 11 December 1968, the Council of the Dutch Employers Federations accepted the NIvRA board's invitation to attend an organizational meeting.

---

[13] Interview with Drs Pieter T. Lakeman, 5 November 1990.

[14] For a discussion of the Enterprise Chamber and the early cases brought by SOBI, see Jan Klaassen, "An Accounting Court: The Impact of the Enterprise Chamber on Financial Reporting in the Netherlands", in *The Accounting Review*, vol. 55, no. 2, April 1980, pp. 327–341. For discussion of the role that SOBI has played as a social pressure group, together with comments on the early Enterprise Chamber cases, see Henk Volten, *Challenges to Financial Reporting in the Netherlands – How Corporate Reporting is Monitored by Social Pressure Groups*, PILOT (Netherlands) 9 (Amsterdam: Nederlands Instituut van Registeraccountants, November 1979).

[15] This citation refers to the minutes of the NIvRA's management board.

[16] There are five sets of minute books that will be cited here. "WV" refers mainly to the minute book dealing with the NIvRA's involvement in the final revision stages of the draft law leading up to the Act on Annual Financial Statements of 1970. "CAJ Perm" refers to the set of minute books containing documents relating to the CAJ's work. "CAJ Werkg" refers to the minute books covering the period from February 1969 through July 1971, when the auditors and employers delegations were holding meetings, before the employees delegation joined. "CAJ Not" refers to the minute books containing the records of CAJ meetings, together with the correspondence sent and received. (The first volume of the minutes of CAJ meetings, through the meeting of 12 November 1969, is labeled "CAJ".) "JO Alg" refers to the minute books for the TO. All of these minute books are housed in the offices of the NIvRA.

5.1.4.2. Initial organization of the TO

On 18 February 1969, a delegation of employers, representing the Council of Dutch Employers Federations, met with a delegation from the NIvRA. The view was expressed by the NIvRA representatives that financial reporting was primarily a responsibility of the employers, but that the auditors had a co-responsibility. A.F. Tempelaar, speaking for the NIvRA group, said that consideration should be given to inviting a delegation of employees as one of the users of financial statements. It was mentioned that the NIvRA had already made an initial contact with the Consultative Council of Trade Unions.

Two alternative approaches to carrying out the minister's suggestion were advanced at the meeting. The first would be the establishment of a broad-based committee, with members representing an array of interested parties, with delegations of equal size, where the NIvRA would be just one of the participating groups. The second would be a more loosely organized arrangement in which a NIvRA committee would produce position papers for discussion and comment by interested parties. Both alternatives presupposed that a consensus would eventually emerge from the deliberations.

It was agreed that the preparatory work would be done by the CAJ, and that its drafts would be commented upon by other interested groups (*andere milieus*). Thereafter, the drafts would be discussed by the parties "sitting together" ("*in gezamenlijk overleg*"). The employers did not want a formal structure for the activity. On this point, the auditors signified their agreement. In this spirit, the procedures to be used when voting on drafts were not discussed. It was also agreed that the results of the study group's deliberations, to the extent they were published, would never have a character other than "knowledgeable advice" ("*deskundig advies*"). During the meeting, the employers expressed the opinion that "acceptability in the economic and social climate" pointed in the direction of "flexible norms" ("*soepele normen*") (CAJ Werkg 2–3).

At the next meeting of the two delegations, on 15 April, the employers confirmed the understanding reached at the February meeting. However, they reported that the Council of Dutch Employers Federations had, at its last meeting, registered a negative reaction to the earlier approach by the NIvRA, in December 1968, to the Consultative Council of Trade Unions to ask that it send a delegation to the study group. The employers Council held the belief that "organized business", as used in the minister's communication, concerned only the employers and the auditors, and it was critical of the initiative taken by the NIvRA.[17]

[17] Several years later, P.C. Louwers, the chief internal auditor of Philips and the 1971 president of the NIvRA, said that "Some people are horrified by the sheer idea that union-representatives should even be involved in the formulation of accounting principles, but so far this joint exercise of the organisations of employers, employees and accountants in my country is working to everybody's satisfaction." P.C. Louwers, *The trend towards fuller disclosure and wider dissemination of financial information*, a paper presented at the 1973 Conference on Company

Also during the April meeting, the employers announced that the Council of Dutch Employers Federations would form a committee similar to the CAJ, and that this committee would carry on discussions with the CAJ (WV 245). The Council's decision to accelerate its participation may have been motivated by the heightened prospect of formal involvement by a delegation of employees.

During the summer of 1969, the NIvRA and the Council of Dutch Employers Federations jointly informed the Justice Minister that, "on the part of the Consultative Council of Trade Unions, there is definitely an interest in these questions, but not to such an extent that they wish to be involved in an organized way from the outset. However, the Consultative Council would appreciate the opportunity to give its opinion on the final result of the deliberations".[18] At this early stage, therefore, the initiative was only bipartite.

5.1.4.3. Initial work program of the CAJ: 1969–71

Two principal tasks were laid before the CAJ as the Act on Annual Financial Statements was nearing final parliamentary approval: (1) to undertake studies leading to judgments or recommendations that would have the effect of giving concrete form to the general principles in the Act, and (2) to draft materials in support of the nascent collaboration between the NIvRA and the Council of Dutch Employers Federations to make an inventory of valuation principles.[19]

Following its installation in June 1969, the CAJ met on a regular basis and began to discuss priorities. Copies of a research study issued by the accounting research division of the American Institute of Certified Public Accountants (AICPA), *A Statement of Basic Accounting Postulates*, by Maurice Moonitz, were distributed to the members.[20]

At the committee's meeting of 20 August, Prof.drs R. Burgert said that either

Financial Reporting in the E.E.C., organized by the *Financial Times*, the Institute of Chartered Accountants in England and Wales, and the *Investors Chronicle*, p. 9.

The employers were of the view that the unions had nothing to do with accounting principles, and that a meeting attended by both to discuss the subject would not be in order. Interview with A.F. Tempelaar, 18 July 1991. Also, interviews with J.A. Burggraaff, 10 September 1990, and with J.P. van Rossem, 12 November 1990.

[18] The quotation has been taken from a letter dated 25 July 1969 from the Nederlands Instituut van Registeraccountants to the Overlegorgaan Vakcentrales (WV 275), which refers to the joint letter, since the joint letter dated 18 June 1969 to the minister has not been preserved.

[19] Verslag van de werkzaamheden van de Commissie van Advies inzake Jaarverslaggeving (C.A.J.) over het jaar 1969/1970, in *Jaarverslag 1969/1970*, Nederlands Instituut van Registeraccountants, pp. 46–47.

[20] This volume had been published as Accounting Research Study no. 1 in 1961 and was used as the basis for the controversial follow-up study, no. 3, written by Moonitz and Robert T. Sprouse, *A Tentative Set of Broad Accounting Principles for Business Enterprises* (New York: AICPA, 1962). This latter study recommended a set of preferred accounting principles, and favored current cost accounting. The study was discarded by the Accounting Principles Board as being "too radically different from present generally accepted accounting principles for acceptance at this time". *Statement by the Accounting Principles Board*, dated 13 April 1962. Both Moonitz and Sprouse were accounting academics.

the NIvRA should provide the CAJ with a large budget to support a scientific staff of four or five persons to be attached to the committee, or the committee should translate the US accounting principles into Dutch, omitting those portions that were not relevant to the Netherlands. He believed that the committee should not repeat work that had already had been done well by others.[21] Burgert proposed that the committee use the recent research study issued by the AICPA's accounting research division, *Inventory of Generally Accepted Accounting Principles for Business Enterprises*, by Paul Grady, as the starting point.[22] Grady's mission had been to take an inventory of principles actually in use, which, in Burgert's view, provided an analogy to the task given to the CAJ.

At the meeting of 1 October, it was agreed that several committee members would prepare discussion memoranda on the main categories of objectives and principles (A through D) in Grady's work, with assignments as follows (CAJ 218):

A. Income and expense – Broertjes.
B. Equity – Breek.
C. Assets – Oosterholt.
D. Liabilities – Burggraaff.

Categories B, C, and D were given priority status in the committee's work. Van Rietschoten asked Oosterholt to write a memorandum on inventories, and van Rietschoten assigned himself the task of drafting a statement on long-term shareholdings (CAJ Perm 484). This subject was also placed on the committee's priority list.

Grady's category E, insofar as it dealt with reporting standards, was considered to be less important, and was not assigned. Nonetheless, two other subjects included in Grady's category E, consolidated statements and the valuation methods used in connection with investments, were, as a consequence of Articles 12 and 13 of the Act on Annual Financial Statements, placed on the priority list.

Much of 1970 was taken up with preparing and debating the various discussion memoranda, which were the starting points for development of the topical sections in the exposure drafts. At the same time, the committee's other activities, arising from assignments begun by the former Advisory Committee on Professional Matters, began to multiply. Subcommittees were formed to deal with the reporting by banks, property insurance companies, and life insurance companies,

---

[21] Burgert's proposal for a budget request for 200 000 to 300 000 guilders was forwarded to the NIvRA's management board, but it was not approved. Interview with Prof.drs R. Burgert, 24 September 1990.

[22] Interview with Prof.drs R. Burgert, 24 September 1990. Grady's book had been published in 1965 as Accounting Research Study no. 7, and was, by far, the largest-selling study in the series. Grady was a retired partner of Price Waterhouse & Co. and was serving as director of the Institute's accounting research division, which had commissioned the study. His book was widely regarded as an authoritative statement of US generally accepted accounting principles.

in the light of recent or expected legislation.

At the meeting on 13 October 1970, the committee decided that the inclusion in a company's annual report of only consolidated financial statements, and not the holding company's statements as well, was not acceptable. However, at the meeting in December there was discussion about the fact that one of the Sijthoff Prizes had just been awarded to N.V. Chemische Fabriek "Naarden", which had presented only consolidated financial statements.(CAJ Not 129)

At the 24 November meeting, the committee discussed a 6-page, double-spaced memorandum prepared by van Rietschoten entitled "*Beschouwingen over de met betrekking tot jaarrekeningen van ondernemingen in het maatschappelijk verkeer toegepaste grondslagen waarop de waardering van de activa en passiva en de bepaling van het resultaat berusten*" ("Considered views relating to the principles used in the economic and social climate, dealing with the valuation of assets and liabilities and the determination of income in the financial statements of enterprises") (CAJ Perm 272–278). This was the first use in the committee's deliberations of the term "Considered Views" (*Beschouwingen*) in this particular sense. "Considered Views" was to become the title of the series of the statements issued by the TO from 1971 to 1979. Van Rietschoten has said that the term was his choice, and was intended to mean "a conclusion by informed people without being a regulation admitting of no exceptions".[23]

At the December and January meetings, the committee discussed successive revisions of van Rietschoten's memorandum, which outlined the nature and scope of the task facing the study group. His plan was that the memorandum, once adopted by the committee, would be forwarded to a study group composed of delegations from the NIvRA and the Council of Dutch Employers Federations. As will be noted below, such a study group began a series of regular meetings in December 1970 under van Rietschoten's chairmanship.

At the 26 January 1971 meeting, the committee also discussed an 18-page, single-spaced introductory memorandum by Burgert (CAJ Perm 379–392), which was submitted as a conceptual underpinning for the series of exposure drafts. Its title was "*Inleiding bij de uiteenzetting van de grondslagen, welke bij de opstelling van de jaarrekening van ondernemingen als in het maatschappelijk verkeer aanvaard kunnen worden beschouwd*" ("Introduction to the exposition of the principles, used in preparing the financial statements, that can be considered as accepted in the economic and social climate"). The memorandum contained a 12-page historical note on the implications of different valuation principles for financial reporting, followed by a discussion of five premises underlying financial statement information: the current state of the economic and social order, going concern, the purchasing power of money, conservatism, and income smoothing. While the committee was impressed with the contents of Burgert's paper, it was

---

[23] Interview with Prof. A.M. van Rietschoten, 23 November 1990.

not accepted, as the committee believed that it was more suitable for a scientific journal than for a publication addressed to the general public. Van Rietschoten believed that it was essential that the committee reach unanimous agreement. The members of the employers delegation, he believed, would be divided along their own company interests, and if there were seen to be a division of views among the auditors, who were the technicians, van Rietschoten believed that the study group might founder. To begin with a highly conceptual statement, he believed, would inevitably lead to controversy and dissent, and would, at the least, delay publication of the first draft. The committee had to lead with a proposal on fairly straightforward issues on which agreement could be obtained. Van Rietschoten made every attempt to prevent the filing of a minority report, and he feared that one was in the making. Burgert, on the other hand, believed that van Rietschoten was in too much of a hurry to issue a publication as soon as possible.[24] In the end, the committee approved van Rietschoten's memorandum, with some minor amendments (CAJ Not 146–147).

By the end of May 1971, the CAJ believed that it had reached a stage at which several of the memoranda intended for the topical sections of the first exposure draft could be forwarded to the study group.

At the CAJ's meeting of 22 June, it was learned that the Consultative Council of Trade Unions had agreed to send several representatives to a meeting with the employers and auditors delegations, to be held on 19 August (CAJ Not 197). Van Rietschoten, who was to be chairman of the TO,[25] admitted that the chairmanship of both the CAJ and the TO would constitute a heavy workload, but he said that it would lead to more effective coordination (CAJ Not 211).

5.1.4.4. Launching of the work of the TO

On 23 January 1970, the CAJ sent a letter to the NIvRA management board, suggesting that it establish contact with the corresponding committee of the Council of Dutch Employers Federations (CAJ Werkg 17–19). The CAJ believed it to be important that the initiative for such a meeting originate with the NIvRA. In its letter, the CAJ proposed ten statements of issues concerning: the interpretation of the draft law that was nearing final approval, accounting principles, and the approach to be used by the committees (for example, should

---

[24] Interviews with Drs J.F. Leeuwerik, 25 June 1990; with Prof.drs R. Burgert, 24 September 1990; and with Prof. A.M. van Rietschoten, 23 November 1990.

In August 1971, Burgert resigned from the committee in order to begin writing a book on the Act on Annual Financial Statements of 1970. He was of the belief that some might see a potential conflict between his continued service on the committee and the writing of his book. Interview with Prof.drs R. Burgert, 24 September 1990.

[25] As noted above, TO will be used for Tripartiete overleg, which is translated by some authors as "Tripartite Study Group". In the next subsection, which begins with a discussion of the early development of the TO, before it became tripartite in August 1971, the term "study group" will be used.

there be a systematic review of published financial statements?). Numbers 2 and 4 in the CAJ's list dealt with current costs and were of particular interest:

> **2.** As a general consequence of the paragraphs in Articles 2 and 3 [of the draft law], it could be maintained that meeting these requirements in subsequent balance sheets and profit and loss statements can be achieved only by periodic (either yearly or otherwise) revaluations in the balance sheet and profit and loss statement.
> **4.** In interpreting the draft law, it is not intended and is not practical as well to explain Article 5 in such a way that the valuation principles of each balance sheet and profit and loss statement must involve so-called current costs.
>
> The use of historical cost certainly represents a great numerical majority [of companies]. Historical cost should remain a legally permitted valuation principle, albeit not without limit.
>
> If valuation based on historical cost differs considerably from that on the basis of current cost, statements in the notes have to be used in order to comply with the general requirement of Article 2 and/or Article 3. This requires an indication of permitted tolerance and of the nature of the information in the notes (CAJ Werkg 18).

According to an earlier version of this list, it was drafted by van Rietschoten and another member of the CAJ on the basis of preceding discussions and, among other sources, the Grady study (CAJ 248). Following an exchange of correspondence between the management board and the CAJ, resulting from the former's suggestion that several of the statements would be better phrased as questions, the management board forwarded the list of issues to the Council of Dutch Employers Federations on 27 March (CAJ Werkg 23–26).

Apparently, the employers were very slow in responding, for it was not until the CAJ meeting of 13 October that an announcement was made that consultations were in progress to set a date for the first meeting with the employers (CAJ Not 96).

On 10 December, delegations from the NIvRA and the Council of Dutch Employers Federations began a series of meetings to discuss the drafts being prepared by the CAJ (CAJ Werkg 28). It was then that the bipartite study group came into existence. P.C. Louwers, who was shortly to become the 1971 NIvRA president, chaired the first meeting. Subsequent meetings were under the chairmanship of van Rietschoten.

At the meeting of 17 February 1971, the study group received van Rietschoten's memorandum from the CAJ, and began its deliberations. In June, a package of drafts on specific topics was transmitted from the CAJ to the study group, built upon on the discussion memoranda prepared along the lines of Grady's work.

During almost all of the study group's meetings, a constant agenda item was how to include a delegation of employees in the deliberations. Furthermore, there was an indication that the Justice Minister had begun to inquire about the absence of published statements resulting from his suggestion made in 1968, and the feeling arose in the meetings of the two delegations that the process should be speeded up. Although the employees had shown an interest in participating in the final stages of the approval of a statement, it was felt that their involvement sequentially, rather than contemporaneously, would attenuate the process (CAJ Werkg 54, 66, 95). On 24 February, the heads of the two delegations jointly wrote the Consultative Council of Trade Unions to solicit the names of some representatives with whom they might continue to discuss the involvement of the unions in the process. On 16 March, the trade union groups responded with three names (CAJ Werkg 50–51, 62). Nonetheless, there seemed to be some ambivalence on the part of the Council of Dutch Employers Federations to bring in the union representatives.

On 26 March, it was announced that a special meeting would be called at which the heads of the two delegations and the presidents of the NIvRA and the Federation of Dutch Industries (VNO)[26] would confer with J. Kraayenhof and H.C. Treffers, the accounting advisers to the Justice Ministry.[27] The concern that lay behind the call for the special meeting stemmed from the parties' reluctance to complete the procedural steps necessary to incorporate the employees into the study group. At the meeting, which was held on 19 April, Kraayenhof suggested that, if no results were soon forthcoming, the minister might install a committee of his own. The Act on Annual Financial Statements was set to go into effect on 1 May, and Kraayenhof was of the opinion that, given the amount of work already invested by the CAJ and the bipartite study group, a draft ought to be ready for publication in three months. Any procedures that might be necessary to involve the employees in the formal deliberations, he added, should not be allowed to delay publication of the first draft. At the close of the meeting, the president of the VNO stated that his organization would shortly announce its position on the participation by the employees (CAJ Werkg 89, 90, 93).

Finally, in the study group's meeting of 10 June the deadlock was broken. The two delegations resolved to invite the three union representatives to attend a meeting in August to discuss the CAJ's drafts, with the full expectation, one supposes, that a three-way deliberative process would begin (CAJ Werkg 135; CAJ Not 197).

At the meeting of 19 August 1971, seventeen persons were present: eight in the employers delegation, six in the auditors delegation, and three in the employees delegation, as follows:

---

[26] The VNO provided the leadership in the Council of Dutch Employers Federations.

[27] As indicated in the section, "Drafting of the Act on Annual Financial Statements", in Chapter 4, the minister's suggestion that "organized business" and the organization of auditors take an inventory of the valuation principles in the economic and social climate, and judge their acceptability, was attributed to Kraayenhof.

Employers (representing the Council of Dutch Employers Federations)

- [C. Bovenberg, board member (i.e., director) of Vihamij-Buttinger N.V. – not present].
- Mr E.J. Egberts, retired board member of Amstel Brouwerij N.V. (head of the delegation).
- P.G.G. Frederiks, head of Central Accounting, Akzo N.V.
- J.A. Hamburger, president of Koninklijke Hamburger B.V.
- Mr R. Hoorens van Heijningen, secretary of the Federation of Dutch Industries (VNO, Verbond van Nederlandse Ondernemingen).
- Mr J.H. Mesker, head of the legal department, C&A (Unicena/Intercena).
- Drs W. Schattinga, retired former chief accountant for the European Continent, Unilever.
- Prof.dr Th.M. Scholten, board member of Steenkolen-Handelsvereeniging N.V. (SHV).
- Mr H.C. Wesseling, member of the legal department, Unilever, and chairman of the board of the Unilever pension fund.

Auditors (representing the NIvRA)[28]

- M.A. Allart, Moret & Limperg
- Drs A.J. Bosman, partner in Vereenigde Accountantskantoren Dijker en Doornbos.
- J.A. Burggraaff, partner in Vereenigde Accountantskantoren Dijker en Doornbos.
- Prof. A.M. van Rietschoten (chairman of the TO).
- J.P. van Rossem, partner in Van Dien, Van Uden, Besançon, Koppenberg & Co.
- A.F. Tempelaar, partner in Vereenigde Accountantskantoren Dijker en Doornbos.

Employees (representing the Consultative Council of Trade Unions)

- J.F. Hoogland, staff of the Dutch Federation of Trade Unions (NVV, Nederlands Verbond van Vakverenigingen).
- Drs J.P.M. Nabbe, staff of the Dutch Catholic Trade Union Federation (NKV, Nederlands Katholiek Vakverbond).
- Drs G.H. Terpstra, staff of the Christian National Trade Union Federation (CNV, Christelijk Nationaal Vakverbond).

---

[28] The affiliation shown for van Rossem was given in the *Ledenlijst 1970* of the NIvRA. In June 1971, Bosman and Burggraaff's firm, Doornbos, De Brey, Spits & Co., had merged with Tempelaar's firm, Vereenigde Accountantskantoren, Dijker, Bianchi & Co., to form Vereenigde Accountantskantoren Dijker en Doornbos. Interview with J.A. Burggraaff, 26 November 1991.

Three members of the employers delegation, Bovenberg, Frederiks and Schattinga, were *registeraccountants*. Bovenberg was a member of the executive committee of VNO's management board. Hamburger and Mesker did not attend any subsequent meetings. (See Appendix 5.1 for a graphical history of the TO's membership.)

Van Rietschoten was head of the auditors delegation, and Burggraaff was deputy chairman. Van Rossem served as the TO's editor, and he handled much of the drafting. Allart was installed as secretary, and was a non-voting member of the delegation. Bosman attended as a representative of the NIvRA's management board.[29]

Although the employees delegation did not formally designate a chairman, Nabbe served as its spokesman.

The first matter taken up at the meeting was whether the union representatives were willing to participate as a delegation in ongoing deliberations with the delegations of employers and auditors. The three union representatives signified their acceptance of the invitation, and, thereupon, the bipartite study group became the TO (JO Alg 4–5).

Without objection from either the employers or employees delegations, the priorities established by the CAJ were accepted, and it was agreed that "Considered Views" ("*Beschouwingen*") would be the title used for the TO's publications. Chairman van Rietschoten spoke on behalf of "Considered Views" as the preferred terminology, since the outcome of the TO's deliberations was to be advice. "*Regelen*" ("rules"), he argued, would be too strict (*klemmend*). Two members of the employees delegation asked how an inventory could be taken and a judgment made on acceptability if no requirements were to be imposed and no preferred treatment was mentioned. Van Rietschoten replied that the objective was to indicate the "boundaries of acceptability". The TO had no power, he said, to set requirements. The choice of the Legislature (*wetgever*) was to issue general criteria within the boundaries of acceptability in economic and social life. A member of the employers delegation offered the view that acceptability in the economic and social climate should be interpreted in the light of the general norms expressed in Articles 2 and 3 of the Act. There was some discussion of the procedures for issuing exposure drafts and the Considered Views. Burggraaff believed that the exposure drafts would be a useful medium for obtaining comment from colleagues, although their cost of printing and distribution had to be considered. There was no discussion of a source of financing for the TO. The

[29] In January 1972, when Burggraaff became chairman of the TO, he suggested to Bosman that it was not really necessary for a representative of the NIvRA's management board to attend the TO's meetings. Interview with Drs A.J. Bosman, 29 November 1991. Burggraaff believed that it would be awkward if his audit firm were to have two partners attending the TO's meetings, and he also believed that members of the NIvRA's management board could not afford the time to attend meetings of a study group. Telephone conversation with Drs A.J. Bosman, 5 December 1991.

NIvRA was providing financial support for the work of both the CAJ and the TO, while the members' firms or employers were supporting their participation.

The spokesman for the employees delegation doubted whether the employees' organizations had sufficient knowledge to contribute to the discussions (JO Alg 12).[30]

Questions were raised, especially by the employers, about how much detail should be included in the TO's statements.

At the next meeting, on 19 October, van Rietschoten worried about the publication schedule. A first publication, he said, should be issued before the end of 1971. The discussions in the TO on the proposed exposure draft, which was based on the discussion memorandum written by van Rietschoten that had been approved by the CAJ, did not require much time, but they were hardly devoid of controversy. The section on inventories gave rise to difficulties, and the employers submitted an alternative draft at the 29 September meeting with fewer details. The employers believed that an abbreviated memorandum was more practicable than a full-fledged statement of Considered Views. In the end, van Rossem and Frederiks collaborated in the writing of the definitive draft, which was issued as a statement of Considered Views. The concept of "economic stock" ("*economische voorraad*"), which would include in inventory the effects of sales and purchase commitments, was discussed, and it was decided that accrued losses on economic stock may, in some circumstances, have to be reflected.(JO Alg 27–28)

5.1.4.5. The first exposure draft

Once all of the delegations had given their approval, the first exposure draft was readied for publication with an issue date of 15 December 1971. Exposure drafts were issued in green covers, and quickly became known as the "green booklets". The title of the first exposure draft was *Voorontwerp van Beschouwingen naar aanleiding van de Wet op de Jaarrekening van Ondernemingen* (Provisional Draft of Considered Views as a Consequence of the Act on Annual Financial Statements of Enterprises), and reflected a rather more conservative rendering of the publication than that originally suggested by the discussion memorandum submitted by van Rietschoten to the CAJ.[31] Rather than place emphasis on the substance of the contents, namely, "the principles ... dealing with the valua-

[30] J.P.M. Nabbe had obtained a degree in *bedrijfseconomie* at the Nederlandse Economische Hogeschool, which had included some study in accounting. At the NKV, he worked in social security, health affairs, and with the works councils. Therefore, Nabbe's duties in the NKV did not bring him into touch with accounting, except, perhaps, in regard to the works councils. Hoogland was a macro-economist, and had even less background in accounting. Interview with Drs J.P.M. Nabbe, 27 September 1990.

[31] That the TO's first exposure draft was labeled as a *voorontwerp* (pre-draft) and not an *ontwerp* (draft) mirrored the cautious and restrained character that its authors sought to associate with its contents. It represented the first foray into uncertain territory by a body whose members were not accustomed to working with each other.

tion of assets and liabilities and the determination of income" (as in the title of van Rietschoten's original memorandum), the TO evidently preferred a title emphasizing the procedural link with the Act. Unlike exposure drafts issued in other countries, which have typically dealt with a single subject, the TO's draft covered a range of unrelated issues, as follows:

- Introduction
- Investments
- Other long-term shareholdings
- Inventories
- Long-term and short-term liabilities
- Liabilities not to be shown in the balance sheet.

On the title page of the exposure draft, the author was said to be the "Annual Reporting Committees" ("*Commissies jaarverslaggeving*"), suggesting a collaboration among co-equal committees representing three constituencies, instead of a single entity integrating three delegations.[32] Throughout the 1970's, the exposure drafts and the statements of Considered Views were officially ascribed to the Annual Reporting Committees, even though the CAJ referred to "*het dusgenaamde tripartite overleg*" ("the so-called tripartite study group") in its annual report of September 1972,[33] and sections in consecutive annual reports of the NIvRA's management board were devoted to the "Tripartite-overleg" beginning in 1972/73.[34]

A total of 6089 copies of the exposure draft were printed, with distribution of 3076 copies to all NIvRA members, 2000 to the VNO, 160 to the Consultative Council of Trade Unions, and 100 to the press; 503 were set aside for sale, and 250 were placed in stock (JO Alg 63).[35] This may have been the first publication arising from a collaborative undertaking by the NIvRA with another organization, and the evident intention was to achieve a wide distribution.

---

[32] The minutes of meetings referred to the "*gezamenlijke vergadering*" (combined meeting) of the three delegations, rather than to a meeting of a single study group.

[33] "Verslag van de werkzaamheden van de Commissie van Advies inzake Jaarverslaggeving (C.A.J.) over het jaar 1971/72", in *Jaarverslag 1971'72*, Nederlands Instituut van Registeraccountants, p. 73.

[34] For the first in the series of such sections in the annual reports of the NIvRA's management board, see *Jaarverslag 1972'73*, Nederlands Instituut van Registeraccountants, p. 15. On p. 12 of the same report, the exposure draft of 15 December 1971 was ascribed to the "Annual Reporting Committees".

For the years 1980 and 1981, the study group published annual reports under the title, *Verslag van de werkzaamheden over het jaar 19– van het TRIPARTIETE OVERLEG* (Report of the Activities for the year 19– of the TRIPARTITE STUDY GROUP). In 1982, as will be seen below, the TO was reorganized as the Council on Annual Reporting (RJ, Raad voor de Jaarverslaggeving).

[35] Another 1275 copies were produced in three series of reprints. All of these were sold (JO Alg 457).

This initial exposure draft, being the TO's first utterance, will be reviewed at some length, both as to approach and content.

"Introduction" to the draft. The keynote for the series of statements of Considered Views was struck in the opening section, the Introduction. It is instructive to examine the contents of this section, including the changes that were made at two stages in the developmental process: from the TO's internal draft to the published exposure draft, and from there to the final statement, which was issued in May 1974. For purposes of this comparison, the three versions will be coded as the Internal, Exposure, and Final drafts. Paragraph numbers refer to the Final version only.[36]

The Introduction was divided into three points treating the approach adopted by the TO, plus six points dealing in general terms with substantive issues, as follows[37]:

- Charge (*Opdracht*)
- Outline of future work (*Indeling van de nadere uitwerking*)
- Premises of the law (*Uitgangspunt van de wet*)
- Equity (*Het vermogen*)
- Income (*Het resultaat*)
- Changes in owners' equity (*Mutaties in het eigen vermogen*)
- Change in values over time (*De verandering van waarden in de tijd*)
- Methods of income determination (*Methoden van resultaatbepaling*)
- What are considered assets and liabilities (*Wat wordt gerekend tot de activa en pasiva*)

In the Introduction, the Considered Views were presented as the TO's response to the minister's charge, and as containing both an inventory and an evaluation of the principles used (*gehanteerd*) in the economic and social climate. In the Exposure draft, a paragraph was added to make clear that the TO's statements should not be seen as prescriptions (*voorschriften*). Giving out rules was not viewed as part of its charge. In the Final draft, the following clarification was added: They [i.e., the committees] do, however, provide guidance to practice by means of these considered views so that financial statements will correspond to the objective stated in the law" (Ia, para. 5). Another sentence added in the Exposure draft and retained in the Final draft stated that "not all principles that are currently in use have been discussed; it may not be concluded that those that are not discussed are unacceptable" (para. 6).

---

[36] The Final drafts of the Considered Views were published in looseleaf format under the title, *Beschouwingen naar aanleiding van de Wet op de jaarrekening van ondernemingen* (Deventer: Kluwer). Subsequent references to the Final drafts of Considered Views will be to this volume.

[37] The core of the Introduction to the exposure draft may be traced directly to the memorandum prepared by van Rietschoten and laid before the CAJ in November 1970.

Two passages were added to the Introduction in Final draft that dealt with coverage and method. In paragraph 3, it was stated that the TO would occasionally pay attention to matters relating to the presentation of financial statements, and in paragraph 4 it was said that, although the TO had to rely on the experience of its members, it intended to begin work on a collection of systematically gathered data.[38] The inclusion of issues dealing with presentation was, strictly viewed, an expansion of the minister's charge.

The December 1971 draft itself addressed matters of presentation, suggesting that the employers delegation had not objected to this wider interpretation of the TO's charge.

The Outline of Future Work listed an ambitious agenda of 27 items. They consisted of a catch-all item for "general topics", 21 items representing account groupings on the asset and equity sides of the balance sheet, two items relating to the profit and loss statement (methods of income determination, and the layout of the statement), an item for liabilities not to be shown in the balance sheet, and a final item for special topics (para. 9). Any impression that the TO had interpreted "valuation principles" narrowly would have been dispelled by this elaborate prospectus.

In the section on the Premises of the Law, in a passage that survived from the Internal to the Final draft with changes mostly in wording, the TO said that it might go so far as to deem a practice as unacceptable:

> The committees [i.e., the TO] focused their considered views primarily on the evaluation of what occurs in the economic and social climate. This evaluation can occasionally lead to the conclusion that something can, under certain circumstances or in the current order of things, not or no longer be considered as acceptable (para. 14).

---

[38] The tangible result of this intention was the series of biennial surveys of financial reporting practices published by the NIvRA under the title *Onderzoek Jaarverslagen*. The first survey was published in 1973 and covered the 1971 financial statements of 129 listed companies. Even though the survey findings were based on published financial statements, the identities of the companies following particular practices were not revealed. For an announcement of its availability and a summary of the contents, see "Maandelijkse notities", in *de Accountant*, vol. 80, no. 9, May 1974, pp. 388–389.

In 1973, the study group asked the Justice Ministry for financial assistance to expand the survey to include non-listed companies (JO Alg 486–487). After considerable discussion of the project, including the possible involvement of Prof.dr R. Slot, of the Rijksuniversiteit Utrecht, a budget of *f* 145 000 was proposed. In December 1975, the Ministry approved a subsidy of *f* 20 000 for "a pilot study of limited scope" (JO Alg 1038). The Limperg Instituut, it was agreed, would conduct the study. The pilot study was published in 1978, followed by an "interim study" in 1980: *Onderzoek gedeponeerde jaarrekeningen 1977* (Amsterdam: Limperg Instituut, May 1980). Although the interim study was concerned primarily with matters of method, it did contain (pp. 44–47) an assessment of the quality of 205 financial statements, mostly those of non-listed companies. The general conclusion was that 56 percent of the surveyed financial statements gave insufficient insight into income and financial position (p. 47).

In the Final draft, the TO allowed for the possibility that, when none of the alternatives could be considered as unacceptable, one alternative must nonetheless be designated as preferable. An occasion for making such a designation might be when the TO were to seek to encourage a particular development in practice (para. 14).

In the sections on equity, income, and changes in owners' equity, short statements were presented on basic, and not particularly controversial, accounting principles, such as going concern and consistency. There were also indications of what subjects would be treated in forthcoming statements of Considered Views: criteria for realization, use of estimates, and the treatment of goodwill.

Of some interest is the section on Change in Values over Time. From the Internal to Final draft, the TO counseled that changes in prices over time (an apparent allusion to the recent spurt of inflation) may make it necessary that information be provided in the financial statements in addition to historical costs. While the Exposure draft was rather unclear about the nature of this additional information, the Final draft was much more specific, calling for information on the basis of "current value" (*actuele waarde*), which was defined in terms of the Limpergian trio of current cost[39], exit value, or present value (*de vervangingswaarde, de directe opbrengstwaarde of de indirecte opbrengstwaarde*) (Ia, para. 31). From time to time, the TO added, advice would be given on the extent of value changes that would necessitate the provision of current value information relating to items in the balance sheet (para. 33). A statement was also promised on the impact of value changes on income, as well as on the question of where in the financial statements or notes such information should be shown (para. 34).

Substantive contents of the exposure draft. The three longest sections dealt with investments[40] (*deelnemingen*), other long-term securities holdings (*beleggingen*), and inventories (*voorraden*). On the subject of accounting for subsidiary investments, the TO said that the publication of consolidated statements is the recommended way of complying with the Act (Art.13, para. 1), rather than pro-

---

39 Although "replacement value" (*vervangingswaarde*) is used in the Dutch literature, the term "current cost" is used here, as being more in line with usage in the Anglo-Saxon literature on the subject of current value/current cost accounting.

40 As mentioned in Chapter 3, the term *deelnemingen*, which is rendered as "participations" or "participating interests" in many translations from the Dutch language into English, is here translated as "investments". According to the Explanatory Memorandum attached to the Act on Annual Financial Statements (paras. 12–15), a *deelneming* is "understood to be a relationship with another enterprise that is meant to be lasting and which results from the ownership of a certain part of the share capital of the latter enterprise ... : the participating company [i.e., the investor] itself has an interest in the activities of the dependent enterprise [i.e., the investee] and thus usually a certain influence on its management". *Wet op de jaarrekening van ondernemingen/Act on Annual Accounts of Enterprises*, NIVRA geschrift nummer 6 (Amsterdam: Nederlands Instituut van Registeraccountants, 1972), p. 67.

In the UK context, "investments" refers to investments in associated companies.

viding separate statements for all investments (IIa3, para. 16). The "intrinsic value" ("*intrinsieke waarde*") method[41] of carrying investments was said to be preferable, but it was permissible to use other methods.[42] (The Act stated that information about the value of an investment, and changes therein, must be given, but no specific valuation principle was prescribed (Art.12, paras. 1, 2).) The valuation of investments at 1 guilder or less was declared to be not "acceptable in the economic and social climate" (para. 25). This was a rare decision by the TO to characterize a practice as unacceptable.

The only dissent ever recorded in either an exposure draft or final statement appeared in the section on investments, where it was said that members disagreed on the meaning of one passage in the Justice Minister's Explanatory Memorandum for Article 12 of the Act on Annual Financial Statements, on the information to be given in the notes when minority investments are not valued by the "intrinsic value" method (IIa3, para. 27).

On the topic of other long-term shareholdings, terms were defined and valuation methods were discussed. Examples of the latter were the effect of interest rate changes on valuation, the amortization of premiums and discounts, and the treatment of unrealized holding gains on listed shares. There was a recital of accepted practices, interspersed with asserted opinions on what was proper.

The section on inventories reflects the most conspicuous influence of Grady's research study. Three historical cost methods (fifo, lifo and base stock) and two current valuation methods (current cost and exit value) were discussed, but only one "ought" statement was advanced: when there was an "important" difference between lifo or base stock and current cost, there must be a note (IIb1, para. 24). The TO also said it would accept either direct costing or absorption costing (para. 19).

---

[41] The "intrinsic value", as defined in the exposure draft, was "the sum of the assets of the subsidiary minus the sum of the liabilities, in which all components are valued according to the valuation system in use by the parent company" (IIa3, para. 19). This may or may not equal the initial amount recorded under the "equity method" of accounting, as it is known in the United States. Subsequently, under both methods, the initial valuation is adjusted for the parent company's share of the subsidiary's profits and dividends.

[42] Included in the CAJ's minute book is a photocopy of the US Accounting Principles Board's exposure draft, "Proposed APB Opinion: The Equity Method of Accounting for Investments in Common Stock", dated 18 December 1970 (CAJ Perm 496–502). This exposure draft led directly to APB *Opinion* no. 18, issued in March 1971, which recommended use of the equity method for significant minority investments. In the UK, *Statement of Standard Accounting Practice (SSAP)* no. 1, "Accounting for Associated Companies", issued in January 1971, contained a similar recommendation, but a copy of that statement is not to be found in the CAJ minute book.

Numerous other APB exposure drafts were included in the CAJ's minute book, suggesting an interest in the agenda and views of that body. The CAJ also monitored the output of the standard-setting program in the UK. A photocopy of Exposure Draft 5, "Extraordinary items and prior year adjustments", issued on 25 August 1971, was included in the study group's minute book.(JO Alg 59–61)

In a short section on liabilities, the TO enumerated accepted practices, and, as with other long-term shareholdings, punctuated the discussion with opinions.

An even shorter, but more enterprising, section on "Liabilities not Shown in the Balance Sheet" addressed Article 25 of the law, and required that information on commitments be displayed in the notes. Broaching the topic of leases, which had been highly controversial in the USA, the TO took a step toward the capitalization of leases on the books of lessees. Perhaps influenced by Grady's reproduction of *Opinion* no. 5, "Reporting of Leases in Financial Statements of Lessee", issued by the Accounting Principles Board (APB) in 1964, the TO distinguished between an "operational lease" and a "financial lease", the first describing an ordinary rental agreement and the second depicting an instrument for financing the acquisition of an economic interest in property (Vb, para. 5). Although the TO conceded that the assets and liabilities corresponding to financial leases need not, under the law, be shown in balance sheets, it nonetheless expressed the "tentative view" that, in general, such inclusion was preferable (para. 6). Moreover, if the sum of the annual rental payments for all noncancelable leases of more than three years should exceed 5 percent of the balance sheet total, the TO advised that information must be provided in the notes about the nature of the commitments, their amount, and their maturities (paras. 7, 8). These norms were roughly comparable to those expressed in APB *Opinion* no. 5, and represented a surprising initiative. The TO's recommendation on this sensitive topic departed from its more cautious stance on the other issues taken up in the exposure draft.[43] Of interest is the fact that, when the proposed Act on Annual Financial Statements was being debated in the Second Chamber, J. Kraayenhof said, in reply to a question about the accounting treatment of leasing agreements, "this is a nice problem for the committee ... of organized business and auditors".[44]

---

[43] That the subject of accounting for financial leases was one of consequence at the time is evidenced by a short article in the press, which said, "There are more and more companies constructing buildings or acquiring machinery that make use of financial leasing: a modern form of instalment purchase .... Nevertheless, in the financial statements of the companies in question there is usually no information, or very insufficient information, concerning the commitments entered into." The paper referred favorably to the recommended treatment of financial leases in the TO's exposure draft. "Huurkoop melden in jaarverslag", *de Volkskrant*, 22 December 1971, p. 7.

[44] As cited in Prof.mr P. Sanders, Prof.drs G.L. Groeneveld and Prof.drs R. Burgert (editors), in *De jaarrekening nieuwe stijl* (Alphen aan den Rijn: Samsom Uitgeverij, 1975), p. 262. Extensive treatment of the Act on Annual Financial Statements (including the parliamentary debate), utterances by the TO/RJ, and commentaries in the professional literature may be found in this volume, now in its fourth edition. A volume written along similar lines, but which refers more extensively to the legal literature, is Mr Th.S. IJsselmuiden, *Wet op de jaarrekening* (Deventer: Kluwer, 1972). A much more expanded treatment may be found in the three-volume, looseleaf handbook service whose original editors were Prof.mr P. Sanders and Prof.drs R. Burgert, *Jaarrekening van ondernemingen* (Alphen aan den Rijn: Samsom Uitgeverij). In subsequent years, much of the editing work has been assumed by Prof.mr C.W.A.

Explanation of the TO's approach. In 1974, van Rietschoten took the occasion of a reply to criticism of the exposure draft by Prof.dr J.L. Bouma and others[45] to discuss his preoccupations during the organization phase of the CAJ.[46] He viewed the NIvRA's decision to create a committee charged with advising its management board and as its representative to meet with "organized business" (as proposed in the Justice Minister's memorandum) as a "problematic and risky thing to do" ("*een vraagstuk en een waagstuk*"). The new committee, he said, had to be careful "not to be reprimanded by the board or the membership meeting" (p. 268). He believed that the TO's first draft had to appear in 1971 in order to be in time to affect the 1971 financial statements, "or, at least, to show its presence" (p. 268). There may have also been a personal reason: van Rietschoten, who had already retired from his firm, had, from the beginning, planned to resign his position on the CAJ shortly after the end of 1971, and he would have wanted to see some tangible production before his departure.

Reflecting, perhaps, on the new institutional role for auditors as a source of the norms of practice, van Rietschoten pointed out that there was an "especially big difference" between giving advice (as the Rijkens and Hamburger committees had done previously) and determining what was acceptable in economic and social life. "The latter", he wrote, "must result in saying what must be considered *un*acceptable" (p. 269). Van Rietschoten viewed his critics as failing to appreciate that the TO's exposure draft could have been stronger only at the risk of increasing the number of dissents, of which there was already one. "As an important policy issue", he wrote, "in order to establish its future authority, [the TO] had to strive for unanimity" (p. 269). He added that, for purposes of taking an inventory, the TO was unable to consult the unpublished financial statements of the large number of "closed" companies, and the only published financial statements that could be examined were those issued in accordance with legislation prior to the effective date of the Act on Annual Financial Statements of 1970. He believed that, by means of an exposure draft, a sample of informed views could come to the TO's attention, although he feared that most respondents might give only their opinions, and not supporting reasons (pp. 269–270).

Organizing the CAJ and the TO had been a difficult task. The members were asked to take stock of valuation principles actually in use, and to determine which principles were "acceptable" in the economic and social climate, evidently

---

Timmermans and Mr H.F.J. Joosten. In 1981, a five-volume, looseleaf service, *Documentatie rond de jaarrekening* (Deventer: Kluwer), edited by Prof.mr drs H. Beckman and O.M. Volgenant jr., made its debut, which includes, among other things, a complete record of the parliamentary debates relating to the laws on financial reporting.

[45] The others were Krens and Bulte, and Groeneveld, whose views are related below in the subsection, "Commentary in the professional literature".

[46] A.M. van Rietschoten, "Weerzien van een voorontwerp", in *Maandblad voor accountancy en bedrijfshuishoudkunde*, vol. 48, no. 6, June 1974, pp. 268–271. Page citations in the text refer to this article.

by the use of their own private criteria.

Bouma's criticism. Should the TO have adopted, as Bouma argued, a scientifically deductive methodology for constructing a theory?[47] After all, "acceptable" implied a normative judgment, not solely a survey of practice. On the empirical side of the TO's work, Bouma complained that "The inventory of principles has an impressionistic character. Mentions in the report rest on 'occurring with some frequency in our experience'. Questions that can arise are: Whose experiences do they have in mind? What is the minimum frequency required to warrant a mention? Wouldn't it have been more convincing to set up a statistically justified inquiry into the valuation methods used in practice?"(p. 102)

While a more rigorous approach to gathering evidence and to building a defensible theory might have yielded research conclusions of great value to a committee of scientists charged with making policy decisions, one could expect that, in view of the backgrounds and temperaments of the members of the CAJ and the TO – practicing auditors, company executives, and employees of trade union federations – such a method would have been dismissed as "academic" and not intuitively appealing. Not surprisingly, Bouma questioned the composition of the TO. He wondered why the TO was confined to employers, employees and auditors. Why, he asked, were capital suppliers and politicians omitted?(p. 103) Bouma lamented that those who were responsible for devising the approach used by the TO missed a precious opportunity to answer the fundamental and enduring questions by the use of a methodologically sound research design.[48]

Rightly or wrongly, van Rietschoten believed that (1) the first exposure draft had to be produced within a short space of time, (2) the subjects selected should be ones on which the three delegations could reach relatively easy agreement, and (3) it was essential that the auditors, at least, stand united behind the draft. There were no financial resources made available for the conduct of extensive research. When inviting the parties to the conference table, the minister did not volunteer any funds to support the undertaking. But the parties could have pointed out that a well-funded research program would not necessarily promote sounder solutions. Even though the APB had invested hundreds of thousands of

[47] Prof.dr J.L. Bouma, "Het rapport van de commissie jaarverslaggeving", in *De Naamlooze Vennootschap*, vol. 50, no. 6, September 1972, pp. 102–104. Page citations in the text refer to this article.

[48] Burgert, who had been an original member of the CAJ, later registered some measure of agreement with Bouma's argument, and seemed to be critical of the TO's ambitious conception of its assignment. Writing in 1980, Burgert reflected on the previous decade, and said that "The three groups – employers, employees and accountants – came together and set themselves a task which by far exceeded the expectations of the government. Instead of restricting themselves to the valuation principles, they tried to prepare a complete set of detailed accounting standards, not on the basis of a well prepared research programme but mainly on the basis of the experience of the accountants participating in the workgroups". Prof.drs R. Burgert, "Current Accounting Practice in the Netherlands", in *Maandblad voor accountancy en bedrijfshuishoudkunde*, vol. 55, nos. 2/3, February/March 1981, p. 54.

dollars in the production of eleven extensive research studies during the decade of the 1960's, only one, the study on pensions, contributed in any significant way to facilitating the issuance of an *Opinion*.[49] The US experience had led some to believe that an ambitious research program might have only a minimal impact on the deliberations of a committee charged with making recommendations on accounting principles.[50]

Commentary in the professional literature.[51] Drs F. Krens and Drs J. Bulte, both of the Nederlandse Economische Hogeschool, maintained that the authority of the organizations behind the TO should have merited a stronger term, such as "recommendations" ("*aanbevelingen*"), to characterize its views.[52] They cited the Hamburger report of 1962 as being a much more forthright document, and, somewhat prophetically, said they would like to see the TO's statements labeled as "*Richtlijnen*" (p. 198).[53] The "Introduction", they said, evoked a comparison with American "generally accepted accounting principles", but it was their view that, in contrast with Grady's inventory, the TO's attempt to list a number of "basic concepts" was fragmentary and unsystematic (p. 199n). They criticized a number of the substantive positions taken in the exposure draft, complaining mostly of a lack of clarity and thoroughness of treatment.

Prof.drs G.L. Groeneveld, a past-president of the NIvA, gave a sketch of the developments leading up to the creation of the TO, and said that the idea of designating a private-sector body to work out the implications of a general law was

---

[49] The pensions study educated the members of the Accounting Principles Board on actuarial principles involved in accounting for pensions, and in this respect it played a constructive role in facilitating the work of the Board. See Stephen A. Zeff, *Forging Accounting Principles in Five Countries: A History and an Analysis of Trends* (Champaign, IL: Stipes Publishing Co., 1972), p. 199.

[50] Maurice Moonitz, the AICPA's Director of Accounting Research from 1960 to 1963, who was in charge of launching the series of research studies for the Accounting Principles Board (APB), has written, "It would certainly be desirable if rational research methods could solve all accounting problems; it is an attractive approach. There is a psychological danger in too heavy a reliance on it, however. Since it will not supply the answers in a firm and conclusive manner, it will disappoint those who put faith in it and they may become disillusioned". Maurice Moonitz, *Obtaining Agreement on Standards in the Accounting Profession*, Studies in Accounting Research # 8 (Sarasota, FL: American Accounting Association, 1974), p. 59. Moonitz' discussion of the APB's reaction to the research studies on basic accounting postulates and broad accounting principles is instructive. *Ibid.*, pp. 18–20.

[51] Curiously, there was hardly any mention in the financial press of the TO's first exposure draft. The authors could find only one article beyond that cited in footnote 43: "Voorontwerp 'Beschouwingen': Praktische wenken voor goede verslaggeving van ondernemingen", in *Handels & Transport Courant*, 22 December 1971, p. 3.

[52] F. Krens and J. Bulte, "Beschouwingen beschouwd", in *TVVS*, vol. 15: Part I, nos. 7/8, July/August 1972, pp. 197–203; Part II, no. 9, September 1972, pp. 218–225. Page citations in the text refer to this article.

[53] The Dutch word "*richtlijn*" can be translated as either "guideline" or "directive", implying very different degrees of force. It is not known which meaning they had in mind.

"almost a stroke of genius" by the Justice Minister.[54] In his view, auditors and employers were the most appropriate parties to undertake such consultations. The representation of trade unions in the TO, Groeneveld added, was a symptom of their emancipation, and resulted from the recognition accorded them by the Act on Works Councils of 1971 as "interested parties" in regard to financial statements. Groeneveld also remarked that the absence of shareholders in the TO, despite their important role, was due to their lack of organization.

Groeneveld noted that the TO had been very careful in its drafting, which had led to a certain vagueness and to a very mild attitude toward dubious practice. Only the valuation of investments at 1 guilder, he said, was clearly rejected by the TO.

As might be expected from a Limperg disciple, Groeneveld was critical of the TO's characterization of current cost accounting as just another system, and of the sloppy way (he said) in which some of the finer points of the theory were presented. But, overall, his opinion was favorable. He expressed his "admiration" for how much had been achieved in a short time, and stated his assurance that the continuing work of the TO would have a great influence on financial reporting.

Sanders, Burgert and Groeneveld, writing in the second edition of their treatise, *De jaarrekening nieuwe stijl*, were aware of the limited resources available to the TO and cautioned readers not to judge its output by reference to what the Americans had done. After quoting Krens and Bulte, and Groeneveld on the vagueness of the exposure draft, and Bouma on its weak methodological base, they said:

> These not-so-favorable judgments should really not cause surprise. One should realize that the Committees [i.e., the TO] had to approach an area that, in our country, was hardly explored systematically. How extensive and varied and how difficult the problems surrounding the financial statements in business are, appears most clearly when one considers the extent of the "codified" American "generally accepted accounting principles", and the care and precision of the wording. For his inventory in 1965, P. Grady needed a book of 445 pages, while the "APB Current Text as of June 30, 1973" takes up two hefty volumes. These books, which, by the way, contain much more than just valuation principles, are the sediment of research activities that took decades, and in which professional auditors were supported by full-time research staff. The Committees have hardly had the benefit of remotely comparable facilities. Perhaps thrift has got the better of wisdom here.[55]

Comment letters on the exposure draft. Thirteen letters were received: seven from audit firms, three from auditors practicing as individuals, and one each from a university, a NIvRA study committee, and an industry association. Curiously,

---

[54] G.L. Groeneveld, book review of the exposure draft, in *Maandblad voor accountancy en bedrijfshuishoudkunde*, vol. 46, no. 8, August 1972, pp. 365–367.

[55] Sanders, Groeneveld and Burgert, *op. cit.*, p. 77.

no letters were received from companies, even though 2000 copies of the exposure draft had been made available to the VNO.

Three of the largest audit firms pressed for stronger and less equivocal guidance. Klynveld Kraayenhof & Co. applauded the decision of the TO to expand its charge to include matters of presentation, and said it was useful that it had gone beyond its own expressed limitations by occasionally stating clear preferences and imperatives. The firm recommended that it should be made explicit in the Introduction that the TO will declare its preferences (JO Alg 167–170). Van Dien & Co suggested that the TO conduct a survey to determine whether a body similar to the APB should be called into existence to issue binding rules. APB *Opinion* no. 20, on accounting changes, was cited as an illustration of the need for a more sophisticated treatment of the subject. The firm also suggested that "the economic and social climate" might include foreign accounting practices for the benefit of international companies (JO Alg 321–326). Moret & Limperg endorsed an even stronger approach:

> The work of the [TO] must, in our opinion, eventually result in a sort of "code" for the principles of valuation and income determination, where the code is understood to refer to a system of norms, not recorded in detail and exhaustively, but expounded in such a way that a violation of the principles would clearly be recognized as censurable or even impermissible (JO Alg 204).

A middle-sized audit firm complained that the TO's exposure draft would do little to reduce the diversity in financial statements. It said that the draft would not succeed in limiting the options available to companies, and that it actually did no more than restate what was acceptable under the old criterion of "sound business practice". The firm urged the TO to come up with a more strict interpretation of what was and was not acceptable, and to strive for a "certain uniformity" (JO Alg 193–194).

The three individual auditors commented only on minor technical issues, and the Federatie Nederlandse Wolindustrie (Federation of the Dutch Wool Industry) expressed appreciation for the contents and structure of the draft. The NIvRA study committee, which had been organized for members not in public practice, requested some clearer guidance on the acceptability of certain practices.

The strongest criticism came from the Rijksuniversiteit Groningen. Following the line in Bouma's article, Drs D.W. Feenstra and his student assistant proposed that the TO construct an "explicitly formulated vision", from which principles could be derived to evaluate what actually occurred in practice. "This explicitly formulated vision", they continued, "should be developed in a combined inductive/deductive iteration of the empirical cycle. Extensive empirical research in the inductive phase is necessary, and should replace the always limited experience of the [TO] members". In view of the composition of the TO and its financial resources, this would have been a tall order.

The TO's reaction to the comments received. During 1973, the TO discussed the reactions to the first exposure draft, and the final statement of Considered Views was issued in May 1974, more than two years after the appearance of the exposure draft.[56] One member of the auditors delegation pointed out in May 1973 that the tentative status of the "green booklets" (two had been issued by then) often led to the comment that they were only drafts, reflecting a certain anxiety that it was important to produce a final statement.

Philosophical differences between the delegations contributed to a slowing of the process, leading to prolonged exchanges during the meetings. At one point, a member of the auditors delegation warned that, if the TO did not nudge companies in the direction of providing information on current cost, the freedom currently enshrined in Article 5 might be taken away. The head of the employers delegation replied that, if such was the case, the TO would have to wait until that happen (JO Alg 453). Plainly, the employers were not of a mind to suggest a voluntary expansion of companies' disclosures of current cost information.

At another point in the deliberations, the head of the employers delegation pleaded against a stipulation that provisions may not be formed to provide for price decreases on inventories held for speculative purposes, using the argument that the tax authorities might, as a result, no longer allow the practice. His argument was rejected as not relevant to the TO's mission (JO Alg 342).

The dissent recorded in the section of the exposure draft on investments was not repeated in the final statement, probably because the member who felt most strongly on the issue was no longer serving on the TO. Nonetheless, it cannot be said that the resulting position was any clearer.

Also, the TO's views on leases were not altered in the final statement.

In a separate publication, the TO conveyed its reactions to the comments received on the exposure draft.[57]

Its general reaction to the comments on the Introduction were as follows:

> The comments received on the introduction concern, to a large extent, the approach to the task. It has been said that the committees [i.e., the TO] have taken a non-binding [*vrijblijvend*] posture, that the principles of the considered views are too vague, that there is no underlying vision, that the sources used in making the inventory were not mentioned, and that too little note was taken of international usage.
>
> After considering these critical comments, the committees have reached the conclusion that there should be no change in the approach and in the principles chosen. They do not consider it part of their task to express an unambiguous

---

[56] A chronology of the TO's final statements, keyed to their earlier exposure drafts, is presented in Appendix 5.2.

[57] *Toelichting op de verwerking in de aflevering 1 van de beschouwingen naar aanleiding van de wet op de jaarrekening van ondernemingen van de op het voorontwerp ontvangen commentaren* [no publisher, undated]. The page number cited in the text refers to this publication.

viewpoint in matters where differences of opinion exist in the economic and social climate, as in the questions, "what is profit" and "what is capital" ... .

In some reactions, the desire has been expressed to include capital suppliers and the academic community in the consultations. In the charge of the Minister of Justice, however, the composition of the [participants in the] consultations has been specified. The approach of the committees (initially through the publication of an exposure draft) has given each interested party sufficient opportunity to make his views known (p. 1).

The TO did indicate, however, that it had inserted some changes in the draft in order to make the intended meaning clearer and more precise.

Much of the character of the TO's statements hinged on van Rietschoten's belief that their future authority depended on the achievement of unanimous agreement. Even though three of the largest auditing firms had announced their support of more forceful and definitive recommendations, there was nonetheless a lack of agreement among the members of the auditors delegation over which accounting practices were to be preferred. Moreover, the employers delegation would not have been an advocate of imposing limitations on companies' freedom to report within the framework of the law. The absence of any letters of comment from individual companies was probably a signal of their lack of interest in the entire proceeding. There was no mechanism for ensuring any measure of compliance with the TO's views, and, after all, Dutch society was one in which conflicts were resolved by compromise and not by crossing swords. In the delicate first years of the tripartite undertaking, which had no precedents on which to rely, the leadership of the TO may understandably have decided that a soft approach with a reliance on consensus was the only feasible course to follow, especially when no one knew what credence the Enterprise Chamber would place on the TO's statements.

5.2. The years 1972–75: Burggraaff as chairman

At the TO's meeting of 26 January 1972, van Rietschoten retired from the CAJ and the TO, and was succeeded by J.A. Burggraaff, the vice-chairman of the CAJ, who had been involved in the work of both bodies since the beginning. As with van Rietschoten, Burggraaff served as chairman of both the TO and the CAJ.

At the CAJ's meeting of 8 February, it was decided to work with the NIvRA's Advisory Committee on Company Law (Commissie van advies inzake Ondernemingsrecht) in formulating comments on the first draft of the European Economic Community's Fourth Directive, which had been published on 16 November 1971.

During 1972 and 1973, the CAJ and the TO reviewed the comments on the first exposure draft (one major auditing firm did not respond until January 1973) and began developing the materials for the second exposure draft, which was published in February 1973. At its September 1972 meeting, the CAJ, after considering the reactions to the December 1971 exposure draft, concluded that the TO's pronouncements (*uitspraken*) should be more concrete and precise. Also, it was felt that the TO should place a limit on the range of acceptable alternatives. Some members believed that the drafts suffered from a lack of a guiding philosophy. One member mentioned that Burgert had attempted to introduce such a philosophy a couple of years earlier.

At its 23 January 1973 meeting, Burggraaff reported to the CAJ that the employees delegation felt that its contribution to the TO did not promote trade union objectives. Further, he said, the employees were frustrated by the policy of the employers to retain as much freedom as possible. The spokesman for the employees delegation, Burggraaff said, saw real progress as coming only through the Fourth Directive. Two members of the auditors delegation confirmed the employees' "irritation" and "uneasiness", especially at the practice of the employers of using inconsistent arguments to achieve their ends (CAJ Not 363–364).[58]

The issue that had provoked a clash between the employees and the employers delegations was the proper way of setting up provisions for reorganization in the context of the choice between the "all-inclusive" and "current operating performance" conceptions of the profit and loss statement. The head of the employers delegation defended the current practice of charging such amounts directly to owners' equity. The spokesman for the employees delegation countered that the position of the Consultative Council of Trade Unions was that charges such as the formation of reorganization provisions should be included in the profit and loss statement as extraordinary items. The employees delegation, he said, would prefer to file a minority opinion. Moreover, he felt it had become necessary to consult with his constituency on whether continued participation by the trade union federations would be useful. The employees were of the view that the only way to change established practice, which was being defended by the employers, was by a change in the law, and that it seemed that the opinions of the employees delegation did not seem to matter very much in the discussions. The head of the employers delegation disagreed, saying that the task of the TO was not the expansion of company law. If the employees, he said, found that the TO's task was too confined, he could understand if they were to withdraw, although he would deplore such a decision. Burggraaff quickly interceded with some conciliatory remarks (JO Alg 310–313). Owing to efforts by the chairman and by members of the auditors delegation, Burggraaff could announce, at the CAJ meeting of 6 March 1973, that matters had cooled down. At the same time, it was said that

[58] The objective of the employers delegation was to preserve as much freedom as possible, as it was felt that the auditors delegation would want stringent rules with few exceptions, for their own "self-protection". Interview with Mr H.C. Wesseling, 10 July 1991. In fact, several of the large audit firms commenting on the TO's first exposure draft called for stronger guidance.

the spokesman for the employees delegation had asked if some auditors might assist in a "brainstorming" session to enable the trade unions to formulate a clearer statement of employees' information requirements. Several auditors volunteered their services, and the resulting discussions led to the preparation of *Open boek: Een nota over de behoefte van werknemers aan informatie over hun onderneming* (Open Book: A Memorandum Concerning the Information Needs of Employees About Their Enterprise), a 23-page booklet published in 1976 by the Federatie Nederlandse Vakbeweging (FNV, Federated Dutch Trade Union Movement).[59]

5.2.1. Second exposure draft

On 28 February 1973, the TO issued its second exposure draft, covering fixed assets, receivables, other current assets, temporary shareholdings, liquid holdings, direct charges and credits to owners' equity, treasury shares, and provisions. The two most controversial issues were direct charges and credits to owners' equity, and fixed assets.

In the TO, the choice between the "all-inclusive" and the "current operating performance" notions of the profit and loss statement excited considerable comment and debate as early as 1971. The CAJ's draft submitted to the bipartite study group in June 1971 contained a strong statement in favor of "all-inclusive" but with exceptions (CAJ Werkg 108–133). The auditors and employees delegations preferred the "all-inclusive" position, while the employers delegation argued in favor of "current operating performance". Everything depended, of course, on the permissible exceptions to either of these two extremes, as there was ample room for gradations of compromise. The disagreement was so difficult to reconcile that the subject was deferred until the second exposure draft. The matter was debated throughout 1972, and, save for Burggraaff's efforts to press for a resolution of the differences, it might have been deferred to the third exposure draft. The depth of feeling among the delegations was suggested above, when, at

[59] Interviews with J.A. Burggraaff, 10 September 1990, and with Drs J.P.M. Nabbe, 27 September 1990. The contents of *Open boek* were summarized in Drs J.P.M. Nabbe, "De informatiebehoefte van werknemers en hun representanten", in *Maandblad voor accountancy en bedrijfshuishoudkunde*, vol. 48, no. 7, July/August 1974, pp. 293–305. For a commentary on the contents of *Open boek*, see H.H.B., "Open boek", in *de Accountant*, vol. 83, no.3, November 1976, pp. 116–117.

Another example of trade union interest in financial statements, together with the voluntary efforts by auditors to further that interest, was the Accountantsdag address delivered in 1975 by W. Kok, president of the Dutch Federation of Trade Unions (NVV, Nederlands Verbond van Vakverenigingen), which was summarized in "De maatschappelijke behoefte aan ondernemingsinformatie", in *de Accountant*, vol. 81, no. 7, March 1975, pp. 422–424. The full paper was published in *Het beroep onder de loep: Verslag Accountantsdag 1975*, NIVRA geschrift nummer 15 (Amsterdam: Nederlands Instituut van Registeraccountants, [1975]), pp. 32–41. Several auditors provided assistance to Kok in the preparation of the address. Interview with Prof.drs J.W. Schoonderbeek, 2 October 1991.

one point, the employees delegation was prepared to consider withdrawing from participation in the TO owing to a difference with employers over the proper treatment of the formation of provisions for reorganization.

In January 1972, copies of APB *Opinion* no. 9, "Reporting the Results of Operations", issued in December 1966 (JO Alg 70–102), in which the APB reversed the accounting profession's long-standing preference for the "current operating performance" notion and acceded to the Securities and Exchange Commission's desire that the "all-inclusive" notion be adopted, were circulated to the members of the TO.[60] Also distributed was Exposure Draft 5, "Extraordinary items and prior year adjustments", issued on 25 August 1971 by the UK's Accounting Standards Steering Committee, in which the "all-inclusive" interpretation was supported. Notwithstanding these precedents, and apparently reflecting the strong preference by the employers delegation, the TO allowed numerous charges and credits to be made directly against owners' equity. The employers and employees delegations were diametrically opposed to each other on what was to be preferred, while the auditors delegation, although favoring "all-inclusive", did not want to make an issue of their preference in the exposure draft (JO Alg 124, 257). In this section of the exposure draft, bold facing was used to say what *must* go through the profit and loss statement, and what *can* be charged or credited directly to owners' equity. The exposure draft specified that "the revenues and expenses that are connected with normal business operations, as well as those revenues and expenses not related to normal business operations that occur with a certain regularity", *must* be included in the profit and loss statement (IIIa1, para. 7). But "large and incidental items" that "will, due to their nature, usually be outside the influence of management and not be related to normal operations" *can* be charged or credited directly to equity (para. 8). This characterization of items that could be omitted from the profit and loss statement, together with the examples of such items given in paragraphs 8 and 9, stamped the position of the TO as more compatible with "current operating performance" than "all-inclusive". This position was, indeed, comparable to that taken by the US Committee on Accounting Procedure in *Accounting Research Bulletin* no. 43, issued in 1953, when it reaffirmed its preference for the "current operating performance" interpretation.[61]

A section of the draft that would have attracted particular attention was the treatment of fixed assets. It was there that the TO's views on current cost accounting were first exposed. Paragraphs 24 through 27 of section IIa1 defined the TO's position:

24 If the valuation in the balance sheet is based on historical data, this valuation

[60] See Zeff, *op.cit.*, pp. 157–158, 200.

[61] Indeed, the TO, like the Committee on Accounting Procedure, began by embracing, in principle, the "all-inclusive" approach and then "political" or sensitive items were, one by one, excluded from income. Interview with Drs J.F. Leeuwerik, 24 October 1990.

can, even though the demand of Article 5, paragraph 1, has been met, after [the passage of] some time, provide too small a foothold for a well-founded opinion [to be formed] on the amount of capital. In so far as, in such cases, no well-founded opinion can be formed, other information must be provided.
25 As far as capital is concerned, the deviations mentioned in paragraph 24 can be remedied by a revaluation in the balance sheet on the basis of current costs, to be credited to owners' equity, or by giving additional information in the notes . . . .
26 In case of an important difference between the depreciation charge in the profit and loss statement based on historical costs, and a higher depreciation based on current cost, information on this [difference] must be provided. This can be done by adjusting the depreciation charge in the profit and loss statement or by disclosing the difference in the notes.
27 The committees [i.e., the TO] have contemplated giving directions for what, in their opinion, must be considered at least as important in this respect. For the time being, they have opted not to do so. In general, a smaller degree of tolerance will apply in determining what is of importance in forming an opinion on income than on capital.[62]

The scars of compromise were everywhere evident in the four paragraphs, reflecting an uneasy coincidence of views between the advocates of current cost and the advocates of historical cost.

5.2.1.1. Comments on the second exposure draft

Of the few commentaries published in the financial press and professional journals, the most noteworthy was an article by Bouma and Feenstra,[63] following up Bouma's earlier article and Feenstra's comment letter submitted to the TO (both mentioned above). The authors said they "could not applaud" the TO's decision to issue a second exposure draft before publishing the final statement based on its first exposure draft, as they would rather have seen how the TO had addressed the methodological issues raised by both authors in regard to the first draft (p. 108). They claimed that the second draft reflected the same kind of vagueness that they found in its predecessor, and they cited the offending phrases. In sum, they noted that the vagueness was a result of working without explicitly formulated criteria (p. 111).

J. Bulte and F. Krens wrote a pair of critical articles, in which they found it deplorable that the TO had not responded to previously voiced criticisms of

62 *Voorontwerp van beschouwingen naar aanleiding van de wet op de jaarrekening van ondernemingen, aflevering* no. 2, 28 February 1973.
63 Prof.dr J.L. Bouma and Drs D.W. Feenstra, "Het rapport van de commissies jaarverslaggeving, aflevering nr. 2", in *De Naamlooze Vennootschap*, vol. 51, no. 7, October 1973, pp. 107–111. Citations in the text to page numbers refer to this article. A typescript of the article was sent to the TO on 30 August 1973 by the journal's editor, since the article was not scheduled for publication prior to the deadline for receiving comments on the exposure draft (JO Alg 413–421).

their approach before proceeding to issue an additional exposure draft.[64] They referred to a debate in Parliament when Kraayenhof had assured questioners that the committee composed of representatives of "organized business" and the organization of auditors would determine the acceptability of accounting principles, so that it would no longer be necessary for the notes to point out corrections of information contained in the body of the financial statements. Bulte and Krens concluded that the TO had failed to meet the expectation raised in Parliament, as its permissive attitude would not lead to the disappearance of undesirable practice (pp. 312–313).

G. Timmer, the chairman of one of the large audit firms, remarked that, despite the TO's adherence to "the neutrality principle", there were more clearly expressed preferences in the second instalment than in the first.[65] As a concluding note, Timmer observed that the TO had, for the time being, skipped some difficult questions, such as goodwill, deferred taxes, and provisions for reorganization (although it had been discussed). Somewhat prophetically, Timmer predicted that these subjects would excite greater controversy than had the items already addressed (p. 56).[66]

Eleven letters of comment were received: seven from audit firms, and one each from an individual auditor, a NIvRA study committee, a pair of academics, and British Gas. Again, no letters were received from Dutch companies. Few of the letters of comment raised significant issues. One large audit firm praised the TO for having made stronger statements on the unacceptability of certain practices. Another large audit firm, while signifying its agreement with the apparent choice, in principle, of the "all-inclusive" approach, said that there should have been a more thorough explanation of the TO's conclusions based on this choice, especially regarding the exceptions enumerated in section IIIa1, paragraphs 8 and 9. The Nederlandse Accountants Maatschap, a large audit firm that did not respond to the first exposure draft, echoed the view expressed by three large firms that had commented on the first draft. The firm wrote,

> In our view, business and auditors would be helped by concrete guidelines concerning the permissibility of valuation norms and matters of presentation.

---

[64] Drs J. Bulte and Drs F. Krens, "Beschouwingen beschouwd (I)", in *TVVS*, vol. 16, no. 11, November 1973, pp. 310–315; and "Beschouwingen beschouwd (II, slot)", in *TVVS*, vol. 16, no. 12, December 1973, pp. 335–341. The page citation in the text refers to this article.

[65] G. Timmer, "Het voorontwerp van beschouwingen naar aanleiding van de wet op de jaarrekening van ondernemingen, aflevering nr. 2", in *Maandblad voor accountancy en bedrijfshuishoudkunde*, vol. 48, no. 2, February 1974, pp. 53–56. The page cited in the text refers to this article. An editor of the journal sent a typescript of the article to the TO on 6 December 1973 in order that it might be considered before the deadline for receiving comments (JO Alg 498).

[66] In 1986, Timmer became chairman of the RJ, and in 1990–91 the subject of intangibles became so difficult for the RJ to resolve that it took the unusual step of issuing a discussion memorandum (*beschouwing*) in order to solicit comments prior to developing an exposure draft.

> Hence, it strikes us that, in certain places in the second series of Considered Views, there is yet again the tone of the very permissive character of the first Considered Views.
>
> We understand that the committees [i.e., the TO] are not to provide concrete guidelines for the rendering of enterprise results (for this would not be consistent with the chosen system of legislation), but it is to be deplored that there are few rejections of faulty presentations in the Considered Views (JO Alg 435).

In their comment letter, Prof.dr L. Traas and Drs J. Klaassen, of the Vrije Universiteit, said that the lack of explicitly formulated criteria to determine acceptability was deplorable (*te betreuren*). The disadvantages of the TO's approach appeared most clearly, they said, in the section dealing with valuation systems, where the statements gave an impression of arbitrariness. They said that a more thorough investigation of what should be understood by "capital" and "income" would lead the TO to the view that it was not possible to meet all information requirements by one set of figures. They recommended that equal weight be given to historical costs and current costs, and that information on both should be required (JO Alg 397–400).

5.2.1.2. The TO's reactions to the comments received

Comparatively few changes from the exposure draft were reflected in the final statement of Considered Views, which was published in May 1976. As with the first statement of Considered Views, published in May 1974, a memorandum was made available in which the TO enumerated and explained the salient changes from the exposure draft (JO Alg 1357–1368).[67]

The section on direct charges and credits to equity was considerably expanded (from 21 to 29 paragraphs), with numerous changes in wording.[68] The only salient change in substance was the report of a compromise on how to classify the formation of provisions for reorganization. In the exposure draft (IIIa1, para. 11), the TO had declined to give an opinion. But in the final statement (IIIa1, para. 20), the TO could refer to a section of the third exposure draft, which had been issued in June 1975, as support for the opinion that the formation of such provisions should go through the profit and loss statement, as an extraordinary item. With this treatment, the employee and employer delegations found a convenient compromise: for the employees, it would not be charged to equity, and for the employers, it would not affect operating profit.

The major change in the section on fixed assets was the deletion of section IIa1, paragraph 27 from the exposure draft, in which it had been suggested that, in the future, specific criteria might be given for judging the difference between

[67] The availability of the TO's "Notes on Revisions" ("*toelichting op herziening*") was announced in *de Accountant*, vol. 83, no. 4, December 1976, p. 163.

[68] The bold facing of "must" and "can" in the section on direct charges and credits to equity was replaced by showing "can" in italics.

historical cost and current cost. There were also a few minor changes in the section.

5.2.2. Kluwer becomes publisher of the considered views

While the exposure drafts were issued in green booklets that were printed by the NIvRA (JO Alg 26) and distributed by the TO, an agreement was entered into with Uitgeverij Kluwer B.V., a major publisher of books and magazines, to print and distribute the final statements of Considered Views as inserts in a set of looseleaf binders. In its letter of April 1974 to prospective subscribers to this service, Kluwer stated, perhaps with a zeal that not all members of the TO would have shared:

> It has been decided not to present these [statements] in the form of "Guidelines" ["*Richtlijnen*"], because this would give them too strict a character. But it is nevertheless clear that – precisely because the "Considered Views" are supported by such representative groupings as indicated above – a great degree of authority can be attached to the form actually chosen as well (JO Alg 614).

5.2.3. The norms for the Sijthoff Prize cite the considered views

In October 1974, a new booklet containing the norms for the annual Sijthoff Prize was published.[69] Serious consideration had been given to discontinuing the Prize following passage of the Act on Annual Financial Statements of 1970, but *Het Financieele Dagblad* had received so many requests for the Prize to be continued that the idea was dropped.[70] Probably because of the greater degree of specification of the contents of the financial statements in the 1970 law, the new booklet ran to only $2\frac{1}{2}$ pages, compared with the 11 pages of the 1956 booklet.

The first demand was that the financial statements meet the requirements of the law, "taking into account the considered views of the 'committees on financial reporting'". In addition, the panel of judges requested that the following information be disclosed:

- clear statements of policy and on the expectations for the current year;
- segmentation of sales and gross income by industry;
- five-year summaries adjusted for accounting changes;
- a statement of source and application of funds;
- recognition of the influence of price changes, through, "for example, use of current cost, price-level adjustments, base stock method, or LIFO";

[69] *Normen voor de beoordeling van Jaarverslagen opgesteld voor de Henri Sijthoff-Prijs* (Amsterdam: *Het Financieele Dagblad*, October 1974), pages unnumbered. The norms were reproduced in *Het Financieele Dagblad*, 16 December 1974, p. 15.

[70] Interview with Hendrik A.H. Sijthoff and H.B.G. Sijthoff, 6 December 1990.

- consolidated financial statements, rather than separate statements for subsidiaries;
- half-yearly reports (an essential norm) or quarterly reports (desirable); and
- immediate announcements of important developments during the financial year.

5.2.4. The TO's reaction to the work of the IASC

On 5 July 1973, a few days after the installation of the International Accounting Standards Committee (IASC),[71] Drs J.W. Schoonderbeek, the 1973 NIvRA president, appeared before the TO to provide some information about the IASC. The NIvRA was one of nine accountancy bodies to sign the agreement setting up the IASC. It was concluded that the formation of the IASC did not hinder or restrict the work of the TO, and it was expected that the TO would provide comments on the IASC's exposure drafts (JO Alg 378–380).

The head of the employers delegation deplored the IASC's choice of the "American and English way", in which auditors tell management what it cannot do, rather than the Dutch way in which auditors and management decide together what can be done. The spokesman for the employees delegation said that he would also like to have seen the participation of other than auditors on the IASC. It was, however, acknowledged, with characteristic Dutch understatement, that it would be difficult to organize a kind of European, let alone worldwide, TO.

In the spring of 1974, IASC's E1 was received, and the TO's views were incorporated in the NIvRA's letter of comment. This procedure was used for subsequent exposure drafts. Usually, two or three members were chosen to prepare a comment, which was then discussed in a plenary meeting of the TO, which, beginning with E3, was augmented to include participation by the CAJ as well (JO Alg 650–657, 740).

Some controversy developed in November 1974, when Burggraaff proposed to the TO that the IASC standards be included as inserts in the Kluwer volume of Considered Views, possibly with notice of the extent to which each standard was supported by the TO. The employers delegation rejected this proposal on the ground that it might lead to confusion between the TO's and the IASC's points of view. Since the employers believed that the Considered Views should be seen more as permissive than as constraining, it is not surprising that they would have opposed the inclusion of an international body's "standards" in the same volume as the Considered Views, as if to suggest that both possessed the same standing in the Netherlands.[72] But the NIvRA took steps of its own to

[71] See "Historic Agreement", in *The Accountant*, vol. 169, no. 5142, 5 July 1973, pp. 1–2; also see p. 5.

[72] Use of the term "standards" was intentionally avoided by the TO, as the term had come to be associated with the program of the UK's Accounting Standards Steering Committeee,

disseminate the IASC's standards, since it was the member body of the IASC in the Netherlands. Beginning in January 1975, IASC standards were published, in Dutch and English, in the NIvRA's journal, *de Accountant*. In 1977, the NIvRA's management board sent copies of the IASC standards to all NIvRA members, together with a notice, prepared by the TO, indicating the differences between the IASC standards and the Considered Views.

5.2.5. The TO's third exposure draft

The third exposure draft was issued in June 1975, and its more important sections treated the materiality of information in the financial statements, the valuation of fixed assets in connection with the threatened discontinuance of enterprise activities, the pensions provision, acceptable principles for income determination, and the allocation of revenue and expense to successive financial years. By far the most controversial section, both inside and outside the TO, was the one dealing with acceptable principles for income determination, which revived the debate over valuation principles.

5.2.5.1. Acceptable principles for income determination

Accounting for general and relative price changes had become a major issue in numerous countries during the 1970's, as inflation was on an upward march. By the end of 1974, exposure drafts calling for the use of general price-level accounting (GPLA) (known as current purchasing power (CPP) accounting in most British Commonwealth countries) had been issued in the United States, Canada, and Australia. Moreover, a provisional *Statement of Standard Accounting Practice* in support of CPP accounting had been issued in the United Kingdom in May 1974, and a committee to inquire into the entire question of inflation accounting (which came to be known as the Sandilands Committee) had been announced by a minister of the UK government in July 1973.[73] In the Netherlands, the inflation rate, which had prevailed at around 5 percent during most of the 1960's, took the following course during the first six years of the 1970's:

1970	5.5%	1973	8.0%
1971	8.5%	1974	10.5%
1972	8.0%	1975	10.5%[74]

begun in 1970, of issuing "standards" that would reflect a narrowing of the areas of difference in accounting practice, and would presuppose that auditors disclose material departures from the recommended positions. Neither of these aims was implied in the work of the TO.

73 For a comprehensive discussion of developments in inflation accounting during the 1970's, see David Tweedie and Geoffrey Whittington, *The debate on inflation accounting* (Cambridge: Cambridge University Press, 1984), Chaps. 3–9.

74 Table 10.2 "Economische kerngegevens", in De Nederlandsche Bank n.v., *Verslag over het jaar 1977*, Statistische bijlage, p. 66.

Work on developing a position on acceptable valuation principles had begun in earnest in 1972. Burggraaff and Drs W. van Bruinessen[75] prepared a memorandum on 12 September 1972 entitled "*De waardering tegen actuele waarde als maatschappelijk aanvaardbare grondslag voor de bepaling van het resultaat en van het eigen vermogen*" ("The valuation at current value as an economically and socially acceptable principle for the determination of income and of equity") (CAJ Perm 1037–1042b, 1491). The memorandum addressed the question of how to apply current value once a decision had been made to adopt it, but not the question of whether or when to use current value. A slightly reworked version, with the reference to equity deleted from the title, was considered at the CAJ's meeting of 6 March 1973, at which it was decided to forward the memorandum to the TO as the second half of a draft covering the entire subject of valuation principles, including historical cost (CAJ Perm 1267–1272; CAJ Not 372–373).

The employers delegation was not pleased with the resulting draft. Even before it was taken up for discussion by the TO on 24 October, the employers delegation had submitted an alternative draft of its own (which eventually appeared in paragraphs 11–13 of section IVa of the exposure draft). The employers objected to the amount of detail in the CAJ draft, but Burggraaff objected to the brevity of the employers' alternative. The employers' displeasure centered on the disparity between the space devoted to historical cost (three pages in the final version) and to current value (six pages), a matter that had already been raised as a possible issue in the CAJ. The employers were concerned that this differential might lead readers to conclude that the TO preferred current cost (CAJ Perm 1491; CAJ Not 359).

For the next six months, further drafts were passed between the CAJ and the TO until, at the meeting of 17 July 1974, two members of the auditors delegation and the spokesman for the employees delegation expressed their belief, evidently the result of their frustrations in dealing with the employers, that the TO should give more weight to stating preferences instead of focusing exclusively on taking an inventory of actual practice. On the specific topic of current value, one of the auditors asked if it was not possible for the Council of Dutch Employers Feder-

---

[75] Van Bruinessen had joined the auditors delegation in January 1972 and remained until October 1984. He was a former student of van Rietschoten's, and was a partner in van Rietschoten's firm, Frese, Hogeweg, Meyer & Hörchner, which merged into Klynveld Kraayenhof & Co. in January 1972. In 1970, he served as the NIvRA president. He was a fervent supporter of current cost, as evidenced by numerous articles and speeches, including several at international conferences and congresses. (See his testimony given at the Financial Accounting Standards Board's public hearing on inflation accounting, held on 23 April 1974: "Reporting the effects of general price-level changes in financial statements," in *de Accountant*, vol. 80, no. 10, June 1974, pp. 423–428.) He was the auditor of Koninklijke Wessanen N.V. In 1959, when Wessanen went public and took up a listing on the Amsterdam Stock Exchange, the company adopted current cost for its fixed assets. At that time, van Bruinessen was an assistant to van Rietschoten, the partner in charge of the engagement. (Information supplied by KPMG Klynveld.)

ations, in 1974, to state a preference for current cost when, in the Hamburger report, it had already done so in 1962. The head of the employers delegation agreed that, in general, the TO should give more attention to preferences, but not on current value. He said that the Netherlands could not go its own way on current value, since some countries in the European Economic Community used historical cost as the only method of accounting. Besides, he added, a number of well-known Dutch companies had recently switched back to historical cost from current value.[76] What the TO could do, he said, was to make a statement that the financial statements must, in one way or another, pay attention to the effects of inflation. He did not want "current value" to be given as a preference, and current cost, he maintained, was only one approach to inflation accounting (JO Alg 672).[77] In the ensuing debate, such factors as "faithfulness" ("*getrouwheid*"), subjectivity v. objectivity, and comparability were invoked. One member of the employers delegation interjected, "comparability is of small use for investors, since shareholders ... take as their starting point the nominal return [i.e., the dividend paid]" (JO Alg 674). At the conclusion of this phase of the discussion, Burggraaff observed that, although the employers delegation was unwilling to state a preference for current value, it was willing to consider a statement to the effect that the difference between income figures on the basis of current value and historical cost should be disclosed. This was the genesis of the TO's so-called "two-track policy" ("*tweesporenbeleid*").[78] The balance of the discussion was concerned with more technical issues, such as, when valuation is based on historical cost but depreciation was based on current value, should the deprecia-

[76] In an article published the following November, Burgert cited three large companies, Akzo, Hoogovens and Nederlandse Dagbladunie, as having wholly or partially renounced current cost in 1972–73. Prof.drs R. Burgert, "De jaarrekening van ondernemingen en inflatie", in *Economisch Statistische Berichten*, vol. 59, no. 2979, 27 November 1974, p. 1061. Volten has written that the companies' motivation was "mainly to enhance their position in comparison with their competitors on the international capital market". H. Volten, "Accountancy and Inflation: Response to Changing Prices", *de Accountant*, vol. 81, no. 10, June/July 1975, p. 647.

[77] At this point in the discussion, the distinction was drawn between current (replacement) cost (*vervangingswaarde*) and current value (*actuele waarde*). The latter, apparently, was intended to allow the use of any of three approaches: current cost, exit value (net realizable value, or net selling price), and discounted present value. While mention was made of the Limpergian model of current value, by which only one of the three approaches would be justified in any given circumstance, it seems unlikely that the employers delegation would have embraced this interpretation of current value.

[78] Burggraaff has taken the view that the two-track policy had a sound theoretical basis, and was not merely an instrument of compromise. Interview with J.A. Burggraaff, 26 November 1991. In an article, he argued that, in the 1930's, when Limperg was developing his current cost theory, he had in mind companies with circumstances that were no longer as applicable to companies in the 1970's. Burggraaff therefore concluded that both current cost and historical cost should be seen as relevant for contemporary enterprise. J.A. Burggraaff, "Vermogens- en winstbepaling in de praktijk", in *Maandblad voor accountancy en bedrijfshuishoudkunde*, vol. 50, no. 2, February 1976, pp. 106–107, 115.

tion be split into two components: historical cost and the excess of current value over historical cost? (The answer was yes.) (JO Alg 674–679)

At the CAJ's meeting on 10 September, it devoted extensive discussion to the matter, and concluded that financial statements should disclose, in whatever way, the amount of income based on current value (which need not be identical to current cost) (CAJ Not 511). When communicating the CAJ's conclusion to the TO, Burggraaff said that the CAJ was of the belief that financial statements that do not show income on the basis of current value do not meet the criteria in Article 2 of the Act on Annual Financial Statements (JO Alg 695). A spokesman for the employers delegation said that, owing to inflationary conditions, his delegation would support a statement that, if the financial statements themselves do not take into account the effect of inflation, information giving this effect must be shown in the notes. The spokesman repeated his delegation's dislike for current cost as the only method of showing this effect. In four meetings held during October, November and December, the TO reached agreement on a preface to section IVa, in which a clear statement was expressed in favor of the two-track policy.

The preface to the section contained the following three paragraphs:

> **5** In the opinion of the committees [i.e., the TO], the financial statements should present, in the profit and loss statement or in the notes, the amount of operating profit (exclusive of interest) calculated on the basis of current values, and the corresponding figure calculated on the basis of historical prices [e.g., by the Fifo method], as well. In this way, the extent to which the results of operations have been influenced by changes in prices of the inventories and fixed assets needed for production will be made known to interested parties.
> **6** In view of the increasing need for information in this respect, it merits consideration that, in the financial statements, information [should] be provided concerning increases in profit and/or capital, expressed in units of constant purchasing power. It is intended to devote a statement of considered views to this subject before long.
> **7** Not all companies have access in a simple way to the data necessary for determining operating income on the basis of current values. The committees are of the opinion that, in the current order of things in the economic and social climate, this information is of great importance to interested parties, and may therefore not be omitted. Not so much an exact determination as a reasonable approximation is what is called for.[79]

In paragraph 47, the TO said that, in regard to accounting for inventories, both historical cost and current value were acceptable bases, but added the proviso that additional information on current value should be provided when there was

---

[79] *Voorontwerp van beschouwingen naar aanleiding van de wet op de jaarrekening van ondernemingen*, *aflevering* no. 3, 30 June 1975, p. 32.

a difference between the two and historical cost was used in the profit and loss statement.

The encouragement (in para. 6) to use general price-level accounting (GPLA) may have been prompted by its use, beginning in 1974, in a supplementary schedule to the annual financial statements of the Royal Dutch/Shell Group.[80] It was the employers delegation that wanted GPLA included in the set of possible options. The delegation's suggestion may have also been inspired by the number of standard-setting bodies, including those in the United States, the United Kingdom, Canada and Australia, that were recommending this approach exclusively. (The report of the UK's Sandilands committee on inflation accounting, which was to reject CPP accounting in favor of current cost accounting, was not published until a few months after the issuance of the TO's exposure draft.) In fact, neither the TO nor its successor, the RJ, ever issued guidance on the use of GPLA. As will be indicated below, in the final statement of Considered Views, published in February 1979, the TO renounced any interest in GPLA, implying that the issue would not be carried further. GPLA has never been an acceptable practice in the Netherlands.

In an article published in November 1974, Burgert urged the TO to give the highest priority to producing a recommendation in support of the publication of supplementary statements in which income and capital were corrected for inflation.[81] As a precedent, he mentioned ED 8 of the UK's Accounting Standards Steering Committee, issued in January 1973, which would require listed companies to publish CPP-adjusted supplementary statements. Burgert added, of course, that a Dutch recommendation would need to allot space to the calculation of the effects of relative price changes. At a time of high inflation, he argued, the TO should take immediate action. However, the TO believed that, in its third exposure draft, it had already taken the step proposed by Burgert. The draft was being printed, and the TO decided to await reactions before proceeding further (JO Alg 855).

---

[80] The Royal Dutch/Shell Group continued to display the GPLA schedule ("Additional Financial Overviews, Adjusted for the Current Purchasing Power of the Pound Sterling" – "*Aanvullende financiële overzichten, aangepast aan de huidige koopkracht van het pond sterling*") as an attachment to its annual financial statements until 1979, when it added current value to the schedule. Both bases, GPLA and current value, were used again in the 1980 report, but only current value was shown in the Group's annual reports from 1981 through 1985, following which the supplementary schedule was discontinued. As is evident from comments contained in its annual reports, the Anglo-Dutch concern was influenced by inflation accounting developments in the United Kingdom, which initially focused on GPLA (or Current Purchasing Power (CPP) Accounting, as it was known in the UK). Following publication of the Sandilands Report in 1975, attention shifted to current cost accounting. In March 1980 (in time for the Group's 1979 annual report), the UK's Accounting Standards Committee (ASC) issued *SSAP* 16, which called for large companies to show current cost (with a gearing adjustment) in the notes if historical cost was used in the financial statements. In 1985, *SSAP* 16 was removed from the ASC's mandatory list. See Tweedie and Whittington, *op.cit.*, Chaps. 5 and 6.

[81] Burgert, "De jaarrekening van ondernemingen en inflatie", *op.cit.*, pp. 1060–1062.

5.2.5.2. Other sections

Two other sections of interest dealt with the materiality judgments about information to be presented in the financial statements, and with pension liabilities. As to the former, the TO provided decision rules for the separate disclosure of items in the balance sheet and profit and loss statement, based on percentages of balance sheet totals, sales revenue, and operating income (Ib1, paras. 5–7). Quantitative rules were supplied concerning the disclosure of the effect of accounting changes (paras. 9–11). The section on pension liabilities was notable for its length and the amount of detail.

A final statement of Considered Views based on this exposure draft was not issued until February 1979, and will be discussed below.

5.2.6. The NIvRA's initiatives on current cost

During 1974, while the TO's three delegations were seeking a common ground on accounting for the effects of changing prices, the NIvRA, long a bastion of current cost accounting, was promoting the concept in other countries. Van Bruinessen gave testimony in April at a public hearing of the Financial Accounting Standards Board, a NIvRA delegation held discussions in May with the UK's Accounting Standards Steering Committee (to advocate current value as being superior to CPP accounting, the method proposed in ED 8), and in November the NIvRA received a delegation from the UK's Sandilands committee on inflation accounting.[82] In June 1975, a NIvRA delegation met with the Institut der Wirtschaftsprüfer.[83] H. Volten, its general director, wrote that the NIvRA

> has used the increased attention for inflation accounting to advocate once more and with doubled effort the solutions of current replacement value accounting which have proven their worth in practice, occasionally even outside The Netherlands.[84]

In meetings of the IASC's board during the latter half of 1975, the Dutch delegation[85] argued that the IASC's exposure draft in favor of general price-level accounting (GPLA) should be amended to provide equal support for current cost accounting. But the accelerating international trend toward current cost led the

---

[82] See van Bruinessen, *op.cit.*; "Accounting for changes in the purchasing power of money", in *de Accountant*, vol. 80, no. 10, June 1974, esp. pp. 406–409; and "Sandilands-commissie", in *de Accountant*, vol. 81, no. 4, December 1974, p. 188.

[83] Prior to the meeting, held in Düsseldorf on 5 June, the NIvRA delegation prepared a set of discussion notes dated 28 May (coded as AS-RVA Doc. 16 in the NIvRA's files).

[84] Volten, (footnote 67) *op.cit.* For extracts from the Sandilands report, where reference is made to the NIvRA's support for current cost accounting, see H. Volten, "Verslaglegging in Groot-Brittannië (2)", in *de Accountant*, vol. 82, no. 3, November 1975, pp. 143–144.

[85] The delegation consisted of H.C. Treffers, P.C. Louwers and I. Kleerekoper, with H. Volten attending as staff observer.

delegation to believe that it might have even a stronger case. Once the West Germans (in a draft recommendation issued by the Institut der Wirtschaftsprüfer), the Australians (in a preliminary exposure draft), the British (in the Sandilands report), and the Americans (in a draft of an SEC release) either had expressed a strong interest in current cost or had rejected GPLA in favor of current cost,[86] the delegation believed that it had sufficient international support to argue that GPLA should be rejected altogether in favor of current cost accounting.[87] The delegation prepared a position statement for submission to the IASC, and H. Volten, the NIvRA's general director and its staff observer to the IASC board, attended the TO's meeting of 12 November 1975 to solicit its endorsement of the statement (JO Alg 955–958, 1038–1039). One of the members of the auditors delegation was van Bruinessen, who had not only steered the drive by the auditors delegation to gain acceptance for current cost accounting in the TO, but who also had been a member of the IASC committee that had prepared the exposure draft on inflation accounting. The TO's reaction to the request from the NIvRA's IASC delegation, especially by the employers and employees delegations, was tepid. The head of the employers delegation wanted the draft to make clear that current cost had been accepted only on a limited scale in the Netherlands. The spokesman for the employees delegation was not prepared to reject GPLA out of hand. Even with these points incorporated in the NIvRA draft, the employees delegation declined to give its support (JO Alg 1085). In the end, the NIvRA sent the statement to the IASC on its own. (In June 1977, the IASC issued IAS 6, "Accounting Responses to Changing Prices", in which it accepted three approaches: "specific price changes" (including current cost and net realizable value), GPLA, or a combination of the two. In its standard, the IASC asked only that enterprises disclose which of these procedures they have adopted, if any, in the preparation of their financial statements.) Nonetheless, by bringing this issue to the meeting of the TO, van Bruinessen would have apprised both the employer and employee delegations of the increasing international support for current cost.

In October 1975, the management board of the NIvRA advised the SEC that it "strongly supports" the SEC's proposal to require the disclosure of certain current cost information in company financial statements. The NIvRA said, how-

[86] The three documents were: draft recommendation, "Accounting for the Purpose of Maintaining the 'Substantialistic Value' of an Enterprise", issued on 15 December 1974 by the Institut der Wirtschaftsprüfer; Preliminary Exposure Draft, "A Method of Current Value Accounting", issued in June 1975 by the Australian Accounting Research Foundation; *Inflation Accounting*, Report of the Inflation Accounting Committee, F.E.P. Sandilands Esq CBE, Chairman (London: Her Majesty's Stationery Office, September 1975); and Proposed Amendment to Regulation S-X, "Disclosure of Certain Replacement Cost Data in Notes to Financial Statements", issued on 21 August 1975 by the Securities and Exchange Commission.

[87] See Drs W. van Bruinessen, "Een IASC-ontwerp over de behandeling van prijsfluctuaties met een begeleidende notitie", in *de Accountant*, vol. 82, no. 5, January 1976, pp. 258–259.

ever, that such information should fall within the scope of the audit, whereas the SEC's proposal was that the disclosure be unaudited. The NIvRA also said that it had "serious doubts" about the merits of GPLA.[88]

5.2.7. Fourth exposure draft

In December 1975, a scant six months after the issuance of the third exposure draft, a fourth draft was issued. Where the first, second, and third drafts had consumed 43, 30, and 54 A4-sized pages, respectively, the fourth draft was much shorter, occupying 24 quarto pages. The topics addressed in the fourth exposure draft were the treatment of accounting changes; the acquisition and disposition of investments, and the accounting for goodwill; and the treatment of taxes in the financial statements.

Accounting changes were defined as (1) changes in the principles used for valuation, income determination and presentation, (2) changes in the criteria used for determining which investee companies should be included in the consolidation, and (3) changes in the methods used for making estimates. In the TO's view, "a company may deviate from the general rule [of consistency] only if the use of an alternative system is clearly preferable to the one used until now. This is the case if a better insight is provided into financial position and income" (Ib2, para. 12). A precedent for the use of preferability in such matters had appeared in *Opinion* No. 20, "Accounting Changes", issued by the Accounting Principles Board (APB) in July 1971. Contrary to *Opinion* no. 20, the TO concluded that, for accounting changes classified as (1) and (2), above, the cumulative effect up to and including the previous year was to be charged or credited directly to equity, and to be shown separately in equity at the beginning of the year (para. 17). *Opinion* no. 20 had confined such retroactive treatment to a very limited number of special cases.

On the subject of goodwill, the TO acknowledged that a wide range of methods were in use: capitalizing the acquisition cost, with or without subsequent amortization; charging purchased goodwill immediately to income; and charging purchased goodwill immediately to equity. Both the capitalizing and non-capitalizing alternatives were said to be supported by the Justice Minister's Explanatory Memorandum to the Act on Annual Financial Statements of 1970 (IIa3, paras. 49, 50). The TO stated a preference for capitalization and amortization over a short period, usually not longer than ten years (para. 52). In a compromised pronouncement in which it was forced to take refuge in a double negative, the TO said that charging goodwill immediately to equity was "not

[88] Letter signed by Henk Volten, General Director, to Mr. George Fitzsimmons, secretary, SEC, dated 15 October 1975, in regard to the SEC's "Notice of Proposed Amendments to Regulation S-X to Require Disclosure of Certain Replacement Cost Data in Notes to Financial Statements (S7–579)".

considered to be unacceptable" (para. 51). Not amortizing capitalized goodwill, the TO added, was unacceptable (para. 54). In the treatment of negative goodwill, the committee counseled consistency: if positive goodwill was charged to equity, negative goodwill should be credited to equity (para. 59).

On taxes, the TO said that there should be a causal relationship between the amount of tax expense[89] and the amount of pre-tax income shown in the profit and loss statement (VI1, para. 7). Deferred tax assets associated with timing differences, the TO said, could be recognized when they could be offset by deferred liabilities, or when "it is reasonable to assume" that future taxable income would indeed be smaller than pre-tax income in the profit and loss statement (para. 19). There was no discussion in the draft, and apparently none in the TO's meetings, reflecting the controversy in the UK (and earlier in the USA) over "comprehensive" versus "partial" tax allocation, since the "comprehensive" method was already widely accepted in the Netherlands.[90] While the TO recommended accounting for the absolute amount of the deferred tax, it did not rule out the use of present values (paras. 20–21). In its discussion of the treatment of taxes arising from the use of current cost, when there was a permanent difference between taxable income and the income shown in the profit and loss statement, the TO accepted most of the possible treatments, including one that would lead to a partial depletion of the revaluation reserve to cover additional taxation charges (para. 13).

5.3. Integration of the 1970 act into the New Civil Code

In 1976, Book 2 of the New Civil Code, incorporating the Act on Annual Financial Statements of 1970, was enacted into law. The project to draft a new civil code had begun in 1947 under the direction of Prof.mr E.M. Meijers. The first installment was published in April 1954 (the so-called Ontwerp Meijers, or Meijers Draft).[91] Meijers died two months later at the age of 73. Thereafter, his work was carried on by a team of lawyers. Owing to the immensity of the project, each of the Books into which the law codes have traditionally been divided was separately drafted, accepted by Parliament, and introduced (i.e., made effective).

The two "*Invoeringswetten*" ("Introduction Laws") for Book 2 of the New Civil Code, with the 1970 Act occupying Title 6 thereof, were presented to the Second

[89] Expense should be distinguished from expenditure, which is the amount actually paid. Expense is the cost to be matched against revenue in the profit and loss statement.

[90] For a later discussion of the deferred tax controversy, see Dr M.A. van Hoepen, *Anticipated and Deferred Corporate Income Tax in Companies' Financial Statements* (Deventer: Kluwer, 1981).

[91] *Ontwerp voor een Nieuw Burgerlijk Wetboek*, opgesteld door Prof.mr E.M. Meijers ingevolge opdracht verleend bij koninklijk besluit van 25 april 1947, no. 20 (Den Haag: Staatsdrukkerij- en Uitgeversbedrijf, 1954)

Chamber of Parliament in the session of 1970/71.[92] These drafts were treated as one in the subsequent process of review by the parliamentary preparation committee and in the parliamentary debates. They were passed by the Second Chamber on 22 April 1975 and by the First Chamber on 6 April 1976, and were introduced into law in 1976.

In large measure, the actions that culminated in approval were confined to technical matters of implementation, although, in the course of parliamentary debate, one substantive amendment to the Act on Annual Financial Statements was approved. In addition, a number of minor changes were effected, and the articles were renumbered from 1 through 38a to 306 through 343.

An amendment introduced by H. Wierenga (PvdA-Labor Party), 11005 no. 46, called upon companies to report a breakdown of their operating income (*bedrijfsresultaat*) by product lines and by operating units (*vestigingen*) with more than 100 employees in the Netherlands. At the suggestion of the Justice Minister, Mr A.A.M. van Agt, the segmentation according to operating units was deleted. As modified, Wierenga's amendment was adopted by the Second Chamber.[93]

During the debates in the Second Chamber, three other amendments were proposed by Wierenga but were not carried. One was a proposal to add a fourth paragraph to Article 5 (of the 1970 Act) on the valuation principle, as follows: "Further rules concerning the acceptability of certain valuation measures can be given by general administrative order" (11005 no. 43). In the meetings of the parliamentary preparation committee, the minister expressed his disapproval of such an amendment. The government, he said, would not know quite what to do with such powers as would be granted by the amendment. His view was that the government would like to see any doubtful cases referred to the Enterprise Chamber.[94] The Second Chamber rejected the amendment.[95]

The second amendment, 11005 no. 44, would have made the disclosure of the remuneration of individual directors and supervisors obligatory. As a result of resistance in the committee, the amendment was altered to require separate disclosure of the remuneration of directors and supervisors as groups.[96] Even in this form, it was rejected by the Second Chamber.

The final amendment, 11005 no. 45, would have required companies to publish absolute sales figures in all cases, except where an explicit exemption had been granted. Article 28 of the 1970 Act allowed companies to use index figures

---

92 *Bijlagen Handelingen Tweede Kamer, Zitting 1970–1971*, nos. 11005 (4 November 1970) and 11416 (11 August 1971), respectively.

93 *Handelingen Tweede Kamer, Zitting 1974–1975*, pp. 3713–3714, 3724.

94 *Vaste Commissie voor Justitie, Zitting 1973–1974*, pp. D40–D42.

95 *Handelingen Tweede Kamer, Zitting 1974–1975*, p. 3724. The rejections of the amendments discussed in the next two paragraphs were recorded on the same page.

96 *Vaste Commissie voor Justitie, Zitting 1973–1974*, pp. D42–D44.

without permission. The amendment was opposed by the minister and was voted down by the Second Chamber.

5.4. The years 1976–81: Schoonderbeek's first six years as chairman

5.4.1. Change in chairmanship

After $5\frac{1}{2}$ years on the CAJ and $4\frac{1}{4}$ years on the TO, Burggraaff retired from both bodies at the end of 1975. He had become chairman of both the CAJ and the TO in January 1972, and in December 1974 he relinquished the CAJ chairmanship to R.J. Ovezall, the director of accounting at Akzo. Hence, in 1975, he was the first chairman of the TO who was not simultaneously chairman of the CAJ, and, in fact, no one occupied the dual chairmanship in later years. In January 1976, Burggraaff became the NIvRA's vice president,[97] and he served a two-year term as president in 1977 and 1978. As will be seen below, in those capacities Burggraaff played a role in the discussions on the status and structure of the TO during the latter part of the 1970's.

Burggraaff's successor was Drs J.W. Schoonderbeek, a partner in the medium-sized Amsterdam audit firm of Pelser, Hamelberg, Van Til & Co., who had served as president of the NIvRA in 1973, and was professor of auditing in the Vrije Universiteit. Schoonderbeek started to attend meetings of both the TO and the CAJ in December 1975, since, as was the custom until the mid-1980's, all of the members of the auditors delegation were also members of the CAJ. As chairman of the TO, Schoonderbeek was also a member of the auditors delegation. Another change in the auditors delegation was the appointment of Drs H. Marseille, a partner in the large audit firm of Van Dien & Co, to succeed van Rossem.

The reconsideration of the status and structure of the TO dominated the period from 1976 to 1979, but other developments were important. Two more exposure drafts were issued, and a third statement of Considered Views was published. In January 1977, the Enterprise Chamber announced its first decision on financial reporting. And in 1977, there was a major change in the composition of the employers delegation in the TO, which was intended to fortify its role.

97 "Tripartite Overleg/CAJ", in *de Accountant*, vol. 82, no. 6, February 1976, p. 314.

5.4.2. Comments received on the third exposure draft[98]

Between October 1975 and May 1976, the TO received a total of 14 letters of comment on its third exposure draft, which had been issued on 30 June 1975. For the first time, comments were received from companies.[99] Six letters came from audit firms, four from companies, two from the life and pension insurance sector, and one each from a trade union and from the NIvRA's "Finad" discussion group of financial accountants.

In regard to the views conveyed from the companies, one must recognize that these may not have represented the official position of the management board. They were, however, written by individuals in position of authority within the enterprise.

Heineken preceded its specific remarks by the following observations:

> In reading the present exposure draft, one senses a certain unevenness; on the one hand, certain topics are treated in great detail, but on the other hand, fundamental problems, especially concerning the discussion [of] current cost/historical cost, are left unresolved.
>
> The question that forces itself [on the reader] is, who is being served by the proposed formalistic rules on all sorts of detailed problems, which would apply only in the Netherlands, when it is known that all kinds of developments are going on internationally.
>
> It is not clear from the exposure draft whether, and to what extent, these international developments have been taken into account (JO Alg 1049).

Referring to the "two-track policy" proposed in the exposure draft, Heineken reproached the TO for "not being able to decide which systems of valuation are acceptable, so that they shift the problem to the readers of financial statements". "It is deplorable", the company added, "that, especially in the Dutch environment, no link is made with the theory of current cost [*vervangingswaarde*], which, after all, gives a scientifically founded solution for the current problems"(JO Alg

98 As the reader will have noticed, the treatment of comment letters and of the deliberations leading up to the preparation of a final statement are not always introduced immediately following treatment of the contents of the exposure draft. Since other issues, such as questions over the status of IASC standards and the status and structure of the TO itself, periodically intervened, the authors have thought it useful to introduce the reaction to exposure drafts and the debate over the final statement in chronological order. Since the reactions received and the debates over final statements may well have influenced the arguments raised on organizational issues, their proper sequencing can be essential to an understanding of the whole.

99 In the 1970's, it was the VNO's practice to send the TO's exposure drafts to the members of its Financial Statements Committee (Commissie jaarrekening), composed of representatives of about a dozen companies. (It was the predecessor of the VNO/NCW's Committee of Information Preparers (Commissie Informatie Verschaffing).) At the same time, a notice would be placed in the VNO's membership newsletter, *Leden bulletin*, that copies of the exposure draft were available at the VNO's office. Apparently, few companies requested copies. (This information was supplied by the VNO.)

1049–1050). Heineken complained that companies that provided "a true picture of income" ("*een juist beeld van het resultaat*"), that is, an income figure corrected for inflation, would also be required to show the "phantom profits" ["*schijnwinsten*"] on the basis of historical cost (JO Alg 1053).

Estel NV Hoesch-Hoogovens recommended that most of the preface on current value be dropped, and regarded the statement that financial statements "ought" to present income on two valuation bases as "undesirable" (JO Alg 1081).

Royal Dutch Petroleum pointed out that it had provided additional information on the effects of inflation since 1974, despite the difficulties of doing so in an international organization consisting of some 900 companies. It did, however, ask the TO to withhold a final statement until more concrete rules could be worked out on a number of problems enumerated in the company's letter, and until there was a sufficient degree of international agreement concerning such rules (JO Alg 1135–1137).

Philips invited the TO to consider that "Good financial reporting cannot come about when one must follow detailed rules that attempt to formulate the requirements for all conceivable circumstances" (JO Alg 1226). On income determination, the company wrote:

> The prescription given in paragraph 5 seems to turn back the clock a number of years. In the light of developments abroad (the United Kingdom, the recently published prescriptions by the SEC), it seems to us that companies that base their valuation and income determination on current value [*actuele waarde*] ought to be no longer required to give figures on a historical [cost] basis in the notes (JO Alg 1232–1233).

It is interesting to observe that the four companies responding to the exposure draft all had a record of accommodating their financial reporting to the effects of changing prices. No letters were received from the many companies that would have objected to a requirement that they use something other than historical cost.

The responding audit firms were, in general, favorably inclined toward the exposure draft. One large firm expressed concern with the TO's decision to prescribe the disclosure of information on the basis of current value even though there was not yet sufficient agreement on the practical rules of application. Once those rules were to be formulated, the firm said, it would fully endorse the use of current value, and there would then be no need to call for additional information on the basis of historical cost (JO Alg 1078). Another large firm was of the view that the request for information on both current cost and historical cost bases was only a temporary solution, with historical cost information being necessary only "in the current phase of developments" (JO Alg 1431). Another large firm recommended that the TO become aware of international developments, and show that it has done so (JO Alg 1097).

At the 27 October 1977 meeting, Schoonderbeek proposed that the TO pay more attention to international developments. But the head of the employers delegation replied that, while the TO should take them into account, he believed that "foreign opinions" ("*buitenlandse opvattingen*"), if they do not agree with Dutch norms, should not be mentioned in the Considered Views. Schoonderbeek added that, in his view, international developments play a role in the formation of opinions of what is acceptable in economic and social life (JO Alg 1707–1708).

The Vervoersfederatie NVV/NKV (Federation of Transport Unions NVV/-NKV) signified its basic agreement with what it considered to be the most important section of the draft, namely, income determination. It argued that the TO should propose the use of current value as an important means for achieving comparability (JO Alg 1109–1110).

In an article published in *MAB*, Drs F. Graafstal, the senior technical partner in a large audit firm, said that the third exposure draft was the most important draft issued thus far, as it showed that the TO no longer shied away from controversial subjects.[100] He applauded this development. Graafstal also noted that the importance attached to the Considered Views was increasing, especially on the part of company managements. He expected more reactions on future exposure drafts from companies (p. 409). He thought that a rewriting of the earlier Considered Views would soon be necessary, to reflect this greater authority, and thought it also desirable to change the name of the statements for this reason (pp. 409–410). Of the several sections in the exposure draft, he said, the one on income determination was the most important: "It is the most far-reaching change in the practice of Dutch financial reporting that the committees have proposed so far" (p. 414). However, he added, it might have been advisable to formulate a more complete set of rules on the practical application of current value before it was actually recommended.

5.4.3. Comments received on the fourth exposure draft

Between July and September 1976, eleven comment letters were received: seven from audit firms, two from companies, and one each from the NIvRA's Finad/Intac study group and an individual auditor. In addition, Mr drs H. Beckman wrote on article on the draft.

A common thread through the letters from the audit firms was that the TO's views were sometimes made without proper motivation (i.e., reasons, arguments and the conceptual underpinnings). It was also believed that some of the views were too general, and did not take into account some possible relevant circum-

[100] F. Graafstal, "Het voorontwerp van beschouwingen naar aanleiding van de Wet op de Jaarrekening van Ondernemingen, aflevering nr. 3", in *Maandblad voor accountancy en bedrijfshuishoudkunde*, vol. 50, no. 8, September 1976, p. 408. Page citations in the text refer to this article.

stances. On accounting changes, two of the large audit firms doubted the usefulness of the "better insight" criterion. One said that its application might not easily lead to a consensus, and the other said that the criterion would be too heavily dependent on subjective judgments by management (JO Alg 1306, 1377).

The TO's proposed treatment of goodwill provoked a number of reactions. Two large audit firms accepted the TO's preference for amortizing goodwill to income, and a third large firm seemed to imply a similar judgment (JO Alg 1313, 1321). Of the two firms explicitly preferring amortization, one argued for a shorter time period than the ten years suggested by the TO, while the other firm counseled against prescribing a maximum amortization period. The latter firm took the view that, even if goodwill were to be charged immediately against equity, it should nevertheless be amortized to income, with corresponding credits made to equity.

As mentioned above, comments from a company may not necessarily have represented the official view of its management board, but were at least the views of the responsible individual writing the letter. Estel NV Hoesch-Hoogovens, which had commented on the third draft, said that it did not see a reason to treat changes in valuation principles differently from changes in methods used to arrive at estimates. The cumulative effect of all material accounting changes, it believed, should be charged or credited directly to equity. On goodwill, the company argued that an immediate charge to equity should be as acceptable as amortization, and not cast in the TO's negative terminology, as "not unacceptable" (JO Alg 1336–1337).

The NIvRA's study group of financial accountants and internal auditors contended that the amortization period for goodwill should correspond to the expected period of surplus profits, and should not be based on an arbitrary ten-year criterion (JO Alg 1300).

The individual auditor considered the charging of goodwill directly to equity to be incorrect, and he deplored the TO's decision not to declare this option as unacceptable (JO Alg 1274).

Beckman's article was mainly a summary of the draft, but in his concluding note he observed that the drafts issued thus far did not excel in offering reasons for the positions taken. They did, however, give a clear overview of current practice (JO Alg 1458).[101]

Owing in part to the time required to advise the government on the proposed draft law to adapt the EEC's Fourth Directive, but mainly to the decision made in May 1977 (see below) to have the Considered Views rewritten, the TO did not convert the fourth exposure draft into a statement of Considered Views by the end of the decade.

---

[101] H. Beckman, "Meningsuitingen van de Commissies Jaarverslaggeving (II)", in *TVVS/Ondernemingsrecht*, vol. 19, no. 12, December 1976, p. 365. Part I of his article was a summary of the third exposure draft.

5.4.4. The fifth exposure draft

In December 1976, the fifth exposure draft, being about twice the length of its immediate predecessor, was published. The contents included discussions of the role of the financial statements in relation to that of the notes; current value; criteria for the inclusion of assets and liabilities in the balance sheet; the breakdown of sales and operating income; interest; and earnings per share.

The section on the relationship between the financial statements and the notes (section Ib3) was significant for being the TO's first attempt to integrate an IASC standard into its series of statements of Considered Views. The TO's discussion drew on the parliamentary debates leading up to the passage of the Act on Annual Financial Statements of 1970, when it was made clear that the notes may not be used to correct the image conveyed by the financial statements. IAS 1, "Disclosure of Accounting Policies", issued in January 1975, was characterized by the TO as expressing the same view (Ib3, para. 3). (In fact, a NIvRA representative, P.C. Louwers, had served on the three-member drafting committee for this IASC standard.[102])

Two paragraphs in this section disclosed a significant shift in the TO's thinking on current value:

> **6** In earlier Considered Views, the committees [i.e., the TO] have made known their opinion that, if the valuation in the balance sheet differs in an important way from current value, there are two options:
>
> - the valuation in the balance sheet is changed to current value; in that case, information on the basis of historical cost must be given in the notes;
> - the valuation in the balance sheet is not adjusted; current value must be disclosed in the notes.
>
> At this time, the committees prefer valuation at current value in the balance sheet.
> **7** Concerning the profit and loss statement, the committees express their preference for current value as the basis for determining cost of goods sold.
>
> The income determination based on historical costs must also be disclosed in the financial statements. In view of the purpose of this provision, there is no objection to an approximation of this income determination in place of an exact calculation, if this appears to be desirable in practice.

The section on current value provided some guidance on how to ascertain and apply current value information once a company had decided to use it. Together with the aforequoted paragraphs, this represented the TO's fourth utterance on current value/current cost (namely, the section on fixed assets in the second

[102] Volten has written that the appearance of this view in IAS 1 was due "in no small way to Louwers' contribution". H. Volten, "IASC en NIVRA", in *de Accountant*, vol. 82, no. 10, June 1976, p. 577.

statement of Considered Views; the section on acceptable principles for income determination in the third exposure draft; and the section on materiality judgments about information to be presented in the financial statements, also in the third exposure draft).

While the CAJ was discussing the breakdown of sales and operating income, the Wierenga amendment on the required segmentation of operating income by product line was being taken up by Parliament. As a result of the amendment, the law required "insight into the degree to which each group of goods or services has contributed to operating income". In the exposure draft, the TO discussed some of the difficulties of presenting such an insight, and said that current financial reporting practices did not offer generally applicable solutions (IVb2, para. 8). On the required disclosure of each group's (i.e., segment's) contribution to operating income, the TO said that gross margin (sales minus cost of raw materials or cost of merchandise sold) had to be provided if the sales figure was not disclosed (para. 26). As the preferred way of providing the "insight" called for by the Wierenga amendment, the TO recommended the disclosure of segmented operating income, although admitting the difficulties likely to be encountered with the allocation of costs and transfer pricing.

Although the law did not have an absolute requirement to disclose sales, the TO said that the non-disclosure of sales would hamper the insight required by the law, and could be justified only when, on objective grounds, it was expected that disclosure would lead to serious damage to the enterprise (para. 12). Furthermore, the TO said that sales should be given by product group for each group contributing 15 or more percent to total sales, with a "miscellaneous" group accounting for no more than 30 percent of total sales (para. 27). The TO also went beyond the law by recommending a breakdown of sales according to geographical area and product groups (paras. 32, 26–27). The disclosure of gross margin by geographical area was also recommended (para. 33). These were forward-looking recommendations.

In treating the influence of interest on valuation, the TO was of the view that, in general, obligations should be stated at their nominal value, with no changes to reflect fluctuations in the interest rate (VI2, para. 10).

As with its immediate predecessor, the fifth exposure draft was not converted into a final statement of Considered Views by the end of the decade.

5.4.5. Origins of the movement for more authoritative statements

Precipitated by the need to define its relationship with the standards that had begun to emerge from the IASC in 1975, the TO began a period of self-appraisal. The NIvRA's management board, partly because the NIvRA was the Dutch professional body that liaised with the IASC, and partly owing to some of its members' disappointment with the TO's record of progress and impact, considered a number of proposals for reform. The direction of reform was toward enhancing the authority of the TO's statements.

The first sign that a reordering of the TO might be in the air became evident at the closing session of the Accountantsdag held on 13 May 1976 in Eindhoven. The chairman of the Accountantsdag, NIvRA President J. Uiterlinden, who was the external auditor of Philips, announced in his closing remarks that the NIvRA management board had agreed on a "forceful" plan by which IASC standards would be integrated into Dutch practice, and he added his own view of the next step that should be taken regarding the work of the TO:

> [The NIvRA] has formulated its point of view in regard to the fulfillment of the obligation it has accepted in association with the IASC. This point of view will be published in the June issue of "de Accountant", and can be discussed at the membership meeting this year. In short, it amounts to this: a forceful endeavor will be made for the acceptance of the pronouncements of the IASC in the economic and social climate. When acceptance on a sufficiently wide scale is apparent, the members of the Institute will be informed that the observance of an international pronouncement is expected from them in their auditing work. Compliance will be monitored, [and] eventually the disciplinary board [*Tuchtrechter*] may be involved. Like measures must be contemplated with respect to definitive [*pertinente*] pronouncements of considered views of the TO.[103]

In the June 1976 issue of *de Accountant*, the NIvRA announced that its management board had reconsidered its obligations toward the IASC based on the agreement that it had signed in 1973.[104] In the future, it would follow a three-step procedure for each IASC standard. In the first phase, the NIvRA would work with the means available to it to gain acceptance of the standard in the economic and social climate, and it expected its members to do the same. A second phase would start when the NIvRA management board announces that a specific standard "must be considered as generally accepted" ("*als algemeen aanvaard moet worden beschouwd*") in the Netherlands. It would do so when a standard was frequently applied in practice or when authoritative bodies such as the TO, the Stock Exchange Association, or the Enterprise Chamber had adopted it in their pronouncements. In this phase, auditors would be expected to draw attention in their report to any departure from the standard that was not explicitly mentioned in the financial statements themselves.[105]

---

[103] J. Uiterlinden, "Slottoespraak voorzitter" ("Chairman's Closing Remarks"), in *Stormen rond normen: De jaarrekening in nationaal, regionaal en mondiaal perspectief* (Storms over Norms: The Financial Statements in National, Regional and International Perspective) (Amsterdam: Nederlands Instituut van Registeraccountants, [1976]), p. 82.

[104] "NIVRA-verplichtingen nopens Internationale Standaarden van het IASC", in *de Accountant*, vol. 82, no. 10, June 1976, pp. 616–617. The announcement was repeated in the November 1976 issue of *de Accountant*, vol. 83, no. 3, pp. 118–119.

[105] The NIvRA's proposal reflected the influence of the standard-setting program in the United

In the third phase, a failure on the auditor's part to disclose a departure would be grounds for a proceeding before the NIvRA's disciplinary board (Raad van Tucht).

At the meeting of the TO on 15 June 1976, Schoonderbeek announced, apparently in relation to the new policy on the status of IASC standards, that the NIvRA management board was striving to bind NIvRA members more closely to the observance of "definitive" ("*pertinente*") pronouncements of both the IASC and the TO. This would entail, he said, a disclosure of any non-compliance in the auditor's report. Two members of the employers delegation objected on the ground that this would exceed the authority of the TO and would not be in accordance with its charge. Schoonderbeek replied that the board was only contemplating "a distillation of the recommendations already appearing in the statements of Considered Views that possess a more binding and restrictive character". He noted that the TO's charge, which included evaluation as well as an inventorying of practice, inevitably involved a degree of regulation (JO Alg 1266).

A possible motivation behind the NIvRA management board's desire to collect the "definitive" statements of Considered Views was the suggestion, made in an article by Volten, that the effectiveness of the NIvRA delegation to the IASC in gaining international acceptance of Dutch opinion could be enhanced if it was able to cite authoritative "national statements" ("*nationale uitspraken*") that served to define Dutch views on proper practice. The IASC's drafting committees, he said, often based their positions on such statements, and it was not helpful that a codified Dutch literature was largely lacking.[106]

The NIvRA's management board continued to discuss the procedures for issuing guidance statements on accounting principles. At the CAJ meeting on 26 January 1977, Chairman Prof. A.B. Frielink[107] announced that the management board had contemplated issuing such guidance on its own, because it had become concerned over the length of time required for the TO to produce final statements. Frielink reported that it was considering either of two plans for the issuance of future statements. Common to both plans was that the CAJ would, as before, do the initial drafting. Under the first plan, the TO would continue to issue statements on its own authority. Under the second plan, the NIvRA

Kingdom, where, since 1970, auditors had been expected to refer in their report to all significant departures from accounting standards, whether or not they were disclosed in the notes to the financial statements. See "Effect of Accounting Standards on Auditors' Reports", in *The Accountant*, vol. 164, no. 5021, 11 March 1971, p. 310; "Accountants lay down the law", in *The Economist* (London), vol. 238, no. 6648, 23 January 1971, p. 71; and Zeff, *op. cit.*, pp. 38–47. This precedent continued to be influential. It was also reflected in the TO's Foreword to the Draft Guidelines issued in June 1980 (see below) and in OTD-15 issued by the NIvRA in January 1982 (see Chapter 6).

[106] Volten, "IASC en NIVRA", *op.cit.*, p. 575.

[107] Frielink had served as NIvRA president in 1975, and had completed his tenure on the NIvRA's management board in December 1976.

would issue the statements itself after consulting the TO. One member of the CAJ said that the second plan would severely diminish the standing of the TO. As in the 15 June 1976 meeting of the TO (see above), the issue of the degree to which pronouncements should be binding again came to the fore. During 1976, the NIvRA had publicly announced a three-step procedure by which IASC standards would become binding in the Netherlands, and it would have been awkward if IASC standards were to have a higher standing than the statements of Considered Views issued by the TO. A member suggested that a summary of the "definitive pronouncements" ("*pertinente uitspraken*") might be an effective way of drawing attention to the opinions that should be expected to command wide respect by companies and auditors. Frielink volunteered to prepare a specimen draft of "definitive pronouncements" already reflected in the two statements of Considered Views, so that the committee might judge the usefulness of such a publication.

Within a month, Frielink had prepared two alternative drafts, in which instances of agreement or disagreement with IASC standards were noted. The drafts were discussed at the CAJ's meeting on 28 February, and it was decided to forward them to the TO for its views, but without the inclusion of "definitive" ("*pertinente*") in the title (CAJ Not 792).

Then the NIvRA stepped up its pressure. During the morning of 15 March, the CAJ held its monthly meeting, and Chairman Frielink announced that the NIvRA's executive committee (i.e., the executive group within its management board) believed that something should be done with "definitive pronouncements" since there was a need to carry out the NIvRA's obligation to use its "best endeavors" to seek members' compliance with IASC standards. Several members suggested that this role could better be performed by the TO, as this would imply a commitment by the business community (*bedrijfsleven*). In reply, a member argued that this would mean a change in the TO's task; rather than inventorying and judging, the TO would issue binding pronouncements. But another member disagreed, saying that judging includes the issuance of binding pronouncements (CAJ Not 794–795).

At its meeting on the afternoon of 15 March, the TO considered Frielink's specimen drafts.[108] The employers delegation reacted cautiously, and was curious to know the motives that had prompted the NIvRA's management board to propose that it might issue final statements in the future. The employees delegation was sympathetic to the idea. The principal danger of a parallel series of "pronouncements", it was said, was that they might begin to lead a life of their

[108]The TO's February meeting had been cancelled owing to a notification received from the Federated Dutch Trade Union Movement (FNV, Federatie Nederlandse Vakbeweging – successor to the Consultative Council of Trade Unions) that it was suspending all contacts with employer representatives until a national conflict over wages and the terms of working conditions was settled (JO Alg 1461).

own and draw attention from the Considered Views themselves. A criticism of the drafts was that the selection of the points to be emphasized seemed to be arbitrary. If the only reason for issuing such "pronouncements" was a better accessibility of the particular points in the statements of Considered Views, then, it was argued, an index could be provided (JO Alg 1520–1521). At the meeting of 17 May, the employers delegation proposed that the integrity of the Considered Views be retained, but that the "affirmative pronouncements" ("*stellige uitspraken*") be denoted by the use of bold facing. References to IASC standards, it was suggested, could be indicated in the margins, and deviations could be mentioned without discussion. Once this proposal was accepted in principle, it was agreed that it would be necessary to rewrite the Considered Views so that the "affirmative pronouncements" could be set apart from those that were purely advisory.[109] The CAJ was asked to recommend the specific procedures (JO Alg 1550–1552).

At the CAJ's meeting of 25 May 1977, it was suggested that the rewriting of the exposure drafts and final statements of Considered Views could be more expeditiously done by an individual than by a committee. Prof.dr J. Klaassen, of the Vrije Universiteit, was mentioned as one who might be able to integrate the rewriting into his university projects. Klaassen, who was a member of the CAJ, was not present at the meeting, but he accepted the assignment at the CAJ's next meeting, by which time the TO had joined in the invitation (CAJ Not 819, 825–826).

5.4.6. Comments received on the fifth exposure draft

Between March and November 1977, the TO received 14 letters of comment on the fifth exposure draft (which had been issued in December 1976): eight from audit firms, four from business circles, and one each from NIvRA's Finad/Intac study group and from the Society of Financial Analysts. In addition, two journal articles were published on the draft. Most of the comments dealt with current value and segmentation.

The audit firms made several points on current value, to-wit: that, for small companies, its cost might exceed the benefits; that further motivation should be given for the TO's change in position toward current value; that more practical guidance should be given on how to apply current value; and that it would be confusing if historical cost information would need to be given in addition to current value. One large firm complained that the TO had gone beyond its charge

[109] Volten has written that "the Enterprise Chamber's decisions were certainly the most important immediate cause of the decision to rewrite the *Considerations*". (See below for a discussion of the first decisions by the Enterprise Chamber, which were announced in January 1977.) Henk Volten, *Challenges to Financial Reporting in the Netherlands – How Corporate Reporting is Monitored by Social Pressure Groups*, PILOT (Netherlands) 9 (Amsterdam: Nederlands Instituut van Registeraccountants, November 1979), p. 20.

(i.e., inventorying and evaluation) by giving "affirmative preferences" ("*stellige voorkeuren*"), an example being the requirement to disclose sales, which, the firm said, "completely abrogated the freedom of choice contained in the law" (JO Alg 1603). Another large audit firm also reproved the TO for exceeding its charge. Its task was not to *develop* the norms that were acceptable in the economic and social climate, the firm said, but the TO did so in proposing segmentation by geographical area. Moreover, the TO went further than the law, the firm said, by calling for disclosure of sales, let alone its segmentation (JO Alg 1635–1636). The other audit firms, however, did not register any fundamental objections to the TO's initiative on the disclosure of sales and segmentation.

Philips conveyed the views of a study group, together with letters from its director of group accounting and its chief of the internal audit department. Taking a tack similar to two of the audit firms, the Philips study group criticized the TO for having exceeded its charge. Further, the TO's approach to implementing the recommended segmentation was found to be defective. Although the study group expressed agreement with the TO's stronger preference for current value, it did not see the necessity of providing historical cost information in the notes (JO Alg 1677).

The group accounting director of Estel NV Hoesch-Hoogovens expressed his "unhappiness" with the more stringent recommendation on current value. Neither in the Netherlands nor abroad, he said, was there sufficient clarity about the future of current value to justify the TO's position (JO Alg 1681–1684).

The letter received from the Society of Financial Analysts (Vereniging van Beleggingsanalisten) was the first communication received from that body, and it dealt solely with the section of the exposure draft on earnings per share (EPS). The Society had published its own views on how to adjust EPS for changes in capital, which it found to be superior to the TO's recommended approach, and it invited the TO to reconsider its view in the light of the Society's statement (JO Alg 1596–1597). One of the audit firms also drew the TO's attention to the Society's statement on EPS, and questioned whether the subject should be treated in the Considered Views (JO Alg 1716).

In one of the journal articles, H.W. Hageman said that he did not see in this exposure draft a continuation of the upward trend in providing more concrete and useful guidance (JO Alg 1774–1781).[110] On current value, Hageman said that the TO should not underestimate the difficulty of implementation, and he noted that the TO had failed to address the most important issue in this regard, namely, how to determine the current value of fixed assets. On segmentation, he echoed several of the comment letters in maintaining that the TO had gone beyond the law, while giving virtually no guidance on the determination of the

[110] H.W. Hageman, "Het voorontwerp van beschouwingen naar aanleiding van de Wet op de Jaarrekening van Ondernemingen, aflevering nummer 5", in *Maandblad voor accountancy en bedrijfshuishoudkunde*, vol. 52, no. 3, March 1978, pp. 145–152.

segments.

In the other article, which dealt exclusively with segment reporting, Beckman concluded that the exposure draft was "very disappointing" (JO Alg 1758).[111] His main concern was that the TO had given hardly any guidance on how to identify segments by product or industry. What resulted, he said, was a recommendation to publish the figures plus an enumeration of some of the problems that might be encountered.

Overall, the criticism of current value and segmentation was the severest thus far received by the TO. One of the common threads, which was also seen in the reactions to earlier exposure drafts, was that auditors and companies wanted more, not less, guidance, especially on the practical problems of implementation. In its early exposure drafts, the TO tended to make fairly general statements, usually avoiding controversial positions. When the TO began to enter more contested areas, such as current value, it was criticized for not supporting its positions with reasons and arguments. But the very composition of the TO, namely, three delegations representing very different constituencies, would have made it difficult enough to arrive at common conclusions, let alone common arugments in support of those conclusions. The TO's practice of adopting positions only with the unanimous consent of the three delegations placed even greater emphasis on the need to find solutions to problems raised by any member, thus complicating the process of developing coherent positions, coherently defended. Assisted by the small secretariat supplied by the NIvRA,[112] the TO was a volunteer body that ordinarily met one afternoon per month to discuss drafts prepared by the CAJ, another volunteer body, which goes some distance toward explaining the pace at which the TO was able to produce drafts and final statements. Another part of the explanation is the fact that one of the three delegations represented companies that, understandably, were not eager to surrender the freedom that the law allowed in fashioning their annual financial statements.

In the absence of greater resources and an active stimulus from government, a private sector body must seek peer approval for the direction and content of its initiatives, else they would have little impact. As will be seen, efforts were made by the NIvRA and within the TO itself to strengthen its hand and provide more ample resources.

[111] Mr drs H. Beckman, "Financiële informatie per produktgroep en de Beschouwingen – Een meningsuiten van de commissies-jaarverslaggeving", in *TVVS/Ondernemingsrecht*, vol. 21, no. 1, January 1978, p. 16.

[112] The secretariat was the equivalent of less than one full-time person. (Information supplied by O.M. Volgenant jr.)

5.4.7. The TO's deliberations from mid-1977 through 1981

During the balance of 1977 and through 1981, the TO addressed a full agenda of items:

- the first decisions of the Enterprise Chamber;
- the procedures for determining the status of IASC standards in relation to the Considered Views;
- the retitling of the Considered Views as Guidelines;
- the issuance of two exposure drafts (nos. 6 and 7) and a statement of Considered Views (no. 3);
- the Foreword to the rewritten Considered Views; and
- the restructuring of the TO.

In late 1977, important changes occurred in the membership of the employers delegation to the TO. In 1979, the spokesman for the employees delegation wrote an article commenting on the evolution of the TO during the 1970's, which provided an interesting historical perspective at the time of the changes in membership in 1977.

5.4.7.1. First decisions of the Enterprise Chamber

In January 1977, the Enterprise Chamber handed down its first opinion on a case involving financial statements that were alleged to be at variance with the law. The defendant was Douwe Egberts B.V. Decisions on cases brought against Homburg B.V., Sekisui Systeembouw N.V., and N.V. Vulcaansoord (the latter being the first decision arising from a proceeding initiated by SOBI) were announced in April and May. In none of these decisions did the court refer to utterances by the TO, and there was concern among some of its members that its views were not seen as carrying any standing with the court. In an article published in June 1977, Burggraaff was critical of the Enterprise Chamber's first verdict. He thought that the court should have referred explicitly to the Considered Views, because that would confirm their authority, which, he argued, would enhance the long-run quality of financial reporting. That the Enterprise Chamber's decisions deviated in only a small degree from the Considered Views nonetheless gave rise to uncertainty.[113] In a later article, J.W. van Aanhold and

[113] J.A. Burggraaff, "Een eersteling: Met gejuich begroet?", in *Maandblad voor accountancy en bedrijfshuishoudkunde*, vol. 51, no. 6, June 1977, p. 275.

Burgert, writing several years later, observed that the Considered Views "continued to suffer after it became clear that during the first legal proceedings the [Enterprise Chamber] did not refer in its Judgements to the [Considered Views] and even made one or two pronouncements in contradiction to them. Moroever, in the first appeal case, the solicitor general of our [High] Court explicitly approved of this attitude and these opinions of the [Enterprise Chamber]". Burgert, "Current Accounting Practice in the Netherlands", *op.cit.*, pp. 54–55. Volten wrote that the failure by the Enterprise Chamber to show why its judgments in certain instances

Drs F. Graafstal agreed with Burggraaff and, referring to the Vulcaansoord decision, deplored the action of the court in finding financial statements insufficient even though, on the matter in question, they complied with the TO's Considered Views. Van Aanhold and Graafstal said they found it difficult to believe that the TO's Considered Views would have been approved without thorough study.[114]

Burggraaff's concern led to a colloquy in the Second Chamber of Parliament in April 1978. Mr A. de Graaf (PvdA) submitted a question on 18 April, in which he asked the Justice Minister for his views on

> the future position, task and authority of the TO ... now that the Enterprise Chamber of the Court of Justice at Amsterdam has in two decisions clearly ignored the published considered views of the TO (JO Alg 1788).

In an attached note, de Graaf cited the Douwe Egberts and Vulcaansoord decisions, and referred to the articles by Burggraaff and by van Aanhold and Graafstal.

In his reply on 9 May, Minister Mr J. de Ruiter (CDA[115]) defined the roles of the two bodies as follows:

> The TO of the financial reporting committees of the organizations of employers, employees and auditors, which exhibits a great deal of activity, performs a valuable function. Through its considered views, this body furthers both the development of a consensus on the requirements that good financial statements must meet, as well as an increase in the general level of [quality of] financial statements. The considered views of the TO, which are not binding, derive their authority from their intrinsic value.
>
> The enterprise chamber of the Court of Justice at Amsterdam is designated as the court that, on suits brought by interested parties, evaluates compliance with the requirements of the law in particular financial statements. How the court wishes to use the considered views of the TO is completely up to its own judgment, on which it does not need to render an account; besides, judicial bodies are not in

differed from the Considered Views "is deplorable in that it endangers the authority of the [TO] and disappointing in view of the government's expectation that the [Considered Views] would serve as a guide for the Enterprises [sic] Chamber". Henk Volten, *Challenges to Financial Reporting in the Netherlands*, *op.cit.*, p. 20.

[114] J.W. van Aanhold and F. Graafstal, "Een vernietiging: Het oordeel van de ondernemingskamer over de jaarrekening 1974/75 van N.V. Vulcaansoord", in *Maandblad voor accountancy en bedrijfshuishoudkunde*, vol. 52, no. 2, February 1978, pp. 45–46. In a later article, Beckman concluded that the Considered Views could be useful to the Enterprise Chamber as reference literature, although he mentioned some inherent weaknesses that might limit this role, such as the absence from the TO of investors' representatives, and the tendency of the TO not to present the arguments in support of its recommendations. Mr drs H. Beckman, "De relatie Ondernemingskamer – Tripartiete overleg", in *de Accountant*, vol. 85, no. 3, November 1978, p. 190.

[115] The CDA is roughly similar to the Christian Democrats in several European Continental countries. For a discussion of the major Dutch political parties, see the section on "National government and political parties" in Chapter 1.

> the habit of ostensibly basing their verdicts on considered views [of professional bodies]. Without doubt, the TO will take the decisions of the enterprise chamber into account in [arriving at] its considered views, insofar as these are of importance outside the scope of the particular financial statements that have been placed before it (JO Alg 1788).[116]

In an earlier question, posed on 26 January 1978, de Graaf had asked the minister to what extent the report of the Limperg Instituut committee on valuation principles used in financial statements (the study for which the Ministry had provided a *f* 20 000 subsidy) would be used to monitor compliance by non-listed companies with the law. On 26 April, an under-secretary replied on behalf of the minister that the Limperg Instituut survey was only a pilot study, and could not be seen as part of the attempt to enforce or monitor compliance (JO Alg 1790).[117]

An author writing in *TVVS* characterized the minister's replies as what "could be expected" but as "not satisfactory", and asked the following rhetorical question:

> Is there a point in going on with the TO in this way, and does not the obligation of the court to motivate its verdicts imply, when, during a suit, an appeal is made to the authority of the Considered Views and this appeal is turned down, that a motivation is provided of why this was done? (JO Alg 1864–1865)[118]

5.4.7.2. Status of IASC standards in relation to the considered views

On 12 September 1977, a special meeting was convoked in 's-Hertogenbosch to discuss the NIvRA's evolving policy on "national norms" in the context of its obligation to the IASC (CAJ Perm 2074–2081). In attendance were Burggraaff, as NIvRA president, and J. Uiterlinden, his immediate predecessor, representing the management board; van Bruinessen from the CAJ, substituting for Frielink, who was unable to attend; three members of the NIvRA's Council on Professional Issues (CBV, College voor Beroepsvraagstukken)[119]: A.C. Bakker (chairman), Drs A.J. Bosman, and Schoonderbeek (who was attending also as TO chairman); and Volten. Burggraaff chaired the meeting.

Schoonderbeek presented the TO's position. He began by reporting that the CAJ's proposal for an abstract of the Considered Views (Frielink's specimen draft) had "evoked resistance", because the link between the statements and the

---

[116] *Bijlagen Handelingen Tweede Kamer, Zitting 1977–1978*, p. 2053.

[117] *Bijlagen Handelingen Tweede Kamer, Zitting 1977–1978*, p. 1953. See footnote 38, above, for a discussion of the project to which de Graaf referred.

[118] W.J.S., "Kamervragen over accountantscontrole op jaarrekeningen en publikatieplicht", in *TVVS/Ondernemingsrecht*, vol. 21, no. 7, July 1978, p. 216.

[119] The CBV was established in 1974 to coordinate the NIvRA's technical committees and to give advice to the NIvRA's management board on various aspects of the auditor's role in society. *Verslag van de werkzaamheden*, 1 september 1973 t/m 31 augustus 1974 (Nederlands Instituut van Registeraccountants), p. 24.

underlying reasoning would be lost. Consequently, the only solution, according to the TO, was a complete rewriting of the Considered Views in such a way that the "affirmative pronouncements" would be immediately clear to the reader. The IASC standards would also be incorporated in the rewriting. He emphasized that the rewriting would not lead to a change in contents, and he urged the NIvRA not to attempt to extract "affirmative pronouncements" from the Considered Views on its own: this could lead, he said, to "the explosion of the TO".

The general reaction to Schoonderbeek's remarks was positive, if the rewriting could be completed in two years. Schoonderbeek replied that it could, but others were skeptical.

On IASC standards, the NIvRA's management board wanted to give shape to its announced intention to bind NIvRA members to their observance, once they were adopted by the TO. The discussion centered on terminology. Should the key phrase characterizing the status of IASC standards in the Netherlands be "generally acceptable" ("*algemeen aanvaardbaar*") or "generally accepted" ("*algemeen aanvaard*")? The former, it was said, would place IASC standards on a par with the TO's Considered Views, that is, as materially binding even though compliance could not be formally enforced by disciplinary measures, while the latter would go much further toward use of the disciplinary sanction. It was agreed that the TO would initially announce the "general acceptability" of the IASC standards issued to date. The NIvRA would then communicate that decision to its members, which would give the IASC standards the same status as the Considered Views (that is, they could not be formally enforced). Once the TO had completed the rewriting of the Considered Views in two years' time, it would announce that the IASC standards had become "generally accepted", which would make them formally binding for NIvRA members.[120]

[120] At about the same time, the TO was working on a public statement of its position to be included in the NIvRA management board's mailing of IASC standards 1–6 to members. Discussions on the exact wording of a draft had been going on since July 1977. At the TO's meeting of 20 September (eight days after the meeting in 's-Hertogenbosch), it was decided to delete all references to acceptability from the TO's statement and the accompanying press release (JO Alg 1688;cf.1663, 1667). The apparent reason was fear on the part of the employers delegation that the IASC standards might start leading a life of their own. In the TO statement released in September, the following sentences appeared:

> The Annual Reporting Committees [i.e., the TO] have found that IASC Standards 1–6 in general represent guidelines that go no further than what is reflected in legal requirements and the Considered Views. This implies that financial statements complying with legal requirements and the Considered Views in general also comply with the aforementioned standards.

The TO's statement then proceeded to point out specific areas in which the Dutch legal requirements and the Considered Views went further than the IASC standards. *Mededeling van de Commissies Jaarverslaggeving van de Raad van Nederlandse Werkgeversverbonden, de Federatie Nederlandse Vakbeweging, het Christelijk Nationaal Vakverbond, het Nederlands*

The final matter taken up at the meeting involved a suggestion that came up in the TO, evidently in the light of the first decisions of the Enterprise Chamber, to invite a legal expert to attend its meetings. It was agreed that Mr drs H. Beckman, who was also a member of the NIvRA, could play this role. The invitation was extended, and Beckman began serving in October.

The following year, a further step was taken to encourage compliance with IASC standards. On 1 August 1978, at the request of the NIvRA management board, the Stock Exchange Association amended its Rules for Securities Trading (Fondsenreglement) to require that listed companies prepare their financial statements in accordance with IASC standards to the extent that they have been "accepted" by the NIvRA.[121] The NIvRA, rather than the TO, was cited as the source, one supposes, because it was the official Dutch representative on the IASC. This action resulted from an initial understanding reached between the NIvRA and the Stock Exchange Association in February 1977. In November, when the TO first learned of this initial understanding, it objected that the TO had not been a party to the request made of the Stock Exchange Association. After receipt of assurance from board level that the TO would be consulted before the NIvRA were to take any further actions relating to IASC standards, the TO's concern subsided (JO Alg 1728–1729;cf.1690, 1691). Then, when the Stock Exchange Association announced its amended rules the following August, without making a reference to the TO, the TO asked the NIvRA management board to publish a statement pointing out, in accordance with the agreement at Den Bosch, that the NIvRA board would act only after the TO were to declare IASC standards as "accepted" (JO Alg 1861–1862). In October 1978, the NIvRA published a statement to this effect.[122]

The IASC standards received further recognition in November 1978, when the

---

Instituut van Registeraccountants betreffende Internationale Standaarden voor Jaarrekeningen (IAS) samengesteld door het International Accounting Standards Committee (IASC) (Kluwer, September 1977), p. IAS-04.

[121] The Stock Exchange Association deleted this requirement on 1 July 1983, when it approved a major amendment of its Rules for Securities Trading to reflect the EEC Directives on securities listings, the framing, supervision and distribution of prospectuses, and interim statements. For a report of the change in the rules, see "New Admission Rules", *The Amsterdam Stock Exchange in 1983* (Amsterdam: Amsterdam Stock Exchange, [1984]), p. 11.

[122] "Internationale standaarden voor de jaarrekening", in *de Accountant*, vol. 85, no. 2, October 1978, p. 84. For further comments on this episode, see H. Volten, "IASC: Internationale standaarden voor de jaarrekening", in *De Naamlooze Vennootschap*, vol. 56, no. 9, September 1978, pp. 153–157; and Mr J.M. van der Beek, "Wanneer worden normen werkelijk normen", in *Maandblad voor accountancy en bedrijfshuishoudkunde*, vol. 53, no. 5, May 1979, pp. 195–202.

Van der Beek's article prompted Mr A. de Graaf (PvdA) to raise a further question in the Second Chamber concerning the TO. On 5 September 1979, he asked the Justice Minister if he thought that the TO should be given legal status in order to enhance the standing of the Considered Views. On 18 September, the minister preferred not to give an answer, but instead to await the outcome of the discussions then going on in the TO (JO Alg 2997).

presiding judge of the Enterprise Chamber said, in an address to the NIvRA's Fall Conference, that his court regarded the IASC standards as having a status equal to that of the Considered Views.[123]

5.4.7.3. Important changes in the TO's membership

The production of five exposure drafts and two final statements of Considered Views was beginning to have an effect. Auditors were referring more frequently to the Considered Views in their discussions with clients, and companies were finding the auditors to be more "difficult". Moreover, the first decisions of the Enterprise Chamber in early 1977 struck some companies with the realization that, perhaps, in a future decision the Considered Views might be accepted as best practice. Companies also were coming to believe that accounting rules might not be so bad as they had once thought. The likely role of the TO in advising government on the eventual adaptation of the EEC's Fourth Directive and the persistent discussions of current value/current cost in a decade of high inflation contributed to the growing awareness in company circles of the importance of active and serious participation by employers in the TO's deliberations.

Within the TO, some had perceived an increasing coincidence of views and mutual sympathy between the auditors and employees delegations, occasionally placing the employers delegation on the defensive. On several occasions, differences between the leadership of the employers delegation and members of either the employees or auditors delegation had flared into pointed exchanges, and, at one point, the employees, irritated with the employers, had even threatened to withdraw from the TO. The leadership of the employers delegation had, since the beginning, been dominated by retired executives who had no daily contact with practice, and there had been no interest in having a technical backup committee, much as the auditors could count on the CAJ.[124]

For one or more of these reasons, key changes were made in the composition of the employers delegation in late 1977. The delegation's constituency believed that it was important to fortify its role in the TO, and especially to bring in some members who were on the management boards of some of the large, progressive companies. In December, two directors of large companies joined the delegation: A. van Putten, of Nedlloyd and a member of the SER, who became head of the delegation, and R.C. Spinosa Cattela, of Philips. J.W. Frijns, who had just retired as accounting and finance director and a member of the management board of Van Doorne's Bedrijfswagenfabriek DAF B.V., the country's most important

123 See Volten, *Challenges to Financial Reporting in the Netherlands*, *op.cit.*, p. 9; and "Najaarsconferentie", in *de Accountant*, vol. 85, no. 6, February 1979, p. 398.

124 Interviews with Drs J.F. Leeuwerik, 24 October 1990; with Mr R. Hoorens van Heijningen, 12 November 1990; with R.C. Spinosa Cattela, 13 November 1990 and 23 September 1991; with Drs J.P.M. Nabbe, 27 September 1990; with E.G. Hoefer, 4 December 1990; with Prof.dr A. van Putten, 8 July 1991; and with Mr H.C. Wesseling, 10 July 1991.

producer of cars and trucks, also joined the employers delegation.[125] At the same time, a support group (study group on financial statements, *werkgroep jaarrekening*) was formed with the participation of members from both the VNO and the Dutch Christian Employers Federation (NCW, Nederlands Christelijk Werkgeversverbond).

An important addition to the employees delegation in late 1977 was Mr J.C.M.G. Bloemarts, a member of staff of the Federated Dutch Trade Union Movement (FNV, Federatie Nederlandse Vakbeweging), who had just been chosen for membership on the SER.[126]

5.4.7.4. Evolution of the climate within the TO

In 1977–78, the temper of the TO was not the same as it had been in 1971. The parties had become more accustomed to the demands of their task, and to collaborating with colleagues from very different constituencies. This change in the working climate of the TO during the 1970's was characterized in a revealing article, "The TO Seen Through the Eyes of an Employees Representative", written in 1979 by J. Nabbe, the spokesman for the employees delegation.[127] At the TO's first meeting in August 1971, Nabbe said there was "a certain tension", as the meeting was, in a way, "an experiment" (p. 746). He felt that some members were thinking, given the presence of labor representatives, "how is it possible that things got this far?" and "what, in God's name, will these people have to say?"(p. 746) Despite some problems on specific issues, Nabbe nonetheless had the impression that the general atmosphere of the meetings was open (p. 747).

In his article, Nabbe discerned three phases in the TO's life. The first phase was "The period of 'defective' codification", during which the TO did not go beyond making a rough inventory of practice on the basis of individual experiences that were judged only on the basis of explicit provisions of the law. He added: "In

---

[125] Van Putten was a professor of *bedrijfseconomie* in the law faculty of Erasmus Universiteit Rotterdam, Spinosa Cattela held a degree in accounting from the University of Melbourne (and was a member of the Australian Society of Accountants), and Frijns was a member of the NIvRA. Spinosa Cattela had returned to the Netherlands in 1974, after spending most of his career with Philips overseas.

[126] In 1976, the Consultative Council of Trade Unions (Overlegorgaan Vakcentrales) was dissolved following the decision of the Christian National Trade Union Federation (CNV, Christelijk Nationaal Vakverbond) to withdraw. In the same year, the FNV came into existence as the vehicle for combining the Dutch Federation of Trade Unions (NVV, Nederlands Verbond van Vakverenigingen) and the Dutch Catholic Trade Union Federation (NKV, Nederlands Katholiek Vakverbond). For further particulars, see J.P. Windmuller, C. de Galan and A.F. van Zweeden, *Arbeidsverhoudingen in Nederland* (Utrecht/Antwerpen: Het Spectrum B.V., 1983), pp. 260–261. In 1976, therefore, the FNV and the CNV replaced the Consultative Council of Trade Unions in the list of sponsoring bodies of the TO. Bloemarts' previous work had been in the NKV.

[127] Drs J. Nabbe, "Het Tripartiete Overleg gezien door de bril van een werknemersvertegenwoordiger", in *de Accountant*, vol. 85, no. 11, July/August 1979, pp. 746–751. Page citations in the text refer to this article.

particular, the employers were constantly thinking about their own financial statements, and sometimes very special situations were presented as if they were frequently occurring practices" (p. 748).

After a few years, the TO entered "The period of non-binding directions". "This development came almost too late, but still in time to keep us involved. At around that time, we had seriously considered dropping out". It was then, he said, that the employees began to formulate explicit goals and principles, as a result of which the FNV published *Open Boek* (see footnote 59, above) was published (p. 748).

The third phase was "The period of binding directions". During this phase, he said, the auditors started "getting used to the idea of regulation", and the employers were becoming "less tenacious in their opposition", changes that Nabbe attributed to general developments occurring outside the TO, such as the IASC standards, the decisions by the Enterprise Chamber, and the EEC's Fourth Directive. The transition to this third phase, he said, had not (by 1979) been completed. The employees' representatives, he said, would like this movement toward more binding rules to be formalized by a legal recognition of the TO, and, preferably, by a better compliance mechanism than the Enterprise Chamber. Nabbe said he would like to see regular supervision of compliance by a special body possessing delegated authority, as was recently suggested by Schoonderbeek (pp. 749–750).[128]

Nabbe also ventured a candid assessment of the performance by the three delegations. He had considerable praise for the work done by the auditors and the NIvRA. It was his belief that the auditors had been able to take a more independent posture in relating to the employers thanks to support from the employees (p. 749).[129] Even so, he thought that the auditors should have shown more persistence in clinging to their points of view, and should not have considered the publication of exposure drafts with dissenting opinions to be a bad thing (pp. 749–780). Nabbe added:

> The *employers* do not function in the TO differently than they do elsewhere; generally speaking, they slacken the pace and avoid coming to grips with problems. They understand that trick very well: they pump their brakes. They regularly make concessions, but force a stop at important moments. This maneuvering requires endless patience by the other parties and especially the chairman. In the end, this tactic is not very clever. Economic and social developments go on. The only thing that the employers can achieve is that things go more slowly. In the

---

[128] Nabbe's reference was to J.W. Schoonderbeek, "Regelgeving voor de jaarrekening, aard en werkwijze", in *De Naamlooze Vennootschap*, vol. 57, nos. 1/2, January/February 1979, pp. 5–8.

[129] An identical sentiment was expressed by Bloemarts a year later. See "Workers and Accounting Standards", in *The Tripartite Accounting Standards Committee*, PILOT (Netherlands) 10 (Amsterdam: Nederlands Instituut van Registeraccountants, December 1980), p. 17.

> meantime, the braking has demanded so much concentration that a contribution to the direction of economic and social developments is hardly possible (p. 750).

Nabbe said he was "not dissatisfied" with the performance of the employees, given the limited resources available for that kind of work, which, he added, is a disadvantage for the party that seeks to effect changes in society (p. 750).

In a subsequent interview, Nabbe said that he found the obstacles raised by the employers delegation to be irritating to both the employees and auditors delegations. But, he said, the auditors, being auditors, were polite. Nabbe could speak more openly in regard to the employers' delaying actions. The auditors, he believed, tried to gain an outlet for their frustrations through Nabbe's expressions made at the meetings. He said that the auditors had told him that, by the mere fact that he was here, they could play the role of mediator between the employers and the employees. He said that he had the opportunity to leave the TO several times. (He remained a member of the TO until June 1980.) There were two reasons why he stayed. First, he felt that "we could reach results there". It would be, he said, "very stupid to leave the auditors alone with the employers: the results would be worse". The need for a more formal arrangement "became overwhelming". Second, he had become acquainted with members of auditors' circles, and began discussing, at various events and occasions, the role of the auditor in society. He said that the auditor has an important role to play in society, and he wanted to make this point. He said that he was also aware of the importance of the auditor's role in relation to the interests of trade unions.[130]

5.4.7.5. Retitling of the considered views as guidelines

The title "Considered Views" had been introduced by van Rietschoten in November 1970, even before the TO came into existence. The full title was: "Considered Views Relating to the Act on Annual Financial Statements of Enterprises". In those early days, when the participants lacked any experience in pronouncing on accounting principles, when it was not known how their pronouncements would be received, and when each of the three delegations was still learning how to deal with one another, a title that understated the authority implied by their pronouncements was understandable. But, as Nabbe had written, the tripartite body had matured as it had developed. Moreover, large audit firms were saying, in their letters of comment on the exposure drafts, that they wanted (as one firm wrote) "concrete guidelines concerning the permissibility of valuation norms and matters of presentation".

At the TO's meeting on 15 November 1977, the title of its statements was raised. The TO was discussing a memorandum from Klaassen on the structure of the Considered Views that he was engaged in rewriting. In his memorandum,

[130] Interview with Drs J.P.M. Nabbe, 27 September 1990. (The contents of the interview have been published with the express permission of the interviewee.)

Klaassen suggested that it would be desirable to change the title to reflect (1) a clearer description of "stringent pronouncements" ("*stringente uitspraken*"), (2) the incorporation of IASC standards in the TO's statements, and (3) the fact that the 1970 legislation had become part of the Civil Code and was no longer cited as the Act on Annual Financial Statements of Enterprises. Klaassen's preference was "Principles of Financial Statements" ("*Grondslagen voor Jaarrekeningen*"), but he encouraged other suggestions (JO Alg 1692). The report of the meeting gave only the outcome, without recapitulating the arguments:

> After some discussion, the meeting agrees with the name "Guidelines for Financial Statements" ["*Richtlijnen voor jaarrekeningen*"] instead of Considered Views, etc.
>
> This reflects that guidance is being given without the appearance of "legislation" (JO Alg 1731).

At the meeting of 13 December, a member of the employers delegation recommended that, since the title of Title 6 of Book 2 of the Civil Code was "The Financial Statements" ("*De Jaarrekening*"), singular and not plural, the title of the TO's pronouncements should be "Guidelines for the Financial Statements" ("*Richtlijnen voor de jaarrekening*"), a suggestion that was accepted without dissent (JO Alg 1740).[131]

During 1978 and 1979, Klaassen's drafts were extensively discussed, an important issue being which sentences and paragraphs should be written in bold face, and therefore qualify as "affirmative pronouncements", and which should be written in light face.

In the course of these discussions, the issue of the title of the TO's statements was reopened on 3 March 1979 by the head of the employers delegation. He had joined the TO at the December 1977 meeting, just after the decision had been made to change to "Guidelines". His strong dislike of the name "*richtlijn*" was probably due to its use for each of the EEC Directives and, in particular, the Fourth Directive (*Vierde richtlijn*), which had been approved in July 1978. Although *richtlijn* could denote either "directive" or "guideline", the fact that it came up every time someone mentioned the Fourth Directive, which was viewed with apprehension in company circles, was enough to make it unsuitable as a title for the TO's statements. Indeed, one of the members of the employers delegation remarked that, because of the influence of the EEC's Directives, the word has "a very binding character" (JO Alg 2209). The head of the delegation said that he doubted that the TO had the authority to give *richtlijnen*. The spokesman for the employees delegation argued that *richtlijn* should be retained, because it would emphasize that part of the TO's work consisted of helping practice

[131] The English translation of both *jaarrekening* and *jaarrekeningen* is "financial statements". Yet the former refers to a single set of financial statements, while the latter refers to more than one set of financial statements.

improve itself. Schoonderbeek said that the *richtlijnen* would not be laws, and that the NIvRA and the CAJ were "very pleased" with the name, and would have serious objections to another name. After some discussion, it was decided to retain *richtlijn* (JO Alg 2209–2210). The ambiguity of *richtlijn* may have commended it as just the right compromise to bridge the very different preferred interpretations of the three delegations.[132]

But the head of the employers delegation raised the matter anew at the meeting of 21 June. He said that, in circles of employers, there was little inclination to accept rules in addition to those in the law. If the TO were to go beyond the law, he said, and did not confine itself to evaluating the acceptability of principles within the framework of the law, the possibility existed that there would be lack of acceptance by employers. The verdicts of the Enterprise Chamber as well as some publications of the TO had, he said, caused a "shock-like increase in the interest in financial statement issues" (JO Alg 2531). He said that, as a consequence, his delegation's support group of company representatives had imposed demands. He gave, as an example, the funds statement, which was a subject scheduled for inclusion in the next exposure draft. He said that the TO would go too far if it were to publish rules on subjects, such as the funds statement, that were not treated in either the law or the EEC Directives.

A member of the auditors delegation said that he might have expected such a remark "years ago" when the TO agreed on segmental reporting (in the fifth exposure draft), which, in some respects, also went beyond what the law required. He said that he thought the employers delegation had agreed with the way things had been going. But the head of the employers delegation said that the greater level of interest displayed by the delegation's constituents, as evidenced by the creation of a support group of company representatives, had changed things. He threw down the gauntlet by asserting that what had been agreed by the employers delegation at a time when there was no support group now lacked validity. He said he could not cooperate in the rewriting of the TO's statements if the name *richtlijn* were to be used (JO Alg 2533).

Schoonderbeek and the spokesman for the employees delegation stated that this declared position by the employers delegation threatened to make it impossible to continue the TO. Klaassen, who was present at the meeting, said that the position of the employers left him with very little inclination to continue his rewriting.

Schoonderbeek came up with a compromise. He proposed to call the rewrit-

[132] Indeed, in 1980, *richtlijn* was translated as "directive" in two accounting publications. The term "directives" was used by Klynveld Kraayenhof & Co. in a booklet prepared for clients, and in a publication of the NIvRA. *Annual Accounts-Developments in 1980*, translation of KKC booklet no. 10 ([Amsterdam:] Klynveld Kraayenhof & Co., January 1981), pp. 11–18; and *The Tripartite Accounting Standards Committee*, *op.cit.*, the addresses by Schoonderbeek and van Putten.

ten statements "Draft Guidelines" ("*Ontwerp-Richtlijnen*"), which would give the employers' support group an opportunity to register a reaction before they were approved as definitive statements. After some discussion, this proposal was accepted. In further discussion, it became evident that the employers very much wanted to have 15 to 25 paragraphs reverted from bold face to light face, so that they would not diverge too much from the EEC Directives (JO Alg 2534). By this stage, however, the question of the title of the TO's statements was finally settled, and attention turned to the broader question of the status and structure of the TO (which will be treated below).

5.4.7.6. ED's 6 and 7, and considered views 3

The sixth exposure draft, which was released in February 1979, addressed a single topic: the accounting implications of the Investment Incentives Act (WIR, Wet op de Investeringsrekening), of 29 June 1978 (Stb. 368), which was intended to stimulate investment in fixed assets. The Act provided that companies purchasing fixed assets would receive a rebate from the government equal to a specified percentage of the asset cost in the year in which the asset was acquired. The concession was known as the "WIR premium" ("*WIR-premie*"), and none of the premium would revert to the government if the asset were held at least eight years.[133] At the TO's meeting on 11 May 1978, shortly before the law received final approval, the head of the employers delegation proposed that the TO recommend a preferred treatment for the WIR in order to prevent a diversity of practice. His proposal was accepted, and the CAJ was asked to prepare a draft (JO Alg 1800).

The CAJ saw the WIR premium as a rare opportunity to deal with a completely new topic. After discussion, it decided that the only proper treatment of the WIR premium was as a subtraction from the cost of the related fixed asset, as if it were a subsidy.[134] Furthermore, the CAJ took the unprecedented step of

---

[133] The exposure draft dealt also with two related investment incentives, the "IPR premium" and the "SIR levy". They were, respectively, a premium to encourage investment in depressed regions, and a levy to discourage investments in the *Randstad*. All three investment incentives were treated as a single accounting question. In this section, therefore, only the WIR premium will be discussed.

[134] In the TO's fourth exposure draft, issued in December 1975 (section VI1, para. 10), a preference had been expressed for amortizing tax benefits associated with the purchase of a fixed asset over the useful life of the asset. But the TO left open the option of crediting the entire benefit to income in the year in which it was realized. Prior to the 1978 Act setting up the WIR premium, the tax benefit had been in the form of an investment allowance (which could be altered at the discretion of the minister) that would be conferred only if the purchasing company had taxable income in the year of purchase. The 1978 Act converted the tax benefit into a rebate that would be granted to a company whether or not it had taxable income in the year of purchase. Although the government did not argue for any preferred accounting treatment, the background papers made it clear that the WIR premium was intended to build up companies' equity and to subsidize the cost of investments in fixed assets. Interview with W.P. Moleveld, 11 July 1991.

publishing its recommendation in *de Accountant*.[135] In the introduction to its published note, the CAJ stated its awareness that, by such a publication, it could not preempt, or diminish the importance of, the decision eventually forthcoming from the TO. At the TO's meeting of 12 October, the head of the employers delegation, evidently not pleased with the CAJ's public announcement, raised the question of the relation between the CAJ and the TO. Once Schoonderbeek had made it clear that the CAJ could not be seen as a subcommittee of the TO, but, rather, as a body with a role within the NIvRA, independent of its preparatory work for the TO, the principle was accepted that the CAJ could make a public statement on its own initiative. Nevertheless, the spokesman for the employees delegation and two members of the employers delegation stated their preference that the CAJ should take a reticient attitude in such matters, but that, if the CAJ were to publish its views in the future, it should not refer to the TO, in order to leave the TO as free as possible to determine its own position (JO Alg 1910–1911).

At the TO's meeting on 20 December, the employers delegation disagreed with the CAJ's preferred treatment. The delegation felt that the WIR premium should be treated as a deferred credit. At issue was the distinction to be drawn between risk-bearing and non-risk-bearing debt. To the employers delegation, the WIR premium was a kind of subordinated capital, closer to owners' equity than to debt. Under a previous ruling of the Enterprise Chamber (the KSH decision, in March 1978), an amount credited directly to owners' equity could not, in future years, be included in income. So, in order to take the WIR premium into future income, it could not be labeled as owners' equity.

It can be seen that several benefits would accrue to companies by treatment as a deferred credit. By not being classified as debt, the "WIR equalization" (as it came to be known) would not burden the debt-equity ratios prescribed in loan covenants, and, in regard to solvency ratios, it would broaden the concept of owners' equity. Moreover, if the WIR premium were subtracted from the cost of the fixed asset, it would be depreciated over the asset's useful life. As a deferred credit, however, it could be amortized to profit over the eight-year minimum holding period. Finally, treatment as a deferred credit might, for some companies, make it unnecessary to calculate depreciation differently for tax purposes than for financial reporting purposes. (For tax purposes, the company would depreciate the gross purchase price.)[136]

The auditors delegation, representing the CAJ, naturally advocated the CAJ's preference. The result was, predictably, a compromise. In the TO's two-page exposure draft, no preference was expressed. The WIR premium could be treated either as a reduction in the cost of the fixed asset or be credited to a "smoothing

---

[135] "Premies ingevolge de Wet Investeringsrekening (WIR)", in *de Accountant*, vol. 84, no. 11, July/August 1978, p. 642.

[136] Interview with Prof.dr J. Klaassen, 27 June 1991.

account" ("*egalisatierekening*") on the equity side of the balance sheet that would be neither a liability nor owners' equity. The auditors delegation did manage to achieve one of its aims: however classified, the WIR premium was to be amortized over its useful life. The head of the employers delegation predicted many reactions on this latter point (JO Alg 2008–2011).

Between March and September 1979, the TO received 17 letters of comment: seven from audit firms, five from companies, two from industry associations, and three from individual auditors. Three audit firms preferred the smoothing account, or at least expressed concern about the practical difficulties of subtracting the WIR premium from the asset cost. A fourth firm opted for subtraction from the asset cost, but recognized the practical benefits of a smoothing account. The three other firms did not express a clear preference, but mainly asked for clarity, a broader framework, and/or the motivations for the TO's position.

The companies and industry associations invariably preferred the smoothing account. None defended subtraction from the asset cost. Three companies and one industry association wanted the option of crediting the WIR premium to income earlier, either immediately upon receipt or at the end of the eight-year minimum holding period.

Two individual auditors preferred the smoothing account, and the third opposed any eventual transfer of the WIR premium to income.

The seventh exposure draft was issued in September 1979, and ran to 28 quarto pages.[137] The subjects were the cash flow statement, events after the balance sheet date, intangible assets, types of provisions, and movements in provisions. The first three sections attracted little discussion in the TO's meetings, partly owing to the amount of committee time needed to advise the government on the proposed adaptation law for the Fourth Directive. The discussion of the final two sections had been concluded as early as March 1977.

The funds statement was not regulated by law. While companies were not required, therefore, to publish such a statement, 88 percent of the 120 listed companies surveyed in *Onderzoek Jaarverslagen 1979* did publish a Statement of Source and Application of Funds (Staat van Herkomst en Besteding der Middelen).[138] In its discussion, the TO provided little explicit guidance on the contents of the statement, except that the definition of funds was to be cash and cash equivalents (Ib6, para. 3). While the auditors and employees delegations wanted to include suggestions on the format and contents of the statement, the employers delegation preferred to leave such matters entirely to the discretion of preparers.[139] The

[137] For a press report, see "Commissies jaarverslaggeving publiceren 7e aflevering voorontwerpen", in *Het Financieele Dagblad*, 25 September 1979, p. 3.

[138] *Onderzoek Jaarverslagen 1979*, NIVRA geschrift nummer 22 (Amsterdam: Nederlands Instituut van Registeraccountants, June 1981), p. 19. It was not stated what proportion of the companies used cash or near-cash as their definition of funds.

[139] Interview with Prof.dr A. van Putten, 8 July 1991.

draft followed APB *Opinion* no. 19 (May 1971) in recommending that investment and financing transactions not directly involving cash (e.g., the acquisition of an investment in exchange for shares) should be shown at their cash equivalents (para. 4).

The section on intangible assets dealt with research and development costs, copyrights, patents, etc., but not with goodwill. The TO did little more than repeat what the law said (Art. 317, para. 1): that such items could be recognized as assets only at historical cost, and that they had to be depreciated. On the subject of research and development costs: research costs were not eligible for capitalization, but development costs could be capitalized if they satisfied certain criteria (that were almost identical to those specified in the UK's *SSAP* 13, "Accounting for research and development", issued in December 1977). The TO had intended to treat goodwill in a separate section (IIa3) of the exposure draft, which had been under discussion for some time, but the section was not included in the draft.

Two paragraphs in the section on types of provisions offered guidance on providing for exchange rate losses. Such a provision was to be limited to cases where there was "a more or less foreseeable and gradual change in exchange rates", leading to losses that could be associated with particular assets and liabilities (IIIb2, paras. 23–24).

Apart from the dispute over guidance for the cash flow statement, none of the subjects treated in the draft was controversial, and in three of the five sections it was stated that the views expressed were in harmony with the relevant IASC standards.

By the end of February 1980, the exposure draft elicited eleven comment letters: eight from audit firms, and one each from the Finad/Intac study group of the NIvRA, an individual auditor and VNO/NCW's support group for the employers delegation. The support group recommended inclusion of an option to define "funds" as working capital, as permitted by IAS 7, "Statement of Changes in Financial Position".

Three of the audit firms, as well as the VNO/NCW support group, pointed out that the exposure draft was not clear whether (1) a cash flow statement should form part of the financial statements, or (2) a cash flow statement, if presented, should be included as part of the financial statements. Where they expressed their preferences, the commentators disagreed among themselves, which perhaps explained the ambivalence in the exposure draft. A fourth audit firm argued for working capital as a permissible definition of funds, and a fifth firm applauded the almost unlimited flexibility of IAS 7: each enterprise should adopt the form of presentation that "is most informative in the circumstances". There appeared to be little sentiment among the commentators for regulating a funds statement.

The third and final set of definitive Considered Views was issued in February 1979. The sections in the third exposure draft on materiality and the allocation of revenue and expense to future years had undergone only minor changes. The section on the valuation of fixed assets in connection with the threatened discontinuance of enterprise activities had been significantly restructured, and the section on the pensions provision had been completely rewritten. But by far the greatest attention had been devoted to the section on acceptable principles for income determination, which included the TO's two-track policy (i.e., using current value as well as historical cost, with a choice of where, as between the body of the statements and the notes, each was to be presented).

In the CAJ, Schoonderbeek proposed inclusion of a strong recommendation that current value information be provided in the financial statements, with a waiver for small companies so long as they gave an explanation in the notes. At the CAJ meeting of 2 May 1977, the members supported Schoonderbeek's proposal, and interpreted it as a step beyond the "preference" for current value stated by the TO in its fifth exposure draft, issued the previous December. They were, however, uncertain about how such a recommendation would be received, since the letters of comment from Hoogovens and Heineken in reply to the third exposure draft had contained conflicting points of view. Nonetheless, in the CAJ's discussions, the auditors expressed the view that current value was "on the march" (CAJ Not 811–816).

The CAJ's current value proposal did not survive in the TO. Surprisingly, the main resistance came from the employees delegation. When the CAJ's draft first came up for discussion, at the TO's meeting on 27 October 1977, the spokesman for the employees delegation drew attention to a policy position recently adopted by the European Federation of Trade Unions (Europees Verbond van Vakverenigingen) to opt for maximum uniformity within a framework of historical cost. At the gathering where this decision was taken, which was apparently dominated by the German advocacy of historical cost, the Dutch delegation had argued for current value, which led to a compromise resolution in favor of some combination of the two approaches. The representatives of the FNV on the TO said that, despite the FNV's consistent record of promoting current value, they would find it difficult to impose an obligation on companies to use current value in their financial statements, in view of the European position to which the FNV had subscribed.[140]

The employees delegation was not the only party objecting to the CAJ draft. The head of the employers delegation felt that the TO should not go beyond the fifth exposure draft: it should express a preference, not impose an obligation (JO

---

[140] Interviews with Drs J.P.M. Nabbe, 27 September 1990 and 17 October 1991. The compromise position adopted by the European Federation of Trade Unions was, in effect, very similar to the TO's two-track policy.

During the meetings in 1977–78 at which current value was discussed, the only members of the employees delegation who attended were Nabbe and Bloemarts, both representing the FNV. P. Kroon, who was a member of the economic staff of the smaller CNV and who had joined the TO in 1972, did not attend any of these meetings.

Alg 1707–1710).

At the TO's meeting of 13 December, the FNV representatives reported that they had consulted their constituents, and were obliged to reiterate their opposition to the CAJ draft. Members of the other delegations expressed dissatisfaction with this "turnabout" by the FNV representatives. Both auditors and employers felt that the credibility of the TO might suffer if it were seen to retreat from the position taken in the fifth exposure draft. The head of the employers delegation, who was about to retire from the TO after six years in the capacity, and who had generally been opposed to changing existing practice, uncharacteristically defended a bold vision for the TO. In the minutes of the meeting, it was stated that

> [the head of the employers delegation] sees guiding the development toward the future [as opposed to a mere inventorying and evaluation] as an important task for the TO. This has been a reason for the speaker to agree in the past with the preference expressed in [the fifth] exposure draft. Against this background, [he] would object to taking a step backwards (JO Alg 1746).

Another member of the employers delegation argued that, in the light of the response to earlier recommendations, little progress would be made in solving the practical problems of applying current value if the stimulus provided by the binding character of the statement were to be removed. The spokesman for the employees delegation then stated that the FNV would be content to register a dissent (JO Alg 1746–1747).

In the CAJ meeting the following day, some degree of bewilderment was expressed: "Earlier [the minutes recorded] the employers were against current value and the employees were in favor, and now it is precisely the other way round" (CAJ Not 879). It was stated that "Schoonderbeek is thinking of a compromise in which the preference would be apparent without being mentioned" (CAJ Not 880). As transmitted to the TO by a letter dated 6 January 1978, Schoonderbeek's proposal was that the strict demand that the financial statements give information on current value could be met either in the statements or the notes.

At the CAJ's meeting of 31 January 1978, Schoonderbeek reported that the FNV representatives had acceded to his proposal, which was essentially a restatement of the TO's two-track policy as first enunciated in its third exposure draft. One member of the auditors delegation, a staunch supporter of current value, reported his displeasure with a compromise that, in his view, represented a 180-degree reversal of the TO's position on current value (CAJ Not 888).

At the TO's meeting of 16 February (at which no one from the employees delegation was present), different members of the employers and auditors delegations took turns at venting their "disappointment with" and "incomprehension of" the changed position of the employees on current value. In the end, the meeting accepted the Schoonderbeek proposal (JO Alg 1767–1768).

5.4.7.7. The foreword to the rewritten considered views

In June 1980, following numerous meetings of the TO at which successive drafts of Klaassen's rewritten Considered Views were discussed in detail, they were published in book format under the title, *Richtlijnen voor de jaarrekening.*[141] In accordance with the agreement reached in the TO the previous year, each of the rewritten final statements was carefully labeled as a "Draft Guideline" ("*ontwerp-Richtlijn*"). For the first time, the "affirmative prouncements" were printed in bold face to emphasize their importance, and much of the discussion within the TO had been about which sentences and paragraphs should be accorded this distinction. Since it was believed, especially by the employers delegation, that the character of the Considered Views had been changed since their original issuance, it was decided that they should be exposed for general comment prior to being approved.[142] Some, however, interpreted this argument as a delaying tactic.

On the whole, the Draft Guidelines were, except for the bold facing, written in the same style as the Considered Views, and the textual differences did not imply significant changes in substance. Klaassen's task had been to reorganize the text so that it would be more accessible to readers, to eliminate inconsistencies, and to introduce the verdicts of the Enterprise Chamber and the IASC standards.[143]

Also included in the book were the financial reporting law, a listing of IASC standards that had not been fully endorsed in the Draft Guidelines, and the fourth through seventh exposure drafts issued between December 1975 and September 1979, which had not been rewritten. Each was labeled as an "Exposure Draft of Considered Views" ("*Voorontwerp van Beschouwingen*").

Once agreement had been reached on the contents of the Draft Guidelines, the remaining discussion centered on the assertive Foreword that was drafted by Schoonderbeek. He sought to emphasize that, once the Draft Guidelines were given final approval, they should be construed as binding, and that the external auditor should report any departures. While the employers delegation, perhaps surprisingly, accepted this characterization of the status of definitive Guidelines, it apparently did not accept the stated role of the external auditor. At the TO's meeting on 5 March 1980, the head of the employers delegation made the point that the definitive Guidelines should be seen as more binding and possess a higher status than the Considered Views. Indeed, in an article published in June 1980, van Putten stated that "the new Guidelines have a different character than the previous Considered Views". He said that the name, Guidelines, had been

---

[141] The book was labeled as "Installment 1" ("*aflevering 1*") of the new series. An English language translation of the volume was published: The Tripartite Accounting Standards Committee, *Netherlands Accounting Guidelines* (Amsterdam: [Nederlands Instituut van Registeraccountants], October 1981). The Shell organization undertook the translation.

[142] Interview with Prof.dr J. Klaassen, 27 June 1991.

[143] Interview with Prof.dr J. Klaassen, 27 June 1991.

chosen deliberately:

> This indicates that, although they do not create a legal obligation, because of their quality and because of the fact that they are backed by the VNO and the NCW they are binding to a high degree.[144]

But the obligation of the auditor to mention deviations in his report was not accepted by the employers.[145] The spokesman for the employees delegation joined in the view that the definitive Guidelines were intended to have a more binding character (JO Alg 3087).

The final version of the Foreword, as published in the book, contained the following key passages:

> With this rewriting, the TO aims to give those who draft, audit and use financial statements a guidebook in which the currently applicable rules and recommendations for financial statements in the Netherlands are included.
>
> In this publication, the name "Considered Views" has been abandoned, because the name suggests, in the current order of things, too much permissiveness [*vrijblijvendheid*].
>
> This publication comes to light under the name "*Guidelines for Financial Statements*". This title has been chosen in order to express the expectation that business and auditors will conform with [its contents]. This expectation naturally has special relevance for the affirmative pronouncements [*stellige uitspraken*] inserted [in the text], recognizable by the bold typeface (pp. VI–VII).
>
> * * *
>
> As soon as the exposure draft phase is completed and the "definitive" [*definitieve*] Guidelines have been published, the TO will assume that the affirmative pronouncements included in the Guidelines (shown in bold face) *will* in principle – as if they were of a binding character – *be applied in all financial statements*. This position implies that a deviation from an affirmative pronouncement is allowed only when the insight into financial position and income required by law is enhanced to a not insignificant degree. Furthermore, it implies that, in the case of noncompliance with affirmative pronouncements included in the Guidelines, this should be mentioned in the financial statements with a specific and, where possible, quantified statement of the deviation(s) and their motivation(s).
>
> The TO expects that organized business, especially the organizations of employers (VNO and NCW), will make an effort to enhance compliance with the Guidelines. The TO expects, furthermore, that the organization of auditors

[144] Dr A. van Putten, "Richtlijnen voor de jaarrekening zijn door niveau in hoge mate bindend", in *Onderneming*, vol. 9, no. 26, 27 June 1980, p. 5. A similar view was expressed in van Putten, "An Entrepreneur's View of Voluntary Cooperation in Formulating Supplementary Rules Regarding External Financial Reporting", in *The Tripartite Accounting Standards Committee*, PILOT (Netherlands) 10 (Amsterdam: Nederlands Instituut van Registeraccountants, December 1980), pp. 11–12.

[145] Interview with Mr H.C. Wesseling, 10 July 1991.

> (NIVRA) will make an effort to assure that those in charge of audits take compliance with the Guidelines into account in their audits of financial statements, and that they mention eventual deviations from what was stated in the previous paragraph in their report on the financial statements (pp. VIII–IX).

The final wording had been toned down somewhat from the draft discussed in March by the TO. In the penultimate paragraph, above, the subjunctive phrase ("as if they were of a binding character") replaced a declarative phrase ("are of a binding character"), and hence softened the assertion. Another moderating change was the insertion of the phrase in which the NIvRA was exhorted "to assure that those in charge of audits take compliance with the Guidelines into account" in place of a categorical statement that "the auditor is bound to check for compliance". Also added in the final drafting was the reference to the "insight" provision in the law.

The TO's Foreword claimed for the definitive Guidelines a status similar to that announced in 1976 by the NIvRA's management board for the IASC standards, namely, that they would constitute authoritative statements, and that auditors would be expected to disclose departures. But no one knew just how seriously companies and auditors would take the TO's admonition in its Foreword.

Restructuring of the TO. In late 1977, the NIvRA and the VNO held a special meeting to discuss the status and financing of the TO's work program. At the CAJ's meeting of 29 November 1977, the CAJ's vice-chairman reported on the special meeting, at which he, the president of the VNO, the head and another member of the employers delegation, and Burggraaff (as NIvRA president) were present. The NIvRA's budgetary problems were discussed, since the NIvRA had been financing the work of the delegation to the IASC, the Groupe d'Etudes des Experts Comptables which had been commenting on the EEC's draft Directives, the biennial survey of the financial reports of listed companies (*Onderzoek Jaarverslagen*), as well as the secretariat of the TO. The status of the Considered Views was also discussed. The parties agreed to propose that the TO be made a committee of the Social and Economic Council (SER, Sociaal-Economische Raad). The VNO promised to give more attention in its publications to the TO's output. The VNO president said he was a proponent of giving prominence to "affirmative pronouncements". The final point taken up was the scope of the TO's statements. Should they pertain to the financial statements or to financial reporting? The practical difference would have been the directors' report. The matter was left open. The VNO said that it would discuss the question in its own circles. It was also said that the organizations of employees would be consulted (CAJ Not 873–874).

Apparently no new developments were reported until the middle of 1978. Burggraaff, in the second year of his two-year NIvRA presidency, used the imminent approval by the EEC of its Fourth Directive as the occasion for reviewing the work of the TO and suggesting possible changes in its structure and procedures in consultation with the government. He made the following points in a memorandum entitled "The Future of the TO", dated 5 May 1978[146]:

- the TO is insufficiently representative because the views of users of financial statement information, as well as middle-sized and small companies, are not given a voice;
- the TO possesses inadequate authority to perform its function, and "the fact that the TO is an informal gathering, without officially granted powers, has the consequence that its utterances do not make a great impression, either on those who have to render account or on the Enterprise Chamber";
- the TO's scope is too limited, since the minister's charge in 1968 referred only to valuation principles; and
- owing to lack of funds, the pace with which the TO's drafts and final statements are published is "slow".

Burggraaff said that there would be a need for further regulation after the adaptation of Dutch law to the Fourth Directive. Since a body (*orgaan*) would be required to issue interpretations, perhaps as a supplement to the legal requirements, he argued that, if those rules were to possess sufficient authority, the government should make compliance with those rules mandatory. Such a body could not be an unstructured, informal gathering like the TO. If the legislature were to delegate authority to such a body, there must be guarantees that it would be independent and perform its functions properly. Burggraaff's specific recommendation for structural reform consisted of three options. First, that the current participants in the TO form a foundation, possibly with the admission of other groups as interested parties. Second, that a public body with regulatory powers be created. Third, that a link be established with the SER. The merits of these three alternatives should, he said, be looked into. He thought that the third option was, for the present, the most promising, because, in contrast with the first option, the SER was an established organization, well-known and with prestige, and, in comparison with the second, the formation of the body could proceed smoothly and quickly. Burggraaff suggested that the following parties be represented in the body: employers, employees (trade unions), users (Stock Exchange Association, Chambers of Commerce, Society for Investor Protection[147]), auditors, and academics. There should be rules and procedures for nomination, appointment, and dismissal; on voting rights; on the qualified majorities neces-

---

146 J.A. Burggraaff, draft, "De Toekomst van het Tripartiete Overleg", dated 5 May 1978 (3 pp.). This document was coded SI Inf 303–305 in the NIvRA archive. "SI" refers to the papers of sector I of NIvRA's management board, being the sector that dealt with professional questions. In order to organize its work, the management board divided itself into four sectors.

147 A curious omission was the Society of Financial Analysts, which was founded in 1961.

sary for approving drafts and final statements; a secretariat and technical staff; and the chairmancy. The increase in costs entailed by this proposed reorganization should be borne by the participating organizations, and possibly by the government and the SER.

Burggraaff's comprehensive memorandum was discussed at a meeting held on 10 October. Those attending were: three members of the NIvRA's management board (including Burggraaff, who chaired the meeting), Chairman Frielink of the CAJ, Chairman Schoonderbeek of the TO, and Volten.

At the meeting, a division of opinion emerged (SI Inf 420–428). While the NIvRA board members favored Burggraaff's third option, both Frielink and Schoonderbeek doubted whether the option of involving the SER was necessary or desirable.[148] They believed that the agreement reached on 12 September 1977 at the meeting in 's-Hertogenbosch (i.e., rewriting the first three Considered Views within two years) continued to be a sound approach, and there was no need for a restructuring of the TO. This rewriting, together with the new name, *Richtlijnen* (Guidelines), which had been adopted by the TO in November 1977, would increase the authority of the TO's pronouncements.

Frielink and Schoonderbeek did not agree with Burggraaff's proposal that government should mandate compliance with the TO's statements. They felt that Burggraaff's goals could be achieved in another way, namely, by securing the participation of the Stock Exchange Association and the NIvRA's Consultative Committee on Published Auditors' Reports (COPA, Commissie Overleg Publieke Accountantsverklaringen[149]), while the NIvRA's management board might issue a statement saying that it would be considered a fault (*misslag*) in the professional conduct of an auditor if a client's financial statements were to reflect a departure from the Considered Views.

No decisions were taken at the meeting. At the end of the discussion, Burggraaff announced that the management board would also be discussing the matter with the organizations of employers and employees. Frielink and Schoonderbeek, however, were opposed to raising the matter of the TO's structure with the other partners.

Within the TO, discussions about a possible restructuring surfaced at the meeting on 12 October 1978, in the context of the dialogue over the relation between the CAJ and the TO, following the CAJ's public announcement of its view on the proper treatment of the WIR premium (see above). The unequal sharing of costs of the TO and the CAJ, which did most of the preparatory

[148] Schoonderbeek was concerned that, if the TO were to become a committee of the SER, its deliberations might be contaminated by the purely political horse trading that occurred during meetings of the SER and its committees on such public-policy issues as taxes, wages, and social security. Interview with Prof.drs J.W. Schoonderbeek, 28 November 1991.

[149] COPA, which was installed in April 1977, had been using quiet persuasion with auditors concerning apparent departures from Considered Views and the law in their clients' financial statements.

work, was raised. It became clear that both the TO and the CAJ could be overburdened when the time came to advise the government on the adaptation of the Fourth Directive. It was agreed that both the employers and employees delegations would prepare memoranda on "the status, structure and procedures" of the TO, with particular reference to funding, including the TO's secretariat (JO Alg 1910–1911).

Within a month, the employees delegation submitted its memorandum.[150] Four circumstances, it said, gave rise to the need for a reorganization of the TO:

- that the Enterprise Chamber had, until then, not made conspicuous use of the Considered Views in its verdicts;
- that the forthcoming adaptation of the law to the Fourth Directive would modernize company financial reporting, would render the minister's 1968 charge to the TO obsolete, and would raise the question before Parliament of the future status of the TO;
- that, because of unequal sharing, the costs of the TO's work had been borne largely by the NIvRA; and
- that there had been a movement toward a more binding character of the TO's statements, stimulated by the issuance of IASC standards.

In order to cope with these circumstances, the delegation proposed that the TO become a committee of the SER, which would provide financial support for its operation (which was customary for committees of the SER). The TO's legal role would be three-fold:

1. To advise the Justice Ministry on matters concerning the financial statements of enterprises (under Title 6, Book 2 of the Civil Code) and institutions (*instellingen*).
2. To promulgate binding rules, either by general administrative order on advice of the SER, or by the SER itself under its public authority.
3. To promulgate non-binding rules or recommendations that would usually be the precursors of binding rules.

The TO would be composed of delegations of equal size from the three groups currently represented. There was no discussion in the memorandum of such matters as voting procedures. The memorandum made clear the employees' belief that the promulgated norms should, in the end, carry express authority to command compliance.

Discussion of the memorandum was put off until the memorandum from the

[150] "*Nota inzake de opzet en werkwijze van het tripartite overleg over de jaarrekening van ondernemingen*" ("Note on the Design and Procedures of the TO in Regard to the Financial Statements of Enterprises"), dated 10 November 1978 (4 pp.). It was signed by P. Kroon, J. Bloemarts and J. Nabbe, the three members of the employees delegation (JO Alg 1923–1926).

employers delegation was in hand. Moreover, on 20 December, Schoonderbeek announced that the auditors delegation would also submit a memorandum on the structure and procedures of the TO (JO Alg 2006). Owing to the extensive consultations and procedural approvals required within the circles of employers and auditors, as well as to some unexplained delays, the two memoranda were not transmitted until eleven months later.

During the hiatus, the financial executives of several Dutch multinationals, realizing that a reorganization of the TO was imminent, sought to make a contribution toward the resolution of the apparently diverse views of the NIvRA, the VNO/NCW and the trade union federations.[151] During August and September 1979, they were engaged in consultations with members of the auditors and employers delegations to the TO. Keeping in mind a desire to coordinate the eventual proposal with a recent submission by Shell to the UK's Accounting Standards Committee,[152] which was also reconsidering its organizational structure, they developed a proposal that called for the establishment of a "TO Foundation" ("Stichting Tripartite Overleg") that would invest the program with a legal personality and, therefore, a degree of stature and independence. The NIvRA, the VNO, the NCW, the FNV and the CNV, together with other organizations involved in financial reporting would be represented on the Foundation's board. Under the Foundation, there would be an "Annual Reporting Committee" ("Commissie Jaarverslaggeving"), which would be composed of about seven experts representing diverse backgrounds, who would be charged with preparing, with the assistance of project groups, draft guidelines. Openness of process was said to be important, and it was proposed that, as far as possible, the committee's meetings be held in public. It was suggested that the Foundation's board would actually publish the guidelines, so long as a qualified majority of the board's

---

[151] One of the multinationals was Shell, whose overriding concern was to promote harmonization among US, UK and Dutch accounting principles, as its group financial statements were based on a "synthesis" of those three countries' norms. In 1979, when the UK's *SSAP* 15 became effective, Shell found itself required to use "comprehensive" tax allocation in the USA and "partial" allocation in the UK. In its 1979 financial statements, the Shell Group adopted "comprehensive" allocation, and disclosed in a note how the result would have been different under "partial" allocation. In their opinion on the financial statements, the group auditors inserted a clause in which they drew attention to the departure from UK standard practice. Shell, which referred to the clause in the auditors' report as a "qualification" (this was a questionable translation of the Dutch *opmerking*, which means "remark"), was, therefore, keenly interested in the process by which statements on accounting standards and principles were developed in the three countries. See the discussion in the *Annual Report of Royal Dutch Petroleum Company 1979*, p. 41; and the address by D. de Bruyne, the president of Royal Dutch Petroleum Company, "International harmonization of accounting and disclosure standards", at the 10th World Congress of the International Association of the Financial Executives Institute, 15 October 1979, Atlanta, Georgia (Royal Dutch/Shell Group of Companies print).

[152] Shell's submission was published in *Submissions on the Accounting Standards Committee's Consultative Document: Setting Accounting Standards* ([London:] The Accounting Standards Committee, 1979), vol. 1, pp. 49–56.

members were to approve of the contents. The final memorandum embodying this proposal was distributed to all of the organizations participating in the TO for their consideration.[153]

The memorandum finally submitted by the employers delegation in November 1979 consisted chiefly of an evaluation of the past work and current position of the TO, followed by some demands that, in the employers' view, must be fulfilled by a restructured TO.[154] It did not offer a detailed blueprint of what the TO should become. In the memorandum, the employers stated that the TO had been set up to make an inventory and evaluation of accounting principles, not to issue standards and guidelines. The importance of the TO, they said, had diminished somewhat as a consequence of the appearance of IASC standards, EEC Directives, guidelines issued by the Organisation for Economic Co-operation and Development (OECD) and the United Nations, and the verdicts of the Enterprise Chamber. Although, the employers continued, it is not possible to give a general statement on the attitude of employers toward the Considered Views, it can be said that many companies would rank them, together with the IASC standards, below the law, company tradition, and the verdicts of the Enterprise Chamber, in that order. The low status of the Considered Views was, they said, attributable to the following factors:

- their non-binding character, which was in line with the Dutch tradition of freedom in financial reporting;
- a style of presentation that diminished their usefulness as a reference guide to sound practice;
- the TO's pace of work, which was seen as "slow" by those outside; and
- the impression they gave of reflecting theory more than practice.

Although, the memorandum went on, Dutch financial reporting stood at a high international level (witness the 1979 *Financial Times* survey), the employers did not rejoice in their position of little influence in the preparation of the Considered Views. Also, especially given the sudden impact of recent decisions by the Enterprise Chamber, employers were looking for greater certainty in their affairs.

Some of these reservations were, the memorandum continued, being addressed by the rewriting of the Considered Views, and by the more structured internal support of the TO delegation being provided by the employers federations. Moreover, the employers federations were now prepared to recommend that their members comply with the definitive Guidelines and disclose and explain material departures. This latter point was an unexpected show of support for the TO, and may have represented a concession by the employers if they could be given a greater role in the shaping of Guidelines that, in consequence of their widespread acceptance by companies, might carry more weight with the Enterprise Chamber.

---

[153] Interview with Prof.dr J. van Helleman, 1 November 1991.

[154] "*Tripartite Overleg: Quo Vadis?*", dated 21 November 1979 (5 pp.) (JO Alg 2814–2818).

In their memorandum, the employers proposed a continuation of the tripartite consultations, on the basis of unanimous decision making. In order to enable the TO to react more quickly to developments like the Fourth and Seventh EEC Directives, it would need a preparatory committee in which all groups were represented. This would be the basis, they said, for a more equitable sharing of costs, but it would also make for a more nearly equal distribution of influence:

> The preparation of the topics to be discussed in the TO is done currently almost exclusively by the NIvRA. In our opinion, such a preponderant influence by one of the parties was not intended, and a more nearly equal contribution of all parties is desirable (JO Alg 2816).

An adequate secretariat was proposed, the costs of which would be divided in a reasonable way among the parties.

The memorandum from the NIvRA actually proposed a blueprint.[155] There would be a foundation (*stichting*) that would be charged with the publication of "Reporting Guidelines" ("*Richtlijnen voor de verslaggeving*"). The foundation's board would be composed of representatives from the participating groups according to a fixed distribution of seats. The board would decide on the issuance of the Guidelines, and would be expected to assure that any published Guidelines were accepted by the constituents.

The actual drafting of the Guidelines would be done by a steering group of, say, ten persons, three from each delegation (plus a chairman), appointed on the basis of their expertise. The foundation's board would approve the list of subjects and their priority; the steering group would handle the drafting and the publication of exposure drafts, and would prepare definitive Guidelines in the light of the comments received. Proposals for definitive Guidelines would be laid before the board, which would have the choice of accepting them by unanimous vote of the delegations, or rejecting them entirely.

The costs would be met from the copyright revenue, contributions from the participating groups, government grants, and other gifts. The memorandum did not elaborate on the financing proposal. One of the justifications for creating a foundation was the need for a legal entity to manage the funds that were being received from Kluwer in respect of publication sales.[156]

It was the NIvRA's view that the authority of the Guidelines would emanate from their inherent quality (based on the expertise of the participants in the process) and by their unambiguous acceptance by the constituents whose representatives had participated in the process.

---

[155] "*NIVRA-nota inzake Werkwijze, werkterrein, samenstelling en status van het TO*" ("NIVRA Memorandum Concerning the Procedures, Scope, Membership and Status of the TO"), dated 29 November 1979 (4 pp.) (JO Alg 2800–2803). In certain respects, the NIvRA memorandum bore a similarity to the proposal developed by the financial executives of several Dutch multinationals, discussed above.

[156] Interview with Prof.drs J.W. Schoonderbeek, 14 June 1990.

In five meetings from January to April 1980, the TO discussed the three memoranda with a view to presenting a proposal to the boards of the participating organizations. Initially, the discussion dealt at a fundamental level with the need to achieve clarity and an eventual consensus on virtually every issue concerning the task and status of the TO: degree of bindingness of pronouncements, compliance, relation to the Enterprise Chamber, extent of involvement of the constituencies, and the link with international developments (JO Alg 2828–2839, 2856–2866). Issues of structure were postponed to the second stage of discussion, although it appeared that the main area of difference was whether or not a relation with the SER should be sought. The employees preferred a link with the SER, while the employers and auditors did not (JO Alg 2836).

Early in February, the outlines of a compromise became discernible in a discussion memorandum prepared by three members of the TO's secretariat and scientific staff (JO Alg 2887–2897). It reflected to a great extent the proposal contained in the earlier NIvRA memorandum: a two-tiered body in the legal form of a foundation, with the foundation's board occupying the upper half, and a committee concerned with drafting and publishing statements occupying the lower half.

At the TO's meetings of 19 February, 5 March and 2 April, the decisions were taken to arrive at a final agreement (JO Alg 3024–3036, 3078–3089, 3114–3121). A member of the employers delegation proposed that the three groups to be represented in the restructured TO be "preparers, auditors and users of information" ("*informatieverstrekkers, -controleurs en -gebruikers*"). In reply, the spokesman for the employees delegation reminded his colleagues that the minister's Explanatory Memorandum in 1968 referred to "organized business", which was understood to mean employers and employees, and to auditors as the constituted parties. He emphasized that, in the TO, the employees delegation participated as employees and not as the representatives of users. This difference in view persisted in the discussions. Schoonderbeek, who sympathized with the suggestion that there be a users group, said that the Stock Exchange Association could play a role as part of the users group (JO Alg 3038, 3040–3041). In the end, the employees delegation accepted its redefinition as a users delegation in return for progress on such matters as a restructuring to give the issuing body greater authority, and the financing of its operations.[157]

On the subject of voting, while the delegations expressed the desire for unanimity, the alternative was proposed of publishing drafts and final versions with a four-fifths majority, and it was accepted. There would be a provision for the publication of minority positions. The head of the employers delegation said

[157] Interviews with R.C. Spinosa Cattela, 13 November 1990, and with Mr J.C.M.G. Bloemarts, 18 October 1991. The employees delegation had a general feeling that, before long, it would be unable to continue active participation by its own functionaries, but it wanted to be able to put forward candidates for the places in the delegation. *Ibid.*

that, in his view, drafts should not be published if the employers, who were the providers of information, were not in agreement. The hope was expressed that, as in the past, actual voting would not be necessary (JO Alg 3081–3083).

Contrary to the blueprint proposed in the earlier NIvRA memorandum, the issuance of exposure drafts and final statements would be handled entirely by the "lower half" of the organization. The foundation's board would not occupy itself with the contents of the statements. The names of "Annual Reporting Foundation" ("Stichting Jaarverslaggeving") and "Council on Annual Reporting" (RJ, "Raad voor de Jaarverslaggeving") were proposed to distinguish between the supervising board and the committee responsible for drafting and publication (JO Alg 3085). A budget of about *f* 500 000 was proposed, to support a staff of four persons and to cover other costs (JO Alg 3083). The decision was made that "Guidelines" ("*Richtlijnen*") would be used as the name of all of the new body's publications, and that there would be a distinction between "affirmative pronouncements" ("*stellige uitspraken*") and "advisory recommendations" ("*aanbevelingen*") (JO Alg 3117).

It should be noted that the original title of the new statements, as decided in 1979, was "Guidelines for the Financial Statements" ("*Richtlijnen voor de jaarrekening*"), whereas the agreed name of the group responsible for issuing the statements was to be contain a reference to "annual reporting". The principal difference between "financial statements" and "annual reporting" was the directors' report, which the employers did not wish to have covered by the series of Guidelines.[158] In the discussions on restructuring, the employers delegation continued to prefer "financial statements", but Schoonderbeek preferred "annual reporting", and, in the end, he won the day. Yet the title of the RJ's statements was not changed from Guidelines for the Financial Statements. The employers were fighting a rear-guard action, since the directors' report was to be regulated under the EEC's Fourth Directive.[159]

While these agreements were reached after a constructive give-and-take in the series of meetings, the question of the possible linkage with the SER could not be resolved. It became clear that the root-cause of the employees' preference for the SER connection was financial. However, Schoonderbeek and a member of the employers delegation argued that any organic connection with the SER was not practicable. They pointed out that the tripartite structure of the SER (employers, employees, and independent experts chosen by the Crown) differed from that of the TO, so that the position of the auditors might become awkward.

[158] Interview with Prof.drs J.W. Schoonderbeek, 17 December 1990.

[159] In the end, it was the imminent adaptation of the law to the Fourth Directive that persuaded the parties to retitle the Guidelines. Since the new law was to have a scope broader than the financial statements alone, it was decided that the statements should be titled "Guidelines for Annual Reporting" ("*Richtlijnen voor de Jaarverslaggeving*"). See *Verslag van de werkzaamheden over het jaar 1982 van de Raad voor de Jaarverslaggeving* (9 March 1983), p. 7.

It was therefore decided to propose a private-sector solution, provided that the financing could be satisfactorily arranged (JO Alg 3119–3120).[160]

The final memorandum of agreement, dated 13 May 1980, was forwarded to the participating organizations.[161]

In subsequent discussions among the representatives of the sponsoring organizations, a compromise was worked out by which there would be a private law foundation but with partial financing from a public law source. The FNV very much wanted the involvement of the SER, which was seen as the only stable and practicable source of funding.[162]

In the TO's annual report for 1980, its first such publication, it was stated that the discussions were continuing within the participating organizations, especially on the legal status and funding of the new body, as well as on the status of its publications.[163] In the TO's minutes, there were virtually no indications about the progress of the discussions. At the meeting of 12 August 1981, it suddenly appeared that the matter of funding was being discussed in the SER (JO Alg 4474–4475). The fact that the funding of the new body was a major issue in these discussions within the SER was also suggested in the NIvRA's annual report for

---

[160] Dr mr P.W. Huizenga, who joined the TO on 29 April 1980 as a member of the employees delegation representing the CNV, filed a memorandum and published an article in opposition to the agreement reached on the restructuring of the TO. He argued that both the employees and the employers should be excluded from the TO. The employees should be left out because they found it difficult to supply delegates with sufficient expertise. The employers should be left out because they were themselves directly involved in preparing financial statements, and could not be expected to be impartial. He wrote:

> Because the employers often want to regulate little in the way of fundamental, politically relevant issues that are of importance as policy matters to the management and employees of enterprise, the regulation could better be left to the auditors alone. Now, the employers have, in fact, a veto on these issues, as a result of which little gets done.

He suggested that the auditors should be assisted by "independent experts". He also said that it might be necessary for the government to establish a Companies Commission (*Vennootschapskamer*), which would officially check financial statements and would draft stricter rules, unless some order was established very soon by the "economic and social climate". P.W. Huizenga, "Werknemers en Jaarrekening (II)-Bezwaren tegen huidige samenstelling Tripartiete Overleg", in *Het Financieele Dagblad*, 9 January 1981, p. 14. Huizenga's two-part article reflected the thoughts expressed in his memorandum dated 5 May 1980 to the TO (JO Alg 3406–3412).

[161] "*Nota bestemd voor de besturen van de deelnemende organisaties van de commissies jaarverslaggeving het Tripartiete Overleg (TO) over zijn doelstelling, struktuur en werkwijze*" ("Memorandum Intended for the Management Boards of the Participating Organizations of the Annual Reporting Committees, the TO, Concerning its Objectives, Structure and Procedures") (JO Alg 3397–3404).

[162] Letter from W.J.L. Spit, vice-voorzitter, Federatie Nederlandse Vakbeweging, to the management boards of the NIvRA, the CNV, and the Council of Dutch Employers Federations, dated 6 October 1980. (A copy of the letter was furnished by the FNV.)

[163] *Verslag van de werkzaamheden over het jaar 1980 van het TRIPARTIETE OVERLEG*, pp. 12, 13.

1980/1981.[164] The NIvRA's annual report, together with the TO's annual report for 1981,[165] contained a description of the outcome of the discussions, the outlines of which were as follows.

The Foundation for Annual Reporting (Stichting voor de Jaarverslaggeving) was established on 18 September 1981, the very day on which the SER decided to fund two-thirds of the cost of its operations (JO Alg 4575).[166] The Foundation's stated goal was

> to enhance the quality of external reporting, especially of the financial statements of legal entities and other economically important organizations within the Netherlands (Art. 2). (JO Alg 4528)[167]

It was to do so through the publication by the Council on Annual Reporting (RJ, "Raad voor de Jaarverslaggeving") of "affirmative pronouncements" and "advisory recommendations".

The Foundation was to be financed in a 1:2 ratio by the NIvRA and the SER, respectively. The total budget for 1982 was estimated at *f* 325 000,[168] well below the estimate of *f* 500 000 proposed in the TO's discussions during early 1980. The articles of incorporation provided that the members of the RJ and the Foundation's board were to receive remuneration (*presentiegeld*) in accordance with the scale established by the SER. A decision was also made on the disposition of the some *f* 70 000 of royalties that had been received from Kluwer. A staff member, thinking that the entire amount should go to the NIvRA, calculated that the NIvRA had incurred costs of approximately *f* 1 million to support the TO since its founding. But the members decided to divide the money among the participating organizations: one-half to the NIvRA, one-fourth to the employers federations, and one-fourth to the trade unions.[169]

The participating organizations were to represent the "preparers, users and auditors of information" ("*verschaffers, gebruikers en controleurs van informatie*"), and they would be entitled to seats on the Foundation's board. These would be the VNO and the NCW, for the preparers; the FNV and the CNV, for the users;

---

164 *Verslag van de werkzaamheden 1980/'81*, Nederlands Instituut van Registeraccountants, p. 8.

165 *Verslag van de werkzaamheden over het jaar 1981 van het TRIPARTIETE OVERLEG*, p. 12.

166 One large audit firm commented that the involvement of the SER "can be regarded as recognition of the significance of the work performed by the [RJ]". *Financial Statements – Developments in 1981*, KKC Booklet no. 14 ([Amsterdam:] Klynveld Kraayenhof & Co., January 1982), p. 6.

167 The statutes, or articles of incorporation, of the Foundation were reproduced in its first annual report: *Verslag van de werkzaamheden over het jaar 1982 van de Raad voor de Jaarverslaggeving* (9 March 1983), pp. 14–22.

168 "Tripartiete Overleg wordt geïnstitutionaliseerd", in *Het Financieele Dagblad*, 16 September 1981 (JO Alg 4525).

169 Interview with O.M. Volgenant jr., 21 November 1991.

and the NIvRA, for the auditors. The SER "cooperated" in the undertaking, but was not represented on the Foundation's board. The organizations were authorized to appoint members to their delegations on the RJ for a renewable term of four years.

A significant step toward elevating the status of the RJ was the decision to name the president of the VNO to the position of chairman of the Foundation's board. In the past, the involvement of the VNO's president in matters concerning the TO had been limited to ad hoc meetings initiated by the NIvRA's management board. In the future, however, the VNO would have a continuing involvement at the highest level.

The RJ would be composed of three delegations of four persons each, plus a chairman who, contrary to the practice in the TO, would not be a member of any delegation. It was authorized to issue exposure drafts and final statements on its own authority.[170] Its decisions would require a four-fifths majority, with the additional requirement that at least one representative of each organization must be in favor.

There was no provision for open meetings or public hearings. These possibilities were apparently never discussed.

The TO would continue to function during the balance of 1981, but would refrain from issuing any definitive Guidelines (JO Alg 4623). In fact, during 1981, six single-issue exposure drafts were issued. One, on accounting changes, called for much more information to be given in connection with changes in accounting policies; it incorporated a number of Enterprise Chamber verdicts by calling for the reasons in support of such changes to be provided. Two drafts dealt with recognition and disclosure criteria. And a further draft was a revision of the section on earnings per share that formed part of the exposure draft issued in December 1976. The new draft was based on a memorandum supplied by the Society of Financial Analysts.

The last meeting of the TO occurred on 9 December 1981, just over ten years after its first meeting on 19 August 1971. The members of the TO at the end of 1981 became the inaugural members of the RJ, after the employers delegation was pared from seven to four. The RJ held its first meeting on 8 January 1982 (RJ Not 5).[171]

5.4.8. Comparison with US and UK statements

As has been suggested, the TO kept a close eye on issues being addressed in the USA and the UK, both for topics to be placed on its agenda and for substantive positions that might be worthwhile adopting or adapting. Some major issues

[170] The proposal by the NIvRA, in its memorandum of 29 November 1979, to give the foundation's board a veto in such matters was not followed.
[171] "RJ Not" refers to the minutes of the RJ.

taken up in the USA and UK, however, did not receive much, or any, attention by the TO. In undertaking such comparisons, one must be cognizant of the very different capital markets and regulatory climates as between the Netherlands and the USA and the UK, as well as the substantial resources furnished to the Financial Accounting Standards Board in comparison with what little was available to the TO.

A few differences, however, stand out. In the USA and the UK, the statement of source and application of funds had been recommended as a basic financial statement in 1971 and 1975,[172] respectively, while the TO did not issue guidance on a funds statement until its seventh exposure draft, published in September 1979, and even then it offered minimal advice and was less than clear on whether it should be considered one of the financial statements. IAS 7, issued in October 1977, also called for the Statement of Changes in Financial Position to be included as an integral part of the financial statements. In view of the unmistakable international trend toward the publication of funds statements, and the fact (as noted above) that almost 90 percent of Dutch listed companies were issuing such a statement, the timidity of the TO on this question, undoubtedly explained by resistance from the employer side, was curious.

Foreign exchange accounting had been addressed in FASB *Statement* no. 8, issued in 1975, and it was the subject of ED 21, issued by the UK's Accounting Standards Committee in October 1977. Yet the TO did not issue any guidance on foreign exchange accounting during its decade of existence (apart from a brief treatment of provisions for exchange rate losses in the September 1979 exposure draft).

Accounting for research and development, which had given rise to US and UK statements in 1974 and 1977[173], respectively, was not taken up by the TO until its seventh exposure draft, issued in 1979. (The issuance of IAS 9, "Accounting for Research and Development Activities", in July 1978, probably brought the issue before the TO.) While the tendency overseas was to charge as much of research and development costs as was practicable directly to income, the TO confined its advice to a recitation of the law.

The desired contents of interim reports, which had been addressed in APB *Opinion* no. 28, in May 1973, was not taken up by the TO, even though the Stock Exchange Association had amended its Rules for Securities Trading in 1971 to call for such statements.

There were, of course, many areas taken up by the TO that had also received considerable attention in the USA and the UK: deferred tax, changing prices, government incentives, leases, pensions, extraordinary items and direct charges

[172] APB *Opinion* no. 19, "Reporting Changes in Financial Position", and *SSAP* 10, "Statements of Source and Application of Funds".
[173] FASB *Statement* no. 2, "Accounting for Research and Development Costs", and *SSAP* 13, "Accounting for Research and Development".

or credits to equity, investments, receivables, merchandise inventories, intangibles, and earnings per share. Dutch recommendations were neither as detailed nor as unambiguous in their prescriptions as were their counterparts in the USA and the UK.

5.4.9. Companies' compliance with the considered views

In 1973, the NIvRA published a survey of selected practices used in listed companies' 1971 financial statements, entitled *Onderzoek Jaarverslagen*, which was the first in a biennial series. This series, together with a survey directed by Prof.dr R. Slot, gave some impression of the degree to which companies actually complied with the TO's recommendations. The NIvRA's biennial surveys indicated that compliance with the TO's recommendations, when they were other than reiterations of what the law already required, was not always satisfactory. As an example, even after the TO issued its strongest declaration that it was "unacceptable" to value investments at *f* 1 or less, between 6 and 8 percent of listed companies showing investments nonetheless continued to do so. That the NIvRA surveys did not attempt a systematic report on compliance with all of the sections in the Considered Views and exposure drafts makes it difficult to render global assessments of the degree to which they were actually followed in practice. The survey reports have tended to emphasize areas of noncompliance rather than areas of compliance.

A study of 1973 financial statements by Slot (and four colleagues) did not show evidence of much compliance either, but by early 1974, when the 1973 financial statements would have been released, only two exposure drafts and no final statement had been issued. Companies were still getting accustomed to a much more specific law and a tripartite body advising them to go even further. Slot's survey examined the financial reports of 50 large industrial and trading companies. After looking for additional information that was not called for by law, he concluded, "Apparently, many companies do not want to go beyond what the law requires."[174] While he occasionally referred to the contents of the exposure drafts, he developed his own list of additional information that companies might have disclosed. Unlike the NIvRA surveys, which have never

---

[174] *Vijftig jaarverslagen – Gewogen en te licht bevonden*, Economisch Instituut der Rijksuniversiteit Utrecht (Leiden: H.E. Stenfert Kroese B.V., 1975), p. 46. For a critical review of the Slot survey, see Prof.drs R. Burgert and Drs J. Dijksma, "Een toetsing van jaarverslagen getoetst", in *Economisch Statistisch Berichten*, vol. 60, no. 3016, 27 August 1975, pp. 815–821; Slot and his colleagues replied on pp. 822–828.

Slot conducted a small follow-up study on the five companies that had shown the worst performance in 1973. It appeared that four of the five had improved their reports in varying degrees, and, by asking questions at the companies' shareholders meetings, Slot learned that his earlier report had played a role in bringing about the improvements. Prof.dr R. Slot, "Vijf van de vijftig", in *Economisch Statistische Berichten*, vol. 61, no. 3071, 22 September 1976, pp. 915–916.

identified complying and noncomplying companies by name, even though all of the information had been taken from published financial statements, Slot's survey associated reporting practices with each company by name. He also named the best and worst companies.

In *Onderzoek Jaarverslagen 1973*, which covered financial statements published during that year, it was stated that "The majority of companies do not in any way indicate the effect of price changes on income and financial position".[175] As an indication of current value, insured value was frequently given, even though its use had been discouraged by the TO in its second exposure draft issued in February 1973.

In *Onderzoek Jaarverslagen 1975*[176], it was reported that "The development in favor of current value applications is going slow"(p. 11), even though the TO's third exposure draft, issued in June 1975, had emphasized the importance of current value. According to the survey, 50 of the 135 surveyed companies gave some information on current value in their financial statements or in the notes, with more doing so in the balance sheet than in the profit and loss statement (pp. 26–27). About half of the companies had made direct charges or credits to equity, but a significant minority of these did not give an adequate explanation in their notes, thus departing from the second exposure draft, issued in February 1973 (pp. 49–51).

In the NIvRA's survey of financial reporting practices in 1977, some general improvement was noted.[177] Current value applications had increased slowly, as 58 out of the 135 surveyed companies gave some form of information (p. 13). Despite the TO's recommendations on accounting changes included in the Considered Views issued in May 1974, half of the changes were not properly motivated. Also, a non-negligible number of companies did not comply with the second statement of Considered Views (issued in May 1976) on direct charges and credits to equity, and with the exposure draft (issued in December 1975) on deferred taxes.

In the 1979 survey, the trend toward gradual improvement continued.[178] Seven percent of the companies used current value for all appropriate items, and 41 percent used a partial application (p. 13). Accounting changes were better motivated, and it was pointed out that the Enterprise Chamber had stressed the importance of doing so (p. 13). The exposure draft on pensions (issued in June 1975) was not followed in important respects in 30 percent of applicable cases

---

[175] NIVRA geschrift nummer 14 (Amsterdam: Nederlands Instituut van Registeraccountants, October 1975), p. 11. The production of the biennial survey was carried out by the CAJ.

[176] NIVRA geschrift nummer 17 (Amsterdam: Nederlands Instituut van Registeraccountants, February 1977). Page citations in the text refer to this publication.

[177] *Onderzoek Jaarverslagen 1977*, NIVRA geschrift nummer 21 (Amsterdam: Nederlands Instituut van Registeraccountants, February 1979). Page citations in the text refer to this publication.

[178] *Onderzoek Jaarverslagen 1979*, NIVRA geschrift nummer 22 (Amsterdam: Nederlands Instituut van Registeraccountants, June 1981). Page citations in the text refer to this publication.

(p. 15).

In the 1981 study[179], the trend toward greater use of current value was reversed somewhat, probably owing to four consecutive years of inflation rates of between 4.5 and 7 percent.[180] Only 4 percent of companies used current value for all appropriate items, while 38 percent used a partial application (p. 12). Motivation of accounting changes continued to be unsatisfactory (p. 12). Compliance with the exposure draft on pensions remained at the same level (p. 13).

In general, compliance with the law was high, although a few provisions in the law met with some resistance. Following adoption of the Wierenga amendment in 1975 on the segmentation of operating income, the following trend in compliance was evidenced in the NIvRA surveys:

	Percentage of Applicable Companies	
Year	Showing Segmented Operating Income	Giving Only Some Quantitative Information
1977	21.3	48.9
1979	44.2	36.0
1981	9.0	49.4

The 1981 study gave as the reason for the significant drop in the percentage of applicable companies showing segmented operating income that companies were anticipating the deletion of the provision from the law, since it had not been included in the Justice Ministry's draft law to adapt to the Fourth Directive.[181]

In April 1979, the NIvRA published the first in a series of comprehensive checklists for use by auditors when examining companies' financial statements.[182] Known as the *Controlelijst jaarrekeningen* (in 1984, renamed *jaarverslaggeving*), the checklist reminded auditors of the legal requirements, the practices recommended in the TO's exposure drafts and Considered Views, IASC standards, and verdicts of the Enterprise Chamber, and every few years an updated checklist has been published. The proposal for the checklist had been made by Schoonderbeek in 1976 (CAJ Not 763).

[179] *Onderzoek Jaarverslagen 1981*, NIVRA geschrift nummer 29 (Amsterdam: Nederlands Instituut van Registeraccountants, June 1983).

[180] In 1974 and 1975, the inflation rate peaked at 10.5 percent, then fell to 9 percent in 1976 and 6 percent in 1977. Prijspeil binnenlandse afzet van bedrijven (Price Level for Domestic Sales by Business Enterprises), Table 10 *Economische kerngegevens*, in De Nederlandsche Bank n.v., *Verslag over het jaar 1980*, Statistische bijlage, p. 40.

[181] *Onderzoek Jaarverslagen 1981*, *op.cit.*, p. 15.

[182] See the brief discussion of this initiative in the *Verslag van de werkzaamheden, 1 september t/m 31 augustus 1979*, Nederlands Instituut van Registeraccountants, p. 9. (Information about the first checklist was supplied by the NIvRA.)

Since 1970, regulations of financial reporting had been coming from several directions, and auditors could have been excused if they were having difficulty keeping up with the latest initiatives. At the same time, the checklist was the NIvRA's way of alerting auditors to the practices favored by the TO and the IASC.

5.4.10. Concluding remarks

The decade of the 1970's was, for auditors and companies alike, a period of intensive regulatory activity, following decades in which the contents of company financial statements had been governed only by a skeletal 1929 law, with later influences coming from such sources as the Stock Exchange Association, two committees sponsored by the employers federations, and the panel of judges for the Sijthoff Prize. For multinationals taking up share trading overseas, the reporting requirements of other countries' capital markets became relevant. But, in general, companies enjoyed very wide latitude in deciding how much and what kind of financial information to present in their annual reports.

Beginning in 1970, however, the world of financial reporting for Dutch companies underwent a profound change. The Act on Annual Financial Statements of Enterprises, which was approved in 1970, took effect in 1971. It required an annual audit for the first time, it effectively ended the use of secret reserves, and it expanded the amount of financial information to be reported by companies. In December 1971, the newly established TO issued its first exposure draft. In 1975, the IASC began publishing accounting standards, and in 1977 the Enterprise Chamber issued its first verdicts in financial reporting cases. In 1978, the Fourth Directive was approved, and the Dutch government began the process of adapting the law to the Directive. A financial reporting environment that was largely unregulated prior to the 1970's suddenly became regulated on all sides.

In the late 1960's and early 1970's, when the groundwork was being laid for the establishment of an ongoing program for giving advice on accounting principles, there was no precedent on which to build. It had never been done before in the Netherlands. But after a few years of conducting negotiations and adjusting to the prospect of working together, the auditors, employers and employees finally launched the TO in August 1971. The TO had a slow and uncertain beginning. No one knew how its drafts would be received by auditors, by companies, and by the Enterprise Chamber. Despite periodic clashes of philosophies and personalities, the TO succeeded in issuing seven exposure drafts and three final statements of Considered Views, covering a range of fairly controversial and sensitive subjects. The language was often heavily compromised, but the very issuance of drafts and final statements was itself an achievement in view of the virtual absence of regulation in previous decades. By the end of the 1970's, there were calls for enhanced status and authority for the TO's work, and even for a stricter monitoring of compliance by companies. These calls stemmed from (1) a disappointment with the level of attention being given (especially by the Enterprise Chamber) to the TO's exposure drafts and final statements, and (2) the NIvRA's need to integrate IASC standards into the process of gaining acceptance for financial reporting norms. There was also a need for a more formal structure than simply three committees coming together in an *overleg* (i.e., a forum for deliberation). In the end, employers as well as the auditors and the employees came to accept a body such as the TO as an entity to be taken seriously in Dutch financial reporting. By the end of 1981, the informal arrangement known as the TO was replaced by a foundation and the RJ. These two new institutions began their work against the background of the ambitious charge to auditors and companies that was included in the TO's Foreword to the rewritten Draft Guidelines in 1980. It remained to be seen whether the auditors and companies would accept the charge.

Appendix 5.1. Membership of the TO and RJ

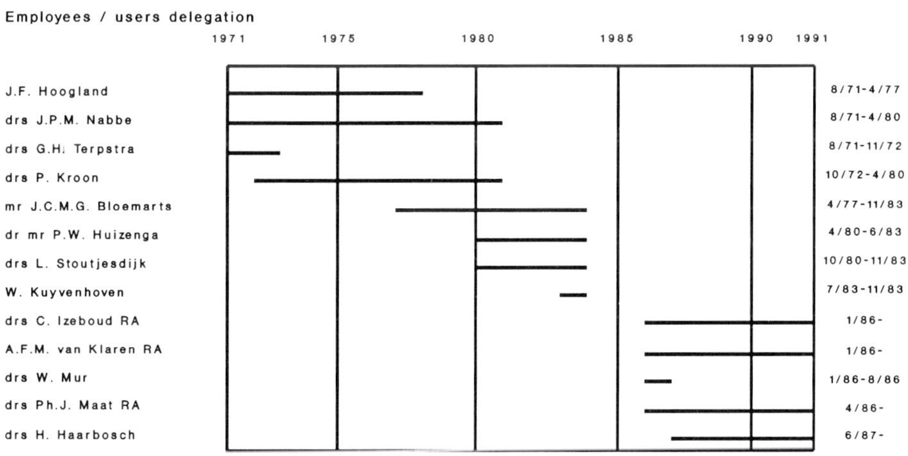

Employers / preparers delegation

Member (1971–1991)	Period
C. Bovenberg RA (Vihamij)	8/71-1/72
Mr E.J. Egberts (Amstel Brouwerij)	8/71-2/78
P.G.G. Frederiks RA (Akzo)	8/71-11/73
J.A. Hamburger (Kon. Hamburger)	8/71
Mr R Hoorens van Heijningen (VNO)	8/71-2/81
Mr J.H. Mesker (C&A)	8/71
Drs W. Schattinga RA (Unilever)	8/71-1/73
Prof.dr Th.M. Scholten (SHV)	8/71-11/71
Mr H.C. Wesseling (Unilever)	8/71-8/86
J.V.M. van Heeswijk (SHV)	11/71-6/76
E.G. Hoefer RA (Chevron)	1/72-12/81
W.J.H. Kuipers RA (C&A)	1/72-12/74
Dr N.L. Ruizendaal RA (Unilever)	5/73-2/75
P.C. Breek RA (Philips)	12/74-10/77
Drs A.J. Rijnvis RA (SHV)	8/76-12/81
J.W. Frijns RA (DAF)	11/77-2/81
Prof.dr A. van Putten (Nedlloyd)	12/77-9/84
R.C. Spinosa Cattela (Philips)	12/77-4/86
Drs G. Verhagen RA (Pakhoed)	3/81-4/88
J. Vos RA (Philips)	3/81-12/81
Drs J.B.H.M. Beks RA (Heineken)	10/84-
J. den Hoed RA (Akzo)	4/86-2/89
Prof.mr M.J.G.C.Raaijmakers (Philips)	9/86-10/87
Drs J.F. Leeuwerik RA (Shell)	11/87-
Drs P. Vergroesen RA (OTRA)	6/88-
Drs M.A. van Alphen RA (Internatio)	6/89-

Auditors delegation

Member (1971–1991)	Period
J.A. Burggraaff RA	8/71-1/76
Prof. A.M. van Rietschoten RA	8/71-1/72
J.P. van Rossem RA	8/71-1/76
A.F. Tempelaar RA	8/71-11/71
Prof.dr W. van Bruinessen RA	1/72-10/84
drs H.F. Oosterholt RA	3/72-12/73
drs H. van der Zee RA	4/74-9/74
Prof.drs J.W. Schoonderbeek RA	12/75-4/86
drs H. Marseille RA	12/75-
drs W.N. Meijer RA	2/80-12/86
drs P.P.M. van der Ree RA	1/82-4/86
drs F. Graafstal RA	10/84-
G. Timmer RA	4/86-
W.P. Moleveld RA	4/86-12/87
P.H. Sneek RA	2/87-1/88
Prof.dr M.A. van Hoepen RA	1/88-
M.H.Th. Steunebrink RA	3/88-

Appendix 5.2. Chronological list of beschouwingen and richtlijnen

Beschouwingen (considered views)

		Exposure Draft
May 1974		
Ia	Inleiding (Introduction)	12/71
IIa3	Deelnemingen (Investments)	12/71
IIa4	Beleggingen op lange termijn (Long-term shareholdings)	12/71
IIb1	Voorraden (Inventories)	12/71
IIIc	Verplichtingen (Obligations)	12/71
IIIc1	Langlopende verplichtingen (Long-term obligations)	12/71
IIIc2	Kortlopende verplichtingen (Short-term obligations)	12/71
V	Niet in de balans opgenomen posten (Liabilities not to be shown in the balance sheet)	12/71
May 1976		
IIa1	Vaste activa (Fixed assets)	2/73
IIb2	Vorderingen (Receivables)	2/73
IIb3	Overige vlottende activa (in het bijzonder overlopende posten) (Other current assets (in particular accruals)	2/73
IIb4	Tijdelijk belegde betalingsmiddelen (Temporary investments)	2/73
IIb5	Betalingsmiddelen (Liquid holdings)	2/73
IIIa1	Mutaties in het eigen vermogen (Direct charges and credits to owners' equity)	2/73
IIIa2	Eigen aandelen (Treasury shares)	2/73
IIIb	Voorzieningen (Provisions)	2/73
February 1979		
Ib	Algemene Onderwerpen (General observations)	6/75
Ib1	Gegevens die voor vermelding in de jaarrekening van belang zijn (Information that is of importance to be shown in the financial statements)	6/75
IIa6	De invloed van (de dreiging van) discontinuïteit op de waardering van vaste activa (Valuation of fixed assets in connection with the imminent discontinuance of enterprise activities)	6/75
IIIa3	Presentatie van het eigen vermogen (Presentation of owners' equity)	6/75
IIIb1	Pensioenvoorzieningen (Provisions for pensions)	6/75
IVa1	Aanvaardbare grondslagen voor de resultaatbepaling (Acceptable principles for income determination)	6/75
IVa2	Toerekening van baten aan de achtereenvolgende verslagperioden (Allocating revenue to successive financial years)	6/75
IVa3	Toerekening van lasten aan de achtereenvolgende verslagperioden (Allocating expense to successive financial years)	6/75
IVb1	Detaillering van de winst- en verliesrekening: Het onderscheid tussen bedrijfsresultaten enerzijds en overige baten en lasten anderzijds (Breakdown of the profit and loss statement: Distinction between operating results and other revenues and expenses)	6/75
Exposure drafts not acted upon by 1980:		
Ib2	Verwerking in de jaarrekening van effecten van stelselwijzigingen (Treatment in the financial statements of the effects of accounting changes)	12/75

Ib3	De verhouding tussen de balans en winst- en verliesrekening enerzijds en de toelichting anderzijds (The relationship between the balance sheet and profit and loss statement on the one hand and the notes on the other)	12/76
Ib4	Actuele waarde (Current value)	12/76
Ib5	Criteria voor het opnemen van active en passiva in de balans (Criteria for the inclusion of assets and liabilities in the balance sheet)	12/76
Ib6	De Staat van Herkomst en Besteding van Middelen (The Statement of Changes in Financial Position)	9/79
Ib7	Gebeurtenissen na balansdatum; datering van de jaarrekening (Events occurring after the balance sheet date; dating the financial statements)	9/79
IIa2	Immateriële activa (Intangible assets)	9/79
IIa3	Het verwerven en afstoten van deelnemingen; de behandeling van goodwill (The acquisition and disposition of investments; the treatment of goodwill)	12/75
IIIb2	Categorieën van voorzieningen (Types of provisions)	9/79
IIIb3	Mutaties in voorzieningen (Movements in provisions)	9/79
IVb2	Detaillering van omzet en bedrijfsresultaat (Breakdown of sales and operating income)	12/76
VI1	Belastingen in de jaarrekening (Taxes in the financial statements)	12/75
VI2	Rente (Interest)	12/76
VI3	Winst per aandeel (Earnings per share)	12/76
VI4	De verwerking van de WIR- en IPR-premies en de SIR-heffingen in de jaarrekening (The treatment of the WIR and IPR premiums and the SIR levy in the financial statements)	2/79

Richtlijnen voor de Jaarrekening (Guidelines for the Financial Statements)

June 1980	
	Voorwoord (Foreword)

Richtijnen voor de jaarverslaggeving (Guidelines for Annual Reporting)

			Former number[1]
January 1984			
1.05	*Criteria voor opname en vermelding van gegevens (Criteria for the recognition and disclosure of information)*		
1.05.1	Criteria voor opname van activa en passiva (Criteria for the recording of assets and liabilities) REVISED 4/86, 6/87, 6/88	1/81	
1.05.2	Criteria voor vermelding (Criteria for disclosure) REVISED 12/84, 4/86, 6/88	6/80	1.05.1

[1] The "former numbers" were those assigned to the "Ontwerp-Richtlijnen" ("Draft Guidelines") that were issued in June 1980. With the first installment of the "Richtlijnen voor de jaarverslaggeving" ("Guidelines for Annual Reporting") in January 1984, the numbering system was changed.

[1.06	Stelselwijzigingen [en de verwerking in de jaarrekening van effecten van stelselwijzigingen] (Accounting changes [and the treatment in the financial statements of the effects of accounting changes]) REVISED 8/89, REPLACED 6/91]	1/81	
1.06	Stelselwijzigingen (Accounting changes) REPLACEMENT	6/91	
2.02	*Materiële vaste activa en afschrijvingen (Tangible fixed assets and depreciation)*		
[2.02.1	Algemeen (General) REVISED 12/84, REPLACED 4/86	6/80]	
2.02.1	Algemeen (General) REPLACEMENT, REVISED 6/88, 8/89	4/86	2.02.1–2
2.02.2	Te hanteren prijsgrondslagen indien het continuïteitsbeginsel niet van toepassing is (Pricing principles to be used when the going concern assumption is not applicable) REVISED 12/84	6/80	2.02.3
2.12	Vorderingen (Receivables) REVISED 12/84, 4/86, 6/88, 8/89	6/80	2.07
2.13	Effecten (Securities) REVISED 12/84, 4/86	6/80	2.04.4
2.14	*Overlopende activa (Deferred charges)*		
2.14.1	Overlopende posten (Accruals) REVISED 4/86, RENUMBERED (2.14) and REVISED 6/87 NEW TITLE: Overlopende activa (Deferred charges)	6/80	2.09.1
2.14.2	Voorwaardelijke baten (Contingent gains) RENUMBERED (2.18) 6/87	1/81	2.09.2
2.15	Liquide middelen (Liquid assets) REVISED 4/86	6/80	2.08
2.51	Verplichtingen algemeen (Liabilities in general) REVISED 6/87, 6/88	6/80	2.11
2.53	*Voorzieningen (Provisions)*		
[2.53.1	Begripsbepaling, presentatie en waardering (Definition, presentation and valuation) REVISED 12/86, 4/86, 6/88, REPLACED 6/90	6/80	2.12]
2.53.1	Begripsbepaling, presentatie en waardering (Definition, presentation and valuation) REPLACEMENT, REVISED 12/90	6/90	
2.53.3	Pensioenvoorzieningen (Pension provisions) REVISED 4/86, 6/88	6/80	2.12.4
[2.53.4	Vervroegde uittreding van personeel en andere non-activiteitsregelingen (Early retirement of personnel and other non-activity settlements) REPLACED 12/90]	6/80	2.12.5
2.53.4	Vervroegde uittreding van personeel en andere non-activiteitsregelingen (Early retirement of personnel and other non-activity settlements) REPLACEMENT	12/90	
2.54	Schulden op lange termijn (Long-term liabilities) REVISED 12/84, 6/87, 6/88, NEW TITLE (6/87): Langlopende schulden	6/80	2.13.1
2.55	Schulden op korte termijn (Short-term liabilities) REVISED 12/84, 6/87, 6/88, NEW TITLE (6/87): Kortlopende schulden	6/80	2.13.2
2.62	Overlopende passiva (Deferred credits) REVISED 6/87, 6/88	6/80	2.14.1
2.65	*Niet in de balans op te nemen verplichtingen (Liabilities not to be shown in the balance sheet)*		
2.65.1	Voorwaardelijke verplichtingen (Contingent liabilities) REVISED 12/84, 6/87, 6/88	6/80	2.11.2

2.65.2	PM-verplichtingen (Liabilities not subject to recognition) REVISED 4/86	6/80	2.11.2
2.71	*De winst- en verliesrekening (The profit and loss statement)*		
2.71.1	Grondslagen voor de bepaling van het resultaat (Principles for determining the result) REVISED 8/89	6/80	2.15.1
2.71.2	Het onderscheid tussen baten en lasten uit de gewone bedrijfsuitoefening enerzijds en de buitengewone baten en lasten anderzijds (The difference between gains and losses from ordinary operations on the one hand and extraordinary gains and losses on the other) REVISED 12/84, 8/89, 6/91	6/80	2.15.2
2.71.3	Rente (Interest) REVISED 10/86, 8/89	6/81	2.15.3
2.81	*De toelichting (Notes)*		
2.81.1	Functie en indeling (Function and layout) REVISED 12/84, 4/86, 6/90, 12/90	1/81	2.16
4.09	Winst per aandeel (Earnings per share) RENUMBERED (4.24) 12/84	1/81	4.09
December 1984			
1.01	*Inleiding (Introduction)*		
1.01.1	Algemene opmerkingen (General comments) REVISED 4/86	6/80	
1.01.2	Opzet (Approach)	6/80	
1.01.3	Status van de Richtlijnen (Status of the Guidelines) REVISED 4/86	6/80	
1.02	Doelstellingen en uitgangspunten (Objectives and premises) REVISED 10/86, 6/88, 8/89	6/80	
1.03	*Prijsgrondslagen (Pricing principles)*		
1.03.1	Inleiding (Introduction)	6/80	
1.03.2	Begripsbepalingen (Definitions) REVISED 4/86	6/80	
1.03.3	Continuïteit (Going concern)	6/80	
1.03.4	Prijsgrondslagen voor materiële en financiële vaste activa en voorraden (Pricing principles for tangible fixed assets, long-term investments and inventories)	6/80	1.03.2
1.03.5	Prijsgrondslagen voor overige activa en passiva (Pricing principles for other assets and liabilities) REVISED 4/86, 10/86	6/80	
1.03.6	Prijsgrondslagen in geval van discontinuïteit (Pricing principles in the case of the discontinuance of activities)	6/80	
1.03.10	Presentatie (Presentation) REVISED 10/86	6/80	
2.11	*Voorraden en kosten van het goederenverbruik (Inventories and costs of goods used)*		
2.11.1	Begripsbepalingen (Definitions) REVISED 10/86	6/80	2.06.1
2.11.2	Waardering (Valuation) REVISED 10/86	6/80	2.06.2
2.41	*Eigen vermogen (Owners' equity)*		
2.41.1	Mutaties in het eigen vermogen (Movements in owners' equity) REVISED 8/89	6/80	2.10.1
2.41.3	Herwaarderingsreserve (Revaluation reserve) REVISED 6/88	6/80	
2.41.4	Eigen aandelen (Treasury shares)	6/80	2.10.2
2.41.5	Presentatie van en toelichting op het eigen vermogen (Presentation of, and the notes for, owners' equity) REVISED 4/86, 6/88	6/80	2.10.3

April 1986

1.03	*Prijsgrondslagen (Pricing principles)*		
1.03.9	Prijsgrondslagen voor vreemde valuta's (Pricing principles for foreign exchange) REVISED 6/87, 6/88	10/83	

October 1986

2.11	Voorraden en kosten van het goederenverbruik (Inventories and costs of goods used)		
2.11.5	Toelichting betreffende voorraden (Notes relating to inventories)	6/80	2.06.3

June 1987

2.01	Immateriële vaste activa en daarmee samenhangende lasten (Intangible fixed assets and associated charges) REVISED 6/88	1/84	

August 1989

2.71	*De winst- en verliesrekening (The profit and loss statement)*		
2.71.6	Detaillering van de netto-omzet (Segmentation of net sales) FORMER TITLE: detaillering van de omzet	12/84	
3.01	Overheidssubsidies en vergelijkbare faciliteiten (Government subsidies and comparable arrangements)	1/84	
4.10	Accountantsonderzoek (Auditor's examination) REVISED 12/90	4/86	

June 1990

2.53	*Voorzieningen (Provisions)*		
2.53.2	Mutaties in voorzieningen (Movements in provisions)	1/84	
2.81	*De toelichting (Notes)*		
2.81.2	Bezoldiging van bestuurders en commissarissen (Remuneration of managers and supervisors)	4/86	

December 1990

1.19	*Overige algemene algemene uiteenzettingen (Other general Observations)*		
1.19.4	Samengestelde transacties ("package deals")	10/86	
2.83	Winstbestemming, verwerking verlies (Income appropriation and treatment of losses)	4/86	
4.02	Overige gegevens (Other information)	4/86	
4.15	Openbaarmaking (Publication of financial statements)	4/86	

June 1991

1.19	*Overige algemene uiteenzettingen (Other general Observations)*		
1.19.1	Geldeenheid en taal (Monetary unit and language) FORMER TITLE: Gebruik van de Nederlandse geldeenheid en de Nederlandse taal (Use of the Dutch monetary unit and the Dutch language)	12/84	
2.81	*De toelichting (Notes)*		

	Bijlage bij hoofdstuk 2.81. Voorbeelden van specificaties [in de toelichting] (Appendix to section 2.81. Examples of analyses [in the notes]) issued as draft Guideline 2.81.9	4/86

Exposure drafts issued since 1984 and not converted into definitive Guidelines by December 1991:

1.19	*Overige algemene uiteenzettingen (Other general Observations)*	
1.19.2	Onderscheid vast/vlottend (Distinction between fixed and current)	6/91
1.19.3	Verbonden partijen (Related parties)	10/86
2.03	*Financiële vaste activa (Financial fixed assets)*	
[2.03.1	Begripsbepaling (Definition) REVISED 4/86, 6/88 REPLACED 6/90]	12/84
2.03.1	Begripsbepaling en enige algemene uitgangspunten (Definition and some general assumptions) REPLACEMENT	6/90
[2.03.2	Waardering van deelnemingen en dochtermaatschappijen (Valuation of minority and majority investments) REVISED 4/86, 6/88 REPLACED 6/90]	12/84
2.03.2	Waardering van deelnemingen (Valuation of investments) REPLACEMENT	6/90
[2.03.3	Groepsjaarrekening en consolidatiemethoden (Group financial statements and consolidation methods) REVISED 4/86, 6/88 REPLACED 6/90]	12/84
2.03.3	Geconsolideerde jaarrekening en consolidatiemethoden (Consolidated financial statements and consolidation methods) REPLACEMENT	6/90
[2.03.4	Waardering overige financiële vaste activa (Valuation of other financial fixed assets) REVISED 6/88, REPLACED 6/91]	12/84
2.03.4	Waardering overige financiële vaste activa (Valuation of other financial fixed assets) REPLACEMENT	6/91
[2.03.5	Resultaatbepaling (Income determination) REVISED 4/86 REPLACED 6/91]	12/84
2.03.5	Resultaatbepaling (Income determination) REPLACEMENT	6/91
[2.03.6	Presentatie (Presentation) REVISED 4/86, 6/88, REPLACED 6/91]	12/84
2.03.6	Presentatie (Presentation) REPLACEMENT	6/91
2.11	*Voorraden en kosten van het goederenverbruik (Inventories and costs of goods used)*	
2.11.3	De verwerking van de economische voorraad in de jaarrekening (The financial-statement treatment of goods purchased or sold but not delivered)	10/86
2.41	*Eigen vermogen (Owners' equity)*	
2.41.2	Verwerking van wettelijke reserves (Treatment of legal reserves) REVISED 4/86, 6/88	1/84
2.53	*Voorzieningen (Provisions)*	
2.53.5	Voorzieningen voor latente belastingen (Provisions for deferred taxes) REVISED 4/86, 6/88, 8/89	1/84
2.53.9	Overige categorieën van voorzieningen (Other types of provisions) REVISED 12/84, 4/86, 6/87	1/84

2.71	*De winst- en verliesrekening (The profit and loss statement)*		
2.71.5	Overige rubriceringen (Other classifications)	12/90	
2.71.6	Detaillering van het bedrijfsresultaat (The segmentation of operating income) FORMERLY: Een beschouwing omtrent ... (A considered view concerning REVISED 6/91 (Balance of 2.71.6 remains a Richtlijn)	12/84	2.71.9
2.71.7	Overige detaillering van de winst- en verliesrekening (Other breakdowns within the profit and loss statement)	6/91	
3.41	*De invloed van de grootte van de rechtspersoon (The influence of the size of legal entities)*		
3.41.1	Indeling naar grootte (Classification according to size)	4/86	
3.41.2	Vrijstellingen (Exemptions)	4/86	
3.42	*Vrijstellingen voor groepsmaatschappijen (Exemptions for group companies)*		
3.42.1	Vrijstelling ten aanzien van de inrichting van de enkelvoudige winst- en verliesrekening (Exemption relating to the layout of a parent company's profit and loss statement)	4/86	
3.42.2	Vrijstelling ten aanzien van een jaarrekening van een tot een groep behorende rechtspersoon (Exemption relating to a financial statement of a legal entity belonging to a group) REVISED 10/86	4/86	
3.42.3	Vrijstelling van deelconsolidatie (Exemption of consolidation requirements for intermediate holding companies)	4/86	
4.01	*Het jaarverslag (The directors' report)*		
4.01.1	Inleiding en algemeen (Introduction and in general)	4/86	
4.01.3	Onderzoek en ontwikkeling (Research and development)	12/90	
4.03	Gebeurtenissen na het einde van het boekjaar en datering jaarrekening (Events occurring after the end of the financial year, and the dating of the financial statements) REVISED 4/86	1/84	
4.20	De Staat van Herkomst en Besteding van Middelen (The Statement of Source and Application of Funds) REVISED 12/84	1/84	
4.22	Kerncijfers, kengetallen en meerjarenoverzichten (Key figures, ratios, and multi-year summaries)	6/90	
4.28	Overzicht toegevoegde waarde (Value-added summary)	6/90	
5.01	Tussentijdse overzichten (Interim statements)	8/89	

Beschouwingen (Discusssion Memoranda)

2.01	Beschouwing inzake een aantal aspecten van de behandeling van immateriële vaste activa (Discussion memorandum on a number of aspects of the treatment of intangible fixed assets)	6/91	

6. The first decade of the Raad voor de Jaarverslaggeving

6.1. Preview of the decade

The period from the early 1980's to 1991 was marked by the adaptations of the law to the Fourth and Seventh EEC Directives, the inception of the Council on Annual Reporting (RJ, Raad voor de Jaarverslaggeving) as successor to the Tripartite Study Group (TO, Tripartiete overleg), an attempt by the NIvRA to strengthen compliance with the RJ's definitive Guidelines, an effort by the NIvRA's management board to screen the CAJ's drafts en route to the RJ, a change in the Foundation's articles to reflect new procedures for voting and a reconstitution of the users delegation, as well as the preparation and issuance by the RJ of a number of exposure drafts, definitive Guidelines and special publications.

The 1980's began under a cloud of uncertainty. Auditors and companies were still unsure of the full meaning of the verdicts by the Enterprise Chamber for company reporting. They were also apprehensive of the possible impact on reporting practices of the imminent adaptation to Dutch law of the Fourth Directive. And there was also a concern that the TO's charge to the organizations of employers and auditors to take steps to enhance compliance with the "affirmative pronouncements" in the forthcoming definitive Guidelines was an attempt to clothe the Guidelines with something like the authority of law. The expanding cloak of regulation was viewed fearfully in a society that, not long before, was virtually free of any such interventions.

6.2. Adaptation of Dutch law to the EEC's Fourth Directive

6.2.1. Background

The object of the series of company law Directives of the European Economic Community had been to achieve a "coordination" of the national legislation of the member countries. The first draft of the Fourth Directive on companies' annual financial statements was published on 16 November 1971. It was based on the Elmendorff proposals of 1967–68. As the drafting work proceeded, Dutch commentators were aware that the Act on Annual Financial Statements of 1970 might enjoy only a limited life before it would need to be revised to reflect the final provisions of the Community's Directive.[1] The first draft was heavily influenced by German thinking, especially in its emphasis on exactness and detail. Use of the term "true" ("*juist*") in the draft, as opposed to "fair" ("*getrouw*"), which appeared in the 1970 Act, was indicative of its tenor. Detailed rules spelled out what the draft meant by "true picture" ("*juist beeld*"). Historical cost was given pride of place, although current cost was permitted in restricted circumstances.[2] Prescribed schedules were to be used for the balance sheet and the profit and loss statement.

The NIvRA's Advisory Committee on Company Law (Commissie van advies inzake Ondernemingsrecht) issued a critical report on the draft.[3] In addition to disapproving of its emphasis on truth and the rigidity in its provisions, the committee argued that equal standing should be accorded to all valuation bases, subject to the criterion in Article 5 of the 1970 Act, namely, that they are considered to be acceptable in the economic and social climate. This was a time of mounting inflation in Western Europe, and organizations of auditors were becoming sensitive to the limitations of historical cost accounting. Moreover, prominent members of the NIvA and the NIvRA had been advocates of current value/current cost accounting for decades.

On 1 January 1973, the United Kingdom and Ireland, together with Denmark, were admitted to the EEC, and the Dutch could count on support from the "true and fair" bloc.

The second draft of the Directive was published on 24 February 1974. Prof.drs R. Burgert, who had been critical of the first draft,[4] commented favorably on the second draft.[5] He welcomed the change from the (German) demand for "complying with the requirement of regular bookkeeping" to the (British) demand of "a true and fair view", together with the requirement to provide additional information where it would be necessary to give a true and fair view (the so-called "true and fair override"). Burgert saw the revised draft as being compatible with the 1970 Act, and in this regard he found it to be a significant improvement.

---

[1] See, e.g., Mr M. Mok, "De EEG en het vennootschapsrecht", in *TVVS*, vol. 11, no. 7, July 1968, p. 170; and Prof.drs R. Burgert, "De vierde richtlijn der E.E.G.-commissie omtrent de jaarrekening", in *Maandblad voor accountancy en bedrijfshuishoudkunde*, vol. 46, no. 2, February 1972, p. 34.

[2] As in earlier chapters, "current cost" (rather than "replacement value") is used to translate "*vervangingswaarde*", while "current value" is used to translate "*actuele waarde*". The authors regard "current cost" as being more in line with international usage than "replacement value".

[3] "Interim-rapport van de commissie ondernemingsrecht over het voorstel voor een vierde richtlijn van de Raad van de Europese Gemeenschappen", in *de Accountant*, vol. 79, no. 1, September 1972, pp. 17–26.

[4] Burgert, *op.cit.*, pp. 34–51.

[5] Prof.drs R. Burgert, "Een gewijzigd voorstel Vierde Richtlijn der E.E.G.-commissie omtrent de jaarrekening", in *Maandblad voor accountancy en bedrijfshuishoudkunde*, vol. 48, no. 5, May 1974, pp. 205–212.

He also praised the explicit prescription of consolidated statements (although there was no regulation of their contents), the recognition of the going concern principle, and the widened scope for deviations from historical cost by allowing various systems of inflation accounting.

Drs W. van Bruinessen has written of the Dutch influence on the drafting process. The Dutch delegation was said to have encountered the difficulty of coping with a German chairman and secretary who tended to interpret all agreements on valuation, a subject on which the Germans and the Dutch had an "almost maximal disagreement", in terms of the German law, while the French and the Belgians tended to side with the Germans, and the Italians had a position that was not clearly defined.[6] Mr P.A. Wessel has written that, during the drafting stage, the Dutch delegation worked assiduously for the inclusion of current value as an acceptable method.[7]

The final version of the Fourth Directive was promulgated on 25 July 1978. In an article written shortly after the publication of the Directive, Wessel ventured the view that the historical cost principle was so firmly implanted in the Directive that there could be no case in which, for the sake of a true and fair view, historical cost would not be allowed (as was equally the case under Article 5 of the 1970 Act).[8]

6.2.2. The initial draft law

A draft adaptation law to the Fourth Directive was submitted to Parliament on 8 September 1980.[9] In writing this law, the Justice Ministry had the assistance of H.C. Treffers and Mr P.A. Wessel, who had also participated in the governmental delegations to the European Commission and Council as the successors to J. Kraayenhof (B2 1979–1980, no. 3, p. 2). It was added that "Advice about the draft has been obtained from the Company Law Committee [Commissie Vennootschapsrecht, a committee of the SER] and the TO; their comments have had

---

[6] Drs W. van Bruinessen, "De grondslagen van de waardering en de winstbepaling in de jaarrekening en de aanpassing van de Nederlandse wetgeving aan de vierde richtlijn", in *De Naamlooze Vennootschap*, vol. 58, no. 10, October 1980, pp. 184–191.

[7] Mr P.A. Wessel, "De waarde en de rechter", in *Maandblad voor accountancy en bedrijfshuishoudkunde*, vol. 57, no. 5, May 1983, p. 201.

[8] P.A. Wessel, "De EEG-Richtlijn voor jaarrekening en jaarverslag van NV's en BV's en vergelijkbare rechtspersonen in andere lid-staten (II)", in *de Accountant*, vol. 85, no. 5, January 1979, p. 345.

[9] *Bijlagen Handelingen Tweede Kamer, Zitting 1979–1980*, no. 16326, "Aanpassing van de wetgeving aan de vierde richtlijn van de Raad van de Europese Gemeenschappen inzake het vennootschapsrecht". The same citational system will be used as was employed in Chapter 4 for the parliamentary process of approval of the Act on Annual Financial Statements of Enterprises. H and B will refer to the Handelingen and Bijlagen, respectively. References to the number 16326 will be omitted, but are implied for all B documents.

a far-reaching influence on the draft" (B2 1979–1980, no. 3, p. 4).[10]

The prominent role of the TO (and its successor, the RJ) in the adaptation process was later confirmed by Volten, who stated that the adoption of many of the TO's recommendations, together with the minister's announcement that the RJ would be consulted on the two administrative orders dealing with the model financial statements and valuation, would have "an extremely beneficial meaning for the position of the [RJ] and the authority of the Guidelines".[11] It is, however, instructive to compare the first draft law with the comments provided by the TO both in the preliminary stage and after the publication of the draft law. In the TO's initial comments of August 1979, four subjects were singled out as "very important": the preeminence of current value, the location of the "economic and social climate" clause, the announced administrative order on valuation, and the definition and treatment of investments.[12] On the first three subjects, the TO's recommendations were not followed, and on the issue of investments its recommendation was accepted only in regard to terminology. As a result, the issues of the required and proper use of current value and, to a certain extent, the treatment of investments had to be raised again in the public comments directed to members of Parliament.

In his Explanatory Memorandum (Memorie van Toelichting), the minister sketched several guiding principles that were followed in the development of the draft law: (1) that what had been already achieved in Dutch law should be preserved, (2) that options provided in the Directive would be retained as options in the draft law, and (3) that the occasion would not be used to introduce any subjects other than those included in the Directive (B2 1979–1980, no. 3, pp. 3–4).

The draft law reflected a number of salient changes from existing Dutch legislation. A short summary of the principal similarities and differences between the draft law and the 1970 Act (as contained in Title 6, Book 2 of the Civil Code) is as follows:

Changes of considerable significance:

- the disclosure rules were significantly increased in number and detail; furthermore, the minister promised an administrative order to require formats to be

[10] "SER" refers to the Social and Economic Council (Sociaal-Economische Raad). For a brief discussion of the SER, see the section on "Aspects of the economy and the capital market" in Chapter 1. The work of the TO was discussed extensively in Chapter 5.

[11] H. Volten, "Aanpassingswet Vierde Richtlijn – Memorie van antwoord en nota van wijziging verschenen", in *de Accountant*, vol. 88, no. 9, May 1982, p. 546.

[12] The recommendations consisted of a general comment and a set of comments on the specific articles, found in the TO's minutes (JO Alg 2671): "Commentaar van de commissies jaarverslaggeving van RNWV, FNV, CNV en NIVRA (Tripartiete Overleg) met betrekking tot het voorontwerp tot aanpassing van wetgeving aan de vierde EG-richtlijn", dated 28 August 1979, and "Artikelsgewijs commentaar" (JO Alg 2611–2668), dated 23 August 1979.

used for the balance sheet and the profit and loss statement.

- the rules for the valuation of investments, including use of the "net equity value" method,[13] were prescribed for the first time, and the size criteria for shareholdings to be classified as investments were altered.
- the requirement to segment operating income by product line (the Wierenga amendment of 1976) was made applicable to sales instead.
- rules were added, for the first time, concerning the contents of the directors' report.
- although the governing criterion of "considered to be acceptable in the economic and social climate" in connection with valuation and income determination was retained, current value was, in effect, required to be disclosed in the notes if not actually used in the financial statements.

Changes of lesser significance:

- the overriding criterion of an "insight" leading to a "well-founded opinion", together with the demands that the contents of the balance sheet and profit and loss statement be "faithfully" and "consistently" expressed were retained, although, in both paragraphs, the criterion of "clearly" ("*duidelijk*"), which was prescribed in Article 2(2) of the Fourth Directive, was added.
- the requirement to disclose changes in reserves was expanded into a statement of changes in owners' equity.
- the option to present separate financial statements as an alternative to consolidated statements was limited to those cases in which insight would be better served thereby.
- the disclosure of the remuneration of directors (as a class) was added to the disclosure of the remuneration of supervisors (also as a class).

By far the most contested issue involving the adaptation of Dutch law to the Fourth Directive was the provision on valuation, and the major portion of this section on the Fourth Directive will deal with this question. Articles 32 (in full) and 33 (in part) of the Fourth Directive provided the framework, as follows:

> **Article 32.** The items shown in the annual accounts shall be valued in accordance with Articles 34 to 42, which are based on the principle of purchase price or production cost.
> **Article 33.** 1. The Member States may declare to the Commission that they reserve the power, by way of derogation from Article 32 and pending subsequent

[13] The "net equity value" ("*netto-vermogenswaarde*") method is substantially the equivalent of the "intrinsic value" ("*intrinsieke waarde*") method, which was discussed in Chapters 4 and 5. It involves showing, as the initial carrying amount of the acquired net assets, the value of the components of the assets and liabilities acquired in accordance with the valuation principles used by the parent company. As with the equity method, which has been practiced for some years in the United States, the initial carrying amount is adjusted for the parent's share of the subsidiary's profits, losses and dividends.

coordination, to permit or require in respect of all companies or any classes of companies:

(a) valuation by the replacement value method for tangible fixed assets with limited useful life and for stocks;
(b) valuation by methods other than provided for in (a) which are designed to take account of inflation for the items shown in annual accounts, including capital and reserves;
(c) revaluation of tangible fixed assets and financial fixed assets.[14]

When the minister prepared the draft adaptation law that was submitted to Parliament on 8 September 1980, his choice as between "permit or require" in Article 33(1) of the Fourth Directive was, disconcertingly to many companies and auditors, more toward the latter than the former. Article 384, paragraphs 4 and 5, of the initial draft law were as follows:

4. Valuation and income determination can take place, subject to the following paragraphs, on the basis of acquisition or construction cost, or on the basis of current value.
5. If the book value of an asset is, to a non-negligible degree, lower than the current value, additional information shall be provided in the notes, in order to enable a well-founded opinion concerning financial position and income. The company must revalue an asset to its current value if the insight that the financial statements should provide according to Article 362, para. 1, sustains serious damage, even when applying the clause contained in the previous sentence, by valuing an asset at lower than the current value.

(Apart from some minor changes in wording, these paragraphs were identical to those on which the TO had commented negatively in exchanges of correspondence with the minister.)

As van Hoepen later wrote, "In effect actual value [i.e., current value] was always allowed; sometimes actual value was compulsory by way of notes, sometimes actual value was compulsory in the balance sheet".[15] A similar view was expressed in the minister's Explanatory Memorandum, where it was said that the criterion of "faithful picture" ("*getrouw beeld*") would not allow the use of historical cost alone under all circumstances (B2 1979–1980, no. 3, p. 21). The

---

[14] "Fourth Council Directive of 25 July 1978 based on Article 54 (3) (g) of the Treaty on the annual accounts of certain types of companies" (78/660/EEC), *Official Journal of the European Communities*, 14.8.78, No L 222/22–23.

[15] M.A. van Hoepen, "The Fourth Directive and the Netherlands", in S.J. Gray and A.G. Coenenberg (editors), *EEC Accounting Harmonization: Implementation and Impact of the Fourth Directive* (Amsterdam: Elsevier Science Publishers B.V. (North-Holland), 1984), p. 72. Van Hoepen's argument that paragraph 5 dealt only with asset valuation and not income determination, thus allowing a company to continue to use historical cost in its profit and loss statement even if it were required to use current value in its balance sheet, may be open to question. Paragraph 4, which dealt with both asset valuation and income determination, was said to be "subject to the following paragraphs".

minister made a more general observation about the valuation principles, and began with a compliment for the work of the TO:

> By a happy initiative on the part of the organizations of auditors (NIvRA) and of employers and employees, the so-called "*tripartiete overleg*" has been started, that presents in its "considered views concerning financial statements" norms that can be considered to be acceptable in the economic and social climate, and in so doing further defines the contents of Article 311, para. 1 [Article 5 in the 1970 Act] .... Although [the considered views] lack binding force, their importance can hardly be overrated: the composition and procedure of the *overleg* [study group] guarantee carefulness and expertise; the published considered views stimulate an improvement in the level of financial reporting .... .
>
> During the preparation of the directive, the danger initially appeared to exist that [the developments that have led to a flexible evolution of accounting principles] in the member states would come to an end, and that in the future only valuation at historical cost would be allowed. The final text of the directive ... still shows that this danger has not been averted without trouble. Nevertheless, Article 33 [of the directive] ... allows the application of other valuation measures. It goes without saying that, in this draft, the Netherlands will, at least to a certain extent, make use of the option in this article (p. 20).

The use of unspecified qualitative criteria to differentiate between the possible situations (historical cost allowed, historical cost allowed with additional current value information, current value only allowed in the financial statements) made different interpretations of this article possible, ranging from obligatory application of current value to the modest view that the article would merely perpetuate current practice.

6.2.3. Reactions to the draft

Several authors were critical of Article 384. It seems that the second sentence of paragraph 5 came to be known as "Kleerekoper's sentence" ("*de zin van Kleerekoper*"), as he was one of the first to ask for its deletion.[16]

The TO issued some comments on the draft law, following up its earlier comments solicited by the Ministry in the preparatory stage. It stated a "fundamental objection" to "the obligatory use of current value". The TO cited its Draft Guideline (*ontwerp-Richtlijn*) 1.03.211 in support of its "two-track policy" ("*tweesporenbeleid*"), which provided that companies should use both valuation bases, one in the financial statements and the other in the notes, so long as there were no technical obstacles and where there was a material difference between the results of the two bases. The TO recommended that a comparable provision be inserted in the new law. It emphasized that the inclusion of information in the notes based on a principle that was not followed in the financial statements

[16] Volten, *op.cit.*, p. 548.

was not a correction of the view given in the statements, but was "indispensable for the insight that should be given by the financial statements" (JO Alg 4067–4079).

The NIvRA devoted its Fall Conference (*Najaarsconferentie*) of 1980 to the subject of the draft law. Sessions were held to hear and discuss addresses by Prof.drs J.W. Schoonderbeek, Mr P.A. Wessel, Drs J.F. Leeuwerik, and Mr drs H. Beckman at the Okura Hotel in Amsterdam and in Eindhoven and Oosterbeek.[17] Two particularly relevant papers were the defense and criticism of the valuation provisions by Wessel and Schoonderbeek, respectively.

Wessel began by pointing out that, although he had participated in the drafting, his opinions were of no importance in interpreting the law. This prerogative was reserved entirely for the judge who applies the law, who might or might not accept any arguments brought forward by Wessel.[18] A few pages later, he turned this same argument against the opponents of Article 384, para. 5, 2nd sentence, as follows:

> It is actually amazing that this second sentence has caused such a storm of protests among the opponents of valuation at current value. In fact, the condition attached in the draft to revaluation (serious damage to insight) should sound like music to the opponents of current value. Because they are, after all, convinced that valuation at historical cost cannot hinder the formation of a proper judgment .... They can calmly ignore that much-abused sentence, smiling with pity about so much naïveté on the part of the authors of the draft, in the certainty that the legal clause contained in that sentence will never be applied. Or are they, perhaps, after all, afraid that the judge might consider the "*bedrijfseconomische*" basis of the historical opinion as insufficient, and would take away with his verdict the legal validity of their opinion, to leave them the empty shell of being "*bedrijfseconomisch*" in the right?
>
> This process, however, could occur as well without this disputed sentence appearing in the law. Because it has been the case, since the approval of the Act on Annual Financial Statements in the beginning of the seventies, that it is no longer the "*bedrijfseconoom*" but the judge who has the final say in cases concerning financial statements. Auditors and "*bedrijfseconomen*" have not, at this time, taken sufficient notice of the significance of the changes that occurred. Perhaps this is the ulterior motive underlying the resistance to which we now find ourselves opposed (p. 73).[19]

[17] Among those present at the Fall Conference were Mr B.C. de Die and Mr S.C.H. Koning, members of the staff of the Justice Ministry who were involved with preparation of the draft law. Wessel was, at the time, the accounting adviser to the Ministry.

The four discussants were Prof.drs G.G.M. Bak, Prof.drs R. Burgert, Prof.dr J. Klaassen, and Prof.dr L. Traas.

[18] P.A. Wessel, "De materiële voorschriften uit het wetsontwerp, in het bijzonder de voorschriften met betrekking tot de waardering", in *Van titel 6 naar titel 8 boek 2 BW*, NIVRA geschrift nummer 24 (Amsterdam: NIVRA/Kluwer, 1981), pp. 67–68. Page citations in the text refer to this volume.

[19] *Econoom* is translated as economist; hence, *bedrijfseconoom* refers to someone who is knowl-

In the meantime, Wessel had clearly stated his own opinion on the meaning of Article 384, para. 5. Giving a "faithful picture", he said, was impossible on the basis of historical costs. Article 384 did no more than clarify the meaning of Article 362, para. 1, which specified that the financial statements should give an insight such that a well-founded opinion could be formed concerning the financial position and income of the enterprise. Without Article 384, para. 5, he argued, the meaning of the law would be the same, but there would only be more uncertainty. According to Wessel, the allowance of historical costs under the 1970 Act as being "acceptable in the economic and social climate" was an error that had to be corrected: "for a long time," he said, "people have practiced too little law and too much bookkeeping" (p. 72). Article 384, para. 5 was therefore meant to limit the scope for interpreting what was "acceptable in the economic and social climate" to what it should have been all along. As far as the TO's position was concerned, Wessel said that the draft did not prohibit a "two-track policy", although he doubted that its use would make for clear and unambiguous financial statements (p. 73).

Schoonderbeek replied with the following points:

- it would be odd to take a position on valuation that was diametrically opposed to that taken by other EEC countries and that was embodied in the Directive;
- the conclusion that a "faithful picture" could be given only on the basis of current value was a "misunderstanding". Current opinion held that historical cost and current value information both have their merits and should be seen as complementary rather than as as opposites;
- this opinion was held not only in academic circles but also in "the economic and social climate" as a whole, as evidenced by the "two-track policy" advocated by the TO; and
- an argument used by the minister in 1968 for not limiting the number of possible valuation systems was that there was as yet no consensus, and that future developments in thinking should not be hindered; this argument had retained its force, as there was still considerable discussion over alternative valuation systems in the Netherlands and abroad.[20]

During the discussion sessions following the presentation of the papers, the audience expressed its dissatisfaction with the valuation provision. Burgert compared it to the choice of color allowed when buying a Model-T Ford: any color so long as it was black (p. 92). Bak expressed some surprise at the negative reaction to (obligatory) current value. Those who pleaded for the usefulness of historical cost information were not prevented, he said, from supplying such information in the notes. Klaassen said (presumably in connection with the valuation provi-

edgeable about *bedrijfseconomie*. *Bedrijfseconomen* is the plural form of *bedrijfseconoom*.

[20] Prof.drs J.W. Schoonderbeek, "De voorschriften van het wetsontwerp met betrekking tot de grondslagen van waardering en resultaatbepaling", in *ibid.*, pp. 81–83.

sion) that he disagreed very much with those who drafted the law, which evoked applause from the audience (p. 13).

That the implications of Article 384, para. 5, were not clear even to close students of the subject was made evident by a series of three articles written by van Bruinessen, who was a member of the TO and had played a large role in the shaping of its position on valuation. In October 1980, he wrote that the draft law "gave a legal basis for the Considered Views of the TO concerning valuation".[21] But in a comment on the draft law the following year, he said that it would not do to rule out historical cost information at a moment when a great difference between the effects of both bases made its disclosure more important. And if it would be necessary to present information on both bases, it should be permissible to have historical cost in the financial statements for reasons of administrative efficiency.[22] Several months later, he actually went so far as to criticize the draft law for making current value mandatory in some cases. Not all companies, he argued, should be required to use current value in their financial statements because the data could sometimes not be produced in a reliable way. Furthermore, to require companies to use current value alone would deprive users of relevant information, that is, data on realized holding gains.[23] Hence, van Bruinessen began by complimenting the draft but eventually became one of its critics.

The Federation of Dutch Industries (VNO, Verbond van Nederlandse Ondernemingen) and the Dutch Christian Employers Federation (NCW, Nederlands Christelijk Werkgeversverbond), the central employers federations, endorsed the objections made by the TO, and submitted their own memorandum as well, dealing also with other issues. There is ground for believing that a number of large companies made forceful representations to the government on the valuation provision. In their written submission, the employers federations agreed with the principle stated in the minister's Explanatory Memorandum, namely, that there should be as much flexibility as possible in applying the options in the Fourth Directive. But they pointed out that the draft law deviated from this principle in a number of important respects, the most important being in connection with current value, which, in their view, had been elevated to the status of a norm.[24]

---

[21] Van Bruinessen, *op.cit.*, p. 189.

[22] Prof.dr W. van Bruinessen, "Grondslagen van de waardering en de winstbepaling in de jaarrekening", in *De Jaarrekening en de Vierde EEG-Richtlijn*, Vennootschaps- en Rechtspersonenrecht, Serie monografieën vanwege het van der Heijden Instituut te Nijmegen, nr. 20 (Deventer: Kluwer, 1981), pp. 13–14.

[23] W. van Bruinessen, "Art 384 van het ontwerp Aanpassingswet vierde richtlijn", in *De Naamlooze Vennootschap*, vol. 60, no. 3, March 1982, pp. 46–47.

[24] Both the TO memorandum and the reaction of the employers federations were discussed, though not quoted, in "Tripartite Overleg van commissies jaarverslaggeving: Principiële bezwaren tegen wetsontwerp tot aanpassing wetgeving aan vierde EG-richtlijn", in *Onderne-*

6.2.4. Reaction of Parliament

Only a small number of members of the Second Chamber took an active part in the work of the parliamentary preparation committee. They represented the four main political parties: the CDA (which headed the government coalition), the PvdA, the VVD and D66.[25] The Justice Minister until November 1982 was Mr J. de Ruiter (CDA), when he was succeeded by Mr F. Korthals Altes (VVD).

In the Provisional Report (*Voorlopig Verslag*) of the parliamentary preparation committee, most of the parties objected to the prominent place given to current value in the draft law. The arguments advanced against the text seemed to a considerable degree to have been derived from outside sources, mainly the TO, as follows (B2 1981–1982, no. 7):

- that it did not agree with the "principle" mentioned by the minister that the law would be as flexible as possible (p. 3);
- that the TO had raised objections against it at an earlier stage (p. 4); and
- that it would not be in the spirit of the Fourth Directive and might therefore hinder harmonization (p. 11).

The CDA members on the committee said they would go so far as to *allow* current value in the notes only, but would *require* additional information in the notes where there were significant differences between current value and historical cost (p. 11).

In his Memorandum of Reply (Memorie van Antwoord) of 19 March 1982, the minister rejected most of these arguments. First, he said, a change in the text would cause "surprise" at home and abroad, because Dutch experts had for years been pleading in international circles for current value,[26] and especially in the European Community, because it was the Netherlands that had pressed for

ming, vol. 10, no. 7, 20 February 1981, p. 8.

[25] The CDA is comparable to the Christian Democrats of other European Continental countries, the PvdA is the Labor Party, the VVD is the Liberal Party, and D66 is a progressive-liberal party. See the section on "National government and political parties" in Chapter 1.

When the draft law was promulgated in August 1980, the government coalition was headed by the CDA (with the VVD as the other partner). As a result of the 1981 national elections, the CDA was returned as the head of the coalition, but with participation by the VVD, PvdA and D66, taking effect in September 1981. In May 1982, the coalition was redefined to exclude the PvdA, and in November 1982 it was further redefined to exclude D66 as well.

[26] Muis has written that the Dutch auditing community had become "a victim of its own propaganda": "When the Dutch legislator, in introducing the 4th Directive into draft law, took the profession at its word on its self-proclaimed expertise in current value theory and applications and effectively opted for current values in the prime accounts, Holland's accounting community was shocked and, believe it or not, ended up strongly opposing the idea. Not too loudly because, as I heard one accounting professor state at a NIVRA conference, we would look so foolish abroad!". Jules W. Muis, "The interface of financial accounting research and practice", in Anthony G. Hopwood and Hein Schreuder (editors), *European Contributions to Accounting Research: The Achievements of the Last Decade* (Amsterdam: VU Uitgeverij, 1984), p. 263.

inclusion of the broader option. Second, it would conflict with the established rule (that had been discussed as well in connection with the 1970 Act) that the notes could not be used to correct wrong practices used in the financial statements (B2 1981–1982, no. 8, p. 10). And third, since the draft law was based on options included in the Directive, it could not really hinder harmonization as defined in the Directive (p. 11).

The minister went on to deny at some length that the draft law meant anything that differed substantially from the TO's point of view.[27] On the contrary, he said, it was only a more direct statement of what had been in the law long before, namely, that the choice of valuation principle was subject to the overriding "insight" criterion. But, given the fact that the choice of words "had apparently caused quite some confusion and concern" (p. 13), he announced a change in wording: Article 384, para. 5 in the current version would be deleted, and a reference to Article 362 (the article containing the overall "insight" criterion) would be inserted in Article 384, para. 1, as follows:

> **Article 384**
> 1. In the choice of principles for valuation of assets and liabilities and for income determination, the legal entity will be guided by the prescriptions of Art. 362, paras. 1–3 (B2 1981–1982, no. 9, p. 3).

Apparently, it was originally intended that the draft law would discourage the view that historical cost could be used in *all* circumstances, without actually requiring that current value be used in the majority of cases. The object was to induce a change in practice away from historical cost.[28] In that light, the minister's contention that neither the original draft law nor the altered version would constitute a change in existing practice was either a tactic used to calm emotions or a concession in disguise.

Outside Parliament, the aforementioned change made by the minister in his Memorandum of Alterations (Nota van Wijzigingen) was not applauded by either side.

According to van Hoepen, the fact that valuation was still to be regulated by administrative order made "the danger not imaginary that current value will be made obligatory once again".[29]

Wessel repeated what he had said earlier, and concluded that the removal of the explicit clause from Article 384, para. 5 concerning the required use of current value had indeed brought about the uncertainty he had predicted:

> There is a chance that the critics have fallen from the frying pan into the fire. Art. 384, para. 5, second sentence, would have allowed an interpretation leading

[27] The attention paid to the TO's report probably said something about the TO's status.
[28] Interview with Mr B.C. de Die, 29 July 1991.
[29] Prof.dr M.A. van Hoepen, "Over verplaatste normen en gelijke waarderingsvoorschriften (1)", in *de Accountant*, vol. 89, no. 3, November 1982, p. 173.

> to a required use of current value in exceptional circumstances only. But now that the reference to exceptional cases has been removed, it is not unthinkable that the judge will be more inclined to consider this requirement to be applicable than would have been the case if the text had not been changed. What is certain is that the text contained in the Memorandum of Alterations states the legal position less explicitly, and this means, in practice, additional risk.[30]

In the Second Chamber, during the exchange of memoranda with the minister following receipt of the Memorandum of Alterations, and during the final debates, members tried, unsuccessfully, to elicit a statement from the minister that it would at all times be possible for financial statements prepared on the basis of historical cost, perhaps with current value information in the notes, to give a "faithful picture". The minister avoided giving a direct answer (B2 1982–1983, no. 12 (Final Report – Eindverslag) and no. 13 (Memorandum Concerning the Final Report – Nota naar aanleiding van het Eindverslag), p. 4; H2 1982–1983, pp. 4467, 4541).

In the First Chamber, the question was raised again, by J.H.B. van der Meer (PvdA). The minister initially made a statement that nothing really had changed with the deletion of Article 384, para. 5, either in regard to existing law or with respect to the original draft law. This reply did not satisfy the questioner, but the minister would not go beyond saying that the criterion of "faithful picture" did not allow general statements to be made on the applicability of any one valuation principle (H1 1983–1984, p. 158, 160).

6.2.4.1. "Economic and social climate"

In the same Memorandum of Alterations in which the minister modified Article 384, he also moved the reference to "principles considered to be acceptable in the economic and social climate" from the article on valuation principles to Article 362, which governed the financial statements as a whole (B2 1981–1982, no. 9, p. 1). This relocation had not been requested by the parliamentary preparation committee, and it was not a necessary consequence of deleting paragraph 5 of Article 384. The change may have been a delayed effect of the suggestion made by the TO in its first set of comments to the minister on the draft law, before being submitted to Parliament. The TO had proposed moving the reference to a separate article in the "general" section, next to Article 362.[31]

No attention was paid to the change in either chamber of Parliament. The depth of appreciation of this change in Parliament may perhaps be illustrated by the fact that one member of the Second Chamber thought it necessary to inquire about the relation between "considered acceptable in the economic and

---

[30] Mr P.A. Wessel, "De aanpassing van het jaarrekeningenrecht aan de vierde EG-richtlijn (I)", in *De Naamlooze Vennootschap*, vol. 60, no. 5, May 1982, p. 83.

[31] Memorandum of 28 August 1979 (JO Alg 2671), *op.cit.*, pp. 1–2.

social climate" and "sound business practice" (*goed koopmansgebruik*), as if the former concept were a novelty (H2 1982–1983, p. 4472).

Volten saw the change as a move on the minister's part to broaden the scope of activities of the RJ, which, in January 1982, had succeeded the TO.[32]

Wessel thought that the change would make the phrase, "is considered acceptable in the economic and social climate", to a certain extent the counterpart of "generally accepted accounting principles" in the United States. But he said that there was a difference: "the normative content of the Dutch phrase is much higher than the Anglo-Saxon one, which reflects a more 'statistically' oriented point of view".[33] As finally approved, paragraphs 1–3 of Article 362, the so-called "general provisions", were as follows:

Article 362
1. The financial statements shall give, in accordance with norms that are acceptable in the economic and social climate, an insight such that a well-founded opinion can be formed concerning the financial position and income, and, insofar as the nature of financial statements allow, concerning the solvency and the liquidity of the legal entity.
2. The balance sheet, together with the notes, shall represent faithfully, clearly and consistently the financial position and its composition of assets and liabilities at the end of the financial year. The balance sheet can represent the composition of the financial position after taking into account the distribution of income or the disposition of a loss, or, if this has not yet been decided, after taking into account the proposed distribution or disposition.
3. The profit and loss statement, together with the notes, shall represent faithfully, clearly and consistently the amount of income for the financial year and its derivation from items of revenues and expenses.

6.2.4.2. Segmentation

As was mentioned in Chapter 5, the Wierenga amendment calling for the segmentation of operating income by product line had been approved in 1976, when the Act on Annual Financial Statements of 1970 was incorporated as Title 6,

[32] Volten, *op.cit.*, p. 548. When, in 1968, the minister had suggested the creation of what eventually became the TO, his charge was that it take an inventory of, and evaluate, the "acceptability of valuation principles in the economic and social climate". As a result of the minister's decision in March 1982, this unique wording ("acceptability ... in the economic and social climate") was relocated to a position where it would apply to the entirety of the financial statements, rather than just to the valuation principles. In fact, the TO had, during the 1970's, expanded the coverage of its statements beyond the valuation principles. Hence, this decision by the minister may have been no more than a recognition of the status quo.

[33] P.A. Wessel, "De aanpassing van het jaarrekeningenrecht aan de vierde EG-richtlijn (I)", *op.cit.*, p. 84. Wessel's suggestion that the American "accepted" is more "statistical" than the Dutch "acceptable" is not shared by the authors. Although the American phrase does refer to "accepted", it is interpreted as meaning *proper* practice as viewed by the standard-setting body and the Securities and Exchange Commission. It does not presuppose a counting of instances of actual use in practice. Hence, it is not "statistical".

Book 2 of the Civil Code. This provision was omitted from the draft law submitted to Parliament in September 1980, but it was replaced by a requirement that, as provided in the Fourth Directive, net sales should be reported on a segmented basis by "categories of activity and into geographical markets" (Art. 43, para. 1(8) of the Directive).[34]

The disappearance of the requirement to report segmented operating income was commented upon by the PvdA and the CDA in the Provisional Report as not being in accordance with the principle of preserving what had been achieved in the Netherlands (B2 1981–1982, no. 7, p. 10). And, they said, there were no indications that Dutch businesses had actually suffered from the existing requirement.

The minister replied that the Dutch delegation to the EEC had argued for inclusion of segmented operating income in the Fourth Directive, but that it had been rejected by the Commission. Besides, the minister said, the Wierenga amendment of 1976 had been accepted only because European regulation of the subject was expected. Now that such was no longer the case, there was no point in placing Dutch business at a competitive disadvantage owing to the required disclosure (B2 1981–1982, no. 2, p. 10).

Predictably, during the debates in the Second Chamber, a number of amendments (nos. 17–20) were introduced to require segmentation of one kind or another. The amendments, all submitted by R.J. Tazelaar (PvdA), called for segmentation of operating income by line of business (no. 17) and by geographical area (no. 19), for "insight into the degree to which fixed and current assets are used for each of [the lines of business]" (no. 18), and for a breakdown of information on capital investments to be provided in the directors' report by line of business (no. 20). The colloquy between Tazelaar and the minister on these issues was extensive, and the arguments turned on the international competitiveness of Dutch enterprises and on the principle of whether the proposed amendments would be a bearable administrative burden for the affected companies. In the end, the minister advised against all four amendments, because they did not match the spirit of deregulation that was the guiding principle of his government. All of the amendments were finally rejected.[35]

---

[34] Beckman had prophesied that the requirement to report segmented operating income would "undoubtedly" be retained in the draft law despite the lack of a corresponding provision in the Fourth Directive. Mr drs H. Beckman, "De EG-richtlijn met betrekking tot de jaarrekening van ondernemingen", in *De Naamlooze Vennootschap*, vol. 57, nos. 1/2, January/February 1979, p. 34. In the same article, he had also predicted that general price-level accounting would "undoubtedly" become part of Dutch law (p. 32).

[35] In November 1983, when a revised booklet of norms for the Sijthoff Prize was published, the request previously made for a segmentation of operating income was converted to a plea to give "as good a quantitative indication of returns as possible in each industry". Otherwise, the specific requirements were not changed. As to the general requirements, the new norms reflected even more of an emphasis on interim reporting. In addition to the general requirement of compliance with the law, taking into account the RJ's Guidelines, a new reference was made

6.2.4.3. Approval of the law

Following the debates in the Second Chamber on 9 and 14 June 1983, the draft law, as revised, was transmitted to the First Chamber (B1 1982–1983, no. 179). The debates in the First Chamber occurred on 6 December 1983. The law was given final approval on 7 December 1983 (Stb. 663),[36] and was entered as Title 8, Book 2 of the Civil Code. It was made applicable to financial years commencing on or after 1 January 1984. The name given to the title was "The Financial Statements and the Annual Report" ("*De Jaarrekening en het Jaarverslag*").[37]

6.2.4.4. The administrative orders

Two administrative decrees, on the formats for the financial statements and on asset valuation, were issued shortly after approval of the law. The decree on the statement formats was based on the layouts set forth in Articles 9–10 and 23–26 of the Fourth Directive. Its full name was "Decree of 23 December 1983 (Stb. 666) to Establish the Formats for the Arrangement of Financial Statements" ("Besluit van 23 december 1983 (Stb. 666) tot vaststelling van modelschema's voor de inrichting van jaarrekeningen").

In regard to the asset valuation decree, the TO had commented in the preparatory stage that it would be very difficult to issue such an order "in a responsible way". It suggested that the announced order should be replaced by a clause in the law stating that the contents, scope and application of the two valuation principles should be in conformity with norms seen as acceptable in the economic and social climate.[38] The TO's suggestion was not taken up.

The decree followed fairly closely the Limpergian value theory by distinguishing three value concepts, together with the circumstances in which they become relevant. In outline, it stated that current cost must be used whenever assets held for use in the business were to be replaced. If this were not the case, but the assets would, during their remaining useful life, be employed in the business, they should be valued at a "going concern value" (which was implicitly assumed to be lower than current cost). If the assets would neither be replaced nor used in the business, they were to be valued at exit prices.

The minister's Explanatory Memorandum to the asset valuation decree stated that no attention had been paid to issues such as the gearing adjustment, since that was part of income determination, and therefore was part of the law. In the specific case of the gearing adjustment, it was said to be covered by the general clauses in Article 362.

to "international standards". *Henri Sijthoff-Prijs: Normen voor de beoordeling van financiële berichtgeving door ondernemingen* (Amsterdam: *Het Financieele Dagblad*, November 1983), unnumbered pages.

36 "Stb." refers to the *Staatsblad*, which is the Statute Book.

37 For an English-language explanation of the new law, see *The new Dutch legislation on annual reporting* (Amsterdam: Klynveld Kraayenhof & Co., 1983)

38 Memorandum of 28 August 1979 (JO Alg 2671), *op. cit.*, p. 2.

The full title of the order was "Decree of 22 December 1983 (Stb. 665) Concerning Rules on the Substance, Scope and Method of the Application in the Financial Statements of Asset Valuation at Current Value" ("Besluit van 22 december 1983 (Stb. 665), houdende regels over de inhoud, de grenzen en de wijze van toepassing in de jaarrekening van waardering van activa tegen actuele waarde").

6.3. The Raad voor de Jaarverslaggeving

6.3.1. Developments from 1982 to 1986

6.3.1.1. Composition of the RJ in January 1982

As indicated at the close of Chapter 5, the newly restructured RJ came into existence in January 1982 as the successor to the TO. Save for the employers delegation (which had to be reduced from seven to four), the members of the TO at the end of 1981 automatically became the charter members of the RJ, as follows (with the year in which they attended their first TO/RJ meeting given in parentheses):

Chairman:

Prof.drs J.W. Schoonderbeek (1975), Klynveld Kraayenhof & Co.

Preparers (VNO/NCW) delegation:

Prof.dr A. van Putten (1977), board member (i.e., director) of Koninklijke Nedlloyd Groep N.V.

R.C. Spinosa Cattela (1977), board member of Philips.

Drs G. Verhagen (1981), board member of Pakhoed Holding N.V. (head of the delegation).

Mr H.C. Wesseling (1971), member of the legal department, Unilever, and chairman of the board of the Unilever pension fund.

Users delegation:

Mr J.C.M.G. Bloemarts (1977), Federated Dutch Trade Union Movement (FNV, Federatie Nederlandse Vakbeweging).

Dr mr P.W. Huizenga (1980), Christian National Trade Union Federation (CNV, Christelijk Nationaal Vakverbond).

Drs L. Stoutjesdijk (1980), FNV.

(One vacancy)

Auditors (NIvRA) delegation:

Prof.dr W. van Bruinessen (1972), Klynveld Kraayenhof & Co.

Drs H. Marseille (1975), Van Dien & Co (head of the delegation).

Drs W.N. Meijer (1980), Moret & Limperg.
Drs P.P.M. van der Ree (1982), Nederlandse Accountants Maatschap/Touche Ross Nederland.[39]

A graphical representation of the membership of the RJ since its founding appears in Appendix 5.1 to Chapter 5.

As to the NIvRA's Advisory Committee on Annual Reporting (CAJ, Commissie van Advies inzake Jaarverslaggeving), which prepared drafts for the RJ, Prof.dr A.B. Frielink continued as chairman, but was succeeded on 1 September 1982 by H.W. Hageman. As had been the custom, all four members of the NIvRA delegation (i.e., the auditors delegation) to the RJ were also members of the CAJ.

In addition to addressing the substantive contents of drafts received from the CAJ and deciding on which of the Draft Guidelines published in June 1980, together with the six additional draft Guidelines published in 1981, would, as suitably revised, be issued as definitive Guidelines, the RJ was also concerned with a number of important procedural and structural issues: the implications of the June 1980 Foreword for compliance with the Guidelines, the interposition of a screening committee by the NIvRA's management board to facilitate the transmission of its views on CAJ drafts prior to their discussion by the RJ, a question over voting rules, and the problems posed by the eventual withdrawal of the trade union representatives from the users delegation. The procedural and structural issues will be addressed first, followed by a general review of the substantive accounting issues taken up during the early and middle 1980's.

6.3.1.2. Compliance with the guidelines: The NIvRA and the VNO/NCW react
In March 1980 (as discussed in Chapter 5), the TO agreed on the Foreword for the rewritten Guidelines, in which the NIvRA was charged with taking steps to enhance compliance by auditors with the Guidelines. In the Foreword, which was published in June 1980, it was stated that

> The TO expects ... that the organization of auditors (NIVRA) will make an effort to assure that those in charge of audits take compliance with the Guidelines into account in their audits of financial statements, and that they mention eventual [undisclosed] deviations from [affirmative pronouncements] in their report on the financial statements.[40]

Within the NIvRA, the Council on Professional Issues (CBV, College voor Beroepsvraagstukken) took up the matter at its meeting on 28 April 1980. While the CBV believed that the legal implications of such a step should be studied,

[39] Van der Ree replaced Schoonderbeek on the auditors delegation, as, under the articles of incorporation, the chairman of the RJ was not to be a member of a delegation.
[40] See the section, "The foreword to the rewritten considered views", in the latter part of Chapter 5.

it was of the view that, if the NIvRA wished to bind its members effectively to report on departures from the Guidelines, it could do so only by issuing an "ordinance" ("*verordening*"), based on Article 19 of the Registered Auditors Act (Wet op de Registeraccountants) (ARTO 16–19).[41] The CBV's deliberations gave the impression that the extent of the NIvRA's authority on such matters was apparently still an open question, notwithstanding the NIvRA management board's 1976 statement calling upon NIvRA members to disclose departures from IASC standards that had been declared by the board to be "generally accepted" in the Netherlands.[42]

At its 2 June 1980 meeting, the CBV reviewed advice that had been received from legal counsel two years earlier in regard to compliance with the IASC statements. The lawyer had argued that an attempt to bind NIvRA members by the IASC standards could be seen by the Justice Ministry and the courts as an attempt to bind the companies as well, which would extend beyond the NIvRA's authority. The legal regulation of the contents of financial statements, he said, was directed to companies, not to their auditors. His advice had been to proceed cautiously in such an undertaking. If it were the NIvRA board's intention to "encourage" auditors to seek company compliance with IASC standards, he said, it would need to do so by issuing "urgent advice from the board" ("*dringend bestuursadvies*"), rather than an ordinance (ARTO 22–30).

After taking the legal counsel's 1978 communication as its point of reference, sector II of the NIvRA's management board, which was also studying the question, decided at its 13 May meeting that it was not in agreement with the board's 1976 statement on auditors' obligations concerning IASC standards. It therefore advised the full board (1) to "refine" its IASC policy by stating that it would not consider an IASC standard as "generally accepted" until it were included in the law or were confirmed in a court decision, and (2) *not* to advise NIvRA members to draw attention to departures from IASC standards and TO Guidelines in their report on financial statements (ARTO 10–12). Notwithstanding this advice, the board's executive committee decided that the board did have authority to declare that NIvRA members should make note of departures from the Guidelines in their report, since non-compliance would lead to a "non-faithful picture" ("*niet getrouw beeld*") (ARTO 14). Mr P.A. Wessel, a dissenting member of the executive committee, succeeded in persuading the executive committee to meet with the CBV in order to set up a small working party to prepare a draft "statement of opinion" ("*meningsuiting*") in which the NIvRA board would issue its

---

41 "ARTO" refers to the Advisory Working Party mentioned below. The minutes of relevant CBV and NIvRA management board meetings were inserted in its files.

42 "NIVRA-verplichtingen nopens Internationale Standaarden van het IASC", in *de Accountant*, vol. 82, no. 10, June 1976, pp. 616–617. See the discussion of this initiative in the section, "Origin of the movement for more authoritative statements", in Chapter 5.

views on compliance with the Guidelines.[43]

In June 1980, the CBV set up a three-member "Advisory Working Party on the Possible Consequences for the Auditor's Report of the Status and 'Expressive Force' of the TO's Guidelines" (ARTO, "Werkgroep advies inzake de eventuele consequenties voor de Accountantsverklaring van de status en 'zeggingskracht' van de Richtlijnen van het Tripartiete Overleg") to develop a proposal in response to the charge in the TO's Foreword. A. van Dongen, a government auditor who had been one of the original members of the CAJ in 1969, was named chairman of the working party. The other members were A.B. Frielink, a partner in Van Dien & Co and chairman of the CAJ, and H.J. Neeleman, a senior partner in Moret & Limperg. Van Dongen and Frielink were also members of the CBV.

At its first meeting on 6 October, the ARTO working party agreed on the following points without apparent difficulty:

1. The obligations assumed by the NIvRA in regard to IASC standards in 1976 "went too far", since their status as "generally accepted" could be confirmed only by their incorporation in statute law or in court decisions.
2. The TO could not issue legally binding rules (*rechtsregelen*).[44]
3. The NIvRA could never go beyond a "strong recommendation" that its members should strive for compliance with the Guidelines.
4. The TO therefore went "too far" in stating the expectation in its Foreword concerning the roles to be performed by the NIvRA and by auditors.
5. The NIvRA board could issue a "statement of opinion" giving its view on the degree to which Guidelines constituted the "demands placed on the financial statements" ("*eisen aan de jaarrekening te stellen*").[45]
6. Any "statement of opinion" should be issued only for a specific Guideline, and not as a "blank check" for all Guidelines (ARTO 51–55).

---

[43] In an article dealing mostly with the Fourth Directive, Wessel argued that the system of enforced compliance with the Guidelines, as delineated in the TO's Foreword, was neither in conformity with the current legal order (in which the legislature and the courts had the exclusive right to propound legal requirements for financial statements) nor wise: it would mean a retreat by auditors to within narrow and formal rules, and thus would downgrade the auditing profession from its current position of exercising "the noble art of truth and fairness". Mr P.A. Wessel, "De aanpassing van het jaarrekeningenrecht aan de Vierde EEG-Richtlijn", in *De Naamlooze Vennootschap*, vol. 58, no. 9, September 1980, p. 168.

[44] The ARTO working party signified agreement with Beckman's recent declaration that "The TO is not a rule-making agency, it has no formal status, it is not representative of all interested parties in financial statements, and the reasoning in its Considered Views is not convincing". Drs Mr H. Beckman, "Het tripartiete overleg en jaarverslaggeving", in *Maandblad voor accountancy en bedrijfshuishoudkunde*, vol. 54, no. 2, February 1980, p. 60.

[45] This was a key phrase in the "Rules of Conduct and Professional Practice for *Registeraccountants*" (GBR, Gedrags- en Beroepsregels Registeraccountants), the professional and ethical guidelines established in 1973 by the NIvRA under its legal authority as a public body. In Article 15 thereof, this phrase was used to characterize, but not to enumerate, the set of norms that, in the economic and social climate, defined a "faithful picture" of financial position and income.

A report largely based on these six points was forwarded to the CBV, and was discussed at its meeting on 25 May 1981. The CBV unanimously agreed that "the NIvRA could not honor the expectation expressed in the Foreword". But the members could not agree on whether the NIvRA should issue "statements of opinion" averring that the contents of specific Guidelines were encompassed within the demands placed on financial statements. Some thought that the issuance of "statements of opinion" for some, but not all, of the TO's Guidelines would cause those not endorsed by the NIvRA to be regarded as "second rate", while others had fundamental objections to auditors having the final word in the determination of the norms for financial statements (ARTO 138–140). In the end, the CBV could do no more than forward a summary of its discussions to the board for its consideration (ARTO 123).

Following discussion by the management board, the NIvRA issued a "Draft Statement of Opinion" ("*Ontwerp-Meningsuiting*") as Discussion Draft 15 (OTD-15, Ontwerp ter discussie 15), entitled "The Meaning of the Guidelines of the TO (now the RJ) for the Auditor's Report" ("*De betekenis van de richtlijnen van het Tripartiete Overleg (thans Raad voor de Jaarverslaggeving) voor de accountantsverklaring*"), dated January 1982. Comments were requested by 1 October 1982.[46] OTD-15 followed fairly closely the text of the ARTO working party's report to the CBV. Yet, at points, it resembled the product of a committee in which a diversity of views had been expressed. While it was stated that the board and the CBV could not honor the charge contained in the TO's Foreword, it was nonetheless conceded that the NIvRA's involvement in the work of the TO implied that both the NIvRA and its members had to exert themselves to ensure compliance with the Guidelines, and especially with the "affirmative pronouncements". The key passage in OTD-15 was as follows:

> Affirmative pronouncements of the TO have, for members of the NIvRA, a meaning similar to that of the statements of opinion of the Board and the CBV. Both aim at giving guidance on the manner in which the profession is exercised by members. They have such a degree of authority that departures must be justifiable by sound reasons.
>
> A departure from an affirmative pronouncement of the TO will compel the auditor [to give] serious consideration whether the financial statements nonetheless meet the demands placed upon them, and, if not, in what way this must be expressed in the auditor's report. A statement in the auditor's report can be omitted if the auditor considers the departure to be justified on the basis of sound reasons (p. 7).

In this way, the NIvRA circumvented the problem of having to ascertain for each "affirmative pronouncement" whether or not it was "generally accepted". The

[46] The parenthetical phrase in the title referred to the fact that, as of 1 January 1982, the RJ had replaced the TO. Page citations in the text refer to this publication.

burden was placed on auditors to determine whether a departure was justified by "sound reasons". The NIvRA had not given *carte blanche* to the new RJ, as it left open the possibility that not all "affirmative pronouncements" would be regarded as coming within the demands placed on financial statements. Nevertheless, it would seem that the NIvRA's statement went further than both the ARTO working party and the CBV in attributing authority to the Guidelines.

In the May 1983 issue of *de Accountant*, it was reported that the reactions to OTD-15 were "diverse", and that the management board had decided to confer with the two employers federations regarding their attitude toward the charge contained in the Foreword.[47] The following month, it was disclosed that a meeting had been held with the VNO.[48] The discussion with the employers evidently resulted from a suggestion by Drs A.J. Bosman, who was president of the NIvRA in the years 1983–84, that it would not be proper for the entire responsibility for disclosing departures to fall on the shoulders of the auditors. The preparers, he believed, should be obliged to disclose any deviations.[49] A principal reason for the meeting on 13 May 1983 with the VNO was to discuss its reaction to this suggestion, especially in view of the generally unfavorable reactions received on OTD-15. At the meeting, the NIvRA representatives (Bosman and H. Volten) explained that there might be a better chance of finding a solution if the VNO and the NCW would issue a recommendation on companies' compliance with the "affirmative pronouncements", or, alternatively, on their disclosure of non-compliance in the notes. The VNO president took the suggestion under advisement (SI Inf 322).

The meeting of the RJ on 5 October was devoted almost entirely to drafting a new Foreword to accompany the first installment of definitive Guidelines scheduled for publication in January 1984. Initially, deep divisions of opinion were evident, but, in the end, compromises were reached. One passage in the draft called upon companies to state that they had complied with the Guidelines, or, if they had not, to report on specific departures in the notes. This passage caught the eye of the employers federations, and a further meeting was held on 7 November at which two members of the NIvRA board and the chairman of the auditors delegation in the RJ met with representatives of the joint VNO/NCW

[47] "Logboek bestuur", in *de Accountant*, vol. 89, no. 9, May 1983, p. 584. The NIvRA advises that the letters of comment received on OTD-15 cannot be located in its archive. It is understood, however, that the replies were generally unfavorable. Evidently, some writers criticized the draft for not going far enough, while others were critical that it went too far.

J. Klaassen, a professor at the Vrije Universiteit, who had given a number of talks in 1981 defending the policy position eventually embodied in OTD-15, said that he was confronted by "frozen stares". The proposal, he said, was seen by auditors as being too dangerous in their commercial relationships with clients. Interview with Prof.dr J. Klaassen, 27 June 1991.

[48] "Logboek bestuur", in *de Accountant*, vol. 89, no. 10, June 1983, p. 659.

[49] Interview with W.P. Moleveld, 10 December 1990, and confirmed in an interview with Drs A.J. Bosman, 29 November 1991.

Committee of Information Preparers (CIV, Commissie Informatieverschaffing). During the meeting, the CIV representatives stated that the passage was not acceptable. In reply, the NIvRA representatives requested that the VNO and the NCW make a commitment to the Guidelines at some level, perhaps involving a publicity campaign in support of the Guidelines. The CIV representatives promised to do "what is necessary in the area of publicity", but gave no further assurances (SB Inf 67–70).[50] Two days later, the RJ held a meeting at which the offending passage was dropped, and one member of the auditors delegation opined that, as a result of the changes between the 1980 version and the new version of the Foreword, the status of the Guidelines had been diminished (RJ Not 360–362; CAJ Not 1240). A revised Foreword signed by Schoonderbeek in November 1983 was published together with the first installment of definitive Guidelines in January 1984. The revised Foreword reflected a much less explicit plan for securing compliance with the definitive Guidelines. The importance of complying with the "affirmative pronouncements" was restated, but neither the auditor nor the company was charged with the specific obligation to disclose any departures. The central passage was as follows:

> By ... making a distinction in the Guidelines between affirmative pronouncements (in bold face) and recommendations, the RJ seeks to place in proper perspective the significance of the Guidelines for the practice of annual reporting. This implies that additional weight is to be given to the affirmative pronouncements shown in bold face. The RJ does not claim that the affirmative pronouncements in the (definitive) Guidelines have binding force, such as provisions in the law. Ultimately, of course, it is the courts that will decide, in each case submitted before them, which principles are considered to be acceptable in the economic and social climate for the financial statements in question. This implies that the reporting enterprise has its own responsibility for its financial statements. The RJ is of the opinion that the Guidelines, and especially the affirmative pronouncements contained therein, contribute generally, by their intrinsic value, to the insight into financial position and income required by law. This means that it can be expected that there will be departures from affirmative pronouncements only when there are sound reasons for doing so.

In the June 1984 issue of *de Accountant*, it was announced that OTD-15 was being withdrawn. The reasons given for this decision were as follows:

> – It cannot be concluded from the reactions received that a definitive statement of opinion can be issued that would obtain sufficient support from the

[50] "SB" refers to sector B of the NIvRA board, formerly sector I.
After a search of *Onderneming*, the VNO's weekly newspaper, through the end of 1984, the authors were unable to find any publicity for the RJ's program of issuing Guidelines. Indeed, there was no mention of the publication in January 1984 of the numerous definitive and draft Guidelines. A factual article did appear after the publication in December 1984 of the second installment of definitive and draft Guidelines. "Tweede aflevering van bundel Richtlijnen jaarverslaggeving", in *Onderneming*, vol. 13, no. 48, 14 December 1984, p. 3.

membership;
- From the foreword to the RJ's Guidelines (1984), it appears that the RJ expects, among other things, that the NIvRA will promote, as far as possible, "that the Guidelines and the affirmative pronouncements contained therein are taken into account in the audit of financial statements". Now that the element relating to the implication of affirmative pronouncements for the auditor's report is no longer included in the currently expressed expectation [by the RJ], the board no longer sees a need to attempt to issue a final statement of opinion on this matter.[51]

No further initiatives were taken on this issue.

6.3.1.3. The BAR: The NIvRA's board monitors the CAJ

In May 1982, the NIvRA's management board, evidently in a desire to have greater influence on the development of drafts dealing with sensitive issues, established a screening committee that would enable it to comment at an earlier stage on the CAJ's drafts. This committee was formed on 21 May 1982 and became known as the BAR (Begeleiding en Advies Richtlijnen – Monitoring and Advisory Committee on Guidelines). In part, it was patterned after the Monitoring Committee on International Accounting Standards (BIAS, Begeleiding International Accounting Standards), which had been set up in the 1970's as the support group for the NIvRA's delegation to the IASC.[52] But whereas BIAS was an informal sounding board for the delegation's members, the BAR was designed to introduce a new step in the decision-making process.

In the past, the NIvRA board had been unable to react to materials prepared by the CAJ for the RJ until the NIvRA delegation met immediately prior to the RJ meeting at which the materials were presented. Occasionally, the board and the NIvRA's CBV had felt it necessary to disagree with the CAJ's positions, but they would have preferred to be able to consult with the CAJ in advance of the RJ meeting date (CAJ Not 1133).

The BAR was to consist of one representative each from both the CBV and sector I of the management board, a representative from the CAJ, and the NIvRA delegation. It was authorized to amend the CAJ's proposals once they had begun to be discussed in the RJ (CAJ Overig 870–871).[53]

At its meeting on 14 June, the CAJ was less than pleased with the role given to the BAR. Several CAJ members expressed their doubts about the wisdom of having a small committee repeat the work already done by the CAJ. They believed that it would probably not increase productivity and might well dampen the motivation of CAJ members.

In recent years, the CAJ's workload, and consequently the workload of those

---

51 "Mededeling inzake OTD-15", in *de Accountant*, vol. 90, no. 10, June 1984, p. 743.

52 Interview with H. Volten, 7 November 1991.

53 "CAJ Overig" refers to the documentary file of the CAJ.

members of the CAJ who also served on the RJ, had become more demanding. The four members serving on both the CAJ and the RJ, were, among other things, reviewing new IASC exposure drafts; advising the Ministry of Justice (on the draft adaptation law for the Fourth Directive), the Insurance Companies Commission, and De Nederlandsche Bank; as well as preparing and revising drafts for the RJ.[54] One member of the NIvRA delegation estimated that he and his three colleagues in the delegation spent between 350 and 400 hours per year on preparation for the meetings and at the meetings themselves. While their need to attend meetings of the BAR represented yet another time commitment, it soon became evident that their participation in the BAR made it unnecessary that they also attend meetings of the CAJ, where the same drafts were being discussed. At the CAJ meeting of 14 June, it was therefore decided that one member of the delegation who had sufficient time to bridge both the CAJ and the RJ would continue to attend CAJ meetings, while the others would attend when they could (CAJ Not 1139).[55]

The BAR's meetings were initially chaired by Drs H. Marseille, the head of the NIvRA's delegation to the RJ, and subsequently by H.W. Hageman, the chairman of the CAJ. The BAR discussed the CAJ's drafts during the interval between the submission of a CAJ draft to the RJ and the meeting, usually several months later, at which the RJ began discussing the draft.

The work of the BAR was assessed in the CAJ meetings of 15 May and 20 June 1983, at which the impression was given that the purpose and place of the BAR in the NIvRA's hierarchy was, at best, unclear. As seen by the CAJ's members, the main problem seemed to be that the CAJ received insufficient feedback from the BAR. When the BAR disagreed with the CAJ's proposals, it did not send them back for reconsideration, but instead amended them without consulting the CAJ. Such amendments struck the CAJ members as being more political than technical, for the BAR would instruct the NIvRA delegation on the departures that would be needed in order to increase the likelihood of eventual acceptance of the entire draft by the RJ (CAJ Not 1197–1199, 1211).

Several alternative approaches to achieving the apparent aims of the NIvRA board and the CBV were considered: sending all materials first to the BAR and then to the RJ; dropping both the BAR and the plenary meetings of the CAJ, and replacing them by meetings at which the CAJ, the NIvRA delegation, and representatives of the board and the CBV were all in attendance; or having

[54] See the report of the CAJ in *Verslag van de werkzaamheden 1981/'82*, Nederlands Instituut van Registeraccountants, pp. 39–40.

[55] The delegation member who continued to attend CAJ meetings was Prof.dr W. van Bruinessen, who had only recently converted from a full-time to a part-time partner in his audit firm. (In December 1980, van Bruinessen had completed a doctorate at the Vrije Universiteit, and the following month he became a professor at the Katholieke Universiteit Nijmegen.) At most meetings of the CAJ during the following two years, only van Bruinessen was in attendance on behalf of the NIvRA delegation to the RJ.

the NIvRA delegation resume its attendance at meetings of the CAJ. None of these options was considered to be practicable. It was decided that the existing arrangement, by which documents were sent simultaneously to the BAR and the RJ, should be retained, but that the BAR would be asked to contact the CAJ at an early stage when principal differences of opinion had arisen (CAJ Not 1215).

Beginning in 1984, the attendance, and thus the number of meetings of the BAR, declined. There was regular attendance by the NIvRA delegation to the RJ and by Hageman, but the CBV and board members attended intermittently. The BAR apparently continued to function as an entity into 1985, but it was not long before the consultations began occurring on a more informal basis, with the consequence that the BAR, as an organizational unit, ceased to exist.[56]

6.3.1.4. A veto by one member forces a change in voting procedures

In 1983, a veto was cast by a single member of the RJ that led to a change in the procedures for approving Guidelines. At the RJ's meeting on 9 February, the subject being discussed was foreign currency translation, which had been under consideration since April 1982. A member of the preparers delegation said that he operated on the premise that "what management is consciously trying to achieve should not be frustrated by bookkeeping". On this basis, he argued that when a loan in a foreign currency has been deliberately hedged, it should be possible to recognize any exchange rate gains or losses as they occur. This premise was not accepted by all members of the RJ, but apparently a compromise was worked out (RJ Not 236). A draft was prepared embodying this compromise which was accepted by all of the RJ's members other than P.W. Huizenga, the lone representative of the Christian National Trade Union Federation (CNV, Christelijk Nationaal Vakverbond). The other two trade union members of the users delegation represented the Federated Dutch Trade Union Movement (FNV, Federatie Nederlandse Vakbeweging).

By the meeting of 9 March 1983, a draft Guideline was ready for publication. It was said to conform with the IASC's E23, "Accounting for the Effects of Changes in Foreign Exchange Rates" (issued in March 1982). But Huizenga had made clear in a memorandum (he was not present at the meeting) that he wanted to exercise his right of veto under the Foundation's articles of incorporation, which provided that at least one representative of every *organization* must be in favor of a decision involving publication. At that point, a member of the preparers delegation announced that he could not work on a body where one

[56] Interview with W.P. Moleveld, 31 October 1991. The BAR may have been impracticable from the beginning, since it placed a much greater demand on its members than did BIAS, upon which the BAR was partly based. The CAJ and the RJ met much more frequently than did the IASC's board and its working parties. In the end, the BAR's members, who were also members of other NIvRA committees, could not keep pace with its agenda. Interview with H. Volten, 7 November 1991.

member could frustrate many hours of work by all of the other members. Unless the articles of incorporation were changed, he said, he would find it necessary to withdraw from further participation in the RJ. A member of the users delegation, representing the FNV, mentioned that it was the preparers who had originally proposed to require the assent of at least one representative of each organization, rather than of each delegation. He argued that, when their plan had been shown not to work, the preparers should not react so negatively. Reviving a suggestion made by the employees on several previous occasions (while serving on the TO), he proposed that dissenting opinions be allowed rather than insisting on unanimity in publication decisions, which had continued to be the RJ's practice even though the articles provided for approval by a four-fifths majority. After further discussion, it was decided to recommend that the articles be changed to require that at least one member of each *delegation* be in favor of all decisions regarding publication (RJ Not 250).

The question of Huizenga's veto was resolved by his decision to retire from the RJ in May 1983, and his replacement, who became known in July, removed Huizenga's veto at the meeting of 14 September (RJ Not 334).

On 29 December 1985, the articles of incorporation were changed to refer to delegations instead of organizations, at the same time at which a change was made in the composition of the users delegation (see below).[57]

6.3.1.5. Reorganization of the users delegation

The trade unions withdraw. Since the middle of 1982, no more than one trade union representative was ordinarily present at RJ meetings, and it was suspected that financial problems at the trade union federations were the reason. The question of the continuing participation by trade union representatives in the users delegation was raised at the 9 June and 15 November 1983 meetings of the Foundation's board. Both the FNV and the CNV announced that they were thinking of replacing their representatives on the RJ by "trusted persons" who would serve on a personal basis with a general mandate from the trade union federations. This prospect was regretted by the employers federations and the NIvRA, as they felt that it might mean a lessening of the unions' commitment, but the change was accepted in principle, because the unions had no other options (BSJ 117–119, 157). The possibility of such a change had apparently also been raised during the discussions relating to the establishment of the RJ in 1980–81 (RJ Not 391).

At the RJ's meeting on 8 February 1984, the issue came up with great urgency. Schoonderbeek announced that he had been intensively engaged with the problems of the users delegation. Owing to declining union membership, the financial situation of the FNV and the CNV made it difficult for them to continue their

[57] *Verslag van de werkzaamheden over het jaar 1985 van de Raad voor de Jaarverslaggeving* (19 February 1986), pp. 22–23.

participation.[58] As had been suggested the previous year, it was proposed that the trade union representatives be replaced by individuals who were trusted by the unions, but who would not actually represent the unions. They would participate in the deliberations without a strict mandate and without consulting the unions on the positions to be taken. Among these experts, it was said, would probably be some external auditors who were known to the unions. This proposal was not welcomed by the preparers delegation. They were not receptive to the idea that auditors might form part of the users delegation. Another concern was that the trade unions' commitment to the Guidelines might diminish since they would no longer be taking part in the deliberations. But at the same meeting, it was made clear that the three trade union representatives (there had been a vacancy since January 1982) could not await a final settlement of their replacements. They would not be attending any further meetings (RJ Not 390–393). Throughout 1984 and 1985, the users delegation was absent in its entirety. Nonetheless, the FNV and the CNV have continued to be represented on the board of the Foundation for Annual Reporting.

At its annual meeting on 6 June 1984, the Foundation's board saw no problem with the RJ's continuing to issue Guidelines with the participation of only two of the three delegations, as the absence of the users delegation was not the responsibility of the RJ (BSJ 183–184).[59] But the preparers delegation did see a problem when the RJ was readying the publication of the second set of draft and definitive Guidelines for publication in December 1984. They were of the view that the articles of incorporation required the participation by all three delegations prior to publication, and that the Foundation's board could not blithely set aside that provision (RJ Not 519, 538). After consultation with the FNV and the CNV, the matter was resolved by the insertion of two paragraphs in the RJ's 1984 annual report, as follows:

> Owing to vacant seats in the RJ, members appointed by the organizations representing users of information have not participated in the decision making over the contents of second installment of (draft-)Guidelines.
>
> The organizations concerned take the position, however, that long-standing vacancies should not block the decision making [leading toward] publication by the RJ, and on that ground publication may proceed. The organizations [of users] have made the proviso that – especially in view of the long-standing vacancies – this aforementioned agreement on publication does not imply that these organiza-

[58] Interview with Mr J.C.M.G. Bloemarts, 20 September 1990. Huizenga, however, has contended that the departure of trade union representatives from the RJ was traceable to their disappointment that (1) OTD-15 fell short of the commitment implied in the January 1980 Foreword, and (2) that the RJ's January 1984 Foreword retreated even further. Dr mr P.W. Huizenga, "De Raad voor de Jaarverslaggeving en de werknemers", in *Maandblad voor accountancy en bedrijfshuishoudkunde*, vol. 61, no. 3, March 1987, p. 113.

[59] "BSJ" refers to the minute book of the board of the Foundation for Annual Reporting (*Bestuur van de Stichting voor de Jaarverslaggeving*).

tions consider the contents of this publication as completely guiding [*richtinggevend*] for the practice of financial reporting, in a similar way as the organizations representing preparers and auditors of information.[60]

Change in the articles. The appointment of a newly constituted users delegation had to await a decision by the Foundation's board to amend the articles of incorporation. The need for the change in the articles arose from the fact that several of the individuals who had been approached to serve on the users delegation believed that it would be inappropriate for the formal appointment to be made by the trade union federations, perhaps because they would not actually be representing the federations. As a compromise, it was agreed that they would be nominated by the federations but appointed by the Foundation. An amendment to the articles was therefore introduced to authorize the Foundation's board to appoint members of a delegation on the basis of nominations submitted by the participating organizations, rather than by filling vacancies, as in the past, through direct appointments made by the organizations themselves. Since the Foundation's board ordinarily held only one meeting a year,[61] it was unable to address the issue until its meeting of 29 May 1985. Although the board decided to amend the articles at that meeting, the change did not take effect until 29 December 1985, owing to a subsequent difference of opinion within the board over the RJ's voting procedures (BSJ 247–249, 271–272).[62] The following changes were reflected in the amended articles:

- the members of each delegation were to be appointed by the board on the recommendation of the relevant organizations (four seats for each delegation);
- an explicit statement was added that members could be dismissed by the board;
- a five-sixths (instead of a four-fifths) majority would be required to approve a publication, and the assent of at least one member of each delegation (instead of organization) would be necessary.

The change in the required majority was a compromise that was intended to offset the greater difficulty of a veto when only one member of each delegation, rather than only one member of each organization, must approve a publication.

Users from the financial community. The possible inclusion of a representative from the financial community in the users delegation had been raised as early as February 1982, when the Society of Financial Analysts (VBA, Vereniging van Beleggingsanalisten) had expressed an interest in becoming involved in the work

[60] *Verslag van de werkzaamheden over het jaar 1984 van de Raad voor de Jaarverslaggeving* (7 February 1985), p. 9.

[61] Except for 1983, when the Foundation's board met twice, it has held one meeting a year since its founding.

[62] For the amended articles of incorporation, see *Verslag van de werkzaamheden over het jaar 1985 van de Raad voor de Jaarverslaggeving* (19 February 1986), pp. 16–24.

of the RJ (BSJ 27–28).[63] The Foundation's board believed, however, that it would not be wise to add any new organizations so soon after the restructuring. It was thought that any representatives from new organizations might best be appointed as observers before being considered for status as full members. The board's preference for a body representing the financial community was the Stock Exchange Association, because of its central role in the Dutch capital market. Both the VBA and the Stock Exchange Association were informed in June 1982 that a joint application from their organizations would be appreciated (BSJ 64–67). The two bodies declined to be treated as a single interested party. They did, however, request separate seats as observers, but no action on these counterproposals was taken by the board (BSJ 75, 103).

On 1 November 1983, a delegation from the Foundation (Mr C. van Veen, president of the VNO and chairman of the Foundation's board; Schoonderbeek, chairman of the RJ; and O.M. Volgenant jr., head of the RJ's secretariat) met with the board of the Stock Exchange Association. It became evident that the latter's principal interest was in closer ties to the VNO so that it might gain some backing in its dealings with listed companies. By then, the Stock Exchange Association had revoked the provision in its Rules for Securities Trading that listed companies should follow IASC standards that had been found to be "generally accepted" by the NIvRA. Moreover, it was stated that the past efforts by the Stock Exchange Association to take over Guidelines issued by the TO/RJ had raised serious objections from listed companies. Hence, the Stock Exchange Association did not wish to participate other than as an observer in the work of the RJ (BSJ 142–143). This reluctance by the Stock Exchange Association to impose financial reporting requirements on listed companies had been commented upon by financial journalists as long ago as the 1950's.[64]

It was clear that the Stock Exchange Association would not send a representative to serve as a full member of the RJ, and there was no longer any support on the Foundation's board for creating observer status. In May 1984, after it had become evident that the trade union representatives would not be returning to the RJ, Schoonderbeek asked the board to consider appointing a representative of investors to the users delegation. While the board agreed with this suggestion in principle, it decided to postpone action on the request until the problems of the trade union federations were resolved (BSJ 170, 183). Contacts with the VBA continued, and at the RJ's meeting of 15 May 1985, Schoonder-

63 The suggestion had been raised even earlier. In an address delivered in 1980, Schoonderbeek said, apparently speaking for the auditors delegation, "We would like to see the participation of investors and investment analysts to further strengthen the Committee's base". "The Dutch Tripartite Accounting Standards Committee", in *The Tripartite Accounting Standards Committee*, PILOT (Netherlands) 10 (Amsterdam: Nederlands Instituut van Registeraccountants, December 1980), p. 9.

64 See the press reaction to the Rijkens report, in Chapter 3, and to the report of the Dr. Wiardi Beckman Stichting study committee, in Chapter 4.

beek announced that the VBA was prepared to propose a candidate for one of the vacant seats. The delegations of preparers and auditors applauded this news (RJ Not 594). Finally, at the board's meeting on 29 May 1985, when the decision was taken to amend the articles of incorporation, it was agreed that one of the amendments would be written in such a way as to allow the VBA to recommend a member of the users delegation without a requirement that it also be represented on the Foundation's board (BSJ 248). The implication was that the trade union representatives on the board would allow the VBA, which would not be formally represented on the board, to recommend a candidate for appointment to the users delegation. The VBA was notified of this arrangement by letter on 19 November 1985 (BSJ 288), and its first representative to serve on the users delegation, Drs W. Mur, who was employed by the Amro Bank, took his seat on 16 January 1986.

The other new members of the users delegation, with the date of their first meeting, were partners in two audit firms, Drs C. Izeboud (16 January), and A.F.M. van Klaren[65] (19 February), and an accounting academic from Erasmus Universiteit Rotterdam, Drs Ph.J. Maat (16 April). All three were nominated by the trade union federations, and were *registeraccountants*.

6.3.1.6. Preparation of drafts and guidelines

During the first five years of the RJ, considerable time was devoted to dealing with EEC Directives as well as with a number of the procedural issues that were discussed above. There was also a growing anxiety among the RJ's members that it had to produce more published work. The last of the Considered Views had been published in February 1979, and the rewritten Considered Views, styled as "Draft Guidelines", had come out in June 1980. The year 1981 was, in effect, a period of interregnum between the TO and the RJ, although draft Guidelines on six subjects were issued. As 1982 began, all of the TO's published utterances were either in the form of exposure drafts of Considered Views (issued between 1975 and 1979) or draft Guidelines. Nothing was labeled as definitive. In some members' minds, there was a need to produce some definitive guidance. This view, however, was not shared by all members. It appeared that a number of large companies held a belief that the Guidelines had run their course and that, especially with the adaptation of the law to the Fourth Directive, there was no further need for Guidelines. Nonetheless, the predominant view in the RJ was that its previous Considered Views (restated as Draft Guidelines), which had been intended as an explanation of the 1970 Act, had to be rewritten in the light of the law adapting the Fourth Directive. In this endeavor, Chairman Schoonderbeek, together with consultants H. Beckman and J. Klaassen, were

[65] Izeboud was a management consulting partner in Van Dien & Co, and van Klaren was an audit partner in Dubois & Co., which was a frequent adviser to works councils.

"explaining and leading".[66]

As part of the RJ's working procedures, the NIvRA delegation proposed the creation of a planning committee, to be composed of one member from each delegation, the chairman, and three members from the secretariat. The committee would plan the work, and would monitor its progress by the use of project committees, each headed by a project leader. The project committees would be made up of RJ and/or CAJ members, plus expert outsiders, if necessary. The project leaders, who would usually be CAJ members, would attend the RJ meetings at which their projects were discussed. The proposal was, with minor changes, adopted at the RJ's first meeting on 8 January 1982.

At the RJ's meeting of 14 July 1982, the decision was made to retitle the series of final statements from Guidelines for Financial Statements (*Richtlijnen voor de jaarrekening*) to Guidelines for Annual Reporting (*Richtlijnen voor de jaarverslaggeving*), evidently to recognize that the directors' report, which would be included in the latter but not in the former, was about to be regulated by the adaptation of Dutch law to the Fourth Directive (RJ Not 99).

Booklet on the Fourth Directive. An activity that took considerable time was the preparation of a booklet containing questions and answers on the new law reflecting the Fourth Directive, which was nearing approval in Parliament. At the RJ's meeting of 14 December 1982, there was mention of the growing uncertainty about the interpretation of parts of the new law, and it was recognized that here was a chance, as the head of the preparers delegation put it, for the RJ "to prove itself". The preparers also saw an opportunity to bring out something quickly, which was considered to be important. It was decided that the preparers would compile a number of questions with tentative answers, and the auditors would prepare more elaborate answers to be discussed in the RJ's meetings. The status of the resulting booklet was left open, except that it should be "guiding" ("*richtinggevend*") (RJ Not 190–191).

The project took longer than was expected, and it occupied sizable parts of the meetings from January through September 1983. A not insignificant cause of the extended discussions was a rehearsal of the debate over the "two-track policy" on current value, which had been adopted in the third installment of Considered Views, published in February 1979. The views of the parties did not seem to have changed, but the debate occurred nonetheless (e.g., RJ Not 232–233). Within the NIvRA, the project was not received very favorably. Both in the BAR (17 January 1983, SI RJ 27)[67] and in the CAJ (7 February 1983, CAJ Not 1180–1181), doubts were raised about the wisdom of maintaining an elaborate procedure for approving definitive Guidelines, while at the same time short-cutting the procedure to issue a set of questions and answers that were to

[66] Interview with Drs P.P.M. van der Ree, 22 November 1990.

[67] "SI RJ" refers to the minutes of the BAR, whose activities were discussed above.

be equally authoritative. Once published, it was said in the CAJ, the RJ could not retract them without losing face. Since all of the drafting was being done in the RJ, without the usual reliance on the CAJ for technical support, the members of the CAJ worried that there might be a greater chance of "accidents", such as contradictions between the questions-and-answers and the Guidelines. The auditors delegation to the RJ defended the questions-and-answers on the ground that "it would at least lead to some publication again"(CAJ Not 1186), and that "it was of vital importance to take a constructive attitude toward the preparers delegation", which had supported the project (SI RJ 27).

Owing to concerns expressed in the CAJ about a tilt away from the two-track policy toward current value in the questions-and-answers project, the final booklet, which was published in October 1983, contained a foreword stating that the questions-and-answers were provisional. The 80-page booklet was said to be an "interim publication" ("*tussentijdse publikatie*") under the general title of *Guidelines for Annual Reporting*.[68] In addition to the 26 questions-and-answers, the booklet contained draft Guidelines on deferred tax and foreign exchange (with correlations to IASC standards) and a text of the draft law.

Draft on deferred tax. The two draft Guidelines included in the booklet both dealt with difficult issues that had been discussed at length by the RJ. The deferred tax draft replaced the corresponding section of the TO's exposure draft of December 1975, which had implicitly accepted "comprehensive" income tax allocation. Indeed, the TO did not even acknowledge the existence of a controversy over "comprehensive" *versus* "partial" allocation, as the latter was hardly seen in practice. Since the issuance of that draft, the UK's Accounting Standards Committee (ASC) had, under considerable industry pressure, reversed its original avowal of "comprehensive" allocation in favor of "partial" allocation (*SSAP* 15, issued in October 1978).[69] In the RJ's meetings, the preparers defended "partial" allocation,[70] while the auditors favored the "comprehensive" approach, even

[68] *Richtlijnen voor de jaarverslaggeving*, gepubliceerd onder verantwoordelijkheid van de Raad voor de Jaarverslaggeving (Deventer: Kluwer, October 1983).

[69] For a discussion of the policy aspects of the ASC's reversal, see Tony Hope and John Briggs, "Accounting Policy Making – Some Lessons from the Deferred Taxation Debate", in *Accounting and Business Research*, vol. 12, no. 46, Spring 1982, pp. 83–96; and Anthony J. Arnold and Brian J. Webb, *The Financial Reporting and Policy Effects of Partial Deferred Tax Accounting*, A report prepared for the Research Board (London: The Institute of Chartered Accountants in England and Wales, 1989), pp. 18–33.

[70] Two companies that would have disagreed with the evident position of the preparers delegation were Shell and Unilever. The former was using a "synthesis" of US, UK and Dutch accounting principles in its group financial statements, and Unilever's group financial statements were prepared in accordance with the UK *SSAP*'s. With "comprehensive" allocation required in the USA and "partial" allocation required (effective in 1979) in the UK, Shell faced a dilemma. In its 1979 group financial statements, Shell used "comprehensive" allocation in the financial statements and disclosed in a note how the results would have been different if "partial" allocation had been used. In their opinion on the 1979 financial statements, the group auditors inserted a clause in which attention was drawn to the departure from UK standard

going so far as to argue that the low valuation yielded by the "partial" approach might not reflect a "faithful picture" (RJ Not 324). One reason why auditors preferred "comprehensive" allocation was that it avoided subjective judgments about when the timing differences would reverse. The preparers had argued that the Seventh EEC Directive, which had been approved on 13 June 1983, allowed "partial" allocation for valuation differences arising on consolidation. The NIvRA delegation to the RJ, however, did not find this to be a sufficient ground for a general approval of "partial" tax allocation (SI RJ 74). In the final wording of the exposure draft, the RJ implied that it regarded "comprehensive" allocation as acceptable, but said that it was not yet prepared to make a pronouncement on the acceptability of "partial" allocation (para. 7 of the draft Guideline).[71]

Draft on foreign exchange. The other draft Guideline was the first substantial utterance, by either the TO or the RJ, on accounting for foreign exchange (*vreemde valuta's*). While the draft was influenced by the FASB's *Statement* no. 52, "Foreign Currency Translation", issued in December 1981, it did reflect certain important differences. The subject had been initially brought up in the TO in 1980, and elements of the argument over the "current operating performance" *versus* the "all-inclusive" notions of the profit and loss statement (preceding the TO's second exposure draft, in 1971–72) were repeated. One of the main issues centered on the balance-sheet translation of foreign subsidiaries, especially if they used historical costs. (If they used current values, it was generally agreed that their balance sheets should be translated at closing rates, with the differences charged or credited directly to equity.) At the meeting of 14 January 1981, the preparers argued that any solution should conform with overseas standards. A member of the preparers delegation representing a multinational cited the dilemma of having to comply with the different prescriptions of different countries (JO Alg 4100). In the end, it was decided that translation gains

---

practice. Beginning in the group's 1981 financial statements, the reference to the departure from UK practice was, in effect, shifted from the auditors' report to the statement of accounting policies. Unilever, in the belief that the use of "partial" allocation would contravene Dutch law, was using "comprehensive" allocation in its financial statements. Neither company would have been able to support a preference for the "partial" approach.

It has been suggested that a motivation behind the preparers' interest in "partial" allocation was that it would produce a higher profit. Interview with J. Vos, 8 November 1991.

[71] In a recent survey of 111 listed companies, it was found that in virtually all cases the "comprehensive" approach was used. See Drs E. van de Gaar and Drs L.G. van der Tas, "De verwerking van belasting naar de winst", in Prof.dr J. Dijksma and Drs C.D. Knoops (editors), *Jaar-in-jaar-uit 5: Verslag van een empirisch onderzoek van jaarrapporten over de jaren 1988 en 1989* (Groningen: Wolters-Noordhoff, 1991), p. 171. While "partial" allocation was rarely used, the preparers nonetheless wanted to keep it open as an option.

Although, by the end of 1991, the draft Guideline on deferred tax had still not emerged from its status as an exposure draft, at its meeting on 19 June 1991 the RJ provisionally approved a preference for "comprehensive" allocation (RJ Not 1183). A factor contributing to this decision was the preference for "comprehensive" allocation expressed in the IASC's E33, "Accounting for Taxes on Income", issued in January 1989.

on short-term assets and liabilities should be taken through income. Exchange rate gains on long-term monetary items may be spread over the duration of the instrument. Exchange rate losses on debts could be postponed if the loans were hedged against a future series of reasonably certain cash flows. For a subsidiary using historical cost accounting, balance-sheet translation would be at current rates, with gains and losses taken directly to equity if it was regarded as an independent entity. If, however, it was seen as a direct foreign activity, assets and liabilities would be translated as if they were owned/owed directly by the parent itself.

The first definitive Guidelines. In January and December 1984, the RJ published the first and second installments of definitive Guidelines, together with 16 single-issue exposure drafts, which, for the most part, were based either on the drafts issued by the TO between 1975 and 1979 or which addressed issues raised in the Fourth Directive.[72] All but one of the sections in the rewritten Draft Guidelines of June 1980, as well as all six draft Guidelines issued during 1981, were declared to be definitive. The section of the Draft Guidelines that was not acted upon in 1984 was eventually converted into a definitive Guideline in 1986. With the exception of Sec. 1.05 on recognition and disclosure, relatively few of the definitive Guidelines occasioned much debate in the RJ. Considerably more discussion time was spent on the new exposure drafts than on the definitive Guidelines. The Draft Guidelines, of course, had been approved as Considered Views in the 1970's, and the discussions over which passages should be boldfaced in the rewritten version had been completed prior to June 1980; hence, little additional debate would have been expected.

Segmentation of operating income. One of the draft Guidelines issued in December 1984, treating the segmentation of operating income, was exceedingly sensitive. The subject had been raised by Schoonderbeek at the RJ's meeting of 10 August 1983, when he proposed that the RJ endorse IAS 14, "Reporting Financial Information by Segment", issued in August 1981, which called for "Enterprises whose securities are publicly traded and other economically significant entities" to show a breakdown of operating income by industry and geographical segments. The preparers delegation replied that the RJ should not limit the freedom of companies that government had granted by removing the segmentation provision from the law. A few months earlier, industry had succeeded in defeating the Tazelaar amendments to the draft law adapting the Fourth Directive, which, among other things, would have reinstituted the segmentation of oper-

[72] These installments were published in an English language version, together with an English translation of Title 8, Book 2 of the Civil Code and the administrative decrees on financial statement formats and asset valuation. See *Council for Annual Reporting: Netherlands Accounting and Reporting Guidelines* (Amsterdam: Council for Annual Reporting, January 1986).

A chronology of the Considered Views and Guidelines, keyed to their exposure drafts, is presented in Appendix 5.2 to Chapter 5.

ating income, and it did not wish to see the matter reopened by the RJ. But a member of the users delegation said that he did not interpret the rejection of the Tazelaar amendments as a sufficient basis for not reaffirming the TO's support for the disclosure of segmented operating income, which had formed part of its fifth exposure draft issued in December 1976. A member of the auditors delegation proposed the issuance of a draft that would carry less weight than a Guideline: it would be styled as a "Considered View" ("*Beschouwing*") and would not contain any recommendations or bold facing. This compromise was accepted (RJ Not 325). The draft that was eventually issued recited the pro's and con's that had been aired during the parliamentary debate (RJ Not 422). While such information, it said, arguably might serve to promote "insight", the specter was raised that it might also damage the international competitive position of Dutch enterprise, since it was not mandated by the Fourth Directive. Entitled "A Considered View Concerning the Segmentation of Operating Income", the draft was careful to avoid the inference that financial statements omitting the segmentation should be regarded as deficient. If segmented operating income were to be disclosed, it was suggested that the usefulness of the disclosure would be furthered if the same segmentation criteria were adopted as for net sales, based on an exposure draft also issued in December 1984, "The Profit and Loss Statement: Segmentation of Net Sales".

Later drafts. No further publications were issued in 1985, but additional draft Guidelines arising from the Fourth Directive were under preparation. Several were issued as exposure drafts in 1986, including: interpretations of the disclosure requirements keyed to company size, guidance on the specific information to be provided in the notes, and advice on how financial statements might be tailored to the exemptions for group companies.[73] Definitive Guidelines on foreign exchange, virtually unchanged from the exposure draft, and on one other subject were published in 1986.

But the RJ's productivity during the period 1984–86 was significantly slowed owing to the need to comment on several time-consuming projects: the draft adaptation law for the Seventh EEC Directive, the EEC proposal for financial reporting by partnerships and other unincorporated entities, and the model of bank financial statements promulgated by De Nederlandsche Bank, among other projects.

Research projects. At the 11 July 1984 meeting, Schoonderbeek broached the possibility that the RJ conduct one or more research projects, but the suggestion was given short shrift by the preparers. Two members of the auditors delegation, however, proposed that a conceptual framework might be one of a number of suitable subjects for research (RJ Not 456). At the meeting of 12 December

[73] *Verslag van de werkzaamheden over het jaar 1986 van de Raad voor de Jaarverslaggeving* (March 1987), p. 19.

1984, the first concrete research proposal, "International Comparison of Financial Reporting Regulation", was, after extensive discussion, voted down as being too broad and not practicable (RJ Not 535–536). At the RJ's 12 March 1986 meeting, a brainstorming session on the RJ's work program led, among other things, to a suggestion for a conceptual framework project, but the idea was not well received. A second research project, on "sound business practice" ("*goed koopmansgebruik*"), was also turned down (RJ Not 708).

While, at various times during the early and middle 1980's, some members of the CAJ expressed interest in pursuing a project on "fundamentals" or "a conceptual framework", and at one time in late 1983 a committee was actually set up to investigate the possibility, the RJ – and especially the preparers – were always cool to the idea (CAJ Not 1056, 1241, 1249, 1299–1300; RJ Not 341). No such project was ever authorized, either by the CAJ or the RJ. There is evidence that the NIvRA's management board considered the drawing up of a conceptual framework as part of its policy plan, but there does not seem to have been any action actually taken (CAJ Not 1218).

Funds statement. The Statement of Source and Application of Funds, on which a mild exposure draft had been issued in September 1979, was the subject of a similarly mild draft Guideline issued in January 1984. One difference was that the 1984 draft recommended that the statement be included in the annual financial statements as part of the notes. No bold-facing, however, was used in the draft, so the recommendation did not have the character of a proposed "affirmative pronouncement". When the subject again came up for discussion in May 1986, the preparers continued to insist that it was undesirable to prescribe any of the statement's contents beyond the elementary points specified in the 1984 draft. After discussion, the matter was referred to the Limperg Instituut for further study (RJ Not 741–742). The Limperg Instituut provided the RJ with a draft in September 1987, but work on a revision has not yet led to a new draft.

6.3.2. Timmer succeeds Schoonderbeek as chairman

In April 1986, Schoonderbeek retired after ten years as chairman of the RJ. Somewhat more than a year before, he had retired from his audit firm. During much of his tenure on the RJ, procedural and organizational issues had dominated the agenda, but substantive issues, such as current value, pensions, segmentation, the WIR premium, deferred tax, and foreign exchange, were extensively debated and eventually found their way into exposure drafts or final statements. All the while, the RJ had spent much of its time giving advice to government and other outside entities.

In July 1985, Schoonderbeek wrote a short booklet on the process of issuing guidance on financial reporting, almost as if it were his valedictory.[74] After exam-

[74] Prof.drs J.W. Schoonderbeek, *Council for Annual Reporting: Setting Accounting Standards*

ining four possible approaches to developing guidance – reviewing best practice, relying on theoretical analysis, studying users' needs, and employing cost/benefit analysis – he concluded that none of the alternatives alone yields a final solution. An important reason, he said, was that the process is political as well as technical. He wrote as follows:

> Perhaps there is no final solution. But the process of standard-setting has to account for all of these elements [i.e., approaches], in particular the interests of suppliers of information and those of users of information – the one often in conflict with the other . . . .
>
> This conflict of interests shows another aspect of the standard-setting process, the political aspect. In a democratic society all parties involved participate, at least ideally, in political processes. This assumption lies at the root of the Dutch formation [and operation] of the standard-setting body . . . (p. 5).

His overall assessment of the work of the TO and the RJ was positive, but not without reservations. He wrote:

> In my opinion, there can be no doubt that the ["Considered Views"] and the "guidelines" have influenced financial reporting practice in the Netherlands. The majority of companies follow most of the [affirmative] pronouncements and recommendations. Important influence is exerted in this respect by auditors recommending compliance with the guidelines. Furthermore, the opinions of the Council have influenced the Dutch government in preparing the adaptation of the law to the Fourth Directive of the European Community. The Enterprise Chamber considers the guidelines seriously, but while it often follows them, it need not do so.
>
> Evaluating the Dutch process of standard-setting, it seems to me rather effective. The guidelines, while not mandatory, are broadly accepted and applied. It is a gradual process. It is a process too, which is subject to delay and acceleration according to social and economic conditions in the business environment. As any political process, it is influenced by motives, arguments and relations of power. In my experience the willingness to extend the accounting standards on the part of the preparers of annual accounts is at this moment less than some years ago. Nevertheless the tripartite structure of the Council is still fruitful (p. 7).

At Schoonderbeek's final meeting as chairman, on 16 April 1986, many kind words were spoken. Perhaps the highest of Dutch compliments was bestowed by the representative of the FNV on the Foundation's board: Schoonderbeek, he said, represented "the epitome of the consensus approach" ("*het vleesgeworden harmoniemodel*") (RJ Not 726).

G. Timmer, the new chairman, was a partner in (and, from 1971 to 1983, chairman of) KMG Klynveld Kraayenhof & Co., and had been a close associate

---

in the Netherlands (Amsterdam: Council for Annual Reporting, July 1985), 9 pp. Page citations in the text refer to this booklet.

of J. Kraayenhof during the 1950's and 1960's, when Kraayenhof was a leading figure in the several initiatives to improve financial reporting. Timmer was to retire from the audit firm at the end of 1986. In the NIvRA, Timmer had served on the management board in 1969–71 and had been on the CBV since 1983, but, as with Schoonderbeek before him, he did not have any prior service on either the CAJ or the TO/RJ.

6.3.3. Developments from 1987 to 1991

As mentioned in the Preface, it is difficult to acquire a historical perspective on very recent developments. Their ramifications are often not fully clear at the time of writing, and, not infrequently, important threads are yet to be unraveled. Furthermore, the participants would not be as willing to comment candidly on contemporary developments as they would on events occurring some years before. From 1987 onward, to complete the record, the authors will focus on a number of the more important developments, but not in quite as much depth as was possible in the 1970's and in the first part of the 1980's.

The major issues on which the RJ issued exposure drafts were the accounting issues raised by the WIR benefit and the capitalization of publishing rights. Another important development, which is briefly treated, is the adaptation of the law to the Seventh EC Directive. A further section deals with the continuing controversy over the authority of the Guidelines. In a final section on the RJ, some comments are made about the RJ's productivity. In the closing section of the chapter, the production of the Enterprise Chamber is briefly reviewed.

6.3.3.1. Metamorphosis of the WIR

Although the TO's exposure draft of February 1979 on the treatment of the WIR premium was never converted into a Guideline, it nonetheless seemed to gain fairly widespread support.[75] But with effect from 1 May 1986, the government changed the form of the investment incentive from that of a premium to a deduction from income tax payable, with the provision that it could be carried forward to the next eight fiscal years, and carried back three years.[76] Prior to 1986, the WIR premium had been payable without regard to whether the purchaser owed any tax.

---

[75] In a survey of the 1984 annual reports of 112 listed companies, it was found that 76 companies followed the TO's recommendation, 32 used a different amortization period for the WIR premium than the asset's useful life, and one took the WIR premium into income immediately. See *Onderzoek Jaarverslaggeving 1984*, NIVRA geschrift nummer 39 (Amsterdam: Nederlands Instituut van Registeraccountants, December 1985), pp. 106–107.

In January 1984, the RJ had issued an exposure draft (Sec. 3.01) that represented an expansion of the February 1979 draft, to embrace all government grants. The equal acceptability of deducting the WIR premium from the cost of the related fixed asset or of treating it as a deferred credit was not disturbed. No further action was taken on the exposure draft.

[76] Wet van 29 April 1986, Stb. 215.

The RJ's first step was to request the CAJ to draft a restatement of the advice given for the WIR premium, as if to suggest that the accounting characteristics of the investment incentive had not fundamentally changed (RJ Not 770). But in a subsequent memorandum, a member of the preparers delegation argued that, since there could be uncertainty for up to eight years over whether a given investment would qualify for the tax reduction, it would be problematic to attempt to associate the WIR benefit with the full useful life of the acquired asset. Hence, he maintained, its nature was such that it should be credited against tax expense in the year in which the WIR benefit was actually realized (RJ Richtl. 3.01/blz.51–52).[77] The effect of this proposal would have been to take the full WIR benefit into a single year's income.

After further discussion in which the preparers delegation was persuaded to modify its position, the RJ decided to lead practice by issuing a quick interpretation.[78] In January 1987, it published a Notice (*Mededeling*) stating its provisional view that the fundamental character of the WIR benefit had not changed, and that the WIR benefit should be allocated over the asset's useful life. The tax receivable carried forward to future years would be recognized as a deferred tax benefit. Comments were requested by 30 June.[79]

Somewhat to the embarrassment of the RJ, the issue was abruptly returned to the drawing-board when, in February 1987, Philips issued its 1986 annual report in which it took the WIR benefits received since 1 May 1986 immediately into income. Evidently, the quickness with which the Notice was issued did not give the preparers delegation sufficient time in which to consult its constituency – or, alternatively, the preparers delegation may not have done its homework. Even without the action taken by Philips, the written reactions to the Notice showed that auditors were divided, even within firms, and that companies were uniformly opposed. From September to November 1987, after the letters of comment had been analyzed, the RJ held lengthy discussions on the treatment of the WIR benefit (RJ Not 921–924, 946–948). This time, the preparers held strongly to the belief that, as with all other tax items, it should be reflected in tax expense. They argued that this tax expense interpretation should not be viewed as second-best, but instead as an alternative of equal standing with the deferral approaches recommended in the 1979/1984 exposure drafts and reaffirmed in the Notice. These discussions led to the issuance of a second Notice in December 1987 in which the tax expense and deferral approaches were presented as equally acceptable alternatives, but only for WIR benefits granted on or after 1 May 1986, when the change in law took effect.[80] On 29 February 1988, the

[77] "RJ Richtl." refers to documents in the RJ's file.

[78] Interview with W.P. Moleveld, 11 July 1991.

[79] *Mededeling aan de abonnees op Richtlijnen voor de jaarverslaggeving* (Raad voor de Jaarverslaggeving, January 1987), 5 pp.

[80] *Mededeling aan de abonnees op Richtlijnen voor de jaarverslaggeving* (Raad voor de

government reduced the rate of the WIR benefit to zero, effectively eliminating its incentive effect.[81] In August 1989, the RJ published a definitive Guideline, Sec. 3.01, "Government Grants and Comparable Arrangements" ("*Overheidssubsidies en vergelijkbare faciliteiten*"), and inserted paragraphs .521 through .521b in a previously issued exposure draft, Sec. 2.53, "Provisions for Deferred Taxes" ("*Voorzieningen voor latente belastingen*"), the collective effect of which was to confirm the equal acceptability of the two approaches allowed by the Notice issued in December 1987.

6.3.3.2. Seventh EC directive and other changes in the Civil Code
The Seventh Directive on consolidated financial statements was approved on 13 June 1983, and Dutch law was adapted to the Directive on 10 November 1988 (Stb. 517). Shortly prior to the adaptation, Klaassen wrote that the Directive would have "only a very limited influence on the practice of financial reporting in the Netherlands", and that seems to have been the case.[82] The RJ prepared a 101-page booklet containing a comparative analysis of differences between the old and new laws, with a commentary on the important changes.[83] The law introduced a slight modification in the criteria for including subsidiaries in consolidated financial statements, but it was not expected to lead to significant changes in practice.[84] In the definition of a subsidiary, there was a shift of emphasis away from percentage of shareownership and toward control, as expressed by actual voting rights. Finally, the new law contained certain prescriptions for the format and contents of consolidated financial statements.

There were no significant debates over accounting matters in the parliamentary approval process.

On 1 January 1989, Title 3 in Book 2 of the Civil Code was assigned to an expanded law on cooperative societies and mutual trusts, which necessitated the renumbering of all subsequent titles. Hence, the law on financial statements was assigned Title 9 in Book 2 of the Civil Code.

On 13 December 1989, a law containing a number of modifications in the fi-

---

Jaarverslaggeving, December 1987), 3 pp.

81 Beschikking van 27 February 1988 (nr 088–621) (*Staatscourant* 40A).

82 Jan Klaassen, "The Netherlands and the Seventh Directive", in S.J. Gray and A.G. Coenenberg (editors), *International Group Accounting* (London: Croom Helm, 1988), p. 127. (In a chapter submitted for the revised edition of the book edited by Gray and Coenenberg, Klaassen has written: "the introduction of the Seventh Directive had a very limited impact on the practice of financial reporting in the Netherlands" (p. 10 of typescript for Chapter 7).) For a similar view, see Christopher Nobes, *Financial Reporting in the UK and the EEC: Mutual Influences*, Certified Research Report no. 6 (London: Certified Accountant Publications Limited, 1986), pp. 67–70.

83 *Extra publikatie inzake Bijzondere bepalingen voor de geconsolideerde jaarrekening en Enige vereenvoudigingen en verduidelijkingen in het jaarrekeningenrecht* (Amsterdam: Raad voor de Jaarverslaggeving, August 1989).

84 *Ibid.*, p. 7.

nancial reporting provisions of Title 9 was passed (Stb.(1990). 1).[85] The law was intended to remove some of the anomalies that had become evident since the existing law had taken effect. The changes involved little controversy, and included a sharper definition of the company size criteria (which define the exemptions for smaller companies), a broadening of the scope for preparing financial statements in a foreign currency, and an option to lengthen the period over which goodwill may be amortized. A member of the Second Chamber introduced a provision to allow Dutch subsidiaries of foreign companies, in restricted circumstances, to prepare their financial statements in accordance with the norms of other EC-member states. Despite opposition from the minister and the RJ, this parliamentary initiative was approved.[86]

6.3.3.3. The RJ reacts to the non-amortization of publishing rights

In a Guideline issued in June 1987, in which the RJ correlated earlier guidance on intangibles with the adaptation law for the Fourth Directive, there was a bold-faced pronouncement that "The amortization [of separate and identifiable intangible fixed assets] must be done systematically" (Sec. 2.01, para. 113). Three years later, this guidance was called into question when the two largest Dutch publishers, Elsevier and VNU, reinstated significant portions of previously written-off goodwill as "publishing rights" ("*uitgaverechten*") and announced, with the evident support of their auditors, that the asset would not be subject to systematic amortization. Included in the Chairman's Message in Elsevier's 1989 annual report was the following passage: "The economic value of publishing rights is, in principle, not subject to periodic diminution. Publishing rights are more akin to land than to buildings or machinery .... This characteristic of publishing rights has led us, following other large European publishers, to depart from the automatic annual amortization of their balance-sheet value".[87] VNU's management board stated in its 1989 annual report that its accounting treatment of publishing rights "corresponds with international developments".[88] Both companies, together with Wolters-Kluwer (which adopted the practice the following year), and their auditors held an unusual meeting at which mutual concerns over implementation were discussed.

The companies' decisions caught the RJ by surprise, and it received advice that the Justice Ministry expected a pronouncement on the matter (RJ Not 1137). A similar controversy had erupted in the United Kingdom in 1988–89, when several companies reinstated previously written-off goodwill as "brands".[89]

---

[85] This law was also discussed in the RJ booklet referred to in footnote 83, above.

[86] *Bijlagen Handelingen Tweede Kamer, Zitting 1988–1989*, 20556, no. 6 (amendment), no. 8 (reply by minister). *Handelingen Tweede Kamer, Zitting 1988–1989*, p. 6174, 9 May 1989 (debate).

[87] Elsevier, *Jaarverslag 1989*, p. 12.

[88] VNU, *Jaarverslag 1989*, p. 12.

[89] See, e.g., Patrick Barwise *et al.*, *Accounting for Brands* (London: The London Business

It quickly became an urgent issue, and the RJ hastily began deliberations in September 1990. A draft styled as a "discussion memorandum" ("*beschouwing*") prepared by the secretariat was considered at the RJ's meeting on 12 December. No recommendation was expressed in the discussion memorandum; instead, it recited arguments for and against the capitalization and systematic amortization of intangible fixed assets such as publishing rights. Since the major publishers and their auditors – the three largest audit firms – had already taken a collective position on the subject, the tenor of the RJ's discussions required more delicacy than was usual in such matters. It was decided at the December meeting to take a sounding of the views of ten professors of financial accounting, by requesting their views on the draft.

The views of the professors were divided, and Chairman Timmer rewrote the discussion memorandum, taking their arguments into account. A 12-page "Discussion Memorandum Concerning a Number of Aspects of the Treatment of Intangible Fixed Assets" ("*Beschouwing inzake een aantal aspecten van de behandeling van immateriële vaste activa*") was issued in June 1991, and comments were requested by December (since extended). It was the first discussion memorandum ever issued by the TO/RJ. In the draft, the RJ modified its earlier view that intangibles *could be* capitalized only if they were separate and identifiable, by stating its provisional view that such assets *might have to be* capitalized. It also interpreted the law to say that intangibles could be capitalized only at their historical cost, and, as the core of the document, gave arguments on both sides of systematic amortization, without offering its own view.[90] Owing to the strong positions already taken on the subject by important companies and audit firms, as well as the failure, thus far, by the UK standard setter to respond effectively to the same question, it was deemed politic to begin the process with the quintessential Dutch *overleg* (consultation).

6.3.3.4. Debate over the authority of the guidelines

Did the ministerial charge of 1968 as well as the broad constituency which its membership represented endow the RJ's Guidelines with authoritative standing? A decision in 1985 by the NIvRA's Board of Appeal (Raad van Beroep) stimulated an exchange of articles, raising the issue afresh.

School and The Institute of Chartered Accountants in England and Wales, 1989).

[90] Bindenga, who is a partner in a firm that audits the financial statements of one of the three publishing companies, has criticized the RJ's discussion memorandum for not dealing with the issue in a fundamental way and for reaching conclusions that are "fragmentary", "confusing", and occasionally inconsistent. He added: "I think it is justifiable to raise the question of whether the RJ has put its credibility at stake". Prof.dr A.J. Bindenga, *Een toekomst voor de Nederlandse accountancy: Een beschouwing over ontwikkelingen in de financiële rapportering en de controle daarvan* (Alphen aan den Rijn/Deurne: Samsom BedrijfsInformatie, 1991), pp. 34–36. In the same *oratie*, Bindenga characterized the tendency to recognize intangibles such as brands and publishing rights as an unfortunate attempt to blend economic and accounting concepts of profit. *Ibid.*, p. 27.

In its ruling, the Board of Appeal said that an auditor, in a case brought before it, should have consulted and, apparently, should have complied with the RJ's Guidelines.[91] In his commentary on the published verdict, J.A. Burggraaff saw the Board's dictum as signaling the end to unrestrained freedom ("*vrijheid, blijheid*"), and he concurred with the ruling. He gave his view that, in the future, all auditors would need to take this verdict into account.[92]

In a widely noticed article, Prof.mr W.C.L. van der Grinten, the *éminence grise* of company law, arrived at an opposite conclusion. He argued that (1) the Guidelines have no binding force whatsoever, and carry no weight other than that of the view of an expert author; (2) the Board should have looked only at compliance with the law; and (3) the Board's verdict cannot bind auditors who were not involved in the actual case (although he conceded that the precedent would have consequences that could not be ignored). Van der Grinten issued the following declaration:

> The RJ would do well if it made clear the character of its pronouncements. It cannot make norms. It does not have the authority to give binding interpretations of the law on financial statements. It can give advice and make recommendations. It may be expected that the RJ would not create confusion over the nature of its guidelines. The use of the word guidelines is already rather unfortunate. This term suggests that the RJ's opinion is more or less binding for business and the auditor.[93]

Mr drs F. van der Wel, in a reply, did not disagree with van der Grinten on the bindingness question, but he nonetheless placed the Guidelines above the general run of literature.[94]

Mr Th.S. IJsselmuiden, however, has argued that considerable authority should be accorded to the Guidelines. To the extent that portions of the Guidelines were seen as constituting "principles that are considered acceptable in the economic and social climate", which might be inferred by their concurrence with international usage, they form part of the legal requirements. Hence, deviations from such Guidelines should be cited by auditors in their report as being departures from the law.[95]

---

91 *Jurisprudentie Tuchtrechtspraak* 1986/3 (20 May 1985).

92 *Ibid.*, "Annotatie", p. 3/11.

93 Prof.mr W.C.L. van der Grinten, "De status van de Richtlijnen voor de Jaarverslaggeving", in *De Naamlooze Vennootschap*, vol. 64, no. 5, September/October 1986, p. 155.

94 Mr drs F. van der Wel, "De status van de Richtlijnen voor de Jaarverslaggeving", in *De Naamlooze Vennootschap*, vol. 65, no. 2, March/April 1987, pp. 73–77. A similar conclusion had been reached by Mr drs J.J. Nagelkerke, "De Stellige Uitspraken van de Raad voor de Jaarverslaggeving – Iets over hun juridische betekenis", in *Maandblad voor accountancy en bedrijfshuishoudkunde*, vol. 56, no. 11, December 1982, pp. 526–541.

95 Mr Th.S. IJsselmuiden, "Bevatten de Richtlijnen voor de jaarverslaggeving rechtens bindende regels", in *TVVS/Maandblad voor ondernemingsrecht en rechtspersonen*, vol. 32, no. 11, November 1989, pp. 277–279. IJsselmuiden was a long-time member of the Enterprise Chamber, and was its chairman from 1984 to 1986.

The legal status of the Guidelines continues to be a contentious question.

6.3.4. Review of the RJ's activities

6.3.4.1. The RJ's productivity

As has been noted several times above, since its founding the RJ has been in continual demand for advice by government and other institutions. These time-consuming but necessary activities have tended to limit the RJ's capacity to develop new exposure drafts and convert earlier drafts into definitive Guidelines.

The RJ's assorted activities not directly related to the production of definitive Guidelines were numerous. During the period from 1987 to 1991, the RJ issued a booklet explaining the important changes in the law resulting from its adaptation to the Seventh Directive; advised fund-raising charities on a set of model financial statements; and advised the Justice Ministry on insurance company reporting in connection with a proposed EC Directive, on a series of draft laws on computer fraud, on financial reporting by banks and other financial institutions, and on the simplification and clarification of the legal requirements for financial statements. In addition, the RJ continued to comment on IASC drafts, and in 1989–90 it spent considerable time on responses to E32, "Comparability of Financial Statements"[96], and E34, "Disclosures in the Financial Statements of Banks and Similar Financial Institutions".[97]

A review of the RJ's production of definitive Guidelines since 1982 shows that, of the 54 entries in Appendix 5.2 to Chapter 5 (the chronological listing of Considered Views and Guidelines), all but 18 had been originally promulgated as definitive Considered Views in the 1970's and had been issued in rewritten format in June 1980. Since 6 definitive Guidelines had their exposure in 1981, which was the final year of the TO, only 12 of the RJ's definitive Guidelines have been based on drafts developed during the tenure of the RJ. To be sure, since 1983 (when it issued its first exposure draft), the RJ has issued 39 exposure drafts: 32 between 1983 and 1986, and 7 since 1987.[98] Of the 39 drafts, 27 were still exposure drafts at the end of 1991, including all 7 that were issued since 1987.[99]

Possible explanations for this record are (1) the considerable time devoted to projects not related to the production of Guidelines; (2) the time required to

---

[96] The RJ's reaction was published as "Commentaar op ED 32 'Comparability of Financial Statements'", in *de Accountant* vol. 96, no. 2, October 1989, pp. 71–73.

[97] The RJ's response was published in *Verslag van de werkzaamheden over het jaar 1990 van de Raad voor de Jaarverslaggeving* (March 1991), pp. 26–27.

[98] The figures refer only to new exposure drafts, and do not include drafts that were replacements of earlier drafts, owing to the need to make extensive revisions.

[99] One must interpret these figures with caution, since some entries in the Appendix refer to significant and lengthy drafts, while others refer to drafts of lesser consequence. Further, while some drafts comprehend a single issue, others are subsections of a larger single-issue statement.

amend previous exposure drafts and definitive Guidelines to reflect the Fourth and Seventh Directives, the model financial statements (*Model jaarrekening*) promulgated by De Nederlandsche Bank, and IASC standards; (3) the part-time nature of the RJ and its almost total reliance on another part-time committee (i.e., the CAJ), which has an agenda of other projects as well, to do the initial drafting; and (4) inhibiting factors in the RJ's voting procedures and staff support. On the matter of voting procedures, although the articles of incorporation, as revised, stipulate a five-sixths majority for the approval of publications, as a practical matter all decisions are based on unanimous consent, without actual voting. In regard to staff support, since the RJ's founding in 1982, the equivalent of somewhat less than one full-time person has been available to manage its technical agenda.[100]

The RJ's practice of holding half-day plenary meetings on a monthly basis may not be the most effective plan for covering its heavy agenda. Each meeting day begins with 90-minute concurrent sessions for the three delegations; the plenary session usually commences at either 10:30 (with a break for lunch) or 1:30, with adjournment at around 6:00. Some RJ members, in interviews with the authors, have complained that the extensive debates during the meetings leave little time for actual decisions. Meetings of comparable bodies in other countries, as well as those of the IASC's board, are scheduled fewer times a year but they occupy two or more days at a time. The ease with which one can commute to meetings in the Netherlands is a factor in planning frequent, short meetings, but longer meetings have the virtue of enabling a full discussion to be followed by ample time for the taking of decisions, without complications posed by members' changing their positions between meetings as well as the need to rehearse previous discussions for the benefit of those who attend irregularly.

6.3.4.2. Sundry observations

Two subjects on which action had been taken many years before in the USA and the UK, deferred tax and the funds statement, had not advanced beyond exposure draft status by the end of 1991. Moreover, the RJ had also not issued any explicit guidance on financial instruments, which had been the subject of several US and UK utterances in the 1980's.

Since the middle of 1987, 12 of the 13 members of the RJ have been *registeraccountants*, the lone exception being Drs H. Haarbosch, the financial analyst (who had replaced W. Mur in July 1987). Omitting two individuals who attended only the inaugural meeting of the TO on 19 August 1971, 16 of the 24 members of the employers/preparers delegation of the TO/RJ have been *registeraccountants*, and all of the members of the users delegation since its reactivation in 1986, other than the occupant of the financial analyst's chair, have been *registeraccountants*.

[100] Interview with O.M. Volgenant jr., 21 November 1991.

Moreover, virtually all of the drafts considered by the TO/RJ have been prepared by the CAJ, a committee of the NIvRA. One can only speculate what effect the backgrounds of the participants may have had on the substantive positions taken.[101]

As a further note, it should be mentioned that the SER, although the source of two-thirds of the RJ's financial support, has never evinced any interest in the RJ's activities, and has never been represented at meetings of the Foundation's board.

The costs incurred by the RJ from 1982 to 1990 have fluctuated in the range of *f* 200 000 to *f* 400 000. A per diem stipend is paid to members, coordinators, and the secretary in accordance with a scale established by the SER for such activities. There was a significant increase in the scale in 1990, which accounted for a rise of about *f* 100 000 in the RJ's costs, to a level of *f* 391 000.[102]

On 15 October 1991, the Foundation sponsored a Conference on the Future of Financial Reporting in the Netherlands, held in The Hague. An audience of about 90 persons was invited to hear presentations by Prof.mr K. Van Hulle, of the EC Commission; Dr A.R. Wyatt, chairman of the IASC; A.V.C. Cook, technical director of the UK's Accounting Standards Board; Prof.dr S.A. Zeff, visiting the Vrije Universiteit; and Prof.dr J. Klaassen, of KPMG Klynveld and a member of the NIvRA's delegation to the IASC.[103] A proceedings volume is being prepared, and it is understood that the conference may lead to discussions about the program and procedures of the RJ.

A final development, which promises a closer relationship between the RJ and the Ministry of Justice, was the request by Mr S.F.M. Wortmann, the staff person in the Ministry who is concerned with the financial reporting law, to attend RJ meetings as an observer.[104] Her request was accepted, and the first meeting at which she was present was on 16 October 1991.

6.3.5. Reprise on the Enterprise Chamber

As noted in Chapter 5, in 1977 the Enterprise Chamber began announcing verdicts in cases dealing with the financial reporting provisions of company law.[105]

---

[101] It has been said that, as seen by the employers/preparers, it was of little concern that the members of their delegation were *registeraccountants*. Interview with E.G. Hoefer, 4 December 1990. That so many of the RJ's members were *registeraccountants* was said to have enabled an easier communication at meetings. Interview with Prof.dr M.A. van Hoepen, 5 July 1991.

[102] Financial information was disclosed for the first time in the RJ's annual report for 1987. The figures for previous years were obtained from the minute books of the Foundation for Annual Reporting.

[103] See the report, "Kritiek op jaarverslag niet gedeeld door de deskundigen", in *Onderneming*, vol. 20, no. 36, 22 October 1991, p. 3.

[104] Interview with G. Timmer, 20 November 1991.

[105] In articles written in English, Klaassen has discussed the procedures for bringing cases before the Enterprise Chamber, and Klaassen and Burgert have discussed the early verdicts

By mid-1991, the Enterprise Chamber had handed down decisions in 45 cases involving financial reporting, of which 21 had been brought by SOBI (Stichting Onderzoek Bedrijfs-Informatie – Foundation to Investigate Company Reporting), and 13 had been brought by shareholders. The remaining were initiated by a variety of interested parties, including employees and trade unions, as well as by the Attorney-General. Based on Berendsen's analysis of the Enterprise Chamber's decided cases through 1986, as updated by the authors,[106] the following is a summary of the outcomes (shown by the Roman numeral in the final column of Berendsen's table):

---

the latter directing some unflattering remarks at SOBI. See J. Klaassen, "An Accounting Court: The Impact of the Enterprise Chamber on Financial Reporting in the Netherlands", in *The Accounting Review*, vol. 55, no. 2, April 1980, pp. 327–341, and Prof.drs R. Burgert, "Current Accounting Practice in the Netherlands", in *Maandblad voor accountancy en bedrijfshuishoudkunde*, vol. 55, nos. 2/3, February/March 1981, pp. 52–64. For comments on the early Enterprise Chamber cases and some observations on SOBI and its founder-chairman, Drs Pieter Lakeman, see Henk Volten, *Challenges to Financial Reporting in the Netherlands – How Corporate Reporting is Monitored by Social Pressure Groups*, PILOT (Netherlands) 9 (Amsterdam: Nederlands Instituut van Registeraccountants, November 1979). For candid remarks on SOBI and Lakeman, see H. Volten, "SOBI's prikkelcampagne", in *de Accountant*, vol. 89, no. 2, October 1982, pp. 77–78.

For commentary on the Enterprise Chamber's decisions, see Prof.mr drs H. Beckman and O.M. Volgenant jr. (editors), *Documentatie rond de jaarrekening* (Deventer: Kluwer), a looseleaf service; and articles regularly appearing in *TVVS* and *De Naamlooze Vennootschap*.

[106] J.G. Berendsen, *Maatschappij, onderneming en accountant: Een onderzoek naar ontwikkelingen in de maatschappelijke positie van de openbare accountant in de jaren na 1945* (Amsterdam: VU Uitgeverij, 1990), pp. 56–59. The authors would add the following decided cases to Berendsen's table on page 58:

24a.	11/10/1984	Jan Molenschot & Zoon B.V.('82)	A	3	2	II
35.	03/11/1988	Van der Giessen-de Noord N.V. ('86)	S	2	1	II
36.	15/12/1988	Aegon N.V. ('86)	S	4	2	II
37.	30/03/1989	Nedlloyd N.V. ('87)	AG	(2)	( )	V
38.	29/06/1989	H&H Beheer B.V. ('86)	A	2	1	II
39.	12/10/1989	Jongeneel Beheer B.V. ('84)	M	6	5	VI
40.	26/10/1989	Sanders Behang N.V. ('87/'88)	AG	( )	( )	V
41.	11/01/1990	NCM-Enkabe ('87)	M	12	12	III
42.	03/05/1990	Nijhuis B.V. ('85)	A	10	10	III
43.	18/10/1990	Schuitema N.V. ('88)	A	( )	( )	V
44.	21/02/1990	KZIJ ('87)	M	10	8	I

The first column of symbols, above, indicates the class of claimant: A – shareholder, S – SOBI, AG – Attorney-General (*Procureur-Generaal*), and M – Miscellaneous. The symbols in the fourth column indicate the class of outcome, as explained in the text. For the meaning of the symbols in the second and third columns, one should consult Berendsen's discussion.

In Berendsen's table, the class of outcome was omitted for Decision no. 10 (KSH case). The authors would designate it as class I. Decision no. 26, which was reported as a class IV outcome in Berendsen's table, would now be reclassified as I, owing to a subsequent verdict announced by the Enterprise Chamber in 1987.

Directions were given for future years' financial statements (II)	13
All claims were rejected (III)	11
The claimant was not accepted as an "interested party" (V)	10
The financial statements as a whole were declared null, owing to their defective contents (I)	7
The current year's financial statements were to be supplemented (VI)	3
The financial statements as a whole were declared null, owing to procedural deficiencies in the process by which they were approved (IV)	1

Of the 45 decided cases, only 23 led to orders for remedial action to be taken. Fully ten of the cases resulted in a decision that the claimant was not an interested party. In the two cases brought by the Attorney-General (both decided in 1989), it was found that he had not demonstrated that the "public interest" ("*openbaar belang*") would be served by remedial action, and, hence, he did not have standing as a claimant.

There has been a drop in the number of financial reporting cases brought to the Enterprise Chamber.[107] In the last several years, SOBI has withdrawn from actively pursuing cases before the Enterprise Chamber.[108] In view of the recent setbacks in the Attorney-General's attempts to achieve standing as an interested party, together with the apparent disinclination on the part of shareholders to bring cases (owing to cost and the length of time required to reach a final verdict), one wonders whether the Enterprise Chamber will continue to be a major player in securing compliance with the financial reporting provisions of company law.

A source of concern to the TO and, subsequently, to the RJ has been the practice by the Enterprise Chamber of not referring in its verdicts to the Considered Views or Guidelines.[109] While the TO and the RJ would have seen explicit references by the Enterprise Chamber to their statements as a confirmation of their importance in the economic and social climate, the Enterprise Chamber has regarded the written law as the authoritative literature for its purposes. Considered Views and Guidelines do not constitute law, written or unwritten. The Enterprise Chamber sees them primarily as guidance for companies and auditors, although it does take cognizance of them in the course of its deliberations.[110]

[107] Interviews with Mr H.F.J. Joosten, 14 September 1990, with Mr Th.S. IJsselmuiden, 14 September 1990, and with Prof.dr M.A. van Hoepen, 5 July 1991.

[108] Interview with Drs P. Lakeman, 5 November 1990.

[109] For the views of those who have been critical of the Enterprise Chamber's practice in this regard, see the section entitled "First decisions of the Enterprise Chamber" in Chapter 5.

It is said that auditors usually refer to the RJ's Guidelines when they appear as a witness in hearings held by the Enterprise Chamber (which are not open to the public). Interview with Prof.dr M.A. van Hoepen, 5 July 1991.

[110] Interviews with Mr H.F.J. Joosten, 14 September 1990, and with Mr Th.S. IJsselmuiden, 14 September 1990.

In his Explanatory Memorandum published in 1968, the Justice Minister, after proposing what was to become the TO, said that "The resulting publications concerning acceptable principles will meet a clear need on the part of enterprise managements, and can serve as a point of reference as well for the Enterprise Chamber when a case in this area is brought before it".[111] As it has turned out, some of the Enterprise Chamber's decisions have been in conformity with the statements issued by the TO and the RJ, while others have been at variance from the statements. But when the Enterprise Chamber has taken positions that depart from those of the TO or the RJ, reasons have not been given.

A number of Enterprise Chamber decisions in the late 1970's had important implications for the TO's Considered Views, but the number of such decisions handed down in subsequent years was decidedly less. One possible reason was the adaptation of Dutch law to the Fourth Directive, which made the financial reporting provisions more explicit and less subject to different interpretations as between the Enterprise Chamber and the RJ.

Some of the financial reporting issues on which the Enterprise Chamber expressed its views were the following:

- in addition to the use of historical cost, in some circumstances current value must be shown in the notes in order to give the insight required by the financial reporting provisions of company law (Homburg, 1977).
- tax loss carryforwards may be recognized as receivables when their realizability can be reasonably assumed (Pakhoed, 1979).
- in the case of "economic stock", not only information about buy and sell contracts, but also the valuation method used, should be shown in the notes (Douwe Egberts, 1977).
- the reasons and the financial effects of accounting changes should be disclosed (Vulcaansoord, 1977; KSH, 1979).
- the Enterprise Chamber will not substitute its judgment for that of the management board and the supervisory board in the estimation of the amounts of provisions (Sijthoff, 1979).

Burgert, writing in 1981, complained of the following deficiencies in the functioning of the Enterprise Chamber:

1. The flexibility of the process is hampered by the excessive length of the proceedings.
2. Owing to the fact that the court can render verdicts only on the cases brought before it, too little progress has been made in the formulation of "accounting standards" that can be authoritatively applied to circumstances beyond the facts of a particular case.
3. Leaving the initiative to "interested parties" has proven to be ineffective, since

[111] *Bijlagen Handelingen Tweede Kamer, Zitting 1967–1968*, no. 3, p. 14.

few such parties have a sufficient intensity of interest to institute an uncertain and costly judicial proceeding.

4. It is not clear that the granting of status as "interested party" has succeeded in balancing the interests of claimants against the interests of the companies (e.g., taking into account the cost of the proceeding and possible negative publicity).[112]

Burgert recommended the creation of a "small companies commission" ("*klein vennootschapskamertje*") that would examine the financial statements of listed companies and would be authorized to initiate court proceedings as a claimant.[113]

Burgert's comments seem not to have lost any of their force ten years later, especially with the departure of SOBI as an active plaintiff. After 20 years of experience, there would seem to be ample justification for a rethinking of the role and function of the Enterprise Chamber.

6.3.6. A question for the 1990's

The uncertainty with which the 1980's began had, by the beginning of the 1990's, dissolved. The business community had weathered the adaptation of the law to both the Fourth and Seventh Directives, the Enterprise Chamber had lost much of its momentum, and the pace and frequency with which the RJ had been issuing Guidelines embodying "affirmative pronouncements" had slowed. The threat of regulation so palpable a decade earlier had clearly receded. A question that remained was, to what extent would the RJ continue to be a force in the improvement of financial reporting?

---

[112] Prof.drs R. Burgert, *Tien jaar wet en rechtspraak omtrent de jaarrekening voor ondernemingen*, Afscheidscollege (Valedictory Lecture), 21 May 1981 (Erasmus Universiteit Rotterdam), pp. 13, 15.

[113] *Ibid.*, pp. 15–17.

7. Comparisons with other countries: National culture, capital market and the legal system and regulatory environment

Meaningful comparisons between the steps taken by different countries to improve company financial reporting are potentially fraught with difficulties unless one takes account of a number of important variables: national culture, the capital market, and the legal system and regulatory environment. In this chapter, we undertake a comparison of the Netherlands with the United States and the United Kingdom, with due attention to these variables.[1]

7.1. Differences in national culture

Discussions of national culture are inevitably intertwined with demographic, social, political, economic and legal considerations.[2] At a high level of generality, there are degrees of reciprocal interactions among all of these factors. The following observations and comments are based on the authors' experiences and observations in the three countries being compared, as well as on relevant writings in the literature.

While the Dutch live in a society in which laws and rules, sometimes in excruciating detail, govern the conduct of individuals and groups, and while they

[1] The discussion will be confined to the financial reporting by profit-seeking enterprise, and will exclude banks and insurance companies.

[2] For discussions of the relevance of national culture to accounting, see Barry E. Cushing (editor), *Accounting and Culture* (Sarasota, FL: American Accounting Association, 1987); S.J. Gray, "Towards a Theory of Cultural Influence on the Development of Accounting Systems Internationally", in *Abacus*, vol. 24, no. 1, March 1988, p. 1–15; M.H.B. Perera, "Towards a Framework to Analyze the Impact of Culture on Accounting", in *The International Journal of Accounting*, vol. 24, no. 1, 1989, pp. 42–56; Robert Bloom and M.A. Naciri, "Accounting Standard Setting and Culture: A Comparative Analysis of the United States, Canada, England, Germany, Australia, New Zealand, Sweden, Japan and Switzerland", in *The International Journal of Accounting*, vol. 24, no. 1, 1989, pp. 70–97; and Gerhard G. Mueller, "Is Accounting Culturally Determined?", paper presented at the EIASM Workshop on Accounting and Culture, June 1985, Amsterdam. For a study of how culture influences the system of corporate reporting regulation in Japan, see Graeme L. Harrison and Jill L. McKinnon, "Culture and Accounting Change: A New Perspective on Corporate Reporting Regulation and Accounting Policy Formulation", in *Accounting, Organizations and Society*, vol. 11, no. 3, 1986, pp. 233–252.

will ordinarily obey these laws and rules, the Dutch nonetheless do not welcome instruments that are created to ensure their compliance. Heavy-handed approaches to securing conformity with laws and rules will be met with opposition. A specific example will be instructive. In the 1960's, a judicial body was preferred to an administrative agency as a means of securing compliance with the Act on Annual Financial Statements, which was approved in 1970. There were, to be sure, legal arguments in support of the choice, but it also could have been expected that a court, which would act only on the initiative of plaintiffs, would be significantly less rigorous a regulator than an agency modeled on the US Securities and Exchange Commission.

Related to the preceding point is the perception that the Netherlands is more a collection of overlapping communities than an impersonal national population. The Netherlands is a small country having a high population density. Much of the country's infrastructure and some 40 percent of its citizens are located in the region delimited by Amsterdam, The Hague, Rotterdam, and Utrecht, known as the *Randstad*, which occupies about 16 percent of the land-space. The securities market is in Amsterdam. In the United States, by contrast, even though the most important securities market is situated in New York, significant markets and major decision-making centers are located in all parts of the sprawling country of 250 million people. In the UK the core of the securities market is in London, although major decision-making centers are to be found in such dispersed cities as Birmingham, Manchester, Leeds, Glasgow, and Edinburgh, among others. Prior to the late 1970's, the London capital market still depended on personal relationships and gentlemen's agreements made within the square mile of the City. This is much less true today than it once was.[3] In London, as well as in New York, many of the major figures in finance and business are not well acquainted with each other. The Netherlands is more like the UK of the pre-1970's. Moreover, the Dutch business community is smaller and more compact. Many of the members of supervisory boards of most of the large companies are known to each other, as quite a number of members belong to the boards of several companies and are on the management board of another. While this network is not as intimately connected as it was 20 to 25 years ago, much of it still remains. The late Allard Jiskoot, then the chairman of the Foundation to Oversee Securities Trading (Stichting Toezicht Effectenverkeer), has said, "We [the Dutch entrepreneurial class] live in a small world where everybody knows everyone else and who is friends with who or was at school with who".[4] The

[3] See Paul J. Rutteman, "A Comparative View of Accounting Regulations", in Robert H. Mundheim and Noyes E. Leech (editors), *The SEC and Accounting: The First 50 Years*, 1984 Proceedings of the Arthur Young Professors' Roundtable (Amsterdam: North-Holland, 1986), p. 96.

[4] As quoted in David Barchard, "Regulation: New powers on the way", in *Financial Times*, 12 June 1990, Section III: "European Finance and Investment – The Netherlands", p. VI.

following remark was made by the audit firm of Coopers & Lybrand in a study recently undertaken for the UK's Department of Trade and Industry:

> The small size of Dutch business society enhances social cohesion and tends to ensure that the main decision makers remain influential.[5]

The securities market is dominated by a small number of commercial banks, merchant banks, and institutional investors whose executives are, for the most part, known to one another. Auditors are also a cohesive community, as a result of contacts made (1) on committees and at conferences of the NIvRA, and (2) through their lecturing and examining at the six universities and at the NIvRA, where students are educated to become *registeraccountants*. It may not be too much of an exaggeration to characterize the Netherlands as a nation of insiders.

There are also important differences among the three countries in the way in which groups make decisions. Prof.dr G. Hofstede's empirical research has shown that the Dutch score very differently than the Americans and the British on the "Masculinity–Femininity" scale.[6] Americans and British rank as quite masculine, while the Dutch are decidedly feminine. In a masculine society, writes Hofstede, "it is important to be assertive, to perform, to achieve something visible, to make money, the public hero is the successful achiever and conflicts are resolved by fighting. In a feminine society, it is important to be modest, not to pretend to be better than someone else ... ; in this society success is suspect and the public hero is the underdog, and conflicts are resolved by negotiation".[7] Shetter writes that "Individual aggressiveness and open expression of emotion [in committees] is not highly valued, but high value is placed on group solidarity".[8]

Americans are more adversarial and confrontational. This applies also to the behavior of their standard-setting bodies, which duly report written dissents and even, during the period 1939–73, written qualified assents. By contrast, the UK's Accounting Standards Committee (ASC)[9] has never announced the tally of votes on its statements, let alone published dissenting opinions. Americans are more

---

[5] *Barriers to Takeovers in the European Community*, A Study by Coopers & Lybrand for the DTI (London: Her Majesty's Stationery Office, 1989), vol. 2, The Netherlands: p. 20.

[6] Geert Hofstede, "American and Dutch Business Cultures – Similarities and Differences", in P. Sanders and J.N. Yanouzas (editors), *Managing in a Global Economy* (Hogeschool Tilburg, June 1985), pp. 11–14. The British score slightly higher on masculinity than do the Americans. See Geert Hofstede, *Culture's Consequences: International Differences in Work-Related Values*, abridged edition (Beverly Hills, CA: Sage Publications, 1984), p. 189.

[7] Hofstede, "American and Dutch Business Cultures", *op. cit.*, p. 14. Medievalist Herman Ploij writes that "the Netherlands prunes anyone who threatens to turn into something of a hero". Herman Pleij, "Culture in a Land of Anti-Heroes", in *International Herald Tribune*, 30 May 1991: The Netherlands/A Special Report, p. II.

[8] William Z. Shetter, *The Netherlands in Perspective: The Organizations of Society and Environment* (Leiden: Martinus Nijhoff, 1987), p. 123.

[9] From 1970 to 1976, the committee was known as the Accounting Standards Steering Committee, and from 1976 to 1990 as the Accounting Standards Committee. To simplify references to the committee, the latter name will be used throughout.

disputatious, while the Dutch prefer a course of consensus and compromise. In this context, the policy of the Tripartite Study Group (TO, Tripartiete overleg) and the Council on Annual Reporting (RJ, Raad voor de Jaarverslaggeving) of not issuing a statement without the unanimous assent of their three delegations can be understood. A certain modesty can be detected in the committees' choice of terminology to describe their statements: Considered Views (*Beschouwingen*) from 1971 to 1979, and Guidelines (*Richtlijnen*) since 1980. These are "soft" terms, being less forceful than such terms as "Recommendations" or "Standards". The committees are aware that their statements need not be heeded by companies or auditors, and they understandably do not wish to overplay their hands.

The lesser degree of outward aggressiveness in Dutch society can also be seen in the behavior of the financial press. Criticisms do appear in the press, but they tend to be couched in more cautious and polite language than is customarily seen in the USA and the UK. In line with the foregoing observation about the Dutch aversion to self-promotion, stronger criticism is more likely to be reserved for those who depart from normal behavior than for those exhibiting proper conduct.

The Dutch are inclined to be more secretive about the workings of their institutions than is the case in the USA and even in the UK. Shetter mentions the tendency of the Dutch to "maintain a discreet public reserve".[10] Specifically, there is less openness of process in the Netherlands than in the USA. In the mid-1960's, the US's Accounting Principles Board (APB) began to meet with interested organizations, and in 1969 started holding symposia, and then public hearings in order to obtain informed comment on their drafts. The rules of the Financial Accounting Standards Board (FASB) require it to hold public hearings on all important projects, and on some especially controversial topics it has held more than one public hearing. The transcripts of the hearings are offered for sale to the public. Since 1977, the FASB has conducted all of its deliberations "in the sunshine", which means that all meetings of the Board, save for discussions of purely administrative matters, are announced in advance and are open to the public. From 1979 to 1981, the UK's ASC experimented with public hearings, but the practice was not continued.[11] Since its formation in 1970, the ASC met

---

[10] *Ibid.*, p. 124.

[11] The ASC held public hearings in 1979 on its self-study and on ED's 25 and 27. See *Setting Accounting Standards*, Report and Recommendations by the Accounting Standards Committee (Accounting Standards Committee, 1981), pp. 3, 12 (even though it was stated on p. 30 that "public hearings have now become an established pattern", they were not continued after Chairman T.R. Watts retired in 1982); "ED 25 public hearing proves its worth", in *Accountancy*, vol. 91, no. 1042, June 1980, p. 20; and "Public hearings on ED 27", in *Accountancy*, vol. 92, no. 1050, February 1981, p. 19. While the press reports were upbeat, disappointingly few interested parties came forward to present their views at the public hearings. Also see T.R. Watts, "Planning the Next Decade", in Sir Ronald Leach and Professor Edward Stamp (ed-

in "plenary session" with interested organizations, which eventually were constituted as its "consultative group".[12] None of the meetings of the ASC or of the current Accounting Standards Board (ASB) and Review Panel are open to the public.[13] The distribution of exposure drafts of proposed pronouncements dates from the 1940's in the USA and from 1970 in the UK.[14] One measure of the contrast between US and UK attitudes toward secrecy of process is captured by the titles of legislation that governs access to confidential government documents: in the United States, the Freedom of Information Act; in the United Kingdom, the Official Secrets Act.

In the Netherlands, all meetings of the TO and the RJ have been held in private, and no consultations have been held with interested organizations on proposed exposure drafts and statements.[15] While the TO began issuing exposure drafts in 1971, letters of comment received in reply to the drafts have not been available for inspection by interested parties. In the USA and the UK, the letters of comment have been publicly available. One could argue that secrecy of process is more consistent than openness with solving conflicts by negotiation. A public airing of disagreements could well encourage a hardening of positions rather than a drive for consensus.

The dual responsibility of private enterprise both to shareholders and employees has occupied a position of much greater importance in the Netherlands than in the United States, although the US position has been changing to take into account the interests of a broader range of parties.[16] Nonetheless, in the USA,

---

itors), *British Accounting Standards: The First 10 Years* (Cambridge: Woodhead-Faulkner, 1981), pp. 30–31, for a discussion of Watts's views on "due process".

[12] Stephen A. Zeff, *Forging Accounting Principles in Five Countries: A History and an Analysis of Trends* (Champaign, IL: Stipes Publishing Co., 1972), pp. 41, 46; and *Setting Accounting Standards*, *op. cit.*, p. 30.

[13] Owing to the public law responsibilities that have been assumed by the Institute of Chartered Accountants in England and Wales, it recently set up a working party to consider the opening up of its working procedures to the public. See "Sun to shine on Institute's work", in *Accountancy*, vol. 108, no. 1177, September 1991, p. 11. Since, as is suggested below, the ASB and the Review Panel have, in effect, been given self-regulatory powers over accounting standards, it is conceivable that their meetings might one day be held "in the sunshine".

[14] Zeff, *op. cit.*, pp. 39, 144–145.

[15] An exception has occurred in the case of regulated industries, such as banking and insurance, where the RJ has consulted De Nederlandsche Bank and a specialist commission on insurance company reporting.

An unusual collective consultation occurred in 1990–91, when the RJ sought the views of ten professors on the issue of the accounting treatment of intangibles. The consultation was conducted by correspondence. See the section, "The RJ reacts to the non-amortization of publishing rights", in Chapter 6.

[16] In the last decade or so, partially as a result of state laws of an anti-takeover nature, some 28 states have passed so-called "other constituency" statutes. Under these laws, directors, when acting in the best interests of the corporation, may take into consideration the interests of a variety of constituencies other than shareholders, including employees, the communities in which the corporation's facilities are located, customers and suppliers. See Charles Hansen, "Other Constituency Statutes: A Search for Perspective", in *The Business Lawyer*, vol. 46,

for most purposes, the stakeholder *par excellence* has been the shareholder. In the UK, the definition of the interested parties in enterprise has been somewhat broader, often seeming to fluctuate according to whether Labour or the Conservatives are in government, a phenomenon that is unknown in the Netherlands. The decision-making hierarchy within Dutch companies – the management board, supervisory board, and works council – is intended to balance shareholder and employee interests, both being stakeholders. Somewhat more than a decade ago, Stamp discussed the difference in stakeholders as between the USA and Europe. In judging his remarks, one must take cognizance of the fact that he was an influential member of the ASC's working party that produced *The Corporate Report*, a discussion paper that emphasized employee interests in company financial reports. The discussion paper was issued in 1975, during the incumbency of a Labour Government. Stamp wrote,

> American standard setters are preoccupied with the needs of investors: in Europe we are more accustomed to thinking of a much wider constituency of users of published financial reports. For this reason alone the nature of the consensus that must be obtained if standards are to be generally acceptable to users will be different in Europe than it is in the United States.[17]

In large Dutch companies, shareholders are not entitled to choose the members of the supervisory board or of the management board[18], a circumstance that would be unthinkable in the USA and the UK with respect to the board of directors. The supervisory board has the legal obligation to act in the interests of the company as a whole: the interests of the company are, by law, not congruent with the interests of the shareholders alone. By the same token, employers and employees have, especially since World War II, participated as social partners in the major decisions relating to the government's social and economic policies and related legislation. The Social and Economic Council was established in 1950 as the principal vehicle for this cooperation. The ferment of the 1950's and 1960's that led to passage of the first modern Dutch companies legislation in 1970 (and also to the Act on Works Councils of 1971) was motivated by the desire to democratize industry from the standpoint of employees and the public. In view of that history, it was no surprise that the Justice Minister's suggestion in 1968 that "organized business" and the organization of auditors should take an inventory of accounting valuation principles that were "considered to be acceptable in economic and social life" led to the founding of a tripartite committee composed of employers, employees and auditors. In 1982, the employees delegation was

no. 4, August 1991, pp. 1355–1376. The authors are grateful to William P. Hackney for alerting them to this article.

[17] Edward Stamp, "A View from Academe", in Leach and Stamp, *op. cit.*, pp. 240–241.

[18] See the section on "Company organization" in Chapter 1 for a discussion of shareholders' rights in choosing members of the supervisory board.

renamed "users delegation", even though the trade unions continued to appoint its members. A financial analyst, representing the interests of investors, was not appointed to the body until 1986.

In the USA, while trade unions have sometimes played a role in movements to amend corporation laws, they have rarely participated in initiatives to improve corporate financial reporting. While, in the UK, employee interests in company financial reporting were addressed in *The Corporate Report*, as mentioned above, employee considerations were never integral to the discussions within the ASC, and employee representatives were never members of the ASC.[19] For a period beginning in 1976, however, the Trades Union Congress (TUC) was represented on the ASC's consultative group.[20] Currently, there is one representative of employees on the 26-member Financial Reporting Council,[21] which oversees the work of the ASB, but none on the ASB itself. It would be fair to say that, in the UK, there has not been much employee interest in standard setting, and the standard setters have done little to stimulate that interest. In this regard, in the Netherlands a greater interest has been evinced in the broad implications of private enterprise, i.e., in the usefulness of financial reporting to the wider community, than has been evident in either the USA or the UK.

A cultural issue that has political and economic dimensions is the long-standing tendency of the Dutch to look outward, and especially overseas. The Dutch economy has always been heavily dependent on export markets, requiring that the country's leaders be sensitive to economic, political and social developments abroad. At the same time, the Netherlands is a small country virtually surrounded by large and politically dominant neighbors. To be effective in international affairs, in capital markets as well as in the markets for goods and services, the Dutch must speak other languages and be attuned to incipient developments. English is an obligatory language in Dutch secondary schools, with four to six years of study required, depending on the kind of school. Many Dutch speak German and French, and a facility with other languages is not uncommon. The Dutch, therefore, are able to read other countries' media and professional literatures, and to participate in international congresses. Their own literature in accounting has, for many years, reflected a keen awareness of developments in the UK and the USA. That several Dutch multinationals are traded in New York has made the Dutch even more aware of US financial reporting standards. But the outside world knows little about the Dutch. Few who are not them-

---

19 Indeed, the ASC ignored *The Corporate Report* in its deliberations.

20 See "ASC Enlarges its Consultative Group", in *The Accountant's Magazine*, vol. 80, no. 842, August 1976, p. 285. It should also be noted that the TUC gave evidence before the Cohen Committee on Company Law Amendment in 1943–44. See Ian C. Stewart, "The Ethics of Disclosure in Company Financial Reporting in the United Kingdom 1925–1970", in *The Accounting Historians Journal*, vol. 18, no. 1, June 1991, p. 43.

21 The employee representative is the general secretary of the Banking, Insurance and Finance Union.

selves Dutch can read the Dutch language. They are therefore precluded from reading Dutch journals and books, and both the print and electronic media are also out of reach. About all that is known overseas about Dutch accounting is the Limpergian theory of current cost accounting and its use by Philips, and the Enterprise Chamber.[22] Much of this knowledge has been learned from Dutchmen who have written articles or books in English. Hence, few from outside the country have been in a position to study and evaluate the Dutch way of doing things, and there has not been a two-way dialogue between the Dutch and students of financial reporting in other countries concerning the evolution of Dutch financial reporting. This circumstance has led to the lack of informed and critical comment by professionals and academics in other countries on Dutch accounting developments. As in other aspects of Dutch society, the Dutch language shields the country from inquiry.

7.2. Differences in capital markets

The demands emanating from capital markets have provided much of the incentive for companies to improve their financial reporting. There are great differences between the Amsterdam capital market and those of New York and London, in scale and vitality. Both the New York and London capital markets are world-class in terms of size and importance, while the Amsterdam capital market has had only a modest impact. On the European Continent, the exchanges (or groups of exchanges) in Germany, Zürich, Paris, Vienna, Basel, and Italy all had a higher dollar-value of turnover in 1990 than did the Amsterdam Stock Exchange.[23] Furthermore, the Amsterdam exchange is not important from the standpoint of new equity issues. Companies go to other markets when raising new equity capital, borrow from their "house banks", or finance their operations via retained earnings.

One manifestation of the broad community interest in company welfare are the high barriers to unfriendly takeovers, as if to emphasize the point that ownership interest is only one of many interests in enterprise performance. In a 1989 study of the European takeover market, it was stated, "Until recently, contested takeover bids were virtually unheard of [in the Netherlands]. Such bids do now occur, but none have succeeded yet".[24] (Since publication of the study, one contested takeover bid has succeeded.) It has been reported that the Amsterdam Stock

[22] As in earlier chapters, "current cost" (rather than "replacement value") is used to translate "*vervangingswaarde*", while "current value" is used to translate "*actuele waarde*". The authors regard "current cost" as being more in line with international usage than "replacement value".
[23] *F.I.B.V. Statistics 1990* (Paris: Fédération Internationale des Bourses de Valeurs, [1991]), Table 1.4.B, p. 20.
[24] *Barriers to Takeovers in the European Community*, *op. cit.*, vol. 2, The Netherlands: p. 21.

Exchange "has long believed that excessive takeover protection depresses Dutch share prices and makes for an imperfect market".[25]

A considerable difference exists in the degree of market penetration among individual investors. According to the New York Stock Exchange's 1990 survey of shareholders, 21.1 percent of Americans are owners of shares.[26] A survey sponsored jointly by the London Stock Exchange and HM Treasury (the SE/HMT survey) in early 1991 found that 11 million people, or about 19 percent of Britons, are shareholders.[27] The doubling in the number of individual shareholders in the UK during the last five years has been driven primarily by the large Government privatizations and the free distribution of Abbey National shares. In the Netherlands, the most recent studies show that between 4 and 6 percent of individuals hold shares.[28] An important reason why a smaller fraction of Dutch individuals are shareholders is the very large contribution that Dutch households make to contractual pension plans, leaving relatively little for free savings.[29] This disparity of participation by individuals in the New York, London and Amsterdam share markets may well influence the degree of interest by the respective stock exchanges in encouraging listed companies to communicate comparable financial information to a wide and diverse readership.[30]

There are also major differences in the comparative development of the three countries' financial communities. In the United States, investment bankers and financial analysts have been organized and active for many decades. The Investment Bankers Association was founded in 1912[31], the *Financial Analysts Journal* was launched in 1945, and the Financial Analysts Federation has traced its history to 1947, although there was an analysts society in New York in the 1920's.[32]

---

[25] Ronald van de Krol, "EC plans erode Dutch defenses", in *Financial Times*, 4 September 1991: "European Finance and Investment – Part 8, The Netherlands", p. 14 (p. 4 of the section).

[26] *Shareownership 1990* (New York: New York Stock Exchange, 1990), p. 10.

[27] "The Current State of Share Ownership", *Quality of Markets Review*, Summer 1991, p. 19.

[28] See the section, "Aspects of the economy and the capital market", in Chapter 1. By way of comparison, it is interesting to note that the first survey carried out by the New York Stock Exchange, in 1952, showed that "barely 4.2% of the population [was] in stock ownership". *Shareownership 1990*, *op. cit.*, p. 7.

[29] Rietkerk refers to the "institutionalization of the management of savings" ("*institutionalisering van het beheer van spaargelden*"), and presents figures to show how large a portion of family savings are dedicated to contractual pension plans. See Dr G. Rietkerk, *Onderneming en vermogensmarkt* (Leiden/Antwerpen: Stenfert Kroese Uitgevers, 1991), pp. 40–42.

It is estimated that pension funds in the Netherlands make up 40 percent of all pension funds in the EC, which gives some indication of the mammoth accumulation of such funds in one small country. See *Barriers to Takeovers in the European Community*, *op. cit.*, vol. 2, The Netherlands: p. 5.

[30] Of some interest is the fact that surveys of the number of individual shareholders are conducted annually in the USA and the UK, but only every five years in the Netherlands.

[31] See David F. Hawkins, *Corporate Financial Disclosure, 1900–1933* (New York: Garland Publishing, Inc., 1986; a doctoral dissertation completed in 1962), p. 168.

[32] See Mildred M. Hermann, "Looking Back – Looking Forward 35 Years for the FAF", in *Financial Analysts Journal*, vol. 38, no. 4, July/August 1982, pp. 15, 17.

A program for chartering financial analysts was launched in the early 1960's.[33] The UK's Society of Investment Analysts was founded in 1955. By contrast, Dutch financial analysts organized in 1961, but it has been only since the late 1970's that they have become professionally dedicated to investment analysis. The Society of Financial Analysts started a journal in 1985.[34]

The scale of the US and UK financial communities, coupled with their active interest in the role played by accounting in investment analysis, is evidenced by the fact that analysts issue (or have issued) several newsletters that deal exclusively with accounting matters. In the USA, there are at least three newsletters regularly published by financial analysts on accounting matters: The *Quality of Earnings Report*, *Accounting Issues* (issued by Bear Stearns, an investment house), and the *Accounting Bulletin* (issued by Merrill Lynch, formerly by Drexel Burnham Lambert). The author of the *Quality of Earnings Report* recently wrote a book on creative accounting.[35] In the UK, Phillips & Drew (the stockbrokers) issued a periodic report entitled "Accounting Research" from the mid-1970's to the early 1980's, mostly on inflation accounting. From 1975 to the early 1980's, de Zoete & Bevan (another brokerage firm) issued a series of reports and analyses on inflation accounting. The authors of both of the firms' reports were chartered accountants. No comparable literature has existed in the Netherlands.

Especially since the 1960's, the US financial press has covered accounting and financial reporting issues with regularity and often with acuity.[36] *Fortune*, *Forbes*, *Business Week*, *The Wall Street Journal*, and *The New York Times* all carry reports on developments in accounting, including controversies over the standard-setting process.[37] For some years, *The Wall Street Journal* and *The New York Times* have each had a journalist who specializes on accounting reportage. Since 1968, *Barron's* has run critical articles on companies' financial reporting practices by Prof. Abraham J. Briloff.[38] On such recent subjects as deferred tax accounting and accounting for other post-employment benefits, the press coverage has been considerable.[39] In 1987, a specialist, biweekly newspaper, *Accounting Today*, began to cover developments in the profession. Even in the much smaller Canadian market, a monthly newspaper, *The Bottom Line*, has

---

33 *Ibid.*, p. 4.

34 See the section, "Aspects of the economy and the capital market", in Chapter 1.

35 Thornton L. O'glove, with Robert Sobel, *Quality of Earnings: The Investor's Guide To How Much Money A Company is Really Making* (New York: The Free Press, 1987).

36 For references to the active coverage by the US financial press in the 1960's, see Zeff, *op. cit.*, pp. 186–191, 212–216 and 221.

37 In almost every issue of *Forbes* an article appears under the title, "The Numbers Game", in which a current issue in financial reporting is discussed.

38 For the list of Briloff's 21 articles in *Barron's* through mid-1984, see George Foster, "Rambo IX: Briloff and the Capital Market", in *Journal of Accounting, Auditing and Finance*, vol. 2, no. 4 (new series), Fall 1987, p. 410.

39 See, e.g., Carol J. Loomis, "Will 'FASBEE' Pinch Your Bottom Line?", in *Fortune*, vol. 118, no. 14, 19 December 1988, p. 93 ff.

specialized in reporting financial and accounting news since 1985.

In the UK, the scrutiny of accounting by the financial press has intensified since the late 1960's, principally as a result of the publicity given to several contested takeovers.[40] The *Financial Times*, *The Independent*, and *The Times*, as well as other dailies, cover newsworthy developments in accounting, including exposure drafts and final statements of the standard-setting bodies. *The Economist* has, for decades, given considerable attention to accounting and auditing issues, and occasionally treats accounting in its leaders.[41] Until 1978, the weekly journal *The Accountant* ran a series of critical commentaries on companies' published financial reports. Similar commentaries have appeared in *Accountancy Age*, a weekly newspaper founded in 1969 (and which is published by the VNU Business Press Group), in addition to its extensive coverage of developments in accounting. As Seidler has written, "No similar regular scrutiny [of companies' financial reports] occurs in the United States".[42] In 1987, the financial editor of *The Independent* wrote a book on creative accounting.[43] When controversies arise concerning such matters as inflation accounting, merger v. acquisition accounting, and goodwill and brands, reports and editorials have appeared frequently in the press.

Also in the UK, in 1976 the *Financial Times* launched *World Accounting Report*, a monthly newsletter on international accounting developments, with Michael Lafferty, its banking and accounting correspondent, as editor. Seven years later, Lafferty left the *Financial Times* and began a series of monthly accounting newsletters, including *International Accounting Bulletin* (since 1983) and *Corporate Accounting International* (since 1989). *European Accounting Focus*, another monthly newsletter, was begun in 1989 by West London Publishing Limited.

In the Netherlands, *Het Financieele Dagblad* is the only newspaper that can be counted on to cover important accounting issues. Since 1955, it has stimulated interest in better financial reporting by offering the annual Sijthoff Prizes. Following each year's ceremony, the critical views of the judging panel are fully reported. No newspaper has reported the exposure drafts or final statements issued by the TO and the RJ with any degree of regularity. However, decisions

---

[40] For references to the active coverage by the UK financial press in the late 1960's, see Zeff, *op. cit.*, pp. 34–37 and 44–45; and for discussion of the evolving role of the press during the 1960's and early 1970's, see *op. cit.*, pp. 62–65.

[41] Indeed, *The Economist* gave testimony to the Cohen Committee on company law amendment in 1943–44. See Leonard W. Hein, *The British Companies Acts and the Practice of Accountancy 1844–1962* (New York: Arno Press, 1978), pp. 261–265, 269.

[42] Lee J. Seidler, "A Comparison of the Economic and Social Status of the Accountancy Profession in Great Britain and the United States of America", in *The Accountant's Magazine*, vol. 73, no. 759, September 1969, p. 494.

[43] Ian Griffiths, *Creative Accounting: How to make your profits what you want them to be* (London: Sidgwick and Jackson, 1986). Two years later, an accountant with a large international company wrote a book along the same line: Michael Jameson, *A Practical Guide to Creative Accounting* (London: Kogan Page, 1988).

handed down by the Enterprise Chamber have typically received considerable attention.

FEM, a financial magazine, has shown an interest in accounting issues. In 1988, R. Nods and Drs P.A. Wieringa, journalists at *FEM*, wrote a lively book, *Wat zeggen de cijfers?*, on financial reporting and financial analysis, in which they complained about "conservative or creative accounting".[44] In recent years more space has been devoted in the press to economic and financial commentary, and there has been more criticism of company financial reporting than in the 1970's.[45] Nonetheless, the extent of coverage, level of criticism and depth of analysis are not comparable to what is seen in the USA and the UK.

In the period from the late 1940's to the late 1960's, there was much more critical reportage about companies' financial reporting in the Netherlands, because the standard was generally low and there was a much greater variation among companies. Since the standard was raised as a result of passage of the Act on Annual Financial Statements of 1970 and the adaptation of the law to the Fourth Directive of the European Economic Community (EEC), company annual reports have adhered to a higher general standard of disclosure and format. Apparently as a consequence, the incidence of critical articles about accounting has declined, even though controversies have flared up on such issues as accounting for the WIR premium, changes in accounting principles, and accounting for publishing rights.

7.3. Differences in legal systems and regulatory environments

As between the Netherlands, on the one hand, and the USA and the UK, on the other, there has been a considerable difference in legal tradition. The Netherlands is a unitary civil code country. The UK is a unitary common law country (as regards company law), while the USA adheres to the common law tradition within a federal framework.

7.3.1. United States

In the USA, the state legislatures enact corporation laws and the Congress approves securities legislation applicable to interstate commerce.[46] Since the states compete with one another in "a race to the bottom" to be seen as the most attractive domicile for corporations, their laws have been very lax in requiring corporations to furnish financial statements or retain external auditors. Even

44 (Utrecht/Antwerpen: A.W. Bruna Uitgevers BV, 1988), pp. 18–20.
45 Interviews with P. van Bakkum, 3 October 1990, and with R. Nods, 13 November 1990.
46 An exception is that national banks are incorporated under Federal statutes.

today, few states have effective requirements in this area.[47] Prior to the 1930's, a number of states passed securities laws, known as "blue sky laws", applicable to their respective jurisdictions, but "Because of inadequate administration or inadequate coverage, they were ineffective to stem the tide of securities frauds that gave rise to federal securities legislation".[48] Hence, in the early 1930's, when it was felt necessary to reestablish investor confidence in the securities markets following the Stock Market Crash, Congress passed the Securities Act of 1933 and the Securities Exchange Act of 1934, the latter creating the Securities and Exchange Commission (SEC). The first law introduced a system of mandatory affirmative disclosure to prospective investors concerning securities offered for sale. The second law established a continuous disclosure system applicable to securities listed on national securities exchanges (such as the New York Stock Exchange), securities traded in the over-the-counter market (chiefly NASDAQ[49]), and corporations that have issued securities in interstate markets and that have met certain size tests.[50] Those enactments represented the first effective regulation of financial reporting, other than for specialized industries.[51] The SEC fits in with the US tradition of entrusting the regulation of vital industries or functions of national importance to independent commissions with large and competent technical staffs, which are endowed with substantial authority to issue rules and

---

[47] It was not until 1979 that the Model Business Corporation Act was amended to provide that corporations should furnish shareholders with annual financial statements, including a reconcilliation of shareholders' equity. But the use of generally accepted accounting principles was not prescribed, nor was a requirement imposed that the financial statements be audited. By November 1990, only nine states had enacted legislation mandating that corporations furnish shareholders with annual financial statements: Alabama, Alaska, Arkansas, Connecticut, Florida, Georgia, Michigan, Mississippi and South Carolina. Most other states require that corporations furnish such statements only upon written request. See *Model Business Corporation Act Annotated*, third edition (Englewood Cliffs, NJ: Prentice Hall Law & Business), vol. 4, Sec. 16.20: 1987 supplement, pp. 1767–1770; 1991 supplement, pp. 1773–1774. US corporations not subject to the jurisdiction of the Securities and Exchange Commission are not required to publish or file their annual financial statements.

[48] Jesse H. Choper, John C. Coffee, Jr., and C. Robert Morris, Jr., *Cases and Materials on Corporations* (Boston: Little, Brown and Company, 1989), p. 347.

[49] NASDAQ is the National Association of Securities Dealers Automated Quotation System, which was introduced in 1971 to computerize the over-the-counter market.

[50] US federal securities legislation provides also for the regulation of broker-dealers, investment companies, investment advisers, public utility holding companies, and stock exchanges. The discussion in this chapter will refer only to the regulation of financial information disseminated by corporations whose securities are subject to the jurisdiction of the SEC.

[51] Prior to then, all states had passed legislation regulating the rates that may be charged to the customers of electric and gas public utility companies, predicated on a "fair rate of return" to shareholders. The companies' financial statements have had to be prepared in accordance with stipulated rules for the purpose of developing a politically acceptable measure of the rate of return. At the federal level, legislation establishing such regulatory commissions as the Interstate Commerce Commission and the Federal Power Commission (superseded in 1977 by the Federal Energy Regulatory Commission) has authorized the commissions to prescribe the measurement rules to be used in the financial statements filed under those laws.

orders without application to the courts.

US state corporation laws, like their counterparts at the national level in the UK and the Netherlands, are applicable to all corporations (or companies) domiciled in their respective jurisdictions.[52] But Congressional securities legislation pertains only to the trading of securities as described above. Currently, approximately 11 000 corporations come under the SEC's jurisdiction, although it is estimated that more than 2.75 million corporations are subject to one or another state corporation law.

During its more than 55 years of operation, the SEC has been a rigorous regulator of the US securities market. It has been especially vigilant concerning corporations' financial disclosures. In the area of accounting principles, the SEC had, until 1973, relied primarily on the Committee on Accounting Procedure (CAP) (1939–1959) and the APB (1959–1973), which were senior technical committees of the American Institute of [Certified Public] Accountants (AICPA), for "substantial authoritative support" of what constitutes "generally accepted accounting principles". In 1973, upon the establishment of the independent FASB, the SEC announced its policy that "principles, standards and practices promulgated by the FASB in its Statements and Interpretations will be considered by the Commission as having substantial authoritative support, and those contrary to such FASB promulgations will be considered to have no such support".[53] The term "generally accepted accounting principles" (GAAP) was coined in the 1930's as the Institute's code phrase for proper accounting practice, and the SEC soon came to refer to the term in its own releases and in the speeches of the Commission's members and staff. Even though the word "accepted" is included in the phrase, the intended meaning is "acceptable". The accounting principles and procedures must be accept*able* to the technical accounting body on which the SEC relies for "substantial authoritative support".

From the beginning, the SEC has operated on the premise that a narrower range of permitted practice is to be preferred over a broader range of alterna-

[52] State corporation laws are invoked to decide (1) accounting questions that are involved when determining the amount of a dividend that can be declared, and the extent to which share purchases or redemptions may be entered into, and (2) the interpretation to be placed on contracts that employ accounting concepts as part of a formula for determining the price of securities, or the amount of a profit-sharing distribution in an employment contract, among other such contracts.

[53] *Statement of Policy on the Establishment and Improvement of Accounting Principles and Standards*, Accounting Series Release no. 150 (20 December 1973). For discussions of the historical development of the SEC's policy on accounting principles, see Carman G. Blough, "Development of Accounting Principles in the United States", in *Berkeley Symposium on the Foundations of Financial Accounting* (Berkeley, CA: Schools of Business Administration, University of California, 1967), pp. 1–14; James F. Strother, "The Establishment of Generally Accepted Accounting Principles and Generally Accepted Auditing Standards", in *Vanderbilt Law Review*, vol. 28, no. 1, January 1975, pp. 201–233; and Zeff, *op. cit.*, pp. 129–221. For a critical view, see Homer Kripke, *The SEC and Corporate Disclosure: Regulation in Search of a Purpose* (New York: Law & Business, Inc./Harcourt Brace Jovanovich, Publishers, 1979).

tives. Comparability among the financial statements of different companies has always been important to the SEC, and it has believed that the fewest number of alternatives, together with a specification of how accounting principles are to be applied in the financial statements, is the best approach to promoting comparability. The SEC's strong preference for comparability was promptly transmitted to the CAP, which, at the SEC's behest, began issuing *Accounting Research Bulletins* in 1939 in order to provide the SEC with "substantial authoritative support" for proper practice. In its first *Bulletin*, the committee made the following observation:

> In the last forty years the outstanding change in the working of the corporate system has been an increasing use of it for the purpose of converting into liquid and readily transferable form the ownership of large, complex, and more or less permanent business enterprises. This development brought in its train certain uses of the processes of law and accounting, which have led to the creation of new controls, revisions of the law, and a reconsideration of accounting procedure.
>
> As a result of this development in the field of accounting, problems have come to be considered more from the standpoint of the current buyer or seller in the market of an interest in the enterprise than from the standpoint of a continuing owner.
>
> One manifestation of [this change] has been a demand for a larger degree of uniformity in accounting . . . .[54]

The CAP's membership consisted of auditors and accounting academics, and it had limited staff support. The membership of its successor, the APB, included CPA's who were financial executives and financial analysts, as well as the staple of auditors and accounting academics, and the APB had a full-time staff of about a half-dozen. Its primary mission to develop a broad conceptual basis for accounting principles foundered at an early stage. As a result, it functioned in much the same manner as the CAP, but it became subject to persistent SEC pressure to "narrow the areas of difference" in accounting practice, else the SEC might issue its own rules, a prospect that has never been welcomed by leaders of the accounting profession. In 1973, the FASB was formed under the aegis of an independent Financial Accounting Foundation, with sponsorship not only from the AICPA but also from organizations of management accountants, financial executives, financial analysts and accounting academics. Its seven members were full-time, and it was given a research and technical staff of more than forty. Its

54 "General Introduction and Rules Formerly Adopted", *Accounting Research Bulletins*, no. 1, September 1939, pp. 1–2. This theme was reiterated in 1953, when *Bulletin* no. 1 was revised and reissued. *Restatement and Revision of Accounting Research Bulletins* (New York: American Institute of Accountants, 1953), pp. 7–8. See Thomas F. Keller, "Uniformity Versus Flexibility: A Review of the Rhetoric", in *Law and Contemporary Problems*, vol. 30, no. 4, Autumn 1965, pp. 637–651; and Barbara D. Merino and Teddy L. Coe, "Uniformity in Accounting: A Historical Perspective", in *The Journal of Accountancy*, vol. 146, no. 2, August 1978, pp. 48–54.

current operating budget is about $14 million. Despite its broader base of support and greatly enhanced resources, the FASB has come under periodic pressure from both the SEC and industry, and on a few occasions the SEC has promulgated its own accounting rules.[55]

The SEC's unquenchable thirst for highly specific advice is, together with the high incidence of litigation in the USA, the most compelling explanation for the many and detailed statements that have been issued by the APB and the FASB. Another explanation is the increasingly sharp competition in capital markets during periods of intense merger activity, coupled with the growing commercialization of the major accounting firms, and their desire not to lose clients to firms with more lenient interpretations of how to apply GAAP.[56] This latter concern has been heightened by the tendency in the last 10 to 15 years for some clients to engage in "opinion shopping", in order to find more "client-friendly" firms. Hence, the accounting firms have, in recent years, welcomed detailed prescription as a measure of self-protection. The FASB's Emerging Issues Task Force, which was established in 1984, was therefore seen as an expeditious means for reconciling differences among firms' interpretations of GAAP.

The SEC has always believed that financial statements reflecting material departures from GAAP are inherently misleading, and any such departures must be rectified or explained before the corporation can remain in good standing with the Commission. The SEC ordinarily does not accept auditors' reports that contain references to a material departure from GAAP. Unless the departure is removed, with the corresponding changes made in the company's financial statements, the SEC will issue an order that trading in the corporation's securities is to be suspended, or that the corporation may not issue securities in interstate markets, penalties that few companies would contemplate with equanimity. An exception is made when, owing to unusual circumstances, the failure to depart from GAAP would result in misleading financial statements.

The reason for the SEC's aversion to departures from GAAP is not difficult to understand, at least in historical context. The SEC was founded in the depths of the Great Depression, when memories of the Stock Market Crash were

---

[55] For an extensive treatment of the FASB's operations, as well as a discussion of its trials and tribulations, see Paul B.W. Miller and Rodney J. Redding, *The FASB: The People, the Process, and the Politics* (Homewood, IL: Richard D. Irwin, Inc., 1988). For a policy-oriented study of the FASB, see David Solomons, *Making Accounting Policy: The Quest for Credibility in Financial Reporting* (New York: Oxford University Press, 1986).

The FASB's influence extends beyond corporations subject to the SEC's jurisdiction. Its standards are also applicable to other corporations that issue financial statements that are audited by independent accountants.

[56] See Stephen A. Zeff, "Recent Trends in Accounting Education and Research in the USA: Some Implications for UK Academics", in *The British Accounting Review*, vol. 21, June 1989, pp. 163–164; and Stephen A. Zeff, "Big Eight Firms and the Accounting Literature: The Falloff in Advocacy Writing", *Journal of Accounting, Auditing and Finance*, vol. 1, no. 2 (new series), June 1986, pp. 145–150.

still vivid in investors' minds, and there was a strong belief that the financial reports released by companies should reflect "full and fair disclosure" of information. Among some of the members and staff of the SEC during its first years, there was a haunting recollection of the free-and-easy 1920's, when large corporations would revalue their fixed assets (including intangibles) without any guiding methodology and, it was suspected, without having adduced any careful and systematic evidential support for the revaluations. Arbitrary revaluations and questionable accounting practices were found to be widespread in a number of the giant public utility holding companies during the 1920's. These practices, many believed, were calculated to mislead investors. A great many write-ups in the 1920's were written down following the Crash of October 1929,[57] raising questions about the credibility of corporations' accounting practices. This was the climate in which the SEC was founded, and leading figures in the Commission resolved not to repeat that embarrassing episode, with loose accounting practices and unlimited discretion given to corporate managements.[58] Primarily for this reason, the SEC has consistently opposed all departures from historical cost accounting in balance sheets and in the determination of net income. As conditions changed and new personnel joined the Commission's staff, this rigid policy eventually was relaxed to some degree in the 1970's, when the SEC required large corporations to display current cost information either in the notes or in a supplementary schedule to their financial statements, which, the Commission said, could be designated as "unaudited".[59]

Prior to the 1970's, the SEC also disallowed corporations from including projections and forecasts in their filings, since they were subjective and not susceptible to audit, and thus might be misleading to investors. But during 1973–74, under the leadership of Chief Accountant John C. Burton, the SEC not only lifted the ban on forecasts, it also began to require corporations to present a narrative statement of "Management's Discussion and Analysis of the Summary of Earnings" (MD&A), so that investors might come to appreciate some of the risks and uncertainties associated with a corporation's financial position and results of operations.[60] In 1980, the SEC amplified the scope of the MD&A requirement

---

[57] See Solomon Fabricant, *Capital Consumption and Adjustment* (New York: National Bureau of Economic Research, 1938) for an extensive study of the revaluations of corporate assets during the 1920's and 1930's.

[58] See Joel Seligman, *The Transformation of Wall Street: A History of the Securities and Exchange Commission and Modern Corporate Finance* (Boston: Houghton Mifflin Company, 1982), pp. 108, 113–117, 197–201.

[59] Securities and Exchange Commission, *Notice of Adoption of Amendments to Regulation S-X Requiring Disclosure of Certain Replacement Cost Data*, Accounting Series Release no. 190 (23 March 1976).

[60] See John C. Burton, "Forecasts: A Changing View from the Securities and Exchange Commission", in Prem Prakash and Alfred Rappaport (editors), *Public Reporting of Corporate Financial Forecasts* (Chicago: Commerce Clearing House, Inc., 1974), pp. 81–98; and Securities and Exchange Commission, *Notice of Adoption of Amendments to Guide 22 of the Guides*

to give more attention to future-oriented variables.[61]

In the 1970's, therefore, the SEC showed signs of placing less emphasis on assurances that the financial statements were not misleading, and more emphasis on their being informative. Nonetheless, the SEC's historic aversion to departures from GAAP has created a climate that has not been friendly to innovation in financial reporting.[62]

Certified public accountants are regulated under state law. The first such law was passed by New York State in 1896, and almost all states passed regulatory legislation by the end of the first quarter of the century. To become a CPA, an individual must pass the Uniform (national) CPA Examination and satisfy the education and experience requirements of his or her state or other jurisdiction.[63] Once an individual becomes licensed as a CPA in one jurisdiction, it is ordinarily not difficult to secure a reciprocal right to practice in other jurisdictions. In each jurisdiction, CPA's have organized a society of certified public accountants as a vehicle for advancing the interests of the profession and its members. CPA's are not required to be a member of the society in their jurisdiction. At the national level, the AICPA, with a membership of about 300 000, is a voluntary association of CPA's. The AICPA has adopted a Code of Professional Conduct, but since the Institute is not a licensing body, it has, in principle, limited control over the actual conduct of its members.[64] Since the 1970's, however, the SEC has delegated self-regulatory authority to the AICPA over firms with SEC clients, including the requirement that such firms undergo periodic peer reviews.

7.3.2. United Kingdom

Rather than make widespread use of government commissions (as in the USA), the UK has opted for the periodic upgrading of financial reporting requirements as a reflection of emerging conceptions of best practice, in response to criticisms of prior legislation, and, since 1981, to adapt UK law to EEC Directives.

The earliest legislation dealing with the financial reporting by limited liability companies occurred in the middle of the 19th century. In 1855, Parliament introduced the right to register companies with limited liability. The Companies Acts passed in 1856 and 1862, while encouraging the publication of financial

---

for Preparation and Filing of Registration Statements Under the Securities Act of 1933 and Adoption of Guide 1 of the Guides for the Preparation and Filing of Reports and Registration Statements Under the Securities Exchange Act of 1934 (textual Analysis of Summary of Earnings or Operations), Accounting Series Release no. 159 (14 August 1974).

[61] See John C. Burton, "Emerging Trends in Financial Reporting", in *Journal of Accountancy*, vol. 152, no. 1, July 1981, p. 56.

[62] See Solomons, *op. cit.*, pp. 194–198.

[63] The other jurisdictions are the District of Columbia, Puerto Rico, the Virgin Islands, and Guam.

[64] The public accountancy boards in the 54 jurisdictions that license CPA's have adopted codes of conduct, and each board has procedures for enforcing its code.

statements and the retention of an auditor, did not impose any requirements to do so.

The Companies Acts of 1900 and 1907 (which were consolidated in an act passed in 1908) established the first requirement for an external audit and the publication of a balance sheet, but no contents were prescribed. (Exemptions were provided for smaller companies.) The Companies Act of 1928 (which was consolidated in 1929 with previous legislation), in addition to specifying the contents of the balance sheet, added a requirement for the publication of a profit and loss statement, but without specifying its contents and requiring that it be audited. The Companies Act 1947 (consolidated in 1948) imposed a requirement for group financial statements, made the profit and loss statement and the group financial statements subject to audit, and required the disclosure of transfers to and from reserves.

Other Companies Acts followed between 1967 and 1980, and in 1981 a Companies Act adapted UK legislation to the Fourth EEC Directive. The Companies Acts were consolidated in 1985.[65]

Some 700 000 companies file their annual financial statements with the Registrar of Companies every year. The Companies Acts have been administered by the Department of Trade and Industry (DTI), but, as regards the provisions on accounting – prior to the Companies Act passed in 1989 (discussed below)–they had regulated "very little".[66]

In 1986, Parliament passed the Financial Services Act which established the Securities and Investments Board to oversee a web of "self-regulatory organizations" and "recognized professional bodies" (among others) in order to provide a more effective supervision of the investment community.[67] This collaboration between an independent regulatory body, responsible to the Secretary of State for Trade and Industry, and self-regulatory entities represented another intermediate step by the UK government toward an eventual state of comprehensive and direct regulation of the capital market.

The Companies Act 1989 provided the statutory framework for a major reform of the standard-setting process. The reform had been precipitated by the Dearing Report, which had been commissioned in 1987 by the Consultative Committee of Accountancy Bodies.[68] On 1 August 1990, the Report's recommendations

---

[65] Most of the information on the succession of UK Companies Acts is based on John Richard Edwards, *A History of Financial Accounting* (London: Routledge, 1989), Chaps. 9, 15–17.

[66] Rutteman, *op. cit.*

[67] See Peter Taylor and Stuart Turley, *The Regulation of Accounting* (London: Basil Blackwell, 1986), pp. 23–32; and Anthony Hopwood, Michael Page and Stuart Turley, *Understanding Accounting in a Changing Environment* (Hemel Hempstead, Herts: Prentice Hall International (UK) Ltd, 1990), pp. 83–86.

[68] *The Making of Accounting Standards*, Report of the Review Committee under the Chairmanship of Sir Ron Dearing CB (London: The Institute of Chartered Accountants in England and Wales, 1988). The Dearing recommendations were substantially patterned on the FASB's

were implemented almost to the letter: the ASC ceased to exist, and it was succeeded by the Financial Reporting Council (FRC), which was to oversee two new entities, the Accounting Standards Board (ASB) and the Review Panel. Of the nine members of the ASB, the chairman and technical director were made full-time appointments, and its budget was increased significantly over that of the ASC.[69] As a result of the 1989 Act and actions since taken thereunder by the Secretary of State for Trade and Industry, "accounting standards" was mentioned for the first time in company legislation, the ASB was designated as the official source of accounting standards. Listed and large unlisted companies must state whether they have prepared their financial statements in accordance with applicable accounting standards and give details of, and the reasons for, any material departures. The Review Panel is charged with determining whether companies' financial statements are, in its view, defective according to the law. If an offending company does not take corrective action following the receipt of notification, the Review Panel may apply to the court for an order requiring the company to issue revised financial statements. If the court approves the order, it may require the directors who approved the defective financial statements to bear the costs of the legal action.[70] In effect, therefore, Parliament has invested the ASB and the Review Panel with self-regulatory authority.

The effect of the 1989 legislation brings the UK very close to the rigorous system of compliance that has existed in the USA, although the mode of ensuring the compliance is different.

In the last 25 years, the comparability of financial statements has become an increasingly important issue in the UK. Since the late 1960's, when a number of financial embarrassments emboldened the financial press to speak out more firmly about the flexibility allowed to companies in the preparation of their financial statements,[71] increased pressure has been brought on the accounting profession,

---

structure and operations, although with significant differences.

[69] The FRC's budget was reported to be £3.4 million, including a provision of £1 million for possible legal costs incident to the work of the Review Panel, compared with the ASC's total budget of £440 000 for 1989. See "Dearing sets up standards shop", in *World Accounting Report*, March 1990, p. 8, and *The Making of Accounting Standards*, *op. cit.*, para. 19.1. Also see Sir Ron Dearing, "Accounting Standards: The New Approach", in *Accountancy*, vol. 105, no. 1162, June 1990, pp. 86–87.

[70] *Guide to the Companies Act 1989*, prepared by Ernst & Young in collaboration with the Institute of Chartered Accountants of Scotland (London: Kogan Page Ltd, 1989), pp. 35–37.

[71] Lee has written that the UK accountancy profession had not been subject to much external pressure and criticism until the late 1960's. Beginning around then, he noted, "the profession as a whole has had to cope with a more sophisticated investment public, a more astute and enquiring financial press, and a far less tolerant academic community". T.A. Lee, "Accounting Standards and Effective Financial Reporting – I", in *The Accountant's Magazine*, vol. 79, no. 823, January 1975, p. 27.

Also see Edward Stamp, "A Crisis in the Accounting Profession", in Edward Stamp and Christopher Marley, *Accounting Principles and the City Code: The Case for Reform* (London: Butterworths, 1970), pp. 68–73, and Stamp's article in *The Times* that played a major role

government, and companies to take steps to lessen the degrees of freedom and, as a result (it is believed), enhance the comparability of financial statements. In the last decade, fueled by the merger movement and the wave of company restructurings, finance directors have spoken out forcefully against accounting standards that are perceived as limiting their companies' freedom of movement. Not surprisingly, the Dearing Report, which laid the foundation for the new accounting standards program, referred to "the strong pressure on auditors from time to time to accept interpretations of accounting standards which conform with the interests of the preparers rather than with the spirit of the standard".[72]

7.3.3. The Netherlands

For reasons set forth above, the regulatory experience in the Netherlands has been guided with a much lighter hand than in the United States and the United Kingdom. The first modern companies legislation was not approved until 1970, and it seems likely that, but for the political agitation behind the movement to democratize enterprise for the primary benefit of employees, legislation calling for improved financial reporting might not have been introduced until the 1980's, when Dutch legislation was adapted to the Fourth EEC Directive.

The Act on Annual Financial Statements of Enterprises of 1970 required that financial statements "give an insight such that a well-founded opinion can be formed concerning the financial position and the income of the enterprise and, to the extent that the annual financial statements permit, on its solvency and liquidity" (Art.2). When interpreting this provision, one should recognize that, in the Dutch cultural climate, stewardship reporting to long-term shareholders occupies a more important position than an orientation to buyers and sellers of securities.[73] This fundamental criterion remains in place today. Comparability is not even alluded to in Dutch companies legislation, and the RJ has stated that comparability is not an issue in its deliberations.[74]

In 1989, there were 6847 NV's and 233 350 BV's, each of which was required to file annual financial statements, full or abbreviated, with the Chamber of Commerce in its district.[75]

---

in prompting the Institute of Chartered Accountants in England and Wales to inaugurate its accounting standards program in 1969–70, pp. 155–159; and Edwards, *op. cit.*, pp. 245–246.

72 *The Making of Accounting Standards*, *op. cit.*, para. 5.20.

73 Schoonderbeek has written that the objectives of financial statements implicit in the general framework laid down by the Act on Annual Financial Statements of 1970 "are to be understood as expressing the underlying philosophy of the stewardship function of management ...". Prof.drs J.W. Schoonderbeek, "The Dutch Tripartite Accounting Standards Committee", in *The Tripartite Accounting Standards Committee*, PILOT (Netherlands) 10 (Amsterdam: Nederlands Instituut van Registeraccountants, December 1980), p. 7.

74 "Commentaar op ED 32 'Comparability of Financial Statements'", in *de Accountant*, vol. 96, no. 2, October 1989, pp. 71–73.

75 These figures were cited in *Barriers to Takeovers in the European Community*, *op. cit.*,

Since the Justice Minister took the occasion in 1968 to suggest that "organized business" and the organization of auditors take an "inventory of valuation principles that are considered to be acceptable in the economic and social climate", and judge their acceptability, the Ministry's only major initiatives in company financial reporting have been the adaptation of the law to the Fourth and Seventh EEC Directives. It has given no further suggestions for the conduct of the process by which the TO and, later, the RJ has been carrying out the charge given to it in 1968.

The mechanism for securing compliance with the financial reporting provisions of the law is a branch of the Court of Justice at Amsterdam, known as the Enterprise Chamber. It acts only when shareholders and other "interested parties" bring cases or when the Attorney-General attached to the Court of Justice at Amsterdam can prove public interest in a proceeding initiated by his office. While it is known that the judges examine the relevant Considered Views/Guidelines in the course of their deliberations, they do not refer to them in their verdicts. Fortunately for the success of the Enterprise Chamber, SOBI, a social pressure group (or public interest group, depending on one's point of view) concerned with the quality of company financial reporting, has been active in bringing cases. Of the 45 cases dealing with financial reporting that were adjudicated by the Enterprise Chamber through the middle of 1991, 21 had been brought by SOBI. In the last few years, SOBI has withdrawn from this activity, and the Attorney-General has not succeeded in demonstrating a public interest in his attempts at initiating judicial proceedings. Shareholders find the process costly, and it can take from two to four years until a decision is announced. Consequently, the number of new cases in recent years has declined to a trickle. Given these circumstances, it is not known whether the Enterprise Chamber will continue to be a force in securing compliance with the financial reporting provisions of company law.

No body acts to enforce compliance with the Guidelines issued by the RJ. The NIvRA does, however, offer some inducements to encourage compliance. Its Consultative Committee on Published Auditors' Reports (COPA, Commissie Overleg Publieke Accountantsverklaringen) has, since its formation in 1977, sought to use quiet persuasion with auditors concerning apparent departures from Considered Views/Guidelines or the law in their clients' financial statements. Since 1974, the NIvRA has published *Onderzoek Jaarverslagen*, a biennial survey of the financial statements of between 120 and 135 listed companies, in which statistics on the use of particular reporting practices, but not the names of companies, are presented. Finally, the NIvRA has, since 1979, issued a checklist of the points contained in the Considered Views/Guidelines to assist auditors in the course of their client engagements.

In the context of the regulatory classification scheme proposed by Puxty et

vol. 2, The Netherlands: p. 11.

al.[76], the Netherlands would reflect the dual influence of Associationism (the initiatives of the RJ) and Legalism (the 1971 Act, as embellished by the adaptations of Dutch law to the Fourth and Seventh Directives, together with the judicial enforcement by the Enterprise Chamber). Since the RJ's predecessor, the TO, was created at the suggestion of the Minister of Justice, and in view of the fact that the SER provides two-thirds of the RJ's financial support, even though the SER has never involved itself in the RJ's policies and operations, the Dutch regulatory environment is also tinged by a shade of Corporatism.

One can therefore discern the following current approaches to the regulation of financial reporting in the three countries:

> *In the United States:* Congressional securities legislation has authorized a government commission to prescribe financial reporting practices, and, in addition to issuing rules (mostly on matters of format and disclosure), the commission has delegated authority to a private-sector body for promulgating accounting standards. Self-regulation occurs in the private sector within the framework created by the government commission: statements of standards are issued, with activist monitoring by the commission. The government commission engages in strict administrative enforcement of compliance with its own rules and with the private-sector promulgations.
>
> Although the government commission's authority extends only to corporations covered by securities legislation, the private-sector body's promulgations are applicable to all corporations that issue audited financial statements.
>
> State corporation laws are applicable to accounting questions relating to the determination of dividends and certain other corporate transactions.
>
> *In the United Kingdom:* Parliamentary companies legislation has prescribed certain financial reporting practices and has provided that a private-sector body is to promulgate accounting standards. Self-regulation occurs in the private sector within the statutory framework: statements of standards are issued, but without close monitoring by the government. There is collaboration between the private sector and government, by use of persuasion and judicial remedies, to enforce compliance with the statutory prescriptions and with the private-sector standards.
>
> *In the Netherlands:* Parliamentary companies legislation has prescribed certain financial reporting practices. Self-regulation stimulated by the government occurs in the private sector, but within a private-sector framework: statements embodying guidelines are issued, but without any monitoring by the government. Interested parties and the Attorney-General (when in the public interest) may initiate a judicial proceeding in a special court to require companies to adhere to the statutory prescriptions; efforts to promote compliance with the private-sector guidelines are limited to confidential discussions with the auditors of companies that apparently are departing from the guidelines.

---

[76] A.G. Puxty, Hugh C. Willmott, David J. Cooper and Tony Lowe, "Modes of Regulation in Advanced Capitalism: Locating Accountancy in Four Countries", in *Accounting, Organizations and Society,* vol. 12, no. 3, 1987, pp. 273–291.

7.4. Consequences for the process of improving financial reporting

Perhaps the clearest implications for accounting of the foregoing discussion of national culture, capital markets, and legal systems and the regulatory environment can be seen in the reasons and arguments that have prompted major changes in the process for improving financial reporting.

In the United States, the reason for setting up the Institute's Committee on Accounting Procedure (CAP) in 1938–39 was to respond to the SEC's criticism of the great diversity in accounting practices used by registrant corporations. The SEC was looking for a means to narrow the areas of difference, thus promoting comparability, and enabling it to use its potent compliance weapons to good effect. In 1959, the APB replaced the CAP in response to criticisms from within the accounting profession, from financial executives, and from the SEC. The arguments were that the committee had been unable to agree on effective solutions in several major problem areas, that preparers *had too much* influence on the committee, that preparers *did not have enough* influence on the committee (depending on whether auditors or preparers were complaining), and that the committee had not done enough to narrow the areas of difference. In 1973, the FASB replaced the APB following a chorus of criticism not only from within the accounting profession but also from a committee of the American Accounting Association.[77] Three of the Big Eight public accounting firms had raised serious questions about the viability of the APB, referring to its apparent inability to withstand partisan pressure from business and government. Moreover, it was questioned whether the members of a part-time body could be truly independent of the interests of their firms' clients or of their employers.[78] At all three junctures, there were criticisms, if not actual crises.

In the United Kingdom, the English Institute began to publish a series of Recommendations on Accounting Principles in 1942 as a result of pressure applied by some of its leading members in industry and commerce, who apparently feared that the expected review of companies legislation might not otherwise have the benefit of advice from a technical committee of the Institute. In the event, the contents of several of the Recommendations were incorporated in the report of

[77] "Report of the Committee on Establishment of an Accounting Commission", in *The Accounting Review*, vol. 46, no. 3, July 1971, pp. 610–613.

[78] See Stephen A. Zeff, "Some Junctures in the Evolution of the Process of Establishing Accounting Principles in the U.S.A.: 1917–1972", in *The Accounting Review*, vol. 59, no. 3, July 1984, pp. 453–466; Maurice Moonitz, *Obtaining Agreement on Standards in the Accounting Profession*, Studies in Accounting Research #8 (Sarasota, FL: American Accounting Association, 1974), and Solomons, *op. cit.* Also see Robert Chatov, *Corporate Financial Reporting: Public or Private Control?* (New York: The Free Press, 1975), Chaps. 8, 12 and 14; and *Establishing Financial Accounting Standards*, Report of the Study on Establishment of Accounting Principles (New York: American Institute of Certified Public Accountants, March 1972), usually referred to as the report of the Wheat Study, after the name of its chairman, Francis M. Wheat.

the review committee and in the ensuing legislation. In 1969–70, the Recommendations series was replaced by a series of *Statements of Standard Accounting Practice* (*SSAP*'s) issued by the newly established ASC, a reform that followed hard on the heels of widespread criticism in the press over flexible accounting principles, both in terms of the number of options allowed and the freedom enjoyed by companies to ignore the Recommendations altogether. There was a sign that the government was restless in the face of the public criticism.[79] From the mid-1980's to 1990, when the ASC was replaced by the FRC, the ASB and the Review Panel, there had again been considerable criticism of the effectiveness of the standard-setting program, from finance directors and from partners in accounting firms, and in the financial press. The government seemed even more concerned than it had been in 1969, and came to the belief that decisive steps should be taken to provide legal backing for accounting standards.

Unlike the US and UK settings, where measures have been taken to secure compliance with recommended norms, enforced compliance has not been accepted in the Netherlands. Nonetheless, ten years ago, the NIvRA proposed that, when an auditor was of the opinion that a company's departure from a definitive Guideline was not justified, he should refer to the departure in his report.[80] Owing to criticism of this proposal from companies and audit firms, it was withdrawn. Measures to promote stricter compliance with the Guidelines have not been proposed by any of the parties to the tripartite committee, or by the government. It is virtually unknown for auditors to draw attention in their reports to a departure from the Considered Views or Guidelines.

Also unlike the US and UK settings, "narrowing the areas of difference" has not been an issue in the Netherlands. In the USA, the efforts to narrow the areas of difference had, in decades of intense merger and restructuring activity (the 1960's and the 1980's), provoked aggressive, organized opposition from the business sector. Companies that were involved in contested takeovers or restructurings were wont to use accounting figures as a tactic in their negotiations and selling documents, and the maximum amount of freedom to do so was regarded as paramount. In the UK, a series of conflicts arose during a similar period of merger and restructuring activity in the 1980's, when industry raised the decibel level of its disagreement with actual or proposed standards in such areas as accounting for inflation, goodwill, mergers and acquisitions, and brands.

In the Netherlands, by contrast, the tripartite committee set up in 1971 was a response to the government's desire that experts in the private sector provide

[79] See Zeff, *Forging Accounting Principles*, *op. cit.*, pp. 33–40.

[80] *De betekenis van de richtlijnen van het Tripartiete Overleg (thans Raad voor de Jaarverslaggeving) voor de accountantsverklaring*, Ontwerp ter discussie 15, Ontwerp-Meningsuiting (Amsterdam: Nederlands Instituut van Registeraccountants, January 1982). This initiative was precipitated by the TO's Foreword to the Draft Guidelines, published in June 1980. See the subsection, "The foreword to the rewritten considered views", in Chapter 5.

interpretations of a provision in the law on valuation principles that was deliberately phrased in general terms. There was no crisis. There had not been much public criticism of the quality of financial reporting. Certainly, the auditing profession had not sought the creation of such a committee. Nor had the employers or trade union federations. Owing to its accepted norm that unanimous consent be obtained for all drafts and final statements, the TO/RJ has laid a broad base of support for its efforts to raise standards. Auditors have undertaken to persuade their clients to adopt the recommendations that they believe are sound, but no compliance mechanism exists to provide a strong stimulus for acceptance.

Why has the Dutch accounting environment been more placid than those in the USA and the UK? A number of reasons have been suggested, but a potent one is the absence of contested takeovers. As mentioned above, the crisis points in the USA and the UK have been related to periods of frequent merger, acquisition and restructuring activity, especially where shareholders and creditors have had to be "sold" on the proposed terms. It is at these times that accounting comes under great pressure, since accounting figures play a prominent role in the selling activity, and companies in such circumstances are tempted to stretch the accounting rules. It is no accident that the pronouncements that precipitated the fall of the APB in the USA and the ASC in the UK were on accounting for mergers and acquisitions, and goodwill. In the late 1960's in the UK, the launching of the ASC's ambitious standards program stemmed directly from press criticism of a large company's use of flexible accounting principles to fend off an unfriendly takeover. In the late 1950's in the USA, "pooling of interests" accounting was the subject of one of the CAP's most criticized bulletins, which contributed to its eventual demise.

Once the European Community's Thirteenth Directive on takeovers is approved in one form or another, the climate for mergers and acquisitions in the Netherlands may undergo a change, perhaps even a profound change, since the barriers against contested takeovers are currently among the highest in the Community.[81] As a consequence of the changed takeover environment, it is prob-

[81] See the table comparing "classic" takeover defenses in Belgium, France, Germany, the Netherlands, and Italy, in "Europe's corporate castles begin to crack", in *The Economist* (London), vol. 321, no. 7735, 30 November 1991, p. 68.

There are signs that the Dutch business and financial community has begun to think about the possible future lowering of takeover barriers. The president of a leading Dutch capital management firm has advised companies to begin cultivating their shareholders, as their support may be the ultimate defense against unfriendly takeovers if companies are eventually obliged by the European Community or other forces to abandon their structural barriers. "Shareholders should be cosseted, says investment chief", in *Het Financieele Dagblad*, 2/4 November 1991, p. 9. Also see the proposal made by Dr H.O.C.R. Ruding, president of the NCW and former finance minister (1982–89), to set limits on the duration of companies' structural defenses against unfriendly takeovers. "Cut-off point for corporate anti-takeover defences", in *Het Financieele Dagblad*, 23/25 November 1991, p. 7. For a development involving the Amsterdam Stock Exchange and the Association of Listed Companies (Vereniging van Effecten

able that the pressures on accounting will begin to mount, and flexibility may no longer be seen as a virtue.

Flexibility can be defended so long as (1) companies do not become aggressive advocates of accounting principles that further their economic and political ends, and (2) auditors do not waver when counseling clients to use accounting principles that promote the statutory "insight". If concerns in other countries over the increasing commercialization of audit firms can be validly raised in the Netherlands, the traditional assumption that auditors will be staunch defenders of the interests of users in their discussions with clients may no longer be tenable.[82]

At the international level, there has been a shift of emphasis from "harmonization" to "comparability", and the International Accounting Standards Committee (IASC) has begun to propose the reduction or elimination of options allowed in its previous standards. It is intended that the flexibility to use any of several alternative treatments will be diminished.[83]

The open question in the Dutch environment is whether, owing to changing demands from the capital market or pressure applied by the movement toward more comparable international accounting standards under the leadership of the IASC, the parameters governing the process of improving financial reporting might be changed. In the absence of (1) influence from these directions, or (2) a major scandal traceable to defective financial reporting, and in view of the cultural and other factors that were discussed in the preceding sections, it seems likely that the Dutch process will not be modified to emulate the changes that have been occurring in the USA and the UK.

Uitgevende Ondernemingen) concerning anti-takeover defenses, see "Akkoord over bescherming beursbedrijven", in *Het Financieele Dagblad*, 14/16 December 1991, pp. 1, 3.

82 See Stephen A. Zeff, "Does the CPA Belong to a Profession?", in *Accounting Horizons*, vol. 1, no. 2, June 1987, pp. 65–68, and "The Decline of Professionalism", in *De Accountant*, vol. 98, no. 5, January 1992, p. 264–267. For the view of a financial journalist on auditor independence and professionalism, see William Sternberg, "Washington: Cooked Books", in *The Atlantic*, vol. 269, no 1, January 1992, p. 20 ff.

83 See the IASC's E32, "Comparability of Financial Statements", and the IASC's "Statement of Intent" on the comparability project, in *International Accounting Standards 1991/1992* (London: International Accounting Standards Committee, 1991), pp. 13–31. For a study of the evolution of the IASC, see R.S. Olusegun Wallace, "Survival Strategies of a Global Organization: The Case of the International Accounting Standards Committee", in *Accounting Horizons*, vol. 4, no. 2, June 1990, pp. 1–22.

8. Conclusions and policy recommendations

In this final chapter, the authors reflect on the regulatory process during the last forty years, and advance several policy recommendations.

Historically, the regulatory process has been dominated by the consensus culture. Two dimensions of the consensus culture have been noteworthy:

a) a political dimension, by which the consensus has been negotiated, as with the TO and the RJ; and
b) a cognitive dimension, by which the educational system has led to the acceptance of assumptions and methodologies, the leading example being the intellectual tradition through which the Limperg doctrines were handed down to generations of auditors and other students of *bedrijfseconomie*.

Even though the political dimension has the shorter history in the Netherlands, it has grown in importance and promises implications for a considerable time to come. The influence of the cognitive dimension can undergo important shifts as intellectual traditions change. By the 1970's, Limpergian thinking began to be supplanted in the Netherlands by ideas and approaches developed overseas, especially in the United States and the United Kingdom.

An unfortunate consequence of the political version of the consensus culture is that the guidance it produces may be characterized by ambivalence and the lack of clear directions for improvement. In committees where a large majority is required for agreement, the inevitable need to accommodate minority positions dilutes the internal consistency, and, to a considerable degree, the intelligibility, of the final report. Unanimous consent is the largest of majorities, and it is especially suited to those members of a committee who would place a high value on retaining the *status quo*. This weakness of a consensus culture in committee deliberations becomes particularly evident in the more controversial subjects, such as deferred tax, foreign exchange, the segmentation of operating income, the cash flow statement, pensions, the WIR premium, and the valuation and amortization of publishing rights. Guidance is heavily compromised; it is expressed in ultra-soft language, with limited bold-facing; it fails to emerge from the exposure stage, even after the passage of a half-dozen or more years; or, in one case where the positions taken by major companies and auditors seem to have prevented a consensus even on an exposure draft, a vehicle that was put to rest more than ten years ago, the *beschouwing* (formerly translated as Considered Views, but newly rechristened as a Discussion Memorandum), was reincarnated.[1]

The actual use of voting procedures, by which a specified majority (significantly less than unanimity) would be sufficient to adopt a recommendation, would lead to guidance that is more clearly expressed and defended, and is more likely to point toward desirable improvements in financial reporting, but it would represent a break from Dutch culture.

Arguments favoring a strengthening of the political process for promoting improvement in financial reporting are often met with the assertion that Dutch reporting is consistently rated as among the best in international surveys, and that the Dutch auditing profession is highly regarded in other important countries. While Dutch financial reporting, especially that of the larger companies, is of a high order, the international surveys have drawn preponderantly on the small set of multinationals, and other very large companies, such as Philips, Akzo, KLM, Hoogovens, Heineken, DSM, Nedlloyd, Océ-van der Grinten, and Buhrmann–Tetterode.[2] The companies in the Dutch contingent that have consistently received the highest scores have been those whose financial reporting has been influenced by the demands of the New York capital market: Philips, Akzo and KLM. These international studies necessarily say very little about the

---

1 Not all would agree with the authors' tendency to draw an important distinction between exposure drafts and definitive Guidelines. In environments such as those in the USA or the UK, where final statements possess a binding character, the difference between an exposure draft and a final statement is crucial. The difference is not crucial in the Netherlands, where compliance with the final statement is not obligatory. Nonetheless, some of our interviewees have said that their audit firms or companies attach greater importance to final statements than to exposure drafts, while others have said that both are treated alike, as representing authoritative advice. While both exposure drafts and Guidelines can be judged by their "intrinsic value", the authors believe that the decision to convert an exposure draft into a Guideline is an important step, as it is represents the culmination of the cognitive and political processes by which tentative positions are revised or confirmed. The history of the TO and RJ suggests that words and terminology are not unimportant, and the consistent practice of the RJ of distinguishing between "draft Guidelines" and "Guidelines" is evidently intended to suggest a hierarchy of meaning.

2 The international studies most commonly cited are Michael Lafferty with David Cairns and James Carty, *1979 Financial Times Survey of 100 Major European Companies' Reports & Accounts* (London: The Financial Times Ltd, 1979); Michael Lafferty and David Cairns, *Financial Times World Survey of Annual Reports 1980* (London: The Financial Times Business Information Ltd, 1980); David Cairns, Michael Lafferty and Peter Mantle, *Survey of Accounts and Accountants 1983–84* (London: Lafferty Publications Limited, 1984); and Dr D.J. Tonkin, *World Survey of Published Accounts* (London: Lafferty Publications Ltd, 1989). It is of interest that, in the 1989 study, the Netherlands ranked fifth, compared with second in the 1979 and 1980 studies. (In the 1983–84 study, the top five countries, which included the Netherlands, were not ranked.) The reasons given for the lower ranking were: the lack of interest in inflation accounting, the "mediocre" accounting scores for the Dutch companies, and their "good but not exceptional" rating on timeliness. *Ibid.*, p. 32.

Shell and Unilever have consistently been rated among the companies with the best annual reports, but they have usually been classified as "international". In the 1989 study, however, Shell was represented by Shell Transport & Trading in the United Kingdom contingent; Unilever was also classified in the UK contingent.

majority of Dutch companies listed on the Amsterdam Stock Exchange or, to be sure, about large but unlisted companies.

The high standing that the Dutch auditing profession enjoys in professional circles overseas undoubtedly owes much to the very able representatives of the Dutch profession who participate with such good effect at international conferences and meetings. The Dutch are probably more alive to accounting and auditing developments overseas than are the professionals of most other important countries, and the NIvA/NIvRA has always arranged for the most informed and most effective *registeraccountants* to represent the Dutch profession at important international events, including meetings of the International Accounting Standards Committee (IASC). This combination of factors, together with the well-known propensity of the Dutch to advocate current cost accounting, has contributed to a very positive image for members of the Dutch auditing profession. While it is not our intention to call this reputation into question, or to doubt the quality of financial reporting by large Dutch companies, neither do we believe that they are grounds for self-congratulation or complacency.

At both the international and domestic levels, a greater degree of comparability is a desirable goal. As national capital markets gradually become integrated into a truly global capital market, the comparability of financial reporting across countries has increasingly become an insistent issue. It is no accident that the International Organization of Securities Commissions (IOSCO), supported by such important regulatory bodies as the US's Securities and Exchange Commission and France's Commission des Opérations de Bourse, has been urging the IASC to eliminate most of the free options in its previously issued standards. While these bodies do not argue that the reduction of alternatives will lead to a state of "true" comparability, they are nonetheless of the view that a multiplicity of alternatives, without reconciliation to an authoritative norm, frustrates users' efforts to make meaningful cross-country comparisons. The implications of this argument for the IASC's future role has been announced in clear terms: Whereas, in the past, it was not very difficult for the NIvRA to show its support of IASC standards that allowed several treatments on most issues, in the future its standards are likely to allow only a single treatment, or, when a free choice is retained, a "benchmark" treatment will be identified.[3] Within a few years, therefore, it is likely that the newly issued IASC standards will, in many areas, call for fewer optional treatments than are currently found in the RJ's Guidelines. Will this curious juxtaposition between IASC and the RJ's Guidelines enable the NIvRA to continue to maintain that it is using its "best endeavors" to gain acceptance for IASC standards in the Netherlands?

It is not clear whether the IASC will one day make regional and national

[3] See the IASC's "Statement of Intent", in *International Accounting Standards 1991/1992* (London: International Accounting Standards Committee, 1991), pp. 13–31.

accounting standards bodies superfluous.[4] For the time being, there continues to be activity at both levels. The European Community (EC) is experimenting with an Accounting Advisory Forum in order to persuade national standard setters to coordinate their agendas through a discussion of common problems. Following discussions at the Community level, it is likely that all will look toward the strongest national standard-setting body for direction. The strongest such body in the Community is the UK's Accounting Standards Board (ASB). The RJ will probably not be successful at formulating a draft Guideline on a controversial subject until the ASB has acted, and even then the preparers delegation in the RJ would be in a position to argue that any such Guideline would place Dutch companies at a competitive disadvantage in comparison with companies in a number of other Community countries. A process such as the RJ's, based on a consensus culture, seems destined to be one of the last in the Community countries to produce a decision.

The long-term interest of the capital market must be seen as consistent with a high standard of financial reporting that promotes the ability of users to make effective comparisons among the securities of different enterprises. Foreign investors accustomed to such financial reporting in other capital markets will not be easily attracted to Amsterdam if they do not perceive Dutch financial information to be of a similar caliber.

It is clear from the history examined in previous chapters that the employers/preparers have played a strong role. From a political perspective, their performance has been excellent. In the Rijkens report, issued in 1955, they anticipated impending developments, and thus acquired a degree of influence, if not actual control, over subsequent calls for reform. Their role in the Teldersstichting report, as the Liberal Party's reply to the report of the Labor Party's Dr. Wiardi Beckman Stichting, together with their sponsorship of the Hamburger report, which created a climate in which the renowned auditor J. Kraayenhof could serve as the linchpin between the Hamburger committee and the Verdam Commission, provided the employers with valuable leverage in the design phase of what was to become the Act on Annual Financial Statements of Enterprises, which was approved in 1970. Moreover, their tactics in the TO and the RJ have demonstrated their ability to set the lines of eventual drafts.

While the auditors, by contrast, have proposed subjects for discussion, testimony from the employees side, as well as our interviews, suggest that, in the meetings of the TO/RJ, the auditors have sometimes shown a reluctance to adopt an independent stance once the employers have marked the turf. The major exception, where the auditors took the lead from the outset, involved current value/current cost accounting, where decades-long teaching of the Limpergian

[4] For a discussion of this and other issues relating to European standard setting, see Anthony G. Hopwood, "The Future of Accounting Harmonization in the Community", in *European Accounting*, 1991, pp. 12–21.

model supplied auditors with a theory and instilled in them a confidence in its superiority.

An issue may be raised about the future leadership role that is likely to be played by the auditing community. In a number of countries, there are signs that the commercial interests of audit firms may have overtaken the traditional concern for the quality of company financial reporting. The *raison d'être* of the audit, namely, to give users confidence in the credibility of the financial statements, may no longer be seen as the premier calling of the audit firm. Firms have seemed to become more inclined to accommodate client interests than to defend the interests of those on whose behalf the independent audit is conducted. The increasing commercialization of audit firms represents a potential threat to the vitality of an independent audit profession.

In the Netherlands, an independent voice from academe has largely been missing, since the great majority of accounting and auditing professors are full-time partners in audit firms. Moreover, in much of their published work, they address practical issues as would audit partners who have no university affiliation. Practical research is important, especially in a practical field. But accounting and auditing are also disciplines of study with a rich intellectual tradition. One can query whether part-time accounting and auditing professors can be expected to engage in the kind of fundamental research – which provides a platform for advancement of the field – that one associates with the mission of the university.

The role performed by information users has been minimal. The Stock Exchange Association, which is responsible for maintaining a market in which investors can rely on the adequacy of published financial information prior to making decisions, has shown scant interest in the norms of financial reporting. Financial analysts have, to be sure, been more forthcoming. But we have often heard it said that, since most analysts are employed by banks – which have "relationships" with a great many companies – they are not encouraged to engage in overt criticism of companies' financial reporting practices. Moreover, the banks themselves still make use of secret reserves.

The composition of the users delegation to the RJ should be reconsidered. Except for one of its members, it is not chosen by, and does not purport to represent, the users of financial statements. In view of the fact that all of the other 12 members of the RJ are *registeraccountants*, it may be difficult for a single user who is not a *registeraccountant* to make an impact. At least several genuine representatives of financial statement users should form part of the delegation.

Perhaps reflecting the air of nonchalance among leading institutions in the capital market, the financial press does not cover financial reporting as fully, as critically, or as analytically as one finds in countries where financial reporting is a topic of active discussion. Since reforms in other countries have frequently been precipitated by complaints registered in the financial press, the comparative silence in the Dutch press could create a climate in which the process of stimulating improvement in financial reporting might enter stagnation. Such an eventuality would be in no one's interest.

The division of responsibilities between the Finance Ministry, which supervises the capital market, and the Justice Ministry, which supervises the financial reporting law, may be less than beneficial. A third ministry, Economic Affairs, supervises the audit profession. A coordination of policies, laws, and institutional oversight in all three spheres would seem to be in the interests of Dutch society.

The authors' impression is that government's concern for financial reporting has diminished, now that the the law has been adapted to both the Fourth and Seventh EC Directives. It has been more than 20 years since the Minister of Justice prompted the formation of the TO. Since then, major changes have occurred in standard setting in countries with two leading capital markets – the United States and the United Kingdom–, the IASC was formed and was recently rejuvenated, Dutch law has been adapted to two major EC Directives, and the Dutch accounting literature has made an important shift from a preoccupation with valuation systems to problem-oriented issues. A great deal has changed, both domestically and internationally. To be sure, the TO was reconstituted as the RJ in 1982, but the changes were more structural than substantive. Government should address the question of whether the RJ, as presently conceived, meets the demands of the 1990's and beyond.

A real and compelling enhancement of quality has come from SOBI. It is striking that this initiative was un-Dutch in two important respects: it promoted conflict, and it depended entirely on one man, Pieter Lakeman. Our assessment is that, while Lakeman sometimes took questionable positions, he nonetheless brought important cases to the Enterprise Chamber. Of the 45 cases on financial reporting that have thus far been adjudicated, 21 were brought by SOBI, and its recent decision to withdraw from this arena will make the Enterprise Chamber a much less vital instrument in the enforcement of financial reporting law. It would be timely for a step to be taken to improve the effectiveness of the Enterprise Chamber. A special committee, such as the Review Panel established in 1990 in the United Kingdom, should be established to conduct an informed and systematic review of large companies' annual financial statements. Its members, who might be auditors, lawyers, financial analysts and economists, would judge whether company financial statements were in material compliance with the general and specific requirements of the law. Companies whose financial statements were found to be defective would be approached informally, and if they were not willing to modify their practices, the Attorney-General would be authorized to initiate proceedings before the Enterprise Chamber.[5]

[5] A similar proposal has been made by Prof.dr J. Klaassen, "Het institutionele kader van de jaarverslaggeving in Nederland", in J.P.C.M. van de Hoeven, A. de Bos and C.D. Knoops (editors), *fMA-kroniek 1991* (Groningen: Wolters-Noordhoff, 1991), pp. 74–75.

Van Hoepen has argued, as did Burgert in 1981, that a small "Companies Commission"

If such a committee is not established, we believe that the authority of the Attorney-General's office should be expanded. His role might be divided into two parts: as a supervisor, and as a prosecutor. The Attorney-General's supervisory role would involve giving informal advice to a company that its financial statements, in his view, fall short of what the law requires. The company would have a choice either of issuing a revised set of financial statements or of possibly facing legal process. The Attorney-General would not be permitted to prosecute the company unless its next year's financial statements were not suitably revised. Alternatively, the Attorney-General could initiate judicial proceedings immediately upon determining the deficiency, without first approaching the company on an informal basis.

Regardless of whether either of the two foregoing alternatives – a committee or a redefinition of the Attorney-General's role – is adopted, the authors believe that the law should be amended to invest the Attorney-General with status as an "interested party", rather than continue to insist that he demonstrate "public interest" in any proceedings relating to deficient financial statements. In the absence of a public interest group such as SOBI, it is evident that comparatively few suits will be brought by interested parties. The Attorney-General holds a public office, and he is in a better position than shareholders to conduct research on the sufficiency of financial statements. At the very least, interested parties (such as shareholders) should be permitted to institute a suit jointly with the Attorney-General's office, so that they would have the benefit of the Attorney-General's legal resources.

European developments, especially the Fourth and Seventh EC Directives, have fundamentally altered the regulatory focus on financial reporting in the 1980's and 1990's. Companies have come to be more attuned to thinking of their relative position in the Community, with their nationality becoming a secondary consideration. A proposal for imposing additional national reporting requirements immediately provokes a complaint from companies that they would be placed at a competitive disadvantage in the Community, a claim that is difficult to assess. In this regard, the EC initiatives have reduced the influence of national governments, who will find it necessary to channel proposed new reporting requirements through the Community's apparatus. This changed perspective provides employers/preparers with a pretext to resist any new reporting requirements in the RJ. It may even lead them to attach less importance to observing

---

should be set up to review the annual reports of large companies, apparently with a view to initiating legal proceedings if the reports were believed to fall short of legal requirements. Such a "Companies Commission", van Hoepen said, would lead to a more systematic accumulation of legal literature, without having to wait until "interested parties" institute legal action. Prof.dr M.A. van Hoepen, "Aandacht voor jaarrekeningarresten sterk overtrokken", in *Account*, vol. 4, no. 4, May 1991, pp. 11–12. Prof.drs R. Burgert's proposal was presented in *Tien jaar wet en rechtspraak omtrent de jaarrekening voor ondernemingen*, Afscheidscollege (Valedictory Lecture), 21 May 1981 (Erasmus Universiteit Rotterdam), pp. 15–17.

the Guidelines in their financial statements. This development, coming at a time when auditors may be less inclined to risk angering clients by pressing for the adoption of Guidelines, could contribute to the impotence of the entire process of giving guidance on financial reporting.

The EC's eventual Thirteenth Directive on takeovers, if it succeeds in lowering the high defenses against hostile takeovers, may have an especially potent impact on the financial reporting climate in the Netherlands (as well as in other countries with high takeover barriers). As has been shown in countries with virtually no such barriers, such as the United States and the United Kingdom, companies engaged in unfriendly takeover struggles are not loathe to use financial figures as an instrument in their campaigns. If, for similar reasons, Dutch companies were to become more heavily committed to the importance of freedom and flexibility in financial reporting, it might be even more difficult to achieve improvements by a consensual process. If flexible financial reporting is seen as enabling companies to take public positions in favor of self-interested takeover objectives, neither the financial community nor the financial press is likely to keep its silence. As was mentioned in Chapter 7, intensive periods of merger and acquisition activity, especially where hostile takeovers were prevalent, have taken a toll on standard-setting programs in both the United States and the United Kingdom. Its possible impact on the Dutch financial reporting climate can, at this stage, only be the subject of speculation. Nonetheless, the prospect of a changed climate in takeover activity, which has drawn comment from some members of the Dutch business and financial community, should be taken seriously.

Another question concerns the role of the NIvRA in financial reporting. As indicated in previous chapters, the NIvRA/NIvA, as a body, did not play an important role in the development of financial reporting until the late 1960's. Since 1971, it has been one of three partners in "the economic and social climate" who have collectively participated in the development of statements issued by the TO and the RJ. But the NIvRA's institutional role in the process of improving financial reporting has been limited to the work of its Advisory Committee on Annual Reporting, which has done the initial drafting of the TO/RJ's statements. The NIvRA has not, however, been a central figure in the developmental process.[6] The authors believe that an organization such as the NIvRA, whose

---

[6] In a report published by the NIvRA in 1980, it was argued that the auditor (and, one supposes, the organization of auditors) should not play a leading role in developing norms for financial reporting. *Neutraal, maar niet passief*, Discussierapport van de Werkgroep Dynamische Functieanalyse (Amsterdam: Nederlands Instituut van Registeraccountants, 1980). It further states:

"Determining the principles of regulation [in the general sphere of reporting] must be done by the interested participants in the economic and social climate. The auditor should be active in preparing and assisting, in so far as these matters are in the area of his professional competence" (p. 34).

R.J. Ovezall, on the other hand, argued as long ago as 1953 that auditors should take the

members are uniquely charged by law to issue an opinion on the credibility of financial statements for the benefit of users, should occupy a pivotal position in the process that produces authoritative literature to support the professional work of auditors. This implies that the NIvRA should perform a clear and understandable function as a forceful intermediary between the users and preparers of financial information. The role must be visible to outsiders, else its effect could be diluted.

Especially at a time when, as in a number of countries, the increasingly commercial environment in audit firms threatens the auditor's steadfast dedication to principle in discussions with clients, the organization of auditors must invigorate the commitment to independence and integrity on the part of the audit profession. The auditor must be viewed as the ultimate arbiter of the attributes of information that should be reflected in a company's financial statements in order that they might be serviceable to users. To this end, the NIvRA and the Limperg Instituut should consider commissioning a study of the objectives of financial reporting.[7] Such a study could enable interested parties to clarify their thinking on the goals to be achieved when taking specific steps to improve financial reporting, and would serve to guide auditors in the advice they give clients in regard to alternative but acceptable treatments. Both the NIvRA and the Limperg Instituut should play leadership roles in the creation of a research literature that could be used not only in educational programs but also as a stimulus for dialogue among auditors and other parties interested in the improvement of financial reporting.

The tripartite body – involving auditors, preparers and users – should also be subjected to a reevaluation of its aims and methodology. While the TO was a perfect fit for the *overleg*-culture in the 1970's, the authors believe that the country has evolved more toward a decision-culture. This evolution calls into

---

lead in the development of improved financial reporting. R.J. Ovezall, "Enige aspecten van het vraagstuk der stille en geheime reserves voor de accountant", in *Maandblad voor accountancy en bedrijfshuishoudkunde*, vol. 27, no. 4, April 1953, p. 174. The authors support the view espoused by Ovezall.

7 A Dutch study of the objectives of financial reporting is not intended to lead to a state where a body concerned with financial reporting would, "relatively autocratically, propose to 'deduce' standards from an elaborate academic framework in which some crucial inferential bottlenecks nevertheless remain", as Muis has warned could occur. In the authors' view, a study of objectives can help to identify the users (who may well represent a different mix in a European continental country than in, say, the USA or the UK) and to understand how they make decisions and what information they require. Those who are concerned with the improvement of financial reporting sometimes speak grandly of the primacy of "user needs", but they typically know little of the users' world. A study of objectives can provide focus and can add clarity to RJ's mission, as well as be of educational value to auditors, company finance directors, the users themselves and students. Such a study is not, however, intended as the first step in the construction of "an elaborate academic framework". See Jules W. Muis, "Accounting Standard Setting: the Pith and the Pendulum", in *Accounting and Business Research*, vol. 7, no. 28, Autumn 1977, p. 294.

question the prevailing climate of consensus within the RJ. At least some formal voting procedures, perhaps providing for majority and minority positions, should be introduced and actually used. This implies a firmer commitment from the participating organizations than currently exists, as it would require the organizations to abide by the Guidelines even in instances where their delegation has been in dissent. Especially as regards the preparers, whether their delegation is in the majority or the minority, there should be an ongoing public commitment to persuade company managements to abide by the Guidelines. In the spirit of the employers federations' Rijkens and Hamburger reports of 1955 and 1962, respectively, the preparers should play an affirmative role in propagating sound financial reporting practices.[8]

The increasing demands placed on the RJ, to give advice as well as to develop guidance on complex accounting questions, require that it be provided with enhanced staff support. At the least, the chairman should be given additional staff. The preparation of initial drafts should not be delegated to a committee of volunteer professionals (as is done now), but should be assigned to full-time technical staff, perhaps on secondment from audit firms or companies, who would work under the supervision of a committee such as the CAJ or a comparable committee from the employers federations. The full-time technical staff could also assist in the evaluation of comment letters, the examination of overseas literature, and the revision of exposure drafts. As has been found in the United States, the United Kingdom, Canada and Australia, service on an accountancy body's technical staff would be valuable experience for technical assignments in audit firms and companies, and for eventual appointment to committees such as the CAJ. It is also important that the audit firms, as well as the companies, undertake to send their leading technical people to the CAJ and the RJ.

The debate in the early 1980's over the possible obligation of auditors to disclose departures from "affirmative pronouncements" was, the authors believe, misdirected. The disclosure of departures from authoritative norms can perform a valuable service to users of financial information, by providing them with a framework with which to infer lines of comparability. Perhaps reflecting overseas developments, the emphasis was placed on the disclosure of departures by auditors. In the authors' view, it would be much more appropriate if the reporting companies themselves were to relate their financial reporting practices to the authoritative norms. It is they who have chosen the practices, and it would seem to be their concomitant obligation, in the first instance, to disclose departures

[8] Drs P.A. van de Paverd, speaking on behalf of the panel of judges for the Sijthoff Prize at the ceremony at which the awards for 1990 were presented, called on company managements "to revitalize the process that, in the 1950's and 1960's, led to a steady improvement of financial reporting in our country". He was also reported to have said that, in the current "tangle of developments", company managements are the only ones who can constructively pick up this gauntlet. "Initiatieven nodig voor betere boeking goodwill", *Het Financieele Dagblad*, 13 December 1991, p. 11. Van de Paverd is a former president of the Society of Financial Analysts.

from authoritative norms. The financial statements are the representations of the company, not the auditor, and an integral part of the duty to communicate with users is to provide them with a *frame of reference* for interpreting the contents of the statements. If a company would depart from an authoritative norm for reasons that it believes are justified, it should explain its decision in the notes or in the directors' report. For the auditor to do so instead of the company is almost as if to suggest that the company did not accept that obligation as a part of its reporting responsibility. If the company were to decline to fulfill this obligation, the auditor should be expected to comment on significant departures. Accordingly, the NIvRA should take appropriate action to make the auditor's role effective in this regard.

The authors believe that the law should contain general provisions and, as in the current law, a limited number of specific provisions concerning financial reporting. Although there is no warrant for the RJ's Guidelines being detailed prescriptions, the RJ should nonetheless express the acceptable principles of reporting in such a way that would establish clear preferences, and where alternative approaches are justified, the distinctive circumstances and factors that would argue for the use of one over the other should be suggested.

As was stated at the outset, the international regulatory environment is changing. The IASC has entered a new phase in which it proposes to eliminate most of the free choices in accounting treatment allowed by its previous standards, and it will provide less flexibility than is allowed by the RJ's Guidelines. It may be questioned whether the financial reporting expected of Dutch companies can, in the future, be decided entirely within the country's borders, and by a consensus culture. But if there is to be an effective program at the national level, it must be entrusted with the necessary resources, be endowed with a process that produces sound guidance, and be supported by a full-fledged commitment by its sponsoring organizations.

Name Index

Subject Index